THE
WESTERN
EXPERIENCE
VOLUME II

SECOND EDITION

PHYSIOGRAPHY OF EUROPE

▨▨▨ Areas Below Sea Level

0   100   200   300   400 Miles

NORWEGIAN SEA

ICELAND

SCANDINAVIAN PENINSULA

SHETLAND I.

KIOLEN MOUNTAINS

GULF OF BOTHNIA

FINNISH LAKE REGION

HEBRIDES

ORKNEY I.

Dal R.

ÅLAND I.

GULF OF FINLAND

Helsinki

BRITISH ISLES

GRAMPIANS

SCOTTISH LOWLANDS

Edinburgh

Oslo

L. Vänern

Stockholm

L. Vättern

L. Peipus

NORTH SEA

Riga

Dvina R.

GOTLAND

ÖLAND

BALTIC SEA

IRELAND

IRISH CENTRAL PLAIN

Dublin

PENNINE CHAIN

IRISH SEA

St. George's Channel

THE WASH

JUTLAND PENINSULA

HELIGOLAND

Copenhagen

Gdansk (Danzig)

Niemen R.

Masurian Lakes

MIDLAND PLAIN

Bristol Channel

FRISIAN I.

Amsterdam

IJsselmeer

Elbe R.

NORTH GERMAN PLAIN

Berlin

Warta R.

Warsaw

Bug R.

Vistula R.

SCILLY I.

London

Thames R.

Strait of Dover

Maas R.

Scheldt R.

Rhine R.

Weser R.

Oder R.

Neisse R.

SUDETEN MTS.

LAND'S END

ENGLISH CHANNEL

CHANNEL I.

Marne R.

Meuse R.

ARDENNES

Moselle R.

Main R.

HARZ MTS.

ERZ MTS.

Prague

BOHEMIAN PLAIN

USHANT I.

BRITTANY PENINSULA

Paris

Seine R.

Vosges Mts.

BLACK FOREST

Danube R.

BOHEMIAN FOREST

Inn R.

Vienna

Budapest

CARPA

PLAIN OF FRANCE

Loire R.

Vienne R.

Saône R.

JURA MTS.

L. Constance

L. Balaton

PLAIN OF HUNGARY

Drave R.

Tisza R.

ATLANTIC OCEAN

BAY OF BISCAY

Bordeaux

Garonne R.

MASSIF CENTRAL

CÉVENNES

Rhône R.

Lyons

Mt. Blanc

L. Geneva

Adige R.

Save R.

TRANSYLVAN

IRON GA

WA

CAPE FINISTERRE

CANTABRIAN MTS.

PYRENEES

PLAIN OF LOMBARDY

Po R.

Trieste

ISTRIA

DALMATIAN ALPS

DINARIC ALPS

Belgrade

Morava R.

Vardar R.

Sofi

RH

IBERIAN PENINSULA

SPANISH

Douro R.

Ebro R.

LIGURIAN SEA

Arno R.

APENNINES

ADRIATIC SEA

BALKAN PENINSULA

PINDUS MTS.

Mt. Olympu

GUADARRAMA

Madrid

CORSICA

ELBA

Rome

Tiber R.

Lisbon

Tagus R.

PLATEAU

Guadiana R.

SIERRA MORENA

Guadalquivir R.

BALEARIC I.

MINORCA

MAJORCA

IVIZA

SARDINIA

ITALIAN PENINSULA

TYRRHENIAN SEA

Mt. Vesuvius

CORFU

IONIAN I.

IONIAN SEA

Athens

MOREAN PENINSULA

SIERRA NEVADA

CAPE TRAFALGAR

Strait of Gibraltar

Gibraltar

Algiers

Mt. Etna

SICILY

Strait of Messina

Tunis

PANTELLERIA

LITTLE ATLAS MOUNTAINS

Féz

MALTA

MEDITERRANEAN SEA

MIDDLE ATLAS MOUNTAINS

SAHARAN ATLAS MOUNTAINS

Tripoli

GULF OF SIDRA

GREAT ATLAS MOUNTAINS

ALGERIAN SAHARA

LIBY

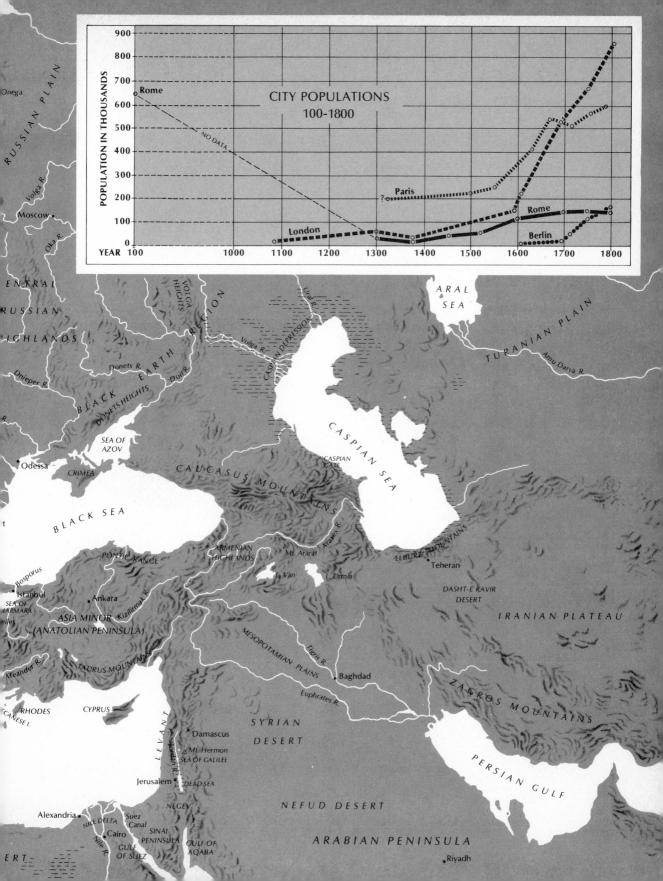

CITY POPULATIONS
100-1800

POPULATION IN THOUSANDS

900
800
700
600
500
400
300
200
100

Rome

NO DATA

Paris

London

Rome

Berlin

YEAR 100 1000 1100 1200 1300 1400 1500 1600 1700 1800

MORTIMER CHAMBERS / *University of California at Los Angeles*

RAYMOND GREW / *University of Michigan*

DAVID HERLIHY / *Harvard University*

THEODORE K. RABB / *Princeton University*

ISSER WOLOCH / *Columbia University*

ART ESSAYS BY H. W. JANSON / *New York University*

ADVISORY EDITOR / EUGENE RICE *Columbia University*
CONSULTANT / ALVIN BERNSTEIN *Cornell University*

THE WESTERN EXPERIENCE

VOLUME II · THE EARLY MODERN PERIOD

SECOND EDITION

ALFRED A. KNOPF NEW YORK

THIS IS A BORZOI BOOK
PUBLISHED BY ALFRED A. KNOPF, INC.

Second Edition
987654321
Copyright © 1974, 1979 by Alfred A. Knopf, Inc.

Library of Congress Cataloging in Publication Data

Main entry under title:
The Western experience
   CONTENTS: v. 1. Antiquity to the Middle Ages.
—v. 2. The early modern period.—v. 3. The modern era.
   Includes index.
   1. Civilization—History. 2. Civilization,
Occidental—History. I. Chambers, Mortimer.
CB59.W38 1978c   909   78-12132

ISBN: 0-394-32139-1 (v. 2)

Book Design by Dana Kasarsky

Cover illustration: Detail from *The Harvesters*, a painting by Pieter Brueghel, the Elder. The Metropolitan Museum of Art, Rogers Fund, 1919.

Map consultant: D. W. Meinig
Maps were executed by Jean Tremblay.

Manufactured in the United States of America

Men and women use their knowledge of the past in legitimately different and sometimes contradictory ways. Two ways especially have satisfied the needs of civilized peoples: the way of the artist and the way of the historian.

The artist, like the scientist and the philosopher, raids his cultural inheritance in order to make something new and personal. Untroubled by anachronism, he repossesses and reshapes only those ideas and images that serve his own work, that nourish his own sensibility, values, and obsessions. The past speaks to the artist, the scientist, and the philosopher in the present tense.

Historians are past-minded. They want to preserve in archives and libraries as complete a record of the past as possible and to transmit the sum of historical sources and knowledge intact to their successors. Sensitive to context and nuance, their professional concern is to avoid anachronism, that is, to understand the past as it really was, in its own terms rather than in present-day terms. They try not to manipulate or distort it but to make it live again in its uniqueness.

The relation of past to present is paradoxical because human beings are both myth makers and truth seekers. As individuals we must be free to use the past as we wish—to plunder it unhistorically, to misunderstand it creatively. This liberty is our guarantee of innovation, our assurance that the past will continue to be used in the interests of the future. As historians, however, our obligation and responsibility are different. We have the duty to correct misconceptions about the past, even fruitful ones, and to expose the myths created by misunderstanding or malice.

The reason for this is not simply that truth is superior to falsehood—as niggling accuracy is to high-minded nonsense—although this is the best reason. We guide our most ordinary thought and action by past experience. The authenticity of what we think and do depends on the accuracy with which our memories reproduce that experience. In the same way the authenticity of our collective lives and the quality of our culture rest on the extent and truthfulness of our memory of history. If our historical memory is defective, it serves the present badly and impoverishes the future.

Sound historical knowledge is useful to us because it makes past experience accessible for our instruction and delight, because it guards us from temporal provincialism and ethnocentrism, and because it helps us understand ourselves better.

Our collective memory is a museum of the mind. Museums preserve the material artifacts of past generations; histories are records of alternatives. Human beings have located the highest good by turns in wisdom, virtue, pleasure, utility, and power, to give a far from exhaustive list. They have worshiped one god, two gods, three gods, many gods, and they have invented a bewildering variety of magical, metaphysical, religious, and scientific hypotheses to

PAST & PRESENT

explain the human condition and the end and purpose of human life. They have considered desirable or necessary alternative kinds of rule—by one, by the wellborn few, by the rich, by priests, by a majority of all; alternative modes of production—craft, capitalist, and socialist; alternative patterns of social stratification—by birth or occupation, education or income; alternative systems of dominance and subjection—slavery, serfdom, or the free exchange of labor for wages. As skeptics of every age have pointed out, nothing is so characteristic of human life as its diversity.

So great is the diversity of mankind and so heterogeneous the possible lessons of the past that we cannot plausibly expect historical precedent to solve our personal or public difficulties in any direct or simple way. If we could the conduct of our affairs would have improved long ago. On the other hand it is precisely the wealth of alternatives preserved in our memory of things said and done that enables us to experiment and suggests the possibility and directions of change. Where there are no alternatives, there can be no choice.

The study of history is a liberating discipline because it offers us, choosing in the present, an ever broadening spectrum of alternatives. This is important. Most people—the exceptions are geniuses, rare in any age—find only what they have been sensitized to see. Transmitting knowledge of past problems and solutions performs the absolutely critical function of alerting each successive generation to a maximum number of possibilities. A clean slate is a wholly unsatisfactory foundation for a better world, and those who wish to free themselves from the past enslave themselves to the present.

The heresies of present-mindedness are temporal provincialism and ethnocentrism. Temporal provincialism is a vulgar conviction that current ways of doing things are normative. It confers a timeless validity on transient contemporary taste. Unlike the present-mindedness of artists, philosophers, and scientists, which manipulates knowledge of the past in the interest of innovation, it is blinkered by ignorance. Ethnocentrism is a cultural bias, the notion (in our own case) that Western civilization is the proper yardstick for judging all others. Knowledge of other cultures and of our own remoter past points up the relativity of the present, induces a healthy skepticism about current arrangements and achievements, and exposes the status quo to continuous critical reappraisal.

Socializing the young, defining the roles of men and women, and preparing for death are permanent human problems. It is narrowing to imagine that our ways of meeting them are the only ones or the best. Knowledge of other ways allows us to reexamine our own with something of the dispassion of foreigners. The hero of one of Voltaire's novels is a Huron Indian traveling in eighteenth-century France. His innocent astonishment at the peculiar customs of the French forced Voltaire's readers to look at themselves with heightened awareness. Not the least benefit of historical study is to make Voltairian Hurons of us all.

History is useful to us in short because it helps us understand ourselves better. By comparing our present behavior and institutions with those of earlier ages and other peoples, we learn more of their real character. Listening to Indian music sharpens our ear to what is distinctive in Western music. A study of feudalism, a system of government in which the exercise of public powers like taxation and the administration of justice rests on the ownership of private property, clarifies the very different nature of the modern sovereign state. Only a comparative investigation of how painters in various periods and cultures have met the problems of representing a three-dimensional world on a two-dimensional surface will turn up the fact that true geometrical perspective is to be found only in Western art between its discovery in Florence in the early fifteenth-century and its abandonment in the first decade of our own. Such a study will show that Western perspective was not the end of a long historical progression, a perfection toward which painters in other times and places worked with greater or lesser success, but rather a stylistic peculiarity of a particular culture during a well-defined period of its history—an alternative open to twentieth-century artists but deliberately rejected by most of them. The same comparative method, by isolating causal variables absent in the ancient Mediterranean world and East Asia but present in late medieval and early modern Europe, offers the best hope of explaining why perspective was unique to Western civilization for roughly five hundred years.

Constantly changing criteria of relevance determine what successive generations will select from the past to illuminate the present. Historians share with everyone else the mental structures of their time and place.   However free they may be of temporal provincialism, however discriminatingly past-minded, they ask questions suggested by the preoccupations of their own day. This does not mean that every man is his own historian or that historical knowledge lacks a solid foundation but rather that every new question gets a new answer. Historical writing is always in flux because historians ask their sources questions newly shaped by changing social and cultural needs.

The questions many historians have been asking for the past twenty years or so have created a distinctive kind of historical writing. Contemporary historians commonly call it "social history." The name is not new; and the impulse behind it goes back a long way too. In antiquity and from the Renaissance until far into the nineteenth century, almost everybody took it for granted that the proper subject of history was past politics, diplomacy, and war. Only gradually were permanently successful efforts made to broaden the subject matter of history to include law, religion, constitutional and economic change, and intellectual and cultural developments. The field of social history and its name emerged at the same time.

But what social history *was* remained vague. It could mean the study of ideas about society. Some narrowed the meaning of "social" to "working class," and social history became the history of labor movements. For others its subject matter was daily life: daily life in ancient Rome, or in Renaissance Florence, or old New York—studies of dress, diet, pots, and pans, salted with anecdote and picturesque detail of manners. Or it was just plain history with the politics left out.

Today historians have a broader notion of social history. They think that the proper object of study is society in all its manifestations. They do not define social history by what it excludes. It can include anything. It certainly includes politics and war. Its defining characteristics are rather ones of emphasis, method, and point of view.

Its sources are anything that records the pulse of human life: pots, coins, paintings, fiscal records, novels and plays, diplomatic correspondence and private letters, account books, publishers' lists, political and theological tracts, and government reports. It tends to be analytical rather than narrative and to emphasize long views. It borrows from the social sciences (as they borrow from it)—terms and ideas such as "growth" and "modernization," categories of stratification, types of family structure —and makes sophisticated use of the techniques and theories of statisticians, demographers, and psychologists. Today's historians are sensitive to the fact that most historical writing has been about the tiny minority of the powerful and rich (they, after all, have left behind the fullest and most accessible records of their activities). The new social history is as mindful of popular culture as it is of the culture of the elite, as interested in the family as in the state, in patronage as in diplomacy, in plague and famine as in political theory. It tries to recover as much as it can of the living experience of ordinary people, to look at a society from the bottom up as well as from the top down.

Another characteristic of today's history is quantification. Counting is important because it helps us test hypotheses and verify generalizations. Even the best historical writing is peppered with words like "typical," "representative," and "widespread." These are implicitly quantitative generalizations. What even a simple quantitative technique enables us to do is to reveal the merits or defects of such impressionistic generalizations by giving them a statistical base. There are problems with quantification, of course, the main one being that before the seventeenth century quantifiable data are scarce; indeed, only from the nineteenth century on can we easily gather samples large enough to make quantitative analysis effective. It is well to remember too that although quantification can often settle what the facts are, it does not often tell us what they mean. Historians must still interpret the results of calculation. Baldly put, though, the message is this: If you wish to generalize about a group or class, it is better to count than to guess; and if you can't count, admit you are guessing (mind you, some guesses are more educated than others).

Equally characteristic of today's history is the way it measures historical time. Since it is typically a study of social and cultural processes, more often a history of structures than a history of events (without abandoning narrative where it is necessary or appropriate), a history of problems rather than of presidencies or reigns, it emphasizes the long haul, moving at the slower tempo of long-term trends in production and consumption, the expansion and contraction of population, or the displacement of one class by another at the levers of political and economic command. Its periodization therefore tends to be different from the familiar one dictated by traditional political and military history. At one level of abstraction, indeed, human history divides plausibly into three periods only: the 100,000 years of prehistory from the emergence of *homo sapiens* to the appearance of the first civilizations in the ancient Near East, when a planned increase in agricultural productivity freed creative energies from the need to supply daily food; the very brief, very recent period initiated by the modern technological and economic revolution at the end of the eighteenth century; and in between virtually the whole of human history, properly speaking, from Sumer and Egypt to the industrial and French revolutions, the many centuries during which the texture of ordinary people's experience remained extraordinarily stable and the rate and character of change extraordinarily slow—slow, that is, by the hectic standards of the modern period.

A minor consequence of living in a rapidly changing society and world is that each generation exaggerates the novelty of what it does. Historians are no exception. The best current work, which seems to us so fresh, its explanations so satisfactory, its subject matter so relevant to our present needs and tastes, its periodization so reflective of what is really important in the Western experience, will no doubt seem to our successors as partial as much of the history written by earlier generations seems to us. In the meantime, though, history speaks directly to us now from the pages that follow.

Eugene Rice

11 / THE WEST IN TRANSITION:
ECONOMY AND INSTITUTIONS 333
   I Economic Depression and Recovery 334
   II Popular Unrest 345
   III The Governments of Europe 348
   IV The Papacy 359

12 / THE WEST IN TRANSITION:
THE RENAISSANCE 367
   I Society and Culture in Italy 368
   II The Culture of the North 379
   III Religious Thought and Piety 383
   IV The Fine Arts 388
   V Science and the Renaissance 393

13 / OVERSEAS EXPANSION AND
NEW POLITICS 397
   I Exploration and Its Impact 398
   II The "New Monarchies" 408
   III The Splintered States 424
   IV The New Statecraft 427

14 / REFORMATIONS IN RELIGION 433
   I Dissent and Piety 434
   II The Northern Humanists 440
   III The Lutheran Reformation 443
   IV The Growth of Protestantism 449
   V The Catholic Revival 454

15 / A CENTURY OF WAR
AND REVOLT 461
   I Warfare 462
   II Revolts 478

16 / CULTURE AND SOCIETY IN THE
AGE OF THE SCIENTIFIC
REVOLUTION 505

CONTENTS

I The Scientific Revolution 507
II Literature and the Arts 523
III Social Patterns and Popular Culture 533

17 / THE TRIUMPH OF ARISTOCRATS AND KINGS 547
I The Absolute Monarchies 548
II The Anti-Absolutists 565
III The Culture of the Age 573

18 / ABSOLUTISM AND EMPIRE 585
I The State System 587
II Absolutism in Central Europe 592
III The Maritime Powers 598
IV The Midcentury Conflagration 608

19 / THE AGE OF ENLIGHTENMENT 615
I The Enlightenment 616
II Eighteenth-Century Cultures 624
III The Enlightenment and the State 636

20 / REVOLUTIONS OF THE EIGHTEENTH CENTURY 645
I The Industrial System 646
II Economics and Demography 652
III Agriculture 656
IV The New Shape of Industry 659
V Constitutional Conflicts 665
VI The French Revolution 671

21 / THE TERROR AND NAPOLEON 685
I The Second Revolution 686
II From Robespierre to Bonaparte 700
III The Napoleonic Imperium 709

INDEX *follows page 724*

COLOR ILLUSTRATION SOURCES follows Index

ART ESSAYS

The Image of Man in Renaissance Art   follows page 408
The Image of Man in 17th and 18th Century Art   follows page 612

MAPS

Physiography of Europe	*ii – iii*
The Black Death	336
The Hundred Years' War	353
Italy 1454	360
The Great Schism 1378–1417	363
Exploration and Conquest in the 15th and 16th Centuries	402
The Growth of Cities in the 16th Century	405
France in the 15th and 16th Centuries	414
The Empire of Charles V	422
Religious Tensions 1560	458
The Netherlands 1579–1609	469
Areas of Fighting 1618–1660	473
Territorial Change 1648–1661	476
Centers of Music 1500–1800	530
Cities of Europe in 1700	534
Speed of News Traveling to Venice	542
The Wars of Louis XIV	553
The Austrian Empire 1657–1718	558
Conflict in the Baltic Area 1660–1721	572
The Expansion of Russia and the Partition of Poland	590
Prussia 1721–1772 and the Hapsburg Empire	597
Overseas Possessions 1713	605
Anglo-French Rivalry in North America and the Caribbean 1754–1763	611
France: Provinces and Regions Before 1789	678
France: Revolutionary Departments After 1789	679
The Revolutionary Republics 1792–1799	706
Europe 1810	717

THE WESTERN EXPERIENCE
VOLUME II

SECOND EDITION

ELEVEN

THE WEST IN TRANSITION: ECONOMY AND INSTITUTIONS

Shadows covered wide areas of European life in the fourteenth and fifteenth centuries. The vigorous expansion into bordering areas which had marked European history since the eleventh century came to an end. The Christian West fought to halt the expansion of the Muslim Turks but did not completely succeed. Plague, famine, and recurrent wars decimated populations and snuffed out their former prosperity. The papacy and feudal government struggled against mounting institutional chaos. Powerful mystical and heretical movements and new critical currents in Scholasticism rocked the established religious and philosophical equilibrium of the thirteenth century.

But for all these signs of crisis the fourteenth and fifteenth centuries were not merely an age of breakdown. The partial failure both of the medieval economy and government and of the established systems of thought and value facilitated change and impelled men to repair their institutions and renew their culture. As Chapter 12 will show, there were vigorous developments in philosophy, religious thought, vernacular and Latin literature, and the fine arts. By the late fifteenth century the outlines of a new equilibrium were emerging. In 1500 Europeans doubtlessly remained fewer in numbers than they had been in 1300. But they also had developed a more productive economy and a more powerful technology than they had possessed two hundred years before. These achievements also equipped Europeans for their great expansion throughout the world in the early modern epoch.

A traditional interpretation of the fourteenth and fifteenth centuries has made them years of renewal, rebirth: the Renaissance. In another interpretation, now equally traditional and reputable, the fourteenth and fifteenth centuries were the "autumn of the Middle Ages," and the somber theme of their history is the decline and death of a formerly great civilization. Today, with our own vastly enlarged fund of information, it is permissible and indeed necessary to consider the age both an autumn and a renaissance. The study of any past epoch requires an effort to balance the work of death and renewal. In few periods of history do death and renewal confront each other so dramatically as in the years between 1300 and 1500.

1. ECONOMIC DEPRESSION AND RECOVERY

The plagues and famines which struck European society in the fourteenth and fifteenth centuries profoundly affected economic life. Initially, they disrupted the established patterns of producing and exchanging goods and led directly to what some scholars now call "the economic depression of the Renaissance." But the effects of this disruption were not entirely negative; in reorganizing the economy under greatly changed demographic conditions, Europeans were also able to make certain significant advances in the efficiency of economic production. To understand this paradox we must first examine how these disasters affected the population of Europe.

DEMOGRAPHIC CATASTROPHE

Scholars have uncovered some censuses and other statistical records which for the first time give an insight into the size and structure of the European population. Nearly all of these records were drawn up for purposes of taxation and they therefore usually survey only limited geographical areas—a city or a province —and are rarely complete. But although they give us no reliable figures for total population, they still enable us to discern with considerable confidence how it was changing.

Almost every region of Europe from which we possess such records shows an appalling decline of population between approximately 1300 and 1450. For example, the population of Provence in southern France seems to have been between 350,000 and 400,000 at about 1310; a century later it had shrunk to something between one-third and one-half its earlier size, and only after 1470 did it again begin to increase. The population of the city and countryside of Pistoia, near Florence, fell from about 43,000 in the middle of the thirteenth century to 14,000 by the early fifteenth. The neighboring city and countryside of San Gimignano had approximately 13,000 residents in 1332 and only 3,100 in 1428; the region still has not regained its maximum medieval size.

For the larger kingdoms of Europe the figures are less reliable, but they cannot be too far from the mark. England had a population of about 3.7 million in 1347 and 2.2 million by 1377.[1] By 1550 it was no larger a nation than it had been in the thirteenth century. France by 1328 may have reached 15 million; it too

was not again to attain its peak medieval size for several hundred years. In Germany, of some 170,000 inhabited localities named in sources antedating 1300, about 40,000 disappeared during the fourteenth and fifteenth centuries. Since many of the surviving towns were simultaneously shrinking in size, the population loss could only have been greater.

Certain favored regions of Europe, however—the fertile lands surrounding Paris or the Po valley—continually attracted settlers and maintained fairly stable populations, but they owed their good fortune more to immigration than to high birth rates or immunity from disease. It can safely be estimated that all of Europe in 1450 had no more than one-half, and probably only one-third, of the population it had had in the thirteenth century.

Pestilence

The great plague of the fourteenth century provides the most evident, although perhaps not the most satisfactory, explanation for these huge human losses. In 1347 a merchant ship sailing from Tana in the Crimea to Messina in Sicily seems to have carried infected rats. A plague broke out at Messina and from there it spread throughout Europe (see Map 11.1).

This Black Death was not so much an epidemic as a pandemic, striking an entire continent. It may not have been the first pandemic in European history (sparse sources mention a general plague from 747 to 750), but it was the first in perhaps six hundred years, and it struck repeatedly during the century. A city was lucky if more than ten years went by without an onslaught; in some part of Europe, in

---

[1] The estimate is based on the pioneering researches of J. C. Russell, *British Medieval Population*, 1948, but there is no national census for England in the period immediately preceding the Black Death and the figure of 3.7 million had to be extrapolated on the basis of presumed mortality rates. Recently, M. M. Postan, in the *Cambridge Economic History*, I, 562, stated that

the preplague population may have been nearer 7 million and that "to most historians abreast of most recent researches the higher estimates may well appear to be more consistent with the economic and social conditions of rural England at the end of the thirteenth century. . . ."

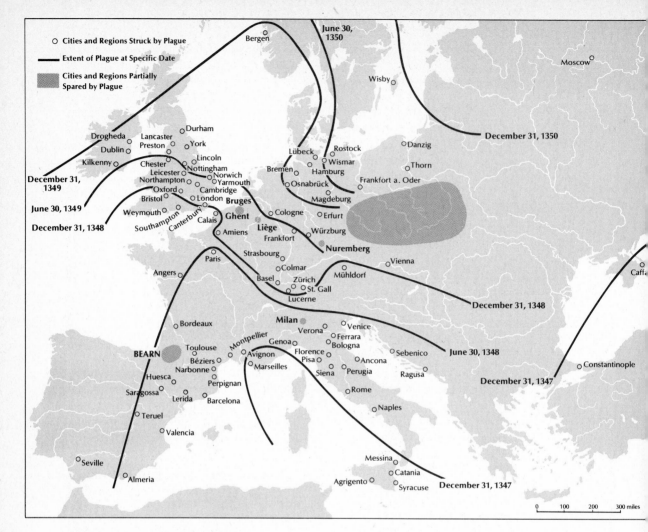

MAP 11.1: THE BLACK DEATH

[Adapted from Carpentier, E., "Autour de la peste noire; famines et épidémies dans l'histoire du XIVe siècle," in *Annales: Economies, Sociétés, Civilisations*, XVII (1962). Used by permission.]

almost every year, the plague was raging. Barcelona and its province of Catalonia, for example, lived through this record of misery in the fourteenth century: famine, 1333; plague, 1347 and 1351; famine, 1358 and 1359; plague, 1362, 1363, 1371, and 1397.

Some of the horror of the plague can be glimpsed in this account by an anonymous cleric who visited the French city of Avignon in 1348:

To put the matter shortly, one-half, or more than a half, of the people at Avignon are already dead. Within the walls of the city there are now more than 7,000 houses shut up; in these no one is living, and all who have inhabited them are departed; the suburbs hardly contain any people at all. . . .

The like account I can give of all the cities and towns of Provence. Already the sickness has crossed the Rhone, and ravaged many cities and villages as far as Toulouse, and it ever increases in violence as it proceeds. On account of this great mortality there is such a fear of death that people do not dare even to speak with anyone whose relative has died, because it is frequently remarked that in a family where one dies nearly all the relations follow him, and this is commonly believed among the people.[2]

Most historians identify the Black Death as the bubonic plague, but they find it difficult to explain how this disease could have spread so rapidly and killed so many, since bubonic plague is more truly a disease of rats and small mammals than of men. If bubonic plague is to spread to a human, a flea must bite an infected rat, pick up the infection, and carry it to a human host through a bite. The infection causes the lymphatic glands to swell but recovery is not uncommon. Only if the infection travels through the bloodstream to the lungs, causing pneumonia, can the disease be spread directly from person to person. The real killer in the fourteenth century seems to have been a pneumonic plague, which infects the lungs directly; it probably was spread through coughing and was almost always fatal.

In spite of the virulence of pneumonic plague it is hard to believe that medical factors alone can explain the awesome mortalities. After all, Europeans had maintained close contact with the East, where the plague had been endemic, since the eleventh century, but not until 1347 and 1348 did it make serious inroads in Europe. In addition, pneumonic plague itself is a disease of the winter months, but the plagues of the fourteenth century characteristically raged during the summer and dissipated with the cooler weather of autumn. Some scholars consider that the weather of the age—it seems to have been unusually cool and humid—somehow favored the disease. Others argue that

acute, widespread malnutrition had severely debilitated the population and lowered resistance to all kinds of infections.

Hunger

A second cause of the dramatic fall of population was hunger. Famines frequently scourged the land; and even if they were less lethal than the plague in their initial onslaught, they were likely to persist for several years. In 1315, 1316, and 1317 a severe famine raged in the north of Europe; in 1339 and 1340 another struck the south. The starving people ate not only their reserves of grain but most of the seed set aside for planting. Only a remarkably good harvest could compensate for the loss of grain by providing both immediate sustenance and seed for future planting in satisfactory quantities.

Why was hunger so rampant in the early fourteenth century? Some historians now locate the root of trouble in the sheer number of people the lands had to support by 1300. The medieval population, they say, had been growing rapidly since about 1000, and by 1300 Europe was becoming the victim of its own success. Parts of the Continent were crowded, even glutted, with people. The county of Beaumont-le-Roger in Normandy, for example, had a population in the early fourteenth century not much below the number it was supporting in the early twentieth century. Thousands, millions even, had to be fed without the aid of chemical fertilizers, power tools, and fast transport. Masses of people had come to depend for their livelihood upon unrewarding soils. Even in good years they were surviving on the slim and uncertain margins of existence; a slightly reduced harvest during any one year took on the dimensions of a major famine. Through hunger, malnutrition, and plague the hand of death was correcting the ledgers of life, balancing the numbers of people and the resources which supported them.

---

[2] *Breve Chronicon clerici anonymi,* quoted in Francis Aidan Gasquet, *The Black Death of 1348 and 1349,* 1908, p. 46.

What effects did the fall in population have on the economy of Europe? Initially, the losses disrupted production. According to the chroniclers, survivors of the plague frequently gave up toiling in the fields or working in shops; presumably, they saw no point in working for the future when the future was so uncertain. But, in the long run, the results were not altogether negative. In agriculture, for example, the contraction of the population enabled the survivors to concentrate their efforts on the better soils. Moreover, in both agriculture and industry the shortage of laborers was a challenge to landlords and entrepreneurs to save costs either by adopting productive routines less demanding of manpower or by increased investment in labor-saving devices. Thus the decline in population eventually taught Europeans to work more efficiently through more rational productive routines and greater capital investment.

Agriculture

Perhaps the best indication of the forces working upon the European economy comes from the history of prices. The evidence is scattered and rarely precise, but it is good enough to reveal roughly similar patterns in price movements all over Europe. Most agricultural products—cereals, wine, beer, oil, and meat—shot up immediately after the Black Death and stayed high until the last decades of the fourteenth century. High food prices in a period of contracting population seem certain evidence that production was falling even more rapidly than the number of consumers.

The beginnings of an agricultural recovery become evident in the early fifteenth century. With a diminished number of Europeans to be fed, the demand for cereals, the cultivation of which dominated agriculture in the earlier centuries, lessened perceptibly and their prices declined; with fewer available workers, the cost of labor pushed steadily upward. Landlords had to compete with one another to attract scarce tenants to their lands and did so by offering lower rents and favorable terms of tenancy. The upward movement of wages and the downward price of cereals led to a concentration on those commodities which would command a better price in the market or were less expensive to produce. Better wages in both town and countryside enabled the population to consume a more varied and more expensive diet. While the price of wheat fell, wine, beer, oil, butter, cheese, meat, fruit, and other relatively expensive foods remained high, reflecting a strong market demand.

One branch of agriculture which enjoyed a remarkable period of growth in the fifteenth century was sheep raising. Labor costs were low, since a few shepherds could guard thousands of sheep, and the price for wool, skins, mutton, and cheese remained high. In England many landlords fenced large fields, converting them from plowland into sheep pastures and expelling the peasants or small herders who had formerly lived on them; this process, called enclosure, continued into the sixteenth century and played an important role in the economic and social history of Tudor England.

By the middle of the fifteenth century, agricultural prices tended to stabilize, and this suggests a more dependable production. Farms enjoyed the advantages of greater size, better location on more profitable soil, and greater capital investments in tools and animals. Agriculture was now considerably diversified, benefiting the soil, lowering the risk of famine through the failure of a single staple crop, and providing more nourishment for the people. Europeans were consuming a healthier diet by the middle of the fifteenth century than had their ancestors two hundred years before.

Industry and Trade

The movement of prices created serious problems for the entrepreneurs within the cities. As the labor force contracted, wages in most towns surged upward and commonly reached levels two, three, and even four times higher than they had been before 1348. Although the prices of manufactured commodities also increased, they did not rise as much as wages, and this worked to reduce profit margins. To offset these unfavorable tendencies, the entrepreneurs sought government intervention. In various enactments from 1349 to 1351, England, France, Aragon, Castile, and other governments tried to fix prices and wages at levels favorable to employers. The English Parliament in the Statute of Laborers, a policy typical of the age, forbade employers to pay more than the customary wages and required laborers to accept jobs at those wages. These early experiments in a controlled economy failed. The price and wage ceilings set by law seem to have had little perceptible influence on actual prices.

A related problem troubled the business climate. Competition grew as population fell and markets contracted. Entrepreneurs tried to protect themselves by creating restricted markets and establishing monopolies. Guilds limited their membership, and some admitted only the sons of established masters. Cities too imposed heavy restrictions on the importation of foreign manufactures.

Probably the best example of the monopoly spirit is the association of north German trading cities, the Hanseatic League. The league was a defensive association formed in the fourteenth century to promote German interests and exclude foreigners from the Baltic trade. The cities initially sought this mutual protection because the emperor was too weak to defend their interests. At its height the Hanseatic League included about seventy or eighty cities under the leadership of Bremen, Cologne, Hamburg, and especially Lübeck. Maintaining its own treasury and fleet, the league supervised commercial exchange, policed the waters of the Baltic Sea, and negotiated with foreign princes. By the late fifteenth century, however, the

The German towns of the Hanseatic League dominated the trade of northern Europe in the fourteenth and fifteenth centuries. The picture shows a bustling port of the period. (Photo: Culver Pictures, Inc.)

league had begun to decline. It failed to meet the growing threat of the Dutch, who were then vigorously competing for leadership in northern commerce. The Hanseatic League was never formally abolished; it continued to meet at lengthening intervals until 1669.

THE FORCES OF RECOVERY

Attempts to raise the efficiency of workers proved to be far more effective than wage and trade regulation in laying the basis for recovery. Employers were able to counteract high wages by adopting more rational production procedures and substituting capital for labor, that is, providing the worker with better tools. Although largely inspired by hard times and labor shortages, most of the technical advances of the fourteenth and fifteenth centuries enabled the worker to practice his trade more efficiently and eventually helped make Europe a richer community.

Metallurgy

Mining and metallurgy benefited from a series of inventions after 1460 that lowered the cost of metals and extended their use in European life. Better techniques of digging, shoring, ventilating, and draining allowed mine shafts to be sunk several hundred feet into the earth, permitting the large-scale exploitation of the deep, rich mineral deposits of Central Europe. Some historians estimate (on slim evidence, to be sure) that the output from the mines of Central Europe—Hungary, the Tyrol, Bohemia, and Saxony—grew as much as five times between 1460 and 1530. During this period miners in Saxony discovered a method of extracting pure silver from the lead alloy in which it was often found (the invention was of major importance for the later, massive development of silver mines in America). Larger furnaces came into use, and huge bellows and triphammers, driven by water power, aided the smelting and working of metals. Simultaneously, the masters of the trade were acquiring a new precision in the difficult art of casting.

By the late fifteenth century, European mines were providing an abundance of silver bullion for coinage. Money became more plentiful, and this stimulated the economy. Beginnings were also laid for the exploitation of the rich coal deposits of the European north. Expanding iron production meant more and stronger pumps, gears and machine parts, tools, and ironwares; such products found wide application in construction work and shipbuilding. Moreover, skill in metalworking contributed to two other inventions: firearms and movable metal type.

Firearms

Men were constantly trying to improve the arts of war in the bellicose Middle Ages; and one weapon, or family of weapons, they sought was a device which would hurl projectiles with great force and accuracy. We do not know how Europeans first learned that certain mixtures of carbon, sulfur, and saltpeter burn with explosive force and could be used to hurl boulders at an enemy, but we do know that cannons were used in the fourteenth century during the Hundred Years' War. Their effect seems to have been chiefly psychological: the thunderous roar merely by frightening the enemy's horses probably did more damage than the inevitably misdirected shots. Still, a breakthrough had been made, and cannons gained in military importance. Their development depended primarily on stronger, more precise casting and on proper granulation of the powder to ensure that the charge would burn at the right speed so that its full force pushed the projectile. With firearms fewer soldiers could fight more effectively; capital, in the

Leonardo da Vinci's concept of a cannon foundry had its ancestry in the Chinese and Byzantine applications of rapid chemical combustion to the weapons of war. The Chinese had used fireworks for centuries; the Byzantines had concocted a "Greek fire" which they sprayed on enemy ships with devastating effect. (Photo: Royal Collection, Windsor Castle)

form of an efficient though expensive tool, was again being substituted for labor.

Printing

The extension of literacy among laymen and the greater reliance of governments and businesses upon records created a demand for a cheap method of reproducing the written word. One important advance was the replacement of expensive parchment by paper, which had originated in the East. But even so, the scribe and copier worked slowly and, like all workmen, were commanding an increased salary. As a solution, printing was first tried by stamping paper or parchment with woodcuts, which were inked blocks with letters or designs carved on them. But the "block books" produced in this fashion represented only a small advance over handwriting, for a separate woodcut had to be carved for each page.

By the middle of the fifteenth century several masters were on the verge of perfecting the technique of printing with movable metal type. The first man to prove the practicability of the new art was Johannes Gutenberg of Mainz, a former jeweler and stonecutter. Gutenberg devised an alloy of lead, tin, and antimony which would melt at a low temperature, cast well in the die, and be durable in the press; this alloy is still the basis of the printer's art. His Bible, printed in 1455, is the first major work reproduced through printing.

In spite of Gutenberg's efforts to keep the technique a secret it spread rapidly. Before 1500 some 250 European cities had acquired presses. German masters held an early leadership, but Italians soon challenged their preeminence. The Venetian printer Aldus Manutius published works, notably editions of the Greek and Latin classics, which are minor masterpieces of scholarship and grace. Manutius and his fellow Italian masters rejected the elaborate Gothic typeface used in the north and developed their own, modeled on the clear script

A page from Johannes Gutenberg's Bible marks one of the most significant technical and cultural advances of the fifteenth century: printing with movable type, a process that made possible a wider dissemination of literature and thought. (Photo: E. Harold Hugo)

they found in their oldest manuscripts. They wrongly believed that it was the style of writing used in ancient Rome; they were in fact imitating the Carolingian minuscule.

The immediate effect of the printing press was to multiply the output and cut the price of books, which meant that the pleasures of reading were no longer the monopoly of the rich and the clergy but were available to a much broader range of the population. Printing also helped to standardize texts, contributing fundamentally to the advance of scholarship, science, and technology.

Printing also could spread new ideas with unprecedented speed and impact, a fact that was appreciated only slowly. The Protestant reformers of the sixteenth century were really the first to take advantage of the potential of printing for propaganda, and Catholics soon followed.

Navigation

Men as well as ideas began to travel more easily in the fourteenth and fifteenth centuries Before about 1325 there was still no regular sea traffic between northern and southern Europe by way of the Atlantic, but it grew rapidly thereafter. In navigation the substitution of capital for labor primarily meant the introduction of larger ships, which could carry more cargo with relatively smaller crews. The large ships were safer at sea; they could sail in periods of uncertain weather, when smaller vessels had to stay in port. They could also remain at sea longer and did not have to sail close to the coastline in order to replenish their supplies. Their voyages between ports could be more direct and therefore speedier.

The larger vessels required more sophisticated means of steering and navigation. Before 1300, ships were turned by trailing an oar over the side. The control provided by this method was poor, especially for sailing ships, which needed an efficient means of steering to take advantage of shifting winds. Sometime during the fourteenth century the stern rudder was developed, enabling the captain to tack effectively against the wind and control his ship more closely entering or leaving ports. Voyages thus were rendered quicker and safer, and the costs of maritime transport declined.

Ocean navigation also required a reliable means for estimating course and position, and here notable progress had been made, especially in the late thirteenth century. Scholars at the court of King Alfonso X of Castile compiled the Alfonsine Tables, which showed with unprecedented accuracy the position and movements of the heavenly bodies. Using such tables along with an astrolabe, captains could shoot the sun or stars and calculate their latitude, or position on a north-south coordinate.[3]

The compass, the origin of which is unclear, was commonly used on Mediterranean ships by at least the thirteenth century. By 1300, and undoubtedly for some decades before, Mediterranean navigators sailed with the aid of maps remarkable for their accuracy. Navigators were further aided by portolani, or port descriptions, which gave an account of harbors and coastlines and pinpointed hazards. All these technical developments gave European mariners a mastery of the Atlantic coastal waters and helped prepare the way for the voyages of discovery in the fifteenth century.

---

[3] Ships could not tell their longitude, or position on an east-west coordinate, until they could carry accurate clocks, which could in turn tell the time of a basic reference meridian (such as that of Greenwich, England) and be compared with the ship's time. Galileo's discovery of the laws of the pendulum made possible the first really accurate mechanical clocks, but they could not function aboard a swaying ship. Not until the eighteenth century were the first accurate "chronometers," or shipboard clocks, developed. Until then navigators such as Columbus who sailed across the Atlantic had no precise idea how far they were traveling.

Business Institutions

The bad times of the fourteenth century also stimulated the development of more efficient business procedures. The mercantile houses in the late fourteenth and fifteenth centuries were considerably smaller in size than those of the thirteenth century, but were more flexible in their structure. The Medici bank of Florence, which functioned from 1397 until 1498, offers a particularly clear example of fifteenth-century business organization. It was not a single monolithic structure; rather, it was founded upon separate partnerships, by which its various branches were established at Florence, Venice, Rome, Avignon, Bruges, and London. Central control and unified management were ensured, since the senior partners—members of the Medici family—were the same in all the contracts; but the branches had autonomy and, most important, the collapse of one did not threaten them all. One scholar has compared this system of interlocked partnerships to a modern holding company.

Banking operations also grew more sophisticated. By the late fourteenth century, "book transfers" had become commonplace; that is, one depositor could pay a debt to another without actually using coin by ordering the bank to transfer credit from his own account to his creditor's. At first the depositor had to give this order orally, but by 1400 such an order was commonly written, making it one of the immediate ancestors of the modern check.

Accounting methods also improved. The most notable development was the adoption of double-entry bookkeeping, which makes arithmetical errors immediately evident and gives a clear picture of the financial position of a commercial enterprise. Although known in the ancient world, double-entry bookkeeping was not widely practiced in the West until the fourteenth century. In this as in other business practices the lands of southern Europe, especially Italy, were precociously advanced, but their accounting techniques eventually spread to the rest of Europe.

Another financial innovation was the development of a system of maritime insurance, without which investors would have been highly reluctant to risk their money on expensive vessels. There are references to the practice of insuring ships in the major Italian ports as early as 1318. In these first insurance contracts the broker bought the ship and cargo at the port of embarkation and agreed to sell them back at a higher price once the ship reached its destination. If the ship sank en route, it was legally the broker's and he assumed the loss. In the course of the fourteenth century the leading companies of Florence, actively interested in providing insurance to shippers, abandoned the clumsy device of conditional sales and wrote explicit and open insurance contracts. By 1400 maritime insurance had become a regular item of the shipping business. It was to play a major role in the opening of the Atlantic.

Insurance for land transport developed a half-century later and never was intensively practiced. The first examples of life insurance contracts come from fifteenth-century Italy and were limited to particular periods (the duration of a voyage) or particular persons (a wife during pregnancy). But without actuarial tables life insurance of this sort was far more a gamble than a business.

The Economy in the Late Fifteenth Century

In the last half of the fifteenth century Europe had fairly well recovered from the economic blows of a hundred years before, and the revived economy differed greatly from what it had formerly been. Increased diversification, capitalization, and rationalization aided production and enterprise in both countryside and city. Europe in 1500 was certainly a much

smaller community than it had been in 1300. Possibly, too, the gross product of its economy may not have equaled the output of the best years of the thirteenth century. But the population ultimately had fallen more drastically than production. After a century of difficult readjustment Europe emerged more productive and richer than it had been at any earlier time in its history.

II. POPULAR UNREST

The demographic collapse and economic troubles of the fourteenth century deeply disturbed the social peace of Europe. European society

This illustration from a printed Italian handbook, which gives instructions to merchants and is dated ca. 1496, shows the interior of a bank or counting house. (Photo: New York Public Library/Picture Collection)

had been remarkably stable and mostly peaceful from the early Middle Ages until approximately 1300, and the chronicles have preserved few notices of social uprisings or class warfare. The fourteenth and fifteenth centuries, however, witness numerous revolts of peasants and artisans against what they believed to be oppression by the propertied classes.

RURAL REVOLTS

One of the most spectacular of the fourteenth-century rural uprisings was the English Peasants' War of 1381. Both the policies of the royal government and the practices of the great landlords angered the peasants. As mentioned earlier, the royal government through the Statute of Laborers (1351) sought to freeze wages and keep the workers bound to their jobs. Although this policy had little practical success, the mere effort to implement it aggravated social tensions, especially in the countryside, where it would have imposed a kind of neoserfdom upon the peasants. In addition the government made several efforts to collect from the rural villages a poll tax (a flat charge on each member of the population). Moreover, the great landlords, faced with falling rents, sought to revive many half-forgotten feudal dues, which had been allowed to lapse when rents were high in the thirteenth century.

Under leaders of uncertain background—Wat Tyler, Jack Straw, and a priest named John Ball—peasant bands, enraged by the latest poll tax, marched on London in 1381. They called for the final abolition of serfdom, labor services, tithes, and other feudal dues and demanded an end to the poll taxes. The workers of London, St. Albans, York, and other cities, who had similar grievances against the royal government, rose in support of the peasants. After the mobs burned the houses of prominent lawyers and royal officials, King Richard II, then fifteen, with considerable bravery personally met with the peasants and was able to placate them by promising to accept their demands. But as the peasants dispersed, the great landlords reorganized their forces and violently suppressed the last vestiges of unrest in the countryside; the young king also reneged on his promises.

The peasant uprising in England was only one of many rural disturbances that occurred between 1350 and 1450, including revolts in the Île de France, Languedoc, Catalonia, Sweden, and another in England (1450). Numerous rural disturbances occurred in Germany in the fifteenth century, and a major peasant revolt there in 1524 played an important role in the history of the early Reformation.

URBAN REVOLTS

The causes of social unrest within the cities were very similar to those in the countryside. Governments controlled by the propertied classes tried to prevent wages from rising and workers from moving and also sought to impose a heavier share of the tax burden upon the poorer segments of society. In the fourteenth and early fifteenth centuries Strasbourg, Metz, Ghent, Liège, and Paris all were the scenes of riots. One of the most interesting, if not perhaps the most typical, of the specifically urban revolts was the Ciompi uprising at Florence in 1378.

Florence was one of the wool-manufacturing centers of Europe; the industry employed probably one-third of the working population of the city, which shortly before the Black Death included probably 120,000 people. The wool industry, like most industries, entered into bad times immediately after the plague. To protect themselves, employers cut production, thereby spreading unemployment. Since many of the employers were also members of the ruling oligarchy, they had laws passed limiting wages and manipulating taxation and other monetary policies to the benefit of the rich. The poorest workers were denied their own guild and had no collective voice which might have influenced the government. In all disputes they were subject to the bosses' judges and the bosses' law.

The poorest workers—principally the wool carders, known as the Ciompi—rose in revolt. They demanded, and for a short time got, several reforms. The employers would produce at least enough cloths to assure work; they would refrain from certain monetary manipulations considered deleterious to the interests of the workers; they would allow the workers their own guild; and they would give them representation in communal government. This was hardly a dictatorship of the proletariat, but it was nevertheless intolerable to the ruling oligarchy. Because the Ciompi did not have the leaders to maintain a steady influence on governmental policy, the great families regained full authority in the city by 1382 and quickly abrogated the democratic concessions. Although the Ciompi revolt was short-lived and ultimately unsuccessful, the incident marks one of the first manifestations of urban class tensions which would frequently disturb capitalistic society in future centuries.

THE SEEDS OF DISCONTENT

Each of the social disturbances of the fourteenth and fifteenth centuries was shaped by circumstances that were local and unique. Nevertheless, there were similarities in these social movements: for example, the fact that misery does not seem to have been the principal cause of the unrest. Indeed, the evidence suggests that the conditions of the working classes in both countryside and city were improving after the Black Death. The prosperity of the thirteenth century, which was chiefly a prosperity of landlords and employers, had been founded in part upon the poor negotiating position, and even the exploitation, of the workers. The depopulation of the fourteenth century radically altered this situation. The workers, now much reduced in number, were better able to bargain for lower rents, higher wages, and a fairer distribution of social benefits.

With the possible exception of the Ciompi the people who revolted were rarely the desperately poor. In England, for example, the centers of the peasant uprising of 1381 were in the lower Thames valley—a region which seems to have been more fertile, more prosperous, and less oppressed than other parts of the kingdom. (Serfdom, for example, was relatively less widespread and onerous here than in other English areas.) Also, the immediate provocation for the revolt was the imposition of a poll tax, and obviously poll taxes, or any taxes or charges, do not alarm the truly destitute, whereas they do alarm men recently arrived at some favorable position and anxious to hold onto their gains.

The principal goad to revolt in both town and country seems to have been the effort of the propertied classes to retain their old advantages and deny the workers their new ones. In the first decades after the Black Death governments failed in their efforts to increase taxes and to peg rents, wages, and prices at levels favorable to landlords and employers; meanwhile they spread hostility among the workers, who felt their improving social and economic status threatened.

The impulse to revolt also drew strength from the psychological tensions characteristic of this age of devastating plagues, famines, and wars. The nervous temper of the times predisposed men to take compulsive action against real or imagined enemies. When needed, ready justification for revolt could be found in Christian belief, for the common teaching of the Christian fathers was that neither private property nor social inequality had been intended by God. In a high-strung world many of these uprisings involved an emotional effort to attain the millennium, to reach that age of justice and equality which Christian belief saw in the past, expected in the future, and put off for the present.

The revolts of the fourteenth and fifteenth centuries brought no radical changes in governments or policies, but underlying social movements were coming to elevate the status of the workers. If the rich wanted tillers for their lands and workers for their shops, they had to offer favorable terms.

By about 1450, after a century of instability, a new equilibrium was emerging in European society, even if slowly and never completely. The humblest classes improved their lot and were fairly secure in their gains. Serfdom all but disappeared in the West; wages remained high and bread cheap. Life of course was still very hard for most workers, but it was better than it had been two centuries before. Perhaps reflective of better social conditions for the masses, the population once more began to grow, equipping Europe for its great expansion within its borders and beyond the oceans in the sixteenth century.

III. THE GOVERNMENTS OF EUROPE

War was a frequent occurrence throughout the Middle Ages but was never so widespread and so protracted as in the conflicts of the fourteenth and fifteenth centuries. The Hundred Years' War between England and France is the most famous of these struggles, but there was fighting in every corner of Europe. The inbred violence of the age manifests a partial breakdown in the governmental systems, their failure to maintain stability at home and peace with foreign powers.

CRISIS AND THE FEUDAL EQUILIBRIUM

The governmental systems of Europe were founded upon multiple partnerships in the exercise of power under the feudal constitutions. The king enjoyed supreme dignity and even a recognized sacred character, but he was far from being an absolute ruler. In return for loyalty and service he conceded a large share

of the responsibility for government to a wide range of privileged persons and institutions: the great secular and ecclesiastical princes, the nobles, religious congregations, powerful military orders such as the Templars, free cities, or communes, and even favored guilds such as the universities.

The growth of the feudal constitution in the eleventh and twelfth centuries had been a major step toward a more ordered political life, but it rested upon a delicate equilibrium. To keep an internal peace, which because of the confused borders of most feudal states often meant international peace, all members of the feudal partnership had to remain punctiliously faithful to their obligations. This governmental system worked well until the beginning of the fourteenth century, but it could not sustain the multiple blows suffered during the period of social crisis. Governments had to be slowly rebuilt, still along feudal lines, still based on shared authority. Many of the new governments that came to dominate the European political scene in the late fifteenth century, although still not absolutistic, conceded far more power for the senior partner in the feudal relationship, the king or prince.

Dynastic Instability

The forces which upset the equilibrium of feudal governments were many. One of the most evident, itself rooted in the demographic instability of the age, was the failure of dynasties to perpetuate themselves. The Hundred Years' War, or at least the excuse for it, arose from the inability of the Capetian kings of France, for the first time since the tenth century, to produce a male heir in direct line. The English War of the Roses resulted from the uncertain succession to the crown of England and the claims which the two rival houses of Lancaster and York exerted for it. In Portugal, Castile, France, England, Naples, Hungary,

Poland, and the Scandinavian countries the reigning monarchs of 1450 were not the direct, male, legitimate descendants of those reigning in 1300. Most of the founders of new lines had to fight for their position.

Fiscal Pressures

The same powerful economic forces that were creating new patterns of agriculture and trade were also reshaping the fiscal policies and financial machinery of feudal governments. War was growing more expensive, as well as more frequent. Better-trained armies were needed to fight for longer periods of time and with more complex weaponry. Above all, the increasing use of firearms was adding to the costs of war. To replace the traditional, undisciplined, unpaid, and poorly equipped feudal armies, governments came more and more to rely on mercenaries, who were better trained and better armed than the vassals who fought in fulfillment of their feudal obligations. Many mercenaries were organized into associations known as companies of adventure, whose leaders were both good commanders and businessmen. They took their enterprise where the market was most favorable, sold their services to the highest bidder, and turned substantial profits. To hire mercenaries, and win battles, was increasingly a question of money, which then became, as it has since remained, the *nervi belli* ("the sinews of war").

While war went up in price, the traditional revenues upon which governments depended sank. Until the fourteenth century the king or prince was expected to meet the expenses of government from ordinary revenues, chiefly rents from his properties; but his rents, like everyone's, were falling in the Late Middle Ages. Governments of all types—monarchies, the papacy, cities—desperately sought to develop new sources of revenue. For example, the papacy, because it could not rely on the

meager receipts from its lands, built a huge financial apparatus that sold ecclesiastical appointments, favors, and dispensations from normal canonical requirements; imposed tithes on ecclesiastical revenues; and sold indulgences. In France the monarchy established a monopoly over the sale of salt (the *gabelle*). In England the king at various times imposed direct taxes on hearths, individuals (the poll tax), and plow teams, plus a host of smaller levies. The Italian cities taxed a whole range of items from windows to prostitutes. Under acute fiscal pressures governments rigorously scrutinized the necessities, pleasures, and sins of society to find sources of revenue.

Surviving fiscal records indicate that in spite of the disturbed times many governments did succeed in greatly increasing their incomes through these taxes. For example, the English monarchy never collected or spent more than £30,000 per year before 1336; thereafter, the budget rarely sank below £100,000 and at times reached £250,000 in the late fourteenth century.

This new reliance on extraordinary taxes had important political consequences. The most lucrative of them were not limited to the ruler's own demesne but extended over all his realm. They were, in other words, national, or at least territorial, taxes. Moreover, the ruler had no established right to their collection but had to seek the consent of his subjects. He therefore frequently summoned territorial or national assemblies of estates, such as Parliament in England or the Estates General in France, to grant the new taxes. But the assemblies in turn often balked at these requests or offered to grant them only in return for political concessions. Even within the Church many reformers maintained that a general council should have ultimate control over papal finances. The extraordinary expansion of governmental revenues thus raised profound constitutional questions in both ecclesiastical and secular governments.

Factional Conflicts

The aristocracy that had developed nearly everywhere in Europe also entered a period of instability in the Late Middle Ages. Birth afforded the principal access to this class, and membership in it conveyed certain legal and social privileges—exemption from most taxes, immunity from certain juridical procedures, such as torture, and so forth. The nobles looked upon themselves as the chief counselors of the king and his principal partners in the conduct of government.

By the fourteenth century, however, the nobles had long since lost whatever economic homogeneity they may once have possessed. Their wealth was chiefly in land, and they, like all landlords, faced the problem of declining rents. Frequently they lacked the funds needed for the new systems of agriculture. They were further plagued by the continuing problem of finding income and careers for their younger sons. In short, the nobles possessed no immunity from the acute economic dislocations of the times, and their class included men who lived on the brink of poverty as well as holders of enormous estates.

To maintain their position some of the nobles joined the companies of adventure to fight as mercenaries. Others hoped to buttress their sinking fortunes through marriage or by winning offices, lands, pensions, or other favors which governments could provide. Amid these social uncertainties the nobles tended to coalesce into factions, which disputed with one another over the control of government and the distribution of its favors. From England to Italy factional warfare, far more than class warfare, constantly disturbed the peace. A divided and grasping nobility added to the tensions of the age and to its taste for violence.

Characteristically, a faction was led by a great noble house and included numerous persons of varying social station—great nobles in alliance with the leading house, poor knights, retainers, servants, sometimes even artisans and peasants. At times the factions encompassed scores of families and hundreds of men and could almost be considered little states within a state, with their own small armies, loyalties, and symbols of allegiance in the colors or distinctive costumes (livery) worn by their members.

ENGLAND, FRANCE, AND THE HUNDRED YEARS' WAR

All the factors that upset the equilibrium of feudal governments—dynastic instability, fiscal pressures, and factional rivalries—helped to provoke the greatest struggle of the epoch, the Hundred Years' War.

The proclaimed issue of the Hundred Years' War was a dispute over the French royal succession. After more than three hundred years of extraordinary good luck the last three Capetian kings (the brothers Louis X, Philip V, and Charles IV) failed to produce male heirs. With Charles's death in 1328, the nearest surviving male relative was his nephew King Edward III of England, son of his sister Isabella. But the Parlement of Paris—the supreme court of France—declared that women could not transmit a claim to the crown. In place of Edward the French Estates chose Philip of Valois, a first cousin of the preceding kings. Edward did not initially dispute this decision, and as holder of the French fiefs of Aquitaine and Ponthieu he did homage to Philip.

More important than the dynastic issue was

A castle under siege during the Hundred Years' War. (Photo: British Museum)

the clash of French and English interests in the county of Flanders, whose cloth-making industry relied on England for wool. In 1302 the Flemings had rebelled against their count, a vassal of the French king, and had remained virtually independent until 1328, when Philip defeated their forces at Cassel and restored the count. At Philip's insistence the count ordered the arrest of all English merchants in Flanders; Edward then retaliated by cutting off the export of wool, which spread unemployment in the Flemish towns. The Flemings revolted once more and drove out the count. To give legal sanction to their revolt they persuaded Edward to assert his claim to the French crown, which would have given him suzerainty over Flanders as well.

The most serious of all points of friction, however, was the exact status of Aquitaine and Ponthieu. Edward had willingly performed ordinary homage for them, but Philip then insisted on liege homage, which would have obligated Edward to support Philip against all enemies. Edward did not believe that, as a king, he could undertake the obligations of liege homage to any man, and refused. Philip began harassing the frontiers of Aquitaine and declared Edward's fiefs forfeit in 1337. The attack upon Aquitaine undoubtedly pushed Edward into supporting the Flemish revolt and was the principal provocation for the Hundred Years' War.

Philip, in his eagerness for glory, had clearly embarked upon a dangerous adventure in his harassment of Aquitaine, and Edward, in supporting the Flemings, reacted perhaps too strongly to the provocation. Both men evidently took their feudal obligation of mutual respect and love very lightly. The coming of this war between the French king and his principal vassal was thus rooted in a breakdown of the feudal constitution of medieval France in both its institutions and its spirit.

The Tides of Battle

The French seemed to have a decisive superiority over the English at the outset of the war. The population of France was perhaps fifteen million; England had between four and seven million. But for most of its course the war was not really a national confrontation. French subjects (Flemings, Gascons, later Burgundians) fought alongside the English against other French subjects. The confused struggle may be fairly divided into three periods: an initial phase of English victories from 1338 to 1360; a phase of French resurgence, then stalemate, from 1367 to 1415; and a wild denouement with tides rapidly shifting from 1415 to 1453.

The series of English victories that opened the war were never fully exploited by the English, nor ever quite undone by the French. An English naval victory at Sluys in 1340 assured English communications across the Channel and determined France as the scene of the fighting. Six years later Edward landed in France on what was more a marauding expedition than a campaign of conquest. Philip pursued the English and finally overtook them at Crécy. The French knights attacked before their forces could be entirely marshaled and organized; the disciplined English, making effective use of the longbow, cut the confused French army to pieces. The scenario was repeated in 1356 at Poitiers. John II, who had succeeded Philip, attacked an English army under Edward's son, the gallant Black Prince, and incurred a defeat even more crushing. English victories, the Black Death, and mutual exhaustion prepared the way for the Peace of Brétigny in 1360. The English were given Calais and an enlarged Aquitaine, and Edward in turn renounced his claims to the French crown.

But the French could not allow so large a part of their kingdom to remain in English

NORTH SEA

E N G L A N D

London

SLUYS 1340
Antwerp
Bruges
DUCHY OF
BRABANT
Calais
COUNTY OF
Cassel
FLANDERS
AGINCOURT 1415
Arras
NAMUR
COUNTY
OF
HAINAUT
*CRECY
1346*

ENGLISH CHANNEL

Rhine R.

Moselle R.

Rouen
Compiègne
Reims
ALSACE

NORMANDY
Seine R.
Paris
Marne R.
CHAMPAGNE
DUCHY OF
LORRAINE

BRITTANY
Rennes
MAINE
Brétigny
Troyes
Domremy

Meuse R.

Angers
ANJOU
Orléans
Loire R.
DUCHY OF
BURGUNDY
*(Supporting
English Claim)*
Dijon
COUNTY
OF
BURGUNDY

Chinon
Bourges

POITOU
POITIERS 1356

BAY OF BISCAY

AUVERGNE

Saône R.

Kingdom of France in 1339

English Areas in 1339

English Controlled Areas in 1429

Burgundian Areas in 1441

★ Battle Site

Bordeaux
Dordogne R.

Garonne

AQUITAINE

Durance R.

Rhone R.

Avignon
PROVENCE

G U I E N N E

Aix

Bayonne
ARMAGNAC
R.
GASCONY

NAVARRE

MEDITERRANEAN SEA

0   50   100 miles

A R A G O N

H O L Y   R O M A N   E M P I R E

MAP 11.2: THE HUNDRED YEARS' WAR

hands. Seven years later, under John's successor, Charles V, they opened the second phase of the war. The French armies succeeded largely by avoiding full-scale battles and wearing down the English forces bit by bit. By 1380 they had pushed the English nearly into the sea, confining them to Calais and a narrow strip of the Atlantic coast from Bordeaux to Bayonne. Fighting was sporadic from 1380 until 1415, both sides content with a stalemate.

The last period of the war from 1415 to 1453 was one of high drama and rapidly shifting fortunes. Henry V of England invaded France and wrought disaster on the French army at Agincourt in 1415. His success was confirmed by the Treaty of Troyes in 1420, an almost total French capitulation. King Charles VI of France declared his son the Dauphin (the future Charles VII) illegitimate, named Henry his successor, appointed him regent of France, and gave him direct rule over all French lands as far south as the Loire River (see Map 11.2). Charles also gave Henry his daughter Catherine in marriage.

The Dauphin of course could not accept this forced abdication, and from his capital at Bourges he led an expedition across the Loire River. Henry drove his forces back and then embarked on a systematic reduction of towns and fortresses north of the river that were loyal to the Dauphin. Then in 1428 the English laid siege to Orléans; its fall would have given them a commanding position in the Loire valley and would have rendered the plight of the Dauphin nearly desperate.

Joan of Arc

The intervention of a young peasant girl, Joan of Arc, saved the Capetian dynasty. Convinced that heavenly voices were ordering her to rescue France, Joan persuaded several royal officials, and finally the Dauphin himself, of the authenticity of her mission and was given an army. In 1429 she marched to Orléans and

forced the English to raise the siege. She then escorted the Dauphin to Reims, the historic coronation city of France. His own coronation there confirmed his legitimacy and enlisted the support of French royalist sentiment in his cause. The tide had turned.

Joan passed from history as quickly and as dramatically as she had arrived. The Burgundians, allies of the English, captured her in 1430 and sold her to the English, who put her on trial for witchcraft and heresy. She was burned at the stake at Rouen in 1431.

Joan was a manifestation of an increasingly powerful sentiment among the people. They had grown impatient with continuing destruction and had come to identify their own security with the expulsion of the English and with a strong Capetian monarchy. This growing loyalty to the king finally saved France from its century of struggle. A series of French successes followed the execution of Joan, and by 1453 only Calais was left in English hands. No formal treaty ended the war, but both sides accepted the outcome: England was no longer a Continental power.

The Effects of the Hundred Years' War

Like all the disasters of that era, the Hundred Years' War accelerated change. With regard to warfare, it stimulated the development of firearms and the technologies needed for them and helped establish that the infantry, armed with longbow, pike, or gun, was superior in battle to mounted knights.

The war also had a significant effect on governmental institutions in England and France. The expense of fighting forced the kings on each side to look for new sources of revenue through taxation. In England the king willingly conceded to Parliament a larger role in return for grants of new taxes. The tradition became firmly established that Parliament had the right to grant or refuse new taxes, to agree to legislation, to channel appeals to the king, and to offer advice on important decisions such as those regarding peace and war. The House of Commons gained the right to introduce all tax legislation, since the Commons could speak, as the Lords could not, as representatives of the shires and boroughs. Parliament also named a committee to audit the tax records, to be sure that its will was respected. Equally important, Commons could also impeach high royal officials, an important early step in establishing the principle that the king's ministers were responsible to Parliament as well as to their royal master. By the end of the Hundred Years' War, Parliament had been considerably strengthened at the expense of royal power.

The need for new taxes produced a somewhat different outcome in France, actually enhancing the power of the French monarchs while weakening the Estates General, the national representative assembly. In 1343 Philip IV established a monopoly over the sale of salt, determining in many French provinces how much each family had to consume and how much they had to pay for it. The tax on salt, called the *gabelle*, was destined to form a major support of French finance for the entire duration of the monarchy, until 1789. In gaining support for this and other proposed taxes Philip and his successors sought the agreement of both the regional, or provincial, assemblies of estates and the national Estates General. The kings' reliance on the provincial estates hindered the emergence of a centralized assembly that could speak for the entire kingdom. By the reign of Charles VII, during the last stages of the war, the monarchy obtained the right to impose national taxes (notably the *taille*, a direct tax from which nobles and clerics were exempt) without the consent of the Estates General. By then, too, the royal government was served by a standing, professional army (the "companies of ordinance")—the first in any European country since the fall of the Roman Empire.

This representation of St. Joan of Arc, done after her death, shows her in battle dress, with the figures of the three saints who instructed her (her "voices") emblazoned upon her banner. (Photo: Archives Nationales/Giraudon)

Both England and France experienced internal dissension during the course of the war. After the death of Edward III in 1377, England faced over a century of turmoil, with the nobles striving to maintain their endangered economic fortunes through factional conflicts—that is, by preying on one another. In time these conflicts led to a struggle between two factions, the Lancastrians and the Yorkists, over the throne itself, with the English nobles quickly aligning themselves on one side or the other. The civil war that followed is known to historians as the

War of the Roses (the Lancastrian emblem was a red rose, that of the Yorkists a white one). It lasted some thirty-five years, ending in 1485, when at Bosworth Field Henry Tudor defeated the Yorkists and acceded to the throne as Henry VII. By this time prosperity had relieved the pressures on the English nobles, and the people in general, weary of war, welcomed the strong and orderly regime which Henry proposed to establish.

In France too the power of the monarchy was threatened by strife between rival factions of nobles, the Armagnacs and the Burgundians. The Armagnacs favored a vigorous prosecution of the war with England, whereas the Burgundians favored accommodation. The territorial ambitions of the Burgundians also posed a threat to the French monarchy. King John the Good of France had granted the huge Duchy of Burgundy to his younger son, Philip the Bold, in 1363. Philip and his successors greatly enlarged their possessions in eastern France, the Rhone and Rhine valleys, and the Low Countries (see Map 11.2). The dukes seem to have taken as their goal the establishment of a Burgundian "middle kingdom" between France and the Holy Roman Empire; such a state would have permanently affected the political geography of Europe and undermined the position of the French monarch. However, this threat ended in 1477 with the death of the last duke, because his daughter and heir, Mary of Burgundy, was unable to hold her scattered inheritance together, and a large part of it came under French control.

With the loss of nearly all its Continental possessions in the course of the war, England emerged from the war geographically more consolidated. It was also homogeneous in its language (English had replaced French as the language of the law courts and administration) and conscious of its cultural distinctiveness and national identity. Freed from its Continental entanglements, England was ready for its expansion beyond the seas and for a great growth in national pride and self-consciousness.

France never achieved quite the territorial consolidation of England, but with the expulsion of the English from the Continent and the sudden distintegration of the Duchy of Burgundy the French king was without a major rival among his feudal princes. The monarchy emerged from the war with a permanent army, a remunerative tax system, and no clear constitutional restrictions on its exercise of power. Most significantly, the war gave the French king greater prestige and confirmed him as the chief protector and patron of the people.

In both France and England, government at the end of the Middle Ages must still be considered decentralized and "feudal," if we mean by that term that certain privileged persons and institutions (nobles, the Church, towns, and the like) continued to hold and to exercise some forms of private jurisdiction. They retained, for example, their own courts. But the king had unmistakably emerged as the dominant partner in the feudal relationship. Moreover, he was prepared to press his advantages still further in the sixteenth century.

THE HOLY ROMAN EMPIRE

With the death of Emperor Frederick II of Hohenstaufen (1250), the Holy Roman Empire ceased to function as a major power in European affairs. The empire continued to link Germany and Italy, but real authority fell to the princes in Germany and the city republics in Italy. In 1273, after a tumultuous period known as the Interregnum, during which several rivals contended for the title, the princes chose as emperor Rudolf of Hapsburg, the first of that famous family to hold the office. Instead of rebuilding the imperial authority, Rudolf rather sought to advance the interests of his own dynasty and its ancestral possessions. His successors also characteristically sought to use the office of emperor for their own narrow dynastic advantage.

A significant event of the fourteenth century was the issuance in 1356 of the Golden Bull, which defined the constitution of the empire as it would largely remain until 1806. Although issued by the pope, the bull reflected the interests of the great German princes. The right of naming the emperor was given to seven electors—the archbishops of Mainz, Trier, and Cologne, the count palatine of the Rhine, the duke of Saxony, the margrave of Brandenburg, and the king of Bohemia. It assigned no role to the popes in naming or crowning the emperor and thus was a victory for imperial autonomy.

A development of major interest in the empire was the emergence of the Swiss Confederation of cantons (districts), which won virtual autonomy in the Late Middle Ages. In the early thirteenth century Emperor Frederick II of Hohenstaufen had recognized the autonomy of two cantons, Uri and Schwyz, and had given them the responsibility of guarding the Saint Gotthard Pass through the Alps, the shortest route from Germany to Italy. The lands of the cantons were technically part of the ancient duchy of Swabia, and in the late thirteenth century the Hapsburg princes, seeking to consolidate their possessions in the duchy, attempted to subjugate the Swiss lands as well. To resist the Hapsburg menace the cantons of Uri, Schwyz, and Unterwalden joined in a Perpetual Compact in 1291. They formed the nucleus of what was eventually to become the twenty-two cantons of present-day Switzerland.

The Swiss had to fight for their autonomy, and they acquired the reputation of being among the best fighters in Europe. Both history and legend, such as the colorful stories of William Tell, celebrate their successes. The confederated governments of the Swiss cantons represent a notable exception to the tendency, evident elsewhere in Europe, for central governments to grow stronger in the fourteenth and fifteenth centuries.

THE STATES OF ITALY

The free city, or commune, was the dominant power in Italian political life at the beginning of the fourteenth century, at least in the center and north of the peninsula. The Holy Roman Empire exerted a loose sovereignty over much of the peninsula north of Rome and the papacy governed the area around Rome, but almost all the principal cities, and many small ones too, had gained the status of self-governing city-states.

However, the new economic and social conditions of the fourteenth century were unfavorable to the survival of the smaller communes. The economic contractions of the times made it increasingly difficult for industries and merchant houses in the smaller cities to compete with their rivals in the larger ones. Moreover, with the rising costs of war the small communes found it equally hard to defend their independence. Finally, in both large and small towns Italian society was deeply disturbed by factional strife which often made political order impossible.

In response to such pressures two principal tendencies become evident in Italian political development. Much stronger governments, amounting at times to true despotisms, tended to replace the weak governments of the free commune. And regional states, dominated politically and economically by a single metropolis, replaced the numerous, free, and highly competitive communes.

Perhaps the most effective Italian despot was the ruler of Milan, Gian Galeazzo Visconti (1378–1402), who energetically set about enlarging the Visconti inheritance of twenty-one cities in the Po valley. Through shrewd negotiations and opportune attacks he secured the submission of Verona, Vicenza, and Padua, which gave him an outlet to the Adriatic Sea. He then seized Bologna, purchased Pisa, and through a variety of ways was accepted as suzerain in Siena, Perugia, Spoleto, Nocera, and Assisi. In the course of this advance deep into central Italy Gian Galeazzo worked with some success to keep his chief enemies, the Florentines and the Venetians, divided, and he seemed destined to forge an Italian kingdom and restore Italian unity.

To establish a legal basis for his power Gian Galeazzo secured from the emperor an appointment as imperial vicar in 1380, and then as hereditary duke in 1395. This made him, in fact, the only duke in all Italy and seemed a step toward the assumption of a royal title. He revised the statutes of Milan, but his chief administrative achievement, and the true foundation of most of his successes, was his ability to wring enormous tax revenues from his subjects. Gian Galeazzo was also a generous patron of Humanism and the new learning, and with his conquests, wealth, and brilliance he seemed to be awaiting only the submission of the truculent Florentines before adopting the title of king. But he died unexpectedly in 1402, leaving two minor sons, who were incapable of defending their inheritance.

Even those states that escaped the despotism of a Gian Galeazzo moved toward stronger governments and the formation of territorial or regional states. In Venice the government was placed under the domination of a small and closed oligarchy. A kind of corporative despot, known as the Council of Ten, looked over and after the Venetian state. Its mandate was the preservation of oligarchic rule in Venice and the suppression of opposition to the government.

Whereas Venice had previously devoted its principal energies to maritime commerce and overseas possessions, it could not now ignore the growth on the mainland of territorial states, which might deprive it of its agricultural imports or jeopardize its inland trade routes. From the early fifteenth century onward Venice too initiated a policy of territorial expansion on the mainland. By 1405 Padua, Verona, and Vicenza had become Venetian dependencies.

Florence, while retaining the outer trappings of republican government, also came under stronger rule. In 1434 a successful banker named Cosimo de' Medici established a form of boss rule over the city. In his tax policies he favored the lower and middle classes of the city, and also cultivated the support of the middle classes by appointments to office and other forms of political patronage. Further, he took peace in Italy as his supreme goal. In guiding the relations between Florence and other cities and states he earned from his fellow citizens the title *pater patriae* ("father of his country"), and most historians would concur in this judgment.

Cosimo's achievements were a preparation for the rule of his more famous grandson, Lorenzo the Magnificent (1478–1492). Under Lorenzo's direction Florence set the style for Italy, and eventually for Europe, in the splendor of its festivals, the elegance of its social life, the beauty of its buildings, and the lavish support it extended to scholars and artists. With good reason, Lorenzo's lifetime is viewed by many as the golden age of Renaissance Florence.

The Papal States and the Kingdom of Naples

The popes, who were now located in Avignon in southern France, sought to consolidate their rule over their possessions in central Italy, but they faced formidable obstacles. The rugged territory with its many castles and fortified towns enabled communes, petty lords, and plain brigands to defy the papal authority easily. Continuing disorders largely discouraged the popes from returning to Rome, and the attempts to pacify the tumultuous region were causing a major drain on papal finances.

Even after its return to Rome in 1378 the papacy had difficulty maintaining authority. Not until the pontificate of Martin V (1417–1431) was a stable administration established, and Martin's successors still faced frequent revolts for the entire course of the fifteenth century.

The political situation was equally confused in the Kingdom of Naples and Sicily. With papal support Charles of Anjou, younger brother of St. Louis of France, had established a dynasty of Angevin rulers over the area. But in 1282 the people of Sicily revolted against the Angevins and appealed for help to the king of Aragon. For the next 150 years the Aragonese and the Angevins battled for dominion over Sicily and Naples. Then in 1435 the king of Aragon, Alfonso V, the Magnanimous, reunited Sicily and southern Italy and made the kingdom the center of an Aragonese empire in the Mediterranean. Alfonso sought to suppress the factions of lawless nobles and to reform taxes and strengthen administration. His efforts were not completely successful, for southern Italy and Sicily were rugged, poor lands and difficult to subdue; but he was at least able to overcome the chaos that had prevailed earlier. Alfonso was an enthusiastic patron of literature and the arts, and his court at Naples was one of the most brilliant of the early Renaissance.

Foreign Relations

Italy, by about 1450, was no longer a land of numerous, tiny free communes. Rather, it was divided among five territorial states: the Duchy of Milan, the republics of Venice and Florence, the Papal States, and the Kingdom of Naples (see Map 11.3). To govern the relations among these states the Italians conceived new methods of diplomacy. Led by Venice, the states began to maintain permanent embassies at important foreign courts.

Moreover, largely through the political sense of Cosimo de' Medici, the Italian states were able to pioneer a new way of preserving stability. The Peace of Lodi in 1454 ended a war between Milan, Florence, and Venice, and Cosimo sought to make the peace a lasting one through balancing alliance systems. Milan, Naples, and Florence held one side of the balance, and Venice and the Papal States the other. Each state felt sufficiently secure in its alliances to have no need to appeal to non-Italian powers for support. During the next forty years the balance was occasionally rocked, but never overturned, and it gave Italy an unaccustomed period of peace and freedom from foreign intervention. This system represents one of the earliest appearances in European history of the concept of the balance of power as a workable means of maintaining both security and peace.

IV. THE PAPACY

The papacy also experienced profound transformations in the fourteenth and fifteenth centuries. It continued to envision as its chief objective a peaceful Christendom united in faith and in filial obedience to Rome. But in fact the international Christian community was beset by powerful forces that worked to undermine its cohesiveness and to weaken papal authority and influence. Although the culmination of these disruptive forces came in the Reformation in the sixteenth century, their roots lie deep within the history of the previous two centuries.

THE AVIGNON EXILE

The humiliation of Pope Boniface VIII by the agents of Philip IV of France at Anagni in 1303 opened the doors to French influence at the Curia. In 1305 the College of Cardinals elected a Frenchman pope, Clement V, who

1 MARCH OF MONTFERRAT
2 MARCH OF MANTUA
3 DUCHY OF MODENA
4 REPUBLIC OF LUCCA
5 COUNTY OF ASTI

THE FIVE GREAT POWERS

Republic of Florence
Duchy of Milan
Kingdom of Naples
Papal States
Venetian Republic

0   50   100 miles

MAP 11.3: ITALY 1454

because of the political disorders in the Papal States settled at Avignon. Though technically a part of the Holy Roman Empire, Avignon was in language and culture a French city. The popes who followed Clement expressed an intention to return to Rome but remained at Avignon, claiming that the continuing turmoil of central Italy would not permit the papal government to function effectively. These popes were, in fact, skilled administrators, and the period witnessed an enormous expansion of the papal bureaucracy, especially its fiscal machinery.

The papal palace at Avignon was the site of what has been termed the papacy's "Babylonian captivity," or the Avignon exile. Rome was without the papacy from 1308 to 1377. (Photo: Photo Boudot-LaMotte)

FISCAL CRISIS

Like many secular governments the papacy at Avignon faced an acute fiscal crisis. But unlike the major powers of Europe it had no adequate territorial base to supply it with funds, because the tumultuous Papal States usually drained off more money than they supplied. The powers of appointment, dispensation, tithing, and indulgences were the only resources the papacy possessed, and it was thus drawn into the unfortunate but perhaps unavoidable practice of exploiting them for financial purposes. For instance, the popes insisted that candidates appointed to high ecclesiastical offices pay a special tax, which usually amounted to a third or a half of the first year's revenues. The popes also claimed the income from vacant offices and even sold future appointments to office when the incumbents were still alive. Dispensation released a petitioner from the normal requirements of canon law. A monastery or religious house, for example, might purchase from the pope an exemption from the visitation and inspection of the local bishop. Tithes were a payment to the papacy of one-tenth of the revenues of ecclesiastical benefices or offices throughout Christendom. Indulgences, remissions of the temporal punishment attendant to a sin, were also distributed in return for monetary contributions to the papacy.[4]

These fiscal practices brought the popes greatly enlarged revenues, but they also had many deplorable results. Prelates who paid huge sums to Avignon tended to pass on the costs to the lower clergy. Parish priests, hardly able to live within the incomes left to them, were the more readily tempted to disordered moral lives. The flow of money to Avignon angered rulers; well before the close of the Middle Ages there were demands for a halt to such payments and even for the confiscation of Church property. Dispensations gravely injured the authority of the bishops, since the exempt persons or houses all but escaped their supervision. The bishops were frequently too weak, and the pope too distant, to deal effectively with abuses on the local level. The fiscal system of the papacy thus helped sow chaos in many parts of the Western Church.

THE GREAT SCHISM

The end of the seventy-year Avignon exile led to a controversy that almost split the Western Church. Pope Gregory XI returned reluctantly to Rome in 1378 and died there a short time later. The Roman people, fearing that Gregory's successor would once more remove the court to Avignon and thereby deprive Rome of desperately needed revenues, agitated for the election of an Italian pope. Responding to this pressure, the College of Cardinals found a compromise candidate who satisfied both French and Italian interests—a Neapolitan of French-Angevin extraction. The new pope, Urban VI, soon antagonized the French cardinals by seeking to limit their privileges and by threatening to pack the College with his own appointments. Seven months after choosing Urban, a majority of the cardinals declared that his election had taken place under duress and was therefore invalid; they then named a new pope, who returned to Avignon. Thus began the Great Schism of the West, the period when two, and later three, popes contended over the rule of the Church. The schism was to last for almost forty years.

Christendom was now confronted with the deplorable spectacle of two pretenders to the throne of Peter, one in Rome and one in Avignon. Princes and peoples quickly took sides (see Map 11.4). The troubles of the papacy were at once doubled. Each pope had his own court and needed still more funds, both to meet ordinary expenses and to pay for policies which he hoped would defeat his rival. And since each pope excommunicated the other and those who supported him, everyone in

---

[4] Both the tithe and the indulgence originated as means of supporting the crusades, but income from them was frequently, and even usually, applied by the pope to his domestic needs.

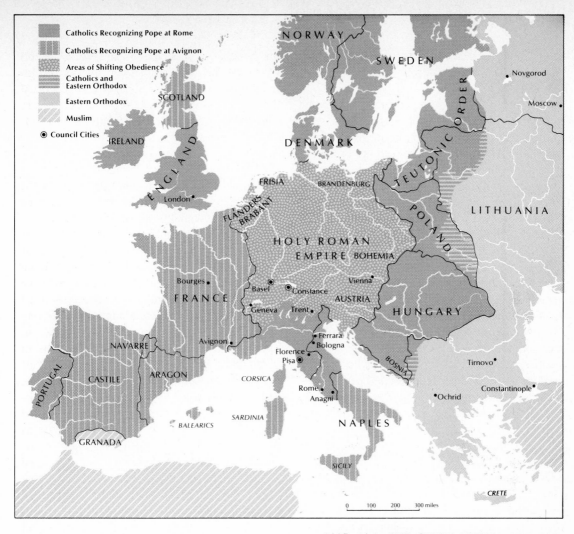

Legend:
- Catholics Recognizing Pope at Rome
- Catholics Recognizing Pope at Avignon
- Areas of Shifting Obedience
- Catholics and Eastern Orthodox
- Eastern Orthodox
- Muslim
- ⊙ Council Cities

MAP 11.4: THE GREAT SCHISM 1378–1417

Christendom was at least technically excommunicated.

THE CONCILIAR MOVEMENT

Theologians and jurists had speculated earlier on who should rule the Church if the pope were to become heretical or incompetent; some concluded that it should be the College of Cardinals or a general council of Church officials. Since the College of Cardinals had split into two factions, each backing one of the rival popes, many prominent thinkers supported the theory that a general council should rule the Church. These conciliarists, as they were called, went even further. They urged that the Church be given a new constitution to confirm the supremacy of a general council. Such a step would have reduced the pope's role to that of a limited monarch. The critical need for correcting numerous abuses, particularly regarding the fiscal support and morality of the clergy, lent further strength to the idea that a general council should rule and reform the Church.

The first test of the conciliarists' position was at the Council of Pisa (1409), which was convened by cardinals of both Rome and Avignon. The council did assert its own supremacy within the Church by deposing the two popes and electing another. But this act merely compounded the confusion, for it left Christendom with three rivals claiming to be the lawful pope.

A few years later another council finally resolved the situation. Some four hundred ecclesiastics assembled at the Council of Constance (1414–1418), the greatest international gathering of the Middle Ages. The council was organized in a fashion novel for the times. The delegates elected to sit and vote by nations to offset the power of the Italians, who constituted nearly half the attendance. The council also gave recognition to the new importance of national and territorial churches, as each national church voted as a unit.

The assembled delegates immediately deposed both the new pope and the pope at Avignon after the latter refused to resign; the Roman pope submitted to the demand of the council and resigned. In his stead the council elected a Roman cardinal, who took the name Martin V. Thus the Great Schism was ended, and the Western Church was once again united under a single pope.

As the meetings continued, the views of the conciliarists prevailed. The delegates formally declared that a general council was supreme within the Church. To ensure a degree of continuity in Church government the delegates further directed that new councils be summoned periodically.

In spite of this assertion of supremacy, the council made little headway in reforming the Church "in head and members," to use the language of contemporaries. Those attending the council, chiefly great prelates, were in large part the beneficiaries of the fiscal system. They were reluctant to touch their own privileges and advantages. The real victims of the fiscal abuses, the lower clergy, were poorly represented. The council could not agree on a general program of reform. This failure illustrates a fatal flaw in the vision of conciliar rule over the Church. The council was too large, too cumbersome, and too divided to maintain an effective ecclesiastical government. The restored papacy quickly reclaimed its position as supreme head of the Western Church.

The practical weaknesses of the conciliar movement were amply revealed at the Council of Basel (1431–1443). Because disputes broke out almost at once with the pope, the council deposed him and elected another to replace him, Felix V. The conciliar movement, designed to heal the schism, now seemed responsible for renewing it. Recognizing the futility of its actions, the council at the death of Felix tried to rescue a semblance of its dignity by "electing" the Roman pope Nicholas V in 1449 and disbanding. This ended the effort to reform the Church through giving supreme authority over it to councils.

The popes retained a suspicion of councils, but in fact they had much more serious rivals to their authority in the powerful lay princes, who were exerting an ever tighter control over their territorial churches. Both England and France issued decrees that limited the exercise of papal powers within their kingdoms. The policy was soon imitated in Spain and in the stronger principalities of the Holy Roman Empire. Although these decrees did not establish national or territorial churches, they do document the deteriorating papal control over the international Christian community.

THE POPES AS PATRONS OF THE ARTS

The papacy in the fifteenth and early sixteenth centuries experienced one of the most troubled and most glorious periods of its history. The popes ruled over a disturbed Christendom, soon to experience one of its greatest crises in the Reformation. Yet never before had the papacy exerted such an influence over artistic and cultural expression in the West. The visitor to Rome today is captivated by the magnificent art which the popes of this age encouraged and supported.

According to his epitaph, Nicholas V (1447–1455) restored the golden age to Rome. A splendid, learned court had become essential to a great prince, and Nicholas intended to make the papal court second to none. The manuscripts that he assiduously collected became the nucleus of the Vatican Library. Pius II (1458–1464) is the only pope to have left us a personal memoir of his reign—his *Commentaries*, which offers a marvelous picture of the psychology of the times.

The Sistine Chapel in the Vatican is the great monument of Sixtus IV (1471–1484). He commissioned the best artists of the day—Botticelli, Perugino, Pinturicchio, and others—to paint the twelve frescoes of the lower walls.

During the reign of Sixtus's nephew Julius II (1503–1513) Michelangelo painted the glorious ceiling of the chapel (see Plate 24), which has remained a true museum of Renaissance artistic genius.

Julius also commissioned the new St. Peter's Church, with the Florentine Bramante (later succeeded by Michelangelo) as architect. Moreover, Julius achieved one of the papacy's main political goals: his military successes and reformed administration had consolidated his authority over the Papal States and ensured stability in central Italy. At this moment of unrivaled splendor and apparent success, the papacy stood on the brink of disaster.

The Reformation, which began during the reign of Julius's successor, makes it hard to judge these magnificent pontiffs fairly. Certainly they do not bear the major responsibility for the Protestant revolt, but they clearly did fail to grasp the depth and danger of the ills afflicting Christendom. The values of the day obscured and limited their vision. They flourished as princes and faltered as popes.

In the fourteenth and fifteenth centuries a series of spectacular catastrophes disrupted European life on almost every level. In the wake of plague, famine, and war, all rooted perhaps in overpopulation, the numbers of Europe's peoples fell drastically, and a severe economic depression gripped the Continent. The European nations were forced to reorganize their economies in accordance with the new scarcity of labor and the new structure of the market. By about 1450 they achieved considerable economic recovery, based upon a greater diversification in production and a marked substitution of capital for labor. In the late fifteenth century Europe was a smaller but richer community than it had been two hundred years before.

Society and government experienced a comparable crisis, as social unrest, factional strife, and war nearly everywhere disturbed the peace of Europe. But here too a new stability was achieved by about 1450, based on better conditions of life for the humbler classes and on the stronger authority claimed by many princes. The papacy also changed; it developed a huge bureaucratic and fiscal apparatus and successfully withstood the challenge of the conciliar movement. However, it failed to lead the Church to the reform many Europeans were demanding.

In European culture as well as institutions a profound crisis occurred in the fourteenth and fifteenth centuries. Yet even in this aspect of the "autumn" of the Middle Ages there was a renaissance, in the sense that out of a crisis of traditional values there emerged new creative efforts to enrich the culture of the West.

RECOMMENDED READING

Sources

Council of Constance. Louise R. Loomis (tr.). 1961.

*Froissart, Jean. *The Chronicles of England, France, Spain and Other Places Adjoining.* 1961. Covers the first half of the Hundred Years' War.

*Pernoud, Regine (ed.). *Joan of Arc: By Herself and Her Witnesses.* 1969.

Pius II, Pope. *Commentaries of Pius Second.* Florence A. Gragg (tr.). 1970. Personal, often acerbic reminiscences; unique document in papal history.

*Vespasiano da Bisticci. *Renaissance Princes, Popes and Prelates.* 1963. Biographies of prominent Italians of the fifteenth century, written by a contemporary.

Studies

*Ady, Cecil M. *Lorenzo dei Medici and Renaissance Italy.* 1952. Readable introduction to the rule and culture of the Medici.

Becker, Marvin B. *Florence in Transition.* 1967 ff. Stimulating and controversial.

*Bridbury, A. R. *Economic Growth in England in the Later Middle Ages.* 1962. Rejects thesis of a "Renaissance depression."

Brucker, Gene A. *Florentine Politics and Society.* 1962–1976. Social and political history of Florence from 1343 to 1420.

De Roover, Raymond. *The Rise and Decline of the Medici Bank.* 1963. Classic study in business history.

Hilton, Rodney. *Bondsmen Made Free.* 1973. A study of peasant violence in the Late Middle Ages.

*Mattingly, Garrett. *Renaissance Diplomacy.* 1964.

*Perroy, Édouard. *The Hundred Years' War.* 1965. Excellent survey by a French scholar.

*Schevill, Ferdinand. *Medieval and Renaissance Florence.* 1963. Readable general history.

---

* Available in paperback.

TWELVE

THE WEST
IN TRANSITION:
THE RENAISSANCE

The Swiss historian Jacob Burckhardt published a book in 1860, which has influenced, as few books have, the understanding that most educated men and women in Europe and America have of their own past. In The Civilization of the Renaissance in Italy *he argued that the fourteenth and fifteenth centuries witnessed a true revolution in values in that country. Men allegedly shook off the religious illusions and institutional restrictions of medieval society and rediscovered both the visible world and their own true selves. The essential novelty of Renaissance culture was the accent it placed on the individual and the delight it took in the beauties and satisfactions of life. The humanistic heritage of Greece and Rome, which stressed similar values, appealed to the men of this age, and the revived interest in that heritage constituted the classical Renaissance. Moreover, according to Burckhardt, the Italy of this period deserves to be considered the birthplace of the modern world.*

Modern historians can easily criticize Burckhardt's sweeping assertions. It is difficult to believe that anyone could attain the full release from his society and its traditions that Burckhardt claimed for the men of the fourteenth and fifteenth centuries. He certainly slighted the achievements of the earlier Middle Ages and exaggerated the originality of the period he called the Renaissance. Also, he confined his vision to Italy, and historians have had difficulty applying his formulas to other regions of Europe. Nevertheless, his fundamental insight still commands the respect and agreement of many scholars.

Historians today still discuss the problems raised by Burckhardt, but they are also learning to view those problems from new perspectives. They are penetrating ever more deeply into archives and attempting to apply stronger analytical methods to the data they are gathering. They are exploring aspects of society and social experience inaccessible to Burckhardt and other earlier historians. How long did men live and how did they grow, marry, raise their children, and meet with death? In the light of these experiences, how did they view the world, and what did they value in life? How and to what extent did their attitudes in fact change? These are the questions for which many scholars today are seeking answers, and which we too shall examine in this chapter.

1. SOCIETY AND CULTURE IN ITALY

In the fourteenth and fifteenth centuries Italy produced an extraordinary number of gifted thinkers and artists, whose collective work constituted the core of the cultural Renaissance and profoundly influenced all areas of European thought and artistic expression. To understand the character of the Renaissance requires, there-

fore, a consideration of the society which, in Burckhardt's estimation, shaped the culture of the modern world.

CITIES

One basic social characteristic clearly distinguished Italy from most European areas: the number and size of its cities, particularly in the northern regions of Tuscany and the Lombard plain. In 1377, for example, only 10 percent of the people in England lived in urban centers with a population greater than 3,200—a percentage fairly typical for most of northern Europe—whereas in Tuscany about 26 percent lived in urban centers. The cities were large. Venice, for instance, counted probably 120,000 inhabitants in 1338; 84,000 in about 1422; 102,000 in 1509; and 169,000 in 1563—a figure it was not to reach again until the twentieth century.

This remarkable urban concentration affected Italian culture. The large nonagrarian population depended for its support on a vigorous commerce and active urban industries. All levels of society participated in commerce, including the great landlords, nobles, and knights —classes which in northern Europe tended to remain on their rural estates. Moreover, success in urban occupations required a level of training higher than that needed in agriculture; therefore, many Italian cities supported public schools to assure themselves of an educated citizenry. Frequently even girls were given an elementary education, since literacy was a nearly essential skill for the wives of shopkeepers and merchants. Finally, many towns were politically independent and offered their affluent citizens the opportunity to participate in governmental decisions. To many great families such participation was essential to the protection of their interests, and required a mastery of the arts of communicating with their fellow citizens. In sum, Italian urban society in the fourteenth and fifteenth centuries was remarkably well educated and committed to active participation in the affairs of business and of government.

FAMILIES

The cities were populous, but the households within them tended to be small and unstable. Average household size roughly followed the general population trends of decline and growth in the fourteenth and fifteenth centuries, but remained small over most of this period.[1] At Florence in 1427, the average household contained only 3.8 persons; at Bologna in 1395, 3.5 persons; at Verona in 1425, 3.7 persons. Restricted household size reflected the numerous deaths in a time of plagues, but marital customs also contributed. In particular, urban males tended to be much older than their brides when they married. At Florence in 1427, most men postponed marriage until they were thirty, and some did not marry at all. Economic factors—lengthy apprenticeships required of males in the urban trades, extended absences from home on commercial ventures, the need to accumulate capital before starting a family—delayed and sometimes precluded marriage for urban men. Florentine women, on the other hand, were on the average less than eighteen years old when they married for the first time; the "modal" (most common) age of first marriage for these urban girls in 1427 was fifteen years.

Several important social and cultural results followed from this distinctive marriage pattern. Because of high mortalities, the pool of prospective grooms (men of approximately thirty years of age) was distinctly smaller than the pool of brides (girls in their middle and late teens). Girls (or rather, their fathers and families) faced acute competition in the search for scarce husbands; brides, in consequence, usually entered marriage under unfavorable terms. In particular they or their families normally had to pay substantial dowries. Families with many daughters to marry faced financial ruin. This was one reason why girls were married so young; their fathers or families were eager to settle their uncertain futures as soon as possible. Those girls who could not be married before the age of twenty had no honorable alternative

---

[1] The data on Florentine families are taken largely from a study by D. Herlihy and C. Klapisch, *Les Toscans et leurs familles* (1978).

but to enter convents. In the words of a contemporary saint, Bernardine of Siena, these unwilling nuns were "the scum and vomit of the world."

Given the wide age difference separating the spouses, the urban marriage was likely to be of short duration, ending usually with the death of the husband. Often, too, the young widow did not remarry. Florentine husbands typically tried to discourage their spouses from remarrying after their own deaths; their widows, once remarried, might neglect the offspring of their earlier unions. Accordingly, the wills of Florentine husbands characteristically gave to their widows special concessions, which would be lost in the event of remarriage: use of the family dwelling, the right to serve as guardians over their children, sometimes a pension or annuity. Moreover, at her husband's death the substantial dowry, paid by her family at her marriage, was returned to the widow to be used as she saw fit. For the first time in her life, she was freed from male tutelage, whether of father, brothers, or husband. Many widowed women obviously relished this new-found freedom. At Florence in 1427, more than one-half of the female population, age forty or over, were widowed. The city teemed with mature women, many of them widows, many attracted to the city from the countryside, some of them wealthy and able to influence urban culture.

Even while her husband lived, the Florentine woman soon attained a special position within the household. Her husband was likely to be fully occupied by affairs of business or politics. The wife assumed primary responsibility for running the household and for bringing up the children. She was also usually destined for longer contact with her children. The average baby in Florence in 1427 was born to a mother of twenty-six; the father was forty. To many Florentines of the fourteenth and fifteenth centuries, the father was a distant figure, routinely praised but rarely intimately known; the

mother dominated the formative years of the children. A friar named Giovanni Dominici, writing in the first decade of the fifteenth century, complained that Florentine mothers were spoiling their children, both girls and boys. They dressed them in elegant clothes and taught them music and dancing, presumably elevating their aesthetic tastes. They did not countenance violent or brutal games or sports. The result, Dominici implies, was an effeminization of Florentine culture. Women served primarily as intermediaries between the urban generations, shaping to their own preferences the values and attitudes which the young received. Elegance and refinement are essential attributes of Renaissance culture; elegant and refined tastes seem to have been assiduously nurtured within the bosom of the urban family.

The short duration of the urban marriage, the reluctance of many widows to remarry, and the commitment of many girls to the convent limited the exposure of urban women to the risk of pregnancy, to use the language of modern demography. In the countryside, men characteristically married in their middle twenties and took as brides girls nearer in age to themselves. The duration of rural marriages was longer, and couples had more children. The urban family was less prolific and usually smaller than its rural counterpart. The city thus ran a demographic deficit in relation to the countryside. This too had an important social repercussion. The city was forced to replenish its numbers by encouraging large-scale immigration from the countryside and small towns. This promoted both physical and social mobility, as the city characteristically attracted and rewarded skilled and energetic immigrants. Many of the leaders of the cultural Renaissance—Boccaccio, Leonardo Bruni, Coluccio Salutati, Poggio Bracciolini, Leonardo da Vinci, and others—were of rural or small-town origins and came to the city to meet its constant need for men. The Renaissance city seems to have been eminently successful in identifying the talented and in utilizing well its human capital.

The unstable character of the urban household and of human relations within it prompted much reflection on the family. Earlier, social thinkers had viewed the family abstractly, in relation to man's ultimate destiny; they affirmed that it was a natural society, but did not examine how it functioned in the real world. In contrast, concern for the welfare, even the survival, of families animates writers of the fifteenth century in Italy. Foremost among them was the Florentine scholar, artist, and architect Leon Battista Alberti, who in the 1430s wrote a tract entitled *Four Books on the Family*. In it he explained how children should be reared, wives chosen, domestic affairs managed, and friends cultivated—all to assure the survival of threatened lineages. Closely related to this examination of domestic policies are numerous tracts devoted to the training of children, many of which advocated a reform of education in the humanistic spirit (see p. 374). These tracts show a new awareness of the special psychology of children. Simultaneously, the artists of the period were presenting young people, even the infant Christ, not as miniature adults, but authentically as children, looking and acting as children do. The playful baby angels known as putti appear in even the most solemn religious paintings. The very fragility of the Italian urban family seems to have inspired a deeper appreciation of the values of family life, and the contribution which every member, even the youngest, makes to domestic contentment.

Finally, the weakness of the urban family forced its members to cultivate ties with outsiders in order to seek supplementary material and moral support. Living in constant contact with the outside world, the inhabitants of the Italian cities grew more sensitive to the canons of good behavior and the art of making friends. The age produced an abundance of essays on good manners, the most famous of which was the *Book of the Courtier*, written in 1516 by Baldassare Castiglione. Castiglione intended to describe proper deportment at court, but his work affected the image of the gentleman and the lady for a much broader range of society and was destined to influence standards of behavior all over Europe.

LEADERSHIP OF THE YOUNG

A principal reason for the instability of the urban family was the high levels of mortality which prevailed everywhere in Europe in the fourteenth and fifteenth centuries. On the basis of family memoirs left to us by Florentine merchants, which record births and deaths in the household, life expectancy from birth for these relatively affluent persons was forty years in about 1300, dropping to only eighteen years in the generation struck by the Black Death, and rising to thirty years in the fifteenth century as the plagues declined in virulence. (Today in the United States a newborn may be expected to survive for some seventy years.) To be sure, the high death rates attributable to plague were strongly "age specific," that is, they varied considerably across the various levels of age. The principal victims were the very young. In many periods, probably between one-half and one-third of the babies born never reached fifteen. Society swarmed with little children, but the death of children was a common occurrence in almost every family.

According to the most recent studies, the plague (as distinct from other causes of death) took greater tolls among young adults than among the aged. In effect, a person who survived one or more major epidemics had a good chance of living through the next onslaught. This phenomenon allowed some few favored persons to reach extreme old age, in the face of the horrendous mortalities. But it also meant that young adults continued to face high risks of dying. Friars, for example, who entered the Dominican convent of Sta. Maria Novella at Florence in the last half of the fourteenth century survived an average of only twenty years after profession, when most would have been in their late teens. Although there are exceptions, the normal adult career was of short duration.

For this reason, on every level and in every activity of life, the leaders of the fourteenth and fifteenth centuries were often very young, and subject to rapid replacement. The young were not frustrated by the lengthy survival of numerous elders, who clung on to the available jobs and blocked their own careers. There was no basis for the kind of generational tensions and conflicts which have disturbed modern societies. The leaders of the age show psychological qualities which may in part at least be attributed to their youth: impatience and imagination; a tendency to take quick recourse to violence; a love of extravagant gesture and display; and a rather small endowment of prudence, restraint, and self-control. High mortality and a rapid turnover of leaders further contributed to making this an age of opportunity, especially within the cities. Early death assured room at the top for the energetic and the gifted, especially in the business and artistic fields, where birth mattered little and skill counted for much.

The power given to the young, the rapid replacement of leaders, the opportunities extended to the gifted, and the thin ranks of an older generation that might counsel restraint worked also to intensify the pace of cultural change. To be sure, notoriously poor communications hampered the spread of ideas. The quickest a man or a letter could travel on land was between twenty and thirty miles per day; to get to Bruges by sea from Genoa took thirty days, from Venice forty days. The expense and scarcity of manuscripts before the age of printing further narrowed and muffled the intellectual dialogue. On the other hand, new generations pressed upon the old at a much more rapid rate than in our own society, and characteristically they brought with them new policies, preferences, and ideas, or at least a willingness to experiment—in sum, ferment. The gifted man was given his main chance early in his life and passed early from the scene. In Italy as in all Europe the stage of the fourteenth and fifteenth centuries with its constantly changing characters often appears crowded, but the drama enacted upon it moves at a rapid, exciting pace.

LEARNING AND LITERATURE

Although university and scholastic learning retained considerable vitality in the fourteenth and fifteenth centuries, Scholasticism did not adequately serve the literate lay population. The curriculum remained largely designed for the training of teachers and theologians, whereas men committed to an active life in business and politics wanted practical training in the arts of persuasive communications: good speaking and good writing. Moreover, many laymen believed that scholastics failed to meet their religious needs. Coldly analytic in its treatment of religious questions, Scholasticism seemed indifferent to the personal, emotional, and mystical aspects of religion. As Petrarch was to note, education should train men in the art of leading a wise, pious, and happy life. The central concern of the cultural Renaissance was to develop a system of education which would do exactly that.

Humanism

One minor branch of the medieval educational curriculum, rhetoric, or the art of good speaking and writing, was concerned specifically with the skill of communicating well. Initially, the art consisted of little more than memorizing Latin formulas by rote for use in letters or legal documents. With time its practitioners began to search through the Latin classics for further

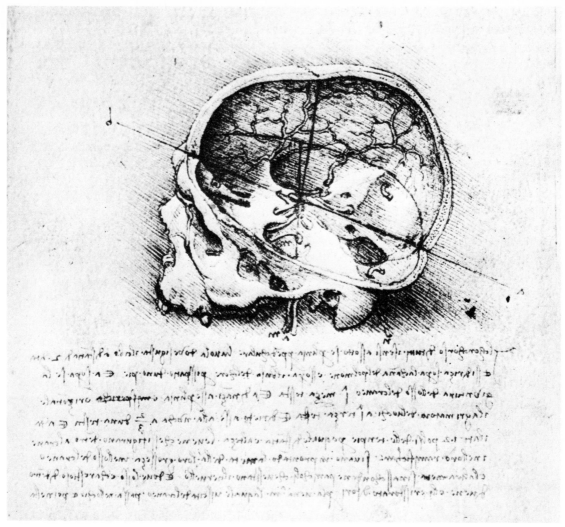

models of good writing. This return to the classical authors was facilitated by the close relationship between the Italian language and Latin, by the availability of manuscripts, and by the visual evidence preserved in countless monuments of the classical achievement. By the late thirteenth century in a number of Italian cities, notably Padua, Bologna, and Florence, writers were calling for new directions in education, urging that the classics be studied inten-

Although the humanists disparaged the narrow professional training of the medieval schools (including medicine), they advocated that all aspects of man were worthy of study: nihil humanum a me alienum, *"nothing human is foreign to me." In this cross section of the human skull, done in 1489, Leonardo da Vinci states in his notes that he sought to illustrate the "confluence of the senses" at the intersection of the diagonal lines. The drawing shows his deep anatomical and psychological interests.* (Photo: Royal Collection, Windsor Castle)

sively and that learning be made morally relevant in the sense of helping men to better lives.

These men were the founders of the intellectual movement known as Humanism. Basically, Humanism means classical scholarship—the ability to read, understand, and appreciate the writings of the ancient world. In classical antiquity, and again in the Renaissance, educators called the curriculum most suitable for the training of free and responsible persons the *studia humanitatis* ("the studies of mankind" or "the humanities").[2] The curriculum was designed to develop in the student primarily those qualities of intellect and will which truly distinguished men from animals. The ideal product of a humanist education was the man, trained in the classics, who possessed both *sapientia* and *eloquentia*—the wisdom needed to know the right path to follow in any situation and the eloquence needed to persuade his fellows to take it.

Renaissance Humanism was marked by three principal characteristics. First, it rejected the emphasis which the medieval schools placed on professional training, whether in theology, law, or medicine, and advocated a liberal education, based on a knowledge of moral philosophy and a command of eloquence. The truly educated person was not identified by technical mastery of a body of learning, but by the capacity to make the right moral judgments in difficult human situations. Second, Humanism stressed the supreme importance of the Latin language (later, Greek also) and the classical authors. These were the models of eloquence and the storehouses of wisdom which offered men the best possible guides to life, apart from religion itself. Third, Humanism affirmed the possibility of human improvement through education and study. Ideally, man should develop

to the fullest all his specifically human faculties—physical, moral, spiritual, aesthetic. There was nothing in this hope for human perfection antagonistic to traditional Christianity and ecclesiastical authority. The modern use of the word "Humanism" to denote a secular philosophy which denies an afterlife has no basis in the history of the Renaissance. Most Renaissance humanists read the Church fathers as avidly as the pagan authors and believed that the highest virtues included piety. Humanism was far more an effort to enrich traditional religious attitudes than a revolt against them.

Petrarch

The man who clarified these humanistic ideals and disseminated them with unprecedented success in Italy and to some extent in Europe was the Tuscan Francesco Petrarch (1304–1374), a writer by profession and one of the most attractive personalities of his age. Petrarch possessed an immense enthusiasm—and generated it in others—for the ancient authors, for educational reform, and for scholarship. He personally sought to save from neglect the ancient authors preserved in monastic libraries and launched an eager search for their manuscripts, a pursuit that was to become an integral part of the humanist movement. Petrarch had a dismal opinion of his own times and held up in contrast the ideal world of ancient Rome, when there supposedly flourished both authentic learning and virtue. For this reason he thought that the Latin classics should be the heart of the educational curriculum.

Petrarch wrote prolifically and with consistent grace and flair in both Latin and Italian. His best Latin works are his five hundred letters, all clearly composed with an eye to a readership beyond the persons addressed. He was the first to discern personality in the great writers of the past, and he directed some of the letters to them—Cicero, Seneca, Vergil, and especially St. Augustine, his favorite literary companion. He also composed an autobio-

---

[2] "Humanism" was not actually coined until the nineteenth century. In fifteenth- and sixteenth-century Italy, *humanista* signified a professor of humane studies (the *studia humanitatis*) or a classical scholar.

graphical "letter to posterity" to future generations—to us. Even today, his warmth and wit win him friends.

Petrarch pretended to disparage his Italian works, but today they are the foundation of his literary reputation. Especially admirable are his 366 sonnets, most of which express his love for a young married woman named Laura, who died in the plague of 1348. In the sonnets written both before and after her death, love represents for Petrarch not so much passion as a way to inner peace; Laura offers him not so much satisfaction as solace.

In his writings, particularly in his imaginative exchanges with St. Augustine, Petrarch examines at length an ethical dilemma characteristic of his age: how should religious people act who aspire to a life of quiet contemplation but feel themselves responsible for the welfare of family, friends, community, Church, and the world in tumultuous times? He does not resolve this dilemma, but probably no one before him explored its dimensions with equal sensitivity.

Petrarch richly deserves his esteemed place in the history of European thought. More than any writer before him, he set a new standard of excellence for Western letters by imitating the simplicity and elegance of classical literary style. He also defined a new aim in education—the art of living happily and well, as distinct from the narrow professional goals of the older Scholasticism. Finally, he helped develop a new vision of human fulfillment. To Petrarch, the ideal man was the one who spent his life in the study of letters, enjoyed them, cherished them, and found God in them.

Boccaccio

A near-contemporary of Petrarch, and second only to him in his influence on fourteenth-century Italian learning, was Giovanni Boccaccio (1313–1375). As a young author, Boccaccio celebrated in poetry the charms of his lady Fiammetta, who, unlike Beatrice and even Laura, did not conduct the poet to idealized

rapture and ultimate peace, but instead delighted him with both her beauty and her wit and sometimes baffled him with her shifting moods. She was the woman, not of mystic love, but of daily experience.

Boccaccio's great work, the short stories known as *The Decameron*, was written probably between 1348 and 1351. It recounts how a group of young Florentines—seven women and three men—fled during the Black Death of 1348 to a secluded villa, where for ten days each told a story. The first prose masterpiece in Italian, and a model thereafter for clear and lively narration, *The Decameron* is often considered a work of literary realism, principally for its frank and frequent treatment of sex. In fact, however, it hardly ever offers a realistic portrait of fourteenth-century life and society, for the narrators are consciously seeking to flee and forget the grim, real world; their servants are even forbidden to repeat unpleasant news within their charming villa. *The Decameron* was composed as an antidote to melancholy—one of the first major works in Western letters intended to divert and amuse rather than edify.

With age this one-time spinner of ribald stories became attracted to the religious life; he took orders in the Church and turned his efforts to the cure of souls. Like Petrarch, he disparaged his vernacular writings and even reprimanded a friend for allowing his wife to read the indecent *Decameron*. He died regretting the work which has earned him immortality.

The Civic Humanists

In the generation after Petrarch and Boccaccio, Florentine scholars were preeminent in the humanist movement, and under the leadership of Coluccio Salutati gave to the revived study of antiquity the character of a true movement. Through the recovery of ancient manuscripts and the formation of libraries Coluccio and his group—Leonardo Bruni, Poggio Bracciolini, and others—made accessible to scholars

Nastagio's tale, from The Decameron, *tells of a rejected suitor who encounters in the woods outside of Ravenna a phantom knight. Every Friday, the knight hunts down and kills the ghost of the lady who, in refusing his love, had caused his death. The suitor invites his own lady and her family to a Friday banquet in the woods, where they too witness the horrifying hunt. The living lady recognizes the cruelty of her ways and accepts the suitor. The depiction of this popular story given here is a detail from panels by the great fifteenth-century Florentine painter, Sandro Botticelli. (Photo: Museo del Prado)*

virtually the entire surviving corpus of classical Latin authors.

These Florentines further sought to reestablish in Italy a command of the Greek language, which, according to Bruni, "no Italian had understood in seven hundred years." In 1396 they invited the Byzantine scholar Manuel Chrysoloras to lecture at the University of Florence. In the following decades—troubled years for the Byzantine Empire—other Eastern scholars joined the exodus to the West, and they and Western visitors returning from the East brought with them hundreds of Greek manuscripts. By the middle of the fifteenth century Western scholars had both the philological skill and the manuscripts to establish direct contact with the most original minds of the classical world and were making numerous Latin and Italian translations of Greek works. Histories, tragedies, lyric poetry, the dialogues of Plato, many mathematical treatises, the most important works of the Greek fathers of the Church—in sum, a large part of the Greek cultural inheritance—fully entered Western culture for the first time.

Coluccio and his contemporary Florentine scholars are now often called civic humanists, since they stressed that participation in public affairs is essential for full human development. They linked their praise of the active life with a defense of the republican liberty of

Florence, then threatened by the despot Gian Galeazzo of Milan. The humanists argued that human advance depends on a kind of community dialogue, which allows men to learn from one another. To participate in such a dialogue the educated citizen needs wisdom founded upon sound moral philosophy and also eloquence, without which his knowledge will remain socially barren. The best education imparts both qualities, which are themselves best exemplified by the ancient classics. Moreover, if human progress depends on dialogue, the best political institutions are those which invite the participation of the citizens in the councils of government. The republican form of government was therefore claimed superior to the despotism represented by Gian Galeazzo. In one integrated argument the civic humanists thus defended the capital importance of training in the classics, the superiority of the active life, and the value of Florentine republican institutions.

Humanism in the Fifteenth Century

As the humanist movement gained in prestige, it spread from Florence to the other principal cities of Italy. At Rome and Naples one of the most able humanist scholars was Lorenzo Valla (1407–1457). Valla conclusively proved that the document known as the Donation of Constantine—one of the documents upon which the papacy based its claim to supremacy in the West—was a forgery concocted in the eighth century. According to the Donation, when Emperor Constantine left Rome in the fourth century to found Constantinople, he gave the pope Italy and the entire Western empire. Drawing on his superb historical knowledge of Latin, Valla pointed out the anachronisms in the document; many of the Latin expressions used were typical of the eighth century, not the fourth. Valla was thus one of the first scholars to develop the tools of historical criticism in interpreting ancient records.

Two fifteenth-century scholars from the north of Italy, Guarino da Verona and Vittorino da Feltre, were chiefly responsible for incorporating the diffuse educational ideas of the humanists into a practical curriculum. Guarino launched a reform of the traditional methods of education and Vittorino brought the new methods to their fullest development in the various schools he founded, especially his *Casa Giocosa* ("Happy House") at Mantua. The pupils included boys and girls, both rich and poor (the latter on scholarships). All the students learned Latin and Greek, mathematics, music, and philosophy; in addition, because Vittorino believed that education should aid physical, moral, and social development, they were also taught social graces such as dancing and courteous manners and received instruction in physical exercises like riding and fencing. Vittorino's Happy House attracted pupils from all over Italy, and his methods were widely imitated even beyond the Italian borders.

By the late fifteenth century, and still more in the sixteenth, Humanism, in the sense of classical literary scholarship, showed a declining vitality in Italy. Like most reform movements Italian Humanism declined principally because its cause had been won. By about 1450, with only a few exceptions, the monastic libraries had yielded their treasures of ancient manuscripts, and in the latter half of the century printing made the texts readily available among the educated public. Humanists were no longer needed to find the ancient authors, copy them, or propagandize for their wider dissemination. Education too had come to recognize, at least partially, the value of training in the classics. By the late fifteenth century the leaders of Italian intellectual life were no longer the humanists but philosophers, who were now able to use a command of the classical heritage to enrich and develop their own philosophical systems.

The Florentine Neoplatonists

One major theme of the cultural Renaissance, perhaps generated by the misery and melancholy of life, was an effort to depict ideal worlds in thought, literature, and art. A good example of what some scholars call the Renaissance religion of beauty is provided by a group of philosophers active at Florence in the last decades of the fifteenth century. The most gifted among them was probably Marsilio Ficino, whose career is a tribute to the cultural patronage of the Medici. Cosimo de' Medici befriended him as a child and gave him the use of a villa and library near Florence. In this lovely setting a group of scholars and statesmen met frequently to discuss philosophical questions. Drawn to the idealism of Plato (and usually called the Platonic Academy), Ficino and his fellows were particularly concerned with the place of the human soul within the Platonic cosmos and with the soul's dignity and immortality, which they passionately affirmed. To spread these ideas among a larger audience Ficino translated into Latin all of Plato's dialogues and the writings of the chief figures of the Neoplatonic tradition. He also made an ambitious effort to reconcile and assimilate Platonic philosophy and the Christian religion.

Another brilliant member of the Platonic Academy was the young Prince Giovanni Pico della Mirandola, who thought he could reconcile all philosophies. In 1486 Pico proposed to dispute publicly at Rome on some nine hundred theses which would show the essential unity of the philosophic experience. But Pope Innocent VIII, believing that the theses contained several heretical propositions, forbade the disputation. By the time of his death at thirty-one Pico had not made much progress toward the "philosophical peace," or reconciliation of philosophical systems, which he sought.

Both Ficino and Pico founded their philosophies upon two essential assumptions: all being is arranged in a hierarchy of excellence with God at the summit. Moreover, each be-ing in the universe, with the exception only of God, is impelled through a "natural appetite" to seek the perfection of its kind; it is impelled, in other words, to achieve—or at least to contemplate—the beautiful. As Pico expressed it, however, man is unique in that he is placed in the middle of the universe linked with both the spiritual world above and the material one below. His free will enables him to seek perfection in either direction; he is free to become all things. A clear ethic emerges from this scheme: the good life should be an effort to achieve personal perfection, and the highest human value is the contemplation of the beautiful.

These philosophers believed that Plato had been divinely illumined and therefore that Platonic philosophy and Christian belief were two wholly reconcilable faces of a single truth. Neoplatonic philosophy has a particular importance for the influence it exerted on many of the great artists of the Florentine Renaissance, including Botticelli and Michelangelo.

The Heritage of Humanism

Fifteenth-century Italian Humanism left a deep imprint on European scholarship and education. The humanists greatly strengthened the command of Latin. They also restored a mastery of the Greek language in the West and elevated a large part of the Greek cultural inheritance to a position of influence in Western civilization. Moreover, they began the systematic investigation of other languages associated with great cultural traditions, most notably Hebrew, and in so doing laid the basis of modern textual and (more remotely) historical criticism. They developed new ways of investigating the character of the ancient world—through archaeology, numismatics (the study of coins), and epigraphy (the study of inscriptions on buildings, statues, and the like), as well as through the study of literary texts. Humanistic influence on the study of history was particularly profound. The medieval chroniclers had looked into the past for evidence of God's saving providence, whereas the humanists were primarily concerned with utilizing the past to illustrate human behavior and provide moral examples. Though their approach was not without its faults—such as an aversion to mundane detail and statistical data, and a sometimes bombastic and obscure rhetorical style—they certainly deepened the historical consciousness of the West and greatly strengthened the historian's technical skill. Humanistic influences on vernacular languages helped bring standardization of spelling and grammar; and the classical ideas of simplicity, restraint, and elegance of style exerted a continuing influence on Western letters.

No less important was the role of the humanists as educational reformers. The curriculum devised by them spread throughout Europe in the sixteenth century; in fact, until the early twentieth century it everywhere defined the standards by which the lay leaders of Western society were trained. Protestants, Catholics, men of all nationalities were steeped in the same classics and consequently thought and communicated in similar fashion. In spite of bitter religious divisions and heated national antagonisms, the common humanistic education helped preserve the fundamental cultural unity of the West.

Whatever the achievements of the movement in the fourteenth and fifteenth centuries, it cannot be concluded that Humanism represented a revolt against the intellectual and religious heritage of the Middle Ages. It would be more accurate to say that the humanists, rather than destroying the heritage of the past, opened it to a new and larger audience. In the thirteenth century learning had remained largely a monopoly of monks and scholastics, and its character reflected their professional and vocational needs. In the fourteenth and fifteenth centuries the humanists introduced a narrow but still important segment of lay society to the accumulated intellectual treasury of the European past, both classical and scholastic, ancient and medieval. Simultaneously, they reinterpreted that heritage and enlarged the function of education and scholarship to serve men in their present life by teaching them, as Petrarch recommended, the art of living wisely and well.

II. THE CULTURE OF THE NORTH

Most areas of Europe beyond the Alps did not have the many large cities and the high percentage of urban dwellers that supported the humanistic movement in Italy. Moreover, unlike those of Italy, the physical monuments and languages of northern Europe did not offer ready reminders of the classical heritage. Humanism and the true classical Renaissance, with a literate, trained laity, did not come to the north until the last decade of the fifteenth century. The court, rather than the city, and the knight, rather than the merchant, dominated northern culture for most of the later fourteenth and fifteenth centuries.

CHIVALRY

In 1919 a Dutch historian, Johan Huizinga, wrote *The Waning of the Middle Ages,* a stimulating study of the character of north European culture in the fourteenth and fifteenth centuries. That culture, Huizinga argued, should be viewed, not as a renaissance, but as the decline of medieval civilization. Paying chief attention to the court of the dukes of Burgundy, who were among the wealthiest and most powerful princes of the north, Huizinga examined courtly life and manners, and described the courtiers' views on love, war, and religion. He found tension and frequent violence in this society, with little of the balance and serenity that had marked medieval society in the thirteenth century. Instead, its members seemed to show a defective sense of reality, an acute inconsistency in their values and actions, and great emotional instability. Many critics now consider that Huizinga probably exaggerated the negative qualities in northern culture, but that his analysis still contains much that is accurate.

The defective sense of reality that Huizinga noted is manifest in the extravagant cultivation of the notion of chivalry. Militarily, the knight was in fact becoming less important than the foot soldier armed with longbow, pike, or firearms. But the noble classes of the north continued to pretend that knightly virtues governed all questions of state and society; they discounted such lowly considerations as money, arms, number of forces, supplies, and the total resources of countries in deciding the outcome of wars. For example, before the Battle of Agincourt, one French knight told King Charles that he should not use contingents from the Parisian townsfolk because that would give his army an unfair numerical advantage; the battle should be decided strictly on the basis of chivalrous valor.

This was the age of the perfect knight and the *beau geste* and grand feats of arms. King John of Bohemia insisted that his soldiers lead him to the front rank of battle, so that he could better strike the enemy; but he needed his soldiers to guide him, for John was blind. The feats of renowned knights won the rapt admiration of chroniclers but affected the outcome of battle hardly at all. The age was marked too by the foundation of new orders of chivalry—notably the Knights of the Garter and the Burgundian Knights of the Golden Fleece.[3] The basic supposition was that these orders would reform the world by the intensive cultivation of knightly virtues.

Princes rivaled one another in the sheer glitter of their arms and the splendor of their tournaments. They waged wars of dazzlement, seeking to confound rivals and confirm friends with spectacular displays of gold, silks, and tapestries. Court ceremony achieved unprecedented excesses.

Extravagance touched the chivalric arts of love as well. A special order was founded for the defense of women, and knights frequently took lunatic oaths to honor their ladies, such as keeping one eye closed for extended periods. Obviously people rarely made love or war in this artificial way. But men still drew satisfaction in speculating—in dreaming—how love and war would be if this sad world were only a perfect place.

THE CULT OF DECAY

Huizinga called the extravagant life style of the northern courts the "cult of the sublime," or the impossibly beautiful. But he also noted that both knights and commoners showed a morbid fascination with death and its ravages. Reminders of the ultimate victory of death and explicit treatment of decay are frequently encountered in both literature and art. One popular artistic motif was the danse macabre, or dance of death, depicting people from all walks of life—rich and poor, cleric and layman, good and bad—joined in their final, intimate dance. Another melancholy theme favored by all European artists was the Pietà—the Virgin weeping over her dead son.

This morbid interest in death and decay in an age of pestilence was not the fruit of lofty religious sentiment. The unbalanced concern with the fleetingness of material beauty shows, if anything, an excessive attachment to it, a

---

[3] Jason, leader of the Argonauts, was the first patron of the order, but the question was soon raised whether a pagan hero could appropriately be taken as a model by Christian knights. It was further pointed out that Jason had treated his wife Medea in a most unchivalrous fashion (he left her for another woman). Jason was therefore replaced as patron by the Old Testament hero Gideon.

kind of inverse materialism. Even more than that, it reveals a growing religious dissatisfaction. In the thirteenth century Francis of Assisi addressed death as a sister; in the fourteenth and fifteenth centuries men clearly regarded it as a ravaging, indomitable fiend. Clearly the Church was failing to provide consolation to many of its members, and a religion that fails to console is a religion in crisis.

Still another manifestation of the unsettled religious spirit of the age was a fascination with the devil, demonology, and witchcraft. The most enlightened scholars of the day argued at length about whether witches could ride through the air on sticks, and about their relations with the devil. (One of the more notable

The danse macabre was a common artistic theme in northern Europe, reflecting a gloomy fascination with death. This woodcut of "Skeleton Dance" is from the Nuremberg World Chronicle of 1493. (Photo: Philip Evola)

witch trials of Western history occurred at Arras in 1460. Scores of people were accused of participating in a witches' sabbath, giving homage to the devil, and even having sexual intercourse with him.) Fear of the devil and perhaps also a widespread cultivation of the occult arts in the lower levels of society are salient departures from the serene, confident religion of the thirteenth century.

Finally, men showed an inordinate desire to reduce religious images to their most concrete form. The passion to have immediate, physical contact with the objects of religious devotion gave added popularity to pilgrimages and still more to the obsession with relics of the saints, which, more often fabricated than authentic, became a major commodity in international trade, and princes accumulated collections numbering in the tens of thousands.

Huizinga saw these manifestations of northern culture as the disintegration of the cultural synthesis of the Middle Ages. Without a disciplined and unified view of the world, attitudes toward war, love, and religion lost balance, and disordered behavior followed. This culture was not young and vigorous but old and dying. However, Huizinga's root concept of decadence must be used with a certain caution. Certainly this was a psychologically disturbed world, which had lost the self-confidence of the thirteenth century; but these allegedly decadent men were not the victims of a torpid spirit. They were dissatisfied perhaps, but they were also passionately anxious to find solutions to the psychological tensions that unsettled them. It is well to recall that passion when trying to understand the appeal and the power behind other cultural movements—lay piety, northern Humanism, and efforts for religious reform.

CONTEMPORARY VIEWS OF NORTHERN SOCIETY

Huizinga wrote about chivalric society from the perspective of the twentieth century. One of the best contemporary historians of that society was Jean Froissart (1333?–1400?) of Flanders, who traveled widely across England and the Continent, noting carefully the exploits of valiant men. His chronicles give the richest account of the first half of the Hundred Years' War, and he has no equal among medieval chroniclers for colorful, dramatic narration. Nonetheless, Froissart has been criticized for his preoccupation with chivalric society; his narrative treats peasants and townsmen with contempt, or simply ignores them. Yet concerns limited to chivalry suited the purposes for which he wrote. He wished to record the wars of his day, lest, as he put it, "the deeds of present champions should fade into oblivion."

The works of contemporary English writers help to round out the picture of northern society in the fourteenth century. One of them, a poet of uncertain identity, probably William Langland, presents the viewpoint of the humbler classes. His *Vision of Piers Plowman*, which was probably written about 1360, is one of the most remarkable works of the age. The poem gives a loosely connected account of eleven visions, each of which is crowded with allegorical figures, and it is filled with spirited comment about the various classes of people, the impact of plague and war upon society, and the failings of the Church.

Geoffrey Chaucer wrote about the middle classes. His *Canterbury Tales*, perhaps the greatest work of imaginative literature produced anywhere in Europe in the late fourteenth century, recounts the pilgrimage of some thirty persons to the tomb of St. Thomas à Becket at Canterbury. For entertainment on the road each pilgrim agrees to tell two stories. Chaucer's portraits sum up the moral and social ills of the day, especially those affecting the Church. His robust monk, for example, ignores the Benedictine rule; his friar is more interested in donations than in the cure of souls; and his pardoner knowingly hawks fraudulent relics. But Chaucer's picture is balanced; he praises the student of Oxford, who would gladly learn and gladly teach, and the rural parson, who cares for his flock while others search out benefices, to the neglect of the faithful. Apart from the grace of his poetry Chaucer was gifted with an ability to delineate character and spin a lively narrative. *The Canterbury Tales* is a masterly portrayal of human personalities and human behavior which can delight readers in any age.

III. RELIGIOUS THOUGHT AND PIETY

The Scholasticism of the thirteenth century, as represented by Thomas Aquinas, was based on the bold postulate that it was within the power of human reason to construct a universal philosophy that would do justice to all truths and would reconcile all apparent conflicts among them. The simultaneous growth in ecclesiastical law had also tended to define Christian obligations and the Christian life in terms of precise rules of behavior rather than interior spirit. This style of thinking changed during the next two centuries. Many scholastics were drawn toward analysis (breaking apart) rather than synthesis (putting together) as they attempted a rigorous investigation of philosophical and theological statements. Many of them no longer shared Aquinas's confidence in human reason. Fundamentally, they hoped to repair the Thomistic synthesis or to replace it by new systems which, though less comprehensive, would at least rest on sound foundations. Piety changed too, as more and more Christian leaders sought ways of deepening interior, mystical experience.

The "Modern Way"

The followers of St. Thomas or of Duns Scotus remained active in the late medieval schools, but the most original of the philosophers were nominalists, that is, those who denied the existence, or at least the knowability, of universal natures —manness, dogness, and the like. The greatest of these late medieval nominalists was the English Franciscan William of Ockham (1300?–1349?). The fundamental principle of his logical analysis later came to be called Ockham's razor. It may be stated in several ways, but essentially it affirms that between alternative explanations for the same phenomenon, the simpler is always to be preferred.

On the basis of this "principle of economy" Ockham attacked the traditional problem of ideal forms, such as manness or dogness. He rejected Aquinas's argument that all beings, apart from God, were metaphysically composite of a principle of unity (act) and a principle of individuation (potency). The simplest way to explain the existence of an individual object is to affirm that it exists. The mind can detect resemblances among objects and form general concepts concerning them; these concepts can be further manipulated in logically valid ways. But they offer no certain assurance that ideal forms—principles of unity in which individual objects participate—exist in the real world.

The area of reality in which the mind can effectively function is thus severely limited. The universe, as far as human reason can detect, is an aggregate of autonomous individual beings, not a hierarchy of ideal forms, natures, or ideas. The proper approach in dealing with this universe is through direct experience, not through speculations about ideal or abstract natures, the very existence of which is doubtful. Any theology based upon observation and reason would obviously be greatly restricted. It would still be possible, thought Ockham, to prove the existence of necessary principles in the universe, but man could not know whether the necessary principle, or God, is one or many.

Ockham and many of his contemporaries were profoundly impressed by the power and freedom of God and by man's absolute dependence on him. They lacked Aquinas's high assessment of human powers and his confident belief in the ordered and autonomous structure of the natural world. Living within a disturbed,

pessimistic age, the nominalists reflect a crisis in confidence, in natural reason and in themselves, which is a major theme of late medieval cultural history.

Nominalism enjoyed great popularity in the universities, and Ockhamite philosophy in particular came to be known as the *via moderna* ("modern way"). Although nominalists and humanists were frequently at odds, they shared certain common attitudes: both were dissatisfied with some aspects of the medieval intellectual tradition; both were impatient with the speculative abstractions of medieval thought; and both advocated approaches to reality that would concentrate upon the concrete and the present and consider them with a stricter awareness of method.

Social Thought

The belief of the nominalists that reality was to be found, not in abstract forms, but in concrete objects had important implications for social thought. Among the social thinkers clearly influenced by nominalism the most remarkable is Marsilius of Padua. In 1324 he wrote *Defender of Peace*, a pamphlet attacking papal authority and supporting lay sovereignty within the Church. In conformity with nominalist principles Marsilius affirmed that the reality of the Christian community, like the reality of the universe, consists in the aggregate of all its parts. The sovereignty of the Church thus rests in its membership—or, as Marsilius phrased it rather vaguely, in its "stronger and healthier part." This part in turn constituted the "human legislator," which represents the collective, sovereign will of the community. The human legislator delegates the functions of government to six great bureaus: the princely office, the

Detail from the Campin Altarpiece. (Photo: The Metropolitan Museum of Art, The Cloisters Collection, Purchase)

treasury, the military establishment, artisans, cultivators, and finally the clergy.

Marsilius is often considered an architect of the modern concept of sovereignty, and even of totalitarianism. He maintained that only those regulations supported by force are true law. Therefore, the enactments of the Church do not constitute binding legislation, because they are not supported by any coercive power. Only the human legislator can promulgate authentic law, and there is no limit on what it may do. The Church has no right to power or property and is entirely subject to the sovereign will of the state. Sovereignty is in turn indivisible, absolute, and unlimited.

Defender of Peace is noteworthy not only for its radical ideas but also for the evidence it gives of deep dissatisfactions within medieval society. Marsilius and others manifested a hostile impatience with the papal and clerical domination of Western political life. They demanded that the guidance of the Church and the Christian community rest exclusively with laymen. *Defender of Peace*, in this respect at least, was a prophecy of things to come.

STYLES OF PIETY

Religion remained a central concern of fourteenth- and fifteenth-century men and women, but new forms of piety, or religious practice, began to appear that were designed to meet the needs of laymen. Mysticism, an interior sense of the presence and love of God, had found its usual expression within the confines of the monastic orders, but by the thirteenth century this monopoly was beginning to break down. The principal mission of the Franciscans and the Dominicans became preaching to laymen, to whom these two mendicant orders hoped to introduce some of the satisfactions of mystical religion. And laymen, wishing to remain in the outside world, could join special branches of the Franciscans or Dominicans known as third orders.

Confraternities, which were religious guilds largely for laymen, grew up in the cities and, through common religious services and the support of charitable activities, tried to deepen the spiritual life of their members. Humanism preserved strong overtones of a movement for lay piety. An abundance of devotional and mystical literature was written for laymen to teach them how to feel repentance, not just how to define it. Translations of the Scriptures into many vernacular languages appeared, although the high cost of manuscripts before the age of printing severely limited their circulation.

This growth of lay piety was in essence an effort to open the monastic experience to the lay world, to put at the disposal of all what had hitherto been restricted to a spiritual elite. Frightened by the disasters of the age, men hungered for emotional reassurance, for evidence of God's love and redeeming grace within them. Moreover, the spread of education among the laity, at least in the cities, made men discontented with empty forms of religious ritual.

The Rhenish Mystics

The most active center of the new lay piety was the Rhine valley. The first of several leading figures in the region was the Dominican Meister Eckhart. A great preacher and a devoted student of Aquinas, Eckhart sought to bring his largely lay listeners into a mystical confrontation with God. The believer, he maintained, should cultivate within his soul the "divine spark." To achieve this he must banish all thoughts from his mind and seek to attain a state of pure passivity. If he succeeds, God will come and dwell within him. Eckhart stressed the futility of dogma and, implicitly, traditional acts of piety. God is too great to be contained in dogmatic categories and too sovereign to be moved by conventional piety.

The Rhenish mystics all stressed the theme that formal knowledge of God and his attributes means little if it is cultivated without love and emotional receptivity. Perhaps the most

influential of all of them was Gerhard Groote of Holland. Groote wrote sparingly, exerting his extraordinary influence upon his followers largely through his personality. After his death in 1384 his disciples formed a religious congregation known as the Brethren of the Common Life. Taking education as their principal ministry, they founded schools in Germany and the Low Countries that imparted a style of lay piety known as the *devotio moderna* ("modern devotion"). Erasmus of Rotterdam and Martin Luther were among their pupils.

The richest statement of the *devotio moderna* appeared about 1425 in *The Imitation of Christ*, a small devotional manual attributed to Thomas à Kempis, a member of the Brethren of the Common Life. *The Imitation of Christ* says almost nothing about fasting, pilgrimages, and other acts of private penitence characteristic of traditional piety. Instead, it emphasizes interior experience as an essential part of the religious life; it is also untraditional in its ethical and social consciousness. The fruit of interior conversion is not extreme acts of personal expiation, but high ethical behavior: "First, keep yourself in peace, and then you shall be able to bring peace to others."

The new lay piety was by no means a revolutionary break with the medieval Church, but it implicitly discounted the importance of many traditional institutions and practices. In this personal approach to God there was no special value in the monastic vocation. As Erasmus would later sharply argue, what was good in monasticism should be practiced by every Christian. Stressing simplicity and humility, the new lay piety was reacting against the pomp and splendor that had come to surround popes and prelates and to mark religious ceremonies. Likewise, the punctilious rules concerning fasts, abstinences, and devotional exercises; the cult of the saints and their relics; and the traffic in indulgences and pardons all seemed peripheral to true religious needs. Without the proper state of soul these traditional acts of piety were meaningless; with the proper state every act was worship.

A generation ago many Protestant scholars considered that the new lay piety was a preparation for the Reformation, while Catholic historians vigorously affirmed that it was authentically Catholic. Today, in our ecumenical age, the desire to enlist Thomas à Kempis among one's spiritual forebears seems pointless. The new lay piety was a preparation for both sixteenth-century reformations, Protestant and Catholic. It aimed at producing a more penetrating religious sentiment. The formal religion of the Middle Ages, for all its grandeur and logical intricacies, no longer fully satisfied the religious spirit and was leaving hollows in the human heart.

Although the *devotio moderna* was a religious movement, it was in many ways similar to Humanism. Both Thomas à Kempis and Petrarch expressed their distaste for the subtle abstractions and intellectual arrogance of the scholastics. Both stressed that the man who is wise and good will cultivate humility and maintain toward the profound questions of religion a "learned ignorance." Both affirmed that it is more important to educate the will to love than the intellect to the mastery of abstruse theology. Finally, both addressed their message primarily to laymen, in order to aid them to a higher moral life. The humanists of course drew their chief inspiration from the works of pagan and Christian antiquity, whereas the advocates of the new lay piety looked almost exclusively to Scripture. But the resemblances were so close that in the late fifteenth and sixteenth centuries, men like Erasmus and Thomas More could combine elements from both in the movement known as Christian Humanism.

Heresies

Efforts to repair the traditions of medieval Christianity also led to outright heretical attacks upon the religious establishment, which of course were strengthened by antagonism toward the papacy, reaction against corruption in the Church, and the social and psychological tensions characteristic of this disturbed epoch. Fundamentally, however, the growing appeal of heresies reflected the difficulties the Church was experiencing in adapting its organization and teachings to the demands of a changing world.

The most prominent of the heretics of the time was the English Dominican John Wycliffe, who was clearly influenced by the national spirit generated by the Hundred Years' War and the apparent subservience of the Avignon papacy to France. In 1365 he denounced the payment of Peter's pence, the annual tax given by the English people to the papacy. Later he publicly excoriated the papal Curia, monks, and friars for their vices.

Wycliffe argued that the Scriptures alone declared the will of God and that neither the pope, the cardinals, nor scholastic theologians could tell the Christian what he should believe. (In 1382 he began to translate the Bible into English, but died two years later without finishing.) He also attacked the dogma of transubstantiation, which asserts that the priest at mass works a miracle when he changes the substance of bread and wine into the substance of Christ. Besides attacking the special powers, position, and privileges of the priesthood in such dogmas as transubstantiation, Wycliffe assaulted with equal vehemence the authority of the pope and the hierarchy to exercise jurisdiction and to hold property. He claimed that the true Church was that of the predestined, that is, those in the state of sanctifying grace. Only the elect could rule the elect; therefore, popes and bishops who had no grace could be justly divested of their properties and had no right to rule. The chief responsibility for ecclesiastical reform rested with the prince, and the pope could exercise only so much authority as the prince allowed.

Wycliffe's adherents, mostly from among the

lower classes, were called Lollards, a name apparently derived from "lollar" (idler). Although this group may have survived in England until the age of the Tudor Reformation, Wycliffe's religious system seems to have had no direct influence on subsequent ecclesiastical history. Still, his ideas show many similarities with later Protestantism. His insistence on a purified Church, a priesthood not sacramentally distinct from the laity, a vernacular Bible, a religion more culturally responsive to the people, and lay direction of religious affairs marks out the major issues which, within a little more than a century, would divide the Western Christian community.

In distant Bohemia a Czech priest named John Huss (1369–1415) mounted an equally dangerous attack upon the dominance of the established Church. Historians dispute how much Huss was influenced by Wycliffe's ideas. Certainly he knew the works of the English heretic, but he was more conservative in his own theology—what can be understood of it. For Huss's ideas are less than clear, and it is hard even to define how he departed from orthodoxy. He seems to have held that the Church included only the predestined and he questioned, without explicitly denying, transubstantiation.

Huss was burned at the stake at Constance in 1415, more for rejecting the authority of the general council which condemned him than for his doctrinal errors. After his death Huss's followers in Bohemia defied the efforts of the emperor and Church to persuade them to submit; however, the Hussites soon divided into several rival sects—in a manner which anticipates the experience of later Protestantism—and civil war raged in Bohemia from 1421 to 1436 with no clear-cut outcome. The Hussite movement represents one of the earliest successful revolts against the medieval religious establishment. It was also the first withdrawal of an entire territory from unity with Rome.

IV. THE FINE ARTS

The social and cultural changes profoundly affected the arts, making the fourteenth and fifteenth centuries one of the most brilliant periods in Western history. Works of art have survived from this age in an unprecedented abundance, a sign that the arts were assuming broader functions in Western society. Princes and townsmen became art patrons, and the artist himself acquired a new prestige.

PATRONS AND VALUES

In the Early Middle Ages architecture, sculpture, painting, and music were primarily liturgical in character, in the sense that their chief function was to enrich Christian worship. There had, of course, always been some lay patronage of the arts—the troubadours, for example, had composed and sung songs for lay patrons—but secular music remained technically behind the music of the Church, and it is difficult today even to reconstruct its sounds.

The Church continued to promote and inspire artistic production in the fourteenth and fifteenth centuries, and many of the greatest creations of the period retained a liturgical character. But the more novel development of the age was the greatly enlarged role which laymen came to play as patrons—notably the princes of Europe and the rich townsmen in Italy and Flanders. In older histories of the Renaissance the growth of lay patronage was often equated with a secularization of art, but such a view is only partially correct. To a large degree lay patrons favored religious themes in the art they commissioned, even though much of it was no longer liturgical in function. Yet the rise of lay patronage did strongly affect the character of art. In works prepared for liturgical purposes the artist could not draw too much attention to his own work, for the Church objected to art or music which overly intruded upon the consciousness of the worshiping Christian.

Moreover, the painter and the sculptor had to accommodate the architecture of the church they were decorating. The lay patronage of religious art—and the use of that art for the decoration of homes as well as churches—in part freed the artist to form his work as he saw fit, knowing that he had the principal attention of the viewer and that the work did not have to be subservient to architecture.

Moreover, the changing religious values that have been mentioned affected artistic styles. Both the humanists and the promoters of the new lay piety insisted that religious values be made more concrete and more immediate to the believing Christian; in terms of art this meant that the viewer should become involved visually and emotionally with the sacred scenes he contemplated. The growth of naturalism in art reflected not a waning interest in religious images, but an effort to view them more intimately.

The interest of fourteenth- and fifteenth-century society in elegant living naturally extended to nonliturgical art, providing artists an abundance of opportunities. Both townsmen and nobles wished to live in attractive surroundings. Architects therefore turned their attention to the construction of beautiful homes, villas, palaces, and châteaus; adding to the beauty of these residences were tapestries, paintings, statuary, finely made furniture, and windows of tinted glass. This pursuit of elegance also gave music a new importance. In the books on good manners characteristic of the age the perfect courtier or gentleman was instructed to develop an ear for music and an ability to sing gracefully and play an instrument. No gathering within the higher levels of society could take place without the participation of singers and musicians.

Art and music also fulfilled other functions. The growing awareness of and concern with the family led patrons to commission portraits of their loved ones. In an often melancholy age art and music offered the same sweetness, delight, and spiritual refreshment which Boccaccio meant to convey in his *Decameron*. In Italy the philosophers of the Platonic Academy maintained that the contemplation of ideal beauty was the highest human activity, and it was primarily in art that the ideal beauty could be found. In the north as well, art and music were essential parts of what Huizinga called the cult of the sublime, the effort to conjure up through the mind and senses images of ideal worlds.

Finally, the social position of the artist himself was changing. In the Early Middle Ages many artists appear to have been either amateurs (in the sense of drawing their support from another career such as the monastic or clerical) or poorly paid artisans. The growing market for works of art, however, widened the ranks of professional artists and gave them greater economic rewards and prestige. The growing professionalism of the artist is perhaps most apparent in music. For example, the great churches of Europe relied more and more on professional organists and singers to staff their choirs, governments employed professional trumpeters to add splendor to their proceedings, and professional musicians entertained at the elegant fêtes of the wealthy. The high technical competence required of singers and musicians in much of the music of the Late Middle Ages probably would not have been within the reach of amateurs. The artist too was often accorded special social status; painters such as Leonardo and Michelangelo were actively cultivated by princes.

TECHNIQUES AND MODELS

The artist was also acquiring a larger array of technical skills. In music the age witnessed accelerated progress in musical notation. More diversified instrumentation became possible as

Rogier van der Weyden, a master of Flemish painting, rendered The Descent from the Cross *about 1435. By placing his figures within a restricted architectural framework he rivets the viewer's attention to the foreground. He is concerned more with the emotional rather than historical significance of the event.* (Photo: Museo del Prado)

new instruments were invented and existing ones improved. Thus in strings there were the lute, viol, and harp; in wind instruments, the flute, recorder, oboe, and trumpet; and in keyboard instruments, the organ, virginal, and clavichord.

Technical advances in painting helped artists to achieve greater depth and realism. The four-teenth-century Florentine Giotto used light and shadow, initiating a technique known as chiaroscuro to create an illusion of depth. Less than a century after Giotto, another Florentine, Masaccio, achieved a complete mastery of the scientific laws of perspective, as evidenced in his *Holy Trinity with the Virgin and St. John,* which seems almost three-dimensional (see Plate 19). The Italians heightened the naturalism of their paintings still further through the scientific study of human anatomy.

The major technical achievement in the north was the development of oil painting in the fifteenth century. Oils provided the artist with richer colors and permitted him to paint more slowly and carefully and to make changes on the painted canvas. To create an illusion of reality, the Flemish masters concentrated on precise detail rather than on perspective and chiaroscuro. Because of their painstaking exactitude the Flemish artists were the leading portrait painters of the age.

The artist was also using new models, and here the most important innovation was the heightened appreciation, especially in Italy, of the artistic heritage of the classical world. Earlier medieval artists had frequently borrowed the motifs of classical art, but they had made no effort to reflect its values—idealized beauty, admiration of the human form, simplicity, restraint, elegance, and balance. An appreciation of classical style and the values it conveyed is the achievement of Italian art, particularly in sculpture, in the fifteenth century. One of the greatest sculptors of the age, the Florentine Donatello, demonstrates those values in his *Annunciation;* though the theme is religious, the treatment is classical (see Plate 17).

In architecture the Italian masters borrowed a variety of forms from the classical style—domes, columns, colonnades, pilasters, and cornices. In the early and middle 1400s the churches and palaces merely combined classical motifs with traditional medieval techniques. A pure classical style did not really triumph until the sixteenth century, when Andrea Palladio fully captured the stateliness and grace of the ancient temples in his villas, palaces, and churches in the lower Po valley.

THE GREAT MASTERS

The two major centers of Western art in the fifteenth century were Italy and the Low Countries, then under the rule of the dukes of Burgundy. In Italy the last decades of the fifteenth century and the opening decades of the six-

teenth are traditionally called the High Renaissance. But most historians of art believe that the term "Renaissance," in the sense of conscious imitation of classical models, is inappropriate in the north of Europe in the fifteenth century, where the chief sources of inspiration remained medieval. All scholars, however, recognize the high level of creativity achieved in the north, especially by the artists and musicians of the Low Countries.

The North

The great period of painting in Flanders began with Jan van Eyck (1385?–1440), whose meticulous concern with detail achieved an intense realism that was to characterize Flemish art. In *The Virgin and Child in the Church,* Van Eyck's precision in depicting the jewels of the Virgin's crown and the fabric of her robe heightens the realism; the Virgin's vivid presence seems almost to envelop the viewer (see Plate 18). In an unstable age, when religious confusion was prevalent in the north, Van Eyck and the other Flemish masters seemed anxious to reassure the viewer of the reality and truth of the scenes they were presenting. Van Eyck's chief rival as the finest representative of Flemish art was Rogier van der Weyden, whose *Descent from the Cross* is a masterpiece of dramatic composition and emotional intensity, related by many critics to the spirit of the *devotio moderna,* then flourishing in the Low Countries.

The Low Countries enjoyed an equal prominence in music in the late fifteenth century. The choirmasters in the cathedral towns such as Cambrai, Bruges, and Antwerp, with the aid of professional singers, carried four-part choral polyphony to a new level of development. With the perfection of the a cappella (unaccompanied) vocal harmony, instrumental music was freed from its traditional subservience to voice. The masters gave their attention almost equally to secular and sacred music.

Leonardo da Vinci's mural The Last Supper *exemplifies an ideal of Renaissance painting with its superb compositional balance and its evocation of what Leonardo called "the intention of man's soul." Leonardo developed perspective by painting the figures first rather than the architectural setting. This enabled him to use architecture symbolically; for example, the large opening in the back wall acts as a halo around the head of Christ.* (Photo: Sta. Maria delle Grazie, Milan)

Among many gifted musicians may be cited Guillaume Dufay of Cambrai, author of several impressive masses as well as secular songs; and Josquin Des Prés, perhaps the most versatile of the northern composers, author of masses, motets, and chansons in almost every current style. These masters, musicians, and composers traveled widely in Europe and many of them spent some time in Italy; they therefore learned from, and deeply influenced, the local and regional musical traditions.

Italy

The art of the High Renaissance in Italy is best represented in the work of three men, each of whom stands among the major artistic geniuses of the Western past: Leonardo da Vinci (1452–1519), Raphael Santi (1483–1520), and Michelangelo Buonarroti (1475–1564).

Leonardo is celebrated for his mechanical designs as well as for his art, but his exact contribution to technology and science remains difficult to assess. He failed to complete most of the projects he contemplated, and he purposely worked in a secretive fashion (he wrote his notes in mirror writing). Although he stands somewhat apart from the mainstream of technical and scientific advance, his inventive imagination produced ingenious speculative designs for an airplane, a tank, and a submarine.

In art Leonardo's accomplishment is unmistakable. Only fifteen paintings survive, but they include some of the greatest masterpieces of Western art. He had two remarkable gifts, an ability to handle groups of people and an extraordinary skill in portraying human psychology, both exemplified by his *Last Supper,* which depicts the psychological reactions of the apostles as they hear Christ say that someone at the table will betray him. The *Mona Lisa,* a portrait of a Florentine matron in her twenties, is a fascinating psychological examination of the lady's personality.

If Leonardo was a master of design, Raphael would have to be called a master of grace. Better than any other artist he reveals the Renaissance admiration for harmony, serenity, pure beauty, and pure form. He was an extremely versatile painter from the point of view of style, readily absorbing the techniques of his masters both in Umbria (his native province) and Florence (where he served his apprenticeship)—the bright colors favored by the Umbrians, the subtle shading of color and the strength of design of Leonardo, and the vitality and power of Michelangelo. Raphael may not be as original a genius as Leonardo or Michelangelo, but he is unsurpassed in the quality of his craftsmanship and the charm of its results.

Michelangelo is probably the best example of the universal genius of the Renaissance, a man of towering accomplishments in architecture, sculpture, and painting. As an artist Michelangelo preferred sculpture to painting, but his work in both mediums is rich with subtle, dramatic vitality. He liked to portray his subjects at the moment of psychological transition. For example, his statue of David catches the young man at the instant he resolves to hurl the stone at Goliath. The statue of

Moses shows the old prophet awakening to anger at the idolatry of the Israelites. Adam, painted on the Sistine ceiling, is represented just as his inert body responds to God's life-giving touch (see Plate 24).

Imbued with the neoplatonic longing to view things not as they are but as they ought to be, Michelangelo did not depict a natural world. His works seem almost a protest against the limitations of matter, from which many of his subjects struggle to be free. There is little that is placid or serene in his art, and this predilection for contorted, struggling, even misshapen figures exercised a profound influence on his successors. His work is traditionally, and justly, considered to mark the bridge between the harmonious art of the Renaissance and the distorted, dynamic style of the Mannerist school.

v. SCIENCE AND THE RENAISSANCE

In the fourteenth and fifteenth centuries numerous changes—social and economic as well as intellectual—prepared the way for the scientific revolution of the early modern epoch. Although the natural philosophers of the period made no dramatic advances in scientific theory, they succeeded in assimilating a large part of ancient science and began the slow process of questioning and revising, which ultimately led to the achievements of Copernicus, Galileo, and Newton.

THE RECEPTION OF ANCIENT SCIENCE

A critical first step toward the scientific revolution was the mastery of the natural science of the ancient world. Ancient science offered philosophers a full and coherent system or model of the natural world (sometimes called a paradigm) against which they could compare their own observations and speculations. In the twelfth and thirteenth centuries the complete corpus of the scientific works of Aristotle, together with the commentary by the Muslim philosopher Averroës, became known in the West and immediately inspired close study and extensive discussion. Albertus Magnus, for example, the teacher of Thomas Aquinas, wrote at length on biological questions; he both reflected and promoted a new interest in the life sciences in Western schools.

In the fourteenth century, nominalists at Paris and Oxford took the first, hesitant steps toward a criticism of Aristotle's world system. At the University of Paris, for example, Jean Buridan proposed an important revision in the Aristotelian theory of motion, or physical dynamics. If, as Aristotle had said, all objects are at rest in their natural state, what keeps an arrow flying after it leaves the bow? Aristotle had reasoned rather lamely that the arrow disturbs the air through which it passes and that it is this disturbance which keeps pushing the arrow forward.

But this explanation did not satisfy the nominalists. Buridan suggested that the movement of the bow lends the arrow a special quality of motion, an "impetus," which stays with it permanently unless removed by the resistance of the air. Although it was inaccurate, Buridan's explanation anticipated Galileo's theory of inertia, according to which an object at rest tends to remain at rest, and an object in motion continues to move along a straight line until it is acted upon by an external force. Buridan and other fourteenth-century nominalists also theorized about the acceleration of falling objects and made some attempt to describe this phenomenon in mathematical terms. Their ideas became the point of departure for other of Galileo's investigations of mechanics. Moreover, their use of mathematics foreshadowed the importance to be given to measurement in scientific work.

The humanists also helped to prepare the way for scientific advance. The growth of textual and literary criticism—a major humanist achievement—taught men to look with greater care and precision at works inherited from the past. Inevitably too, they acquired a sharper critical sense concerning the content as well as the language of the ancient texts. The revival of the classics placed at the disposal of Europeans a larger fund of ancient ideas, and this increased the awareness that ancient authors did not always speak in unison. Could the ancients therefore always be correct? Furthermore, the idealism of Plato and the number mysticism of Pythagoras maintained that behind the disparate data of experience there existed ideal forms or harmonies, which the philosopher should seek to perceive and describe. Once this assumption gained credence, it was natural to assume that the cosmic harmonies might be described in mathematical terms.

The Middle Ages also nourished traditions of astrology and alchemy; men sought not only to understand natural processes but also to turn that knowledge into power. Natural science and the scientists themselves would for a long time maintain close connections with these intellectual forms of magical practice.

Finally, technological and economic changes contributed to the birth of exact science. The improvement of ships stimulated, for navigational purposes, more accurate observation of the heavenly bodies. Changes in warfare raised interest in the ballistics of cannon balls, in the design of war machines and fortifications, and in military engineering generally. Artists were able to depict with high levels of accuracy the human anatomy, maps, or astronomical charts. Printing assured that ideas could be disseminated cheaply, accurately, and quickly across wide geographical areas. Craftsmen working in metal and glass were growing more skilled in the course of the Late Middle Ages. Eyeglasses became ever more popular in Europe in the thirteenth century, and glass workers ground lenses more accurately and experimented with their uses. Although the telescope was a seventeenth-century invention, the technical basis for it was laid in the Late Middle Ages.

The scientific revolution was, in sum, supported by a whole range of developments in European cultural life, many of which occurred in the fourteenth and fifteenth centuries. It remained for the fathers of modern science to draw upon these various traditions in the sixteenth and seventeenth centuries, and to form out of them and their own observations new systems or models of the natural world.

The culture of the West was changing profoundly in the fourteenth and fifteenth centuries, as it responded to new social needs. In Italy a literate lay aristocracy had come to dominate society. Traditional cultural interests and values seemed too abstract, too removed from the lives of these men, who daily faced concrete problems and wanted moral guidance. To meet this need Italian humanists developed a system of education which emphasized rhetoric and moral philosophy and looked to the works of classical antiquity for the best models of wisdom and persuasive language.

In the north of Europe the ideals of chivalry continued to dominate the culture of the lay aristocracy until late in the fifteenth century; but those ideals had become exaggerated, and they began to distort reality. The overripe chivalry of the north has helped give the Late Middle Ages its reputation for decadence.

Nominalist philosophers in the universities were effecting a critical reappraisal of the principles of thirteenth-century Scholasticism in the interest of defining precisely the borders between reason and faith. Also evident is a new style of piety which stressed the need to cultivate an interior sense of the presence and love of God.

The humanists, nominalist philosophers, and advocates of the new piety were not revolting against the accumulated cultural heritage of the Middle Ages. Rather, they wished to enrich it and make it accessible to a broader spectrum of the population. Learning, literature, art, and religion, they believed, should help men lead lives which would at once be more cultured, more contented, more pious, and more human.

The fine arts flourished during these years of change. In both Italy and the north artists adopted new techniques and gave brilliant expression to a much fuller range of values. The scientific achievements of the age were more modest, but they foreshadowed the revolutionary changes in science that were to take place in the sixteenth and seventeenth centuries.

RECOMMENDED READING

Sources

*Boccaccio, Giovanni. *The Decameron*. G. H. Mc-William (tr.). 1972.

*Cassirer, Ernst, P. P. Kristeller, and J. H. Randell, Jr. (eds.). *The Renaissance Philosophy of Man*. 1953. Selections from Petrarch, Valla, Ficino, Pico, and others.

Eckhart. *Meister Eckhart, a Modern Translation*. Raymond Bernard Blakney (tr.).

Froissart, Jean. *Chronicles of England, France, Spain and the Adjoining Countries*. Thomas Johnes (tr.). 1901.

Kempis, Thomas à. *The Imitation of Christ*. William Benham (tr.). 1909. Great classic of late medieval piety.

Langland, William. *The Vision of Piers Plowman*. Henry W. Wells (tr.). 1959.

*Marsilius of Padua. *Defender of Peace*. Alan Gerwith (tr.). 1956.

Studies

*Baron, Hans. *The Crisis of the Early Italian Renaissance: Civic Humanism and Republican Liberty in the Age of Classicism and Tyranny*. 1966. Fundamental analysis of Florentine "civic humanism."

*Berenson, Bernard. *The Italian Painters of the Renaissance*. 1968. Classical essays in the history of art.

*Burckhardt, Jacob. *The Civilization of the Renaissance in Italy*. 1958. One of the great works in European history.

Cartellieri, Otto. *The Court of Burgundy*. 1929.

Clark, J. M. *The Great German Mystics: Eckhart, Tauler and Suso*. 1949.

Crombie, Alistair C. *Medieval and Early Modern Science*. 1961.

*Herlihy, David. *The Family in Renaissance Italy*. 1974.

*Huizinga, Johan. *The Waning of the Middle Ages*. 1953.

*Kristeller, Paul Otto. *Renaissance Thought: The Classic, Scholastic and Humanistic Strains*. 1961. One of many works by a leading student of Renaissance thought.

Leff, Gordon. *William of Ockham*. 1975. Recent, authoritative examination of a difficult philosopher.

Martines, Lauro. *The Social World of the Florentine Humanists*. 1963. The humanists examined in the light of their social origins.

---

* Available in paperback.

THIRTEEN

OVERSEAS EXPANSION
AND NEW POLITICS

Between the last quarter of the fifteenth century and the middle of the sixteenth century, a renewed sense of confidence spread through Europe, accompanying a revival of prosperity, authority, and stability. The vigor that returned to economic life was particularly remarkable; this was a period of rising prices, population growth, and a rapid expansion of trade. Overseas the results of this surge of enterprise were even more spectacular: the discovery of new lands and riches, and the founding of colonies which grew into massive empires that endured into the nineteenth and twentieth centuries.

The question of why it was Western civilization that eventually spread around the globe has long fascinated historians. In the fifteenth century Europeans were less advanced in technology than Asians, and their leading rulers had none of the wealth of Indian moguls or Chinese emperors. Some scholars have suggested that Oriental societies, being much larger, were more self-sufficient and that therefore neither explorers nor international traders achieved the status they gained in the West.

Another reason the Europeans seem to have been able to launch the expansion was the restoration of stability in political life. A new assurance permeated the government of the rulers of three leading kingdoms: England, France, and Spain. Often called "new monarchs" by historians, they merited the title because of their potent reassertion of royal preeminence in their domains. Their aims were still largely personal and dynastic—they were concerned more with the fortunes of their own families than with the destinies of the people they ruled—but to this end they raised their power at home, particularly against the nobility, to new levels. By the 1550s the new monarchs had emerged from the uncertainties of the Late Middle Ages as the main political force in their realms.

The Germans, Italians, and Eastern Europeans, by contrast, began to fall behind their Western neighbors in this crucial respect. They lacked strong, unifying central governments, and thus local nobles or small political units frag-  *mented political authority. The result was the eventual decline of these countries. From the mid-sixteenth century until the mid-nineteenth century, they slipped to lesser roles in international affairs, victims of the chief political lesson of this period: only a capable central authority could marshall the resources of a territory and win prominence on the international scene.*

1. EXPLORATION AND ITS IMPACT

Few great changes in the history of the world have owed so much to the exploits of a handful of daring men as did the overseas expansion of Europe. The origins of the movement can be traced back to the crusades, the Europeans' first outward steps after centuries of defensiveness and shrinkage. Travelers such as Marco Polo and traders in the Levant had also contributed to this interest in far-off places. But the enlargement of the Ottoman Empire during the fifteenth century threatened to cut overland contacts with Asia. It was therefore necessary to find an alternative: a sea route such as the one being opened up by the explorers who were inching their way around Africa toward the Indian Ocean.

THE OVERSEAS EXPANSION

The most spectacular evidence that a long period of contraction in the West had come to an end was the territorial and economic expansion that began in the fifteenth century. The explorers, colonists, and merchants of this period transformed an inward-looking Europe into the booming and vigorous founder of empires that stretched from East Asia to the Americas.

The Portuguese

The pioneers in this transformation were the Portuguese, occupants of an inhospitable land, whose seafarers had always held an important place in the country's economic life. The need for better agricultural opportunities had long turned their eyes toward the Atlantic islands and the territories held by the Muslims (Moors) to the south. But this ambition had to be organized into a sustained effort if it was to achieve results, and in the early fifteenth century, Prince Henry the Navigator, a younger son of the king, undertook that task.

A talented leader, Henry participated in the capture of the North African port of Ceuta from the Arabs in 1415, a crusading expedition that only whetted his appetite for more victories over the infidels. At Ceuta he probably received information about legendary Christians (the fabled kingdom of Prester John) and mines of gold somewhere in the interior. A mixture of motives—profit, religion, and curiosity—spurred him on, and in 1419 he founded a center for sailors, mapmakers, astronomers (because their contributions to celestial navigation were vital), shipbuilders, and instrument makers at Sagres, at the southwestern tip of Portugal. Here men interested in discovery—mainly Ital-

ians—gathered, hoping to find a way around Africa in order to reach India. The early adventurers did not succeed, but during their gradual advance down the West African coast, they opened a rich new trade in ivory, gold, and slaves.

Then, in 1487, one Portuguese captain, Bartholomeu Dias, returned to Lisbon after an incredible voyage. He had been blown out to sea by a northerly gale and spent thirteen days without sight of land. As soon as possible he had headed east, but when he made his landfall it proved to be on the east coast of Africa, beyond the Cape of Good Hope, which thus far no one had been able to pass.

The way to India now seemed open, but before the Portuguese could send out their first expedition the news arrived that a sailor employed by the Spaniards, one Christopher Columbus, had apparently reached India by sailing west. To avoid conflicting claims, Portugal and Spain signed the Treaty of Tordesillas in 1494, which gave Portugal possession of all the lands to the east of an imaginary line about 300 miles west of the Azores, and Spain a monopoly of everything to the west. Portugal thus kept the only practical route to India (as well as the rights to Brazil, which one of her sailors may already have discovered). Three years later Vasco da Gama took the first Portuguese fleet across the Indian Ocean.

At first, he found it very hard to trade, because the Arabs, who had controlled these waters for centuries, tried to keep out all rivals. Within the next fourteen years, however, the Portuguese merchants had established themselves. The key to their success was naval power, for their ship designers had learned to combine their old square sails, which provided speed, with the Arabs' lateen sails, which increased maneuverability. The Portuguese were also the first to give their fleets effective fire power, realizing that cannon, not soldiers, won battles at sea. In addition, they deployed their ships in squadrons rather than individually, a tactic that further increased their superiority. The result was rapid and overwhelming success. A series of victories at sea reduced Arab naval strength, and bombardments brought recalcitrant cities to submission. Guided by the military skill and superb strategic sense of a brilliant commander, Affonso de Albuquerque, the Portuguese established tradings posts in the East that by 1513 extended to the rich Spice Islands, the Moluccas (see Map 13.1).

The empire Portugal created remained entirely dependent on sea power; she rarely tried to colonize overseas areas. Instead she set up a chain of trading bases, consisting of warehouses combined with forts that could be supplied and defended by sea, from West Africa to China. Generally the Portuguese restricted contacts with Africans and Asians to maintaining friendly relations and missionary and trading rights; they made no attempt to conquer. By the mid-fifteenth century, they were beginning to profit from their explorations—between 1442 and 1446 almost 1,000 slaves were brought home from Africa—and in the sixteenth century their wealth multiplied as they became major importers of luxuries from the East such as spices, which were in great demand as medicines, preservatives, and tasty delicacies. By dominating commerce with the rich Oriental civilizations, Portugal's merchants controlled Europe's most valuable trade.

The Portuguese achievement displayed all the ingredients of the West's rise to worldwide power: driving ambition, technical superiority in guns and ships, tactical skills, commercial expertise supported by military force, and careful planning and organization in the home country. Their expansion was sustained by the political and economic revival that was spreading through Western Europe at this time and by the added spur of competition. For Spain soon determined to emulate her neighbor, and when later the Dutch, English, and French took

the lead in empire building, they sought to outdo their predecessors and each other. This competition gave the Europeans the crucial stimulus that other peoples had lacked, and it projected them into a dominance over the rest of the globe that would last for more than 450 years.[1]

The Spaniards

Inspired by the same centuries-old crusading ambitions as the Portuguese, the Spaniards rode the second wave of expansion to wealth and glory overseas. Because she was a much larger nation and because she happened to direct her attention toward a more sparsely populated continent than did Portugal, Spain founded her empire on conquest and colonization, not trade. But she got her start from a stroke of luck.

Christopher Columbus, an experienced Genoese sailor who had some contact with the leading Italian geographers of his day, seems to have believed (it is difficult to know for certain, for he was always a secretive man) that Asia lay only 3,500 miles beyond the Canary Islands. He arrived at this figure as the result of two mistakes: he relied on the ancient Ptolemaic estimate that the circumference of the world was 18,000 miles—6,000 miles too short—and on Marco Polo's estimate that Asia extended 1,500 miles farther east than in fact it does.

Convinced that sailing across the Atlantic to the East was perfectly feasible, Columbus took his proposal in 1484 to the Portuguese government, which refused to underwrite the venture. With a mystic belief in his own destiny, he persisted, gained the financial backing and blessing of Ferdinand V and Isabella I of Spain, and

---

[1] Current discussions of the differences that led Europe, rather than another civilization, to expand throughout the world are excellently surveyed in Joseph R. Levenson (ed.), *European Expansion and the Counter-Example of Asia, 1300–1600* (1967). See also Robert O. Collins, *Europeans in Africa* (1971), Ch. 1.

set sail in 1492. He was an excellent navigator (one of his discoveries on the voyage was the difference between true and magnetic north), and he kept his men going despite their horror of being so long at sea without sight of land. After thirty-three days he reached the Bahamas, and though disappointed that he found no Chinese or Japanese as he investigated Cuba and the west coast of Hispaniola (today's Haiti), he was certain that he had reached Asia, notwithstanding the lack of resemblance between the few natives he encountered and those whom travelers such as Marco Polo had described.

Columbus crossed the Atlantic Ocean three more times, but he made no further discoveries of significance. By the end of his life, in 1506, it was becoming apparent that he had found islands close by a new continent, not Asia. The Treaty of Tordesillas reserved the exploration of these lands for the Spaniards, who soon began to perceive them as an asset, not an obstacle.

Other Spanish voyages of discovery followed those of Columbus. In 1513 Vasco de Balboa saw the Pacific Ocean from Central America, and this rekindled the notion that an easy westward passage might be found to East Asia. But the last remaining hopes were finally dashed in 1522, when the one surviving ship from a fleet of five that had set out under Ferdinand Magellan three years before returned to Spain after the ordeal of having sailed around the world (see Map 13.1).

Magellan's ninety-eight-day crossing of the Pacific stands as a supreme accomplishment of seamanship in the age of discovery. But the perilous voyage persuaded the Spaniards that Portugal clearly had the best route to the East, and in 1529 they finally renounced all claims to trade with the Spice Islands for a payment of 350,000 ducats. The world had been divided, and Spain could concentrate on the Americas, those unexpected continents that were to become possessions of unbelievable richness.

Volunteers were amply available. When the

This facsimile of a wood engraving depicts the discovery of Santo Domingo by Christopher Columbus. It is based on a sketch attributed to the explorer himself. (Photo: New York Public Library/Picture Collection)

Muslim kingdom in southern Spain was conquered by the Castilians in 1492, a group of men with a long tradition of military service found themselves at loose ends. These were the younger sons of noble families, who were kept from inheriting land because Spanish law allowed only the eldest son to inherit. Naturally the prospect of unlimited land and military adventure across the Atlantic appealed to them, and thus the conquistador, the conqueror,

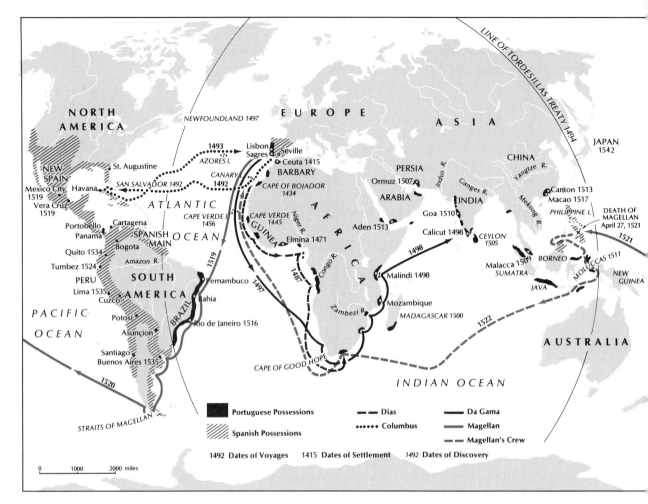

MAP 13.1: EXPLORATION AND CONQUEST IN THE 15TH AND 16TH CENTURIES

was born. There were not many of them—less than 1,000 at most—but they overran much of America in search of wealth and glory.

The first and most dramatic of these leaders was Hernando Cortés, who in 1519 landed on the Mexican coast and set out to overcome the splendid Aztec civilization in the high plateau of central Mexico. His army consisted of only 600 men, but in two years, with a few reinforcements, he had won a complete victory. Guns alone made no important difference be-

cause Cortés had only thirteen muskets and some unwieldy cannon. More effective were his horses, his clever manipulation of Aztec superstitions, and the unshakable determination of his men. The Mexican Mayas also surrendered to Cortés, while the Incas of Peru fell to Francisco Pizarro. Other conquistadors repeated these successes throughout Central and South America. By 1550 the conquest was over, and the military men, never very good at governing the territories they had won, gave way to administrators who began to pull the huge empire into organized shape.

The Spanish government established in the New World the same pattern of political administration that it was setting up in its European territories (see section II). Representatives of the throne, viceroys, were sent to administer the empire and to impose centralized control. Each was advised by a local *audiencia*, a kind of miniature council that also acted as a court of law, but the ultimate authority remained in Spain.

To the rest of the world, the overwhelming attraction of Spanish America was its mineral wealth, especially its silver. In 1545 a major vein of silver was discovered at Potosí, in Bolivia, and from those mines—worked by Indian forced labor—came the treasure that made fortunes for the colonists, sustained wars that Spain was fighting against her neighbors, and ultimately enriched all of Western Europe (see accompanying table). For the balance of the sixteenth century, however, despite the efforts of other countries, Portugal and Spain remained the only conspicuous promoters and the major beneficiaries of Europe's expansion.

IMPORTS OF TREASURE TO SPAIN FROM THE NEW WORLD, 1511–1600

DECADE	TOTAL VALUE*
1511–1520	2,626,000
1521–1530	1,407,000
1531–1540	6,706,000
1541–1550	12,555,000
1551–1560	21,437,000
1561–1570	30,418,000
1571–1580	34,990,000
1581–1590	63,849,000
1591–1600	83,536,000

* In Ducats

Adapted from J. H. Elliott, *Imperial Spain, 1469–1716* (New York, 1964), p. 175.

ECONOMIC GROWTH

Most of the silver from the New World went beyond Spain to Italian and German merchants who financed the wars of the Spanish kings and also controlled the American trade. Although other sources of supply, mainly silver mines in Austria, were appearing at this time, the New World was primarily responsible for the end of the crippling shortage of precious metals, and hence of coins, that had plagued Europe for centuries. By the middle of the seventeenth century, the Continent's holdings in gold were to increase by one-fifth, and, more important, its stock of silver was to triple.

In 1556 a Spanish professor named Azpilcueta suggested that this flow explained a phenomenon that was beginning to cause wide concern —a tremendous rise in prices. The inflation was sharpest in Spain, where money lost three-quarters of its 1500 value by 1600; the depreciation elsewhere was serious but less marked —in England for example it was about two-thirds. Recent historians, however, have shown that the upward movement of prices began before substantial amounts of silver were shipped and that the rate slowed at the very time that imports from South America rose sharply. Although it is still acknowledged that the supply of precious metals directly influenced price levels and contributed to Europe's economic revival, an exclusive correlation can no longer be accepted.[2] Other factors must be taken into consideration to explain the startling changes of the late fifteenth century.

At the simplest level what happened was a gradual revival of confidence. After a century and a half of hard times, economic conditions were improving. Much of the credit for this must be given to the restoration of political sta-

[2] There is a good introduction to the problem of explaining the rise in prices in J. H. Elliott, *Imperial Spain, 1469–1716* (1964), pp. 172–191.

bility. Merchants were more inclined to risk long-distance trading under strong governments. Rulers could make treaties with foreign powers for commercial advantage and guarantee that such agreements would be upheld. The growth of population in the sixteenth century was the most dramatic result of the new sense of confidence, and the surge in the number of people was a prime contributor to the inflation because it increased the demand for goods. In general the businessman, encouraged by the discovery of new sources of silver, enlarged markets, and the improved profits generated by rising prices, was now able to widen the scope of his investments.

Records are far too poor to permit a measurement of the increase in population, but it is likely that by the early seventeenth century, Europe's population was perhaps 50 percent larger than it had been in the late fifteenth. And cities grew much faster than did the population as a whole: London for example had approximately 50,000 inhabitants in the early sixteenth century but over 200,000 a hundred years later (see Map 13.2). Significantly, wide areas of marginal farmland were reoccupied, having been abandoned in the fourteenth and fifteenth centuries because a shrinking population had provided no market for their produce. Now there were more mouths to feed, and the extra acres again became profitable.

The population rise was followed by a staggering jump in food prices. By the early 1600s wheat cost approximately five times more than in the late 1400s, an increase that far outpaced the movement of prices in general. It is not surprising, therefore, that this period witnessed the first wave of enclosures in England: major landowners put up fences around common tilling or grazing ground, traditionally open to all the animals of the locality, in order to reserve it for their own crops or their sheep, whose wool was also in increasing demand. By 1600 about an eighth of England's arable land had been enclosed.

As markets began to grow in response to population pressures, the volume of trade also shot upward; commercial profits thus kept pace with those of agriculture. Customs receipts rose steadily, as did the yield of tolls from ships entering the Baltic Sea, one of Europe's leading trade centers. In many areas, too, shipbuilding boomed. This was the heyday of the English cloth trade and the great Spanish sheep farms, of the central German linen industry and the northern Italian silk industry. Printing became a widespread occupation, and gunmaking and glassmaking also expanded rapidly. The latter had a major effect on European society, because the increasing use of windows allowed builders to divide houses into small rooms, thus giving many people a little privacy for the first time.

Leading financiers who invested in the growing volume of trade of course accumulated large fortunes. For centuries the Italians had been in the vanguard of economic advance but in the sixteenth century firms of other nations were achieving international prominence. The most successful of the new enterprises was run by a family descended from a fourteenth-century weaver, Johannes Fugger of Augsburg. The sixteenth-century Fuggers financed the Spanish King Charles I's campaign for the throne of the Holy Roman Empire and his later wars when he became the Emperor Charles V. Great bankers were thus often closely allied with monarchs, and like all merchants, they gained from the mounting power of central governments. Rulers encouraged commerce in the hope of larger revenues from customs duties and taxes, and they gave leading entrepreneurs valuable privileges. Such alliances were eventually the undoing of some houses, which were ruined by royal bankruptcies, but until the late sixteenth century, Italian and German bankers controlled Europe's finances.

The continued importance of Italy, and of the Mediterranean in general, indicates that the overseas expansion did not change Europe over-

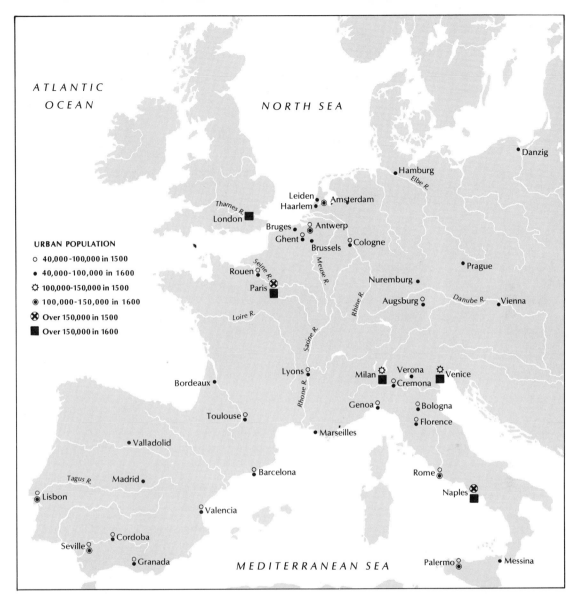

MAP 13.2: THE GROWTH OF CITIES IN THE 16TH CENTURY

URBAN POPULATION
- ○ 40,000–100,000 in 1500
- ● 40,000–100,000 in 1600
- ✿ 100,000–150,000 in 1500
- ◉ 100,000–150,000 in 1600
- ⊗ Over 150,000 in 1500
- ■ Over 150,000 in 1600

ATLANTIC OCEAN

NORTH SEA

MEDITERRANEAN SEA

Danzig
Hamburg
Elbe R.
Leiden Amsterdam
Haarlem
Thames R.
London
Bruges Antwerp
Ghent
Brussels Cologne
Prague
Rouen
Seine R.
Meuse R.
Nuremburg
Paris
Augsburg
Danube R. Vienna
Rhine R.
Loire R.
Saône R.
Lyons Milan Verona Venice
Bordeaux Cremona
Rhône R.
Genoa Bologna
Toulouse Florence
Marseilles
Valladolid
Tagus R. Madrid
Barcelona Rome
Lisbon Naples
Valencia
Cordoba
Seville Palermo Messina
Granada

night. In fact, Italy's overland spice trade across Asia continued as it had for centuries, even though the Portuguese found it much cheaper to bring the goods west by sea. But rather than try to squeeze Italy out of the trade, Portugal simply charged the same prices and thus made a larger profit. Not until Dutch and English fleets began to enter the Mediterranean around 1600, and at the same time gained control of eastern spice shipments, did the balance shift away from the Italians. In the meantime, the boom benefited all areas of Europe.

Indeed, every level of trading activity offered opportunities for advancement. The guild sys-

OVERSEAS EXPANSION AND NEW POLITICS / 407

tem expanded in the sixteenth century to incorporate many new trades, while the whole structure of mercantile enterprise developed in new ways. The idea took hold that a business firm was an impersonal entity, larger than the man who owned it and vested with an identity, legal status, permanence, and even profits that were not the same as those of its members. Here was yet another indication of the creativity and energy at work in economic affairs.

SOCIAL CHANGE

Not everyone shared in the new prosperity. Naturally landowners and food producers benefited most from the inflation and could amass considerable wealth. The tenant could also do well, because rents did not keep pace with food prices. But wages lagged miserably. By the early seventeenth century, a laborer's annual income had about half the purchasing power it had had at the end of the fifteenth, a decline that made its most drastic impact on Eastern Europe, where serfdom reappeared. In the West, large numbers of peasants had to leave the land, which could no longer support all of them; others were forced off by enclosures and similar "improvements." These displaced people turned to begging and wandering across country, often ending up in towns, where crime became a serious problem. Peasant uprisings directed at tax collectors, nobles, or food suppliers were almost annual affairs in one region of France or another after the mid-sixteenth century, and in England the unending stream of vagrants gave rise to a belief that the country was overpopulated. The extreme poverty was universally deplored, particularly as it promoted disorders; local nobles, not as strong as they had once been, could no longer restrain potential troublemakers, and the two centuries from

Antwerp on market day, ca. 1600. (Photo: Koninklijke Museum voor Schone Kunsten, Brussels)

the mid-sixteenth to the mid-eighteenth were the great days of the highwayman. Nobody could understand, much less control, the forces that were transforming society.

The newly strong governments of the period tried to relieve the distress, but their efforts were not always consistent. They regarded the beggars sometimes as shirkers who should be punished and at other times as unfortunates who needed to be helped. Not until the end of the sixteenth century did the more compassionate view begin to prevail.

Vagrancy was only one of the signs that Europeans were witnessing the beginnings of modern urbanization, with all of its dislocations. Major differences also developed between life in the country and life in the town. The rural worker may have led a strenuous existence, but he escaped the worst hazards of the urban dweller. Whole sections of most large cities were controlled by the sixteenth-century equivalent of the underworld, which offered sanctuary to criminals and danger to most citizens. Plagues were much more serious in towns—the upper classes soon learned to flee to the country at the first sign of disease—and famines more devastating because of the far poorer sanitation in urban areas and their remoteness from food supplies.

On the other hand the opening of economic opportunities offered many people a chance to improve their status dramatically. At courts, in royal administrations, in law, in the burgeoning cities, and overseas in growing empires, men won fortunes and titles and founded new aristocratic dynasties. The means of advancement varied: the English monarchy sold to the newly rich the lands it confiscated from monasteries after the religious struggle that split the kingdom from the Church of Rome (see section II); France put government offices on the market to raise revenue and build the bureaucracy; the New World gave minor Spanish nobles the chance to acquire vast estates; and everywhere the long boom in commerce encouraged social mobility. By the 1620s, when the upward movement began to subside, a new aristocracy had been born that was destined to dominate Europe for centuries.

It seems a paradox that the disruptive economic and social changes of the sixteenth century should have happened at a time when the "new monarchs" of England, France, and Spain were asserting their control and imposing order in their realms. The two processes were not unrelated—strong central governments gave vital support to economic growth, overseas expansion, and attempts to relieve social distress, while prosperity provided rulers with the tax revenues that were essential to their power—but they clearly had somewhat contrary effects. In the long run, however, it was the restoration of political stability that permitted the solution of the problems that arose during the sixteenth century. The creation of well-organized states, structured around powerful central governments, was even more decisive than the economic boom in shaping the future of Western Europe.

II. THE "NEW MONARCHIES"

During the last quarter of the fifteenth century, England, France, and Spain were governed by remarkable rulers, whose accomplishments have led historians to call them "new monarchs": Henry VII, Louis XI, and Ferdinand and Isabella.[3] Their reigns are generally regarded as marking the end of more than a century of fragmentation and the beginning of a revival of royal power that would ultimately create the bureaucracies characteristic of the modern state. Moreover the successors to their thrones not only inaugurated more active and aggressive policies in international affairs but also—and

this was of momentous significance—gradually gained ground over traditional competitors for power such as the Church.

TUDOR ENGLAND

The English monarchs had relied for centuries on local cooperation to run their kingdom. Unlike other European countries, England contained only fifty or sixty families out of a population of perhaps 2.5 million who were legally nobles. But many other families, though not technically members of the nobility, had large estates and were dominant figures at the parish, county, and even national level. They were known as gentry, and it was from their ranks that the crown appointed the local officers who administered the realm—notably the justices of the peace (usually referred to as J.P.s). These voluntary, unpaid officials served as the principal public servants in the more than forty counties of the land.

For reasons of status as well as out of a feeling of responsibility, the gentry had always sought such appointments. From the crown's point of view, the great advantage of the system was its efficiency: enforcement was in the hands of those who could enforce, for as a "great man" in his neighborhood, the justice of the peace rarely had trouble exerting his authority. By the Late Middle Ages, the king had had at his disposal an administrative structure without rival in Europe. This cooperative approach to the task of governing had created a strong sense of duty among the members of the ruling class, and the king had come to consult them more frequently over the years.

In the sixteenth century an institution that had developed from this relationship, Parliament, began to take on a general importance as the chief representative of the country's wishes;

---

[3] An excellent introduction to the scholarship on the "new monarchs" is Arthur J. Slavin (ed.), *The "New Monarchies" and Representative Assemblies: Medieval Constitutionalism or Modern Absolutism?* (1964), which also covers some subjects not treated in this chapter—for example the rise of representative assemblies in the Low Countries and the establishment of a strong central government in Sweden during the sixteenth century.

THE
IMAGE
OF
MAN
IN RENAISSANCE ART

It has been said of the Renaissance that there are as many ways of defining it as there are branches of historic study and that the one point of agreement among experts is that the new era began when people realized they were no longer living in the Middle Ages. The Renaissance, in other words, was the first period in history to be aware of its own existence. Not only did it coin a name for itself—Renaissance means "rebirth"—but also for its predecessor, the "thousand years of darkness," which it thought followed upon the fall of ancient civilization. Both names have stuck, although today we no longer regard the Middle Ages as dark and are less sure what the Renaissance was a rebirth of.

To those who first thought in these terms—a tiny minority even among the educated in fourteenth-century Italy—"rebirth" meant the revival of the classics, the language and literature of ancient Greece and Rome; in the course of the next hundred years, however, the concept came to embrace the entire range of cultural life, including the visual arts. From this the Italian humanists distilled a new philosophy of man designed to reconcile what seemed to them two equal sources of authority: Christian revelation and the wisdom of the ancients. Its basis is still the biblical account of man's creation by the Lord "in our image and likeness," but the emphasis is now on man's freedom of will rather than his dependence on God. Thus Gianozzo Manetti, in his treatise "On the Dignity and Excellence of Man," proclaims him not only the most beautiful and perfect of all creatures but a second creator: "After that first, new and rude creation of the world [by God], everything seems to have been discovered, constructed and completed by us . . . all homes, all towns, all cities, finally all buildings in the world which certainly are so many and of such a nature that they ought rather to be regarded as the works of angels than of men. . . . Ours are the paintings, ours the sculptures, ours the arts, ours the sciences. . . ." Is it any wonder, Manetti asks, that "the first inventors of the various arts were worshiped as gods by the early peoples"?[1] In Pico della Mirandola's oration on the same theme, the Lord speaks to the newly created Adam as follows: "The nature of all other beings is limited . . . within the bounds of laws prescribed by Us. You, constrained by no limits, in accordance with your own free will . . . shall ordain for yourself the limits of your nature. . . . We made you neither of heaven nor of earth, neither mortal nor immortal, so that with freedom of choice . . . you may fashion yourself in whatever shape you prefer. You shall have the power to degenerate into the lower forms of life, which are brutish. You shall have the power . . . to be reborn into the higher forms, which are divine."[2] The humanists, then, saw man as endowed by God with gifts that make him the master of his own fate.

If Pico's exalted vision of man's potential seems to anticipate Michelangelo (see Plate 24), Manetti's celebration of man as the active and self-confident shaper of his world, with special pride in his achievements in the visual arts, suggests the new poise of Donatello (see Plate 17) and the clarity and order of Masaccio (see Plate 19). Scientific perspective, the means by which Masaccio achieved these qualities, was far more than a technical accomplishment; it permitted the painter, for the first time in the history of art, to define, exactly and measurably, man's relation to his spatial setting within the picture and at the same time to treat the fictitious painted space as an extension of the real space of our sense experience. This new structuring of space also demanded a more precise knowledge of the structure of the human body. The skeleton in Masaccio's mural, unlike those in earlier art, is anatomically correct, and in the figure of Christ we sense the same interest in the body as an organic entity. Compared to older, less consistent methods of creating pictorial space, such as that used by Jan van Eyck (see Plate 18), scientific perspective is something of a paradox: subjective and impersonal at the same time. Its system, based on a central vanishing point that corresponds to the eye of a single beholder, expresses the individualism of the new era. It was this individualism that made portraiture, neglected since the fall of the Roman Empire, once more a major concern of painters and sculptors (see the kneeling donors in Plate 19 as well as Plates 20 and 28–30). On the other hand, the effectiveness of scientific perspective depends on mathematical rules that leave little scope for personal interpretation. Perspective boasts of setting a standard of objective truth and thus allies the artist with the scientist. To Leonardo da Vinci, who was both, "seeing" was equivalent to "knowing." The ultimate result of this alliance was to be the invention of photography in the early nineteenth century, which to the painters of the time seemed at first a threat, then a liberation that permitted them to abandon the Renaissance goal of truth to nature.

"Truth to nature," however, could be interpreted in radically different ways even by Renaissance artists. Comparing the paintings by Bellini and Botticelli (Plates 22 and 23), we realize how little the two pictures have in common, although both were painted in the 1480s. Bellini's view of nature, despite its abundance of detail, is as firmly structured as the architecture in Masaccio's "Trinity," and man's place in it is defined with equal precision. What we see here is the familiar nature of everyday experience transfigured by the saint's ecstasy. Botticelli's picture, in contrast, looks as flat and patterned as a playing card. It bears out Leonardo's remark that Botticelli "paints very dull landscapes." What concerns Botticelli is man's relation not to nature but to an ideal of formal perfection embodied in the art of antiquity and reflecting man's desire, in Pico's words, "to be reborn into the higher forms, which are divine." His goal is nature perfected rather than nature observed; and since, according to Pico's God, such perfectibility is vouchsafed only to man, the rest of the natural world holds little interest for him. This unconcern with objective truth is still more evident in Parmigianino (see Plate 26) and in Bronzino (see Plate 28). The problem of reconciling ideal and real nature haunted artists and critics for centuries to come.

The conflict of ideal and reality in art, like the humanists's new view of man, originated in Italy. But whereas humanism found a ready response north of the Alps and profoundly influenced the religious Reformation, Italian Renaissance art did not become a model for the rest of Europe until the sixteenth century, and even then its authority was far from absolute. Jan van Eyck, Masaccio's contemporary, was an equally great innovator in his way, yet he perceived the visible world in terms of light and color rather than of its underlying structure (compare Plates 18 and 19). He founded a tradition so powerful that Altdorfer (see Plate 31), painting a century later, still owes more to Jan van Eyck than to any Italian source, despite the classical subject of the picture. Other Northerners, such as the remarkable Dutch painter Hieronymus Bosch (see Plate 21), mirror the conflict between the medieval and Renaissance concepts of man in their pessimistic visions of a sinful humanity remote from any hope of redemption. When, soon after 1500, Northern artists began to visit Italy in order to study classical antiquity and the "classic" masters of their own day, the new image of man they came to know tended to remain an alien element in their own work, like quotations in an unfamiliar language. Pieter Bruegel, the greatest Northern painter of the second half of the century, acknowledges the humanist vision in an oddly backhanded way; his "Land of Cockaigne" (Plate 32) is a sermon on the dignity of man, but in reverse, by showing the fate of those who fail to heed it. It was not until 1600 that the heritage of Italian Renaissance art was fully shared by the rest of Europe.

---

[1] Charles Trinkaus, *In Our Image and Likeness: Humanity and Divinity in Italian Humanist Thought* (1970), vol. 1, p. 247.
[2] *The Renaissance Philosophy of Man*, edited by Ernst Cassirer et al. (1948), p. 225.

Among the founding fathers of Renaissance art, it was Donatello who first formed the new image of man demanded by the new era. His *Annunciation* in Plate 17 shows more strikingly than any of his other works why the Renaissance proclaimed itself the rebirth of antiquity, for nowhere else does he approach the classic Greek ideal of human beauty as closely as he does here. The two figures are carved in high relief rather than in the round, but they move with such complete ease and freedom that they seem in no way constrained by their architectural setting; and their response to each other—the reverential greeting of the angel, the Virgin's gentle gesture of surprise—is equally well-balanced and natural. For the first time in a thousand years, body and spirit seem to be in complete harmony. The contrast with the Romanesque *Annunciation* in Plate 12, done three centuries earlier, could hardly be more striking.

How Donatello achieved this is little short of miraculous. Although he was an ardent admirer of ancient sculpture, he knew it only from late and inferior examples. Yet he perceived in them, with the clairvoyance of genius, the underlying ideal of classical perfection and recreated it in his own work. The framework, too, bespeaks the rebirth of antiquity: its forms derive from the ornamental vocabulary of ancient Greece and Rome, although Donatello's way of combining them is uniquely his own.

Plate 17. Donatello, THE ANNUNCIATION
ca. 1430–1435, limestone,
height of niche 7'2"
Santa Croce, Florence

The revolutionary change that took place in northern European painting about 1420 becomes strikingly evident if we compare Jan van Eyck's panel in Plate 18 with the *April* miniature in Plate 16. Suddenly the bright fairytale world of the International Gothic style has given way to an art that brings us face to face with visible reality in all its richness and depth, as if the picture surface had been turned into a window. The difference between the two is technical as well as artistic: the miniature is painted in tempera (pigments mixed with diluted egg yolk) and the panel is an early instance of the use of oils. Tempera is thin, opaque, and quick-drying; oil viscous and slow-drying. Unlike tempera, oil permits the smooth blending of tones on the picture surface, and its body may vary from translucent colored glazes to thick layers of creamy, saturated paint. Jan van Eyck knew how to exploit the greater flexibility of the new medium to full effect. Yet the panel contains a contradiction: the lovely Virgin is far too big for the architecture. Only if we recognize this mistake and its hidden purpose can we understand the subtlety of Jan van Eyck's art. Realism to him did not limit the symbolic meaning of his pictures, but rather it actually enhanced it. In this panel, the church building stands for the Church and so does the

Plate 18. Jan van Eyck
THE VIRGIN AND CHILD IN THE CHURCH
ca. 1425—1430, oil on wood, height 12"
Staatliche Museen Preussischer
Kulturbesitz, Gemäldegalerie, Berlin (West)

Virgin; therefore, the interior is just tall enough to hold her. For final proof we need only look at the altar in the background, attended not by priests but by angels.

In Masaccio's mural in Plate 19, the surface is also treated as a window. Here, however, everything is lifesize, and the painted space seems a direct continuation of the actual space surrounding the beholder. This has been achieved by means of scientific perspective, one of the great discoveries of the Italian Early Renaissance, which is a system of projecting three-dimensional shapes onto a flat surface, analogous to the way the camera lens projects them onto a piece of film. Masaccio's entire composition embodies his faith in rational order and clarity. The figures are as massive as Giotto's and as fully articulated and self-sufficient as Donatello's; the architecture resembles the classically inspired framework of Donatello's *Annunciation* rather than the Gothic interior of Jan van Eyck's panel. Like the latter, Masaccio's mural was done for a private patron; he and his wife are kneeling in prayer just outside the sacred precinct. The step on which they kneel coincides with the beholder's eye level. It is also the dividing line between time and eternity: above it, salvation; below it, a skeleton to remind us of the brevity of man's life on earth.

Plate 19. Masaccio
THE HOLY TRINITY WITH
THE VIRGIN AND ST. JOHN
*ca. 1425, wall painting,
height 21'10"*
Santa Maria Novella, Florence

The exploration of visible reality in fifteenth-century painting has its counterpart in the daring sea voyages beyond the limits of the known world that culminated in the discovery of America. The Portuguese led the way in these ventures. It was they who explored the west coast of Africa and opened the sea route to India; they who first circumnavigated the globe. What was the impulse behind their journeys? A quest for riches and power, surely, but also a quest for knowledge, and, equally important, a sense of religious duty, as attested by Nuño Gonçalves' panel in Plate 20. Here St. Vincent displays to the reverently kneeling king a Gospel text concerning the Apostles' mission among the infidels, and in so doing appoints him their spiritual heir. The older man with hands folded in prayer is the king's uncle, Prince Henry the Navigator, the earliest royal sponsor of voyages of discovery. Gonçalves must have learned his art in close contact with the great Flemish realists, such as Jan van Eyck. Although a less subtle painter than Van Eyck, he was a portraitist of exceptional power who has left us an unforgettable record of the rulers of Portugal.

Plate 20. Nuño Gonçalves
SAINT VINCENT COMMANDING KING
AFFONSO V OF PORTUGAL TO SPREAD
THE CHRISTIAN FAITH IN AFRICA
1471—1481, oil on panel,
height 6'9½"
National Museum of Ancient Art, Lisbon

The Dutchman Hieronymus Bosch was a pioneer of another sort, venturing farther into the unexplored regions of man's imagination than any artist before him. His vision of Hell in Plate 21 is a nightmare world of burning cities and icy rivers where sinners are punished by being surfeited with the vices they had enjoyed on earth. Thus, in the center of our panel, a huge stomach houses a devilish inn; below it, musical instruments are engines of torture (secular music was "the food of love" and hence a sinful pleasure); and in the lower right-hand corner, a sow embraces a man who is vainly trying to escape. The interpretation of Bosch's pictures has proved extremely difficult, but enough is known about them to assure us that he intended every detail to have a precise didactic meaning, however strange his imagery may seem today. He was haunted—indeed mesmerized—by the power of evil to corrupt mankind; its counterweight, the promise of redemption, is barely hinted at in his work. This state of mind reflects the conflict between the other-worldly goals of traditional Christianity and an ever greater openness to the attractions of life on earth, a crisis of conscience that was to erupt soon in the Reformation.

Plate 21. Hieronymus Bosch
HELL WING (*from the triptych,*
THE GARDEN OF EARTHLY DELIGHTS)
ca. 1500, oil on wood panel, height 7'2½"
Prado Museum, Madrid

The work of the great Flemish realists was known and admired in fifteenth-century Italy. Although it had little immediate effect in Florence, birthplace of the Early Renaissance, it left a lasting imprint on Venice. Before long, the use of oils and an emphasis on light and color became hallmarks of Venetian Renaissance painting. Venetian masters, such as Giovanni Bellini, also raised landscape to a new level of importance. In Plate 22,

St. Francis is so small compared to the setting that he seems almost incidental, yet his mystic rapture before the beauty of nature sets our own response to the glorious view that is spread out before us. He has left his wooden clogs behind and stands barefoot, thus indicating that the ground is hallowed by the presence of the Lord. The soft, glowing colors, the warm late-afternoon sunlight, the tender regard for every detail, recall the art of Jan van Eyck. Unlike the Northerners, however, Giovanni Bellini knows how to define the beholder's relationship to the space within the picture; the rock formations of the foreground are clear and firm, like architecture rendered by the rules of scientific perspective.

In Florence, meanwhile, the revival of antiquity kindled a new interest in the pagan deities, who now began to appear once more in their original form. The Venus in Botticelli's famous painting in Plate 23 is modeled on a classical statue of the goddess. Could such a subject be justified in a Christian civilization? How did artist and patron escape the charge of being neo-pagans? Part of the answer to these questions is provided by the Neo-Platonic philosophers of the time. They believed that the life of the universe, including that of man, was linked to God by a spiritual circuit continuously ascending and descending so that all revelation, whether from the Bible, Plato, or classical myths, was one. Thus they could invoke the celestial Venus interchangeably with the Virgin Mary as a source of divine love. Once we understand this quasi-religious meaning of Botticelli's picture, we may find it less strange that the figures look so ethereal. They are embodiments of poetic and philosophical ideas rather than creatures of flesh and blood—exquisitely beautiful but accessible only to a select and highly educated circle of initiates.

Plate 23. Sandro Botticelli
THE BIRTH OF VENUS
ca. 1480, oil on canvas, height 69"
Uffizi Gallery, Florence

Plate 24.
Michelangelo, THE CREATION OF ADAM *(detail of the Sistine Ceiling), 1508–1512, wall painting*
Sistine Chapel, Vatican

The early sixteenth century—the High Renaissance—has been called the age of genius, for it was the time that formed the concept of artistic genius. Until then, even the greatest of artists were mere makers; now they were creators, set apart from ordinary men by divine inspiration. No less exalted term would fit men such as Leonardo da Vinci, who was both artist and scientist yet full of mystery like a magician, or Michelangelo, who was driven by a truly superhuman ambition. Their works immediately became classics, equal in authority to the most renowned works of the ancients, and their spell persists even today. This is certainly true of Michelangelo's masterpiece, the Sistine Ceiling, which had so vast an impact that it changed the course of Western art for several centuries to come. In this huge expanse of vaulted surface with its hundreds of figures, Michelangelo proclaimed a new ideal image of man: heroic, nude, and beautiful as the gods of Greece but, unlike them, troubled by inner conflicts and unfulfilled yearnings. Thus Adam, in Plate 24, reaches out for contact with the Divine (characteristically, Michelangelo does not

show the physical making of Adam's body); at the same time, however, his glance meets that of Eve, who nestles yet unborn in the shelter of the Lord's left arm. No other artist ever achieved so dramatic a juxtaposition of Man and God.

Some of the figures in Titian's *Bacchanal* in Plate 25 have the muscular build, the animation, the complex poses of Michelangelo's (the influence of the Sistine Ceiling had reached Venice within a few years after its completion), but they form part of a very different world: a richly sensuous, untroubled pagan paradise, inspired by classical poetry. Titian clearly owes a good deal to Giovanni Bellini as well (compare Plate 22), although his brushwork is broader and more fluid, his colors deeper, and the play of sunlight and shadow more dramatic. These figures, unlike those in Botticelli's *Birth of Venus,* are full-blooded human beings who bring antiquity back to life with all the vigor and immediacy we could demand. If Titian lacks the heroic vision of Michelangelo, his works have a vitality whose direct appeal has hardly been dimmed by the passage of time.

In its twin centers, Florence and Rome, the High Renaissance lasted barely two decades, ending with the death of Leonardo in 1519 and that of Raphael in 1520. Michelangelo, it is true, lived until 1564, but his later work no longer had the radiant energy and assurance of the Sistine Ceiling. The next generation of artists reacted to the classic style of their great predecessors in strange and unexpected ways. Some, such as Parmigianino, pursued an ideal of unearthly grace; the long-limbed, languid figures in the *Madonna with the Long Neck* in Plate 26 have a formal perfection that defies any comparison with actual human beings. Characteristically, the meaning of the picture is so intricate that it went unrecognized until very recently. The crystal vessel displayed by the angel on the far left symbolizes the Virgin's purity; its surface, however, reflects a cross (now barely visible), and the Infant Christ, who has seen it, is frightened by this prophecy of his future suffering, while Mary, not yet aware of it, smiles at him tenderly.

The forms in Rosso's *Descent from the Cross* in Plate 27 are as jagged and angular as Parmigianino's are smooth and sinuous. The entire composition seems filled with unbearable anguish whether we look at the latticework of figures engaged in lowering the body of Christ to the ground or at the frozen grief of those at the foot of the cross. The colors, too, appear to be deliberately off-key, designed to reinforce the harsh expressiveness of the artist's style. How are we to understand this deliberate rejection of balance and rationality? By High Renaissance standards, the frantic Rosso and the elegant Parmigianino are equally anticlassical. The new trend they represent, known as Mannerism, has been explained as a symptom of the spiritual crisis brought about by the Reformation. It can be viewed equally, however, as a response to the perfection of High Renaissance art, which had assumed an authority greater even than nature and thus had established style as an ultimate value, an end in itself. Be that as it may, Mannerism was to dominate much of Italian as well as Northern art from the 1520s to the end of the century.

Plate 27. Rosso Fiorentino
THE DESCENT FROM THE CROSS
1521, oil on wood panel, height 11'
Pinacoteca Comunale, Volterra

Plate 28.
Agnolo Bronzino
ELEANORA OF TOLEDO AND HER SON GIOVANNI DE' MEDICI
ca. 1550, oil on canvas, height 38″
Uffizi Gallery, Florence

The elegant phase of Mannerism appealed particularly to aristocratic patrons and produced splendid portraits like that of Eleanora, the wife of Cosimo I de'Medici, by Cosimo's court painter Bronzino. The sitter in Plate 28 appears as the member of an exalted social caste rather than as an individual personality. Congealed into immobility behind the barrier of her lavishly ornate costume, Eleanora seems more akin to Parmigianino's Madonna (compare Plate 26) than to ordinary flesh and blood. Her masklike features betray no hint of inner life; she permits us to admire her, but under no circumstances would she deign to acknowledge our presence.

The ideal type underlying portraits of this kind reflects a development that was to reach its climax a hundred years later: the absolute monarchy, with all strands of state power gathered in the hands of the sovereign. El Greco's portrait in Plate 29 is based on an altogether different scale of values. The last and greatest of Mannerists, El Greco was born on the Greek island of

Crete. As a youth, he acquired the rich heritage of Venetian painting (he worked under Titian for a while), went to Rome, and finally settled in the Spanish town of Toledo. Spain had long been the home of the Counter-Reformation, and El Greco's mature work was decisively shaped by the spiritual climate of that movement. Unlike Bronzino, whose portrait of Eleanora conveys a sense of awed distance between artist and sitter, El Greco was on intimate terms with Paravicino, a scholar and poet who has left us several sonnets in praise of El Greco's genius. The contrast between the two pictures could hardly be more striking: Bronzino's forms are rigidly immobile, while El Greco's every brush stroke communicates a quivering movement; Eleanora's coldness is matched by Paravicino's emotional ardor. His frail, expressive hands and the pallid face, with its sensitive mouth and burning eyes, project an ideal image of the saints of the Counter-Reformation—mystics and intellectuals at the same time.

Plate 29.
El Greco
FRAY FELIX HORTENSIO PARAVICINO
ca. 1605, oil on canvas, height 44½"
Museum of Fine Arts, Boston

When the young German painter Albrecht Dürer visited Venice in 1495, two experiences made an indelible impression on him: the high esteem accorded to Italian artists, and the clarity and rationality of Italian art. In his own work, Dürer spread the gospel of the Italian Renaissance with an almost religious zeal. However, the flowering of the Northern Renaissance which he had helped to bring about was as brief as the High Renaissance in Italy. By the mid-1520s, Germany and her neighbors were in the grip of the Reformation crisis; and since Protestantism opposed religious imagery, artists found themselves deprived of their principal task. The career of Holbein, Germany's greatest artist after Dürer, is characteristic of the times. When the city of Basel went Protestant he was saved by his gift for portraiture: he emigrated to England and became court painter to Henry VIII. His picture of the king in Plate 30 has the immobile pose, the air of unapproachability, and the emphasis on costume and jewelry familiar to us from Bronzino's court portraits (compare Plate 28). Its rigid frontality and physical bulk create an overpowering sensation of the king's ruthless, commanding presence. Here, we realize, stands not only the temporal sovereign, but also the creator and head of the Church of England.

Plate 30. Hans Holbein the Younger, HENRY VIII *1540, oil on wood panel, height 32½" National Gallery of Ancient Art, Rome*

Other northern artists tried their hand at subjects from classical antiquity, although more often than not they drew them from literary rather than from visual sources. Nothing could be less classical than Altdorfer's picture in Plate 31 of the battle in which Alexander defeated Darius, with its ant-like mass of sixteenth-century soldiers spread over an Alpine valley. In fact, the only classical element is the inscribed tablet in the sky, which enables us to identify the subject. The painting might well show some contemporary battle except for the spectacular sky, where we see the sun triumphantly breaking through the clouds and defeating the moon. This celestial drama, obviously correlated with the human contest below, raises the scene to the cosmic level.

Plate 31. Albrecht Altdorfer, THE BATTLE OF ISSUS
1529, oil on wood panel, height 62"
Alte Pinakothek, Munich

Plate 32.
Pieter Bruegel the Elder, THE LAND OF COCKAIGNE
1567, oil on wood panel, height 20½"
Alte Pinakothek, Munich

Although the Netherlands suffered more than any other country in the struggle between Protestants and Catholics, it was Dutch painters who led the field in developing new secular themes to replace the traditional religious subjects. The greatest of them, Pieter Bruegel, explored landscape, peasant life, and moral allegory. *The Land of Cockaigne* in Plate 32 is a fool's paradise, based on a folk tale, where tables are always laden with tasty dishes, houses have roofs made of pies, and pigs and chickens run about roasted to a turn. To reach it, one must eat his way through a mountain of gruel (see the upper right-hand corner). The lesson Bruegel teaches here is a philosophical comment on human nature; the men under the tree are not sinners in the grip of evil like those in Bosch's Hell (compare Plate 21), they are simply not wise enough to know what is best for them. By becoming slaves to their stomachs, they relinquish all ambition for the sake of a kind of animal happiness—the knight has dropped his lance, the farmer his flail, the scholar his books. "Beware of the fool's paradise," the artist seems to say; "it is more dangerous than hell because people *like* going there." And the impressive composition, in the shape of a great wheel turned on its side, shows that he must have thought the subject serious and important.

it was increasingly considered to be the only body that could give a ruler's actions a wider sanction than he could draw from his prerogatives alone. Although for a long time to come it would remain firmly subordinated to the crown, England's kings already realized that they could not take such measures as raising extraordinary taxes without Parliament's consent.

Another of the monarch's assets was England's common law, the uniform country-wide system of justice based on precedent and tradition. Like Parliament, the common law would eventually be regarded by opponents of royal power as an independent source of authority with which the crown could not interfere. But under the conditions facing the "new monarch" in the 1480s, it proved an effective tool in his work of restoring the authority of the throne after two centuries of weakness.

Henry VII

Henry VII (1485–1509), who founded the Tudor dynasty, came to the throne as a usurper in the aftermath of more than thirty years of civil conflict, the Wars of the Roses. England's nobles had been fighting one another for decades, and the situation hardly looked promising for a reassertion of royal power. Yet Henry both extended the authority of the crown and restored order with extraordinary speed.

His first concern as he set about establishing a stable rule was finances. The crown's income was about £52,000 a year, but Henry's immediate expenses were considerably higher.[4] He knew that unless he could balance his budget, his position would remain insecure. Yet extra taxes were the surest way to alienating subjects who expected a king to "live of his own," that is, from the income his lands provided, customs payments, and the traditional contributions made to him at special times such as the marriage of his daughter. It is a testimony to the care with which he nurtured his revenues that by the end

of his reign he had paid off all his debts and accumulated between one and two million pounds as a reserve.

Part of his success was due to his beginning his reign with more property than any of his predecessors, a consequence of forfeitures and inheritances during the civil wars. But Henry also sharply increased the profits of justice—fees and fines—which had the added advantage of cowing unruly subjects. Moreover he radically improved his financial administration by taking the tasks of collection and supervision out of the cumbersome office of the Exchequer and placing them in his own more efficient household. By careful management of this kind, he was able to "live of his own."

Where domestic order was concerned, the main impetus behind the revival of royal authority was clearly the energy of the king and his chief servants. Henry increased the powers of the justices of the peace, thus striking severely at the independence attained by leading nobles during the previous two centuries. Under his leadership, too, the council became a far more active and influential body. The ministers not only exercised executive powers but also resumed hearing legal appeals, primarily because the government was determined to exert all its force to quell disorder. Plaintiffs could be sure that at such a hearing, where there was no jury and where deliberations would not be influenced by the power of a local lord, decisions would be quick and fair, and the popularity and business of the councillors' court grew rapidly.[5]

The dual objective of government stability and fiscal responsibility guided Henry's foreign policy. He never became involved in costly adventures, and he allowed no challenge to the Tudor dynasty's claim to the crown. In 1492 for example, after Henry half-heartedly invaded

---

[4] To give a sense of scale, a man who made £100 a year was considered very rich.

[5] The room where the royal council met had stars painted on its ceiling; the council sitting as a court eventually came to be known by the name of the room, the Star Chamber.

France as a protest against the French annexation of Brittany, Charles VIII signed a treaty promising to pay him £160,000 and guaranteeing not to support any claimants to the English throne. A succession of agreements with other rulers from Denmark to Florence bolstered the position of England's merchants, whose international trade was essential to the crown's customs revenues. Henry encouraged the manufacture and export of the country's great staple product, cloth, and protected shipping with a navigation act. Turning to more distant possibilities, he granted an Italian sailor, John Cabot, a patent to search for a westward route to China. The result of this undertaking was the discovery of enormous fishing banks off Newfoundland whose exploitation was to be the basis of the growing prosperity of many English ports in the sixteenth century.

Henry VIII and His Successors

The first Tudor was a conservative, building up his authority and finances through traditional methods and institutions that had long been at the disposal of England's kings but that the founder of the new dynasty applied with exceptional determination and vigor. The young man who followed him on the throne, Henry VIII (1509–1547), was an expansive, dazzling figure, a strong contrast to his cold and careful father (see Plate 30). Early in his reign he removed a longstanding threat from England's north by inflicting a shattering defeat on an invading Scots army at Flodden in 1513, and the following year he brought a sporadic war with France to a favorable conclusion. With his prestige thus enhanced, he spent the next fifteen years taking only a minor part in European affairs while he consolidated royal power at home with the capable assistance of his chief minister, Cardinal Thomas Wolsey.

Wolsey was not an innovator but a tireless and effective administrator who continued the consolidation of royal power begun under Henry VII. To meet the rising demand for royal justice, he expanded the jurisdiction and activities of the Star Chamber and guided another offshoot of the king's council to independent status: the Court of Requests, or Court of Poor Men's Causes.

Wolsey fell from power in 1529, ruined by the king's wish to obtain a divorce from his wife, who had failed to produce a surviving male heir. Henry had married his brother's widow, Catherine of Aragon, under a special papal dispensation from the biblical law that normally prohibited a union between such close relatives. Obsessed with continuing his dynasty, for which a male heir seemed essential—and infatuated with a young lady at court, Anne Boleyn—Henry had urged Wolsey to ask the pope to declare the previous dispensation invalid. Under ordinary circumstances there would have been no trouble, but at this moment the pope was in the power of Charles V, king of Spain and emperor of the Holy Roman Empire, who not only had a high sense of rectitude but also was Catherine's nephew. When all Wolsey's efforts ended in failure, Henry dismissed him.

For three years thereafter the king tried in vain to get his divorce. He called Parliament and gave it free rein to express bitter anticlerical sentiments; he sought opinions in European universities in favor of the divorce; he attacked his own clergy for having bowed to Wolsey's authority; he even extracted a vague recognition from the clergy of his position as "supreme lord" of the Church. Finally he placed his confidence in Thomas Cromwell, a former servant of Wolsey, who suggested a radical but simple solution: that Henry break with the pope, declare himself supreme head of the Church, and divorce Catherine on his own authority. The king agreed, thus unleashing a revolution that dramatically increased the powers of the royal government.

The instrument chosen to accomplish the

break with Rome was Parliament, the only body capable of giving the move legal sanction and an aura of national approval. Henry called the assembly in 1529 and did not dissolve it until 1536. During its sessions it acted on more matters of greater importance than a Parliament had ever considered before. It forbade litigants from making ecclesiastical appeals to Rome, thus allowing Henry to obtain his divorce and remarry, and finally declared him supreme head of the Church in England in 1534. Royal power gained enormously from these acts, but so too did the stature of Parliament, thanks to its unprecedented responsibilities and length of meeting.

Previously, election to Parliament had been considered a chore by the townsmen and landed gentry in the House of Commons, who found the expense of unpaid attendance and its encroachments on their time more irksome than did the nobles in the House of Lords (so named during Henry VIII's reign). But this attitude began to change in the 1530s as members of the Commons, returning to successive sessions, came to know one another and in time developed a remarkable esprit de corps as jealous guardians of Parliament's traditions and privileges.

Following his successful suggestion for solving Henry's conflict with Rome, Thomas Cromwell rose rapidly in his monarch's service. He was a tireless bureaucrat; he reorganized the administration of the country into six carefully distinguished departments with specific functions and gave himself the chief executive position, the secretaryship. A Privy Council, consisting of the king's principal advisers, was also established to coordinate and direct the administration.

Unquestionably the principal beneficiary of the events of the 1530s was the crown. Royal income rose markedly when Henry became head of the English Church and took over the ecclesiastical fees that previously had gone to the pope. He gained an even larger windfall when he dissolved all English monasteries and confiscated their immensely valuable lands, which were sold over the next few decades. Fortunes were made by speculators, and new families rose to prominence as major landowners.

For all the stimulus he gave to parliamentary power, Henry now had a much larger, wealthier, and more sophisticated administration at his disposal, and he left no doubt where ultimate authority lay. He did not establish a standing army, as some of the Continental kings did, but he had no need for one. He was fully capable of awing ambitious nobles or crushing an uprising.

Royal power was put to the test very soon. Where doctrine and the structure of the Church were concerned, Henry was a conservative; he allowed few changes in dogma or liturgy. As the Lutheran reform movement on the Continent created a serious split in Christendom, Henry tried to restrain the spread of Reformation ideas and persecuted heresy, but he could not avoid compromises. Perhaps realizing the shape of things to come, he had his son, Edward, tutored by a committed reformer. Moreover in the 1540s a leading Continental reformer, Martin Bucer, spent a few years in Cambridge, deeply influencing a number of future leaders of the English Church.

During the reign of Edward VI (1547–1553), who died while still a minor, the nobility attempted to resume some of their old powers in government, and the Reformation advanced rapidly in England. But Edward's half-sister Mary I tried to reestablish Roman Catholicism when she became queen in 1553, forcing many Englishmen into exile and others into two major revolts during her five-year reign. Royal power, however, was strong enough to survive these strains. The revival of the nobles was short-lived, and Mary's death, in 1558, brought an end to the reversal of religions. She was succeeded by Henry VIII's last surviving child,

Elizabeth, a woman of determination who demonstrated that the growth of the monarchy's authority had been but briefly interrupted under Edward and Mary.

VALOIS FRANCE

The rulers of France in the fifteenth century, unlike their English counterparts, lacked a well-formed organization for local government. Aristocrats dominated many sections, particularly those farthest from Paris, and great nobles had become virtually independent rulers. They had their own administrations and often their own courts and taxation, leaving the crown little say in their affairs. The size of the kingdom also placed restraints on royal power; it took more than a week to travel from Paris to the remoter parts of the domain—almost double the time for the equivalent English journey. Delays of this size inevitably hampered central authority.

The monarchy had tried to resolve the problem of ruling distant provinces by granting close relatives appanages, large blocs of territory that came into royal hands. Theoretically the kinsman would devote full attention to these lands and execute the monarch's wishes more effectively than he himself could from Paris. In practice, however, an ambitious family member often became just as difficult to handle as any powerful noble. After 1469 the crown kept control over such acquisitions—an indication that it was becoming capable of exercising authority even in areas far from the capital.

The administrative center of the government in Paris was the royal council and its chief departments: the Chancery, which had charge of all formal documents, and the Treasury. The greatest court of law in the land was the Parlement of Paris, whose members were appointed by the crown and which had remained a judicial body, unlike the English Parliament. As the central administration grew in the fifteenth and early sixteenth centuries, various provinces received their own parlements from the crown, a recognition of the continuing strength of local autonomies. The countervailing force was the dominant system of Roman law, which enabled the monarch to govern by issuing ordinances and edicts. They had to be registered by the parlements in order to take effect, but usually this was a formality.

Representative assemblies, the estates, also reduced the power of the throne. A number of provinces had local estates, and matters such as the raising of taxes had to be arranged through them. But the national representative body, the Estates General, to which clergy, nobles, and townsmen sent delegates, never attained the prestige of the English Parliament and was never able to bind the country together or function as an essential organ of government.

Moreover French kings had a degree of independence that English monarchs never achieved in a critically important area: finances. For centuries they had supplemented their ordinary sources of income, from lands and customs duties, with extraordinary levies in the form of a sales tax (*aide*), a hearth tax (*taille*), and a salt tax (*gabelle*). Consequently the average Frenchman who was subject to taxation (all nobles and many towns were exempt) usually bore a heavier burden than his English counterpart. In earlier days the consent of the localities had been required before such demands could be made, but after 1451 the taxes could be raised on the king's authority alone, although he still had to negotiate the exact rate with provincial estates and be careful not to go beyond what would seem reasonable to his subjects.

But the most decisive contrast with England lay in France's standing army. The upkeep of the troops accounted for more than half the royal expenditures in Louis XI's reign, mainly because their numbers grew with increases in revenues. In the 1480s a force probably larger than 15,000 men, chiefly professional mercenaries and military-minded nobles, was held in permanent readiness every campaigning season from spring to fall. With the invention of the arquebus, a primitive handgun, and the need for large concentrations of pikemen to protect the gunners, the size of armies had to be increased; moreover, the development of cannon demanded the expensive skills and logistics of heavy artillery. These innovations added to the advantages of the central government because it alone could afford the cost of the new technology. At the same time, much larger resources were needed to support the army in the field. Troops were billeted in various provinces, and often the local estates had to contribute to their maintenance. As a result all Frenchmen eventually had the indirect burden of heavier taxation, and many regions of France had direct contact with royal soldiers. Although frequently short of pay, the troops were firmly under royal control and hence a vital device—rarely used but always a threat—in the strengthening of royal authority.

Louis XI and Charles VIII

When Louis XI (1461–1483) began his reign, he faced a situation as unpromising as that of Henry VII at his succession, for the country had just emerged from the Hundred Years' War, and royal powers were much reduced. English troops, present in France for most of the war years, had finally departed in the 1450s; but a new and equally dangerous menace had arisen in the east: the conglomeration of territories assembled by the dukes of Burgundy.

By the 1460s the dukes, though vassals of the French crown in their southern holdings, were among the most powerful lords in Western Europe. They ruled a loosely organized dominion that stretched from the seventeen separate provinces of the Low Countries to the Swiss Confederation, and their Burgundian capital, Dijon, had become a major cultural and political center. In 1474 Louis XI put together a coalition against Duke Charles the Bold, who had been at war with him for some seven years, and in 1477 Charles was killed in battle with the French king's Swiss allies. Louis then reannexed the duchy of Burgundy itself; but Mary, the duke's daughter, retained the Low Countries, which would later form part of the imperial inheritance of her grandson, the Holy Roman Emperor Charles V.

The Burgundian lands added considerably to Louis's sphere of authority. His masterful maneuvering in the tortuous diplomacy of his day soon won him other territories; he was appropriately nicknamed "the Spider," because the prizes he caught in his web were more often the result of waiting or shrewd negotiation than of victories on the battlefield. Such was the case at the beginning of his reign when, by a typical combination of force and fraud, he pried two provinces on his southern border away from Spain. Simple luck enlarged his realm as well: in 1481 he inherited the enormous Angevin lands—the provinces of Anjou, Maine, and Provence. The result was that by the end of his reign, though government procedures had not noticeably changed, royal power had penetrated into massive areas where previously it had been unknown; only one major region, Brittany, remained completely beyond the crown's influence (see Map 13.3).

Louis XI's son and successor, Charles VIII (1483–1498), was equally dedicated to increasing the territories under the Valois dynasty's command. For a start he married the heiress of the duke of Brittany, thereby securing the last independent region of France, though it was not officially incorporated into the royal domain for another half-century.

In 1494, seeking further gains, Charles invaded Italy at the request of the duke of Milan, who was afraid of being attacked by Florence and Naples. After some initial successes the French settled into a prolonged struggle with the Hapsburgs for control of the rich Italian

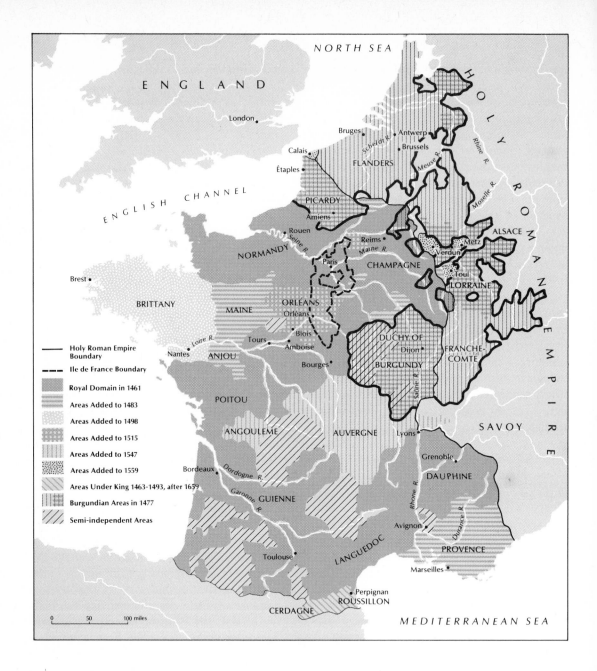

MAP 13.3: FRANCE IN THE 15TH AND 16TH CENTURIES

This map shows in detail the successive stages whereby the monarchy extended its control throughout France.

peninsula. The conflicts lasted for sixty-five years, ending in defeat for the French. Although the Italian wars failed to satisfy the territorial ambitions of Charles and his successors, they provided an outlet for the restless French nobility and gave the monarchy an opportunity to consolidate royal power at home.

The Growth of Government Power

After Charles VIII's reign France's financial and administrative machinery grew in both size and effectiveness, largely because of the demands of the Italian wars. There was rarely enough money to support the adventure; the kings therefore relied heavily on loans from Italian bankers, who sometimes helped shape France's financial policies. At the same time the crown made a determined and notably successful effort to increase traditional royal revenues.

But expenses were also rising. France was a rich country of 15 million people with the most fertile land in Europe; yet the financial needs of the monarch always outstripped his subjects' ability to pay. Nobles, many towns, royal officeholders, and the clergy were exempt from the *taille* and the *gabelle*. Thus the bulk of the taxes had to be raised from the very classes that had the least to give. Other means were therefore needed to supplement the royal income.

One solution was found in the sale of offices. The kings sold positions in the administration, the parlements, and every branch of the bureaucracy to purchasers eager to obtain both the tax exemption and the considerable status (sometimes a title of nobility) that the offices brought them. From modest and uncertain beginnings under Louis XII (1498–1515), the system widened steadily; by the end of the sixteenth century, it would provide the crown with one-twelfth of its revenues.

Many other rulers were adopting this device, and everywhere it had similar effects: it stimulated social mobility, creating dynasties of noble officeholders and a new administrative class; it caused a dramatic expansion of bureaucracies; and it encouraged corruption. The system spread most rapidly and the effects were most noticeable in France, where the reign of Francis I (1515–1547) witnessed a major increase in the government's power as its servants multiplied. Francis tried hard to continue the widening of royal control by expeditions into Italy, but in fact he contributed more to the development of the crown's authority by his actions at home.

One of the earliest and perhaps most remarkable of Francis's accomplishments was the power he gained over his formidable rival, the Church. Early in his reign he was highly successful in his Italian campaigns, and he used his position to persuade the pope in 1516 to give France's king the right to appoint all her bishops and abbots. According to this concordat, the first year's income after a new bishop took office still went to the Vatican, but in effect Francis now controlled the French Church. Its enormous patronage was at his disposal, and he could use it at will to reward servants or raise money. Since his wishes had not been blocked by the pope, he did not need to break with Rome in order to obtain the authority over the clergy that Henry VIII was soon to achieve in England.

In the 1520s he also began a major reorganization of the government. Francis formally legalized the sale of offices, and gradually the purchasers replaced local nobles as the administrators of the various sections of France. He also formed an inner council, more manageable than the unwieldy royal council, to act as the chief executive body of the realm. As part of this streamlining, in 1523 all tax-gathering and accounting responsibilities were centralized in one agency. Against the parlements, meanwhile, the king invoked the *lit de justice*, a prerogative which allowed him to appear before an assembly that was delaying the registration of any of his edicts or ordinances and declare them registered and therefore law. The Estates General was no problem because none met between 1484 and 1560.

With the monarchy's authority extended throughout his country, Francis's interests began to move outside of Europe. Jacques Cartier's voyages to North America in the 1530s and a French challenge to the Portuguese monopoly of West African trade were the first stirrings of a maritime effort that was cut short only by civil wars in the late sixteenth century.

By the end of Francis's reign, royal power was thus stronger than ever before; but signs of disunity had begun to appear that would intensify in the years to come. The Reformation was under way in the Holy Roman Empire, and it soon produced religious divisions and social unrest in France. As the reign of Francis's son Henry II (1547–1559) came to a close, the Italian wars ended in a French defeat, badly damaging the prestige of the monarchy. The civil wars that followed came perilously close to destroying all that the monarchy had accomplished during the previous hundred years.

UNITED SPAIN

The Iberian Peninsula in the mid-fifteenth century was divided into three very different kingdoms. Portugal, with some 1.5 million inhabitants, was in the midst of an expansion around the coast of Africa that was soon to bring her great wealth from the East. Castile, in the center, with a population of more than 8 million, was the largest and richest of the kingdoms. Sheep farming was the basis of her prosperity, and her countryside was dominated by powerful nobles. Castile was the last kingdom still fighting the Moors, and in the ceaseless crusade against the infidels the nobles played a leading part. They had built up both a great chivalric tradition and considerable political strength as a result of their exploits, and their status was enhanced by the religious fervor that the long struggle had inspired. The third kingdom, Aragon, approximately the same size as Portugal, consisted of three areas: Catalonia, the heart of the kingdom and a great commercial region centered on the city of Barcelona; Aragon itself, which was little more than a barren hinterland to Catalonia; and Valencia, a farming and

fishing region south of Catalonia along the Mediterranean coast.

In October 1469, Isabella, future queen of Castile, married Ferdinand, future king of Sicily and heir to the throne of Aragon. Realizing that the marriage would strengthen the crown, the Castilian nobles opposed the union, precipitating a ten-year civil war. But the joined monarchy emerged victorious, more powerful, and in control of a new political entity: the Kingdom of Spain.

Ferdinand and Isabella

When Ferdinand and Isabella jointly assumed the thrones of Castile in 1474 and Aragon five years later, they made no attempt to create a monolithic state. Aragon remained a federation of territories, administered by viceroys, who were appointed by the king but who allowed local customs to remain virtually intact. The traditions of governing by consent and preserving the subject's rights were particularly strong in this kingdom, where each province had its own representative assembly, known as the Cortes. Ferdinand left the system untouched, but he did make the viceroys a permanent feature of the government and created a special council for Aragonese affairs, through which he controlled the kingdom. In Castile, however, the two monarchs were determined to assert their superiority over all possible rivals to their authority. Their immediate aims were to restore the order in the countryside that had been destroyed by civil war, much as it had been in England and France, and to reduce the power of the nobility.

The first objective was accomplished with the help of the Cortes of Castile, an assembly dominated by urban representatives who shared the wish for order because peace benefited trade. The Cortes established special tribunals to pursue and try criminals, and by the 1490s it had succeeded in ending the widespread lawlessness in the kingdom.

To reinforce their authority, Ferdinand and Isabella sharply reduced the number of great nobles in the royal council and overhauled the entire administration, particularly the financial agencies, applying the principle that ability rather than social status should determine appointments. As the bureaucracy spread, the hidalgo, a lesser aristocrat, who was heavily dependent on royal favor, became increasingly important in government. Unlike the great nobles, whose enormous wealth was little affected by the reforms that reduced their role, the hidalgos were hurt because they lost their tax exemptions. The new livelihood they found was in the service of the crown, and they became essential figures in the centralization of power in Castile as well as the overseas territories.

The monarchs achieved final control over the nobles in the 1480s and 1490s, when they took over the rich and powerful military orders into which the aristocracy was organized. The great nobles could not be crushed completely; nor did the king and queen wish to destroy them. But like the kings of England and France, Ferdinand and Isabella wanted to reduce their autonomy to a level that did not seem to threaten central authority—a process that was accomplished by 1500.

The rulers also succeeded in weakening the Spanish bishops and abbots, who were as strong and wealthy as leading nobles. After Ferdinand and Isabella destroyed the power of the Moors in Castile, the pope granted the monarchy the right to make all major ecclesiastical appointments in the newly won territory, and this right was extended to the New World shortly thereafter. In the following reign the monarchy would gain complete control over Church appointments, making Spain more independent of Rome than any other Catholic state.

Mastery over the towns and the Cortes of Castile did not pose much of a problem. Where local rule was concerned, an old official, the *corregidor*, was given new powers and a position of responsibility within the administrative

hierarchy. Usually a hidalgo, he became the chief executive and judicial officer in his region, rather like the justice of the peace in England, and he also supervised town affairs. The Cortes did not seriously restrict the crown because Spanish taxes, like French, could be raised without consent. The Castilian assembly met frequently and even provided additional funds for foreign wars, but it never challenged royal supremacy during this reign.

The king and queen supervised the system of justice directly, hearing cases personally once a week. All law was considered to come from the throne, and they had full power to overrule the decisions of local courts, often run by nobles. Centralized judicial machinery began to appear, and in a few decades Castilian law was organized into a uniform code—always a landmark in the stabilization of a state.

Considering the anarchy at the start of their reign and the absence of central institutions, Ferdinand and Isabella performed greater wonders in establishing royal power than did any of the other new monarchs. A good index of the effectiveness of their growing bureaucracy is the increase in their revenues. As soon as the main administrative reforms were completed, in the 1490s, the yield of the sales tax (the *alcabala*), which was the mainstay of royal income, began to rise dramatically. Total annual revenue is estimated to have soared from 80,000 ducats in 1474 to 2.3 million by 1504, the year Isabella died.[6] Religious affairs, too, helped in the consolidation of the crown's authority. After the civil wars in Castile had come to an end, Ferdinand had turned his energies to driving the Moors from the peninsula. The reasons for his aggressive policy were clear: first, it complemented the crown's drive for power at home; second, war was a traditional

---

[6] There were approximately four Spanish ducats to the English pound, which means that Ferdinand and Isabella had an income nearly five times that of Henry VII or half that of Louis XII.

INQVISITION

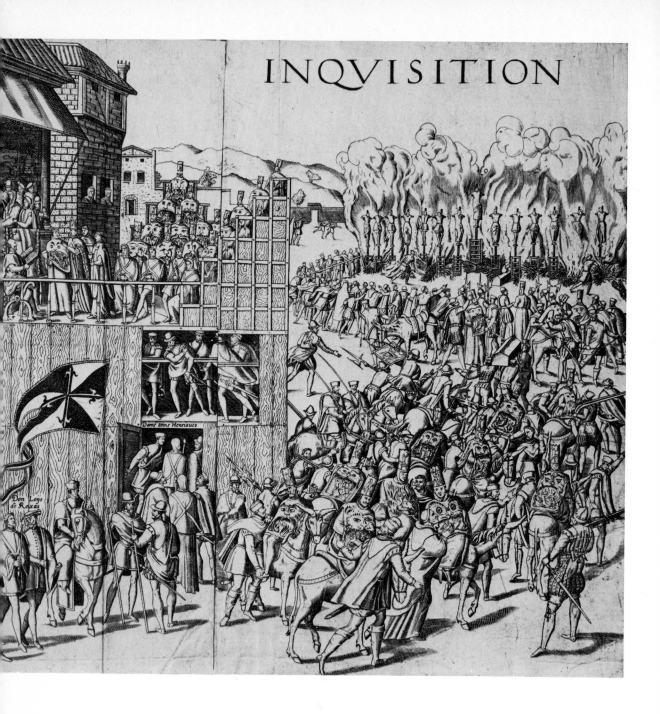

At the dread auto-da-fé a public judgment of guilt was passed on those whom the Spanish Inquisition had tried. Then followed the punishment, which was carried out by the civil authorities—usually burning the heretics, as shown in this engraving. (Photo: Giraudon)

interest for an ambitious ruler, and it helped keep restless nobles occupied; and finally, the element of crusade in the struggle against non-Christians stimulated the country's religious fervor, which in turn promoted enthusiasm for its rulers.

The tide of religious zeal swept on after the last Arab stronghold, Granada, capitulated in 1492. Less than three months later, all Jews were expelled from Spain. Some 150,000 of the most enterprising people in Aragon and Castile, including many leading doctors, government officials, and others who had made a vital contribution to economic and cultural life, departed overnight. It was only natural that the rulers' determination to remove anything that stood in their way should have focused on a group that did not share the popular religious passion sustaining their authority. The campaign against the Jews thus went hand in hand with growing royal power.

The same drive to consolidate their strength had prompted Ferdinand and Isabella to obtain permission from the pope in 1478 to establish their own Inquisition. Since 1483 this indigenous body had been run by a royal council and given a mandate to root out Marranos and Moriscos—Jews and Moors who under coercion had pretended to accept Christianity but in fact retained their original beliefs. After the fall of Granada, the Spanish Church attempted to convert the Moors, and in 1502 all Arabs who were not officially Christian were expelled from the country. Nonetheless suspected Moriscos and Marranos kept the Inquisition busy. The persecution welded the country into a religious unity that paralleled and supported the political centralization achieved by the monarchy. Religious policy was thus as much an instrument of political power as it was of ideological conformity.

Foreign Affairs

The fall of Granda extended Spain's dominion southward, but there were also lands to be captured to the north and east. It was in this undertaking that Ferdinand took the lead, because men controlled diplomacy and warfare, and he emphasized these activities during the twelve years he ruled on his own after Isabella's death. His first success had come in 1493, when Charles VIII rewarded Spain's support of the French expedition into Italy by returning to her the two provinces on the French border that Louis XI had taken thirty years before. Two years later, however, fearful that France's Italian invasion was threatening his Kingdom of Sicily, Ferdinand decided to enter the war in Italy.

His achievements in the next two decades were due to a combination of military and diplomatic skills unusual even among the highly capable rulers of the age. A reorganization of Spain's standing army made it the most effective force in Europe, and it rapidly achieved a commanding presence in Italy: by 1504 it had conquered Naples, and Spain had become a major power in the peninsula. Ferdinand also built the strongest diplomatic service of his time, setting up five permanent embassies—at Rome, Venice, London, Brussels, and the Hapsburg court. The ambassadors' reports and activities made him the best-informed and most effective maneuverer in the international politics of the day.

Thus by the time of his death, in 1516, the united Spain that he and Isabella created had gained enormously in territory and status both at home and abroad. The successor to the throne inherited a monarchy fully as dynamic and as triumphant over its rivals as those of England and France.

Charles V, Holy Roman Emperor

To bolster their dynasty the joint rulers had married their five children to members of the leading families of Europe. Their daughter Joanna became the wife of the Hapsburg Archduke Philip of Austria, and her son Charles became heir to both the royal throne of Spain and the Hapsburg dukedom.

A Jew kneeling before Queen Isabella during the Inquisition. (Photo: Museo Provincial, Zaragoza/Photo MAS)

Early in his reign as king of Spain, however, Charles (1516–1556) had to withstand a major onslaught on the crown's position. Educated in Flanders, he spoke no Castilian, and when he arrived in Spain late in 1517, he soon aroused the resentment of the local nobility, particularly when members of the large Flemish entourage he brought with him were given positions in the government. The young king stayed for two and a half years, during which time he was elected emperor of the Holy Roman Empire (1519). This enhanced his prestige, but it also intensified his subjects' fears that he would become an absentee ruler with little interest in their affairs. The Cortes, in particular, showed open hostility when Charles requested additional tax funds so that he could leave the country with Spanish troops for imperial purposes. As soon as he left, in 1520, revolts began to break out in Spain's towns, and the risings of these communes racked the country for two years. The troubles Charles now endured were one of the first of many major clashes during the next 150 years between the traditional dynastic aims of the leading European monarchs and the jealous sense of distinctiveness felt by their subjects.[7]

Fortunately for the crown, the communes lacked positive aims; their resentments and hopes were deep but vague. They wanted to reverse the growth of royal power and to restore their traditional autonomy—a grievance that central governments were bound to encounter as they extended their authority. To this end communes asked for the removal of Flemish royal officials and a reduction in taxation, and at first they had the strong sympathy of the Spanish nobles, who particularly disliked the foreign ruler. But the movement soon took on social overtones: the communes launched attacks on the privileged orders of society, especially the nobility, and this lost the revolt its only chance for success. For now the nobles turned against the communes and defeated them in battle even before Charles returned to Spain.

The king took warning from the uprisings and made sure that his administration was now kept entirely in Spanish hands. Henceforth the energies of his subjects were channeled into imperial missions overseas, where the conquest of Mexico was under way, and against the Ottoman Turks in the Mediterranean. Once again foreign excursions bought a monarch peace at home.

The one notable extension of royal power during Charles's reign was the large empire Spaniards were establishing in Central and South America. Closer to home, however, there was little that gave him or his Spanish subjects cause for pleasure. As Holy Roman Emperor and king of Spain, Charles ruled almost all of Continental Europe west of Poland and the Balkans, with the major exception of France, and he was almost ceaselessly at war defending his territories (see Map 13.4). To the Spaniards most of the wars helped imperial ambitions and were thus irrelevant. As far as they were concerned, aside from the widening acquisitions in the New World, Charles did little to further the expansion started by Ferdinand and Isabella.

The recurrent crises and wars outside of Spain kept Charles away from his kingdom for more than two-thirds of his forty-year reign. But in his absence a highly talented administrator, Francisco de los Cobos, shaped and clarified the government's position. He established the complete supremacy of the crown by greatly enlarging the bureaucracy and elaborating the system of councils that Ferdinand and Isabella had begun. In the 1520s this structure, which was to survive for centuries, received its final form.

There were two types of council. One was responsible for each of the departments of the

---

[7] Although this feeling cannot be called nationalism, it was certainly an ancestor of that powerful modern force. Incidentally, the word "communes" as used here refers to the towns and cities of Spain that had distinct legal privileges and some degree of self-government; they were the center of the revolt. Their inhabitants are called, in Spanish, "comuneros."

MAP 13.4: THE EMPIRE OF CHARLES V

This map indicates both the vastness of Charles's empire and the extent of the fighting in which he became involved. Almost every battle his troops fought—against Spanish communes, German Protestants, the Turks, and the French—is included so as to show the full measure of the emperor's never-ending ordeal.

government—finance, war, the Inquisition, and so on. The other supervised each of the territories ruled by the crown: Aragon, Castile, Italy, the Indies, and later in the century the Low Countries. At the head of this system was the Council of State, the principal advisory group, consisting of leading officials from the subsidiary councils. All the subsidiary councils reported to the king or to his deputy when he was away, but since each controlled its own bureaucracy, they were perfectly capable of running the empire in the monarch's absence.

What emerged was a vast federation, with Castile standing at its heart but with the parts, though directed from the center, allowed considerable autonomy. A viceroy in every major area (there were nine altogether from Naples to Peru) ran the administration under the supervision of the *audiencia*—the territorial council—and while on the whole these officials were left to do as they wished, they had to report to Castile in minute detail at regular intervals and refer major decisions to the central government.

Although corruption was widespread and delays in communications (it took at least eight months to send a message from Castile to Peru) made the system unwieldy, the centralization gave the monarch the power he wanted. The enormous bureaucracy was carefully staffed, primarily by hidalgos and townsmen, while great nobles were given only vice-royalties or high army posts. Flexibility was allowed at the local level, but through the hierarchy of loyal servants the crown could exercise unhampered control. As a result, Spain's administrative machine was one of the most remarkably detailed structures ever devised for ruling so vast an empire.

The Financial Toll of War

The only serious strain on Charles's monarchy was financial, the result of the constant wars the Hapsburgs had to support. A large portion of the money for the fighting came from Italy and the Low Countries, but Spain had to pay a growing share of the costs. As the sixteenth century progressed, the Spaniards increasingly resented the siphoning away of their funds into foreign wars. It was the tragedy of their century of glory that so much of the fantastic wealth they discovered in Latin America was exported to support hostilities from which they drew almost no benefit.

The burden was by no means equally distributed. The stronger Cortes of Aragon was able to prevent substantial increases in taxation, which meant that Castile had to assume the brunt of the payments. To some extent this was balanced by a monopoly of trade with the New World that was granted to the inhabitants of Castile, but eventually the basic inequality among different Spanish regions led to civil war in the next century.

Charles's finances were saved from disaster only by the influx of treasure—mainly silver—from Latin America. Approximately 40 percent of the bullion went into the royal coffers, while the rest was taken by merchants in the Castilian city of Seville, mainly Genoese, who were given the sole right to ship goods to and from America. Starting with an annual inflow of some 20,000 ducats at the beginning of the century, Charles was receiving approximately 800,000 ducats' worth of treasure each year by the end of his reign. Unfortunately it was always mortgaged in advance to the Italian and German bankers whose loans sustained his armies.

The country and the monarchy faced increasing difficulties as the wars continued for more than a century and a half. Seville's monopoly prevented the rest of the nation from gaining a share of the new wealth, and foreigners—notably representatives of Italian and German financiers—came to dominate her economy and her commerce. Spain was squeezed dry by the king's financial demands; yet he only just kept his head above water. In 1557, the first year of the reign of Charles's successor, Philip II, the monarchy had to declare itself bankrupt, a self-defeating evasion of its mammoth debts that it had to repeat seven times in the next 125 years. There has never been a better example of the way that ceaseless war can sap the strength of even the most formidable nation.

III. THE SPLINTERED STATES

The rulers of England, France, and Spain in the mid-sixteenth century came to thrones strengthened domestically and internationally. Their predecessors had centralized their governments, largely subdued the rivals to royal power, engaged in a huge expansion overseas, and brought a fair measure of prosperity and safety from lawlessness to their subjects. Above all they had begun to free the individual from subjection to his local lord. But in the European domains east of these three kingdoms, such developments took place fitfully and only within small territorial units such as city-states. Here the centrifugal forces retained the control they had enjoyed for centuries.

THE HOLY ROMAN EMPIRE: AUTONOMOUS PRINCES

The Holy Roman Empire is a classic example of weak institutions preventing the emergence of a strong central government. Members of the leading family of Central Europe, the Hapsburgs, had been elected to the imperial throne since the thirteenth century, but they lacked the authority and machinery to halt the fragmentation of the lands they nominally ruled. In addition to some 2,000 imperial knights, some of whom owned no more than four or five acres, there were 50 ecclesiastical and 30 secular princes, more than 100 counts, some 70 prelates, and 66 cities, all virtually independent politically though officially subordinate to the emperor.

The princes, who reigned over most of the area of the Holy Roman Empire, rarely had any trouble resisting the emperor's claims; their main concern was to increase their own power at the expense of their subjects, another prince,

or the cities. The cities themselves also refused to remain subordinate to a central government. Fifty of them contained more than 2,000 inhabitants in 1500—a sizable number for this time—and twenty had over 10,000. Their wealth was substantial, because many were situated along a densely traveled trade artery, the Rhine River, and many were also political powers. But their fierce independence meant that the emperor could rarely tap their manpower or wealth.

The only central institution apart from the imperial office itself, the Diet, consisted of three assemblies: representatives of the cities, the princes, and the electors (the seven princes who elected each new emperor). Given this make-up, the Diet in effect became the instrument of the princes; with its legislation they secured their position against both the cities and the lesser nobility within their own domains.

By the end of the fifteenth century, most of the princes had achieved considerable control over their own territories. Only in the southwest of the empire were they significantly restricted by representative assemblies led by the lesser nobility. The princes were thus enjoying a success that paralleled the accomplishments of the monarchs of England, France, and Spain except that the units were much smaller. Although the Hapsburgs tried to develop strong central authority, they exercised significant control only over their personal dominions, which in 1500 comprised Austria, the Low Countries, and so-called imperial Burgundy, or Franche-Comté. To the rulers of other states of the empire, they were feudal overlords in theory but powerless in practice.

Nevertheless the need for effective central institutions met with some response in the late fifteenth century, particularly in the west and southwest of the empire. In 1495 for example a tribunal was established to settle disputes between local powers. Controlled and financed by the princes, the chief beneficiaries of its work, it made considerable headway toward ending the lawlessness that had marked the fifteenth century, an achievement similar to the restoration of order in France, Spain, and England at the same time. The tribunal's use of Roman law had a wide influence on legislation and justice throughout the empire, but again only to the advantage of the princes, who interpreted its endorsement of a leader's authority as referring only to themselves.

Further attempts at administrative reform had little effect, because ecclesiastical and secular princes reacted by tightening their hold on the multitude of territories that constituted the empire. The religious dissensions of the Reformation worsened the rivalries, dividing the empire and making Charles V no more than the leader of one side in the conflict, incapable of asserting his authority over his opponents. Charles's many commitments elsewhere diverted him repeatedly, but even when he won decisive military victories over the princes, he could not break the long tradition of local independence.

EASTERN EUROPE: RESURGENT NOBLES

In the late fifteenth century, the dominant force in Eastern and Central Europe was the Kingdom of Hungary, under the leadership of Matthias Corvinus (1458–1490). He was exactly in the mold of the other new monarchs of the day: he restrained the great nobles, expanded and centralized his administration, dramatically increased the yield of taxation, and established a standing army. The king's power thus grew spectacularly both at home and abroad. He gained Bohemia and some German and Austrian lands, and he made Vienna his capital in 1485.

Immediately after his death, however, royal authority collapsed. To gain Hapsburg recognition of his right to the throne, his successor gave up the conquests of Austrian and German territories and arranged dynastic marriages with the Hapsburgs. This retreat provided the nobles of Hungary with an issue over which to reassert their position. First they forced the king to dissolve the standing army by refusing him essential financial support. Then, following a major peasant revolt against increasing repression by landowners, they imposed serfdom on all peasants in 1514 at a meeting of the Hungarian Diet, the governing body, which was controlled by the aristocracy. In the course of the next thirty years, the country was overrun by the Ottoman Empire, whose system of rule—reliance on local powers who would give allegiance to Constantinople—strengthened the nobility further at the expense of both the monarchy and the peasantry. By the middle of the sixteenth century, a revival of central authority had become impossible.

In Poland royal power began to decline in the 1490s, when the king turned to the lesser nobles to help him against the greater nobility. He issued a statute in 1496 that strengthened the lower aristocrats against those below them, the townsmen and the peasants. The latter virtually became serfs, for they were forbidden to buy land and were deprived of freedom of movement. In 1505 the national Diet, consisting only of nobles, was made the supreme body of the land, without whose consent no laws could be passed. Shortly thereafter the Diet officially established serfdom.

Royal and noble patronage produced a great cultural efflorescence in Poland in these decades, most famously represented by the astronomer Nicolaus Copernicus. Yet the monarchy was losing influence steadily, as was revealed by the failure of its attempts to found a standing army. At the end of Sigismund II's reign, his kingdom was the largest in Europe; but his death, in 1572, ended the Jagellon dynasty, which had ruled the country for centuries. The Diet immediately made sure that succession to the crown, which technically had always been elective and in the hands of the nobles, would henceforth depend entirely on their approval. Thus the aristocracy confirmed both its own dominance and the ineffectiveness of royal authority.

The Hungarian and Polish patterns were repeated throughout Eastern Europe. By the early sixteenth century, serfdom had been officially imposed in all the territories east of the Elbe River. In the West at the same time, labor shortages caused by the plagues of the fourteenth and fifteenth centuries had brought a permanent end to this kind of subjection. Peasants who were needed to work the land became scarce, and since estates were relatively small, desperate landowners, competing with one another for labor, had to offer the remaining serfs freedom in exchange for services. In the East much of the territory was newly settled and divided into very large holdings. Here the lords could achieve economies of scale and make do with fewer laborers per acre; consequently, they did not feel the need to make concessions. Moreover, these great landowners also held the keys to political power, and hence they could combine influence in the government with economic pressure to ensure the repression of the lowest levels of society.

The political and social processes at work in Eastern and Central Europe thus contrasted strongly with developments in England, France, and Spain in this period. Nevertheless, although the trend was toward fragmentation in the East, one class, the aristocracy, did share the vigor and organizational ability that in the West was apparent primarily in the policies of kings. To that extent, therefore, the sense of renewed vitality in Europe during these years was also apparent beyond the borders of the new monarchies. The critical difference lay in the leaders of the revival. When kings were in command, their states gained strength and status; when the nobles dominated, countries lost ground in the fierce competition of international affairs.

ITALY: INDEPENDENT CITY-STATES

The cultural and economic leader of Europe, Italy, had developed a unique political struc-
ture. In the fifteenth century five major states had managed to consolidate themselves among the numerous warring principalities and towns of the peninsula: the Kingdom of Naples; the Papal States, centered on Rome; the duchy of Milan; and two republics based on cities, Florence and Venice. The Treaty of Lodi in 1454 established a balance among them that was preserved without serious disruption for the next forty years.

This long period of peace was finally broken in 1494, when Milan asked Charles VIII of France to help protect it against Florence and Naples. Thus began the Italian wars, which soon revealed that these relatively small territories were totally incapable of resisting the force that a new political organization, the national monarchy, could bring to bear.

Venice and particularly Florence had long been regarded by Europeans as model republics —reincarnations of classical city-states and centers of freedom governed with the consent of their citizens. In truth Venice was controlled by a small merchant oligarchy and Florence by the Medici family, but the image was still widely accepted. Moreover the Italians were regarded as masters not only of politics but also of culture and manners.

It was a considerable shock to Europe therefore when the Italian states crumbled before the onslaught of French forces and then of the Spaniards and the Hapsburgs. Charles VIII drove the Medicis out of Florence in 1494 and established a new republic, but in 1512 Ferdinand of Aragon engineered their return, and eventually the Hapsburgs set up the Medici family as hereditary dukes. Ferdinand had annexed Naples in 1504, and Emperor Charles V ultimately took over Milan. The fighting finally ended in 1559 with the Hapsburgs in control; they would dominate the Italian peninsula for the next century. Only Venice and the Papal States remained independent, the former somewhat battered by a series of defeats and the latter the one gainer from the Italian wars. Julius II (1503–1513), known as the Warrior Pope, carved out a new papal territory in central and eastern Italy by force of arms.

The critical lesson of this disastrous sequence of events was that the small political unit could not survive in an age when governments were consolidating their authority in large kingdoms. No matter how brilliant and sophisticated, a compact urban state could not withstand such superior force. Italy's cultural and economic prominence took a long time to fade, but by the mid-sixteenth century, her political independence had disappeared, not to return for 300 years.

iv. THE NEW STATECRAFT

At the same time as European political life grew more elaborate and complex, innovations appeared in the relations among states and the perspectives of political observers. The newly powerful central governments were confronted by an international situation radically different from that of only a century before. Rulers had achieved levels of military and economic strength and a freedom of action that required equivalent transformations in the techniques of diplomacy. Theorists and historians who witnessed these changes began to see politics in a different light. Two Italians in particular, Niccolò Machiavelli and Francesco Guicciardini, opened the way to a totally new understanding of the phenomenon of political leadership.

Hans Holbein's The Ambassadors *shows the worldliness that was expected of diplomats (many of whom were also soldiers) in the sixteenth century. The two men are surrounded by symbols of the skills, knowledge, and refinement their job required—geography, mathematics, literature, and music. But despite this emphasis on material concerns, Holbein reminds us (in the optically distorted skull across the bottom of the painting) that death and spiritual needs cannot be forgotten.* (Photo: National Gallery, London)

INTERNATIONAL RELATIONS

The Italian states of the fifteenth century, in their intensive machinations and competition, developed various new ways of pursuing foreign policy. During the Italian wars these techniques spread throughout Europe and caused a revolution in diplomacy. Any state hoping to play a prominent role in international affairs worked under a serious disadvantage if it did not adopt the new methods.

The essential innovation was the resident ambassador. Previously rulers had dispatched ambassadors only for specific missions, such as arranging an alliance, declaring war, or delivering a message, but from the sixteenth century on, important states maintained their representatives in every major capital city or court continuously. The permanent ambassador could not only keep his home government informed

of the latest local and international developments but could also move without delay to protect his sovereign's interests.

As states established embassies, procedures and organization became more sophisticated: a primitive system of immunities evolved, formal protocol developed, and embassy officials were assigned different levels of responsibility and importance. Considerable advances were still to come, but by the mid-sixteenth century the outlines of the new diplomacy were already visible —yet another reflection of the growing powers and ambitions of central governments.

The great dividing line between established arrangements and the new diplomacy was the Italian wars, the first Europe-wide crisis of modern times. Rulers as distant as the English King Henry VIII and the Ottoman Sultan Suleiman II were drawn into the conflict between the Hapsburgs and the Valois, and gradually all states recognized that it was in the interests of everyone to accept a system in which no one power dominated the rest. In later years this interdependence, this prevention of excessive aggression, was to be known as the balance of power, yet by the mid-sixteenth century the glimmerings of the idea were already affecting alliances and peace treaties. The lesson again came from the Italians, who on a smaller scale had tried to create a balance among the leading states of the peninsula with the Treaty of Lodi.

For Charles V, ever on the defensive and an instinctive peacemaker, such orderliness had much to recommend it. But Francis I considered the Hapsburgs far too powerful, and he pursued his ambitions in Italy with all the means at his disposal, undeterred by repeated defeats. In 1535 he shocked Europe by concluding a treaty with the Muslim Suleiman, the Hapsburgs' most formidable enemy. And the sultan even paid the papacy a pension to help it pursue its own opposition to Charles V. Thus common political interests brought religious opponents together.

In military affairs the new monarchs took similar initiatives. A recent historian has called the period of Charles V's reign "more decisive for the evolution of the art of war" than any thereafter until the late eighteenth century. During this time the crossbow was finally superseded, armies combined artillery with infantry and cavalry, the division emerged as the basic military unit, city wall bastion fortification was devised, and the siege became the essential tactic of warfare. Logistics were now as important as any other military art, and strategists laid out careful systems of supply and command. An amazing feature of this military revolution was that it advanced uniformly throughout Europe. No ruler could afford to be left behind in the deadly race.

CONTEMPORARY APPRAISALS: MACHIAVELLI AND GUICCIARDINI

Political commentators soon began to seek theoretical explanations for the new authority and aggressiveness of rulers and the collapse of the Italian city-states. Turning from arguments based on divine will or contractual law, they looked to pragmatism, opportunism, and effective government as an end in itself.

The earliest full expression of these views came from the Italians, the pioneers of the methods and attitudes that were revolutionizing politics. When all military efforts proved futile in face of the superior forces of France and Spain, they naturally wanted to find out why. The most disturbing answer was given by an experienced diplomat, Niccolò Machiavelli, who was thrown out of his job when the Medicis took control of Florence in 1512. With a bitter pen he immediately set about analyzing exactly how power operated.

The result, *The Prince*, is one of the few radically original books in history. To move from his predecessors to Machiavelli is to enter a world that even the immediate Italian background does not foreshadow; Roman jurists talking of kings as the source of law and writers asserting that a monarch was not subordinate to the pope were still thinking in legalistic or moral terms. Machiavelli swept away all these conventions. If he came out of any tradition, it was the Renaissance fascination with style and method that had produced manuals on cooking, dancing, fencing, and manners. But he wrote on a subject never previously approached: power.

Machiavelli showed not why power does or should exist, but how it works. In the form of advice to a prince and without reference to divine, legal, or natural justification, the book explains what a ruler needs to do to win and maintain complete control over his subjects. Machiavelli did not deny the force of religion or law; what concerned him was how they ought to be *used* in the tactics of governing— religion for molding unity and contentment, and devotion to law for building the ruler's reputation as a fair-minded man. *The Prince* outlines the particular methods of a conqueror, legitimate heir, or usurper as well as the proper ways to deal with insurrection and the many other problems that a ruler is likely to encounter. Fear and respect are the bases of his authority, and he must exercise care at all times not to relax his control over either potential troublemakers or the image he conveys to his people.

Very few contemporaries of Machiavelli dared accept his view of politics. To men of the sixteenth century and long thereafter, "Machiavellianism" was synonymous with evil and cunning. Secular and pragmatic considerations might be gaining prominence, but Europe was not yet ready to abandon its reverence for law, divine providence, and natural morality.

The change in the perspective on power became noticeable in historical writings too.

Machiavelli's other masterpiece, the *Discourses*, developed a cyclical theory of every government moving inexorably from tyranny to democracy and back again. His conclusion, drawn particularly from a study of Roman history, is that healthy government can be preserved only by the active participation of all citizens in the life of the state. He attributed the Italians' defeat to the fact that his countrymen had relied on mercenary troops and abandoned their civic responsibilities. The vigor of the Roman republic had depended on its citizen army.

Another Italian, Franceso Guicciardini, writing in the 1530s, saw the root of the problem as the lack of unity in Italy. His great work, a *History of Italy*, rose above the particularism of previous narratives, which had dealt with events in only one city-state or region. Guicciardini's comparative analysis of the Italian states led him to conclude that government should be left in the hands of an intelligent ruler. There are no basic principles at work in history; experience, flexibility, and the ability to meet a situation on its own terms make a good ruler.

Guicciardini was the first major historian to rely heavily on original documents rather than secondhand accounts. If the conclusions he reached from his study of the sources seem dauntingly cynical—he attributed even less to underlying historical forces than did Machiavelli—the reasons for his pessimism are not far to seek. The actions of kings and princes in the early sixteenth century hardly gave much room for optimism, and shrewd observers like Machiavelli and Guicciardini must have found it difficult to avoid pessimism about public events. They were exposing the atmosphere of the times, capturing in print the obsession with power and pragmatism that drove Europe's newly powerful rulers as they extended their authority both at home and abroad.

Beginning in the late fifteenth century, the kings of England, France, and Spain consolidated their realms into strong polities with power centralized under their own command. These new monarchs, as historians have called them, extended their authority at home by undermining their traditional domestic rivals, the nobility and the Church, and pursued aggressive dynastic ambitions abroad. The Holy Roman Empire, Eastern Europe, and Italy did not experience this development. Instead local powers—cities, nobles, and princes—remained autonomous, preventing their countries from marshaling their resources and organizing themselves like the new monarchies. Ironically, though the Italian city-states were too small to retain their independence, their politicians were teaching the rest of Europe new methods of conducting international relations; and their political analysts and historians, perceiving the trends in statecraft before anyone else, broke new ground in their analysis of how power works and why states rise and fall.

Parallel to the political developments were remarkable economic advances and an expansion to other continents that reflected the vigor of a newly confident age. Europe's population was increasing, its prices were rising, and its trade was multiplying—all unmistakable signs of a healthy society. Yet the social consequences were not always benevolent, for the revival had paradoxical results. Social mobility did increase, but so did poverty. Strong central governments restored order, but they also provoked resentment. And rapid change by its very nature caused considerable bewilderment, producing signs of disquiet in the culture of the age. Of all the causes of tension, however, none equaled in impact the most shattering disruption of the sixteenth century, an upheaval that brought an end to more than a thousand years of Western Christian unity—the Reformation.

RECOMMENDED READING

Sources

*Guicciardini, Francesco. *The History of Italy and Other Selected Writings.* Cecil Grayson (tr.). 1964.

*Machiavelli, Niccolò. *The Prince and the Discourses.* Luigi Ricci (tr.). 1950.

Studies

Blum, Jerome. "The Rise of Serfdom in Eastern Europe." *American Historical Review,* Vol. 62, No. 4 (July 1957), 807–836. A discussion of why serfdom disappeared in Western Europe at the very time that it was becoming firmly established in the East.

Boxer, Charles R. *The Portuguese Seaborne Empire.* 1970. An excellent overview of the rise and structure of the Portuguese empire.

*Brandi, Karl. *The Emperor Charles V.* C. V. Wedgwood (tr.). 1968. This is a long and detailed biography, but the narrative is well written and flows easily. Moreover, in the course of the book just about every political problem that arose in Europe during Charles's lifetime is discussed.

Cipolla, Carlo M. *Guns, Sails, and Empires: Technological Innovation and the Early Phases of European Expansion 1400–1700.* 1965. This is a lively study of the reasons the expansion succeeded, with particular emphasis on weaponry.

*Elliott, J. H. *Imperial Spain, 1469–1716*. 1964. The best introduction to Spanish history in this period, covering mainly political and economic developments.

*Elton, Geoffrey R. *The Tudor Revolution in Government*. 1959. An important study of how government worked, and how its operations were expanded, during the reign of Henry VIII.

*Gilmore, Myron P. *The World of Humanism, 1453–1517*. 1952. A thorough introduction to the entire period, with a full, though somewhat out-of-date, bibliography. For more recent work, see the bibliography in Rice, below.

*Hale, J. R. *Machiavelli and Renaissance Italy*. 1963. The clearest and most straightforward short account of Machiavelli and his times.

*Jensen, DeLamar (ed.). *The Expansion of Europe: Motives, Methods, and Meanings*. 1967. A collection of writings on the expansion, reflecting the different views historians have held about the overseas movements.

*Mattingly, Garrett. *Renaissance Diplomacy*. 1971. An elegant account of the changes that began in international relations during the fifteenth century.

*Morison, Samuel Eliot. *Admiral of the Ocean Sea: A Life of Christopher Columbus*. 1942. An exciting story, well told, that brings to life Europe's most remarkable explorer.

*Parry, John H. *The Age of Reconnaissance*. 1963.

The most complete history of Europe's expansion through 1620.

Parry, John H. *The Spanish Seaborne Empire*. 1966. Published in the same series as Boxer's book on the Portuguese empire, this is a good review of the establishment of the Spanish empire.

Potter, G. R. (ed.). *The New Cambridge Modern History*. Vol. I: *The Renaissance, 1493–1520*. 1964. The most thorough and detailed history of the period.

Raab, Felix. *The English Face of Machiavelli: A Changing Interpretation 1500–1700*. 1964. A well-written study of the people who read Machiavelli, what they thought of him, and how his reputation changed over two hundred years.

*Rice, Eugene F., Jr. *The Foundations of Early Modern Europe, 1460–1559*. 1970. The best of the recent short surveys of the period, with three pages of suggested readings that list the main books that have been published since Gilmore's bibliography.

Rich, E. E., and C. H. Wilson (eds.). *The Cambridge Economic History of Europe*. Vol. IV: *The Economy of Expanding Europe in the Sixteenth and Seventeenth Centuries*. 1967. A comprehensive survey of recent works in the field.

Wolfe, Martin. *The Fiscal System of Renaissance France*. 1972. An account of the way a central government raised money and exercised power during this period.

---

* Available in paperback.

FOURTEEN

REFORMATIONS
IN RELIGION

To the sixteenth-century European, the most momentous revolution of the time was not the growth of royal power, the rise of prices, or the discovery of new lands overseas but the movement that destroyed the West's religious unity: the Reformation. Two sides began to form, to be called Catholic and Protestant, each resolutely convinced of its own righteousness and the other's error, and their confrontation inspired wars for more than a century.

The new ideas of the religious thinkers Martin Luther, Ulrich Zwingli, John Calvin, and their successors stimulated a radical rethinking of traditional views of God, man, and society. At issue in the Reformation was the balance between the role of the Church and the piety of the individual in the answer to the fundamental question of Christian history: How can sinful humans gain salvation? The traditional answer was that the Church was the essential intermediary through which man could be saved. This laid the stress on community, on outward participation in rituals, and particularly on the seven sacraments, the principal channels of grace. But there was another answer that had been advocated by distinguished Church fathers such as St. Augustine: that man could be saved by his faith in God and love of him. This view emphasized the inward and personal and focused on God as the source of grace.

The two traditions were not incompatible; for centuries they had coexisted without difficulty, and elements of each would be retained by both Protestants and Catholics after the Reformation. Indeed, one of the problems theologians faced around 1500 was the absence of precise definition in many areas of doctrine. It was often difficult to tell where orthodoxy ended and heresy began. This indeterminacy might have been an asset had it reflected a commitment to flexibility and comprehensiveness by the leaders of the Church. In fact, however, as the papacy and the Church had grown in power and im-portance during the High Middle Ages, official attitudes had shifted decisively toward the outward, sacramental, institutional view and away from the inward and personal approach. The main purpose of the Reformation was to reverse this trend. What was not clear at the outset was whether the change would be accomplished by reform from within or by a revolution and schism in the Church.

I. DISSENT AND PIETY

Dissatisfaction with the Church was evident at all levels of society in the early sixteenth century. For more than 200 years the prestige of the papacy had been steadily eroding, and increasing numbers of deeply pious people were finding the Church's growing emphasis on ritual and standardized practices unhelpful in their personal quest for salvation. What they sought was spiritual renewal and a return to the basic values of early Christianity. Their religious grievances were the root of the ferment; once the Reformation had begun, however, political, economic, and social issues influenced its course.

SOURCES OF MALAISE

The spiritual authority of the papacy had been declining for more than two centuries. During the seventy years of the Babylonian captivity, when the pontiffs had lived in Avignon, they had no longer seemed to be symbols of the universal Church but rather captives of the French monarchs. Far more demoralizing, the Great Schism that followed had threatened to undermine the unity of Western Christendom, as two and then three pretenders each claimed to be the true pope. The Council of Constance had closed this breach by 1418 but had also encouraged the conciliar movement. This attempt to subordinate papal power to the authority of Church councils ultimately failed, but it was yet another direct challenge to the pope's supremacy. Only the refusal of secular rulers to protect the reform movements that arose around 1400—in particular, the efforts of John Wycliffe and John Huss and their followers—prevented a major split like the Reformation 100 years before it actually occurred.

The papacy had also lost spiritual influence because of its secularization. Increasingly popes were conducting themselves like Italian princes. With skillful diplomacy and even military action, they had consolidated their control over the papal lands in the peninsula. They had surrounded themselves with an elaborate court and become patrons of the arts, taking over for a time the cultural leadership of Europe. But this concern with political power and grandeur had eclipsed religious duties to the point where popes used their spiritual powers to raise funds for their secular activities. The fiscal measures developed at Avignon, which furnished the papacy with income from appointments to Church offices and from dispensations and indulgences, had enlarged revenues but led to widespread abuses. High ecclesiastical offices could be bought and sold, and men (usually sons of nobles) were attracted to them by the opportunities they provided for wealth and power, not by a religious vocation.

Abuses were widespread at lower levels in the Church as well. Some prelates held several offices at a time and could not give adequate attention to any of them. The ignorance and moral laxity of the parish and monastic clergy also aroused antagonism. The lower clerical orders, particularly the ordinary parish priests, were little better off than the peasants among whom they lived, and many of them used indulgences as a fund-raising device—granting the remission of some of the temporal punishment for sin to anyone who made a donation to the Church. Many laymen found this practice a shocking attempt to sell divine grace.

These abuses provoked two major responses: anticlericalism and a call for reform within the Church. Both reactions were symptomatic of a broader quest for genuine piety that was running throughout European society by the early 1500s.

The deepest source of discontent with the Church was its failure to meet spiritual needs. The institution had grown more formal, its doctrines supported by an elaborate system of canon law and theology and its services filled with pomp and ceremony. Increasing importance was being attached to the sacraments, the role of the priest, and the doctrine that salvation could be achieved only if faith was accompanied by good works—fasting, abstinence, and similar acts of denial or expiation.

Lay people sought a more personal piety than the official devotions provided. Observation of Church rituals meant little, they felt, unless the believer could cultivate an interior sense of the love and presence of God. They looked for nourishment, therefore, to those, like the mystics, who emphasized religious individualism. Rejecting the theological subtleties of Scholasticism, they sought divine guidance in the Bible and the writings of the early Church fathers, especially St. Augustine. Lay religious fraternities dedicated to private devotions and charitable works proliferated in the cities, especially in Germany and Italy. The most widespread of them in Germany, the Brotherhood of the Eleven Thousand Virgins, consisted of laymen who gathered together, usually in a church, to sing hymns. In the mid-fifteenth century, 80 such groups had been established in Cologne, a city of some 35,000 people, and more than 100 in Hamburg, which had slightly more than 10,000 inhabitants. Churchmen, unhappy about a development over which they had no control, had tried to suppress such activities but to no avail. Itinerant preachers still roamed Central Europe in considerable numbers, urging direct communication between believers and God free from ritual and complex doctrine. To the vast crowds they drew, they seemed to echo the words of St. Augustine: "God and the soul I want to recognize, nothing else."

The most spectacular outburst of popular piety around 1500 was the ascendancy over the city of Florence of Girolamo Savonarola, a zealous Dominican who wanted to banish the irreligion and materialism he saw everywhere about him. The climax of his influence came in 1496, when he arranged a tremendous bonfire, in which the Florentines burned cosmetics, light literature, dice, and other such frivolities. But Savonarola's attempts at internal reform eventually brought him into conflict with the papacy. At that point the Church intervened, and eventually he was executed for heresy.

The widespread search for a more intense devotional life was a sign of spiritual vitality. Had the hierarchy responded by adapting religious teachings and practices to meet this need, the Church might have been spared the upheavals of the Reformation. Instead churchmen gave little encouragement to ecclesiastical reform and the evangelization of the laity. They reacted with vigor only when they detected a clear threat to their authority—when

for example they condemned the teachings of John Wycliffe and John Huss as heretical. Only in Spain was there a deliberate attempt to eradicate abuses and encourage religious fervor, and there the leadership in the effort came not from Rome but from the head of the Spanish Church, Cardinal Francisco Ximenes de Cisneros. When the papacy finally did attempt to revitalize the Church in the mid-sixteenth century, the revolt of the reformers was an accomplished fact.

PIETY AND PROTEST IN LITERATURE AND ART

Popular piety received unexpected assistance from technology. The invention of the printing press made reading material available to a much broader segment of the population and new ideas traveled with unprecedented speed. Perhaps a third of the professional and upper classes—townsmen, the educated, and the nobility—could read, but books reached a much wider audience. Throughout Europe, peddlers began to carry printed materials in their packs, selling them in country towns in all regions. Here they could be bought by a local person for reading out loud at a gathering of villagers. These evening readings to a group of people who would never have had access to written literature in the days of manuscripts became an important means of spreading new ideas.

Some publishers took advantage of this new market by printing almanacs filled with homely advice about the weather and nature that were written specifically for simple rural folk. And translated Bibles made Scripture available to ordinary people in a language that, for the first time, they could understand. For the Reformers, therefore, books were a powerful weapon, but they were used by both sides in the religious conflict and revealed the general interest in spiritual matters. Devotional tracts, lives of the saints, and the Bible itself

were the most popular titles—often running to editions of around 1,000 copies.

Printing may thus have lessened the layman's dependence on the clergy; whereas traditionally the priest had read and interpreted the Scriptures for his congregation, now many could consult their own copy. By 1522 eighteen translations of the Bible had been published. Some 14,000 copies had been printed in German alone, enough to make it easy to buy in most German-speaking regions.

This sixteenth-century painting depicts the torture and execution of Savonarola and his chief followers in the main square of Florence in 1498. (Photo: Museo di San Marco, Florence/Alinari)

Many books were profusely illustrated, and thus accessible to the illiterate as well. Perhaps the most famous was the German Sebastian Brant's *Ship of Fools* (1494), a long satire in verse describing life as a voyage. The poem

THE SPREAD OF PRINTING THROUGH 1500
Number of Towns in which a Printing Press Was Established for the First Time, by Period and Country

PERIOD	GERMAN-SPEAKING AREAS	ITALIAN-SPEAKING AREAS	FRENCH-SPEAKING AREAS	SPAIN	ENGLAND	NETHER-LANDS	OTHER	TOTAL
Before 1471:	8	4	1	1	–	–	–	14
1471–1480:	22	36	9	6	3	12	5	93
1481–1490:	17	13	21	12	–	5	4	72
1491–1500:	9	5	11	6	–	2	8	41
Total by 1500:	56	58	42	25	3	19	17	220

Adapted from Lucien Febvre and Henri-Jean Martin, *The Coming of the Book: The Impact of Printing 1450–1800*, translated by David Gerard, London, NLB, 1976, pp. 178–179 and 184–185.

(*Note:* Printing did not spread to other towns in England because the government, to ensure control over printers, ordered that they work only in London.)

dissects each passenger—the beggar, the friar, and so on—lampooning his lack of true faith or morality.

The most gifted satirist of the age, however, was François Rabelais, an incisive critic of the clergy and morality of his day. He was a monk (as well as a doctor), but he was deeply unhappy that traditional religious practices had diverged so far from the ideals of Jesus. Rabelais is most famous for his earthy bawdiness, but again and again he returned to clerical targets. His *Gargantua* and *Pantagruel* (1533 and 1535) contain numerous sardonic passages:

"Don't [monks] pray to God for us?" "They do nothing of the kind," said Gargantua. "All they do is keep the whole neighborhood awake by jangling their bells. . . . They mumble over a lot of legends and psalms, which they don't in the least understand; and they say a great many paternosters . . . without thinking or caring about what they are saying. And all that I call a mockery of God, not prayer."

Scurrilous broadsides no less stinging in tone became very popular during the Reformation. These were single sheets, often containing vicious attacks on religious opponents and usu-

ally illustrated by cartoons that used obscene imagery so that the point would be unmistakable. These propaganda pieces were the product of partisan hostility, but their broader significance should not be ignored (see illustration, p. 445). Even the most lowly of hack writers could share with a serious author like Rabelais a common sense of outrage at indifference in high places and a dismay with the spiritual malaise of their time.

This concern with spiritual and religious themes, so evident in European literature, also permeated the work of Northern artists in the late fifteenth and early sixteenth centuries. The gruesome vision of Hieronymus Bosch, for example, depicts the fears and dangers his contemporaries felt threatening them. He put on canvas the demons, the temptations, the terrible punishments for sin that men considered as real as their tangible surroundings (see Plate 21). Bosch's younger contemporary Mathias Grünewald conveyed the same mixture of ter-

Grünewald's Temptation of St. Anthony *bears witness to the terrifying impact of the supernatural on the thought of Northern artists.* (Photo: Lauros-Giraudon)

ror and devotion. Like Bosch, he painted a frightening *Temptation of St. Anthony* showing the travails of the saint who steadfastly resisted horrible attacks by the devil. These artists explored the darker side of faith, taking their inspiration from the fear of damnation and the hope for salvation—the first seen in the devils, the second in the redeeming Christ.

The supreme innovation of the finest Northern artist of this period, Albrecht Dürer, was not in painting but in the art of the woodcut. Developed in the mid-fourteenth century, the technique of cutting a picture into wood so that it could be inked and reproduced grew in importance with the invention of printing. Until touched by the genius of Dürer, however, it remained a stiff and primitive art form. His hand transformed it into a subtle, versatile means of expression, a superb vehicle for the religious themes he portrayed.

The depth of piety conveyed by these artists reflected the temper of Europe (see, for example, the religious meaning put even into a secular painting like Holbein's *The Ambassadors*, reproduced on p. 427). In art and literature as in lay organizations and the continuing popularity of itinerant preachers, men showed their concern over individual spiritual values and their dissatisfaction with a Church that was not meeting their needs. But no segment of society expressed the strivings and yearnings of the age more eloquently than the Northern humanists.

II. THE NORTHERN HUMANISTS

The salient features of the humanist movement in Italy—its theory of education, its emphasis on eloquence, its reverence for the ancients, and its endorsement of active participation in affairs of state—began to win wide acceptance north of the Alps in the late 1400s. But the Northerners added a significant religious dimension to the movement by devoting considerable attention to early Christian literature —the Bible and the writings of the Church fathers. The greatest of the Northern humanists, Erasmus, urged a return to the "philosophy of Christ," but he eventually found that the simple piety he advocated was leading in a new and, in his eyes, unacceptable direction: toward a split in the Church.

CHRISTIAN HUMANISM

The first major center of Northern Humanism was the University of Heidelberg, but by the end of the fifteenth century the influence of the movement was almost universal. As it grew, there was a quickening of activity in the world of letters and thought that paralleled the new energy in economic life, politics, and overseas enterprise. The ease of communication created by the printing press helped accelerate the exchange of ideas, for by 1500 there was at least one press in every city of any size along the Rhine River from Basel to Leiden.

The driving force behind Northern Humanism came to be a determination to probe early Christianity for the light it could throw on the origins of current religious belief. But this scholarly pursuit soon produced a conflict that arrayed humanist intellectuals against more traditional scholars.

At issue was the danger inherent in the study of Jewish writings. The protagonists were a bitter ex-Jew, Johannes Pfefferkorn, who considered Hebrew works pernicious and wanted them condemned, and Johann Reuchlin, a humanist and brilliant Herbraist, who advocated research that would illuminate the parent faith of Christianity. The controversy inspired scores of polemical pamphlets. The most famous, the *Letters of Obscure Men* (1515 and 1517), a stinging defense of Reuchlin that ridiculed his opponents, was the creation of a group of aggressive young humanists; one of them, Ulrich von Hutten, was to be among Luther's most ardent supporters. Thus Northern Humanism's broad examination of religious issues helped create the atmosphere in which Luther's much more serious criticisms could flourish.

This new direction was especially noticeable in the work of the leading French humanist of the period, Jacques Lefèvre d'Étaples, who was one of the most important biblical scholars of his day. In his commentary on St. Paul (1512), he applied the humanist principle of seeking the straightforward, clear meaning of the text and in this way built a powerful case for a return to the simple godliness of early Christianity and for the primacy of biblical authority. The revival of interest in the apostle St. Paul was a major step on the road to Reformation, and it is notable that a number of Lefèvre's comments on Paul anticipated Luther's pronouncements.

Christian Humanism, as modern scholars call the phase of the movement represented by men like Reuchlin and Lefèvre, retained an interest in classical authors and continued to utilize the methods of the Italian humanists—analysis of ancient texts, language, and style. But its purpose was different: to answer questions about the message of Jesus and the apostles so as to offer contemporaries a guide to true piety and morality. This was a deeply religious undertaking, and it dominated the writings of the most famous Christian humanists, one English and one Dutch.

THOMAS MORE AND ERASMUS

Sir Thomas More (1478–1535), a lawyer and statesman, was the central figure of English Humanism. His reputation as a writer rests primarily on a brief work, *Utopia*, published in Latin in 1516, which describes an ideal society on an imaginary island. In it More condemned war, poverty, religious intolerance, and other evils of his day and defined the general principles of morality that should underlie human society.

The first book of *Utopia* asks whether a man of learning should withdraw from the world to avoid temptation, or actively participate in affairs of state so as to guide his fellow men. The Italian civic humanists had established commitment to public responsibilities as an essential part of the humanist movement. More reopened the question from the standpoint of religious as well as ethical values and answered with a warning against evading public duties, even though rulers rarely heed the advice they are given.

The second and more famous book of *Utopia* describes the ideal commonwealth itself. In political and social organization, it is a carefully regulated, almost monastic community that has succeeded in abolishing private property—together with greed and pride—and has achieved true morality. The Utopians are non-Christian, and More implies that a society based on Christian principles can attain even greater good. Asceticism is his answer to the fall of man: weak human nature can be led to virtuousness only if severely curbed.

True to his prescriptions, More, though a layman, subjected himself to the strict discipline of a Carthusian monastery in his twenties, after which he entered public life as a member of Parliament in 1504. He rose high in government service, succeeding—against his will—to the lord chancellorship on Wolsey's fall in 1529. He gave his life for remaining loyal to the pope and refusing to recognize Henry VIII as head of the English Church. His last words revealed his unflinching adherence to the Christian principles he pursued throughout his life: "I die the King's good servant, but God's first."

The supreme representative of Christian Humanism was the Dutchman Desiderius Erasmus (1466?–1536). Erasmus early acquired a taste for ancient writers, and he determined to devote himself to classical studies.

For the greater part of his life, he wandered through Europe, writing, visiting friends, occasionally working for important patrons. He always retained his independence, however, for unlike More, his answer to the question of whether a scholar should enter public life was that he should avoid the compromises he would have to make in the service of a ruler.

Erasmus became so famous for his learning and his literary skills that he dominated the world of letters in Europe. Constantly consulted by scholars and admirers, he wrote magnificently composed letters that reflected every aspect of the culture of his times. The English humanists, particularly More, were among his closest friends, and it was during his first visit to England, in 1499, that his interests were turned away from purely literary matters toward the theological writings that became the main focus of his scholarship.

Erasmus' most famous book was *The Praise of Folly* (1509), inspired by the already popular *Ship of Fools*, but a subtler work with a deeper moral commitment. Some of it is gay, light-hearted banter that pokes fun at the author himself, his friends, and the follies of everyday life, suggesting that a little folly is essential to human existence. But in other passages Erasmus launched sharply satirical attacks against monks, the pope, meaningless ceremonies, and the many lapses from what he perceived to be the true Christian spirit.

At the heart of Erasmus' work was the message that he called the "philosophy of Christ." He believed that the life of Jesus himself and especially the teachings in the Sermon on the Mount should be the model for Christian piety and morality. For ceremonies and rigid discipline he had only censure: too often they served as substitutes for genuine spiritual concerns. People lit thousands of candles for Mary but cared little about the humility she is supposed to inspire, for they forgot that what counts is the spirit of religious devotion, not the form. By simply following the precepts of Jesus, a Christian could lead a life guided by sincere faith. Because of his insistence on ethical behavior, Erasmus could admire a truly moral man even if he was a pagan. "I could almost say 'Pray for me, St. Socrates!'" he once wrote.

Erasmus believed that the Church had lost sight of its original mission. In the course of fifteen centuries, traditions and practices had developed that obscured the intentions of its founder, and the only way purity could be restored was by studying the Scriptures and the writings of the early Church fathers. Here the tools of the humanists became vitally important, because they enabled scholars to understand the meaning and intention of an ancient manuscript. Practicing what he preached, Erasmus spent ten years preparing a new edition of the Greek text of the New Testament so as to correct errors in the Latin Vulgate, which was the standard version, and revised it repeatedly for another twenty years.

But the calm, scholarly, and tolerant moderation Erasmus prized was soon left behind by events. The rising fanaticism of the reformers and their opponents destroyed the effort he had led to cure the ills of the Church from within. Despite its surface plausibility, the famous saying, "Erasmus laid the egg that Luther hatched," misses the fundamental difference between the two men: Erasmus, a classic nonrevolutionary, wanted a revival of purer faith, but within the traditional structure of the Church.

The final irony of Erasmus' career was that he inspired reformers in both camps and yet in the end was rejected by both. He was condemned by Catholics as heretical and by leaders of the Reformation as half-hearted. In an age of confrontation, it was impossible to keep a middle course, and Erasmus found himself swept aside by forces that he himself had helped build but that Luther unleashed.

III. THE LUTHERAN REFORMATION

That the first religious conflict should have erupted in the Holy Roman Empire is not surprising. Here popular piety had been noticeably strong, as evidenced by the waves of Rhineland mysticism and the lay religious movements. In addition the chief local authorities in many areas were ecclesiastical princes, usually aristocratic bishops such as the ruler of the important city of Cologne on the Rhine. As a result no strong intermediaries like the rulers of England, France, and Spain stood between the papacy and the people, and the popes regarded the empire as their surest source of revenue. This situation may help explain why a determined reformer, Martin Luther, won such swift and widespread support; but the reasons he made his stand must be sought in the personal development of a highly sensitive, energetic, and troubled man.

MARTIN LUTHER

Martin Luther (1483–1546) was born into a simple workingman's family in Saxony in central Germany. The household was dominated by the father, whose powerful presence some modern commentators have seen reflected in his son's vision of an omnipotent God. The boy received a good education and decided to become a lawyer, a profession that would have given him many opportunities for advancement. But in his early twenties, shortly after starting his legal studies, he had an experience that changed his life. Crossing a field during a thunderstorm, he was thrown to the ground by a bolt of lightning, and in his terror he cried to St. Anne, the mother of Mary, that he would enter a monastery.

Although the decision may well have been that sudden, it is clear that there was more to Luther's complete change of direction than this one incident, however traumatic. He was obviously a man obsessed with his own sinfulness, and he joined an Augustinian monastery in the hope that a penitential life would help him overcome his sense of guilt. Once in the order he pursued every possible opportunity to earn worthiness in the sight of God. He overlooked no possible discipline or act of contrition or self-denial, and for added merit he endured austerities such as self-flagellation that went far beyond normal requirements. To no avail: at his first mass after his ordination, in 1507, he was so terrified at the prospect of a sinner like himself transforming the wafer and wine into the body and blood of Christ that he almost failed to complete the ritual.

Fortunately for Luther his superiors took more notice of his intellectual gifts than of his self-doubts and in 1508 assigned him to the faculty of a new university in Wittenberg, the capital of Saxony. It was from his scholarship, which was superb, and especially from his study of the Bible, that he was able at last to draw comfort and spiritual peace.

A second episode that probably took place when he was in his mid-thirties marked another crucial turning point in Luther's life. Until "the experience in the tower," as it is usually called, he could see no way that he, a despicable mortal, could receive anything but the fiercest punishments from a God of absolute justice. Now, however, he suddenly understood that he had only to rely on God's mercy, a quality as great as his justice. He later described the experience in these words:

> I greatly longed to understand Paul's Epistle to the Romans and nothing stood in the way but that one expression, "the justice of God," because I took it to mean that justice whereby God is just and deals justly in punishing the unjust. My situation was that, although an impeccable monk, I stood before God as a sinner troubled in conscience, and I had no confidence that my merit would assuage him. . . . Night and day I pondered until I saw the connection

between the justice of God and the statement [Romans 1:17] that "The just shall live by his faith." Then I grasped that the justice of God is that righteousness by which through grace and sheer mercy God justifies us through faith. Thereupon I felt myself to be reborn and to have gone through open doors into paradise.[1]

The many advances in Luther's thinking thereafter came ultimately from this insight: that justification—expiation of sin and attainment of righteousness through a gift of grace—is achieved by faith alone.

The Indulgence Controversy

In 1517 an event occurred that was ultimately to lead Luther to an irrevocable break with the Church. In the spring a Dominican monk, Johann Tetzel, began to sell indulgences a few miles from Wittenberg as part of a huge fund-raising effort to pay for the new Church of St. Peter in Rome. Originally an indulgence had been granted to a person who was unable to go on a crusade and who gave sufficient money to permit a poor crusader to reach the Holy Land. The indulgence itself released a sinner from a certain period of punishment in purgatory before going to heaven, and was justified doctrinally as a sort of credit that could be drawn from the treasury of merit built up by Jesus and the saints. But the doctrine had not been defined exactly, and clerics had been taking advantage of this vagueness to sell indulgences indiscriminately. Tetzel, an expert salesman, was offering complete releases from purgatory without bothering to mention the repentance demanded of everyone as the condition for forgiveness of sin.

The people of Wittenberg were soon flocking to Tetzel to buy this easy guarantee of salvation. For Luther, a man groping toward an evangelical solution of his own doubts, it was unforgivable that people should be deprived of their hard-earned money for spurious, worthless promises. On October 31, 1517, he nailed to the door of the university church in Wittenberg ninety-five theses, or statements, on indulgences that he offered to debate with experts in Christian doctrine.

This was no revolutionary document. It merely described what Luther believed to be correct teachings on indulgences: that the pope could remit only the penalties that he himself or canon law imposed, that therefore the promise of a general release was damnable, and that every true believer shared in the benefits of the Church whether or not he obtained letters of pardon. Within a few weeks the story was all over the empire that a monk had challenged the sale of indulgences. The proceeds of Tetzel's mission began to drop off, and the Dominicans, rallying to the defense of their brother, launched an attack against this presumptuous Augustinian.[2]

The controversy soon drew attention from Rome. At first Pope Leo X regarded the affair as merely a monks' quarrel. But in time Luther's responses to the Dominicans' attacks began to deviate radically from Church doctrine, and by 1520 he had gone so far as to challenge the authority of the papacy itself in three pamphlets outlining his fundamental position.

In *An Address to the Christian Nobility of the German Nation*, Luther made a frankly patriotic appeal to his countrymen to reject the foreign pope's authority. The Church, he said, consisted of all Christians, including laymen; hence the nobles were as much its governors as the clergy, and they had the responsibility to remedy its defects. Indeed, Emperor Charles V had an obligation to call a council to

---

[1] Quoted in Roland Bainton, *Here I Stand: A Life of Martin Luther* (1955), pp. 49–50.

[2] The Dominicans, long-time rivals of the Augustinians, were the traditional upholders of orthodoxy and prominent in the Inquisition. Luther liked to refer to them by using an old joke that split their Latin name into *Domini canes,* "dogs of the Lord."

end the abuses. *The Babylonian Captivity*, the most radical of the three works, attacked the system of the seven sacraments, the basis of the Church's power.[3] In *The Liberty of the Christian Man*, a less polemical work, Luther explained his doctrine of faith and justification, stressing that he did not reject good works but that only the faith of the individual believer could bring salvation from an all-powerful, just, and merciful God.

There could no longer be any doubt that Luther was embracing heresy, and in 1520 Leo X issued a bull excommunicating him. Luther publicly tossed the document into a bonfire, defending his action by calling the pope an Antichrist. In 1521 Charles V, theoretically the papacy's secular arm, responded by summoning the celebrated monk to offer his defense against the papal decree at a Diet of the Empire at Worms, a city on the Rhine. The journey across Germany was a triumphant procession for Luther, who had evoked widespread sympathy. Appearing before the magnificent assembly dressed in his monk's robe, he offered a striking contrast to the display of imperial and princely grandeur. First in German and then in Latin, he made the famous declaration that closed the last door behind him: "I cannot and will not recant anything, since it is unsafe and wrong to go against my conscience. Here I stand. I cannot do otherwise. God help me. Amen." On the following day the emperor gave his reply: "A single friar who goes counter to all Christianity for a thousand years must be wrong."

Charles added legality to the papal bull by issuing an imperial edict calling for Luther's

In this broadside (see p. 438), a single sheet printed in thousands of copies and sold cheaply at fairs and stalls throughout Germany, Johann Tetzel is ridiculed for his greed. The poem describes him as a breaker of the faith who became a thief and was stopped only by the blessed Dr. Luther. The fifth and sixth lines of the second column quote the claim attributed to Tetzel: "As soon as the coin clinks in the box, the soul flies straight to heaven." (Photo: The Granger Collection)

arrest and the burning of his works. At this point, however, the independent power of the German princes and their resentment of foreign ecclesiastical interference came to the reformer's aid. Elector Frederick III of Saxony,

---

[3] The seven sacraments are baptism, confirmation, matrimony, the eucharist, ordination, penance, and extreme unction. Apart from some special exceptions, these ceremonies are considered by Catholics to require the attendance of a priest, because his presence (and hence the mediation of the Church) is believed to be essential to the proper administration of the sacrament.

who had never met Luther and who was never to break with the Catholic Church, nonetheless determined to protect the rebel who lived in his territory. He had him taken to the Wartburg castle, one of his strongholds, and here Luther remained for almost a year, safe from his enemies.

Lutheran Doctrine and Practice

While at the Wartburg Luther, together with his friend Philipp Melanchthon, developed the elements of Lutheranism and shaped them into the independent set of beliefs which formed the background for most of the subsequent variations of Protestant Christianity.

It is important to realize, however, that some of these positions had roots in the nominalist theology taught at Luther's old monastery. Two of the teachings in particular left a lasting impression on Luther and later reformers. First, in opposition to Aquinas and the thirteenth-century attempts to unite reason and faith, the nominalists stressed the primacy of faith, the inadequacy of reason, and the unknowableness of God. Second, as a natural corollary to his mystery, they emphasized the overwhelming power and majesty of God. Both of these beliefs were to reappear frequently in the reformers' writings. Their importance was hardly surprising, for Nominalism was by far the most influential philosophical and theological movement of the fourteenth and fifteenth centuries.

This influence is apparent in the two fundamental assertions that lay at the heart of Luther's teachings. First, faith alone—not good works, nor the receiving of the sacraments—justifies man, that is, makes him righteous in the eyes of God and wins him redemption. Man himself is a helpless and unworthy sinner who can do nothing to cooperate in his own salvation; God bestows faith on those he chooses to save. Second, the Bible is the sole source of religious authority. It alone carries the word of God, and Christians must reject all

other supposed channels of divine inspiration: tradition, commentaries, or the pronouncements of popes and councils.

These two doctrines had important implications. According to Luther all men are equally capable of understanding God's word as expressed in the Bible and can gain salvation without the help of intermediaries; they do not need a priest endowed with special powers or an interceding church. Luther thus saw God's chosen faithful as a "priesthood of all believers," a concept totally foreign to Catholics, who insisted on the distinction between clergy and laity. The distinction disappeared in Luther's doctrines, because all the faithful now shared the responsibilities formerly reserved for the priests.

True to his reliance on biblical authority, Luther denied the efficacy of five of the Catholics' sacraments. Only baptism and the eucharist are mentioned in Scripture, therefore they alone can be the means by which God distributes grace. Moreover the ceremony of the eucharist was now called communion (literally "sharing") to emphasize that all worshipers, including the officiating clergyman, were equal. Confession was abolished, which reduced the priest's importance yet again, and the last sign of his distinctiveness was removed by allowing him the right to marry.

The new teachings on the sacraments transformed the mass, the ceremony that surrounds the eucharist, or Lord's Supper. According to Catholic dogma, when the priest raises the host during the mass and recites the words *Hoc est corpus meum* ("This is my body"), the sacrifice of Jesus on the cross is reenacted. The wafer and the wine retain their outward appearance, their "accidents," but their substance is transformed into the body and blood of Christ—in other words, transubstantiation takes place.

Luther asserted that the wafer and wine retain their substance as well as their accidents and undergo *con*substantiation at the moment the priest says "This is my body." The real presence of Christ and the natural substance *coexist* within the wafer and wine. Nothing suddenly happens, no miraculous moment occurs; the believer is simply made aware of the real presence of God, who is everywhere at all times. Again, it is the faith of the individual, not the ceremony itself, that counts.

Luther reduced the mystery of the Lord's Supper further by allowing the congregation to partake of the wine, which was reserved for the priest in the Catholic ceremony—a change that also undermined the position of the priest. The liturgy in general was simplified—by abolishing processions, incense, votive candles, and the like—to make it more approachable for ordinary people, and services were conducted in the vernacular.

Given the priest's reduced stature, it was vital to make God's word more readily accessible to all worshipers. To this end Luther began the gigantic task of translating the Bible. He was to complete the work in 1534, creating a text that is a milestone in the history of the German language. By then, however, his work of forming the new faith was done, for his doctrines had been put together systematically in the Augsburg Confession of 1530. Although he was to live until 1546, henceforth the progress of the revolution he had launched would rely on outside forces: its popular appeal and the actions of political leaders.

It is usually said that Lutheranism spread from above, advancing only when princes and rulers helped it along. Although this view has some basis, it does not adequately explain the growth of the movement. The response to Luther's stand was immediate and widespread. Even before the Diet of Worms, heretical preachers were drawing audiences in many parts of the Holy Roman Empire, and in 1521 there were waves of image smashing, reports of priests marrying, and efforts to reform and simplify the sacraments.

Soon men were conducting services according to Luther's teachings throughout the empire and in Sweden, Denmark, Poland, Prussia, and Hungary. Broadsides and pamphlets fresh from the printing presses spread the news of the reformer's message with breathtaking speed, stimulating an immediate response from thousands who saw the opportunity to renew their faith.

As long as his own doctrines were adhered to, Luther was naturally delighted to see his teachings spread. But from the start people were drawing inferences that he could not tolerate. Early in 1522 for example three men from the nearby town of Zwickau appeared in Wittenberg claiming to be prophets who enjoyed direct communication with God. Their ideas were both radical and, in Luther's eyes, damnable. When he returned from the Wartburg, therefore, he preached eight sermons to expose their errors—a futile effort, because the reform movement was now too dispersed to control. Capitalizing on mass discontent, radical preachers incited disturbances in the name of faith, and it was only a matter of time before social as well as religious protest exploded.

DISORDERS IN THE NAME OF RELIGION

The first trouble came in the summer of 1522, when fighting broke out between a number of princes of the empire and a group of imperial knights. The knights occupied a precarious position in the social hierarchy. Usually their holdings consisted of little more than a single castle, but they owed official allegiance to no one but the emperor himself, and inevitably they came to resent the growing power of cities and territorial rulers.

Posing as the true representatives of the imperial system—that is, as loyal supporters of the emperor's authority in contrast to the cities and princes, who wanted to be independent—

and pointing to Lutheranism as further justification, the knights launched an attack on one of the leading ecclesiastical rulers, the archbishop of Trier. The onslaught was crushed within a year, but it was now easy for the Lutherans' opponents to suggest that the new religious teachings undermined law and order.

The banner of the new faith rose over popular revolts as well. A peasant uprising began in Swabia in 1524 and quickly engulfed the southern and central parts of the empire. Citing Luther's inspiration, the peasants published a list of twelve demands the next year. However, ten of their grievances concerned social, not religious, injustices: they wanted an end to serfdom, tithes, and the restrictions and burdens imposed by their overlords, including prohibitions on hunting and fishing, excessive rents and services, and unlawful punishments. In religious matters they demanded the right to choose their own pastors and insisted that only Scripture could determine the justice of their cause.

Luther sympathized with the last two claims, and at first he considered the peasants' demands reasonable. But when it became apparent that they were spreading anarchy through the empire—burning, looting, and murdering as they went—he wrote a vicious pamphlet, *Against the Rapacious and Murdering Peasants*, calling on the nobility to cut them down without mercy so as to restore peace. A few months later the rebels were defeated in battle, and thereafter Luther threw his support unreservedly on the side of the princes and the established political and social order.

This is not to say that there was never again popular support for Lutheranism; the advance of the movement, particularly in northern Germany and Scandinavia, still depended on its appeal to the ordinary believer. Nonetheless, after the mid-1520s popular enthusiasm alone would not have sufficed; Lutheranism could not have stood up to the Catholic opposition had it not been defended by powerful princes in the empire and the kings of Denmark and Sweden.

One of the reasons the new set of beliefs could attract a number of princes was its conservatism. As long as a person accepted the doctrines of justification by faith alone and Scripture as the sole authority, he could be accepted as a Lutheran. Consequently the new congregations could retain much from the old religion: most of the liturgy, the sacred music, and, particularly important, a territorial church that, though less hierarchic, was still organized so as to provide order and authority.

Some rulers were swept up by the emotions that moved their subjects, but others were moved by more material interests. Since ecclesiastical property was abolished when reform was introduced, princes could confiscate the rich and extensive holdings of monasteries and churches in their domains. Furthermore, they now had added reason for flaunting their independence from Emperor Charles V, an unwavering upholder of orthodoxy. It was risky to adopt this policy, for Charles could strip a prince of his title. On the other side, a prince loyal to Catholicism could blackmail the pope into offering him almost as many riches as he could win by confiscation. Nevertheless, the appeal of the new faith eventually tipped the balance for enough princes to create a formidable party capable of resisting Charles' power. Gathered together at the imperial Diet of Speyer in 1529, they signed a declaration "protesting" the Diet's decree that no further religious innovations were to be introduced in the empire, and thereafter they were known as Protestants. The following year, at another imperial Diet, the Lutheran princes announced their support of the Augsburg Confession, a statement of the doctrines of the reformed faith drawn up by Melanchthon and approved by Luther; it is still the official creed of the Lutheran Church. Charles V now realized that military force would be needed to crush the heresy, and in the face of this threat, the Lutherans formed a defensive league in 1531 at the small Saxon town of Schmalkalden. Throughout the 1530s this alliance grew in strength, consolidated Protestant gains, brought new princes into the cause, and in general amassed sufficient strength to deter Charles from immediate action.

The reform party became so solidly established that it negotiated with the pope—on equal terms—about the possibility of reconciliation, but the talks collapsed, and the chances for a reunification of Christendom evaporated. Yet not until 1546, the year of Luther's death, was battle finally joined. Then, in a brief war, Charles won a crushing victory. But matters had advanced too far for the entire movement to collapse merely because of a single defeat on the battlefield. The new faith had gained acceptance among a large part of the German people, particularly in the north and the east, farthest away from the center of imperial power. Some of the great cities of the south, such as Nuremberg, which had been centers of Humanism, had also come over to the Lutheran side. By the 1550s Lutheranism had captured perhaps half the population of the Empire.

The Catholic princes also played a part in assuring the survival of the new faith. Fearful of Charles V's new power, they refused to cooperate in his attempt to establish his authority throughout the empire, and he had to rely on Spanish troops, who further alienated him from his subjects. The Protestants rallied, and in 1555 the imperial Diet at Augsburg drew up a compromise settlement that exposed the decline of the emperor's power. Henceforth each ruler was allowed to determine the religion of his territory, Lutheran or Catholic, without outside interference. Religious uniformity was at an end, and the future of Lutheranism was secure.

The influence that this first Protestant Church was to exert on all of European life was immense. The equality of believers in the eyes of God was to inspire revolutionary changes in thought and society: the appearance of antimonarchical constitutional theories, the acceptance of economic life as worthy, and the undermining of the hierarchic view of the universe. But the most immediate effect of the new faith was on religious life itself: before the century was out, the dissent led by Luther had given birth to a multitude of sects and a ferment of ideas without precedent in the history of Europe.

IV. THE GROWTH OF PROTESTANTISM

Hardly had Luther made his stand in 1517 when heresy in many different forms suddenly appeared. It was as if no more was needed than one opening shot before a volley of discontent broke out—a testimony to the deep and widespread striving for individual piety of the times. The Peasants' War, in particular, gave scores of fiery preachers the opportunity to gain a wide hearing, and their teachings were much more radical than Luther's. As new ideas proliferated, it seemed that the fragmentation of the reform movement might lead to chaotic disunity. But the work of John Calvin gave the Reformation the organization that its further advance required.

ZWINGLI

Less than two years after Luther posted his ninety-five theses, another reformer defied the Church in the Swiss city of Zurich: Ulrich Zwingli (1484–1531). A priest, a learned humanist, and a disciple of Erasmus, Zwingli began to develop a system of doctrine between 1519 and 1522 that was quite similar to Luther's. Like the Saxon reformer, he based his ideas entirely on Scripture, excluding all non-biblical authorities. He rejected the role of the Church as mediator between the believer and God, the celibacy of the clergy, and the belief in purgatory after death. However, Zwingli was less concerned than Luther to demonstrate man's inadequacy. Instead he sought chiefly to simplify religious belief and practice, freeing them from complexity and ceremony. To this end he asserted that none of the sacraments were channels of grace; they were merely signs of grace already given. Baptism does not regenerate the recipient, and communion is no more than a memorial and thanksgiving for the grace bestowed by God, who is present only in spirit—not in actuality, as Luther believed.

Despite his obvious debt to Luther, Zwingli's divergences were significant. When he met Luther in 1529, hoping to iron out differences in order to present a united front, their inability to agree on a doctrine of communion kept them apart. Zwingli had founded a new form of Protestantism, more thoroughly dependent on the individual believer and more devoid of mystery and ritual than anything Luther could accept.

Taking a line of argument closer to Sir Thomas More's than Luther's, Zwingli held that man is innately good but needs constant correction to lead a godly life. Since he recognized no distinction between secular and religious authority, he established a tribunal of clergymen and magistrates to enforce discipline among the faithful. It supervised all moral questions, from compulsory church attendance to the public behavior of amorous couples. The court could excommunicate flagrant transgressors, and it maintained constant surveillance—through a network of informers—to keep the faithful on paths of godliness.

Because Zwingli considered it vital for discipline that the faithful should receive a continuing education, he also founded a theological school and authorized a new transla-

tion of the Bible. He revealed a similar intent when he established the practice of lengthy sermons at each service. Worship was stripped bare, as were the churches, and preaching began to assume tremendous importance as a means of instructing the believer and strengthening his faith. Zwingli also revived the ancient Christian practice of public confession—yet another reinforcement of discipline.

Zwingli's ideas spread rapidly in the Swiss Confederation, helped by the virtual autonomy each canton enjoyed. By 1529 six cantons had accepted Zwinglianism. As a result two camps formed in the country, and a war broke out in 1531 in which Zwingli himself was killed. Thereafter Switzerland remained split between Catholics and reformers. Zwinglianism as such never grew into a major religion, but it had a considerable effect on subsequent Protestantism, particularly Calvinism.

THE RADICALS

Both Luther and Zwingli wanted to retain a territorial church, and therefore insisted that infant baptism was the moment of entry into the church, even though this had no biblical sanction. Some radical reformers, however, extending Luther's logic, believed that as in biblical times baptism should be administered only to mature adults who could make a conscious choice for Christ, not to infants who were incapable of understanding that they were receiving grace. Soon they were contemptuously called Anabaptists ("rebaptizers") by their enemies. The term is often used to describe all radicals, though in fact it applied only to one conspicuous group.

Diversity was inevitable among these extremists, who refused to recognize church organization, rejected priests, and gave individual belief free rein, sometimes to the point of recognizing only personal communication with God and disregarding Scripture. Many groups of like-minded radicals formed sects—

voluntary associations of adult believers (rarely more than a hundred or so)—in an effort to achieve complete separation from the world and avoid compromising their ideals. They wanted to set an example for others by adhering fervently to the truth as they saw it, regardless of the consequences.

Some sects established little utopian communities, holding everything in common, including property and wives. Others, direct descendants of the mystics, disdained all worldly things and lived only for the supreme ecstasy of a trance in which they made direct contact with God himself. Many, believing in the imminent coming of the Messiah, prepared themselves for the Day of Judgment and warned their fellow men of the approaching Armageddon.

Such divergence in the name of a personal search for God was intolerable to Luther, Zwingli, and later to Calvin, each of whom believed that his doctrines were the only means of salvation. Once the major branches of Protestantism were firmly entrenched, they became as deeply committed as the Catholic Church to the status quo and to their hierarchies and traditions. The established reformers thus regarded the radicals' refusal to conform as an unmistakable sign of damnation; Heinrich Bullinger, Zwingli's successor, put it bluntly when he wrote that individual interpretation of the Bible allowed each man to carve his own path to hell. Indeed, Lutherans, Zwinglians, and Calvinists alike saw it as their duty to persecute these people who refused salvation.

The assault began in the mid-1520s and soon spread through most of Europe. The imperial Diet in 1529 called for the death penalty against all Anabaptists, and most members of a group of more than thirty Anabaptist leaders who met to discuss their ideas in 1533 eventually met a violent death. Finally, in the Rhine city of Münster, a particularly fiery sect known as the Melchiorites provoked a reaction

that signaled doom even for the more moderate dissenters.

The Melchiorites had managed to gain considerable influence over both the ordinary workers of Münster and the craft guilds. Early in 1534 they gained political control of the city and began to establish their "heavenly Jerusalem" on earth. They burned all books except the Bible, abolished private property, introduced polygamy, and in an atmosphere of abandon and chaos dug in to await the coming of the Messiah.

Here was a sufficient threat to society to force Protestants and Catholics into an alliance, and they captured the city and brutally massacred the Melchiorites. Thereafter the radicals were savagely persecuted throughout the empire. To survive, many fled first to Poland, then to the Low Countries and England, and eventually to the New World.

JOHN CALVIN AND HIS CHURCH

The one systematizing force among the varied Protestant movements in the 1530s was the creation of a second-generation reformer, John Calvin (1509–1564). Born in Noyon, a small town in northern France, he studied both law and the humanities at the University of Paris. In his early twenties he apparently had a blinding spiritual experience that he later called his "sudden conversion," an event about which he would say almost nothing else. Yet from that moment on all his energy was devoted to religious activity.

In November 1533 Calvin was indicted for heresy, and after more than a year in hiding, he took refuge in the Swiss city of Basel. There in 1536 he published a little treatise, *Institutes of the Christian Religion*, outlining the principles of a new system of belief. He would revise and expand the *Institutes* for the remainder of his life, and it was to become the basis of the most vigorous branch of Protestantism in the sixteenth century.

This contemporary caricature of John Calvin mocks the subhuman character of the stern religious leader. (Photo: Gripsholm Castle, Sweden)

Later in 1536 Calvin settled in Geneva, where, except for a brief period, he was to remain until his death. The citizens of this prosperous market center had just overthrown their prince, a bishop. In achieving their independence they had allied with other Swiss cities—notably Bern, a recent convert to Zwinglianism. Rebels who had just freed themselves with the help of heretics from an ecclesiastical overlord would obviously be receptive to new religious teachings.

Outwardly Calvinism seemed to have much in common with Lutheranism. Both emphasized man's sinfulness, lack of free will, and helplessness; both rejected good works as a means of salvation; both accepted only two sacraments, baptism and communion; both regarded all positions in life as equally worthy in the sight of God; both strongly upheld established political and social authority; and both leaned heavily on St. Paul and St. Augustine

in their views of faith, man's weakness, and God's omnipotence. But the emphases in Calvinism were very different.

Luther's belief in justification by faith alone assumed that God can predestine a man to be saved but rejected the idea that damnation can also be preordained. Calvin's faith was much sterner, however, for it recognized no such distinction: if a man is damned, he should praise God's justice because his sins certainly merit such a judgment; if a man is saved, he should praise God's mercy because his salvation is not a result of his own good deeds. Either way the outcome is predestined, and nothing can be done to affect his fate. It is up to God alone to justify a person; he then perseveres in his mercy despite the person's sins; and finally he decides whether to receive the sinner into the small band of saints, or elect, whom he wishes to save. Calvin's was a grim but powerful answer to the age-old Christian question: How can sinful human beings gain salvation?

Calvin believed that the life a man leads on earth is no indication of his fate. He did suggest that someone who has been justified by God is likely to be upright and moral, but such behavior is not necessarily a sign of salvation. However, because man has to try to please God at all times, he should make every effort to lead the kind of life that will be worthy of one of the elect.

Calvin therefore developed a strict moral code for the true believer that banned frivolous activities like dancing in favor of constant self-examination, austerity, and sober study of the Bible. To help the faithful observe such regulation, he reestablished public confessions, as Zwingli had, and required daily preaching. He made services starkly simple: stripped of ornaments, they concentrated on uplifting sermons and the celebration of communion. His doctrine of communion occupied a middle ground between Luther's and Zwingli's. He rejected Zwingli's interpretation, saying instead that Christ's body and blood were actually and not just symbolically present. But unlike Luther, he held that they were present only in spirit and were consumed only spiritually, by faith.

In order to supervise the morals of the faithful more closely, Calvin gave his church a strict hierarchical structure. It was controlled by deacons and lay elders, who could function even in the hostile territories where many Calvinists found themselves. A body of lay elders called the consistory served as the chief ecclesiastical authority. They enforced discipline and had the power of excommunication, though they always worked together with the secular magistrates, who imposed the actual punishments for failures in religious duties.

Calvin's genius produced a cohesiveness and organization achieved by no other Protestant church. The *Institutes* spelled out every point of faith and practice in detail—an enormous advantage for his followers at a time when new religious doctrines were still fluid. A believer's duties and obligations were absolutely clear, as was his position in the very carefully organized hierarchy of the church. In France for example there was a cell in each town, a local synod (or council) in each area, a provincial synod in each province, and a national synod at the top of the pyramid. Tight discipline controlled the entire system, with the result that Calvinists felt themselves to be setting an example that all the world would eventually have to follow. They were part of a very privileged group, not necessarily the elect but at least possessors of the true faith. Like the children of Israel, they had a mission to live out God's word on earth, and their sense of destiny was to be one of Calvinism's greatest strengths.

Preachers from Geneva traveled through Europe to win adherents and organize the faithful wherever they could. In 1559 the city opened a university for the purpose of training them, because Calvin regarded education

as an essential means of instilling faith. Moreover, soon after the elector of the Palatinate converted to Calvinism in 1556, he turned the great university in his lands, Heidelberg, into a similar training center. From Geneva flowed a stream of pamphlets and books, which strengthened the faith of all believers and made sure that none who wished to learn would lack the opportunity.

By 1564, when Calvin died, his church was well established: more than a million adherents

The disillusionment resulting from religious conflict is reflected in this French engraving of 1600, which shows the disputes among the Pope, Calvin, and Luther, depicted as three old men pulling each other's hair, oblivious to the crucifixion and martyrdom of St. Sebastian behind them. (Photo: Giraudon)

CALVIN · LE PAPE · LUTHER

in France, where they were called Huguenots; the Palatinate converted; Scotland won; and considerable groups of followers in England, the Low Countries, and Hungary. Despite its severity Calvin's coherent and comprehensive body of doctrine proved to have wide and powerful appeal in an age of piety that yearned for clear answers.

V. THE CATHOLIC REVIVAL

Those with Protestant sympathies usually refer to the Catholic revival that started in the 1530s as the Counter Reformation, implying that action came only as a result of criticisms by Luther and others. Catholic historians call it the Catholic Reformation, implying that the movement began within the Church and was not merely a reaction to Protestantism. There is justification for both views. Certainly the papacy was aware of its loss of control over millions of Christians, but a great deal of the effort to put the Catholic Church's house in order came from men of deep faith who were determined to purify their institution for its own sake. This internal purification can quite properly be called the Catholic Reformation.

CRISIS AND REFORM IN THE CHURCH

There could be no doubt that a revival within the Catholic Church was badly needed. The first half of the sixteenth century was the lowest point in its history, and by the 1560s few observers could have expected it ever to recover. Much of Europe had been lost and even in areas still loyal the papacy was able to exercise little control. The French Church for example had a well-established tradition of autonomy, typified by the concordat of 1516, which had given Francis I and his successors the right to make ecclesiastical appointments. In Spain, too, the monarchy retained its independence and even had its own Inquisition. In the Holy Roman Empire, those states that had rejected Protestantism gave the pope no more than token allegiance.

Moreover there was still no comprehensive definition of Catholic doctrine on justification, salvation, and the sacraments. Worse yet, the Church's leadership was far from effective. Although one pope, Leo X, had attempted to correct notorious abuses such as simony in the early sixteenth century, the Vatican simply did not have the spiritual authority to make reform a vital force in the Catholic Church.

The situation changed with the pope elected in 1534: Paul III, a man not renowned for saintliness himself, but a genius at making the right decisions for the Church. By the end of his reign, in 1549, the Catholic revival was well under way.

The heart of Paul's strategy was his determination to assert papal responsibility throughout the church. Realizing that uncertainties in Catholic doctrine could be resolved only by a reexamination of traditional theology, he decided within a few months of taking office to call a church council for that purpose, despite the danger of rekindling the conciliar movement. It took ten years to overcome resistance to the idea, but in the meantime Paul relentlessly attacked abuses throughout the church, disregarding both vested interests and tradition. He aimed his campaign at all levels of the hierarchy, undeterred by powerful bishops and cardinals long used to a lax and corrupt regime. And he also founded a Roman Inquisition to destroy heresy throughout society.

Paul realized that in the long run the revival of Catholicism would depend on whether his successors maintained the effort. Within a few years therefore he made a series of appointments to the College of Cardinals, which elected the popes, that transformed it into possibly the most illustrious group that has ever held that honor at one time. Many were famous for their piety, others for their learning.

They came from all over Europe, united by their devotion to the church and their resolve to see it once again command the admiration and reverence it deserved. The result of this far-sighted policy was to be a succession of popes through the early seventeenth century who would fully restore the atmosphere of spirituality and morality that had long been missing from the papacy.

THE COUNCIL OF TRENT

The ecumenical, or general, council that Pope Paul finally succeeded in opening met at Trent, a northern Italian city, in 1545, and met irregularly until the delegates managed to complete their work in 1563. The council's history was one of stormy battles between various national factions. The non-Italians pressed for decentralization; the Italians, closely tied to the papacy, advocated a consolidation of power. Because the Italians were a large majority of the delegates, time after time the authority of the pope's office was confirmed and reinforced. The threat of a revival of conciliarism thus never materialized.

In keeping with Paul's instructions, the Council of Trent gave most of its time to the basic issue of doctrine, devoting little attention to the problem of reform. Almost all its decisions drew on the interpretations put forward by Thomas Aquinas, who now became the central theologian of the Catholic Church. Significantly the one major subject left unsettled was a definition of the extent of papal authority on matters of faith and morals.[4]

Trent's most important decrees affirmed the truth of precisely those teachings the Protestants had rejected. Catholicism from then on would be committed primarily to the outward, sacramental heritage of Christianity. In this view the Bible is not the exclusive authority—tradition also holds a place in establishing the true faith. Man's will is free; good works as well as faith are means of salvation; all seven sacraments are channels of grace; and Christ's sacrifice is reenacted in every mass. The Council of Trent endorsed the special position of the priest and insisted that God be worshiped with appropriately elaborate ceremonies and rites.

These were the principal decisions at Trent, but hundreds of minor matters also had to be settled. Thus for the first time the priest's presence was declared to be essential at the sacrament of marriage, a further reinforcement of his importance. The Vulgate, the Latin translation of the Bible prepared chiefly by St. Jerome, was decreed to be a holy text, which rebutted humanists and other scholars who had declared the Greek and Hebrew versions superior. And in direct contrast to the Protestants, gorgeous ritual was heavily stressed, which encouraged artists to beautify church buildings and ceremonies.

What the council was doing was adjusting the church to the world—an aim shared by Vatican II in the 1960s. Many ordinary people, troubled by the stern self-denial and predestination taught by most Protestant churches and sects, were delighted to embrace the traditional faith, now infused with new vigor, for the council had not hesitated to deal with morality and discipline as thoroughly as with belief. In fact, it had given its approval to the Inquisition and the "Index of Forbidden Books," which informed all Catholics of works with heretical content that they were not allowed to read.[5]

---

[4] Not until 1870, at the council known as Vatican I, was this matter settled by the assertion of the dogma of papal infallibility.

[5] The Index became a major weapon, used particularly effectively against borderline cases such as Erasmus. Later distinguished entries in the list included Michel de Montaigne, René Descartes, and Edward Gibbon. In the twentieth century, though, considerable relaxation has been allowed.

The Aftermath of Trent

The new atmosphere of spiritual dedication swept through the Catholic Church, inspiring thinkers and artists throughout Europe to lend their talents to the cause. In many ways Baroque art was to be the genre of the Counter Reformation: painters, architects, and musicians caught up by the new moral fervor in Catholicism expressed their faith in brilliant and dramatic portrayals of religious subjects and in churches that were designed to dazzle the observer in a way that most Protestants could not allow.

This outpouring was of course far more than a reflection of the decisions of a few hundred prelates assembled in a council. It was also one of many indicators of the new vigor of Catholicism. Spain experienced a great flowering of mysticism. In France the new generation of church leaders who appeared in the late sixteenth century were distinguished for their piety, learning, and observance of their duties. In Italy a similar group of talented theologians and religious writers gathered around the revitalized papal court. The inheritors of the traditional scholastic philosophy multiplied, and in the late sixteenth and early seventeenth centuries they were to become influential throughout Europe, particularly in the Holy Roman Empire, Italy, and Spain.

The most conspicuous examples of this new energy, however, were the popes themselves. Paul III's successors used their personal authority and pontifical resources not to adorn their palaces but to continue the enormous cleansing operation within the church and to lead the counterattack against Protestantism. If a king or prince refused to help, they would try to persuade one of his leading subjects to organize the struggle (for example, the Guise family in France or the dukes of Bavaria in the empire). Their diplomats and agents were everywhere, ceaselessly urging the faithful to stamp out Protestantism wherever it was found. And the pontiffs insisted on strict morality in order to set the best possible example: one pope even ordered clothes painted on the nudes in Michelangelo's *Day of Judgment* in the Sistine Chapel.

With the leaders of the church thus bent on reform, the restoration of the faith and the reconquest of lost souls could proceed with maximum effect. And they had at their disposal an order established by Ignatius Loyola in 1540 specifically for these purposes: the Society of Jesus.

IGNATIUS LOYOLA: THE MAKING OF A REFORMER

The third of the great religious innovators of the sixteenth century, after Luther and Calvin, was Ignatius Loyola (1491–1556), but unlike his predecessors he sought to reform the Catholic Church from within.

Loyola was the son of a Basque nobleman, raised in the chivalric and fiercely religious atmosphere of Spain, and he was often at the court of Ferdinand of Aragon. In his teens he entered the army, but when he was thirty a serious wound ended his career. While convalescing he was deeply impressed by a number of popular lives of the saints he read, and soon his religious interests began to take shape in chivalric and military terms. He visualized Mary as his lady, the inspiration of a Christian quest in which the forces of God and the devil fought in mighty battle. This was a faith seen from the perspective of the knight, and though the direct parallel lessened as his thought developed, it left an unmistakable stamp on all his future work.

In 1522 Loyola gave up his knightly garb and swore to become a pilgrim. He retired to a monastery for ten months to absolve himself of the guilt of a sinful life and to prepare spiritually for a journey to the Holy Land. At the monastery he had a momentous experience that, like Luther's and Calvin's, dominated the rest of his life. According to tradition it was a vision lasting eight days, during which he first saw in detail the outline of a book, the *Spiritual Exercises,* and a new religious order, the Society of Jesus.

The first version of the *Spiritual Exercises* certainly dated from this time, but like Calvin's *Institutes,* it was to be revised thoroughly many times. The book deals not with doctrines or theology but with the discipline and training necessary for a God-fearing life. The believer must undertake four weeks of contemplation and self-examination, culminating in a feeling of union with God in which he surrenders his mind and his will to Christ. If successful, he is then ready to submit completely to the call of God and the church and to pursue the commands he receives without question.

The manual was the heart of the organization of the Society of Jesus, and it gave those who followed its precepts a dedication and determination that made them seem like the Church's answer to the Calvinists. But while the end might be similar to Luther's and Calvin's—the personal attainment of grace—the method, the emphasis on individual effort and concentration, could not have been more different. For the *Spiritual Exercises* prepared a man's inward condition for grace through a tremendous act of will, and its severity relied on the belief that the will is free and that good works are efficacious.

During the sixteen years after he left the monastery Ignatius led a life of poverty and study. He traveled to Jerusalem and back barefoot in 1523–1524, and two years later he found his way to the University of Alcalá, where he attracted his first disciples, three fellow students. Suspected by the Inquisition, the little band walked to Paris, where they were joined by six more disciples. Ignatius now decided to return to the Holy Land, but the companions found themselves unable to travel beyond Venice because of war. Instead they preached in the streets, visited the poor and

the sick, urged all who would listen to rededicate themselves to piety and faith, and in 1537 achieved ordination as priests. Their activities were beginning to take definite shape, and so they decided to seek the pope's blessing for their work. They saw Paul III in 1538, and two years later, despite opposition and suspicion at the Vatican, the pope gave his approval to a plan Ignatius had drawn up for a new religious order that would owe allegiance only to the papacy.

The Jesuits

The Society, or Company, of Jesus had four principal functions: preaching, hearing confessions, teaching, and founding and maintaining missions. The first two were the Jesuits' means of strengthening the beliefs of individual Catholics or converting heretics. The third became one of their most effective weapons. Loyola, much influenced by the Christian humanists he had encountered, was convinced of the tremendous power of education. The Jesuits therefore set about organizing the best schools in Europe, an endeavor in which they succeeded so well that some Protestants sent their children to the Society's schools despite the certainty that the pupils would become committed Catholics. The instructors followed humanist principles and taught the latest ideas, including for a while the most recent advances in science. The Jesuits' final activity, missionary work, brought them their most spectacular successes among both non-Christians and Protestants.

A number of qualities combined to make the Jesuits extraordinarily effective in winning converts and turning Catholics into militant activists. First, they had a remarkable knowledge of Scripture and traditional teachings and were usually more than a match for any serious opponent. In addition they were carefully selected and received a superb training that fashioned them into brilliant preachers and excellent educators. Their discipline, de-

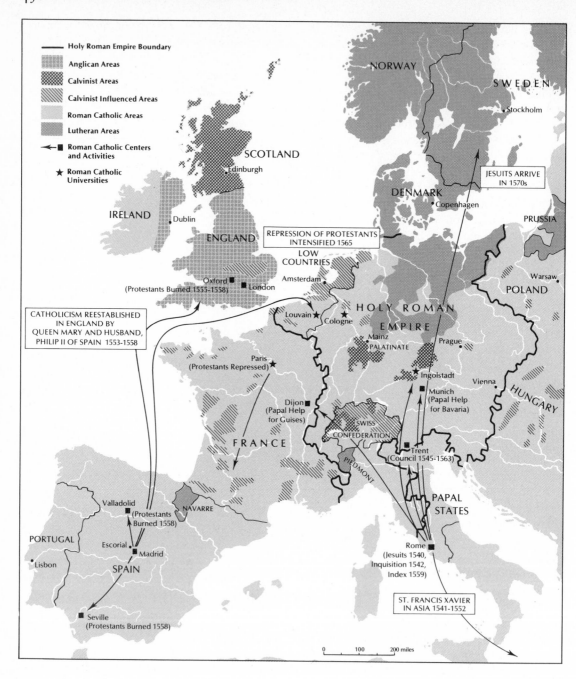

Holy Roman Empire Boundary
Anglican Areas
Calvinist Areas
Calvinist Influenced Areas
Roman Catholic Areas
Lutheran Areas
Roman Catholic Centers and Activities
Roman Catholic Universities

NORWAY

SWEDEN

Stockholm

JESUITS ARRIVE IN 1570s

DENMARK

Copenhagen

PRUSSIA

SCOTLAND

Edinburgh

REPRESSION OF PROTESTANTS INTENSIFIED 1565

Warsaw

IRELAND

Dublin

LOW COUNTRIES

Amsterdam

POLAND

ENGLAND

Oxford ■ ■ London

(Protestants Burned 1555-1558)

HOLY ROMAN

Louvain ★ ★ Cologne

EMPIRE

Mainz
PALATINATE

Prague

CATHOLICISM REESTABLISHED IN ENGLAND BY QUEEN MARY AND HUSBAND, PHILIP II OF SPAIN 1553-1558

Paris ★
(Protestants Repressed)

★ Ingolstadt

Vienna

HUNGARY

Dijon ■
(Papal Help for Guises)

Munich ■
(Papal Help for Bavaria)

FRANCE

SWISS CONFEDERATION

Trent ■
(Council 1545-1563)

PIEDMONT

PAPAL STATES

Valladolid ■
(Protestants Burned 1558)

NAVARRE

Rome ■
(Jesuits 1540, Inquisition 1542, Index 1559)

PORTUGAL

Escorial • ■ Madrid

SPAIN

Lisbon •

ST. FRANCIS XAVIER IN ASIA 1541-1552

Seville ■
(Protestants Burned 1558)

0   100   200 miles

MAP 14.1: RELIGIOUS TENSIONS 1560

termination, and their awareness of the contemporary world allowed them to make clever use of their fearsome reputation, whose darker side—they were accused of the most sinister conspiracies—had little foundation in fact. But of their successes there could be no doubt; they had no equal in the forcefulness with which they advanced the aims of the Council of Trent and the papacy.

It is not inappropriate to regard the Jesuits as the striking arm of the Counter Reformation; indeed, their organization was to some extent modeled on the medieval military orders. A Jesuit at a royal court was often the chief inspiration for a ruler's militant support of the faith, and in many areas the Society was the main conqueror of heresy. Yet it must be noted that in this age of cruel persecution, the Jesuits always opposed execution for heresy; they far preferred to win a convert than to kill a man. Their presence was soon felt all over the world—as early as the 1540s, one of Loyola's first disciples, Francis Xavier, was conducting a mission to Japan. Despite many enmities (some of them richly deserved), their unswerving devotion to Catholicism was a major reason for the revival of the Roman Church.

One of the saddest spectacles in history is the diversion of the wish for a purer, simpler religion, freed from abuses and material concerns, into fanaticism and bloodletting in the late sixteenth century. What had started as a desire to improve religious practice and belief within existing institutions soon became, in Luther's hands, a determination to start anew. Inevitably the ideas of those who broke with Rome became increasingly radical, and when they received the organization provided by Calvin, they had extraordinary success in winning new adherents.

Within the Catholic Church, meanwhile, a reform movement begun by Pope Paul III in the 1530s raised that institution's moral stature and gave it the organization and aggressive force to meet its opponents on equal terms. Spearheaded by the Jesuits, Catholic reformers made many gains and ensured that Protestantism would not engulf the Continent.

But it was not enough for either side to remedy religious deficiencies and abuses. Each had to launch a fanatical and unrelenting attack on the enemy religion. In this atmosphere of hatred and violence, voices of moderation such as Erasmus' were ignored, and pleas for toleration went unheard. For there was a rare ferocity to the conflicts that now racked European civilization.

As the religious upheavals multiplied, the sources of hostility broadened, and revolutionary thought and action erupted on many other planes of society. Subjects challenged their governments; writers and artists expressed deep discontents. Lacerated by vicious warfare, Europe entered one of its most tormented centuries.

RECOMMENDED READING

Sources

* Calvin, John. *On God and Political Duty.* J. T. McNeill (ed.). 1950.
* ———. *On the Christian Faith.* J. T. McNeill (ed.). 1957.
* Erasmus, Desiderius. *Essential Works of Erasmus.* W. T. H. Jackson (ed.). 1965.
* Loyola, Ignatius. *The Spiritual Exercises of St. Ignatius.* R. W. Gleason (ed.). 1964.
* Luther, Martin. *Martin Luther: Selections from his Writings.* John Dillenberger (ed.). 1961.

Studies

* Bainton, Roland H. *Here I Stand: A Life of Martin Luther.* 1955. The standard biography in English, with many quotations from Luther's writings.
*Cohn, Norman. *The Pursuit of the Millennium: Revolutionary Messianism in Medieval and Reformation Europe and its Bearing on Modern Totalitarian Movements.* 1961. A study of radical and extreme religious movements which indicates the kind of popular piety that existed in Europe during the medieval and Reformation periods.
* Davis, Natalie Zemon. *Society and Culture in Early Modern France.* 1975. A collection of essays about popular beliefs and attitudes, particularly on religious matters, during the sixteenth century.
*Dickens, A. G. *The Counter Reformation.* 1969. A clear and thorough introduction to the subject, handsomely illustrated.
Elton, Geoffrey (ed.). *The New Cambridge Modern History.* Vol. II: *The Reformation, 1520–1559.* 1965. The most detailed and thorough survey of European history during this period.
* Fülop-Miller, René. *Jesuits: A History of the Society of Jesus.* 1963. The only account in English of the full history of the order.

Hexter, J. H. *More's Utopia: The Biography of an Idea.* 1965. A fascinating study of the way the book developed in More's mind, and the problems he was trying to solve.
* Huizinga, Johan. *Erasmus and the Age of Reformation.* 1957. A warm and sympathetic biography, beautifully written.
Koenigsberger, H. G., and G. L. Mosse. *Europe in the Sixteenth Century.* 1968. The best overall introduction to the period—compact, well written, and equipped with useful bibliographical notes.
*McNeill, J. T. *The History and Character of Calvinism.* 1967. A clear short history of the movement that Calvin founded.
*Strauss, Gerald. *Nuremberg in the Sixteenth Century.* 1966. A study of a German city, showing how its people lived and how they responded to Luther.
* Tawney, R. H. *Religion and the Rise of Capitalism.* 1947. A lively and powerfully argued study of the links between Protestantism and economic behavior.
* Weber, Max. *The Protestant Ethic and the Spirit of Capitalism.* Talcott Parsons (tr.). 1958. Originally published in 1904 and 1905, this study of the way in which the Reformation helped create the modern world has become a classic and has influenced much of the historical thinking about the Reformation.
Wendel, François. *Calvin: The Origins and Development of his Religious Thought.* Philip Mairet (tr.). 1963. The best overall introduction to the reformer's work.
Williams, George H. *The Radical Reformation.* 1962. A comprehensive history of the many sects and radical ideas that sprung up during the Reformation.

---

* Available in paperback.

FIFTEEN

A CENTURY OF
WAR AND REVOLT

In the wake of the rapid and bewildering changes of the early sixteenth century—the dislocations caused by the activities of the new monarchs, the rises in population and prices, the overseas discoveries, and the Reformation—Europe entered a period of fierce upheaval. It was difficult to come to terms with such radical alterations in so many elements of society: the increasing interference in local affairs by bureaucrats from distant capitals, the sudden soaring of food costs, or the questioning of hallowed authorities like the pope. Many people, often led by nobles who saw their power dwindling, revolted against their monarchs. The poor launched hopeless rebellions against their social superiors. And the two religious camps struggled relentlessly to destroy each other. From Scotland to Russia, the events of the century following the Reformation, from about 1560 to 1660, were dominated by warfare.

The pivot of the conflict was the Hapsburg family, which ruled most of southern and central Europe. Until the 1590s its chief representative was Philip II, King of Spain, whose ambitions and world-wide commitments lay at the center of forty years of international disputes. Then, after a short respite, the Thirty Years' War began and involved large areas of Europe in the bloodiest fighting the Continent had ever seen. Domestic tensions, peasant revolts, and civil wars added to the perpetual upheaval. The constant military activity had widespread effects on politics, economy, society, and thought. No country was untouched, because phenomena as diverse as population increase and political theory or taxation and the proliferation of bureaucracies were transformed by the impact of the wars. The fighting was in fact a crucial element in the long and painful process whereby Europeans came to terms with the revolutions that had begun about 1500. Almost imperceptibly, fundamental economic, political, social, and religious changes took root, and troubled Europeans managed to come to terms with their altered circumstances. At last, in the mid-seventeenth century, the long struggle seemed to ease as conflict shifted to different issues. But by the time the long adjustment finally ended, countless lives had been sacrificed and endless suffering had been caused.

I. WARFARE

Western Europe was the scene of almost constant fighting during the late sixteenth century and the succeeding era of the Thirty Years' War. Warfare was so widespread between 1600 and 1650 that no country was immune to the effects of the mounting brutality. The effects of war were to be felt in all areas of political and social development, intensifying the sense of disorder and upheaval that had arisen during the first half of the six-

teenth century and causing basic shifts of power in political and economic structures.

THE MILITARY REVOLUTION

Dramatic changes took place in the way battles were fought and armies were organized between the early 1500s and the middle of the seventeenth century. At the beginning of the period gunpowder first came into general use. The result was not only the creation of a new

(top) *A view of the siege of Magdeburg during the Thirty Years' War. Cannon are pouring fire into the city. Star-shaped bastions are visible in the lower right and at the far left.* (Photo: New York Public Library Picture Collection) (left) *A typical system of trenches approaching a bastion.* (Photo: The Granger Collection)

type of industry, cannon and gun manufacture, but also a transformation of tactics. Individual castles could no longer be defended against explosives; even towns had to build heavy and elaborate fortifications if they were to resist the new fire power. Sieges became complicated, expensive operations, whose purpose was to bring explosives right up to a town wall so that it could be blown up. This required an intricate system of trenches, because walls were built in star shapes so as to multiply angles of fire and make any approach dangerous. Although both attack and defense thus became increasingly costly, sieges remained essential to the strategy of warfare until the eighteenth century.

In open battles, the effects of gunpowder were equally expensive. The new tactics that appeared around 1500, perfected by the Spaniards, relied on massed ranks of infantry, organized in huge squares, and made the traditional cavalry charge obsolete. Around the edge of the square were soldiers carrying pikes. They fended off horses or opposing infantry while the men with guns—in the center of the square—tried to mow the enemy down. The squares with the best discipline usually won, and for over a century after the reign of Ferdinand of Aragon, the Spaniards had the best army in Europe. Each square had about 3,000 troops, and to maintain sufficient squares at full strength required an army numbering approximately 40,000. The cost of keeping that many men clothed, fed, and housed, let alone equipped and paid, was enormous. But worse was to come: new tactics emerged in the early seventeenth century that required even more soldiers.

Since nobody could outdo the Spaniards at their own methods, a different approach was developed by their rivals. The first advance was made by Maurice of Nassau, who led the Dutch revolt against Spain from the 1580s. He relied not on sheer weight and power, but on flexibility and mobility. Then one of the geniuses of the history of warfare, Gustavus Adolphus, king of Sweden, found a way to achieve mobility without losing power. His main invention was the salvo—instead of having his musketeers fire one row at a time, like the Spaniards, he had them all fire at once. What he lost in continuity of shot he gained in a fearsome blast that, if properly timed, could shatter enemy ranks. Huge, slow-moving squares were simply no match for smaller, faster units that riddled them with well-coordinated salvos. To add to his fire power, Gustavus had his engineers devise a light, movable cannon that could be brought into action wherever it was most needed on a battlefield.

These changes brought about a further increase in the size of armies because the more units, the better they could be placed on the battlefield. Although the Spanish army hardly grew between 1590 and 1600, remaining at 40,000 to 60,000 men, the Swedes had 175,000 men by 1632; and at the end of the century, Louis XIV considered a force of 400,000 essential to maintain his dominant position in Europe.[1]

This growth had far-reaching consequences. Rulers knew the risks of relying on mercenary troops, who might change sides for a raise in pay, and Gustavus introduced conscription in the late 1620s so that his army, consisting largely of his own subjects, would be easier to control. Because it also made sense not to disband such huge forces each autumn, when the campaigning season ended, the armies were kept permanently ready.

The need to maintain so many soldiers the year round caused a rapid expansion of supporting administrative personnel. Taxation mushroomed. All levels of society felt the impact but especially the lower classes, who paid the bulk of the taxes and provided most of the recruits. To encourage enlistment rulers made military service as attractive as possible—not a difficult task at a time when regular meals, clothing, housing, and wages were not always easy to come by. Social distinctions were reduced; an able young man could rise high in the officer corps, though the top ranks were still reserved for nobles. Even the lower echelons were given important responsibilities because the new system of small, flexible units required that junior officers, who were sometimes in command of only fifty men, be given considerable initiative. The decline of the cavalry, which had always been an aristocratic preserve, similarly reduced social differentiations.

Life in the army also changed. Maneuverability demanded tighter discipline, which was achieved by the introduction of drilling and combat training. The order of command was clarified, and many ranks familiar today—major, colonel, and the various levels of general—appeared in the seventeenth century.

---

[1] An excellent analysis of the military revolution and its implications can be found in Michael Roberts' "Gustav Adolf and the Art of War" and "The Military Revolution, 1560–1660," in his *Essays in Swedish History* (1967), pp. 58–81 and 195–225.

Gustavus Adolphus, the Swedish monarch whose domestic and military policies gained his country a position of considerable power in the early seventeenth century, is here shown landing in Germany with his men and immediately thanking God for his success thus far. (Photo: National-museum, Stockholm)

The distinctions were reinforced by uniforms, which became standard equipment. These developments created a sense of corporate spirit among military officers, an international phenomenon that was to occupy an important place in European society for three centuries.

As Gustavus himself put it, war nourishes itself. With ever-larger armies, stimulated by national ambitions and governments in search of wider powers, it was inevitable that the devastations of warfare would proliferate. Gustavus himself enunciated the strategy of devastation—an opponent can be brought to his knees, he said, only if his strength is totally destroyed. This is a brutal concept, and it spilled over into the writings of Hugo Grotius, a great Dutch jurist who tried to lay down order and rules for international affairs. Though Grotius hoped to control war, he said that the law permits combatants to kill prisoners of war, to treat noncombatants (including women and children) as belligerents, and to ravage an enemy's territory. Such conclusions clearly reflected the appalling slaughter of the era that has come to be known as the age of religious warfare.

THE WARS OF RELIGION

Although many other issues were involved in the wars that plagued Europe from the 1560s to the 1640s, religion was the burning motivation, the one that inspired fanatical devotion and the most vicious hatred. A deep conviction that heresy was dangerous to man and hateful to God made Protestants and Catholics treat one another callously and cruelly. Even the dead were not spared; corpses were sometimes mutilated to emphasize how dreadful their sins had been in their lifetimes. This was the bitter emotion that blended in with political and other ambitions to give Europe a century of almost ceaseless war.

Spain's Catholic Crusade

During the second half of the sixteenth century, the conflict was ignited by the leader of the Catholics, Philip II of Spain (1556–1598), the most powerful monarch in Europe. He ruled the Iberian peninsula, much of Italy, the Netherlands, and a huge overseas empire, but his main obsessions were the two enemies of his church, the Muslims and the Protestants.

Against the Muslims in the Mediterranean, Philip's successful campaigns seemed to justify the financial strains they caused. In particular, his naval victory at Lepanto, off the coast of Greece, in 1571 made him a Christian hero at the same time as it rid the western Mediterranean of Muslim interference. But elsewhere he found little but frustration. He tried to prevent a Protestant, Henry IV, from succeeding to the French crown, and after he failed he continued to back the losing side in France's civil wars even though Henry converted to Catholicism.

Philip's policy toward England was similarly ineffective. After the Protestant Queen Elizabeth I came to the throne in 1558, he remained uneasily cordial toward her for about ten years. But relations deteriorated as England's sailors and explorers tried to take some of the wealth of Philip's New World possessions for themselves. The last straw came in 1585 when Elizabeth began to help the Protestant Dutch in their rebellion against Spain.

Philip decided to end all these troubles with one mighty blow: in 1588 he sent a mammoth fleet—the Armada—to the Low Countries to pick up a Spanish army, invade England, and crush his Protestant enemies. By this time, however, English seamen were among the best in the world; and their ships, which had greater maneuverability and fire power than the Spaniards', made up in tactical superiority what they lacked in size. After several skirmishes with the Armada, they set fire to a few vessels with loaded cannon aboard and sent them drifting toward the Spanish ships, anchored off Calais. The Spaniards panicked, and some of the fleet was lost. The next day the remaining ships retreated up the North Sea. The only way home was around Scotland and Ireland, and wind, storms, and the pursuing English ensured that no more than a few stragglers reached Spain safely. This shattering reversal was comparable in scale and unexpectedness only to Xerxes' disaster at Salamis more than 2,000 years earlier.

The defeat spelled the doom of Philip's foreign policies. Though he improved the defense of the Spanish Empire, English raids multiplied in a tremendous wave of privateering in the 1590s, and his possessions were under almost constant attack thereafter. Enemies to the bitter end, both Elizabeth and Philip died before peace came in 1604.

The Dutch Revolt

Philip's most serious reversal was the revolt of the provinces he had inherited from his father in the Netherlands. Here his single-mindedness provoked a determined reaction that grew into a successful struggle for independence, the first major effort in Western Europe to resist the new authority of a monarchy.

The original focus of opposition was Philip's reorganization of the ecclesiastical structure so as to gain control over the country's Catholic church, a change which deprived the aristocracy of important patronage. The billeting of troops meanwhile aroused the resentment of ordinary citizens. Using this situation, the nobles, led by William of Orange, threatened mass disorder, but Philip kept up the pressure: he put the Inquisition to work against heretics, and summoned the Jesuits to combat religious unorthodoxy. These moves had a disastrous effect because they further undermined local autonomy and threatened the Protestants of the country.

Philip's interference in religion provoked violence in 1566: Protestant mobs swept through cities, sacking Catholic churches as they went. He therefore tightened the pressure, appointing as governor the ruthless duke of Alva, whose Spanish troops were used to suppress heresy and treason. Protestants were hanged in public, small rebel bands were mercilessly decimated, and two nobles who had been guilty of nothing worse than demanding that Philip change his policy were executed.

The reaction of one observer, the great painter Pieter Brueghel, was a searing indictment of the persecution. When he painted the famous biblical subject, the Massacre of the Innocents, he set the scene in a village in the Netherlands during the harshest season, winter. His own countrymen were the victims, and the murderers were Spanish soldiers, watched over by the sinister figure of the duke of Alva, dressed entirely in black.

Organized revolt broke out in 1572, when a small group of Dutch seamen flying the flag of William of Orange seized the fishing village of Brill, on the North Sea. The success of these "sea beggars," as the Spaniards called them, stimulated uprisings in towns throughout the Low Countries. The banner of William of Orange became the symbol of resistance, and under his leadership full-scale rebellion gathered momentum.

After the sea beggars' capture of Brill, the Spaniards advanced into the province of Holland, but they were stopped in 1574 by the opening of the dikes when they were only twenty-five miles from Amsterdam.[2] Following two more years of fighting, Philip's troops

---

[2] Most areas of the provinces of Holland and Zeeland lay below sea level and were protected by dikes. Defenders could flood them at very short notice by opening sluices in the sea walls. The forewarned population would take to boats, and the enemy soldiers, caught unawares, would have to beat a hasty retreat.

This detail from Brueghel's Massacre of the Innocents *shows the brutality of Spanish soldiers toward the local population. The figure in black at the center of the detachment of cavalry has been identified as the duke of Alva.* (Photo: Kunsthistorisches Museum, Vienna)

mutinied and rioted in Antwerp. In reaction sixteen out of seventeen provinces united behind William to drive out the Spaniards. The next year, however, the ten southern provinces again gave their allegiance to Philip because he had restored political power to the nobility.

In 1579 the remaining seven formed the United Provinces (Map 15.1). Despite the assassination of William in 1584, they managed to hang on, for various reasons: they could always open up the dikes; Philip was often diverted by other wars, and in any case never placed total confidence in his commanders; and the Calvinists, though still a minority, became the heart of the resistance with their determination to establish freedom for their religion as well as their country. William was succeeded by Maurice of Nassau, his son, a brilliant military commander who won a series of victories in the 1590s. The Spaniards could make no progress and agreed to a twelve-year truce in 1609, but final recognition of the independence of the United Provinces did not come until the Peace of Westphalia, in 1648, after twenty-seven more years of fighting. The new state, bound together by religious, economic, and military ties, demonstrated the occasional positive effects of warfare in this period: it could unite a people and give them the means to achieve dignity and full autonomy.

Civil War in France

The warfare that religion inspired had no such redeeming effects in France. By the 1550s Calvinism was widespread among the peasants and poorer middle classes in the southern and southwestern section of the country, and its leaders had virtually created a small, semi-independent state within France. To meet this threat, a great noble family, the Guises, assumed the leadership of a Catholic party, and in response the Bourbons, another noble family, championed the Calvinists. The ensuing war split France apart.

It was ominous that in 1559, the year that Henry II, France's last strong king for a generation, died, the Protestant Huguenots organized their first national synod, an indication of impressive strength. During the next thirty years, a period when factional disputes among the nobles and religious passions overwhelmed the country, the throne was occupied by Henry's three ineffectual sons. The power behind the crown was Henry's widow, Catherine de Médicis (see the accompanying genealogical table), who tried desperately to preserve royal authority. But she was often helpless because the religious conflict intensified the factional struggle for power between the Catholic Guises and the Protestant Bourbons, both of whom were closely related to the monarchy and hoped eventually to inherit the throne.

The fighting started in 1562, and lasted for thirty-six years, interrupted only by short-lived peace agreements. Catherine first turned to the Catholics for help but later switched to the Calvinists. When they became too powerful at court, she changed sides again, and she probably gave tacit approval to a massacre in

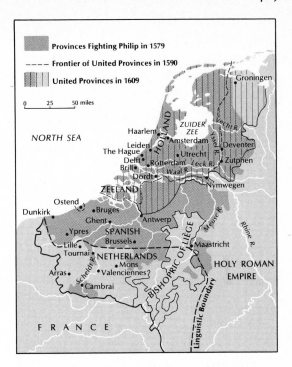

MAP 15.1: THE NETHERLANDS 1579–1609

The seventeen provinces making up the Netherlands, or the Low Countries, were detached from the Holy Roman Empire when Charles V abdicated in 1556. As the map indicates, their subsequent division into two states was determined not by the linguistic difference between French-speaking people of the south and Dutch-speaking people of the north, but rather by geography. The great river systems at the mouth of the Rhine eventually proved to be the barrier beyond which the Spaniards could not penetrate.

Paris on St. Bartholomew's Day, August 24, 1572, which destroyed the Calvinist leadership. Henry of Navarre, a Bourbon, was the only major figure who escaped. When Catherine switched again and made peace with the Calvinists in 1576, the Guises, in desperation, formed the Catholic League, which for several years virtually ran the government. In 1584 the league made an alliance with Philip II to

THE KINGS OF FRANCE IN THE SIXTEENTH CENTURY

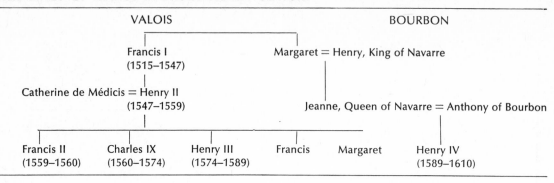

destroy heresy in France and deny the Bourbon Henry's legal right to inherit the throne.

The defeat of the Armada proved to be the turning point in France's civil war. The duke of Guise lost his principal support, Spain; and Henry III, who had been a pawn of the league, ordered Guise's assassination and threw in his lot with the Bourbons. Within a few months he in turn was assassinated, and Henry of Navarre inherited the throne.

Henry IV (1589–1610) had few advantages as he began the reassertion of royal authority. The Calvinists and Catholics had formed almost independent governments, controlling large sections of France. The Catholic League was in command of the east, including the capital, Paris; the Calvinists dominated the south and southwest, remote from the central government. In addition the royal administration was in a sorry state, for power had returned to the crown's oldest rivals, the great nobles, who were now unchallenged in their domains.

Yet largely because of the assassination of the duke of Guise, Henry IV survived and recovered. The duke had been a forceful leader, a serious contender for the throne. He was succeeded by his brother, who had agreed to support a Spanish candidate for the crown. The prospect of a foreign ruler, the loss of a charismatic leader, and war weariness destroyed much of the support for the Catholic League, which finally collapsed as a result of revolts in eastern France against the Guises in the 1590s. The uprisings, founded on a demand for peace, increased in frequency and intensity after Henry IV renounced Protestantism in 1593 to win acceptance by his Catholic subjects. The following year Henry had himself officially crowned, and all of France declared its allegiance to the monarchy so as to join in the effort of repelling the Spanish invader.

When Spain finally withdrew and signed a peace in 1598, the fighting came to an end. To complete the reconciliation, Henry issued (also in 1598) the Edict of Nantes, which granted toleration to the Huguenots. Although it did not create complete religious liberty, it made Calvinism legal, protected the rights of the minority, and opened public office to Protestants.

But the effects of decades of strife could not be brushed aside. A basic change in political thought, for example, was an inevitable response to the civil wars, because a number of

From a portrayal of the Massacre of St. Bartholomew's Day by a Huguenot survivor. (Photo: Andre Held)

theorists felt obliged to reassess the relationship between a king and his subjects.

The Huguenots were the first to justify resistance to a monarch. Seizing on a vague passage in Calvin's writings about the sanctity of conscience and ignoring his endorsement of obedience to authority, they asserted that when a king goes against God's wishes and disturbs the faith, he breaks his contract with his people, thus making revolt permissible. Catholics took up a similar argument when they were fighting the king. The Jesuits developed the idea of a contract between ruler and ruled and found excellent biblical support for the overthrow of a tyrant (for example pharaoh) who turned against true religion.

These extreme positions soon lost appeal when order was restored, however, and a group whose views had previously gone unheeded gained the ascendancy: the politiques. Although most were Catholics their main premise was that peace, security, and national unity were far more important than the claims of rival churches. Representing the forces of nationalism and central authority, the politiques were the heralds of a more stable future.

Their most famous representative, Jean Bodin, made his case by examining the basic structure of the state, and his analysis influenced political theorists for centuries. His principal work is *The Six Books of the Republic* (1576), in which he tried to define the nature and the limits of authority. By aiming for a balance between power and restraint, Bodin was seeking a principle for restoring stability in an age of shattering upheaval. But in the process he also exposed the paradox that has been the primary focus of political theory ever since: control versus freedom, the need for authority and yet the equal need for individual rights. Bodin never really tried to resolve the problem, but in emphasizing this equilibrium as the essential difficulty of political thought, he not only mirrored the uncertainties of his age but also influenced everyone who grappled with the issue thereafter.

THE THIRTY YEARS' WAR

In the Holy Roman Empire fierce religious antagonisms were particularly dangerous because the empire lacked a central authority and unifying institutions. Small-scale fighting broke out repeatedly after the 1550s, always inspired by religion. And though in most of Western Europe the first two decades of the seventeenth century were a time of relative peace, which seemed to signal a decline of confessional conflict, in the empire the stage was being set for the bloodiest of all the wars fired by religion.

Known as the Thirty Years' War, this ferocious series of encounters began in the Kingdom of Bohemia in 1618 and continued until 1648. The principal battleground, the empire, was ravaged by the fighting, and eventually every major ruler of Europe became involved in the struggle. Political ambitions soon began to replace religious motives as the prime concern of the combatants, but the devastation continued to spread until international relations seemed to be sinking into total chaos. The chief victims were of course the Germans, who, like the Italians in the sixteenth century, found themselves at the mercy of well-organized states that used another country as the arena for settling their quarrels.

The immediate problem was typical of the situation in the empire. In 1609 Emperor Rudolf II promised toleration for Protestants in Bohemia, one of his own domains. When his cousin Ferdinand, a pious Catholic, suc-

This map reveals both the extent and the fluctuations of fighting in Europe from the outbreak of the Thirty Years' War to the end of the Civil War in England. The principal battles are listed so as to give a more precise indication of the timing and location of major encounters. A look at the route followed by Spain's troops as they marched to the Netherlands, always staying close to friendly Catholic territories, will pinpoint the vital importance of the Valtellina, a vulnerable pass through the Alps that they had to cross.

MAP 15.2: AREAS OF FIGHTING 1618–1660

NORWAY

SWEDEN

RIGA 1621

SCOTLAND

DUNBAR 1650

NORTH SEA

DENMARK

• Copenhagen

BALTIC SEA

PRUSSIA

IRELAND

DROGHEDA 1649

• Dublin

ENGLAND

STRALSUND 1628

LÜBECK 1627

STETTIN 1630

Elbe R.

Weser R.

Vistula R.

WARSAW 1656

UNITED PROVINCES

Amsterdam •

SCHEVENINGEN 1654

WORCESTER 1651

NASEBY 1645

EDGEHILL 1642

• London

SCHEVENINGEN 1654

BREDA 1625, 1637

DUNKIRK 1658

Thames R.

MAGDEBURG 1631

STADTLOHN 1623

LUTTER 1626

DESSAU 1626

BREITENFELD 1631

LUTZEN 1632

SAXONY

Oder R.

POLAND

ENGLISH CHANNEL

LENS 1648

Scheldt R.

SPANISH NETHERLANDS

Brussels •

Rhine R.

HOLY ROMAN EMPIRE

HOCHST 1622

WHITE MOUNTAIN 1620

PRAGUE 1648

CORBIE 1636

PERONNE 1654

ROCROI 1643

LOWER PALATINATE

PILSEN 1622

NUREMBERG 1622

Seine R.

Meuse R.

PHILIPPSBURG 1635

WIMPFEN 1622

Paris •

ST. ANTOINE 1652

WIESLOCH 1622

NORDLINGEN 1634

AUGSBURG 1635

BAVARIA

MUNICH 1632

UPPER AUSTRIA 1626

AUSTRIA

Vienna •

PRESSBURG 1619

BREISACH 1638

Loire R.

FRANCE

SWISS CONFEDERATION

HUNGARY

VALTELLINA 1622-1637

Danube R.

LA ROCHELLE 1628

SAVOY

CASAL 1629

THE MILANESE

Milan •

MANTUA 1630

Venice •

PINEROLO 1630

CHERASCO 1631

PIEDMONT

Genoa •

ADRIATIC SEA

SPAIN

PERPIGNAN 1642

CORSICA

PAPAL STATES

Rome •

	Conflict Areas 1618-1630
	Conflict Areas 1630-1648
	Conflict Areas 1648-1669
	Occupied by Spain in 1621
→	Route of Spanish Soldiers
Boundaries in 1618	★ Battle Site

Barcelona •

KINGDOM OF NAPLES

SARDINIA

BALEARICS

MEDITERRANEAN SEA

0   100   200 miles

ceeded to the Bohemian throne in 1617, he refused to honor Rudolf's promise, and the Bohemians rebelled. Since the crown was technically elective, they declared Ferdinand deposed, replacing him with the leading Calvinist of the empire, Frederick II of the Palatinate. Frederick accepted the crown, an act of defiance whose only possible outcome was war between the two religious camps.

For more than a decade, little went wrong for the Hapsburgs. Ferdinand became emperor (1619–1637), and the powerful Catholic Maximilian of Bavaria put his army at the emperor's disposal. Within a year the imperial troops won a shattering victory over the Bohemians at the Battle of the White Mountain. Leading rebels were executed or exiled, and Ferdinand II confiscated all of Frederick's lands. Half were given to Maximilian as a reward for his army, and the remainder were offered to the Spaniards, who occupied them as a valuable base for their struggle with the Dutch. It seemed as though the Catholic and imperial cause had triumphed. But in 1621 the truce between the Spaniards and the Dutch expired, hostilities reopened in the Netherlands, and religious warfare resumed in Germany (see Map 15.2).

Until 1630, however, the Protestants could do little in the face of the armies of the Hapsburgs and Bavaria. In 1622 the Spaniards occupied the Valtellina, a Swiss valley that was the best route for their troops traveling to the Netherlands. And in the empire all attempts by Protestants to help Frederick were beaten back. By 1630 Hapsburg power, bolstered by the creation of a new army, had reached its height.

The man who put together the new imperial army was Albrecht von Wallenstein, a minor Bohemian nobleman and a remarkable opportunist who had become one of the richest men in the empire. In 1624 Wallenstein, realizing that the emperor's great weakness was that he lacked his own army, offered to raise a force if he could billet it and raise its supplies among the population in whatever area it happened to be stationed. Ferdinand agreed, and by 1627 his army had begun to conquer the northern region of the empire, the last major center of Protestant strength. To emphasize his supremacy, Ferdinand issued the Edict of Restitution in 1629, ordering the restoration to Catholics of all the territories they had lost to Protestants—mainly in the northern empire—since 1552.

But these successes were more apparent than real because it was only the extreme disorganization of the empire that permitted a mercenary captain like Wallenstein to achieve such immense power. Once the princes realized their danger, they united against the Hapsburgs; and the forced contributions exacted by Wallenstein's army strengthened their determination to curb this growing menace to their independence. At an electoral diet in 1630, they made Ferdinand dismiss his general by threatening to keep his son from the imperial succession. The emperor's submission proved fatal to his cause, for Sweden and France were now preparing to unleash new aggressions against the Hapsburgs, and Wallenstein was the one man who might have been able to beat back the onslaught.

The year 1630 marked the beginning of a change in fortune. In the spring France, disturbed at Hapsburg power—both Austrian and Spanish—on her eastern border, attacked the duke of Savoy, a Hapsburg ally, and occupied his lands. Then early in 1631 Gustavus Adolphus of Protestant Sweden, fearing that Swedish territories around the Baltic Sea might be threatened, and alarmed at Ferdinand's treatment of Protestants, signed alliances with France and the elector of Saxony. In July he crossed the Baltic, and at the head of a Swedish-Saxon army destroyed the imperial force at Breitenfeld in one of the few decisive battles of the war.

Ferdinand hastily recalled Wallenstein,

whose troops finally met the Swedes in battle at Lützen in 1632. Although Gustavus' soldiers won the day, he himself was killed, and his death saved the Hapsburg dynasty from total destruction. Nothing, however, could restore Ferdinand's former position. The emperor was forced to turn against Wallenstein once more; a few months later he had him assassinated. The removal of the great general marked the end of an era, for he was the last man in more than three centuries capable of establishing unified authority throughout what is now Germany.

Encouraged by Gustavus' success, the empire's princes began to raise new armies, and by 1635 Ferdinand had to make peace with them at the Treaty of Prague. In return for their promise of assistance in driving out the Swedes, Ferdinand agreed to suspend the Edict of Restitution and to grant amnesty to all but Frederick of the Palatinate and a few Bohemian rebels. Ferdinand was renouncing most of his ambitions, and it seemed that peace might return to the battle-scarred land.

But the French could not let matters rest. In 1635 they finally declared war on Ferdinand and occupied the Valtellina. For the next thirteen years, the French and Swedes rained unmitigated disaster on Germany. Peace negotiations began in 1641, but not until 1648 did the combatants agree to lay down arms and sign the treaties of Westphalia. Even thereafter the war between France and Spain, pursued mainly in the Spanish Netherlands, continued for another eleven years; and hostilities around the Baltic among Sweden, Denmark, Poland, and Russia, which had started in 1611, did not end until 1661.

The wars killed off more than a third of Germany's population. They caused serious economic dislocations, because a number of princes—already in serious financial straits—sharply debased their coinage. Their action worsened the continent-wide depression that had begun around 1620 and had brought the

great sixteenth-century boom to an end, causing the first drop in prices since 1500. Few contemporaries perceived the connection between war and economic troubles, but nobody could ignore the interminable drain on men and resources or the widespread effects of the conflict on the life of the time.

THE PEACE OF WESTPHALIA

By the 1630s it was already becoming apparent that the fighting was getting out of hand, and that it would not be easy to bring the conflicts to an end. There had never been such widespread or devastating warfare; in the view of many diplomats, the settlement had to be far more decisive and of far greater scope than any negotiated before. And they were right. When at last the treaties were signed, after seven years of negotiation in the German province of Westphalia, a landmark in international relations was passed—remarkable not only because an anarchic situation was brought under control, but because a new system for dealing with wars was created.

The most important innovation was the gathering at the peace conference of all the participants in the Thirty Years' War, rather than the usual practice of bringing only two or three belligerents together. The presence of ambassadors from Bavaria, Brandenburg, Denmark, France, the Holy Roman Empire, Saxony, Spain, Sweden, Switzerland, and the United Provinces made possible, for the first time in European history, a series of all-embracing treaties that dealt with nearly every major international issue at one stroke. Although the Franco-Spanish and the Baltic wars continued for more than ten years, the Peace of Westphalia in 1648 became the first comprehensive rearrangement of the map of Europe in modern history (Map 15.3).

The principal beneficiaries were France and Sweden, the chief aggressors during the last decade of the war. France made important

MAP 15.3: TERRITORIAL CHANGE 1648–1661

This map shows the territorial changes that took place after the Thirty Years' War. The treaties of Westphalia (1648) and the Pyrenees (1659) arranged the principal transfers, but the settlements in the Baltic were not confirmed until the *treaties of Copenhagen, Oliva (both 1660), and Kardis (1661). The arrows indicate the direction of conquests and the date at which they were accomplished.*

gains on her northeastern frontier, notably the provinces of Alsace and Lorraine; and Sweden obtained extensive territories in the Holy Roman Empire, among them Eastern Pomerania, Bremen, and Verden. The main loser was the House of Hapsburg, since both the United Provinces and the Swiss Confederation were recognized as independent states and the German princes, who agreed not to join an alliance against the emperor, were otherwise given almost complete independence.

However, the princes' autonomy was not officially established until 1657, when they elected as emperor Leopold I, the head of the House of Hapsburg, in return for two promises. First, Leopold would give no help to his cousins, the rulers of Spain; and second, the empire would be a *Fürstenstaat*, a prince's state, in which each ruler would be completely free from imperial interference. This freedom permitted the rise of Brandenburg-Prussia and the growth of absolutism within the major principalities. In addition the Hapsburgs' capitulation prepared the way for their reorientation toward the east along the Danube River —the beginnings of the Austro-Hungarian Empire.

For more than a century the settlement reached at Westphalia was regarded as the basis for all international negotiations. The Treaty of the Pyrenees in 1659, ending the war between France and Spain, and the treaties of Copenhagen and Oliva in 1660 and Kardis in 1661, ending the Baltic struggles, were considered only to have rounded out the agreements made at Westphalia. Even major new accords, such as the one that ended yet another series of wars in 1713, were viewed primarily as adjustments of the decisions of 1648.

In practice of course multinational conferences were no more effective than brief, limited negotiations as means of reducing international tensions. Wars continued to break out with monotonous frequency, and armies grew in size and skill. But diplomats did believe that the total situation was under better control and that the anarchy of the Thirty Years' War had been replaced by something more stable and more clearly defined.

Confidence was reinforced as it became clear after 1648 that armies were trying to improve discipline and avoid the excesses of the previous thirty years. The treatment of civilians became more orderly, and on the battlefield the casualty rate went from as high as one death per three soldiers in the 1630s down to one death in seven at worst, or one in twenty at best, during the early 1700s. As religious passions declined, combat became less vicious, and the aims of warfare changed significantly.

The most obvious difference after the Peace of Westphalia was that France replaced Spain as the Continent's dominant power, and that northern countries—especially England and the Netherlands—took over economic leadership from the Mediterranean, where it had been centered for 2,000 years. But behind this outward shift a more fundamental transformation was taking place. What had become apparent in the later stages of the Thirty Years' War was that Europe's states were interested in fighting only for economic, territorial, or political advantages. Dynastic aims were still important—and were to remain so for centuries —but supranational goals like religious advancement could no longer determine foreign policies.

The Thirty Years' War was the last major conflict in which two religious camps organized their forces as blocs. After 1648 such connections gave way to more purely national interests. Despite the universal wish for peace, Pope Innocent X, furious at the Catholics' compromises, denounced the treaties of Westphalia, but his voice went unheard. The declining influence of ideology meant that men would henceforth pursue the glory of their nation or ruler—not the advantage of their faith. This shift marked the final stage of a process that had long been under way: the emergence of the state as the basic unit and object of loyalty in Western civilization.

If the new aims of foreign policies, such as economic advantage, could not yet arouse the same passions as religion, they nevertheless revealed that commitment to one's country, and an interest in the way it was run, was becoming important throughout Europe. Indeed, at the very time that tensions were lessening in international affairs, they reached a new height in the internal affairs of a number of countries. Just as the mid-seventeenth century witnessed the most intense phase and also the settlement of the difficulties among states, so too did it mark the climax and the resolution of an era of upheaval and revolt within states.

II. REVOLTS

The warfare of the century from the 1560s to the 1660s affected the relations between rulers and their subjects no less than relations between countries. The additional taxes and bureaucrats required by the military created burdens that provoked the resistance to governments that was a major feature of the century. Some of these domestic conflicts had international dimensions—the Dutch revolt, the French civil wars, and the upheavals in Bohemia and Germany all blended in, as we have seen, with much wider wars—but they were equally important in shaping the internal administration of Europe's states. By the time the conflicts died away, after a particularly acute outburst in the mid-seventeenth century, they had helped create the national political structures that endured until the age of the French Revolution.

ENGLAND

The one attempt at a radical transformation of politics and society—a revolution—occurred in England. Compared to her neighbors, England seemed relatively calm during the second half of the sixteenth century and the early years of the seventeenth. But tensions were rising that were to produce the most far-reaching upheaval of the age.

Elizabeth I
The tranquillity of the period from the 1560s to the 1630s had several causes. With only occasional fighting to support, and that largely at sea, England was far less affected by war than the Continental states. Furthermore the people were already united by such common bonds as a national reformation and the institution of Parliament, so the crown did not experience the severe challenges that plagued royal authority in contemporary Spain and France. And the monarch also happened to be extraordinarily clever at the task of calming discontent.

Elizabeth I (1558–1603) has been an appealing figure to every generation because she combined shrewd hard-headedness and a sense of the possible with a charming appearance of frailty. Her qualities are easily appreciated: her dedication to the task of government; her astute choice of advisers—with the one exception of the handsome young earl of Essex, for whom she developed a disastrous infatuation near the end of her life; her careful and usually successful handling of political problems; and her ability to feel the mood of her people, to catch their spirit, to inspire their unquestioning enthusiasm.

Her concern for loyalty made Elizabeth reluctant to break openly with those who opposed her, but this also led to an indecisiveness that had unfortunate consequences, notably where the succession was concerned. Her refusal to marry caused serious uncertainties, and it was only because of the astute planning of Elizabeth's chief minister, Robert Cecil, that a crisis was avoided when she died in 1603 without naming a successor. Thanks to Cecil's diplomacy, the king of Scotland, James Stuart, succeeded without incident.

The advisers Elizabeth appointed to the Privy Council, the chief government body, were essential to her success. They distilled the flow of administrative business and worked closely with the queen, but they also represented different views. Some advocated caution, inaction, and discretion in international affairs, whereas others favored an aggressive foreign policy. Elizabeth had great skill in balancing the contrasting viewpoints and her clever maneuvering assured her of her ministers' loyalty at all times.

Even more important than her approval of a policy was the patronage that accompanied her pleasure. Because the government's powers and hence its need for officials had grown rapidly since the 1530s, dozens of new posts were being created for the crown to bestow. Whoever was the queen's favorite therefore had the best chance of nominating a successful candidate for a vacancy in the bureaucracy. But as a result of the patronage system, a swarm of parasites descended on London, hopeful of advancement. Many Englishmen viewed this development with distaste, and after Elizabeth's death it became the cause of serious cleavage between crown and subjects.

Economic and Social Change

Another force with dangerous implications for the future was the result of rapidly shifting patterns in English society. With new methods of warfare, nobles no longer had a vital military role to play. Moreover they were losing their preeminence in government; nearly all the chief ministers were new men in national life, and the House of Commons was becoming at least the equal of the House of Lords in Parliament. The nobles were also not benefiting as much from England's rising prosperity as were other sections of society. Thus they were losing their hold over the power, wealth, and government of the country.

The gentry, the new group that joined them at the head of society, ranged from people considered great men in a parish or other small locality to courtiers considered great men throughout the land. There were never more than sixty nobles during Elizabeth's reign, but the gentry may have numbered close to 20,000 by the time she died.

The majority of the gentry were doing well economically, primarily from the purchase of land that the crown had confiscated when the monasteries were dissolved, in the 1530s. They also benefited from spiraling food prices and rising rents. Many profited too from crown offices; a number became involved in industrial activity; and hundreds invested in new overseas trading and colonial ventures. The gentry's participation in commerce made them unique among the landed classes of Europe, whose members were traditionally contemptuous of business affairs, and it testified to the enterprise and vigor of these Englishmen. Long important in local administration, they wanted power at the center of government, and they flocked to the House of Commons, for they regarded Parliament as the instrument of their drive for power. Their ambitions were to pose a serious threat to the monarchy, especially when linked with the effects of rapid economic change.

In the 1550s, stimulated by the general boom in trade and by the help of leading courtiers who recognized the importance of opening new markets, England's merchants began to transform her economic situation. During the next half-century, they started commerce with Russia, the Baltic and Mediterranean lands, the Levant, and East Asia. Although cloth remained the dominant export until the middle of the seventeenth century, it was joined by a growing trade in the reexport of overseas goods, such as Newfoundland fish, which were distributed throughout Europe.

Early attempts at colonization were not successful, with the exception of those in Ireland;

but vital experience was gained, and the financial rewards were sometimes significant. Within England, moreover, there was significant industrial development. The mining and manufacture of a whole variety of commodities, from alum to wire, grew at a rapid pace, and shipbuilding became a major industry. The production of coal alone increased fourteenfold between 1540 and 1680, creating many new fortunes and an expertise in industrial and commercial techniques that took England far ahead of her neighbors.

The most revealing evidence of England's new position was the founding of nearly fifty companies devoted to overseas exploration, commerce, or colonization between 1600 and 1630. The more successful ones laid the foundations for the British Empire. In India, the Caribbean islands, Bermuda, Virginia, Maryland, New England, and Canada, colonies were started that within a century were to become the most populous offshoots of any European nation.

The economic vigor and growth that ensued, apparent also in industrial and agricultural advances, gave the classes that benefited the most—the gentry and the merchants—a cohesion and a sense of purpose that made it dangerous to oppose them when they felt their rights infringed. They increasingly regarded themselves as the leaders of the nation, second only to the nobility, whose importance was diminishing. They wanted respect for their wishes, and they bitterly resented the economic interference and political high-handedness of Elizabeth's successors.

What made the situation particularly dangerous was that many of the gentry were sympathetic to the Puritans. These religious reformers believed that the Protestant Anglican Church established by Elizabeth was still too close to Roman Catholicism, and they wanted further changes. Elizabeth had refused, and although she had tried to avoid a confrontation, in the last years of her reign she had had to silence the most outspoken of her critics. As a result, the Puritans had become a disgruntled minority, ready to add their demands to those of the gentry (some of whom were themselves Puritans). By the 1630s, when the government tried to repress such religious dissent more vigorously, there were many Englishmen who felt that the monarchy was leading the country astray and was ignoring the wishes of its subjects. Leading parliamentarians in particular soon came to believe that only revolution could restore justice to England.

Parliament and the Law

The place where the gentry made their views known to the government was Parliament, the nation's supreme legislative body. Three-quarters of the lower chamber, the House of Commons, consisted of members of the gentry. These men were better educated than before; at the end of the sixteenth century, more than half of them had attended a university, and slightly less than half had legal training. Through the House of Commons, they were beginning to make a bid for their share of government, and since the Commons had to approve all taxation, these members had no compunction about using the power of the purse to promote their ambitions.

The monarchy was still the dominant force in the country when Elizabeth died in 1603, but Parliament's challenge to that supremacy was gathering momentum. Although the queen had been known for her care with money, in the last twenty years of her reign, her resources had been overtaxed by the war with Spain and an economic depression. Consequently she bequeathed to her successor, James I, a huge debt— £400,000, the equal of a year's royal revenue—and the struggle to pay it off gave the Commons the leverage to expand their powers even further.

Trouble began to mount in 1604, at the first meeting of Parliament in the reign of James I (1603–1625). Puritans who still hoped to

change the Anglican Church by legislation and gentry who wanted to extend the powers of the House of Commons led the opposition to the king. They began to dominate proceedings, and through 1629 (after which there was no session for eleven years) they engaged in a running battle with the monarchy. They blocked the union of England with Scotland that James sought. They drew up an "Apology" explaining his mistakes and his ignorance,

The decisions and policies of English monarchs had often been challenged by Parliament, but these challenges were strongest and most successful during the reigns of James I and Charles I in sessions of the House of Commons such as the one shown here in 1624. (Photo: Historical Pictures Service, Chicago)

as a Scotsman, of English traditions. And they wrung repeated concessions from him until in

1624 they gained the unprecedented right to discuss foreign policy.

The parliamentarians used the law as justification for their resistance to royal power. The basic legal system of the country was the common law—justice administered on the basis of precedents and parliamentary statutes, decided with the assistance of juries. This system stood in contrast to Roman law, prevalent on the Continent, where royal edicts could make law, and decisions were reached by judges without juries. Such practices existed in England only in a few royal courts of law, such as the Star Chamber. Proceedings here were popular, because they were quicker, and powerful men could not influence the decisions of the judges who were usually prominent men themselves.

Common lawyers, whose leaders were also prominent in the House of Commons, resented the growth of this rival system, and they attacked royal courts in Parliament. Both James and his successor were accused of putting pressure on the judges to gain their ends—particularly after they won a series of famous cases involving a subject's right to criticize the monarch. Thus the crown could be portrayed as disregarding not only the desires of the people but the law itself. Technically the king had extensive rights, but when he exercised them without regard to Parliament's wishes, his actions began to take on the appearance of tyranny.

Rising Antagonisms

The confrontation in Parliament grew worse during the 1620s. In 1621 the House of Commons forced the king's lord chancellor, Francis Bacon, out of office for accepting bribes, and in reaction to their attacks, James had some of the members sent to prison. Under his son Charles I (1625–1649), the hostilities intensified. At the Parliament of 1628–1629, the crown faced an open challenge, whose climax was the Petition of Right, an appeal that has

become a landmark in constitutional history. The petition demanded an end to imprisonment without cause shown, to taxation without the consent of Parliament, to martial law in peacetime, and to the billeting of troops among civilians. Charles agreed, in the hope of gaining much-needed subsidies, but then broke his word.

The issue was now clearly whether Parliament, as the representative of the nation, would hold an essential position in the government alongside the king. To stop further confrontation Charles ordered Parliament dissolved, but in a move of great daring, two members denied the king even this hallowed right by holding the speaker of the House in his chair while they passed a final angry resolution.

Resentful subjects were clearly on the brink of open defiance of their sovereign. Puritans, common lawyers, and disenchanted country gentry had captured the House of Commons, and Charles could avoid further trouble only by refusing to call another session of Parliament. This he managed to do for eleven years, all the while increasing the repression of Puritanism and resorting to unpopular extraordinary measures to raise revenues.

But the smooth sailing could not last long. The leaders of the Puritan and parliamentary opposition met regularly after 1630, and they finally had the opportunity in 1639 to extract from the king the concessions they sought when the Calvinist Scots took up arms rather than accept the Anglican prayer book. Religious persecution had once again sparked military combat: the Scots invaded England, and Charles had to raise an army. To obtain the necessary funds, he turned to Parliament, which demanded that he first redress its grievances. When he resisted, civil war followed.

The English Civil War

The Parliament that met in 1640 was dominated by John Pym, a Puritan and a prominent critic of the monarch for nearly twenty years, who opened the session with a two-hour speech outlining the long-standing grievances against both church and government. Charles refused to change his policies and the Commons refused to grant a subsidy, and so the king angrily dissolved the session. But there was no way to pay for an army without taxes. By the summer of 1640, the Scots occupied most of northern England, and Charles had no alternative but to summon a new Parliament. This one sat for thirteen years, earning the appropriate name of the Long Parliament.

Pym was in complete control of Parliament for the first year. The House of Commons passed legislation abolishing the royal courts, such as Star Chamber, and establishing the writ of habeas corpus (which prevented imprisonment without cause shown) as mandatory; it declared taxation without parliamentary consent illegal; and it ruled that Parliament had to meet at least once every three years, with the additional proviso that the current assembly could not be dissolved without its consent. Meanwhile, the Puritans were preparing to reform the church. Oliver Cromwell, one of the leading members of the House, demanded abolition of the Anglican Book of Common Prayer and strongly attacked the institution of episcopacy. The climactic vote came the next year, when the Commons passed their Grand Remonstrance, outlining for the king all the legislation they had put through and asking that bishops be deprived of their votes in the House of Lords.

This was the prelude to a more revolutionary assault on the structure of the church, but significantly the Grand Remonstrance passed by only 11 votes. A moderate party was detaching itself from Pym, and the beginning of a royalist party was appearing. The nation's chief grievances had been redressed, and there was no longer a uniform desire for change. Still Charles misjudged the situation and tried to arrest five leaders of the opposition, including Pym, ostensibly for plotting treason with the Scots. But Parliament refused to order their arrest, and the citizens of London, now openly hostile to Charles, sheltered the five.

In June 1642 the king received the Commons' final demands: complete parliamentary control over the church, the appointment of ministers and judges, and the army. This would have meant the abdication of all effective royal authority, and Charles refused. Gradually England began to split in two. By the late summer both sides had assembled armies, and the Civil War was under way.

The fascination of this great revolution that sought to transform English government and society has been endless. Much attention has been given to religion and politics, to the motives of Puritans and parliamentarians; it is now clear that simple differentiations cannot be made. Half the parliamentarians joined the king; the Puritans were split; and many members of the gentry, not noticeably committed to either of these opposition groups, fought against Charles.

What made so many people overcome their habitual loyalty to the monarchy? One interesting distinction is that the royalists in Parliament were considerably younger than their opponents; this suggests that it was long experience with the Stuarts and nostalgia for Elizabethan times that created dedicated revolutionaries. Another clear division was regional. The south and east of England were primarily antiroyalist while the north and west were mostly royalist. What this implied was that the more cosmopolitan areas, which were closer to the Continent and also the principal centers of Puritanism, were primarily on Parliament's side. Frequently the decision was very much a personal matter: a great man would take his locality to one side because his old rival, the great man a few miles away, had chosen the other. Those who opposed the Church of England were unequivocally antiroyalist, but they were a minority in the country and hardly even a majority in the House of Commons. Like all revolutions, this one was animated by a small group of radicals (in this case Puritans) who alone kept the momentum going.

The Stuarts' long alienation of their subjects can account for the situation in 1640, when Charles could find no support anywhere, but by the end of 1641 many felt that the necessary remedies had been obtained. Thus apart from Puritanism—or to put it more generally, apart from opposition to the Church of England—

This contemporary Dutch engraving of the execution of Charles I shows the scaffold in front of the Banqueting House in Whitehall—a building that still can be seen in London. On the far right of the scaffold, the executioner displays the severed head for the crowd. (Photo: The Granger Collection)

the historian can point to no basic cause but only to the influence of local circumstances to explain how two sides came into being in the summer of 1642.

The Course of Conflict

The first round of fighting was indecisive—a year of small successes on both sides. Then in 1643 the antiroyalists, supported by the Scottish army, gained the first military advantage. The alliance with the Scots was Pym's last accomplishment, because shortly thereafter he died, and the first major split in the antiroyalist ranks occurred.

Increasingly during the last months of Pym's life, a group known as the Independents urged that the Anglican Church be replaced by the congregational system, in which

each local congregation, free of all central authority, would decide its own form of worship. The most important representative of the Independents in Parliament was Oliver Cromwell (1599–1658). Opposed to them were the Presbyterians, who wanted to establish a strictly organized Calvinist system, much like the one that had been created in Scotland, in which local congregations were subject to centralized authority, although laymen did participate in church government. Since both the Scots, whose alliance was vital in the war, and a majority of the members of the Commons were Presbyterians,[3] Cromwell agreed to give way, but only for the moment. In addition to the religious issue, there was also a quarrel over the goals of the war because the antiroyalists were unsure whether they ought to attempt to defeat Charles completely. This dispute crossed religious lines, though on the whole the Independents were more determined to force him into total submission, and in the end they had their way.

Meanwhile the fighting continued. Hoping to create a more potent fighting force, Cromwell persuaded the House of Commons early in 1645 to create a completely reorganized army, the New Model Army, to bring the war to an end. Whipped to fervor by sermons, prayers, and the singing of psalms, the New Model Army became a formidable force. At the Battle of Naseby in June, it won a major victory over the royalists and a year later Charles surrendered.

The next two years were chaotic. The Presbyterians and Independents quarreled over what to do with the king, and finally the Civil War resumed. This time the Presbyterians and Scots backed Charles against the Independ-

ents. But even with this alliance the royalist forces were no match for the New Model Army; Cromwell soon defeated his opponents and captured the king.

At the same time, in 1647, the Independents abolished the House of Lords and removed all Presbyterians from the House of Commons, leaving behind a "rump" of less than 100 men, about a fifth of the original membership of the Long Parliament. The Rump Parliament tried to negotiate with Charles but discovered that he continued to plot a return to power. With Cromwell's approval the Commons decided that their monarch, untrustworthy and a troublemaker, would have to die. A trial without legality was held, and though many of the participants refused to sign the death warrant, the "holy, anointed" king was executed by his subjects in January 1649, to the horror of all Europe and most of England.

England Under Cromwell: The Interregnum
Oliver Cromwell, the hero of the New Model Army, was now master of England. The republic established after Charles' execution was officially ruled by the Rump Parliament, but a Council of State led by Cromwell controlled policy, with the backing of the army. Military activity was far from over because first an Irish rebellion had to be crushed—and it was, brutally—and then the Scots revolted in support of Charles II, the executed monarch's son. This last threat was not suppressed until late in 1651.

At home Cromwell had to contend with a ferment of political and social ideas. One group, known as the Levellers, demanded the vote for nearly all adult males and parliamentary elections every other year. The men of property among the Puritans, notably Cromwell himself, were disturbed by the political egalitarianism implied by these proposals and insisted that only men with an "interest" in

---

[3] This was a majority of a depleted House, however, because a few dozen royalists had departed from the Commons during 1641, especially after the Grand Remonstrance, and they never returned.

England—that is, land—should be qualified to vote.[4]

Even more radical were the Diggers, a communistic sect that sought to implement the spirit of primitive Christianity by abolishing personal property; the Society of Friends, which stressed personal inspiration as the source of faith and all action; and the Fifth Monarchists, a messianic group who believed that the "saints"—themselves—should rule because the Day of Judgment was at hand. Men of great ability contributed to the fantastic flood of pamphlets and suggestions that poured forth in these years—the poet John Milton, Cromwell's secretary, was one of the most prominent pamphleteers—and their ideas inspired many future revolutionaries. But at the time they merely put Cromwell on the defensive, forcing him to maintain control at all costs.

Cromwell himself—as an Independent among the Puritans, a staunch parliamentarian, and a country gentleman—fought for two overriding causes: religious freedom (except for Anglicanism and Catholicism) and constitutional government. But neither came within his grasp, and he grew increasingly unhappy at the Rump's refusal to enact reforms. When the assembly tried to perpetuate itself, he dissolved it in 1653 (the final end of the Long Parliament).

During the remaining five years of his life, Cromwell tried desperately to lay down a new constitutional structure for his government. He always hoped that Parliament itself would establish the perfect political system for England. In fact, though, the three Parliaments he called during these five years seemed to have no inclination to undertake such reforms. Cromwell refused on principle to influence proceedings—except to dismiss the assembly when he felt a selfish faction was seeking its own ends—but in so acting he ignored the realities of politics and left his ideals unfulfilled.

Cromwell was driven by noble aspirations, but he adhered to them so intensely that he could make few compromises. Finally, when he felt he had no other recourse since nobody else was as high-minded as he was, he created a blatant military dictatorship, because the alternatives seemed worse. From 1653 on he was called lord protector and ruled through eleven major generals, each responsible for a different district of England and supported by a tax on royalist estates. To quell dissent he banned newspapers, and to prevent disorder he took such measures as enlisting innkeepers as government spies.

Cromwell always remained a reluctant revolutionary; he hated power and sought only limited ends. Some revolutionaries, like Lenin, have a good idea of where they would like to be carried by events; others, like Cromwell, move painfully, hesitantly, and uncertainly to the extremes they finally reach. It was because he sought England's benefit so urgently and because he considered the nation too precious to abandon to irreligion or tyranny that he remained determinedly in command to the end of his life.

Those final years, however, were filled with plots led by Levellers, royalists, and other dissidents of every shade of belief. The court that gathered around the young Stuart heir, Charles II, who had been in exile on the Continent since 1648, was a breeding ground of conspiracy. Only a superb counterespionage system, organized by the head of Cromwell's postal services (who simply read the mails), enabled him to quench all the plots.

Gradually more traditional forms reap-

---

[4] It should be recalled that voting rights were still tightly restricted; parliamentary elections by no means assured every Englishman a voice in government. In a town only the freemen (a small group, rarely more than about 20 percent of the population) and in the country only owners of land worth at least 40 shillings in rent a year (considerably less than 10 percent) were entitled to vote.

peared. The Parliament of 1656 offered Cromwell the crown, and though he refused, he took the title of "His Highness" and ensured that the succession would go to his son. Cromwell was monarch in all but name; only he assured stability. After he died his quiet, retiring son Richard proved no match for the scheming generals of the army. To bring an end to the chaos, General George Monck, the commander of a well-disciplined force in Scotland, marched south, assumed control, invited Charles II home from exile, and thus in May of 1660 brought the interregnum to an end.

The Results of the Revolution

Cromwell's chief success had been in foreign policy: he had strengthened the navy, captured Jamaica, gained Dunkirk, and in general reasserted England's importance in international affairs. But at home only the actions taken during the first months of the Long Parliament, in 1640 and 1641—the abolition of leading royal courts, the prohibition of taxation without parliamentary consent, and the establishment of the writ of habeas corpus—persisted beyond the interregnum. Otherwise everything was much the same as before: bishops and lords were reinstated; the repression of religious dissent was resumed; Parliament was called and dissolved by the monarch; and though many old feudal rights were annulled, the king got a set annual income in their place. Inertia and tradition reasserted themselves in the end.

The obvious long-term political and social changes were so minor that one might well question whether this had indeed been a revolution. By comparison with the French and Russian revolutions, its legacy was slim at best. And yet in one fundamental way it had altered the structure of government and society. Henceforth the gentry could no longer be denied a decisive voice in politics. In essence this had been their revolution, and they had succeeded. When in the 1680s a king again tried to impose his wishes on the country without reference to Parliament, there was no need for another major upheaval. A quiet, bloodless coup reaffirmed the new role of the gentry and Parliament.

Thus a new settlement was reached after a long period of growing unease and open conflict. The English could now enjoy untroubled a system of rule that with only gradual modification was to remain in force for some two centuries.

FRANCE

Before 1789, the civil wars of the sixteenth century were the closest France came to a revolutionary situation, but the tensions did not disappear when Henry IV brought the fighting to an end. Although the monarchy managed to extend its powers over the next fifty years, resistance continued until a final violent confrontation between the central government and its opponents in the 1640s and 1650s ended in victory for the crown. That confrontation, known as the Fronde, did not develop into a radical attempt to reorganize society, but it did parallel the contemporary English revolution in that its outcome settled the political and social structure of the country for over a century.

Henry IV

Henry IV began the process of strengthening royal power as soon as the civil wars were over. During the remaining years of his reign, from 1598 to 1610, opposition was muted, and he was able to establish his authority in a variety of ways. He mollified the traditional landed aristocracy, known as the nobility of the sword, by giving its leaders places on the chief executive body, the Council of Affairs, and then, when he felt strong enough, by shunting them off to their country estates with large financial settlements that were little better than bribes.

The principal bureaucrats, known as the nobility of the robe, required more careful treatment. They were a formidable group, in control of the country's administration, and led by great officeholding dynasties that were highly suspicious of newcomers. Henry did not try to undermine their position, but he made sure to turn their interests to his benefit. Since all crown offices had to be bought, he used the system both to raise revenues and to confirm the bureaucrats in their loyalty to the king. His tactics involved not only an acceleration in the sales of offices, but also the invention of a new device, an annual fee known as the *paulette*. Regular payments of the *paulette* ensured that an officeholder's job would remain in his family when he died. This not only increased royal profits (by the end of Henry's reign, receipts from the sales accounted for one-twelfth of crown revenues), but also reduced the flow of newcomers and thus strengthened the commitment of existing officeholders to the status quo, that is, to the crown.

By 1610 Henry had succeeded in imposing his will throughout France to a degree that would have been unimaginable in 1598. His treasury was solvent, neither great nobles nor Huguenots gave him trouble, and he was secure enough to plan an invasion of the Holy Roman Empire to extend his power even further. He was assassinated as he was about to leave Paris to join his army, but he had already brought about a quite extraordinary revival of royal authority.

Economic Affairs

In economic affairs the religious wars had taken a toll that was not so quickly remedied. In the 1550s a most fruitful alliance in trading ventures had developed between merchants and nobles. Significant advances had been made overseas, where the French had begun to encroach on the Portuguese monopoly of slaves, gold, and ivory in West Africa. Great ports such as Bordeaux and Marseilles and trade centers such as Lyons had enjoyed unprecedented prosperity. France possessed more fertile agricultural land than any other country of Europe, and her manufactured goods, notably clothes, had been sought throughout the Continent.

The civil war had changed this rosy situation. Trade had suffered heavily, particularly in the once-bustling coastal areas along the Channel. The overseas effort had come to a halt, and the French had soon been replaced by the Dutch and the English as the principal challengers to the Spanish and Portuguese empires. Taxes had mounted, and a large part of the burden had fallen on the merchants in the form of heavy customs dues. Naturally men had abandoned commerce as soon as they could afford to enter the nobility and gain a tax exemption by buying a royal office. The result was that capital had been diverted from trade to unproductive expenditures, and by the end of the century the nobility had developed a lofty contempt for commerce. French trade did not recover its vitality for more than a hundred years. Agriculture had suffered less, but uprisings of peasants, the main victims of the tax system, occurred almost annually in some part of France from the 1590s until the 1670s.

Although the restoration of stability ended the worst economic disruptions, Henry could do little about the fundamental problems that faced the merchants and the peasants. Nevertheless, once the process of centralization started, the assumption developed that the government was also responsible for the health of economic affairs. This view was justified by a theory known as mercantilism that became an essential ingredient of absolutism.

Mercantilism was more a set of attitudes than a systematic economic theory. Its basic premise—an erroneous one—was that the world contained a fixed amount of wealth and that each nation could enrich itself only at the expense of others. To some thinkers this meant hoarding as much bullion (gold and silver) as possible; to others it required a favorable balance of trade—more exports than imports. All mercantilists, however, agreed that state regulation was necessary for the welfare of a country. A strong, centralized government was the only power that could encourage native industries, control production, set quality standards, allocate resources, establish tariffs, and take other measures to promote prosperity and improve trade. Thus mercantilism was as much a political as an economic viewpoint and fitted in perfectly with Henry's restoration of royal power.

The Regency and Richelieu

Unrest reappeared, however, when Henry's death left the throne to his nine-year-old son, Louis XIII (1610–1643). The widowed queen, Marie de Médicis, serving as regent, dismissed her husband's ministers, and changed his aggressive foreign policy into friendship with the Hapsburgs. The Calvinists feared for their safety, and their stronghold, the southwest, came close to open revolt. The nobles too began to reassert themselves, infuriated because Marie, an Italian, took advice from her fellow countrymen and not from the aristocrats of the kingdom. Led by the prince of Condé, a cousin of Henry IV's, they demanded an investigation of the Council of Regency and particularly of its financial dealings. In the face of these mounting troubles, Marie summoned the Estates General in 1614.

This was the last meeting of the Estates General for 175 years, until the eve of the French Revolution, and its failings demonstrated that the monarchy was the only institution around which the nation could be united. The session revealed only the impotence of those who wished to oppose the throne, and Marie put the issue beyond doubt by declaring her son to be of age and the regency dissolved. There was now nothing left

to investigate, for the Estates General could only offer advice to a king; it had no legislative powers. The remaining aristocratic dissidents were silenced by large bribes, which consumed the entire treasure left by Henry IV, and the Calvinists were partially appeased by guarantees that their status would not be changed.

For a decade after the crisis, the court lacked the energetic direction that was needed to continue the consolidation of power begun by Henry IV. But in 1624 one of Marie's favorites, Armand du Plessis de Richelieu, a churchman who rose to the cardinalate through her favor, took control of the government. For the next eighteen years, there was once more an ambitious and determined head of the central administration.

Many forces pressed on the monarchy as it concentrated its power, and it was Richelieu's great achievement that he kept them in balance. The strongest group was the bureaucracy, whose ranks had been swollen by the sale of office. Richelieu was a classic example of the great ministers of the seventeenth century in that he always paid close attention to the wishes of the bureaucrats and could then face the monarchy as the head of a vast army of indispensable royal servants. He achieved a similar balance with the nobles, whom he integrated into the regime by giving them posts as diplomats, soldiers, officials, and administrators of local regions. With prominent positions in government, the nobility was as eager as the monarch for domestic security.

But the Huguenots still stirred uneasily. Since the death of Henry IV, they had feared new repressions and had engaged in sporadic fighting with the monarchy. The conflict reached a new intensity in the mid-1620s, and the royal army embarked on a systematic destruction of their military power in their stronghold, the southwest, capturing their chief bastion, the port of La Rochelle, in 1628. Richelieu then imposed strict terms. All the guarantees established by the Edict of Nantes were abolished, and though the Huguenots were allowed freedom of worship, they no longer were permitted local independence, which might threaten the unity of the state.

Richelieu also hoped to reduce administrative expenses, but when money was needed for aggression abroad, the good intentions disappeared. The sale of office was allowed to break all bounds: by 1633 it accounted for approximately one-half of the royal revenue. Ten years later more than three-quarters of the crown's direct taxation was needed to pay the salaries of the officeholders. It was a vicious circle, and the only solution was to increase the ordinary taxes, which fell most heavily on the lower classes.

As the burden of taxation mounted, Richelieu had to improve the government's control over the realm to obtain the revenue he needed. He increased the power of the *intendants*, the government's chief agents in the localities, and established them as the principal representatives of the monarchy in each province of France—a counterpoise to the traditionally dominant nobility. The *intendants* recruited for the army, arranged billeting, supervised the raising of taxes, and enforced the king's decrees. They soon came to be hated figures because the rising taxes were creating constant unrest.

In almost every year of the seventeenth century but with greatest intensity from the 1620s to the 1670s, there was a peasant uprising in some area of France, and the main grievance was taxation. But there were other issues too, notably a dislike for the growth of the central government. The peasants were frequently led by local notables who resented the widening powers of the monarchy because the increase in taxes and the rise of the *intendants* threatened their own jurisdictions.

Thus, when Richelieu decided to ignore domestic problems and concentrate on foreign ambitions, he took a major gamble, which almost failed in 1636: troops sent to quell a peasant uprising left a serious gap in France's eastern defenses, allowing Spanish troops to invade to within 100 miles of Paris. But disaster was avoided, the French went on to increasing military success, and when Richelieu died in 1642, it appeared that the twin ambitions of absolutism at home and preeminence abroad were close to realization.

Yet it was clear that the costs of France's foreign policy during the early seventeenth century intensified her domestic problems. Those who resented the growing power of the central government were only waiting for the right moment to reassert themselves. Yet the centralization was so successful that when the moment came, in the Fronde, there was no major effort to reshape the social order or to reorganize the state into a new political system. The Fronde was certainly a strident clash between opposing forces, but it took place within the traditional political and social forms. The principal expressions of discontent came from the upper levels of society: the nobles, townsmen, and members of Parlements. Only occasionally were these groups joined by peasants, who had bitter grievances against taxation and royal officials, and only for a brief while in the city of Bordeaux was there a foretaste of the sweeping revolution that was eventually to overtake France in 1789.

The Fronde

The death of Louis XIII, in 1643, followed by a regency because Louis XIV was only five years old, provided the opportunity for those who wanted to hold back the rise of absolutism. The immediate issues strikingly resembled those of Louis XIII's own minority, under the regency of Marie de Médicis. Louis XIII's widow, Anne of Austria, took over the government and placed all the power in the hands of the Italian-born Cardinal Giulio

Mazarin, a protégé of Richelieu's who symbolized the influence of foreigners and the Catholic Church that both nobles and parlementaires disliked. Moreover, Mazarin used his position to amass a huge fortune. He was therefore a perfect target for the expression of a deep-seated resentment: anger at the encroachment of central government on local authority.

Early in 1648 Mazarin sought to gain a respite from the monarch's perennial financial trouble by withholding payment of the salaries of some royal officials for four years. In response the members of various administrative and legal institutions in Paris, including the Parlement, drew up a charter of demands. They wanted the office of *intendant* abolished, no new offices created, power of approval over the raising of taxes, and enactment of a habeas corpus law. The last two demands reflected what the English Parliament was seeking at this very time, but the first two were long-standing French grievances, intensified by the officers' fear for their class identity and authority in the face of royal power, and by general opposition to newly created officials and taxes.

Mazarin reacted by arresting the Paris Parlement's leaders, thus sparking a popular rebellion in the city that forced him and the royal family to flee from the capital—an experience the young Louis XIV never forgot. In the spring of 1649, Mazarin promised to redress the parlementaires' grievances, and he was allowed to return to Paris. But the trouble was far from over; during that summer uprisings spread throughout France, particularly among peasants and in the old Huguenot stronghold, the southwest.

The most turbulent developments took place in the city of Bordeaux, where the parlementaires lost control and minor artisans and lawyers, furious at the taxes imposed by the crown and eager to revenge themselves on the less-burdened upper orders of society, took over the municipal government. Peasants and street mobs roamed the city, directing their hostility as much at the rich and powerful as at the representatives of the king.

From Mazarin's point of view, however, a more direct threat was posed by two generals who had turned against the government: Henri de Turenne and Louis II of Bourbon, prince of Condé, who had won a series of brilliant military victories in the 1640s and paved the way for France's gains at Westphalia in 1648. Condé was particularly dangerous because he was the head of the greatest noble family in France, and many aristocrats followed his lead. Their aims had not changed much since the days of the Guises eighty years before: they wanted Mazarin removed, their local powers restored, and a more influential position at court. Some nobles made brief alliances with the regional parlementaires, but each group wanted power for itself, and thus they soon drew apart.

Capitalizing on the disillusionment that soon resulted from the perpetual unrest, Mazarin began to reassert the position of the monarchy. Turenne was simply bought over; military force and the threat to use it subdued Paris and most of the rural rebels; Condé, losing support, fled to Spain; and the vulnerable regency was brought to an end by the declaration that Louis was of age in 1652. When Bordeaux finally fell to royal troops the next year, the Fronde was virtually over. Although peasants continued their occasional regional uprisings for many years to come, no other element in French society seriously challenged the crown as the basis for order in the realm.

Mazarin's remaining years in power, until his death in 1661, were relatively free of trouble. In foreign affairs he brought the war with Spain to a triumphant conclusion at the Treaty of the Pyrenees in 1659. At home the nobles had now been weakened as never before; the royal administration, centered on the *intend-ants*, faced no significant resistance; and the parlements subsided into quiescence, their demands all rejected when Louis was declared of age. This outcome was very different from the situation across the Channel in 1661, but just as surely as England, France had found a stable solution for long-standing conflicts.

SPAIN

For Spain the upheavals of the mid-seventeenth century were little short of disastrous. Until they erupted, she was the most powerful state in Europe; when they were over, she had lost her preeminence and was on her way to becoming a second-class power. Yet the seeds of her difficulties—primarily administrative and financial—were already visible in the sixteenth century.

Stresses in the Reign of Philip II

Philip's chief problem was the lack of unity in his diverse domains. From his father he inherited the Low Countries, Naples, Sardinia, Sicily, and Spain and her New World territories. In 1580 Portugal and her possessions also came under his control.

To hold this sprawling empire together, Philip developed an elaborate bureaucracy. But he was an obsessively suspicious man, and he therefore determined to maintain close control over the administrative structure by keeping in touch with every decision. As a result proceedings were agonizingly slow and inefficient in both important and trivial matters. The effect on military affairs was crippling; commanders in the field were often paralyzed, waiting for orders from home before taking action. Moreover the bureaucracy was run by Castilian nobles, who were resented as outsiders in other regions of the empire.

The standing army also caused the king

problems. Although the military gave the throne potent support, it was the regime's single largest expense. The cost was readily undertaken since the logistic and administrative needs of the army stimulated the growth of bureaucracy and government authority. But the populace was less appreciative of these outlays, particularly when, to meet some of the expense and to emphasize the might of the crown, soldiers were lodged in the homes of ordinary citizens without recompense. This aroused bitter resentment, especially in the Low Countries, where the Spanish troops were regarded as foreigners.

Within the Iberian peninsula, however, Philip was able to overcome the resentment by using religious belief to arouse his subjects' loyalty. Spaniards regarded their country as the bastion of Catholicism, and Philip's devoutness reflected their mood perfectly. He eradicated any sign of heresy, and his enmity toward unorthodoxy affected even the great flowering of Spanish mysticism, led by St. Theresa of Avila. Neither the king nor the ecclesiastical hierarchy could feel comfortable about the mystics because such extremes of personal faith seemed to weaken the position of the Catholic Church. Nonetheless Philip's emphasis on the nation's faith powerfully stimulated Spain's political cohesion, which was promoted rather than hindered by the military activity in behalf of the Church.

Economic Problems

In other areas, notably the economy, there was little Philip could do to relieve the strains of constant warfare. Spain was a rich country in Philip's reign, but the most profitable activities were monopolized by limited groups, often foreigners. Because royal policy valued administrative convenience above social benefit, the city of Seville was arbitrarily given control over commerce with the New World so as to simplify supervision of this enormous source of income. Other lucrative pursuits, such as wool and wine production, were dominated by a small coterie of insiders who made large profits but needed little manpower. And the pasturage rights throughout Castile that the crown granted sheep breeders removed vast areas of land from use by growers of foodstuffs. The only important economic activity whose income spread beyond a restricted circle was the prosperous Mediterranean trade. This commerce, centered in Barcelona, brought wealth to much of Aragon.

The profits made by non-Spaniards were the most obvious example of the limited domestic benefit of Spain's vast wealth. Most of the American treasure was sent abroad to repay German and Italian bankers whose loans kept Philip's troops in the field. Apart from Seville the cities that gained most from the new wealth were Genoa and Antwerp. And the Genoese mercantile community, with long experience in international finance, dominated Seville's economic life and played a crucial role in financing Philip's campaigns. Antwerp, always important as the meeting place for traders from the Mediterranean and the North, now gained prominence as the focus of Spanish activity in the Low Countries.

Thus even though the influx of silver into Spain continued to rise (it quadrupled between the 1550s and 1590s), the money was not profitably invested within the country. Drastically overextended in foreign commitments, the king declared himself bankrupt three times during his reign. His misguided policies, especially his continuing military involvements, were causing a slow economic deterioration.

Spain's futile struggles with the Dutch and later with the French proved to be the final blows in a succession of multiplying difficulties—economic, political, and military. For a while it seemed that the problems might be overcome because the second half of Philip III's reign (1598–1621), following the truce signed with the Dutch in 1609, was a time of peace. But in fact Philip's government was incompetent and corrupt, capable neither of dealing with the serious consequences of generations of excessive war spending nor of broadening the country's limited list of exports beyond wool and wine. Moreover, when the flow of treasure from the New World began to dwindle after 1600, the crown was deprived of a major source of income that it was unable to replace (see accompanying table). The decline was caused partly by a growing use of precious metals in the New World colonies but more importantly by a demographic disaster that overtook the Indians who worked as laborers and miners. Disease, overwork, and a drastic fall in the birth rate

IMPORTS OF TREASURE TO SPAIN FROM THE NEW WORLD, 1601–1660

DECADE	TOTAL VALUE*
1601–1610	66,970,000
1611–1620	65,568,000
1621–1630	62,358,000
1631–1640	40,110,000
1641–1650	30,641,000
1651–1660	12,785,000

* In ducats
Adapted from J. H. Elliott, *Imperial Spain 1469–1716*, New York, 1964, p. 175.

reduced their numbers with incredible speed. In Mexico and northern Guatemala alone, there had been approximately 25 million natives when the Spaniards first arrived in 1519. By the 1650s there were only 1.5 million.

In the meantime tax returns at home were shrinking, and at best they never covered expenses. The most significant factor in this decrease was a drop in the population of Castile and Aragon from 10 million in 1600 to 6 million in 1700. No other country in Europe suffered a demographic reversal of this proportion during the seventeenth century. The decline began when a terrible bout of plague carried off half a million people in five years around 1600, a loss that Spain never recovered. In addition, though the wine and wool industries continued to prosper, their spectacular growth had come to a halt by the early seventeenth century, and no other important industries took their place. Worse still, Spain had to rely increasingly on the importation of expensive foodstuffs to feed her people.

It was under these conditions that Spain resumed large-scale fighting under Philip IV (1621–1665), first reopening hostilities against the Dutch in 1621 and then starting an escalating involvement in the Thirty Years' War. With her dwindling resources the burdens now became too much to bear. Through the 1620s a brilliant general, Ambrogio di Spinola, maintained the Spaniards' tradition of military victory, but his death, in 1630, removed their last able commander. The effort to continue the government's commitment to war during the subsequent decades in defiance of totally inadequate financial means was finally to bring the greatest state in Europe to its knees.

Revolt and Secession

The final crisis was brought about by the policies of Philip IV's chief minister, the Count of Olivares. His aim was to unite the kingdom, to "Castilianize" Spain. He wanted all the territories to bear equally the burden of maintaining their country's dominant position in the world. Laws would be uniform, expenses would be apportioned equitably among the provinces, and each province would receive its fair share of the nation's gains. Although Castile would no longer dominate, she would also not have to provide the bulk of the taxes and army.

Olivares' program was called the Union of Arms, and though it seemed eminently reasonable, its implementation caused a series of revolts in the 1640s that split Spain apart. The reason was quite simple. For more than a century, Castile had controlled the other provinces, which had felt increasingly that local independence was being undermined by a centralized regime. The Union of Arms was regarded as the last straw because it added new substance to this long-standing grievance. Moreover Olivares undertook his plan at a time when Spain's military and economic fortunes were noticeably in decline. France had declared war on the Hapsburgs in 1635, and thereafter Spain's position had deteriorated. The funds to support an army were becoming harder to raise, and in desperation Olivares pressed more vigorously for the Union of Arms. But all he accomplished was to provoke crippling revolts against the Castilians in Catalonia, Portugal, Naples, and Sicily.

The precipitant was France's invasion of Catalonia in 1639. Thinking that the Catalans would not refuse to share some of the effort of repelling the invaders from their own territory, Olivares ordered the troops fighting the French to be billeted in Catalonia. But instead of strengthening the government, the order provided the people with the issue that finally goaded them into open defiance in 1640.

Olivares tried to meet the revolt by asking the Portuguese to help subdue the Catalans, but this attempt to bind together the components of the Spanish Empire only aroused further defiance. By the next year both Catalonia and Portugal declared themselves independent republics and placed themselves under French protection. Plots began to appear against Olivares, and Philip dismissed the one minister who had understood Spain's problems but who, in trying to solve them, had made them worse.

The Catalonian rebellion continued for another eleven years, and it was thwarted in the end only because the peasants and town mobs transformed the resistance to the central government into an attack on the privileged and wealthy classes in the province. At this point the Catalan nobility abandoned the cause and joined the government side. About the same time the Fronde forced the withdrawal of French troops. Thus when the last major holdout, Barcelona, fell to a royal army in 1652, the Catalan nobles returned with their rights and privileges guaranteed, and the revolt was over.

The Portuguese, on the other hand, though not officially granted independence from Spain until 1668, were fully capable of defending their autonomy and even invaded Castile in the 1640s. Their revolt against the central government never became tinged with the social unrest that undermined the Catalans' unity. Portugal's nobles maintained their authority throughout the struggle and dominated the government thereafter.

The revolts in Sicily and Naples, aimed at the Castilians who ruled and taxed both provinces, took place in 1647. In Naples the unrest soon developed into a tremendous mob uprising, led by a local fisherman. The poor turned against all the representatives of government and wealth they could find, and chaos ensued until their leader was killed. The violence in Sicily by contrast was more exclusively the result of soaring taxes and was directed almost entirely against government representatives. Severe countermeasures were taken in both

Naples and Sicily, and within a few months the government regained control.

Spain had experienced a period of great cultural brilliance during Philip IV's reign, but even this died away as grim times descended on the country. Overextension in foreign war, financial and economic shortcomings at home, and the excessive reliance on Castile all had helped sap the nation's strength. The revolts during the 1640s were the result of decades of growing resentment at the monarch's inability to solve these basic, pressing problems; but the domestic unrest finally brought Spain's international ambitions and thus the worst of her difficulties to an end. Like England and France, she found a new way of life in the 1660s. She was to be a stable, second-level state, heavily agricultural, and run by her nobility.

THE UNITED PROVINCES

Although the United Provinces remained locked in a struggle for survival against Spain until 1648, and in various ways became a unique state, the Dutch did not escape the domestic tensions of the seventeenth century. Despite the remarkable fluidity of their society, they too went through a period of confrontation in the mid-seventeenth century that determined the structure of their government for over a century.

The Structure of the United Provinces

The United Provinces became a unique state for a number of reasons. Other republics existed in Europe, but they were controlled by small oligarchies; the Dutch, who had a long tradition of a strong representative assembly, the estates, founded a country in which many citizens participated in their own government through elected delegates. Although powerful merchants and a few aristocrats close to the House of Orange did create a small elite,

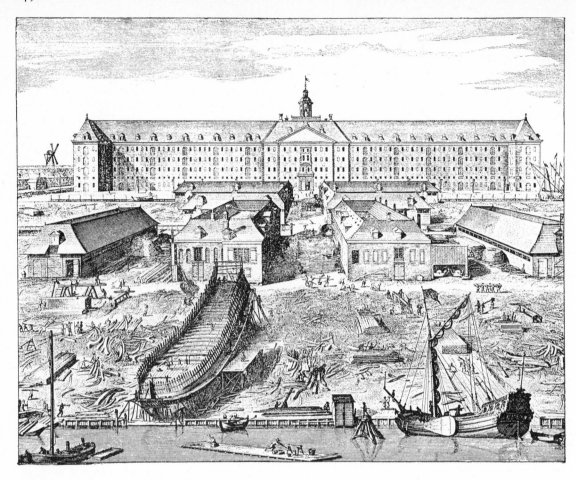

The Dutch became the best shipbuilders in Europe in the seventeenth century; the efficiency of their ships, which could be manned by fewer sailors than those of other countries, was a major reason for their successes in trade and commerce. (Photo: The Granger Collection)

the ordinary citizenry, participating in politics and united by a common cause, reduced the social differentiation prevalent elsewhere in Europe. The resultant openness and homogeneity colored the two most remarkable features of the United Provinces: economic mastery and cultural brilliance.

The most striking accomplishment of the Dutch was their rise to supremacy in the world of commerce. Amsterdam displaced Antwerp (and Genoa) as the Continent's financial capital and gained control of the trade of the world's richest markets. And in 1609 the Bank of Amsterdam was established, the first semiofficial financial institution of its kind in modern history; it made a vital contribution to the country's economy by offering the lowest interest rates in Europe. This encouraged native industries, such as shipbuilding, as well as overseas ventures, such as the East India Company, which needed substantial investments. In addition, the Dutch rapidly emerged as the cheapest shippers in international trade. As a result, by the middle of the seventeenth century they had become the chief carriers of European trade.

The openness of Dutch society permitted the freest exchange of ideas of the time. An official church, the Reformed Church, was established, but no religious groups were forbidden as long as they worshiped in private. The new state therefore gave refuge to dissenters of all kinds, whether extreme Protestant radicals or Catholics who wore their faith lightly, and the city of Amsterdam became the center of a brilliant Jewish community. This freedom attracted some of the greatest minds in Europe, and fostered remarkable artistic creativity. Patrons were easy to find among the wealthy merchants, and Dutch painting in the seventeenth century is one of the glories of Western culture. Yet it was not the result of the taste or sensibility of a few patrons and geniuses but an outpouring from many directions; and it was not the climax of a long tradition but a sudden outburst whose greatest expressions appeared in the first generation. The energy that produced the wealth and creativity reflected the pride of a tiny nation that was winning its independence.

Domestic Tensions

From the earliest days of the revolt against Spain, there had been a basic split within the United Provinces. The two provinces of Holland and Zeeland dominated the Estates General because they supplied a majority of its taxes. Their representatives formed a mercantile party, which advocated peace abroad so that their trade could flourish unhampered, government by the Estates General so that they could make their power felt, and religious toleration. In opposition to the mercantile interest was a party centered on the House of Orange, which sought to boost that family's leadership of the Dutch. This party stood for war to strengthen a popular national leader, centralized power for the House of Orange, and (after William died) strict religious orthodoxy.

The differences between the two factions came to a head in 1618, when Maurice of Nassau used the religious issue as a pretext for executing his chief opponent, Jan van Oldenbarneveldt, the principal representative of the province of Holland. Oldenbarneveldt opposed the resumption of war with Spain when the truce of 1609 expired in 1621, and his removal left Maurice in full control of the country. The mercantile party had been defeated, and war could resume in 1621.

For more than twenty years, the House of Orange remained in command, unassailable because it led the army in time of war. Not until 1648, when the family was headed by a new leader, could its opponents reassert themselves and sign the treaty of Westphalia that officially recognized the independence of the United Provinces. It then seemed that the mercantile party had gained the upper hand. But the outcome remained in the balance (there was even the threat of a siege of Amsterdam by troops loyal to the House of Orange) until William II suddenly died in 1650, leaving as his successor a posthumously born son, William III.

With serious opposition removed, the mercantile interest could now assume full power, and Jan De Witt, the representative of the province of Holland, took over the running of the government in 1653. De Witt's aims were to leave as much authority as possible in the hands of the provinces, particularly Holland; to weaken the executive in this way and prevent a revival of the fortunes of the House of Orange; to pursue trading advantage; and to maintain peace so that the economic supremacy of the Dutch would not be endangered. For more than a decade, he guided the country in its golden age. But in 1672 French armies overran the southern provinces, and De Witt, with his mercantile inclinations, lacked the military instinct to fight a dangerous enemy. The Dutch at once turned to the family that had led them to independence; a mob murdered De Witt; and the House of Orange, under William III, resumed the centralization that henceforth was to characterize the political structure of the United Provinces. The country had not experienced a mid-century upheaval as severe as those of its neighbors, but it had nevertheless been forced to endure unrest and violence before the form of its government was securely established.

SWEDEN

The Swedes, too, reached basic decisions in the mid-seventeenth century about political relations and administration of the state. Violence was avoided, but tensions had to be resolved nonetheless.

The Achievement of Gustavus Adolphus

In the early 1600s Sweden, a Lutheran country of a million people which had gained its independence from Denmark less than a century earlier, was one of the backwaters of Europe. A feudal nobility dominated the countryside and sought to control the government, a barter economy made money almost unknown, and both trade and towns were virtually nonexistent. Moreover the Swedes found themselves in a running battle with the Danes, whose well-organized, well-armed, and prosperous monarchy dominated the Baltic Sea. Sweden, by contrast, lacked a capital, central institutions, and government machinery. The task of ruling was thus entirely dependent on the king and a few courtiers; officials were appointed only to deal with specific problems as they arose.

Gustavus Adolphus (1611–1632) trans-formed this situation. At the start of his reign, he faced a war that was to involve all the states in the area—his own, Denmark, Poland, and Russia—in a struggle to control the lands around the Baltic. Without his nobles' help, however, Gustavus could not raise an army. He therefore arranged an alliance with the nobles and gave them dominant positions in a newly organized bureaucracy. By winning their support he not only staffed an administrative machine but organized an army, thus equipping himself both to govern and to fight.

During the two decades of his reign, Gustavus engaged in a remarkable series of conquests abroad. By 1629 he controlled the coastline of the eastern Baltic, making Sweden the most powerful state in the area. He then entered the Thirty Years' War, advancing victoriously through the Holy Roman Empire until his death, in 1632, during the showdown battle with Wallenstein. Although without their general the Swedes could do little more than hang on to the gains they had made, they remained for a century a force to be reckoned with in international affairs.

The system of government that Gustavus and his chief adviser, Axel Oxenstierna, established in 1611 was to be the envy of other countries until the twentieth century. At the heart of the system were five administrative departments,[5] each led by a nobleman, with the most important—the Chancellery—run by Oxenstierna, who supervised diplomacy and internal affairs. Gradually an administrative center emerged in Stockholm where, under Oxenstierna's capable leadership, the bureaucracy proved that it could run the nation, supply the army, and implement policy even during the last twelve years of Gustavus' reign, when the king himself was almost always

---

[5] They were the Chancellery, the Ministry of Justice, the Treasury, the Department of War, and the Department of the Navy.

abroad. During his absence Oxenstierna took charge, though executive power was officially vested in the Rad, an assembly of nobles.

Another major institution, the Riksdag, consisted of representatives of four estates: the nobility, the clergy, the townsmen, and (unique in Europe) the peasants. Although officially it was the highest legislative authority in the land, real power was retained by the nobles and the crown. For centuries the Riksdag functioned as no more than a sounding board that gave the appearance of popular approval to royal and aristocratic rule, which by the 1630s was already operating with an efficiency unparalleled on the Continent.

A major cause of Sweden's amazing rise was the development of the domestic economy. Early in Gustavus' reign new discoveries made possible the mining of huge deposits of copper, an important metal for cannon and coin manufacture. With the only other major source of copper being Japan, a Continental monopoly was assured. The crown maximized its profits by taking over the mining itself. To avoid dependence on one commodity, the government also encouraged iron mining. Foreign experts were brought in, and the discovery of a new smelting process made Swedish iron highly prized. At the same time, the country's traditional tar and timber exports were stepped up, and a fleet was built. By 1700 Stockholm had become an important trading and financial center, growing in the course of the century from fewer than 5,000 to more than 50,000 inhabitants—a phenomenal rise and further evidence of the general northward shift of European economic activity.

The Role of the Nobles

The one source of tension amidst this remarkable progress was the position of the aristocracy. They had been Gustavus' partners and after he died they tightened their control over the government and society.

Between 1611 and 1652 nobles more than doubled the proportion of land they owned in Sweden, and increased sixfold their holdings in Finland, which Sweden ruled. Much of this growth was at the expense of the crown, which granted away or sold its lands to help its war efforts abroad. Both peasants and townsmen viewed the developments with alarm. Peasants always fared much worse under nobles than as direct tenants of the king because the great landowners sought the maximum possible return from their possessions. And the towns felt that their place in national affairs was being completely destroyed by an excessively powerful aristocracy. Both groups were frightened when the Danish nobles took advantage of the death of their country's strong king, in 1648, to gain control of government.[6] Two years later the showdown came in Sweden.

The ruler of Sweden was Gustavus' daughter Christina, an able but erratic young queen who usually allowed Oxenstierna to run the government. In the late 1640s she was becoming increasingly hopeful that she could abdicate her throne, become a Catholic, and leave Sweden—an ambition she fulfilled in 1654. She wanted her cousin Charles recognized as her successor, but the aristocracy threatened to create a nobles' republic if she abdicated. The queen therefore summoned the Riksdag, Sweden's representative assembly, in 1650, and taking advantage of the grievances of townsmen and peasants, she encouraged the three lower estates to mount a campaign against the aristocracy. Believing that they might now gain a new importance in national affairs, the townsmen and peasants demanded the return of nobles' lands to the crown, freedom of

---

[6] In 1660 the Danish king engineered a countercoup that firmly established absolutism in that country. Denmark was thus yet another state whose political structure was settled for a long time to come during this period.

speech, and real power in the Riksdag so that the lower estates could outvote the nobles. Under this pressure the nobility gave way and recognized the future Charles X Gustavus as successor to the throne—a good choice, because Charles was an able soldier who consolidated Gustavus Adolphus' gains and confirmed Sweden's mastery of northern Europe.

But the confrontation of 1650 proved to be short-lived. Once Christina had won the argument over her successor, she removed her support from the Riksdag and rejected the demands of the lower estates. Only gradually did power shift away from the great nobles toward a broader elite of lesser nobles and bureaucrats.

EASTERN EUROPE

The major powers of eastern Europe, the Ottoman Empire, Poland, and Russia, were as affected by warfare as their western neighbors. And in Poland and Russia there were also upheavals in the mid-seventeenth century that helped determine these states' future political development.

The Ottoman Empire

In the Ottoman Empire central control was highly effective by the early 1500s. The first signs of a decline of strength at the center began to appear after the death of Suleiman, in 1566. Harem intrigues, corruption at court, and the loosening of military discipline became increasingly serious from the late sixteenth century onward. Yet the Ottomans remained·an object of fear and hostility throughout the West—their constant wars with the Hapsburgs devastated Hungary, where most of the fighting took place, and in the eastern Mediterranean they remained a formidable force, though the English and Dutch were coming to play a dominant role in the area after 1600.

The Turkish rulers had unparalleled powers. A crack army of more than 25,000 men stood ready to serve the sultan at all times, and within his domains his supremacy was unquestioned. He was both spiritual and temporal head of his empire, completely free to appoint all officers, issue laws, and raise taxes. But these powers, geared to military conquest and extending over enormous territories, never became a focus of cohesion among the disparate races of the Balkans and the Middle East who were ruled from Constantinople, because the sultan left authority in the hands of local nobles and princes as long as his ultimate sovereignty was recognized. Whenever questions of loyalty arose (as they did sporadically in the Balkans), they revealed that the authority of the central government rested on its military might. That was more than enough to prevent any serious challenges to the power of the Ottomans until they began to lose ground to the Hapsburgs in the eighteenth century.

Poland

The largest kingdom in Europe, Poland, was as disorganized as the Holy Roman Empire. The king could exercise control over his personal lands but elsewhere the country was entirely in the hands of powerful nobles, who from 1572 onward confirmed their independence by ensuring that the monarchy would be strictly elective. The Diet, an assembly of nobles, was required to meet at least once every two years, and without the approval of this body no policy could be enforced.

In Poland as elsewhere, religion was a major issue during the second half of the sixteenth century. Sigismund III (1587–1632), with the help of some members of the aristocracy and the Jesuits, crushed Protestantism. But not all the nobles favored Roman Catholicism; some belonged to the Greek Orthodox Church. Attempts were made to unite the Roman Catholics with the Greek Orthodox, and one group, known as the Uniate Church, agreed to acknowledge papal supremacy while retaining traditional Greek rites. When the Jesuits tried to increase their influence, however, the adherents of the Orthodox and Uniate churches formed a coalition for common defense that split the country into two religious camps.

Although Poland was constantly at war, Sigismund and his successors were never able to use the military situation to overcome the fragmentation of political authority and create a strong central government. Instead, the religious divisions and the power of local nobles became increasingly serious problems until, in the mid-seventeenth century, the Poles, like so many Europeans, faced a major internal clash.

The crisis arose in the Ukraine, the borderland in the southeast of Poland that had long been occupied by the soldier-farmers known as Cossacks. Like their Russian counterparts, these Cossacks were allowed considerable independence because of their importance in protecting the countryside against turbulent neighbors to the south and east. Firm adherents of the Greek Orthodox Church, they became increasingly annoyed at the government for encouraging Catholicism. Finally in 1648 they rebelled, took control of the eastern Ukraine, and in 1654 offered their allegiance to the Greek Orthodox tsar of Russia.

The Polish monarchy was much too weak to combat the revolt, and the nobility had little wish to undertake a long assault on this frontier region. Thus the Ukraine was lost—yet another casualty of the upheavals of the age—though internally Poland continued much as before, a country dominated by a small yet powerful aristocracy. Once again, the storms that swept political life had been succeeded by a sense of settlement.

Russia

The power of the central authority in Russia was already apparent in the reign of Ivan IV (1547–1584)—called the Terrible—who used his considerable military strength both at home and in conquests that extended Muscovite rule along the length of the Volga River to the southeast.

Ivan's autocracy was hampered by fewer limitations than any other ruler in Europe. Russia was still feudal; her peasants were serfs, and her great lords, known as boyars, controlled local areas but had little say in national affairs. Jealous of their regional powers, Ivan launched a vicious campaign against the boyars and enormously increased the areas of Russia under his direct control. He enlarged his bureaucracy to meet the new administrative tasks created by his conquests, but the authority of the central government was now a divisive rather than a unifying force, discredited and hated because it had grown by military might.

The reaction came after Ivan's death, when the country entered a thirty-year period that would later be called the Time of Troubles. Ivan's son Feodor, the last of the Rurik dynasty, which had ruled since the ninth century, lacked his father's vigor and could not prevent the boyars from reasserting their power. From 1591 onward he virtually handed over control of the government to his brother-in-law, Boris Godunov, whom the boyars regarded as an upstart. When Feodor died in 1598 Boris became tsar and major revolts soon broke out.

For fifteen years the country was in chaos as peasants, townsmen, and petty nobles joined in various coalitions against the government and the boyars. The final confrontation took place when the leading boyars supported a Polish claimant to the throne, and a popular army, led by townsmen and lesser nobles who had been excluded from political prominence by the higher nobility, drove the Polish claimant from Moscow. In his place a national assembly, consisting of nobles and townsmen,

elected as tsar a grandnephew of Ivan the Terrible, Mikhail Feodorovich (1613–1645),
founder of the Romanov dynasty.

The central government emerged from
these disruptions with its powers essentially
unimpaired. The boyars had been unable to
weaken the tsar's ability to take firm military
measures against his opponents, and under
Mikhail they returned to docile inaction.
They now depended on the throne for their
control over local areas, and many had to serve
the tsar in order to retain their estates. During
the half-century after the Time of Troubles,
the monarchy organized its administration systematically, codified Russia's laws, and continued the extension of its authority by the use or
threat of armed force.

But the potential for domestic upheaval was
not entirely removed, and indeed it was during this half-century that the groundwork for
new turmoil was laid as the boyars gradually
closed the last loopholes in the system of serfdom. Previously an escaped serf who remained uncaptured for a certain number of
years was automatically liberated, but in 1646
the boyars persuaded Tsar Alexis (1645–1676)
to abolish the limit. Now a serf remained in
his status for life—a hopeless fugitive even if he
did escape his master.

The result was constant agrarian unrest, met
by harsh repression, which inspired even more
violent uprisings. The disturbances were fed
by increasing financial demands on both serfs
and townsmen from the central government
and local lords, and in 1648 the boiling point
was reached. A major riot broke out in Moscow, the tsar was forced to hand over to the
rebels a number of his financial administrators,
and by the end of the year almost every large
city in Russia had experienced virulent disorders, quelled only by the intervention of
royal troops. This year of upheaval, as fierce
in Russia as in England and France, marked the
beginning of a period of more than two decades when the lower classes made a major effort, for the last time in centuries, to restrain
the growing power of the central government
and the landowners.

The popular discontent intensified in the
1650s and 1660s, and finally in 1668 the major
revolt that had long been brewing exploded in
the southern provinces of Russia, led by a Cos-
sack, Stenka Razin, who terrorized the area
and launched a fleet that caused chaos on the
Caspian Sea. In 1670 Razin led two expeditions up the Volga River, capturing a succes-
cession of towns and handing them over to
mob rule. His very approach incited peasants
to violence, for his troops included thousands
of escaped serfs who hoped to bring liberty to
all their oppressed brethren. There was open
advocacy of what amounted to class war: the
poor against the rich, the weak against the
powerful. Eventually royal troops shattered
the poorly equipped army; and though marauding bands continued to harass the inhabitants of central Russia for years, the major
threat was ended in 1671, when Razin was
executed in Moscow.

Compounding Russia's troubles was serious
dissension within the national Greek Orthodox
Church. The dispute arose over the decision
of the patriarch of Moscow, the head of the
Russian Church, to correct the traditional liturgical books of the faith, which contained
errors introduced by copyists over the centuries. A group calling itself the Old Believers,
refusing to change usages hallowed by custom,
objected to the revision and broke away from
the established church. The schism was accompanied by violence, which forced the patriarch and his followers to become entirely
dependent on the secular power to maintain
their authority. This reliance on the state undermined the clergy's spiritual leadership and
helped the monarchy on its way to assuming
complete control over all facets of Russian
society.

Having overcome two potential threats to his authority—peasant unrest in areas far from Moscow and the rivalry within the church—Alexis began to feel strong enough in his last years to pay less attention to the boyars. It was clear that a determined ruler could once again make the tsar the dominant figure in Russian society, and in the late seventeenth century it was Peter the Great who was to be that ruler.

Throughout Europe in the mid-seventeenth century long-standing tensions which had just passed through an especially virulent phase were resolved, and a period of relative stability began that was to last for over a century. In international affairs a vicious circle of brutality was broken as a degree of restraint was imposed on the anarchy of warfare. Within Europe's states, the resistance to central governments, usually the result of regional loyalties, traditional aristocratic independence, or resentment at soaring taxes, was effectively brought to an end. Whatever the outcomes—and they ranged from England's parliamentary system to France's absolutism—each country's political situation now settled into accepted forms, just as warmaking and diplomacy did after Westphalia.

Because the disturbances had been so widespread, historians have called the mid-seventeenth century an age of "general crisis." It is a rather vague term, but it does convey the flavor of a period when upheaval was common, reached crisis proportions, and then subsided into relaxation. To the extent that the crisis was general, however, one would expect it to be reflected not merely in politics but in thought, art, and society. And indeed, the mid-seventeenth century was the time when, for example, the ideas of the scientific revolution became, after much doubt, an essential part of European civilization. One must not push the connections too far, because simple parallels distort the complexities of the period; nevertheless, the progression from turbulence to calm in politics was not without its analogies in the cultural and social developments of the sixteenth and seventeenth centuries.

RECOMMENDED READING

Sources

* Franklin, Julian H. (tr. and ed.). *Constitutionalism and Resistance in the Sixteenth Century: Three Treatises by Hotman, Beza, & Mornay.* 1969. Three of the most radical tracts of the period, each justifying rebellion.

Studies

* Aston, Trevor (ed.). *Crisis in Europe 1560–1660: Essays from Past and Present.* 1965. This is a collection of those essays in which the "general crisis" interpretation was initially put forward and discussed.

Doolin, P. R. *The Fronde*. 1935. Still the best account in English of the French upheaval.

Elliott, John H. *The Revolt of the Catalans*. 1963. The standard history of the growing troubles of the Spanish monarchy in the seventeenth century.

* Forster, Robert, and Jack P. Greene (eds.). *Preconditions of Revolution in Early Modern Europe*. 1972. An excellent series of essays on resistance to central governments, and its causes, in a number of European countries.

Hellie, Richard. *Enserfment and Military Change in Muscovy*. 1971. This study shows the links between military affairs and social change in Russia during the early modern period.

Howell, Roger. *Cromwell*. 1977. The clearest and most reliable short biography of the revolutionary leader.

Koenigsberger, H. G. *Estates and Revolutions: Essays in Early Modern European History*. A most useful set of articles, primarily on political history; of particular interest is a fascinating comparison of the revolutionary parties in France and the Netherlands.

* Mattingly, Garrett. *The Armada*. 1959. This beautifully written book, which was a best seller when it first appeared, is a gripping account of a major international crisis.

* Neale, J. E. *Queen Elizabeth I: A Biography*. 1934. A lucid and affectionate account of the reign by its most distinguished twentieth-century historian.

* Pagès, Georges. *The Thirty Years' War: 1618–1648*. 1971. The most straightforward history of a highly complex period.

Parker, Geoffrey. *The Army of Flanders and the Spanish Road, 1567–1659: The Logistics of Spanish Victory and Defeat in the Low Countries' Wars*. 1972. A study of the way Spain kept the route to the Netherlands open and the methods of warfare in this period.

* ———. *The Dutch Revolt*. 1977. This brief book gives a good introduction to the revolt of the Netherlands and the nature of Dutch society in the seventeenth century.

* Rabb, Theodore K. *The Struggle for Stability in Early Modern Europe*. 1975. An assessment of the "crisis" interpretation, including extensive bibliographic references.

Roberts, Michael. *Gustavus Adolphus and the Rise of Sweden*. 1973. This is the best biography of the Swedish king, emphasizing especially his military and administrative achievements.

* Salmon, J. H. M. *The French Wars of Religion: How Important Were Religious Factors?* 1967. A collection of interpretations of the causes and nature of the civil wars.

* Shaw, Howard. *The Levellers*. 1968. This brief introduction to the ideas and activities of the most famous radical group in the English revolution is accompanied by extracts from their writings.

Stone, Lawrence. *The Causes of the English Revolution, 1529–1642*. 1972. A short but comprehensive assessment of the reasons for the outbreak of the seventeenth century's most far-reaching revolution.

Tapié, V. L. *France in the Age of Louis XIII and Richelieu*. D. McN. Lockie (tr. and ed.). 1974. The standard history of the twenty-year period when the basic development of French absolutism took place.

* Walzer, Michael. *The Revolution of the Saints: A Study in the Origins of Radical Politics*. A provocative interpretation of the revolutionary impulse in English Puritanism.

---

* Available in paperback.

SIXTEEN

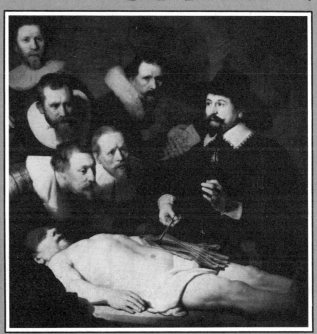

CULTURE AND SOCIETY IN THE AGE OF THE SCIENTIFIC REVOLUTION

The sense of upheaval and then crisis followed by a settling down that dominated European politics and international relations from the mid-sixteenth to the mid-seventeenth century is also visible in other areas of life. Indeed it is remarkable how well cultural and social patterns reflect the progression from uncertainty to stable resolution. Here, too, the doubts of more than a century, from the days of the Reformation, the discovery of new worlds, and the beginnings of the scientific revolution, were gradually overcome.

Not only the clearest but also the most important development along these lines was the scientific revolution. Starting with tentative and disturbing questions about the theories of ancient authorities, whose views had been accepted for centuries, scientists eventually created a completely new way of looking at nature and a new way of thinking and arguing about physical problems. Their successes were remarkable, and they became very influential, because the certainty and orderliness of their results appealed to a Europe that was seeking relief from uncertainty.

The central event in the confrontation between the old and the new was the trial and condemnation by the Roman Inquisition of one of the greatest of the seventeenth-century scientists, Galileo. But in the next generation the ideas he represented triumphed, as part of a renewed sense of settlement that descended on European society. Stability was visible throughout intellectual life: in literature as well as in art, in painting as well as in poetry. Where the Mannerist painters and the writers of the late sixteenth century emphasized doubts, upheaval, and insecurity, their successors in the Baroque period gave themselves up to enormous, grandiose ambitions, but the artists after the mid-seventeenth century increasingly stressed calm, restraint, and order. It was the exact equivalent to the resolution of tension one could see elsewhere in society.

Although for ordinary men and women these high intellectual movements had little meaning, their lives were changed in a similar direction as central governments gained considerable control over them, severely reducing the restlessness and rebelliousness that had been prevalent since the early sixteenth century. Even the inhabitants of country villages found that they were no longer as isolated and self-contained as they had once been. One of the most obvious symptoms of their unease, the tremendous outburst of witchcraft during this period, was curbed from above. And when religion no longer caused disruptions throughout Europe, the common people lost a major occasion for self-expression and violence. In general, with the powers of repression growing and their traditional local independence—and their wages—declining, ordinary people took an unavoidable part in the universal quieting down that characterized Western society in the late seventeenth century.

I. THE SCIENTIFIC REVOLUTION

To contemporaries the wars and crises of the sixteenth and seventeenth centuries seemed to dominate their lives. To us it is clear that European civilization was affected no less deeply in this period by the quiet revolution in ideas about nature that was accomplished by a handful of scholars and experimenters. We call such people scientists, but at the time they were known as natural philosophers. They were specialists in an area of philosophy then considered less important than theology; but by the time their revolution was complete, their ideas had become central to Western thought.

ORIGINS OF THE SCIENTIFIC REVOLUTION

The study of nature by Europeans took its point of departure from the ancient Greeks whose interests shaped subsequent work until the sixteenth century—Aristotle in physics, Ptolemy in astronomy, and Galen in medicine. The most dramatic advances during the scientific revolution came in the fields the Greeks had pioneered, and were to some extent caused by increasing evidence that their theories did not cover all the facts. For instance, Aristotle's belief that all objects in their natural state are at rest created a number of problems, such as explaining why an arrow kept on flying after leaving a bow; while grappling with this question, some fourteenth-century scientists came up with a new explanation, the belief that a moving body possessed impetus, which kept the motion going until it died out. Similarly, observations revealed that Ptolemy's picture of the heavens, in which all motion was circular around a central earth, could not account for the peculiar motion of some planets, which at times seemed to be moving backward. Moreover Galen's theories, often based on mistaken

anatomical information, were shown by dissections to be inadequate.

Still, it is not likely philosophers would have abandoned their cherished theories—they far preferred making adjustments than beginning anew—if it had not been for various other influences at work in the fifteenth and sixteenth centuries. First was the humanists' rediscovery of the work of a number of ancient scientists, which showed that classical writers themselves had not all agreed with the theories of Aristotle or Ptolemy. One particularly important rediscovery was Archimedes, whose studies of dynamics were an important inspiration for new ideas in physics. A second influence was an increasing interest in what we now dismiss as "magic," but which at the time was regarded as a serious intellectual enterprise. There were various sides to magical inquiry. Alchemy was the belief that by mixing substances and using secret formulae the nature of matter could be understood. A related interest was the theory of atomism, the idea that all matter was made up of tiny particles, whose composition could be changed—again a theory newly recovered from ancient writers. One of the most famous sixteenth-century alchemists, Paracelsus, was also a proponent of new medical theories, notably the belief that diseases were separate entities with lives of their own. Another magical favorite was astrology, which claimed that natural phenomena became understandable and predictable if planetary movements were properly interpreted. A similar easy key to the mysteries of nature was promised by Hermeticism, a school of thought that asserted that all of knowledge had once been given to man, that it was contained in some obscure writings, and that with the right approach and intelligence, a complete insight into the structure of the universe could be achieved.

What linked all this magic was the conviction that the world could be understood and that the answers to traditional questions consisted of simple, comprehensive keys to nature. The theories of Neoplatonism, which became very influential during the Renaissance, supported this conviction, as did some of the mystical beliefs that attracted attention in the fifteenth and sixteenth centuries. One of the latter, derived from a system of Jewish thought known as cabala, suggested that the key to the universe might consist of magical arrangements of numbers. For all its irrational elements, it was precisely this longing for new, simple solutions to ancient problems that made natural philosophers capable, for the first time, of discarding the honored theories they had inherited from antiquity, trying different ones, paying greater attention to mathematics, and eventually creating an intellectual revolution.

Two other influences deserve mention. The first was Europe's long fascination with technological invention. The architects, navigators, engineers, and weapons experts of the Renaissance were important pioneers of the belief in measurement and careful observation. For example, at the Arsenal in Venice, where huge cannon were moved and devices invented for handling great weights, Galileo got ideas and made experiments that helped his study of dynamics. A related interest was followed by the anatomists at the nearby university of Padua who created a school famous for its work in dissections and its direct investigations of nature; many of the leading figures of the scientific revolution received their training in methods of experiment and observation at Padua. It was not too surprising, therefore, that the period of the scientific revolution was marked by the invention of important new instruments which often made the discoveries possible: the telescope, the thermometer, the barometer, the vacuum pump, and the microscope. These instruments encouraged the development of a scientific approach that was

entirely new in the seventeenth century—it did not go back to the ancients, to the practitioners of magic, or to the engineers. It was pioneered by Francis Bacon and consisted of the belief that in order to make Nature reveal her secrets, she had to be made to do things she did not do normally: in Bacon's phrase, one had to "twist the lion's tail." What this meant was that one did not simply observe phenomena that occurred normally in nature—for instance, the apparent bending of a stick when placed in a glass of water—but created conditions that were *not* normal. With the telescope one could perceive secrets hidden to the naked eye; with the vacuum pump one could begin to understand the properties of air.

The influences that combined to create the scientific revolution varied greatly. Yet there is no doubt that the heart of the change lay in purely intellectual breakthroughs. A small group of brilliant men, grappling with ancient problems of physics, astronomy, and anatomy—motion, heavenly phenomena, and the structure of the body—came up with persuasive discoveries that changed Western thought forever.

THE FIRST BREAKTHROUGHS

The earliest advances were in astronomy and anatomy. By coincidence, both were contained in books published in 1543, which was also the year when the first printed edition of Archimedes appeared. *The Structure of the Human Body*, by Andreas Vesalius, a member of the Padua faculty, pointed out errors in the work of Galen, the chief medical authority for over a thousand years. Although Vesalius himself did not always follow strictly the findings of dissections—like Galen, he showed the liver as having five lobes, which is true of some animals but not of humans, though in a corner of the picture he also showed a small

An engraving of Copernicus' conception of the universe shows the sun rather than the earth at the center, the spheres to which planets were attached, and the moons of Jupiter discovered by Galileo. (Photo: British Museum)

two-lobed liver, perhaps to indicate that he knew what the human one really looked like—he opened a new era of careful observation and experimentation in studies of the body.

On the Revolutions of the Heavenly Bodies, by Nicolaus Copernicus, a Polish cleric who had studied at Padua, had far greater consequences. A first-rate mathematician, he felt that the calculations of planetary movements under Ptolemy's system had grown too complex. In Ptolemaic astronomy, the planets and the sun, attached to transparent, crystalline spheres, revolved around the earth. All motion was circular, and observed irregularities were accounted for by epicycles—movement around small spheres which were attached to the larger spheres and which themselves re-

Kepler, surrounded by the instruments of the astrologer and the astronomer, discussing his work with his patron, the emperor Rudolf II. (Photo: New York Public Library, Picture Collection)

volved. Much influenced by Neoplatonic and related ideas, Copernicus believed that a simpler picture would reflect more accurately the true structure of the universe. In good Neoplatonic fashion, he argued that the sun, as the most splendid of celestial bodies, ought rightfully to be at the center of an orderly and harmonious universe.

Copernicus' system was in fact no simpler than Ptolemy's—the spheres and epicycles were just as complex—and he had no way of proving that his theory was correct. But he was such a fine mathematician that his successors had to use his calculations even if they rejected his assumptions. He thus became part of intellectual discussion, drawn upon when Pope Gregory XIII decided to reform the calendar in 1582. The Julian calendar, in use since Roman times, counted century years as leap years, thus adding extra days which caused Easter—whose date is determined by the position of the sun—to drift further and further away from its normal occurrence in

March. The reform produced the Gregorian calendar, which we still use—ten days were simply dropped, and since then three out of every four century years have not been leap years (1900 had no February 29, but 2000 will have one). The need for calendar reform had been one of the motives for Copernicus' studies, which proved useful even though his theories remained controversial.

What developed during the half-century following the publication of his *Revolutions* was a growing sense of uncertainty. The greatest astronomer of the period, Tycho Brahe, made the most remarkable observations of the heavens before the telescope, plotting the paths of the moon and planets every night for decades. But the only theory he could come up with was an uneasy compromise between the Ptolemaic and Copernican systems. It was a disciple of his, the German Johannes Kepler, who made the first major advance on the work of Copernicus and who helped resolve the uncertainties that had arisen in the field of astronomy.

Kepler

Like Copernicus, Kepler believed that only the language of mathematics could describe the movements of the heavens. He was an open advocate of the latest magical ideas of his day —a famous astrologer, he also speculated about such subjects as the mystical meaning of geometric shapes—and he was convinced instinctively that Copernicus was right. He threw himself into the task of confirming the sun-centered (heliocentric) theory, and as a result of his study of Brahe's observations, he discovered three laws of planetary motion (published in 1609 and 1619) that opened a new era in astronomy.

The first law states that the orbits of the planets are ellipses, with the sun invariably at one focus of the ellipse. This was an enor-

KEPLER'S SECOND LAW

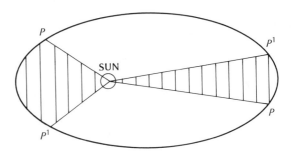

P *and* P¹ *are any two points on the orbit between which the planet passes in equal time. The area described by Sun–P–P¹–Sun is always equal.*

mous break with the past, for the assumption that circular motion is the most perfect and natural motion had been an essential part of the study of nature since Aristotle. Even Galileo was unable to reject this assumption, but Kepler followed wherever his data and his mathematics took him. The second law states that if a hypothetical line is drawn from the sun to the planet, equal areas will be swept by that line in equal times. What this means is that the planet moves faster—that is, it has to cover more of the orbit in a given period— when it is closer to the sun than when it is farther away (see figure).

The third law enters an entirely different area, describing not the motion of an individual planet, as do the first two, but a relationship among the movements of all planets. It states that the square of the ratio of the *time* it takes any two planets to complete their orbits equals the cube of the ratio of these planets' average *distance* from the sun. Formulated as an equation, $(T_1/T_2)^2 = (D_1/D_2)^3$, where T_1 and T_2 are the two planets' orbiting times and D_1 and D_2 are their average distances from the sun. This third law was Kepler's most elegant and subtle discovery, a worthy monument to his mathematical skills. However, it had little direct impact on the study of astronomy until Sir Isaac Newton used it late in the century as the foundation for his construction of a new system of the heavens.

Kepler's last major achievement was the publication in 1627 of the *Rudolfine Tables*, named after his patron, Emperor Rudolf II. The tables combined Brahe's observations of planetary positions with Kepler's theories of planetary motion and made it possible to predict celestial movements far more accurately, to the great benefit of navigators as well as astronomers. They demonstrated that Copernicus' and Kepler's discoveries had a practical value, and it became increasingly difficult to ignore or doubt the new findings. Adherents of Ptolemaic cosmology continued to hold firm for decades, but among serious observers of the heavens they were a rapidly dwindling group after the 1620s. A theory that at the beginning of Kepler's career had been uncertain at best had been transformed by the end of his life into a plausible explanation of planetary motion.

Galileo

A contemporary of Kepler's, the Italian Galileo Galilei, took the breakthrough a stage further when he became the first to perceive the connection between planetary motion and motion on earth, and his studies revealed the importance to astronomy not only of observation and mathematics but also of physics. Moreover he was the first to bring the new understanding of the universe to the attention of a wider public. Galileo's concern with technique, argument, and evidence marks him as one of the first scientists recognizable as such to modern eyes.

The study of motion inspired Galileo's most fundamental scientific contributions. When he began his investigations, the Aristotelian view that a body is naturally at rest and needs to be pushed constantly to keep moving dominated the study of dynamics. Kepler for example believed that some steady force emanating from the sun maintains the planets' motion. Galileo broke with this tradition, developing instead a new type of physical explanation that was perfected by Newton half a century later.

Unlike Kepler, who was concerned with the strictly limited phenomena of planetary movements, Galileo wanted to uncover the principles of all motion. His observations were prolific. At the Arsenal in Venice, he watched the techniques workmen used to lift huge weights; adapting a Dutch lensmaker's invention, he built himself a primitive telescope to study the heavens; and he devised seemingly mundane experiments, employing anything from pendulums to little balls rolling down inclined planes, to test his theories. Moving from observations to abstraction, Galileo arrived at a wholly new way of understanding motion: the principle of inertia.

This breakthrough could not have been made on the basis of observation alone. For the discovery of inertia depended on mathematical imagination, the ability to conceive of a situation that cannot be demonstrated to the senses because it cannot be created experimentally: the motion of a perfectly smooth ball across a perfectly smooth plane, free of any outside forces, such as friction. Galileo's conclusion was that "Any velocity once imparted to a moving body will be rigidly maintained as long as external causes of acceleration and retardation are removed. . . . If the velocity is uniform, it will not be diminished or slackened, much less destroyed."

This insight completely undermined the Aristotelian view. Physics would never be the same again, because Galileo demonstrated that only mathematical language could describe the underlying principles of nature.

The most immediate impact of Galileo's work was on astronomy. He first became famous when in 1609 he published his discoveries that Jupiter has satellites and the moon has mountains. Both these revelations were further blows to traditional beliefs, which held that the earth is changing and imperfect while the heavens are immutable and unblemished. Now, however, it seemed that other planets have moons, just like the earth, and that these moons might have the same rough surfaces as the earth.

This was startling enough, but Galileo also sought a complete change in the methods of discovery, believing, unlike his predecessors, that the principles he had uncovered in terrestrial physics could also be used to explain phenomena in the heavens. His purposes became apparent when he calculated the height of the mountains on the moon by using the geometric techniques of surveyors, when he described the moon's secondary light—seen while it is a crescent—as a reflection of sunlight from the earth, and when he explained the movement of sunspots by referring to the principles of motion that he had found on earth. In all cases Galileo was treating his own planet simply as one part of a uniform universe. Every physical law, he was saying, is equally applicable on earth and in the heavens, including the laws of motion. As early as 1597 Galileo had told Kepler that some of his discoveries in physics could be explained only if the earth was moving, and during the next thirty years he became the most famous advocate of Copernicanism in Europe.

Galileo conveyed his arguments with devastating logic. Citing Aristotle's principle that the simplest explanation is the best explanation, Galileo asked how anyone could conceivably accept all the complexities and effort needed to keep the entire universe revolving around the earth when all the motions could be explained by the rotation of only one planet, the earth.

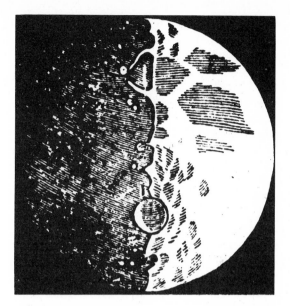

This sketch of the moon's surface appeared in Galileo's Starry Messenger (1610). *It shows what he had observed through the telescope and was interpreted as proof that the moon had a rugged surface because the lighted areas within the dark section had to be mountains. These caught the light of the setting sun longer than surrounding lower terrain and revealed, for example, a large cavity in the lower center of the sketch.* (Photo: New York Public Library Picture Collection)

When academic and religious critics pointed out that the moon looks smooth, that we would feel the earth moving, or that the Bible says Joshua made the sun stand still, he reacted with scorn to their inability to understand that his observations and proofs carried more weight than their traditional beliefs. And in response to religious objections, he asserted that "in discussions of physical problems we ought to begin not from the authority of scriptural passages, but from sense experience and necessary demonstrations."

For all the brilliance of his arguments, Galileo was now on dangerous ground. Although traditionally the Catholic Church had not concerned itself with the theories used in investigations of nature, in the early seventeenth century the situation was changing. Now deep in the struggle with Protestantism, the church was responding to the increased challenge to its authority by seeking to control any potentially questionable views held by its followers. Moreover Galileo had antagonized Jesuit and Dominican astronomers. These two orders were the chief upholders of orthodoxy in the church in this period, and it was they who referred Galileo's views to the Inquisition and then guided the attack on Copernicanism and its most brilliant proponent.

In 1616 the Inquisition forbade Galileo to teach the heretical doctrine that the earth moved; but when one of his friends was elected pope in 1623 he thought he would be safe in writing a great work on astronomy. The result was Galileo's masterpiece, the *Dialogue on the Two Great World Systems*, published in 1632 (with the approval, probably accidental, of the Inquisition). A marvelously witty, elegant book, the *Dialogue* is one of the few monuments in the history of science that the layman can find constant pleasure in reading. And so it was intended. Galileo wrote it in Italian, not the Latin that had always been used for scholarly works, because he wanted it to reach the widest possible audience.

In April 1633 he was brought before the Inquisition for having defied the order not to teach Copernicanism. In a trial that has caused controversy ever since, the aged astronomer, under threat of torture, abjured the "errors and heresies" of believing that the earth moved. Legend has it that as he left the hall, he murmured, "*Eppur si muove!*" ("And yet it does move!") and he certainly was not docile for the remainder of his life even though he was under perpetual house arrest and progressively lost his eyesight. He had his principal

work on physics, the *Two New Sciences*, published in tolerant Holland in 1638, while many of his letters ridiculed his opponents.

Galileo's condemnation discouraged further scientific activity by his countrymen. Italy had been the leader of the new discipline, but now her supremacy rapidly passed northward, to the English, Dutch, and French. Yet this only showed that the rise of science, once begun, could not be halted for long. By the late 1630s no self-respecting astronomer could deny that Galileo's findings and his *Dialogue*, added to Kepler's laws and the *Rudolfine Tables*, had established the correctness of the Copernican theory beyond reasonable doubt.

In a progression of events remarkably similar to the movement from upheaval to resolution that was taking place in politics at this very time (see Chapter 15), scientists had started out by causing tremendous bewilderment and doubt, but had ended up by creating a new kind of certainty that had far-reaching influence. And this was true not only in physics and astronomy, but also in anatomy. For with Vesalius there had begun a period in the study of the human body when many questions were raised but few answers were found. Finally, though, in 1628, another genius of the scientific revolution, the English doctor William Harvey, provided a new and more certain understanding of anatomy when he identified the function of the heart and proved that the blood circulated.

SCIENTIFIC METHOD: A NEW EPISTEMOLOGY

Both Copernicus and Galileo stressed that their discoveries rested on a way of thinking that had an independent value, and they refused to allow traditional considerations, such as the promptings of common sense or the assumptions of theology, to interfere with their conclusions. What the scientists were moving toward was a new epistemology, a new theory of how to obtain and verify knowledge, based on experience, reason, and doubt, rejecting all unsubstantiated authority. Their methods required a revolutionary definition of what could be accepted as a true description of physical reality.

The process the scientists followed after they formulated a hypothesis consisted, in their view, of three parts: first, observations; second, a generalization induced from the observations; and third, tests of the generalization by experiments whose outcome had to conform with the conclusions deducible from the generalization. A generalization remained valid only as long as it was not contradicted by experiments specifically designed to test it. The scientist used no data except the results of strict observation, and his reasoning was confined to the perception of the laws, principles, or patterns that emerged from the observations. Since measurement was the key to the data, the observations had a numerical, not a subjective, value, and the language of science naturally came to be mathematics.

Perhaps the most famous example of the method was the series of experiments Galileo conducted with inclined planes. His original hypothesis was that all objects fall at the same speed and that the difference we see between the time it takes for a stone and a feather to fall is the result only of friction and air resistance (a hypothesis recently confirmed by astronauts on the moon). He first showed that acceleration is a function of time, a proposition which he proved geometrically and then demonstrated by rolling a ball down a plane, noting the time required to make the descent: "We [then] rolled the ball only one-quarter the length of the [plane]; and having measured the time of its descent, we found it precisely one-half of the former [descent]." He

repeated such experiments a hundred times, and always the ratio of the distances was a square of the ratio of the times. From this basic regularity he proceeded to a proof, similarly resting on both geometry and experiment, that regardless of the angle of a descent, a body always reaches the bottom in the same interval of time if the vertical height of its descent remains the same.

This was a classic application of the new scientific method. Mathematics, in this case geometry, allowed Galileo to measure and describe natural phenomena. Carefully controlled experiments then verified conclusions that might seem contrary to common sense. And the progression—hypothesis, observation, generalization, and tests, conducted in the language of mathematics—provided him with a logical structure that could be defeated only on its own terms. Nothing was accepted as given. It was a self-contained mode of demonstration whose conclusions could be rejected solely if disproved by identical procedures.

Scientists in fact rarely move through all the steps toward a conclusion in the exact way this idealized scheme suggests. The French scientist Blaise Pascal, for instance, described an experiment at the foot of a deep vat filled with water that would have been impossible to perform at the time. However, he understood the relevant physical theory so well that he knew what would have happened. In other words, experiments as well as hypotheses can occur in the mind; the essence of scientific method still remains a special way of looking at and understanding nature.

THE WIDER INFLUENCE OF SCIENTIFIC THOUGHT

The principles of scientific inquiry received attention throughout the intellectual community only gradually; it took time for the power of the scientist's method to be recognized. For decades, as Galileo found out, even investigators of nature continued to use what he would have considered irrelevant criteria, such as the teachings of the Bible, in judging scientific work. If acceptance of the new method was to spread, then the literate public would have to be educated in the techniques being employed. This growing understanding was eventually achieved by midcentury as much through the efforts of ardent propagandizers as through the writings of the great innovators themselves.

Francis Bacon

Although not an important scientist himself, Francis Bacon was the greatest of these propagandists, and he inspired an entire generation with his vision of what the discipline could accomplish for mankind. His description of an ideal society in the *New Atlantis*, published in 1627, the year after his death, was the most famous of a series of seventeenth-century descendants of Sir Thomas More's *Utopia*, all af which placed the constant and fruitful advance of science at the center of their schemes. *New Atlantis* is a vision of science as the savior of the human race. It predicts a time when those doing research at the highest levels will be regarded as the most important people in the state and will work on a vast government-supported project to gather all known facts about the physical universe and its properties. By a process of gradual induction, this information will lead to universal laws that in turn will enable man to improve his lot on earth.

Bacon's view of research as a collective enterprise whose aim is the discovery of practical benefits for all made a powerful impact on a number of later scientists, particularly the founders of the English Royal Society. Many cited him as the chief inspiration for their work. Moreover Bacon advocated a total overhaul of the traditional educational curriculum: an end to the study of venerated philosophers and more attention to practical concerns. By the mid-seventeenth century, his ideas had entered the mainstream of European thought, an acceptance that testified to the broadening interest in science and its protagonists.

René Descartes

The French philosopher René Descartes made the first concentrated attempt to apply the new methods of science to theories of knowledge, and in so doing he laid the foundations for modern philosophy. The impulse behind his work was his realization that for all the importance of observation and experiment, man can be deceived by his senses. In order to find some solid truth, therefore, he decided to apply the principle of doubt—the refusal to accept any authority without strict verification—to all knowledge. He began his investigations with the assumption that he could know unquestionably only one thing: he was doubting. This allowed him to proceed to the observation, "I think, therefore I am," because the very act of doubting proved he was thinking, and thinking in turn demonstrated his existence.

The cardinal point of his philosophy was contained in the statement that whatever is clearly and distinctly thought must be true. This was a conclusion drawn from the proof of his own existence, and it enabled him to construct a proof of God's existence. We cannot fail to realize that we are imperfect, he argued, and we must therefore have an idea of perfection against which we may be measured. If we have a clear idea of what perfection is, then it must exist; hence there must be a God.

The proof may not seem entirely convincing to modern readers, particularly since one suspects that a major reason for its prominence

The portrait of René Descartes by the Dutch painter Frans Hals shows the austere thinker who fitted well into the sober atmosphere of Amsterdam. Descartes spent a number of years in the United Provinces, where the exchange of **ideas** *was much freer than in his native France. (Photo: Hubert Joesse/EPI, Inc.)*

was the desire to show that the principle of doubt did not contradict religious belief. Nevertheless the argument is a good illustration of Descartes' assertion that the activity of the mind is the vital element in the search for truth. The title he gave his great work, *Discourse on the Method of Rightly Conducting the Reason and Seeking Truth in the Sciences* (1637), is thus entirely appropriate.[1] Thought is a pure and unmistakable guide, and only by reliance on its operations can man hope to advance his understanding of the world.

Descartes developed this view into a fundamental proposition about the nature of the world and of knowledge—a proposition that philosophers have been wrestling with ever since. He stated that there is an essential dichotomy between thought and extension (tangible objects) or, put another way, between spirit and matter. Various writers, including Bacon and Galileo, had insisted that science, the study of nature, is an undertaking separate from and unaffected by faith or theology, the study of God. But Descartes turned this distinction into a far-reaching principle, dividing not only science from faith but even the reality of the world from our perception of that reality. There is a difference, in other words, between a chair and our understanding of that chair in our minds.

So insistent was he that matter and spirit remain distinct that he undertook a careful examination of human anatomy to discover the seat of the soul. He had to find a part of the body that had no physical function whatsoever, because only there could the soul, a thing of spirit, reside. His candidate was the tiny

pineal gland, which did absolutely nothing, according to the medicine of the day; modern investigations still have not disclosed the function of the hormone it secretes.

The emphasis Descartes placed on the operations of the mind gave a new direction to epistemological discussions. A hypothesis gained credibility not so much from external proofs as from the logical tightness of the arguments used to support it. The decisive test was how lucid and irrefutable a statement appeared to be to the thinking mind. Descartes thus applied what he considered to be the methods of science to all knowledge. Not only the phenomena of nature but all truth had to be investigated according to the strict principles of the scientist.

Descartes' own contributions to the research of his day were theoretical rather than experimental. In physics he was the first to perceive the distinction between mass and weight, and in mathematics he was the first to apply algebraic notations and methods to geometry, thus founding analytic geometry. When he turned to astronomy, however, he formulated a theory of planetary motion based on enormous whirling vortexes, rather like the cones of tornadoes, that has come to be regarded as one of the curiosities of the scientific revolution.

The failings of specific theories, however, do not detract from Descartes' position as a prime mover of the revolution in Western thought during the seventeenth century. His emphasis on the principle of doubt irrevocably undermined such traditional assumptions as the belief in the hierarchical organization of the universe. Possibly he put too much trust in the powers of the mind, but it is undeniable that he laid down the strict procedures that philosophy—and in fact any speculation about man or his world—had to follow. And the European intellectual community accepted

---

[1] Like Galileo's *Dialogue*, Descartes' *Discourse* was written in a vernacular language. It thus had a much more popular audience than a Latin book would have received, though after a few years it was translated into Latin so that scholars from all European countries could read it.

this approach with enthusiasm. The admiration he inspired indicated how completely the methods he advocated had captured his contemporaries' imagination.

Thomas Hobbes

A notable example of the borrowings inspired by the scientists were the writings of Thomas Hobbes, who used their method to make an extraordinarily original contribution to political theory.

A story has it that Hobbes once picked up a copy of Euclid's *Elements* and opened the book in the middle. The theorem on that page seemed totally without foundation, but it rested on a proof in the preceding theorem. Working his way backward, he discovered himself finally having to accept no more than the proposition that the shortest distance between two points is a straight line. He thereupon resolved to use the same approach in analyzing political behavior. The story is probably apocryphal because as a young man Hobbes was secretary to Francis Bacon, who doubtless gave him his first taste of scientific work. Nevertheless it does capture the essence of Hobbes' approach, for he did begin his masterpiece, *Leviathan* (published in 1651), with a few limited premises about human nature from which he rigorously deduced major conclusions about political forms.

Hobbes' premises, drawn from his observation of the strife-ridden Europe of his day, were stark and uncompromising. Man, he asserted, is selfish and ambitious; consequently, unless he is restrained, he fights a perpetual war with his fellows. The weak man is more cunning and the stronger more stupid. Given these unsavory characteristics, the state of nature—which precedes the existence of society —is a state of war, in which life is "nasty, brutish, and short." Hobbes' conclusion was that the only way to restrain this instinctive ag-

gressiveness is to erect an absolute and sovereign power that will maintain peace. Everyone must submit to the sovereign because the alternative is the anarchy of the state of nature. The moment of submission is the moment of the birth of orderly society.

In a startling innovation Hobbes suggested that the transition from nature to society is accomplished by a contract that is implicitly accepted by all who wish to end the chaos. They agree among themselves to submit to the sovereign, thus the sovereign is not a party to the contract and is not limited in any way. A government is totally free to do whatever it wishes to keep the peace. However tyrannous, this solution is always better than the turmoil it has replaced.

Both contemporaries and later writers were strongly influenced by Hobbes, not only because his logic was compelling but also because he seemed so much like a scientist. From his observations of men, he had induced general propositions about human behavior, and from these he had deduced certain political lessons that were verified by European politics. Moreover he had applied a mechanistic view to man more thoroughly than ever before, reducing all that human beings do to simple appetites and aversions.

In doing so he contributed to the popularity of the mechanistic view of the universe, a theory derived in part from the materialistic implications of Descartes' philosophy. In its simplest form mechanism holds that the entire universe, including man himself, can be regarded as a complicated machine and thus subject to strict physical principles. The arm is like a lever, the elbow like a hinge, and so on. Even an emotion is no more than a simple response to a definable stimulus.

But this approach also aroused hostility. Although they were deeply affected by his ideas, most of Hobbes' successors denounced him as godless, immoral, cynical, and unfeeling. These were charges that could be leveled at all practitioners of science, but for a long time they were not raised, largely because the scientists dealt with areas that seemed to have nothing to do with human behavior.

Blaise Pascal

At midcentury only one important voice still protested against the new science. It belonged to a young Frenchman, Blaise Pascal, one of the most brilliant mathematicians and experimenters of the time. Before his death at the age of thirty-nine, in 1662, Pascal's investigations of probability in games of chance led him to the theorem that still bears his name, and his research in conic sections helped lay the foundations for integral calculus. He also explored the properties of the vacuum and invented a versatile calculating machine.

In his late twenties, however, Pascal became increasingly dissatisfied with scientific research, and he began to wonder whether his life was being properly spent. His doubts were reinforced by frequent visits to his sister, a nun at the Abbey of Port-Royal, where he came into contact with a new spiritual movement within Catholicism known as Jansenism.

The movement took its name from Cornelis Jansen, a bishop who had written a book suggesting that the Catholic Church had forgotten the teachings of its greatest father, St. Augustine. Jansen insisted that man was not free to determine his own fate, that salvation was entirely in the hands of an all-powerful God, and that unswerving faith was the only path to salvation. These doctrines sounded ominously like Protestant teachings, and during the years after Jansen's death, the Catholic Church and especially the Jesuits, who placed great emphasis on freedom of will, made various attempts to suppress his beliefs.

Jansenism was not a particularly popular movement at the time, and its adherents consisted of little more than the immediate circle of a prominent family of magistrates, the Arnaulds, one of whom was the head of Port-Royal. But Pascal was profoundly impressed by the piety, asceticism, and spirituality at Port-Royal, and in November of 1654 he had a mystical experience that made him resolve to devote the rest of his life to the salvation of his soul. He wrote a series of devastating critiques of the Jesuits, accusing them of irresponsibility and, as he phrased it, of placing cushions under sinners' elbows.

During the few remaining years of his life, Pascal put on paper a collection of reflections —some only a few words long, some many pages—that were gathered together after his death and published as the *Pensées* (or "reflections"). These writings revealed not only the beliefs of a deeply religious man but also the anxieties of a scientist who feared the growing influence of science. He did not wish to put an end to research; he merely wanted people to realize that the truths uncovered by science were limited and not as important as the truths perceived by faith. In the words of one of his more memorable phrases, "The heart has its reasons that the mind cannot know."

Pascal was warning against the replacement of the traditional understanding of man and his destiny, gained through religious faith, with the conclusions reached by the methods of the scientists. The separation between the material and the spiritual would be fatal, he believed, because it would destroy the primacy and even the importance of the spiritual. Pascal's protest was unique, but the fact that it was raised at all indicates how high the status of the scientist and his method had risen by the 1650s. A scant quarter-century earlier, such a dramatic change in fortune would have been hard to predict, but now many intellectuals, seeing an opportunity of ending

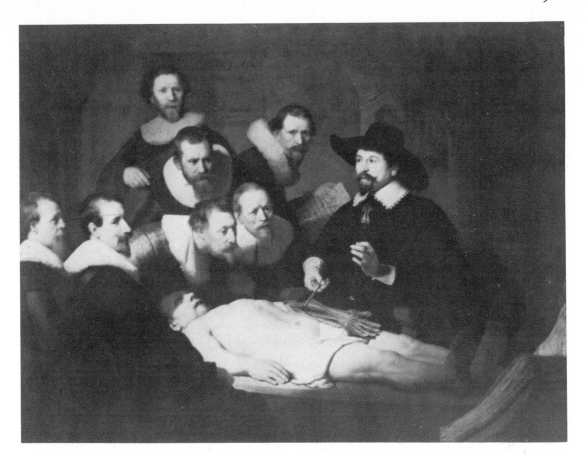

Among the many representations of the public anatomy lessons so popular in seventeenth-century Holland, the most famous is one of Rembrandt's greatest paintings, The Anatomy Lesson of Dr. Nicholaas Tulp. (Photo: A. Dingjan)

the uncertainties that had bedeviled their work for decades, eagerly adopted the new epistemology. Turmoil was once again giving way to assurance.

SCIENCE INSTITUTIONALIZED

There were many besides Bacon who realized that scientific work should be a common endeavor, pursued cooperatively by all its practitioners, and that information should be exchanged so that researchers might concentrate on different parts of a project instead of wasting time and energy following identical paths. The first major effort to apply this view was undertaken by the Lincean Academy,[2] founded under the patronage of a nobleman in Rome in 1603. Organizations of scientists had existed before, but this was the first assemblage interested in all branches of science and in

---

[2] The academy was named after Linceus, reputedly the most keen-sighted of the legendary Argonauts of ancient times.

publishing the findings of its members. After the decline of research in Italy, however, the academy gradually lost its importance.

More fruitful beginnings were made in France, where in the first decades of the seventeenth century a friar named Marin Mersenne became the center of an international network of correspondents interested in scientific work. He increased the dissemination of news by also bringing scientists together for discussions or experiments. The meetings were sporadic, but out of them developed procedures that led to a more permanent organization of scientific activity.

The first important steps toward establishing a permanent body in England were taken at Oxford during the Civil War when the revolutionaries captured the city and replaced many traditionalists at the university. A few of the newcomers formed what they called the Invisible College, a group that met to exchange information and discuss one another's work. What was important was the enterprise, not its results, for the group included only one first-class scientist: the young chemist Robert Boyle. In 1660 twelve members, including Boyle and the architect Sir Christopher Wren, formed an official organization, the Royal Society of London for Improving Natural Knowledge, with headquarters in the capital and a council to supervise its affairs. In 1662 it was granted a charter by Charles II.

The Royal Society's purposes were openly Baconian. Its aim for the first few years—until everyone realized it was impossible—was to gather all knowledge about nature, particularly whatever might be useful. For a long time the members continued to offer their services for the public good, helping in one instance to develop the science of social statistics ("political arithmetic" as it was called) for the government. Soon, however, it became clear that their principal function was to serve

as a headquarters and clearing center for research. Their secretaries maintained an enormous correspondence, encouraging foreign scholars to transmit their discoveries to the society. And in 1665 they began the regular publication of *Philosophical Transactions*, the first professional scientific journal.

As a stimulus to new discoveries, the Royal Society was without peer in seventeenth-century Europe. Imitators were soon to follow. In 1666 Louis XIV gave his blessing to the founding of the Royal Academy of Sciences, and similar organizations were established in Naples and Berlin by 1700. Membership in these societies was limited and highly prized, a symptom of the glamour that was beginning to attach itself to the new studies. By the 1660s there could be no doubt that science, secure in royal patronage, had triumphed. Its practitioners were extravagantly admired, and throughout intellectual and high social circles, there was a feverish scramble to apply its methods and its mode of thought to almost every conceivable activity.

Descartes himself had applied the techniques of science to epistemology and more broadly to philosophy in general; Bacon and Hobbes had put them at the service of social and political thought. But the borrowings were not only at these exalted levels. Formal gardens were designed to exhibit the order, harmony, and reason that science had made the most prized qualities of the time. And the arts of fortification and warfare were transformed by the adoption of principles learned from the new investigations, such as accurate measurement.

As the scientists' activities grew in popularity, amateurs known as virtuosos began to proliferate. These were usually aristocrats who spent their time playing at science. Herbariums and small observatories were added to country estates, and parties would feature an evening of star gazing. Some virtuosos took their tasks quite seriously—an early Italian enthusiast, Prince Federigo Cesi, joined in the first investigations with a microscope, a study of bees; and one English country gentleman inundated the Royal Society with meticulous observations of local sand dunes. But by and large these frivolous scientists are interesting primarily because they reveal the awe and delight aroused by a new discipline that had revolutionized man's understanding of nature.

Science was also beginning to have an impact on the general populace. Among the most eagerly anticipated occasions in seventeenth-century Holland was the public anatomy lesson. The body of a criminal would be brought to an enormous hall, packed with students and a fascinated public. A famous surgeon would dissect the cadaver, announcing and displaying each organ as he removed it.

On the whole, the influence of the scientists on laymen was not dependent on the technological improvements from their work. And by our standards much of what they did, even at the theoretical level, seems primitive at best. What this suggests is that the reverence for science and its methods developed not from a broad understanding of actual accomplishments or their potential consequences but from the fame of the spectacular discoveries which enabled a few brilliant men to provide startlingly convincing solutions to centuries-old problems in astronomy, physics, and anatomy. Thus the disturbing implications of a Hobbes, like the protests of a Pascal, could be ignored, and the new discipline could be given unblemished admiration. The entire world was coming to be viewed through the scientist's eyes —a striking victory for a recently struggling member of the intellectual community—and the qualities of regularity and harmony that he stood for began to appear in the work of playwrights and poets, artists and architects.

II. LITERATURE AND THE ARTS

Changes in culture were not as clear-cut as in politics or science, but certain parallels are evident. During the second half of the sixteenth century and into the 1610s, the tensions and uncertainties of the age were visible in the paintings of the Mannerists, and in the writings of Montaigne, Cervantes, and Shakespeare. Thereafter, two major styles dominated Europe: the Baroque, which consciously sought to arouse the emotions and achieve dramatic effects, and the Classical, which epitomized discipline, restraint, and sometimes decorum. Very gradually over the course of the seventeenth century, the emphasis moved from the values of the Baroque to those of the Classical. This shift in artistic aims bore a distinct resemblance to the sense of settlement that descended over other areas of European civilization at midcentury.

THE CULTURE OF THE LATE SIXTEENTH CENTURY

One response to the upheavals of the sixteenth century was the attempt to escape reality, to devise a distorted view of the world. It was especially noticeable in the work of the great painters of the age. Acutely sensitive to the disruptions and changes that surrounded them, they created a strange and uneasy vision of human existence.

The Mannerists

As early as the 1520s, a reaction had set in against the balance and serenity of the High Renaissance style. The artists involved in this movement, which lasted about eighty years, are generally called Mannerists. No specific characteristics united them, but they all wished to go beyond reality and to develop theatrical and disturbing qualities in their paintings. They undermined perspectives, distorted human figures, and devised unnatural colors and lighting to create startling effects. Even the great figures of the High Renaissance were affected by this orientation. Michelangelo, who lived until 1564, began to create tortured, agonized figures writhing in violent action; Titian, who died in 1576, placed a shrieking Magdalene in his last painting, a subdued Pietà.

The movement was embodied, however, in Parmigianino, an Italian, and El Greco, a Greek living in Spain. Parmigianino's *Madonna of the Long Neck* (see Plate 26), named after its most salient feature, typifies his efforts to unsettle the viewer with tricks of perspective, odd postures, and an unbalanced composition. El Greco, a man whose compelling and disturbing vision symbolized the uneasy age in which he lived, took these devices even farther. His elongated human beings, cool colors, and eerie lighting make him one of the most distinctive painters in the history of art (see Plate 29).

Michel de Montaigne

The man who expressed the most vivid concern about the upheavals and uncertainties of his age was Michel de Montaigne, the greatest humanist and philosopher of the late sixteenth century. Born into the French petty nobility, he suffered a shock at the age of thirty—the death of his closest friend—that changed the course of his life. Obsessed by death, he began one of the most moving explorations in European intellectual history.

Determined to overcome his fears, Montaigne retired to a tower in his country home in order to "essay," or test, his innermost feelings by writing short pieces of prose even about subjects he did not fully comprehend. In the process he created a new literary form, the essay, and shaped the development of the French language. But his chief influence was philosophical: he has inspired the search for self-knowledge since his time, from René Descartes and Blaise Pascal to the Existentialists of the twentieth century.

In the 1570s Montaigne's interests turned to Skepticism, which appeared in full flower in his longest essay, "An Apology for Raymond Sebond." Sebond was a Spanish theologian who tried to prove the truth of Christianity by the use of reason. Montaigne firmly rejected Sebond's belief in the power of the mind and emerged from this essay with the total uncertainty of the motto *"Que sais-je?"* ("What do I know?")

In his last years Montaigne struggled toward a more confident solution of his uncertainties, taking as his model the ancient saying, "Know thyself." By looking into his own person, each human being can find answers and values that hold true at least for himself: all truths and customs are relative, but by looking into himself, he can look into all humanity. Montaigne even came close to a morality without theology, because good and self-determination were more important to him than doctrine, and he saw everywhere religious people committing inhuman acts. Man, he argued, can know good and can achieve it by an effort of will. Trying to be an angel is wrong; being a good man is enough.

This process of self-discovery was a radical and totally secular individualism. It required a joyous acceptance of the world that finally gave Montaigne the optimistic answer to his anguish—though it was a unique, personal answer that gave comfort to few other people.

Cervantes and Shakespeare

In Spain the disillusionment that accompanied the decline of Europe's most powerful state was perfectly captured by Miguel de Cervantes (1547–1616). He was heir to a brilliant satirical and descriptive tradition that had already produced a classic literature in the sixteenth century in the writings of Erasmus and Rabelais. Cervantes saw the wide gap between the hopes and the realities of his day—in religion, in social institutions, in human behavior—and made the dichotomy the basis of the scathing social satire in his novel *Don Quixote*.

At one level Cervantes was ridiculing the excessive chivalry of the Spanish nobility in his portrayal of a knight who was ready to tilt at windmills, though he obviously admired the sincerity of his well-meaning hero and sympathized with him as a perennial loser. On another level the author brought to life the Europe of the time—the ordinary people and their hypocrisies and intolerances—with a liveliness rarely matched in literature. His view of that society, however, was far from cheery. "Justice, but not for my house," says Don Quixote as he experiences the foibles of mankind, particularly of those in authority. Cervantes avoided politics, but he was clearly directing many of his sharpest barbs at the brutality and disregard for human values that were characteristic of his fanatical times. What were Spain's repeated crusades accomplishing? Were Quixote's dreams as worthy as Sancho Panza's blunt and sensible pragmatism? These were not easy questions to answer, but they went to the heart of the dilemmas of the age. And in Spain's great enemy, England, another towering figure was grappling with similar problems.

For the English-speaking world, the most brilliant creative artist of this and all other periods was William Shakespeare, whose plays capture every conceivable mood—searing grief, airy romance, rousing nationalism, uproarious and farcical humor. Despite little education he disclosed in his imagery a familiarity with subjects ranging from astronomy to seamanship, from alchemy to warfare. It is not surprising therefore that some have doubted that one man could have produced this amazing body of work.

Shakespeare started writing in the 1590s, when he was in his late twenties, and continued until his death, in 1616. During most of this time, he was also involved with a theatrical company, and he often had to produce plays on very short notice. He thus had the best of all possible tests as he gained mastery of theatrical techniques—audience reaction.

Shakespeare rose far above his setting to timeless statements about human behavior: love, hatred, violence, sin. Of particular interest to the historian, however, is what he tells us about attitudes that belong especially to his own era. For example the conservatism of his characters is quite clear. They believe firmly in the hierarchical structure of society, and throughout the long series of historical plays, events suggest that excessive ambition does not pay. The series begins with Richard II, a legitimate monarch who is overthrown by a usurper, with catastrophic results. Repeated disasters follow as the chronicle is taken through the War of the Roses to the restoration of order by the Tudors. Again and again legality and stability are shown as fundamental virtues—a natural reaction against turbulent times. Shakespeare's expressions of nationalism are particularly intense; when in *Richard II* the king's uncle, John of Gaunt, lies dying, he pours out his love for his country in words that have moved Englishmen ever since:

> This royal throne of kings, this sceptered isle,
> This earth of majesty, this seat of Mars,
> This other Eden, demi-paradise, . . .
> This happy breed of men, this little world,
> This precious stone set in the silver sea, . . .
> This blessed plot, this earth, this realm, this
>   England.
>
> [*Richard II*, act 2, scene 1]

The uncertainties of the day appear in many of the plays. In *Julius Caesar* the optimistic "There is a tide in the affairs of men, which, taken at the flood, leads on to fortune" celebrates vigor and decisiveness but also warns against missing opportunities. And Hamlet offers the sober conclusion, "There's a divinity that shapes our ends, rough-hew them how we will." Shakespeare's four most famous tragedies, *Hamlet, Lear, Macbeth,* and *Othello,* end in disillusionment: the heroes are ruined by irresoluteness, pride, ambition, or jealousy. He is reflecting the Elizabethans' interest in the fatal flaws that destroy great men and in dramas of revenge, but the plays demonstrate as well his deep understanding of human nature. For all the promise of the future, one cannot forget man's weakness, the inevitability of decay, and the constant threat of disaster. The contrast appears with compelling clarity in a speech delivered by Hamlet:

> What a piece of work is man! how noble in reason! how infinite in faculties! in form and moving how express and admirable! in action how like an angel! in apprehension how like a god! the beauty of the world, the paragon of animals! And yet to me what is this quintessence of dust? Man delights not me.
> [*Hamlet*, act 2, scene 2]

Despite such pessimism, despite the deep sense of human inadequacy, the total impression Shakespeare gives is of immense vigor, of a restlessness and confidence that recall the many achievements of the sixteenth century. Prospero, the hero of his last play, *The Tempest*, has often been seen as the symbol of the new magician-cum-scientist, and references to the discoveries overseas are abundant. Yet a sense of decay is never far absent. Repeatedly men seem utterly helpless, overtaken by events they cannot control. There is a striking lack of security in the world Shakespeare's people inhabit. Nothing remains constant or dependable, and everything that seems solid and reassuring, be it the love of a daughter or the crown of England, is challenged. In this atmosphere of ceaseless change, where all solid, safe landmarks disappear, Shakespeare forcefully conveys the tensions of his time.

THE BAROQUE AND CLASSICISM

From around 1600 onward, new concerns began to gain prominence in the arts and literature. First, in the Baroque there was an attempt to drown uncertainty in a blaze of grandeur and drama. But gradually the aims of Classicism, which emphasized formality, balance, and restraint, came to dominate European culture.

The Baroque

The word "Baroque" has been taken to indicate ornateness, grandeur, and excess as well as all the traits, including the Classical, of seventeenth-century art. Historians have applied it to music, literature, politics, and even personality traits. Its usage here will be restricted to its most precise meaning: the characteristics of a style in the visual arts that emanated from Rome in the first half of the seventeenth century. Passion, drama, mystery, and awe are the qualities of the Baroque: the viewer must be involved, aroused, uplifted. Insofar as these characteristics are reflected in other kinds of creative work, such as literature and music, it is reasonable to discuss the various examples together; but to regard all manifestations of dramatic splendor or grandiose extravagance as Baroque is to depart from the essentially visual meaning of the term.

The Baroque was closely associated with the Counter Reformation's emphasis on gorgeous display in Catholic ritual. The patronage bestowed by leading church figures and the presence of art treasures accumulated over centuries made Rome a magnet for the major painters of the period. Elsewhere the Baroque flourished primarily at the leading Catholic courts of the seventeenth century, most no-

The contrasting postures of victory and defeat are masterfully captured by Diego Velázquez in The Surrender of Breda. *The Dutch soldiers droop their heads and lances, but the victorious Spaniards hardly show triumph, and the gesture of the victorious general, Ambrosio Spinola, is one of consolation and understanding.* (Photo: Prado Museum)

tably the Hapsburg courts in Madrid, Prague, and Brussels and the ducal court of Bavaria, since the style expressed perfectly the pomp of seventeenth-century princes. Few periods have conveyed so strong a sense of grandeur, theatricality, and ornateness.

Peter Paul Rubens (1577–1640) was the principal ornament of the brilliant Hapsburg court at Brussels. His major themes typified the Baroque style: glorification of great rulers (see Plate 37) and exaltation of the ceremony and mystery of Catholicism. His secular paintings convey, by their powerful depiction of human bodies and vivid use of color, the awe-inspiring might of his subjects; his religious works similarly overwhelm the viewer with the majesty and panoply of the church and excite the believer's piety by stressing the dramatic mysteries of the faith. Toward the end of his life Rubens' paintings became more lyrical, especially on mythological subjects, but he never lost his ability to generate strong emotions.

Other artists glorified rulers of the time through idealized portraiture. The greatest court painter of the age was Diego Velázquez, some twenty-two years Rubens' junior. His portraits of members of the Spanish court depict rulers and their surroundings in the stately atmosphere appropriate to the theme (see Plate 38). Yet occasionally Velázquez hinted at the weakness of an ineffective monarch in his rendering of the face, even though the basic purpose of his work always remained the exaltation of royal power. And when he painted a celebration of a notable Hapsburg victory, *The Surrender of Breda*, he managed to suggest the sadness and emptiness as much as the glory of war.

Giovanni Lorenzo Bernini was to sculpture and architecture what Rubens was to painting,

and like Rubens he was closely associated with the Counter Reformation. Pope Urban VIII commissioned him in 1629 to complete both the inside and the outer setting of St. Peter's, extending and elaborating Michelangelo's original architectural plan. For the interior Bernini designed a splendid papal throne that seems to float on clouds beneath a burst of sunlight, and for the exterior he created an enormous plaza, surrounded by a double colonnade, that is the largest and most imposing square in all Europe.

The glories of Baroque Rome owe much to the work of Bernini. The elaborate fountains he sculpted can be seen throughout the city; his busts of contemporary Roman leaders set the style for portraiture in marble or stone; and his dramatic religious works reflect the desire of the Counter Reformation popes to electrify the faithful. The sensual and overpowering altarpiece dedicated to the Spanish mystic St. Theresa makes a direct appeal to the emotions of the beholder that reveals the excitement of Baroque at its best (see Plate 35). And drama is also immediately apparent in his *David*, which shows the young warrior at his supreme moment, just after he has unleashed his slingshot at Goliath. Bernini emphasized the intense exertion and concentration of this moment as an expression of human vigor, and with a touch that was characteristic of the bravado of the times he gave the figure his own face.

Similar qualities can be seen in the architecture of the age. Ornate churches and palaces were built on a massive scale that paralleled exactly the concerns of painting and sculpture. And it is significant that the three most conspicuous centers of the Counter Reformation—Rome, Munich, and Prague—were also major centers of Baroque architecture.[3]

David *by Bernini*. (Photo: Alinari–Art Reference Bureau)

---

[3] A good survey of Baroque architecture can be found in Nikolaus Pevsner, *An Outline of European Architecture* (1943 and later editions), Chap. 6.

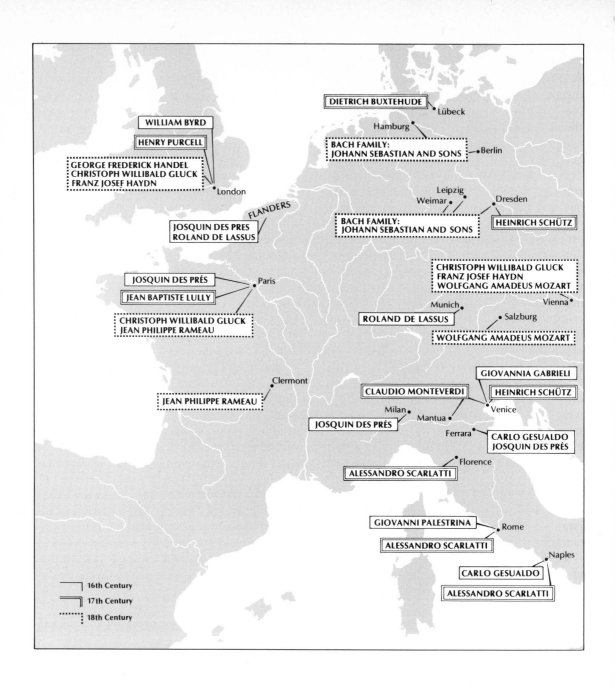

MAP 16.1: CENTERS OF MUSIC 1500–1800

Map labels:

DIETRICH BUXTEHUDE — Lübeck

Hamburg

BACH FAMILY: JOHANN SEBASTIAN AND SONS — Berlin

WILLIAM BYRD

HENRY PURCELL

GEORGE FREDERICK HANDEL
CHRISTOPH WILLIBALD GLUCK
FRANZ JOSEF HAYDN — London

Leipzig
Weimar
Dresden

FLANDERS

BACH FAMILY: JOHANN SEBASTIAN AND SONS

HEINRICH SCHÜTZ

JOSQUIN DES PRES
ROLAND DE LASSUS

JOSQUIN DES PRÉS

JEAN BAPTISTE LULLY — Paris

CHRISTOPH WILLIBALD GLUCK
FRANZ JOSEF HAYDN
WOLFGANG AMADEUS MOZART

Munich
Salzburg
Vienna

ROLAND DE LASSUS

CHRISTOPH WILLIBALD GLUCK
JEAN PHILIPPE RAMEAU

WOLFGANG AMADEUS MOZART

Clermont

GIOVANNIA GABRIELI

JEAN PHILIPPE RAMEAU

CLAUDIO MONTEVERDI

HEINRICH SCHÜTZ

Milan
Mantua
Venice

JOSQUIN DES PRÉS

Ferrara

CARLO GESUALDO
JOSQUIN DES PRÉS

Florence

ALESSANDRO SCARLATTI

GIOVANNI PALESTRINA — Rome

ALESSANDRO SCARLATTI

Naples

CARLO GESUALDO

ALESSANDRO SCARLATTI

16th Century
17th Century
18th Century

The seventeenth century was significant, too, as a decisive time in the history of music. New instruments were developed, notably in the keyboard and string families, that enabled composers to create richer effects than had been possible before. Musicians also began to explore the potential of a form that first emerged in these years: the opera. Drawing on the resources of the theater, painting, architecture, music, and the dance, an operatic production could achieve a panoply of splendors beyond the reach of any one of these arts on its own. The form perfectly attuned to the courtly culture of the age, to the love of display among the princes of Europe.

The dominant figure in seventeenth-century music was the Italian Claudio Monteverdi, one of the most innovative composers of all time. He has been called with some justification the creator of both the operatic form and the orchestra. His masterpiece *Orfeo* (1607) was written for his patron, the duke of Mantua, whose court provided Monteverdi with the many skilled professionals needed to mount an opera, from scene painters to singers. The result was a tremendous success, and in the course of the next century, the opera gained in richness and complexity, attracting composers, as well as audiences, in ever increasing numbers.

There was a similar extension of the range of instrumental music. The accompaniment to *Orfeo* was still scored primarily for plucked instruments like the lute, which (except for the harp) were soon to disappear from the orchestra, but in his later works Monteverdi began to rely increasingly on strings and woodwinds. He became much freer in his use of extended melodies and readier to introduce unexpected discords, which give his works a flavor decidedly different from the music of earlier composers and reasonably familiar to modern ears.

Classicism

Classicism, the second major style of the seventeenth century, attempted to recapture the aesthetic values of ancient Greece and Rome. What this usually meant in practice was an acceptance of the strict forms embodied in the works of antiquity. Like the Baroque, Classicism aimed for grandiose effects, but it achieved them through restraint and discipline, within the bounds of a formal structure. The gradual rise of the Classical style in the seventeenth century echoed the trend toward stabilization that was taking place in other areas of intellectual life and in politics.

The epitome of disciplined expression and conscious imitation of classical antiquity is the work of Nicolas Poussin (1594–1665), a French artist who spent much of his career in Italy among the relics of Rome's glory. Poussin was no less interested than his contemporaries in momentous subjects and dramatic scenes, but the atmosphere in his canvases is always more subdued than in those of Velázquez or Rubens. The colors are muted, the figures are restrained, and the settings are serene. Peaceful landscapes, men and women in stately togas, and ruins of classical buildings are consistent features of his work, even his religious paintings (see Plate 43).

In the United Provinces different forces were at work, but they too led to a style that was much more subdued than the powerful outpourings of Rubens and Velázquez. Two aspects of Dutch society had a particular influence: Protestantism and republicanism. The Reformed Church frowned on religious art and thus reduced the demand, both ceremonial and private, for paintings of biblical scenes. Religious works therefore tended to be expressions of personal faith, not glorifications of the church. The absence of a court meant that the chief patrons were sober merchants, who were far more interested in precise, dignified portraits than in ornate displays. The result, notably in the work of the most powerful Dutch master, Rembrandt van Rijn, was an epic and compelling art whose beauty lies in its calmness and restraint.

Rembrandt explored an amazing range of themes, but his greatest paintings are his portraits. He was fascinated by human beings—their personalities, emotions, and self-revelations. Whether children or old people, simple servant girls or rich burghers, they are presented without elaboration or idealization; always the personality is allowed to speak for itself.

His most remarkable achievement in portraiture—and one of the most moving series of canvases in the history of art—is his depiction of the changes in his own face over his lifetime. The brash youth turns into the confident, successful, middle-aged man, one of the most sought-after painters in Holland. But in his late thirties the sorrows mounted: he lost his beloved wife, and commissions began to fall off. Sadness fills the eyes in these pictures. The last portraits move from despair to a final, quiet resignation as his sight slowly failed (see Plate 40). Taken together, these paintings bear comparison with Montaigne's essays as monuments to man's exploration of his own spirit—a searching appraisal that brings all who see it to a deeper understanding of human nature.

Rembrandt's large-scale, grandiose undertakings, like his smaller works, avoided startling effects. His many religious works, for example, are subdued and reverential in their approach, reflecting his own faith. The atmosphere differs sharply from the swirling passion conveyed by Rubens, who emphasized the drama of an event, whereas Rembrandt entered into the overwhelming emotions of the people present.

One could argue that Rembrandt cannot be fitted into either of the dominant styles of his time. Except for his powerful use of light, his work is far more introspective than most of the Baroque. On the other hand he did not adopt the forms of antiquity, as did Poussin and other Classical painters. Yet like the advocates of Classicism, Rembrandt in his restraint seemed to anticipate the art of the next generation. After his death, in 1669, serenity, calm, and elegance became the watchwords of European painting. An age of repose and grace was succeeding a time of upheaval as surely in the arts as in other spheres of life.

By the middle of the seventeenth century, the formalism of the Classical style was also being extended to literature, especially drama. This change was most noticeable in France, but it soon moved through Western Europe, as leading critics demanded that new plays conform to the structure laid down by the ancients. In particular they wanted the three unities observed: unity of place, which required that all scenes take place without change of location; unity of time, which demanded that the events in the play occur within a twenty-four hour period; and unity of action, which dictated simplicity and purity of plot.

The work of Pierre Corneille, the dominant figure in the French theater during the mid-century years, reflects the rise of Classicism. His early plays resemble rather complex Shakespearean drama, and even after he came in contact with the Classical tradition, his effervescent genius did not accept its rules easily. His masterpiece Le Cid (1636), based on the legends of a medieval Spanish hero, technically observed the three unities but only by compressing an entire tragic love affair, a military campaign, and multitudinous other events into one day. The play won immediate popular success, but the critics, urged on by Richelieu, an advocate of Classical drama, condemned Corneille for imperfect observance of the three unities. Thereafter he adhered to the Classical forms, though he was never entirely at ease with their restraints.

Passion was not absent from the strictly Classical play; the works of Jean Racine, the model Classical dramatist, portrayed some of the most intense emotion ever seen on the stage. But the exuberance of earlier drama, the enjoyment of life and of human nature, was disappearing. Only the figure of Molière was to retain these qualities, and even he respected the formalism of the Classical style. Nobody summed up the values of Classicism better than Racine in his obituary eulogy of Corneille:

> You know in what a condition the stage was when he began to write. . . . All the rules of art, and even those of decency and decorum, broken everywhere. . . . Corneille, after having for some time sought the right path and struggled against the bad taste of his day, inspired by extraordinary genius and helped by the study of the ancients, at last brought reason upon the stage.[4]

This was exactly the progression—from turbulence to calm—that was apparent throughout European culture in this period.

III. SOCIAL PATTERNS AND POPULAR CULTURE

It is difficult to draw analogies between, on the one hand, changes in the way ordinary people lived or in their customs and, on the other hand, the movement of ideas among a small, highly literate group of intellectual and artistic geniuses. There were points of contact and influence, to be sure. The magical interests of astrologers and alchemists were not far removed from the belief in hidden mysteries and spirits that influenced the inhabitants of every European village. In the late seventeenth century the first collections of folk tales were published, put together by writers who assumed that ancient wisdom was revealed in the sayings and stories of peasants. And ordinary men and women could not help but be affected by the attitudes and instructions imposed on them by their rulers. Nevertheless, one must not make the connections too close. Popular culture had roots of its own, and if we see certain trends toward restraint and order that parallel what was happening in politics and literate culture, they must not be overdrawn. Apart from anything else, the absence of social mobility and the effects of demographic trends were basic determinants of the life and outlook of the peasant and the poor; these limitations must be understood before one can even begin to consider the place of popular behavior and belief in the history of the times.

HIERARCHY AND RANK IN THE SOCIAL ORDER

Seventeenth-century men occupied well-defined places in society. According to a common view, they formed links in the great chain of being, which, ascending by degrees, united all of creation with the angels and God. Man stood in the middle of the chain between animals and angels, and within mankind there were also degrees, rising from the peasant through the well-to-do landowner or professional and the noble to the king. It was considered against the order of nature for someone to move to another level of society.

---

[4] Jean Racine, *Discours Prononcé à l'Académie Française à la Réception de M. de Corneille* (1685), in Paul Mesnard (ed.), *Oeuvres de J. Racine*, IV (1886), p. 366. Translation by Theodore K. Rabb.

URBAN POPULATION

○ Cities of Over 40,000 in 1700

● Cities of Over 100,000 in 1700

■ Cities of Over 200,000 in 1700

MAP 16.2: CITIES OF EUROPE IN 1700

In fact, though, the people of the seventeenth century divided themselves into multiple groups and strata. Perhaps the clearest way to describe this structure is to liken society to a set of four ladders, each representing a distinct group: those on the land (about four-fifths of the population), those in the clergy, those in commerce (including artisans and shopkeepers), and those in the professions (mainly lawyers, doctors, and teachers). Within each ladder there was a sharply differentiated hierarchy, but most positions on each ladder had rough equivalents on the others. While all four were parallel, the landed ladder was clearly superior in that it rose higher and included the leaders of society, the courtiers and the great magnates.

Mobility and Privilege

The determinants of status in modern times —wealth, family background, and education —were viewed rather differently in the seventeenth century. Wealth was significant chiefly to merchants, education was important mainly among professionals, and background was vital primarily to the nobility. But in this period the significance of these three social indicators began to shift. Wealth grew increasingly respectable as ever-larger numbers of successful merchants bought their way into the nobility. Education was also becoming more highly prized; throughout Europe attendance at institutions of higher learning soared after 1550 because a smattering of knowledge was now considered to be a mark of gentility.[5] And background was being scrutinized ever more carefully (though to less effect) by old-line nobles, who were dismayed at the multiplication of "new" aristocrats.

---

[5] See Lawrence Stone, "The Educational Revolution in England, 1560–1640," *Past & Present*, July 1964, pp. 41–80.

The growing social importance of wealth and education indicates that mobility was possible despite the great chain of being. Thanks to the expansion of bureaucracies during the sixteenth and seventeenth centuries, it became easier for men to move to new levels, either by winning favor at court or by buying an office. High status conferred important privileges: great landowners could demand services and taxes from their tenants; city freemen, nobles, and bureaucrats were frequently exempt from taxes; and courtiers controlled portions of the vast patronage that the government disbursed. This period witnessed the rise of some of the most successful self-made men in history, particularly among the ministers who served the kings of England and France.

Somewhat different patterns were emerging in Europe's colonies. From their earliest days, the overseas settlements had reflected their countries of origin. Both the Portuguese and the Dutch for example had concentrated almost exclusively on commerce. They had small populations and were incapable of conquering large areas; instead they established a network of trading posts linked by sea that were marked by an effort to live amicably amid the native populations. The French followed a similar practice for a different reason: because the home country was rich in land and prosperous, few of its inhabitants were willing to emigrate. Spaniards and Englishmen by contrast flocked to new settlements in search of gold, land, and religious freedom. They remained overseas, occupying vast territories, subduing the natives, and creating extensive political structures that were far more elaborate than the earlier commercial outposts.

The common problem of all the colonies was their vulnerability. They were exposed to attack from the local population and from rival colonizers, and they rarely had the defensive capability to feel completely secure.

Under this pressure they often created societies imitative of but even more rigid than those of the countries they had left behind. Representatives of church and king dominated Portugal's settlements, and in her one major colony, Brazil, a few powerful landowners dominated in a way that no noble could in the homeland. Among the Dutch, as might be expected, the merchants took charge completely; and the French were subjected to strict supervision by the government—there was even an *intendant* for Canada. Spain's empire was also focused on the crown, and if its extent and remoteness permitted the emergence of a fairly independent society, great nobles and the church still stood at its head, as at home. And the English created a system in which landed gentry, such as the plantation owners of Virginia, and thriving merchants remained the leading citizens, though independent-minded New England diverted significantly from this pattern, reflecting the challenge to the traditional hierarchical view of social structure posed by Protestantism's egalitarian implications.

All the colonies, however, were distinguished from the mother countries by one institution which was vital to their economies but also degrading to its participants: slavery. The slaves posed yet another military threat to the settlers, thus reinforcing their inclination toward rigid social control.

It is important to realize that, both in Europe and in the colonies, the lower levels of society scarcely participated in the mobility caused by the growth of commerce and bureaucracy. Peasants throughout Europe were in fact entering a time of increasing difficulty at the end of the sixteenth century. Their taxes were rising rapidly, but the prices they could get for the food they grew were stabilizing. Moreover landowners were starting what has been called the "seigneurial reaction" —making additional demands on their tenants, raising rents, and taking as much as they could out of the land. The only escape was to cities or armies, both of which grew rapidly in the seventeenth century. A few lucky people improved their lot by such a move, but for the huge majority a life of poverty in cities caused even more misery and hunger than one on the land. Few were allowed to become apprentices, and day laborers were poorly paid and usually out of work. As for military careers, armies not only destroyed the well-being of the rural areas they passed through but were hardly less dangerous for their own troops. They were carriers of disease, frequently ill fed, and subject to constant hardship. For many, therefore, the only alternative to starvation was crime. In London in the seventeenth century, social events like dinners and outings took place during the daytime, because the streets were unsafe at night.

DEMOGRAPHIC PATTERNS

During the last twenty years, a number of historians have developed a new technique called family reconstitution, which uses analyses of the records of births, marriages, and deaths in parish registers to re-create the patterns of seventeenth-century life.[6] Some of the contrasts they have revealed are startling. For example in France illegitimacy appears to have accounted for only 1 percent of births in the countryside, about 4 or 5 percent in towns, and somewhat more in Paris. In England, however, illegitimacy accounted for 20 percent of births, and the rate reached 40 or 50 percent after 1700. In New England in the same period the proportion evidently rose from 10 to 50 percent. The view that sets the loose French against the proper English or re-

---

[6] An excellent introduction to the work of the historical demographers is E. A. Wrigley, *Population and History* (1969).

pressed New Englanders is thus the reverse of the truth.

Once the babies were born, no more than 25 percent reached the age of one, only 50 percent survived to be twenty, and less than 10 percent lived to be sixty. This was a society dominated by those in their twenties and thirties, able to rise because their predecessors died earlier than they do in modern times. Because only one child in two reached adulthood, a couple had to produce four children merely to replace themselves.

The likelihood that they would be able to do so was not improved by the practice of marrying relatively late or the fact that women lost the capacity to bear children in their late thirties. The average age of marriage for men was around twenty-seven and for women close to twenty-five. On the average therefore a woman would have some twelve years in which to give birth to four children if the population was to be maintained. Because of lactation the mean interval between births was almost two and a half years, which meant that the average married couple was only just raising two adults. And in fact population levels were barely being maintained for most of the seventeenth century. There had been an enormous increase before 1600, and a slight rise was sustained thereafter, but the real resumption of growth did not come until the eighteenth century.

The causes of the high mortality rate were simple but insuperable: famine, poor nutrition, disease, and war. The plague, erupting every few years from the fourteenth century on, swept away mainly the young and the old and it did not disappear until the 1720s. The upper classes, better fed and able to get away from plague centers, had a better chance for survival; but the odds were often equalized by their resort to dangerously incompetent doctors.

How and why the general population trend

changed is impossible to know for certain. It is fairly clear that as early as the fifteenth century, the upper levels of society had begun limiting the size of their families in order to preserve their wealth—dowries for a daughter were expensive, and younger sons might not be able to live from family resources. Whether self-limitation was understood, let alone practiced, by other classes is difficult to say, though it is hard to offer an alternate explanation of the fact that the average gap between children sometimes rose to double the usual thirty months, particularly in troubled times. Late marriage for the upper classes was another means of controlling family size. For the lower levels of society, such postponement was a traditional economic defense: children had to work for their families until their parents' death allowed them to strike out for themselves.

Because of late marriages and low life expectancies, two married generations were rarely contemporary. Thus the extended family—more than one nuclear group of mother, father, and children living together—was extremely uncommon. Almost everyone who survived married, so there were few bachelors and spinsters, and usually each family could live on its own.

These features and consequences of demographic behavior give a sense of the basic patterns of seventeenth-century society, but we still do not know why the population grew so markedly in the sixteenth century, so little in the seventeenth, and then again so rapidly in the eighteenth. One can but suggest that repercussions were felt from the political, economic, and intellectual upheavals of the seventeenth century.

In only one area, the link between war and life expectancy, were the effects obvious. At the simplest level the Thirty Years' War alone caused the death of more than 5 million people. It also helped plunge Western Europe into a

EUROPE'S POPULATION, 1600–1700, BY REGIONS

REGION	1600*	1700	PERCENT-AGE CHANGE
Spain, Portugal, and Italy	23.6	22.7	−4
France, Switzerland, and Germany	35.0	36.2	+3
British Isles, Low Countries, and Scandinavia	12.0	16.1	+34
Total	70.6	75.0	+6

* All figures are in millions
Source: Jan de Vries, *The Economy of Europe in an Age of Crisis, 1600–1750*, Cambridge, 1976, p. 5.

debilitating economic depression, which in turn decreased the means of relieving famine. These were mighty blows at the delicate balance that maintained population growth, and disasters of such magnitude could not easily be absorbed. The few regions that managed to avoid decline were to become the leaders of Europe's economy (see accompanying table).

If the seventeenth century was almost everywhere a time of stagnation or decline in population, a period of harsh weather and recurrent famines and plagues, it was so especially for the poorest members of society. The low life expectancy, the frequent deaths of children, and the struggle to survive were constant and desperate pressures. It is small wonder that their culture embraced beliefs in dark forces and rituals of violence and protest. Nor is it surprising that as governments extended their hold over their subjects, they reduced the autonomy of ordinary villagers and limited the extremes of popular self-expression.

POPULAR CULTURE

As is natural for people living close to the land and dependent for their livelihood on the kindness of nature—good weather, health, fertility of soil—peasants in sixteenth- and seventeenth-century Europe assumed that outside forces controlled their destinies. Particular beliefs varied from place to place but there was general agreement that a mere human being could do little to assure his own well-being. The world was full of spirits and powers, and all one could do was to encourage the good, defend oneself as best one knew how against the evil, and hope that the good would win. Nothing that happened—the death of a calf, lightning striking a house, a toad jumping through a window into a home—was accidental. Everything had a purpose. Any unusual event was an omen, part of a larger plan, or the action of some unseen force.

To strengthen themselves against trouble, people used whatever help they could find. One device was to organize special processions and holidays to celebrate good times (such as harvests), to lament misfortunes, to complain about oppression, or to poke fun at scandalous behavior. These occasions, known as "rough music" in England and "charivari" in France, often used the theme of "the world turned upside down" to make their point. In the set pieces in a procession, a fool might be dressed up as a king, a woman might be shown beating

Adrianus Hubertus

her husband, or a tax collector might appear hanging from a tree. Whether ridiculing a cheating wife or lamenting the lack of bread, the community was expressing its solidarity in the face of difficulty or distasteful behavior through these rituals. It was a way of letting off steam and declaring public opinion.

This engraving reveals the popular image of witches in early modern Europe—in this case Germany. They are shown preparing for a ride, either on broomsticks or on the goats that were symbols of the devil, while the woman in the center boils up one of their evil concoctions. (Photo: Culver Pictures)

The potential for violence was always present at such gatherings, especially when religious or social differences became entangled with other resentments. The viciousness of ordinary Protestants and Catholics toward one another—it was not uncommon for one side to mutilate the dead bodies of the other—revealed a frustration and aggressiveness that was not far below the surface. When food was scarce or new impositions had been ordered by their rulers, peasants and townsmen needed little excuse to show their anger openly. In many cases women took the lead, not only because they had first-hand experience of the difficulty of feeding a family but also because troops were more reluctant to attack them. This tradition was still alive in 1789, in the early days of the French Revolution, when a band made up primarily of women marched from Paris to the royal court at Versailles to demand bread.

There was a peasant uprising in one location or another in France every year during the century up to 1675. But ordinary people also had other outlets for their problems. Recognizing their powerlessness in face of outside forces, they resorted to their version of the magic that the literate were finding so fashionable at this very time. Where the rich patronized astrologers, paying fortunes for horoscopes and advice about how to live their lives, the peasants and the poor consulted popular almanacs or sought out "cunning men" and wise women for secret spells, potions, and similar remedies for their anxieties. Even religious ceremonies were closely related to the rituals of the magical world, in which so-called "white" witches—the friendly kind—gave assistance when a ring was lost, when a new bride could not become pregnant, or when the butter would not form out of the milk.

For most Europeans, such support was all too necessary as they struggled with the un-predictability of nature. Misfortunes, they believed, could never be just plain bad luck; rather, there was intent behind everything that happened. Events were *willed*, and if they turned out badly, they must have been willed by the good witch's opposite, the evil witch. Such beliefs went back to the ancient world and for centuries had been the cause of mass scares and cruel persecutions of innocent victims—usually helpless old women, able to do nothing but mutter curses when taunted by neighbors, and easy targets if someone had to be blamed for unfortunate happenings.

In the sixteenth and seventeenth centuries, the hunt for witches intensified to levels never previously reached. This has been called the era of "the great witch craze," and for good reason. There were outbursts in every part of Europe, and tens of thousands of the accused were executed. The patterns varied—in some areas they were said to dance with the devil, in others to fly on broomsticks, in others to be possessed by evil spirits—but always the punishment was the same: burning at the stake. And the hysteria was infectious. One accusation could trigger dozens more until entire regions were swept with fear and hatred. Political and religious authorities, which often encouraged witch hunts as expressions of piety or as means of stamping out disorder, found themselves unable to stop the flow once it started. It was the perfect symptom of an age of disruption, uncertainty, and upheaval.

By the middle of the seventeenth century, however, the wave was beginning to recede. The rulers of society came to realize how dangerous to authority the witchcraft campaigns could become, especially when accusations were turned against the rich and privileged classes. Increasingly, therefore, cases were not brought to trial, and when they were, lawyers and doctors cast doubt on the validity of the testimony. Gradually, excesses were restrained and control was reestablished; by 1700 there was only a trickle of new incidents.

The decline reflected not only the more general quieting down of society but also the growing proportion of Europe's population that was living in cities. Here, less reliant on good weather or the luck of fertility, people could feel themselves more in control of their own fates. If there were unexpected fires, there were fire brigades; if a house neverthe-less burned down, there might even be insur-ance—a new idea, just starting in the late seven-teenth century. A notable shift in the world view of popular culture was under way, the inevitable result of basic changes in social or-ganization.

CHANGE IN THE TRADITIONAL VILLAGE

A number of forces were combining to trans-form the atmosphere of the traditional village. Over three-quarters of Europe's population still lived in these small communities, but their structure was not what it once had been. In the east peasants were being reduced to serf-dom; in the west—our principal concern—fa-miliar relationships and institutions were changing.

The essence of the traditional village had been its isolation. Cut off from frequent con-tact with the world beyond its immediate re-gion, it had been self-sufficient and closely knit. Everyone knew everyone else, and mu-tual help was vital. There might be distinc-tions among villagers—some more prosperous, others less so—but the sense of cohesiveness was powerful. It extended even to the main "outsiders" in the village, the priest and the lord. The priest was often indistinguishable from his parishioners: almost as poor and sometimes hardly more literate. He adapted to

local customs and beliefs, frequently taking part in semipagan rituals so as to keep his au-thority with his flock. The lord could be ex-ploitative and demanding, but he considered the village his livelihood, and he therefore kept in close touch with its affairs and did all he could to ensure its safety, orderliness, and well-being.

The first intrusion onto this scene was eco-nomic. As a result of the boom in agricultural prices during the sixteenth century, followed by the economic difficulties of the seven-teenth, differences in the wealth of the vil-lagers became more marked. The richer peas-ants began to set themselves apart from the poorer, and the feeling of unity began to break down. For hundreds of years, most villages had governed themselves through elected councils drawn from every part of the popu-lation. Toward the end of the seventeenth century, however, these councils started dis-appearing as the commitment to common in-terests declined.

Some of the other outside influences were more direct. In a few areas of Europe, espe-cially in England and the Netherlands, the iso-lation of the villages was broken down by merchants who were experimenting with new ways of organizing labor. Traditionally, a vil-lage would raise sheep, shear them, and sell the wool at market to traders who would have it finished into cloth in towns. Now, aiming at greater efficiency, merchants were organizing production on a larger scale in a new industry that has been called the rural "putting-out" system or "cottage industry." What they were doing was buying up the raw wool in sheep-raising villages, distributing it to other villages that were now geared entirely to weaving and producing cloth, and then taking the finished material to market for sale. Entire areas came to be in the employ of merchants, dependent on them for materials and a liveli-

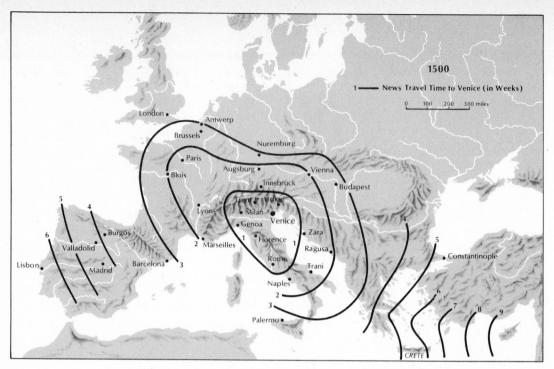

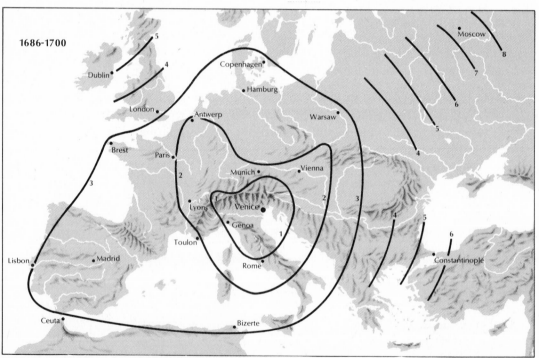

MAP 16.3: SPEED OF NEWS TRAVELING TO VENICE

hood. This created a new set of relationships, based on piecework rather than services, which again helped redirect the traditional patterns of life in the village, reducing independence and the ties of friendship and mutual help.

The isolation was also lessened as cities grew, not only because large urban centers needed ever wider regions to provide them with food and goods, but also because they attracted people who could not make ends meet in the countryside. Long-range communications became more common, especially as localities were linked into national market and trade networks, and immigrants in cities came to know fellow countrymen from distant villages (see Map 16.3).

Noneconomic forces, too, hastened the loss of autonomy. Over the course of the seventeenth century, nobles were looking more and more to central courts and capital cities, rather than to their local holdings, for position and power. Pursuing the seigneurial reaction, they treated the villages they dominated as sources of income and began to distance themselves from the inhabitants. Relations became impersonal where once they had been close and supportive. Charity, for example, was no longer thought to be the responsibility of neighbors: it was the duty of the church or the government.

The churches were taking on new roles, but these only had the effect of encouraging conformity. In Catholic countries the Counter Reformation produced better-educated priests who were trained to impose official doctrine instead of tolerating local customs. Among Protestants, ministers were similarly well-educated and denounced traditional beliefs as idolatrous or superstitious. Regardless of church, the outside world was intruding yet again. Habits did not change overnight, but in the long run the villagers were being forced to accept new values and to abandon their old beliefs.

The final blow was the growing presence of representatives of central government. In 1500 few villagers would have known what a servant of the king was, let alone have seen one. By 1700 they would all have had considerable experience with bureaucrats of one sort or another: tax collectors, recruiting officers, or army suppliers. Villagers no longer lived on their own in a small corner of the land. They were a part of the territorial state, important resources that the national government had to tap if it was to increase its power. Institutions (such as charity) had to be uniform; order had to be maintained. With their autonomy fragmenting and their customs and coherence under assault, the villages had no capacity to resist the integrating forces that were blending them into their nation states and subduing their eccentricities and traditions.

As Europeans entered the last decades of the seventeenth century, they had reason to feel that the upheavals and uncertain times they had gone through for more than 100 years were behind them. An extraordinarily successful intellectual movement, the scientific revolution, had solved many ancient problems about nature. Artists and writers had developed a new confidence. And throughout society an atmosphere of orderliness was returning

after over a century of change, disruption, and excesses like the witch craze. Religion had lost much of its power to arouse hatred and aggression; a calmer time seemed to be dawning, taking as its model the respect for reason that the scientists were encouraging.

The natural beneficiaries of these tendencies were the upper classes throughout Europe. Ordinary villagers may not have felt reconciled to the order being imposed upon them, but they proved unable to resist the forces—economic, political, and cultural—that were pressing them to conform. On the other hand, the sense of order was perfectly suited to the needs of aristocrats. They could now relax, confident that their power was secure. At dazzling princely courts, especially in France, they could enjoy the absence of turmoil and set their stamp on the culture of a new, less troubled age.

RECOMMENDED READING

Sources

* Drake, Stillman (tr. and ed.). *Discoveries and Opinions of Galileo.* 1957. The complete texts of some of Galileo's most important and readable works.
* Hall, Marie Boas (ed.). *Nature and Nature's Laws: Documents of the Scientific Revolution.* 1970. A good collection of documents by and about the pioneers of modern science.

Studies

* Butterfield, Herbert. *The Origins of Modern Science.* 1949. An elegantly written history of the scientific revolution, with a good bibliography.
* Caspar, Max. *Kepler.* C. Doris Hellman (tr.). 1959. A lucid biography of a complicated man, half-scientist, half-magician.
* Davis, Natalie Z. *Society and Culture in Early Modern France.* 1975. A fascinating set of essays on popular culture in the sixteenth and seventeenth centuries.
  Frame, Donald M. *Montaigne: A Biography.* 1965. The best biography of this influential thinker.
* Geymonat, Ludovico. *Galileo Galilei.* Stillman Drake (tr.). 1965. A straightforward and clear biography.
* Hibbard, Howard. *Bernini.* 1965. A graceful account of the life and work of the artist who was the epitome of the Baroque.

Kamen, Henry. *The Iron Century: Social Change in Europe 1550–1660.* 1971. This thorough, almost encyclopedic overview of the social history of the period also has a good bibliography.
* Kuhn, Thomas S. *The Copernican Revolution: Planetary Astronomy in the Development of Western Thought.* 1957. The most comprehensive account of the revolution in astronomy.
* ———. *The Structure of Scientific Revolutions.* 1962. A suggestive interpretation of the reasons the scientific revolution happened.
* Ladurie, Emmanuel Le Roy. *The Peasants of Languedoc.* John Day (tr.). 1966. A brilliant evocation of peasant life in France in the sixteenth and seventeenth centuries.
  Maland, David. *Culture and Society in Seventeenth-Century France.* 1970. This survey of art, drama, and literature contains a good discussion of the rise of Classicism.
  Palisca, Claude. *Baroque Music.* The best survey of this period in the history of music.
* Popkin, Richard H. *The History of Scepticism from Erasmus to Descartes.* 1964. Taking one strand in European thought as its subject, this lively study places both Montaigne and Descartes in a new perspective.
* Shearman, John. *Mannerism.* 1968. The best short introduction to a difficult artistic style.
  Tapié, V. L. *The Age of Grandeur: Baroque Art and Architecture.* A. R. Williamson (tr.). 1960. Although concentrating primarily on France and

Austria, this is the most comprehensive survey of this period in art.

* Thomas, Keith. *Religion and the Decline of Magic*. 1971. The most thorough account of popular culture yet published, this enormous book, while dealing mainly with England, treats at length such subjects as witchcraft, astrology, and ghosts in a most readable style.

White, Christopher. *Rembrandt and his World*. 1964. A brief but wide-ranging introduction to the artist's work and life.

————. *Rubens and his World*. 1968. As good on Rubens as the previous title is on Rembrandt.

---

* Available in paperback.

SEVENTEEN

THE TRIUMPH OF
ARISTOCRATS AND KINGS

Ever since the time that effective central governments had coalesced in Europe in the Late Middle Ages, nobles and rulers had engaged in a running struggle for power. After the upheavals of the mid-seventeenth century, however, it became clear that central administrations—now highly complex and commanding large bureaucracies—would dominate political life. Yet no ruler could govern without the help of the aristocracy. Of the main orders, or estates, into which society was divided—aristocrats, churchmen, townsmen, and peasants—only the aristocrats had the education, experience, and status essential for the running of a state.

The actual control they wielded over policy varied widely. In the absolutist realms they were most powerful in Austria, less so in France and Brandenburg-Prussia, and least in Russia. Moreover influence in the government was usually restricted to a small group; the class as a whole benefited only indirectly. But in England (where the ruling elite was being penetrated by members of the untitled gentry), the United Provinces, Sweden, and Poland, virtually no major decision could be executed without their approval. In effect, the aristocracy had taken possession of the administration of Europe's states and no longer had to compete with towns, representative assemblies, or the ruler himself for the fruits of power.

By the end of the seventeenth century, therefore, Europe's nobility was moving toward a new type of leadership. Historians have called this the domestication of the aristocracy, a process in which great lords who had once drawn their status primarily from the antiquity of their lineage or the extent of their lands gradually came to see service to the throne and royal favor as the best source of power.

To central administrations, eager to restore or confirm orderly government after over a century of disruptions, this alliance was more than welcome, and the rewards they bestowed—whether in patronage, privilege, or perquisites—were enormous. New power structures thus emerged in the age of Louis XIV, though the forms differed from country to country, and the fortunes of the lower classes fluctuated accordingly. Yet throughout Europe the quest for order was the underlying concern, a preoccupation that was already evident in the mid-seventeenth century and that pervaded not only political and social developments, but also thought and taste during the subsequent fifty years.

I. THE ABSOLUTE MONARCHIES

In countries that were ruled by absolutist monarchs—where all power was believed to emanate from the untrammeled person of the king—the center of society was the great court.

Here the leaders of government assembled, and around them swirled the most envied social circles of the time. At the court of Louis XIV in particular, an atmosphere of ornate splendor arose that, though primarily intended to exalt the king, inevitably glorified the aristocracy too. No other ruler could match its scale and magnificence, but many tried to imitate its style. Even at courts where nobles played a somewhat different role, this influence was inescapable.

LOUIS XIV AT VERSAILLES

In the view of Louis XIV (1643–1715), absolutism and the building of both the state and the government went hand in hand. But all three had to have a focus, preferably away from the turbulent city of Paris. To this end Louis, at a cost of half a year's royal income, transformed a small chateau his father had built at Versailles, twelve miles outside of Paris, into the largest building in Europe, surrounded by vast and elaborate formal gardens.

The splendor of the setting was designed to impress the world with the majesty of its principal occupant, and a complex ritual of daily ceremonies centered on the king gradually evolved. The name "Sun King" was another means of self-aggrandizement, symbolized by coins that showed the rays of the sun falling first on Louis and then by reflection onto his subjects, who thus owed life and warmth to their monarch. Versailles also provided an appropriate physical setting for the domestication of the nobility. Each year those who sought Louis' favor had to make an ostentatious appearance at court, and endless factions and plots swirled through the palace as courtiers jockeyed for position, competing for such privileges as handing the king his gloves in the morning. Louis regarded all men as his servants, and they were kept constantly aware of their vulnerable status.

Government and Foreign Policy

Yet this system was not merely a device to satisfy one man's whim, for Louis was a gifted state builder. In creating or reorganizing government institutions to reflect his own wishes, he strengthened his authority at home and increased his ascendancy over his neighbors. In fact the most durable result of absolutism in seventeenth-century France was the state's winning of final control over three critical activities: the use of armed force, the formulation and execution of laws, and the collection and expenditure of revenue. These functions in turn depended on a centrally controlled bureaucracy responsive to royal orders and efficient enough to carry them out in distant provinces over the objections of local groups.

In its ideal form an absolute monarch's bureaucracy was insulated from outside pressure by the king's power to remove and transfer appointees. In the case of France, this involved creating new administrative officials—commissioners—to supersede some existing officers or magistrates who claimed their positions by virtue of property or other rights.[1] The process also required training programs, improved administrative methods, and the use of experts wherever possible. This approach was considered desirable both for the central bureaucracy in the capital and for the provincial offices.

At the head of this structure, Louis XIV was able to carry off successfully a responsibility that few monarchs had the talent to pursue: he served as his own first minister, actively and effectively overseeing administrative affairs. He thus filled two roles—as king in council and king in court. Louis the administrator coexisted with Louis the courtier, who cultivated the arts, hunted, and indulged in gargantuan banquets. In his view the two roles went together, and he held them in balance.

Among his numerous imitators, however,

---

[1] The *intendants*, who remained the chief provincial administrators, provided the model for the commissioners, because their success derived from dependence on royal approval. It should be noted that all bureaucrats were called officers, but those with judicial functions were known as magistrates.

this was not always the case. Court life was the pleasanter, easier side of absolutism. It tended to consume an inordinate share of a state's resources and to become an end in itself. The display performed certain useful functions, of course; it stimulated luxury trades, supported cultural endeavors, and thus exercised a civilizing influence on the nobility of Europe. But beyond this it tended to be frivolous and wasteful, lending an undeserved prestige to the leisure pursuits of the upper classes, such as dancing, card playing, and hunting, while sapping the energies of influential figures. Louis was one of the few who avoided sacrificing affairs of state to regal pomp.

Like court life, government policy under Louis XIV was tailored to the aim of state building. As he was to discover, there were limits to his absolutism; the resources and powers at his disposal were not endless. But until the last years of his reign, they served his many purposes extremely well. Moreover Louis had superb support at the highest levels of his administration—men whose viewpoints differed but whose skills were carefully blended by their ruler.

The king's two leading ministers were Jean Baptiste Colbert and the marquis of Louvois. Colbert was a financial wizard who had been raised to prominence by Mazarin and who regarded a mercantilist policy as the key to state building. He believed that the government should give priority to increasing France's wealth. This meant in turn that the chief danger to the country's well-being was the United Provinces, Europe's great trader state, and that royal resources should be poured into the navy, manufacturing, and shipping. By contrast Louvois, the son of a military administrator, consistently emphasized the army as the foundation of France's

power. He believed that the country was threatened primarily by land—by the Holy Roman Empire on its flat, vulnerable northeast frontier—and thus that resources should be allocated to the army and to an extensive border fortification program.

Louis shifted back and forth between these considerations, but the basic tendencies of his policy can always be traced. In his early years he relied heavily on Colbert, who moved gradually toward war with the Dutch when all attempts to undermine their control of French maritime trade failed. But the war, occupying most of the 1670s, was a failure, and so the pendulum swung toward Louvois. Adopting the marquis' aims, in the early 1680s Louis asserted his right to a succession of territories on France's northeast border. No one claim seemed important enough to provoke the empire to military action; moreover its princes were distracted by a growing Turkish threat from the East. Thus France was able to annex large segments of territory, ultimately extending her frontier to Strasbourg, near the Rhine River (see Map 17.1). Finally, however, the defensive League of Augsburg was formed against Louis, and another war broke out in 1688. This one too went badly for him, and when he decided to seek peace, Louvois fell from favor. In a move that surprised all of Europe, Louis then brought back to power a former foreign minister named Simon de Pomponne, who had always stood for peace and careful diplomacy. It was characteristic of the Sun King to use his servants this way—raising and discarding them according to their position on his policy of the moment. But even this balancing process broke down in the last two decades of his reign, when France became involved in a bitter, drawn-out war that brought famine, wretched poverty, and humiliation. Louis was seeking the succession to the Spanish throne for his family, and he was determined to pursue the fighting until he achieved his aim.

The Palace of Versailles in 1668. (Photo: Louvre)

Louis XIV (seated) is shown here in full regal splendor surrounded by three of his heirs. On his right is his eldest son, on his left is his eldest grandson, and, reaching out his hand, his eldest great-grandson, held by his governess. All three of these heirs died before Louis, and thus they never became kings of France. (Photo: Wallace Collection, London)

Legend (inset top-left):
— French Boundary at 1661
······· Boundary of the Greatest Gains of Louis XIV
☐ France at 1713

SCOTLAND

NORTH SEA

ENGLAND

SPANISH NETHERLANDS

Rhine R.

BAR

LORRAINE

Stras-bourg

ALSACE

Paris

Seine R.

FRANCHE-COMTÉ

Rhone R.

SAVOY

TERRITORIAL CHANGES 1661 to 1713

UNITED PROVINCES

Calais
Boulogne
Antwerp
Brussels
Cologne
Arras
Rhine R.

Rouen

HOLY ROMAN EMPIRE

Verdun
Philippsburg
Paris
Metz
Versailles
Strasbourg
Fontainebleau
Kehl
Breisach
Freiburg
Seine R.
Dijon

FRANCE

SWISS CONFEDERATION
Geneva

Grenoble
SAVOY
THE MILANESE
Casale
Rhone R.

Antibes • Nice

PORTUGAL

Madrid

SPAIN
(TO BOURBONS 1713)

PAPAL STATES

NAPLES

Boundaries at 1661
◆ ◇ Cities Fortified by Vauban
/// Conflict Areas

MEDITERRANEAN SEA

0   100   200 miles

MAP 17.1: THE WARS OF LOUIS XIV

This final and ruinous enterprise revealed both the new power of France and her limits. By launching an all-out attempt to establish his own and his country's supremacy, he showed that he felt capable of taking on the whole of Europe; but by then he no longer had the economic and military base at home or the weak opposition abroad to assure success.

The strains had begun to appear in the 1690s, when shattering famines throughout France reduced both tax revenues and manpower at home, while enemies began to unite

THE SPANISH SUCCESSION, 1700

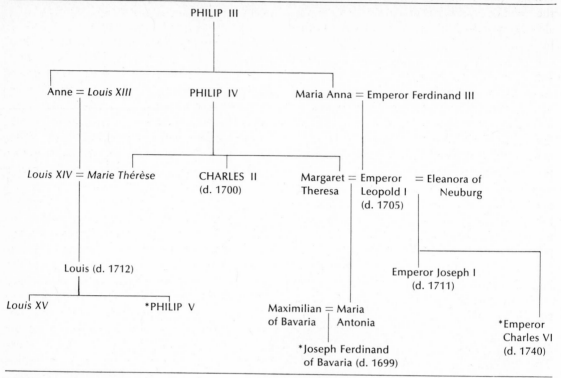

NAMES IN CAPITALS = Kings of Spain
Names in italics = Kings of France

*People designated at various times as heirs of Charles II

abroad. Louis had the most formidable army in Europe—400,000 men by the end of his reign—but both William III of the United Provinces and Leopold I of the Holy Roman Empire believed that he could be defeated by a combined assault. They worked persistently to this end, particularly after the Turkish threat to Leopold ended with the failure of the siege of Vienna, in 1683, and William gained the English throne six years later. The League of Augsburg, transformed into the Grand Alliance after William and other rulers joined it, fought a successful holding action against Louis' attempt to intervene across the Rhine, and the final showdown was precipitated when

the Hapsburg king of Spain, Charles II, died without an heir.

There were various possible claimants to the throne, and Charles himself had changed his mind a number of times, but at his death his choice was Philip, Louis XIV's grandson (see the accompanying table). Had Louis been willing to agree not to unite the thrones of France and Spain, Charles' wish might well have been respected by the rest of Europe. But Louis refused to compromise, insisting that there were no conditions to Charles' bequest. The rest of Europe disagreed and declared war on France so as to prevent Philip's unrestricted succession. Thus Louis found himself fighting virtually the entire Continent in the War of the Spanish Succession, not only at home but also overseas, in India, Canada, and the Caribbean.

Led by brilliant generals, the Englishman John Churchill, duke of Marlborough, and the Austrian Prince Eugène, the allies won a series of smashing victories. France's hardships were increased by a terrible famine in 1709. Yet the Sun King's hold over his subjects was unimpaired. Nobody rose in revolt against him; his policies were not seriously challenged; and despite military disaster he succeeded in keeping his nation's borders intact and the Spanish throne for his grandson (though he had to give up the possibility of union with France) when peace treaties were signed at Utrecht in 1713 and 1714. In sum his great task of state building, both at home and abroad, had faced and withstood the severest of all tests: defeat on the battlefield.

Domestic Affairs

The assertion of royal supremacy at home was almost complete by the time Louis came to power, but he extended the principle of centralized control to religion and social institutions. Religion was a major area of activity because two groups, the Protestant Huguenots and the Catholic Jansenists, interfered with the spiritual and confessional uniformity that the king considered essential in the absolutist state.

Of the two the Huguenots were the more obviously unintegrated. Government pressures against them mounted after 1668, when their greatest adherent, the famous Marshal Turenne, converted to Catholicism. Finally in 1685 Louis revoked the century-old Edict of Nantes, thus forcing France's 1 million Protestants either to leave the country (four-fifths did) or to convert to Catholicism. This was a political rather than a religious act, taken for the sake of unity despite the economic conse-

quences that followed the departure of a vigorous and productive minority.

Jansenism posed a more elusive problem. It had far fewer followers, though among them were some of the greatest figures in the land, such as the playwright Racine; and it was a movement within Catholicism. But the very fact that it challenged the official church hierarchy and had been condemned by Rome made it a source of unrest and disorder. What was worse, it was beginning to gain support among the magistrate class—the royal officers in the parlements, which had to register all royal edicts before they became law. The Parlement of Paris was the only governmental institution that offered Louis any real resistance during his reign. The issues over which it caused trouble were usually religious, and the link between parlementaire independence and dislike for court frivolity on the one hand, and Jansenism on the other, gave Louis more than enough reason for displeasure. He razed the Jansenists' headquarters, the Abbey of Port-Royal, and then persuaded the pope to issue a bull condemning Jansenism. He was prevented from implementing the bull—over parlementaire opposition—only by his death, in 1715.

The drive toward uniformity that lay behind these actions was reflected in all aspects of domestic policy. Louis rapidly crushed what little parlementaire protest there was; an attempt by peasants in central France to resist the government was ruthlessly suppressed; Parisian publishers came under bureaucratic supervision; and the *intendants*, the government's chief provincial officers, were given increased authority, particularly in connection with the ever-growing needs of the army.

At the outset of his rule, Louis used the government's power to improve France's economy. In this he followed a pattern familiar from earlier monarchs' reigns: an initial burst of reform measures to cure the country's economic ills, which were gradually forgotten because foreign policy demanded instant funds. In the early years, under Colbert's ministry, major efforts were made to stimulate manufacturing, agriculture, and home and foreign trade. Some industries, notably those involving luxuries like the silk production of Lyons, received considerable help and owed their rise to prosperity to royal patronage. Colbert also tried, not entirely effectively, to reduce the crippling effects of France's countless internal tolls. These were usually nobles' perquisites, and they could multiply the cost of goods shipped any distance. The government divided the country into a number of districts within each of which shipments were to be toll-free, but the system never removed the worst abuses. And finally, Louis made a concerted attempt to boost foreign trade, at first by financing new overseas trading companies and later by founding new port cities to strengthen maritime forces. Here he achieved notable success, particularly in the West Indies, which became a source of immense wealth for western France.

Louis' overall accomplishments were remarkable, and France became the envy of Europe. Yet ever since the Sun King's reign, historians have recalled the ruination caused by famine and war during his last years and have contrasted his glittering court with the misery of Frenchmen at large. Particularly after the famines of the 1690s and 1709, many contemporaries remarked on the dreadful condition of peasants in various regions. Even at Versailles there was disenchantment, expressed not only by a shrewd critic like the duke of Saint-Simon, who looked on the emptiness of court life with disdain, but also by concerned men who had not previously found fault with Louis' policies. A notable example was the great fortifications expert Sébastien le Prestre, marquis of Vauban, who had made a vital contribution to the military successes of

the reign (see Map 17.1). Late in life he called on the government to end its obsession with war because taxation was bringing the ordinary Frenchman to a state of hopeless despair.

Such warnings of course went unheeded, but in recent years historians have questioned whether France was in fact so badly off. That there was hardship cannot be denied, but its extent and lasting effect are open to question for two reasons. First, the difficulties caused none of the uprisings that were the normal reaction in the countryside either to excesses on the part of the central government or to severe food shortages. Second, France's quick recovery and unprecedented economic and demographic growth in the years following 1715 could never have taken place if the country had been as shattered as the dramatic tales of catastrophe suggest.

Nonetheless the reign of Louis XIV can be regarded as the end of an era in the life of the lower classes. In the early eighteenth century, the terrible subsistence crises, with their cycles of famine and plague, came to an end; both manufacturing and agriculture entered a period of great prosperity; and cities enjoyed spectacular new growth. It is likely that the hand of the central government seemed heavier in 1715 than a hundred years before, but the small landowner and urban worker had been struggling with taxes for decades, whether the payee was king or noble. And the Counter Reformation Church, growing in strength since the Council of Trent, provided a measure of blessing, for it began to bring into local parishes better-educated and more dedicated priests who, as part of their new commitment to service, exerted themselves to calm the outbreaks of witchcraft and irrational fear that had swept the countryside for centuries. The fortunes of Jacques Bonhomme, the symbolic French everyman, had risen noticeably by 1715.

The improvement was also apparent in the

mercantile class, which was about to enjoy a level of prosperity that outstripped even the sixteenth-century boom. Discontent at the government's interventions may have been felt by magistrates and parlementaires, who bewailed their lack of power, but these were voices in the wilderness. That there were some strains nobody could deny, but on the whole the absolutist structure had achieved its ends—a united, prosperous, and powerful France.

THE HAPSBURGS AT VIENNA AND MADRID

The pattern set at Versailles was repeated at the court of the Hapsburg Leopold I, the Holy Roman emperor (1658–1705). Heir to a reduced inheritance that gave him effective control over only Bohemia, Austria, and a small portion of Hungary, Leopold nonetheless maintained a magnificent establishment. His plans for a new palace, Schönbrunn, that was to have outshone Versailles were modified only because of a lack of funds. And his promotion of the court as the center of all political and social life turned Vienna into what it had never been before: a city of noble as well as burgher houses.

Nevertheless, Leopold himself did not display the pretensions of the Sun King. He had been a younger son and had inherited his crown only because of the death of his brother. An indecisive, retiring, deeply religious man, he had little fondness for the bravado Louis XIV enjoyed. He was a composer of no small talent, and his patronage laid the foundation for the great musical culture that was to be one of Vienna's chief glories. Whatever his inclinations, however, he found himself the holder of considerable royal authority: for more than a century, except during the Bohemian resistance of 1618 to 1621, the Hapsburg rulers had had few serious challenges to

their power. This was a tradition that Leopold felt obliged to continue, though unlike Louis XIV he relied on a small group of leading aristocrats to implement policy and run the administration.

The Thirty Years' War had revealed that the elected head of the Holy Roman Empire could no longer control the princes who nominally owed him allegiance, but within his own dominions he could maintain complete control with the cooperation of the aristocracy. The Privy Council, which in effect ran Leopold's domain, was largely filled with members of aristocratic families, and his chief advisers were always prominent nobles. But he did not switch about among representatives of various policies as Louis XIV did. Instead he carefully consulted each of his ministers and then came to decisions with agonizing slowness, even when all of them were agreed.

Unlike the other courts of Europe, Schönbrunn did not favor only native-born aristocrats. The leader of Austria's armies during the Turks' siege of Vienna in 1683 was Charles, duke of Lorraine, a prince whose duchy had long ago been taken over by the French. His predecessor as field marshal had been an Italian, and his successor was to be one of the most brilliant soldiers of the age, Prince Eugène of Savoy. None of these men were members of the Austrian nobility until Leopold gave them titles within his own dominions, but they all fitted easily into the aristocratic circles that controlled the government and the army.

Prince Eugène was a spectacular symbol of the aristocracy's continuing dominance of European politics and society. A member of one of the most distinguished families on the Continent, he had been raised in France but found himself passed over when Louis XIV awarded army commissions, perhaps because he had been intended for the church. Yet he was determined to follow a military career and therefore volunteered to serve the Aus-

MAP 17.2: THE AUSTRIAN EMPIRE 1657–1718

trians in their long struggle with the Turks. His talents soon became evident: he was field marshal of Austria's troops by the time he was thirty. For the next forty years, though foreign-born, he was a decisive influence in Hapsburg affairs, the man primarily responsible for the transformation of Vienna's policies from defensive to aggressive.

Until the siege of 1683, Leopold's innate cautiousness kept Austria simply holding the line, both against Louis XIV and against the Turks. In the 1690s, however, he tried a bolder course at Eugène's urging and in the process laid the foundations for a new Hapsburg empire along the Danube River: Austria-Hungary (see Map 17.2). He helped create the coalition that defeated Louis in the 1700s, intervened in Italy so that his landlocked do-

mains could gain an outlet to the sea, and began the long process of pushing the Turks out of the Balkans. Leopold did not live to see the advance more than started, but by the time of Eugène's death, the Austrians were within a hundred miles of the Black Sea.

However, the power of the aristocracy blocked the complete centralization of Leopold's dominions. Louis XIV supported the nobles after he had subdued their independent positions in the provinces; Leopold by contrast gave them influence in the government without first establishing genuine control over all his lands. The nobility did not cause him the troubles his predecessors had faced during the Thirty Years' War, but he had to limit his ambitions in territories outside of Austria. Moreover, as Austrians came increasingly to dominate the court, the nobles of Hungary and Bohemia reacted by clinging ever more stubbornly to local traditions and rights. Thus Leopold's was an absolutism under which the aristocracy retained far more autonomous power—and a far firmer base of local support, stimulated by nationalist sentiments—than was the case in France, despite the increased centralization achieved during his reign.

Madrid enjoyed none of the success of its fellow Hapsburg court. Its king, Charles II, was a sickly man, incapable of having children; and the War of the Spanish Succession seriously reduced the inheritance he left. Both the southern Netherlands and most of Italy passed to the Austrian Hapsburgs, and Spain's overseas possessions were already virtually independent territories, paying little notice to the homeland.

The Spanish nobility was even more successful than the Austrian in turning the trappings of absolutism to its advantage. In 1650 the crown had been able to recapture Catalonia's loyalty only by granting the province's aristocracy considerable autonomy, and this pattern recurred throughout Spain's Continental holdings. Parasitic, unproductive nobles controlled the regime almost entirely for their own personal gain. The country had lapsed into economic and cultural stagnation, subservient to a group of powerful families, and reflecting its former glory only in a fairly respectable navy.

THE HOHENZOLLERNS AT BERLIN

The one new power that emerged to prominence during the age of Louis XIV was Brandenburg-Prussia, and here again a close alliance was established between a powerful ruler and his nobles. In this case, however, thanks to effective leadership, the results were very different than in Spain.

Frederick William (1640–1688), known as the "great elector," was the ruler of scattered territories that stretched 700 miles from Cleves, on the Rhine, to a part of Prussia on the Baltic. (See Map 17.3.) Taking advantage of the uncertainties and hopes for a new order that followed the chaos of the Thirty Years' War, he made his territories the dominant principality in northern Germany and at the same time strengthened his power over his subjects. His first task was in foreign affairs, because when he took over as elector most of his possessions were devastated by war, with troops swarming over them at will. Frederick William realized that by determination and intelligent planning, even a small prince could emerge from these disasters in a good position *if* he had an army. With some military force at his disposal, he could become a useful ally for the big powers, who could then help him against his neighbors, while at home he would have the strength to crush his opponents.

By 1648 Frederick William had 8,000 troops, and he was backed by both the Dutch and the French at Westphalia as a possible restraint on Sweden in northern Europe. Without having done much to earn new territory, he did very well in the peace settlement, and he then took brilliant advantage of the Baltic wars of the 1650s to confirm his gains by switching sides at crucial moments. In the process his army grew to 22,000 men, and he began to use it to impose his will on his own territories. The fact that the army was essential to all of Frederick William's successes—giving him status in Europe and power within his territories—was to influence much of Prussia's and thus also Germany's subsequent history.

The presence of the military, and its role in establishing the elector's supremacy, was apparent throughout Brandenburg-Prussia's society. In 1653 the Diet of Brandenburg met for the last time, sealing its own fate by giving Frederick William the right to raise taxes on his own authority, though previously he had had to obtain its consent. The War Chest, the office in charge of financing the army, took over the functions of a treasury department and collected government revenue even when the state was at peace. The execution of policy in the localities was placed under the supervision of war commissars, men who were originally responsible for military recruitment, billeting, and supply in each district of Brandenburg-Prussia, but who now became the principal agents of all government departments.

Apart from the representative assemblies, Frederick William faced substantial resistance only from the cities of his realm, which had long traditions of independence. Yet once again sheer intimidation swept opposition aside. The last determined effort to dispute his authority arose in the rich city of Königsberg, which allied with the Estates General (representative assembly) of Prussia to refuse to pay taxes. But this resistance was brought to a swift conclusion in 1662, when Frederick William marched into the city with a few thousand troops. Similar pressure brought the towns of Cleves, along the Rhine, into submission after centuries of proud independence.

The nobles were major beneficiaries of this policy. It was in fact the alliance between the nobility and Frederick William that made it possible for the Diet, the cities, and the representative assemblies to be undermined. The leading families saw their best opportunities for the future in cooperation with the central government, and both within the various representative assemblies and in the localities, they worked for the establishment of absolutist powers—that is, for the removal of all restraints on the elector. The most significant indicator of their success was that by the end of the century, two tax rates had been devised, one for cities and one for the countryside, to the great advantage of the latter.

Not only did the nobles staff the upper levels of the elector's bureaucracy and army; they also won a new prosperity for themselves. Particularly in Prussia they used the reimposition of serfdom and their dominant political position to consolidate their land holdings into vast, highly profitable estates. This was a vital grain-producing area—often called the granary of Europe—and they made the most of its economic potential. To maximize their profits they eliminated the middleman by not only growing but also distributing their produce themselves. Efficiency became their hallmark, and their wealth was soon famous throughout the Holy Roman Empire. Known as Junkers, these Prussian entrepreneurs were probably the most successful group within the European aristocracy in their pursuit of both economic and political power.

Unlike Louis in France, however, Frederick William did not force his nobles to lead a life of social ostentation revolving around his person. The court at Berlin became a glittering focus of society only under his son, Frederick III (1688–1701). The great elector himself was more interested in organizing his administration, increasing tax returns, building up his army, and imposing his authority at home and abroad. He began the development of his capital, Berlin, into a major city and cultural center—he laid out the famous double avenue Unter den Linden, and he founded what was to become one of the finest libraries in the world, the Prussian State Library, in his palace —but this was never among his prime concerns. His son by contrast enjoyed the pomp of his princely status and set about encouraging the arts with enthusiasm.

Frederick III lacked only one attribute of royalty: a crown. He hungered for the distinction, and he gained it when Emperor Leopold I, who still retained the right to confer

This early eighteenth century engraving of Berlin shows a skyline marked by the many new churches with which the Electors were beautifying their capital. Yet the view also reminds us that, for all their rapid growth, eighteenth century European cities (with the exception only of the three or four largest, which were surrounded by expanding suburbs) were still very close to the agriculture of the nearby countryside. (Photo: New York Public Library Picture Collection)

titles in the empire, needed Brandenburg's troops during the War of the Spanish Succes-

sion against Louis XIV. Although none of Frederick's territories had been a kingdom previously, he was allowed to call himself "king in Prussia" (a technicality; the title soon became "king of Prussia"). At a splendid coronation in 1701, Elector Frederick III of Brandenburg was crowned King Frederick I, and thereafter the court, now regal, could feel itself to be on equal terms with the other monarchical settings of Europe.

Frederick undertook a determined campaign to improve the social and cultural atmosphere in his lands. He founded the Order of the Black Eagle to encourage aristocratic ambitions, and he made his palace a center of art and polite society to compete, he hoped, with Versailles. A major construction program in Berlin beautified the city with seven churches and a number of huge public buildings, making it an important center of Baroque architecture. Following English and French models, Frederick also created an Academy of Sciences in Berlin and persuaded the most famous German scientist and philosopher of the day, Gottfried Wilhelm von Leibniz, to become its first president. All these activities obtained generous support from state revenues, as did the universities of Brandenburg and Prussia. By the end of his reign, in 1713, Frederick could take considerable satisfaction from the transformation he had brought about. He had given his realm the prestige of a throne, the reputation derived from important artistic and intellectual activity, and the elegant manners of an aristocracy at the head of both social and political life.

PETER THE GREAT AT ST. PETERSBURG

One of the reasons the new absolutist regimes of the late seventeenth and eighteenth centuries seemed so different from their predecessors was that many of them consciously created new settings for themselves. Versailles, Schönbrunn, and Berlin were all either new or totally transformed sites for royal courts. The palaces·were far larger and grander and provided a more impressive backdrop than previous seats of government. But only one of the autocrats of the period went so far as to build an entirely new capital: Peter I of Russia, called the Great (1682–1725), who named the city St. Petersburg after his patron saint. Not

surprisingly he was also the only man among his contemporaries to declare himself an emperor.

None of the monarchs of the period had Peter's terrifying energy or ruthless resolve. A man of fierce temper, he was determined to impose his will without regard for opposition, though his decisions were often made in anger and then blindly implemented. The supreme example of his callousness was the torture of his own son, a quiet, retiring boy, who was killed by the inhumane treatment he received after trying to escape from his overbearing father.

Peter left no doubt about his intention to exercise absolute control in his realm. Of all the changes brought about in his reign, the most unprecedented was the destruction of ecclesiastical independence. When the patriarch of the Russian Church died in 1700, the tsar simply did not replace him. The government took over the monasteries, using their enormous income for its own purposes, and appointed a procurator (the first one was an army officer) to supervise all religious affairs. The church was in effect made a branch of government.

In the government itself Peter virtually ignored the Duma, the traditional advisory council, and concentrated on strengthening his bureaucracy. He carried out change after change, few of which lasted any length of time, but their cumulative effect was the creation of an administrative complex many times larger than the one he had inherited. Copying Western models, especially the Swedish system, he set up carefully organized executive departments, some with specialized functions, such as finance, and others with responsibility for geographic areas, such as Siberia. The result was an elaborate but unified hierarchy of authority rising from local agents of the government through provincial officials up to the

In the eighteenth century Peter the Great of Russia outstripped the grandeur of other monarchs of the period by erecting an entirely new city for his capital. St. Petersburg (now Leningrad) was built by forced labor of the peasants under Peter's orders; they are shown here laying the foundations for the city. (Photo: Tass from Sovfoto)

staffs and governors of eleven large administrative units and finally to the leaders of the re-

gime in the capital. Peter's reign marked the beginning of the saturating bureaucratization that was to characterize Russia ever after.

In the process the tsar laid the foundations for a two-class society that persisted until the twentieth century. Previously a number of ranks had existed within both the nobility and the peasantry, and a group in the middle, known as the *odnodvortsy* (roughly, "esquires"), were sometimes considered the lowest nobles and sometimes the highest peasants. Under Peter such mingling disappeared. All peasants were reduced to a uniform level, their equality emphasized by their universal liability to a new poll tax, military conscription, and forced public work, such as the building of St. Petersburg. Below them were the serfs, whose numbers were steadily increased by harsh legislation and who spread throughout the southern and western areas of Peter's dominions where previously they had been relatively unknown. The peasants possessed a few advantages over the serfs, but their living conditions were often equally dreadful.

At the same time Peter created a homogeneous class of nobles by substituting status within the bureaucracy for status within the traditional hierarchy of titles and ranks. In 1722 he issued a table of ranks that gave everyone his place according to the bureaucratic or military office that he held. Differentiations still existed under the new system, but they were no longer unbridgeable, as they had been when antiquity of family was decisive. The result was a more tightly controlled social order and greater uniformity than in France or Brandenburg-Prussia. By definition the Russian aristocracy was the bureaucracy and the bureaucracy the aristocracy.

But this was not a relatively voluntary alliance between nobles and government, such as existed in the West; in return for his support and his total subjection of the peasantry, Peter required the aristocrats to provide manpower for his rapidly expanding bureaucracy and officers for his growing army. When he began the construction of St. Petersburg, he also demanded that the leading families build splendid mansions in his new capital. In effect the tsar was offering privilege and wealth in exchange for what was virtual conscription into public service. Thus there was hardly any sense of partnership between aristocracy and

throne—the tsar often had to use coercion to ensure that his wishes were followed.

On the other hand Peter did a good deal to build up the nobles' fortunes and their ability to control the countryside. As one recent interpreter of the tsar's policy put it, he wanted "the landowning nobility to be rich and powerful; but it must nonetheless be composed of his personal servants who were to use their wealth and power in his services."[2] It has been estimated that by 1710 he had put under the supervision of great landowners more than 40,000 peasant and serf households that had formerly been under the crown. And he was liberal in conferring new titles—some of them, such as count and baron, an imitation of German examples.

In creating an aristocratic society at his court, as in much else that he did, Peter mixed imitations of what he admired in the West with native developments. He forced the nobility to follow the ritual surrounding a Western throne; he founded an Academy of Sciences in 1725; and he encouraged the beginnings of a theater at court. Italian artists were imported, along with Dutch ship builders, German engineers, and Scandinavian colonels, not only to apply their skills, but to teach them to the Russians. St. Petersburg, unquestionably the finest example of a city built in the Classical style of eighteenth-century architecture, is mainly the work of Italians, and the Academy of Sciences long depended on foreigners for whatever stature it had. But gradually the Russians took over their own institutions—military academies produced native officers, for example—and by the end of Peter's reign the nobles had no need of foreign experts to help run the government. Within little more than half a century, the Russian Court would become the elegant, French-

---

[2] M. S. Anderson, *Peter the Great* (1969), p. 24.

speaking gathering so penetratingly described in Tolstoy's *War and Peace*. Peter the Great had laid the foundations for the aristocratic society by which his people were to be ruled for two hundred years.

The purpose of these radical internal changes was not only to consolidate the tsar's power at home but to extend it abroad. He established a huge standing army, more than 300,000 strong by the 1720s, and imported the latest military techniques from the West. One of Peter's most cherished projects, the creation of a navy, had limited success, but there could be no doubt that he transformed Russia's capacity for war and her status among European states. He extended the country's frontier to the south and west, beginning the destruction of Sweden's empire at the battle of Poltava in 1709 and following this triumph by more than a decade of advance into Estonia, Lithuania, and Poland. By the time of his death Russia was the dominant power of the Baltic region and a major influence in European affairs.

II. THE ANTI-ABSOLUTISTS

The abolutist regimes provided one model of political and social organization, but an alternative model, in most cases no less committed to uniformity and order, also flourished in the late seventeenth century: governments dominated by aristocrats or merchants. The contrast between the two was perceived by contemporary political theorists, especially opponents of absolutism, who compared France unfavorably with England. And yet the differences were often less sharp than such commentators suggested, primarily because the position of the aristocracy was similar throughout Europe. The same elite dominated both politics and society, whether in England or in France. That there were genuine differences

in social structure cannot be denied, but they were subtle and often below the surface.

THE TRIUMPH OF THE GENTRY IN ENGLAND

To outward appearances Charles II (1660–1685) was restored to a throne not radically changed from the one on which his father had sat before the interregnum. He still summoned and dissolved Parliament, he made all appointments in the bureaucracy, and he signed every law. But the crown's effective power had changed drastically. The royal courts (such as Star Chamber) had been abolished, thus lessening the king's control over judicial matters. He also could not interfere in parliamentary affairs: he could no longer arrest a member of Parliament and he could not create a new seat in the Commons. Even two ancient prerogatives, the king's right to dispense with an act of Parliament (give an exemption to a specific individual or group) and to suspend an act completely, crumbled when Charles tried to exercise them. And he could no longer raise money without parliamentary assent—instead, he was given a fixed annual income, financed by a tax on Englishmen's favorite beverage, beer.

The real control of the country's affairs had by this time passed to that large, somewhat amorphous group known as the gentry. Between 100 and 200 members of this class held hereditary titles, such as duke or earl, that made them members of the peerage who sat in the House of Lords in Parliament. About 700 other men held baronetcies, which were inheritable knighthoods (but not considered peerages); and a few hundred more were knights, which meant that they could call themselves "sir" but could not pass the honor on to their heirs. Beyond these, in a country of some 5 million people, perhaps 15,000 to

Court life under Charles II of England was similar to that of the absolute monarchs in that formal, elegant, aristocratic gatherings dominated the social scene. The occasion shown here is Charles dancing at The Hague. (Photo: The Mansell Collection)

20,000 other families were considered gentry, these being people of importance in the various localities throughout England.[3] This

---

[3] These totals are based on the estimates made by an early statistician, Gregory King, in 1696. His calculations were performed with remarkable accuracy, and they produced the oldest figures that historians still accept today.

proportion, approximately 2 percent, was probably not significantly different from the percentage of the population that belonged to the nobility in most Continental states.

What set the gentry apart from the nobles of other countries was their ability to determine national policy. Whereas in France, Austria, Brandenburg-Prussia, and Russia aristocrats depended on the monarch for their power and were subservient to him, the English gentry regarded themselves as an independent force. Their status was hallowed by custom, upheld by law, and maintained by their representative assembly, the House of Commons, which was both the supreme legislative body in the land and the institution to which the executive government was ultimately responsible.

Not all the gentry took a continuing, active interest in affairs of state, and no more than a few of their number sat in the roughly 500-member House of Commons. Even the Commons did not always exercise a constant influence over the government. All that was necessary was for the ministers of the king to be prominent representatives of the gentry, whether lords or commoners, and that they be able to win the support of a majority of the members of the Commons. Policy was still set by the king and his ministers. But the Commons had to be persuaded that the pol-

icies were correct, for without parliamentary approval a minister could not long survive.

Despite occasional conflicts this structure worked relatively smoothly throughout Charles II's reign. The gentry's main fear was that his brother, James, next in line for the succession and an open Catholic, might try to restore Catholicism in England. To prevent this they even managed to force Charles to exclude James from the throne for a few years, during a confrontation known as the Exclusion Crisis. But in the end the instinctive respect for legitimacy that was characteristic of the age, combined with some shrewd maneuvering by Charles, ensured that there would be no tampering with the succession.

THE ENGLISH SUCCESSION FROM THE STUARTS TO THE HANOVERIANS

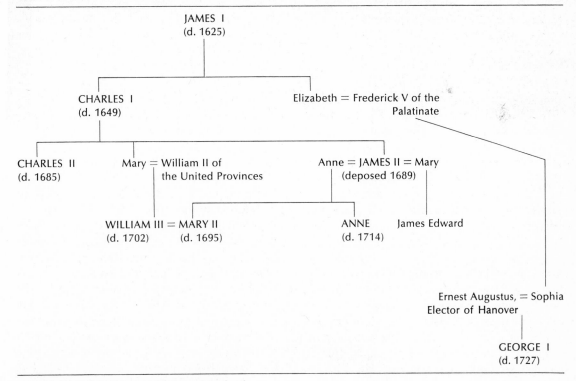

NAMES IN CAPITALS = Monarchs of England

Very quickly, however, the reign of James II turned into a disaster. Elated by his acceptance as king, James rashly attempted the very encouragement of Catholicism that Englishmen had feared. This was a direct challenge to the gentry's newly won power, and in the fall of 1688, seven of their leaders—including members of some of the oldest families in the realm—invited the Protestant ruler of the United Provinces, William III, to invade the country and take over the throne. Although William landed with an army half the size of the king's, James, uncertain of his support, decided not to risk battle and fled to exile in France.

The new king gained what little title he had to the crown through his wife, Mary (see the table on page 567), and the couple were therefore proclaimed joint monarchs by Parliament early in 1689. The Dutch ruler had taken the throne primarily to bring England into his relentless struggles against Louis XIV, and he willingly accepted a settlement that outlined the essential position of Parliament in the government of the country. The Bill of Rights was passed, settling the future succession to the throne, defining Parliament's powers, and establishing the basic civil rights of individuals; the Act of Toleration put an end to all religious persecution, though members of the official Church of England were still the only people allowed to vote, sit in Parliament, hold a government office, or attend a university; and in 1694 a statute laid down that Parliament had to meet and new elections had to be held at least once every three years.

Despite the restrictions on his authority, William exercised strong command. He guided England into a new, aggressive foreign policy, picked the ministers favorable to his aims, and never let Parliament sit when he was out of the country to pursue the war or to attend to Dutch affairs. But unlike James, William recognized his limits. He tried to

have the Bill of Rights reversed and a standing army established, but he gave up these attempts when they provoked major opposition. By and large, therefore, the gentry were content to let the king rule as he saw fit. For they had shown by their intervention in 1688 that ultimately they controlled the country.

Politics and Prosperity

The political system in England now reflected the social system: a small elite controlled both the country's policy and its institutions. This group was not monolithically united, however, as was apparent when a party system began to appear in Parliament during Charles II's reign. Its most concrete early manifestation was during the Exclusion Crisis, from 1678 to 1680, when the Whig party emerged in opposition to royal prerogatives and Catholicism. The Whigs were largely responsible for the passage of the exclusion legislation. Their rivals, the Tories, stood for the independence and authority of the crown and favored a ceremonial and traditional Anglicanism.

Because the Whigs were the prime force behind the removal of James II, they controlled the government for most of William III's reign. They naturally supported him in his vendetta against Louis XIV, since France harbored both James and his followers, the romantic but ill-fated Jacobites, who tried for decades to restore James' line to the throne. The Whigs were only too happy to give England what seemed her proper place in the restraining of France's ambitions. But on the whole this was a nonpartisan issue.

Where the sustained rivalry between the Tories and the Whigs was most evident was in their competition for voters. Because the qualification for voting—owning freehold land worth 40 shillings a year in rent—had become less restrictive as a result of inflation and was not to be increased until the late 1700s, this period witnessed the largest electorate in English history before the mid-nineteenth century. It has been estimated that almost 5 percent of the population, or more than 15 percent of the adult males, could vote.[4] Although results were usually determined by the influence of powerful local magnates, as they had been for centuries, fierce politicking took place in many constituencies. And in one election—that of 1700—it brought about a notable reversal: the Tories won by opposing further war, because for the previous three years France seemed to have been contained.

Within two years, however, and despite William's death, England was again at war with Louis XIV, and soon the Whigs were back in power. Not until 1710 did a resurgence of war weariness work in the Tories' favor. Queen Anne made peace with France at Utrecht in 1713, and it was only because the Tories made the mistake of negotiating with the Jacobites after Anne died the next year without heir that the Whigs regained power when the first Hanoverian, George I, came to the throne. They then entrenched themselves, and under the leadership of Robert Walpole, they began almost a century of political control.

The system within which these maneuverings took place remained essentially unchanged until the nineteenth century, though it allowed considerable flexibility. The crown was still the dominant partner: the monarch could dismiss ministers and could influence votes in the House of Commons through the patronage at the throne's disposal. But there were strict limits to royal power. Despite party struggles the gentry as a whole retained

the upper hand. They were quiescent most of the time, but on major issues, such as war or peace, no government could survive without their support.

In this same period England was winning for herself unprecedented prosperity, and the foundations of her world power were being laid. During the reigns of the later Stuarts, the navy was built up and reorganized—largely under the direction of Samuel Pepys, the famous diarist—into the premier force on the sea, the decisive victor over France during the world-wide struggle of the early eighteenth century. In Charles II's time important new colonies were established, particularly along the North American seaboard, where the aristocracy provided the main impetus for the settlement of New Jersey and the Carolinas. The empire expanded rapidly, so that when England and Scotland joined into one kingdom in 1707, the union created a Great Britain ready for its role as a world leader.

This growth was accompanied by a rapid economic advance both at home and in world trade. A notable achievement was the establishment of the Bank of England in 1694. The bank was given permission to raise money from the public and then lend it to the government at 8 percent interest. Within twelve days its founders raised more than a million pounds, demonstrating not only the financial security and stability of England's government but also the commitment of the elite to the country's political structure.

The success of the Bank of England, the rise of the navy, and the overseas expansion were not the only symptoms of England's mounting prosperity. London was becoming the financial capital of the world, and British merchants were gaining control over maritime trade from East Asia to North America. And perhaps most significantly, the benefits of this boom helped the lower levels of society.

[4] J. H. Plumb, "The Growth of the Electorate in England from 1600 to 1715," *Past and Present*, November 1969, pp. 90–116.

There can be little doubt that with the possible exception of the Dutch, the ordinary Englishman was better off than any of his equivalents in Europe. Poverty was admittedly widespread, and London, rapidly approaching half a million in population, contained frightful slums and miserable, crime-ridden sections. Even the terrible fire of London in 1666 did little to wipe out the appalling living conditions because the city was rebuilt much as before, the only notable additions being a series of magnificent churches, including St. Paul's, designed by Christopher Wren. But the grim picture should not be overdrawn.

Compared to the sixteenth century, these years saw little starvation. The system of poor relief may have often been inhumane in forcing the unfortunate to work in horrifying workhouses, but it did provide them with the shelter and food that they had long lacked. After more than a century of crippling inflation the laborer could once again make a decent living, and the craftsman was meeting a growing demand for his work. Higher up in the social scale, more men had a say in the political process than ever before, and more could find opportunities for advancement in the rising economy of the period—in trade overseas, in the bureaucracy, or in the growing market for luxury goods. England had better roads than any other European country, lower taxes, a more impartial judicial system, and a freedom from government interference—especially since there was no standing army—that was unique for the times.

One thing is clear, however: these gains could not compare with those that the gentry had made. In fact many of the improvements, such as fairly administered justice and low taxes, were indirect results of what the upper classes had won for themselves. There is no question that the fruits of the seventeenth century's progress belonged in the first place to the aristocracy, now more surely than in previous centuries the dominant element in society.

ARISTOCRACY IN THE UNITED PROVINCES, SWEDEN, AND POLAND

In the Dutch republic the fall of Jan De Witt seemed to signal a move in the direction of absolutism rather than aristocratic control. William III, who took over the government in 1672 and led the successful resistance to Louis XIV in a six-year war, was able to concentrate government in his own hands. Soon, however, the power of the merchant oligarchy and the provincial leadership in the Estates General reasserted itself. William did not want to sign a peace treaty with Louis when it became clear that the French invasion had failed. Like his forebears in the House of Orange, he wanted to take the war into the enemy's camp and reinforce his own authority by keeping the position of commander in chief in a time of war. But the Estates General, led by the province of Holland, brought the war to a conclusion.

A decade later it was only with the approval of the Estates General that William was able to seek the English throne and thus bring the two countries into limited union—limited because the representative assemblies, the effective governing powers of the two countries, remained separate. And when William died without an heir, the Dutch provincial executive offices remained unfilled. His policies were continued by Antonius Heinsius, who now held the position of grand pensionary of Holland that Jan De Witt had once occupied. Heinsius had been a close friend of William's, but to all intents and purposes, policy was determined by the Estates General.

The representative assembly now had to

preside over the decline of a great power. In finance and trade the Dutch were gradually overtaken by the English, while in the war against Louis XIV they had to support the crippling burden of maintaining a land force, only to hand command over to England. Within half a century Frederick II of Prussia was to call the republic "a dinghy boat trailing the English man-of-war."

The aristocrats of the United Provinces differed from the usual European pattern. Instead of ancient families and bureaucratic dynasties, they boasted merchants and mayors. The prominent citizens of the leading cities were the backbone of what can be called the Dutch upper classes. Moreover social distinctions were less prominent than in any other country of Europe. The elite was comprised of hard-working financiers and traders, richer and more powerful but not essentially more privileged or leisured than those farther down the social ladder. The situation discussed in much eighteenth-century literature and political writing—the special place given to nobles, which sometimes led even to immunity from the law—was far less noticeable in the United Provinces. There was no glittering court with elegant trappings. Although here, as elsewhere, a small group controlled the country, it did so for largely economic ends and with a totally different style.

In Sweden the conditions of court life and political power more closely resembled those of Louis XIV's France, though the reigns of Charles XI and XII, the last half-century in which Sweden was still an imperial power, were marked by a continuing struggle between king and nobility. The nobles eventually established themselves as the dominant force, but not until they had gone through a long and sometimes bitter struggle with the monarch.

The chief issue was the policy of rever-

sions, whereby Charles XI forced great lords to return huge tracts of land they had received as rewards for loyalty during the precarious years of Gustavus Adolphus and Christina. The aristocrats strongly opposed the policy, but the king had the bulk of the population on his side because the crown was always a more lenient landlord for peasant tenants. By clever maneuvering Charles not only had the reversion legislation passed by the Riksdag but also had himself proclaimed virtually an absolute monarch in 1682.

The remainder of his reign was spent consolidating the power of his government at home. He stayed out of war and strengthened both his administration and his finances. The great copper mines of Sweden gave out in the 1680s, and alternatives to this lucrative source of revenue had to be built up—primarily iron and timber products, such as cannon and tar. Tolls and taxes from captured territories helped sustain the empire, but it was clear that Charles' strength depended on his avoiding the strains of war.

His successor, Charles XII, had a different set of priorities. Harking back to the glorious days of Gustavus Adolphus, he wanted to cover Sweden in military glory. His ambitions and those of Peter I of Russia embroiled the Baltic in what came to be known as the Great Northern War. At first the fighting went Sweden's way, mainly because of a brilliant victory over the Russians at Narva in 1700, which immediately established Charles as one of the ablest commanders of his day. But he then decided—the first of a series of generals to do so—that he was capable of conquering Russia. His communications and logistics broke down, and at Poltava in 1709 his invading army was shattered. The dismemberment of the Swedish Empire now began: by the time Charles was killed in battle nine years later, the Danes, Prussians, and

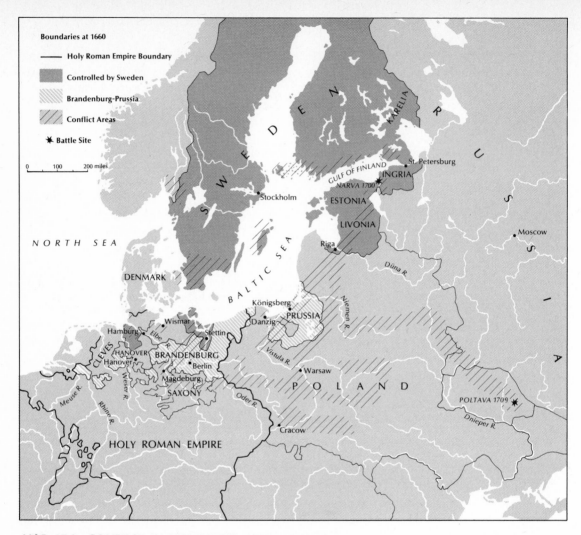

MAP 17.3: CONFLICT IN THE BALTIC AREA 1660–1721

Russians had begun to overrun Swedish possessions in Germany, Poland, and around the Gulf of Finland. (See Map 17.3.) At a series of treaties signed from 1719 to 1721, the empire was parceled out, and Sweden reverted to roughly the territory she had a century before.

Naturally the nobles took advantage of Charles XII's frequent absences to reassert their power. They ran Sweden while he was campaigning and forced his successor to accept a constitution that gave the Riksdag effective control over the country. The new structure was consciously modeled on England's political system, and the nobility came to occupy a position analogous to that of the English gentry—as the leaders of society and the controllers of politics. A splendid court arose, and Stockholm became one of the more elegant and cultured aristocratic centers in Europe.

Warsaw fared less well. In fact the strongest contrast to the French political and social model in the late seventeenth century was provided by Poland. No better object lesson can be found to demonstrate what Louis XIV was preventing in France. The sheer chaos and disunity that plagued Poland until she ceased to exist as a state in the late eighteenth century were the direct result of continued dominance by the old landed aristocracy, which blocked all attempts to centralize the government.

There were highly capable kings of Poland in this period—notably John III, who achieved Europe-wide fame by relieving Vienna from the Turkish siege in 1683. These monarchs could quite easily gather an enthusiastic army to fight (and fight well) against Poland's many foes: Germans, Swedes, Russians, and Turks. But once a battle was over, the ruler was rarely in a position to exercise anything more than nominal leadership. Each king was elected by the assembly of nobles and had to agree not to interfere with the independence of the great lords, who were growing rich from serf labor on fertile lands. The crown had neither revenue nor bureaucracy to speak of, and so the country continued to resemble nothing so much as a feudal kingdom, where power remained in the localities.

If Poland seemed a nobleman's paradise, she nonetheless produced no important cultural center like Berlin or Vienna. For that to happen some degree of central authority was necessary, a hub around which national life could revolve. Two cities in particular—London and Paris—occupied such a position, and therefore at the very beginning of the eighteenth century, they became the heart of Europe's intellectual and artistic activity.

III. THE CULTURE OF THE AGE

The quest for regularity, order, and decorum which was the most notable feature of late seventeenth-century culture contrasted strongly with the grandiose and dramatic strivings of the preceding age. The change in aesthetics offers striking evidence of the growing sense of settlement and calm in Europe after the crises of midcentury. And it was paralleled by the emergence of new kinds of cultural institutions—formal, regulated, and controlled from above unlike any that Europe had ever seen before. Not only the standards of taste but the success of individual writers, artists, and scientists reflected the preferences of a society dominated by its aristocracy.

THE ACADEMY AND THE SALON

A clear indication that the cultural atmosphere was becoming more ordered and restrained was the rise of academies and salons as mechanisms which organized intellectual life. The most carefully institutionalized setting was the official academy established under royal patronage to supervise cultural affairs. Such bodies were not entirely new—their pedigree went back to the Platonic academy, and there had been more immediate predecessors in sixteenth-century Italy—but their purpose, to set standards for artistic creations, was a departure from tradition.

France led the way in this development. The French Academy, founded by Richelieu in 1635, became the leading upholder of classical drama, while the Royal Academy of Painting and Sculpture, the Royal Academy of Architecture, and the Academy of Inscriptions and Literature, established over the next thirty-five years, performed equivalent functions in other fields. These bodies marked the beginning of a system that in France did not crumble until attacked by such nineteenth-century rebels as the Impressionists.

The cultural institutions that were founded in other countries (mostly in Italy) during this period were less prestigious but no less reflective of cultural trends. The academies were intended to preserve and promote the standards that were considered essential to good art. Just as the Royal Society was regarded as an arbiter of scientific truth, a promoter of proper method, so too in art and literature academies would set the style.

The origins of the salon were diverse and its predecessors many. Artists have frequently united in coteries when they have shared a common outlook, and rich and noble patrons have often given them encouragement. The particular form that developed in seventeenth-century France was a small, intimate gathering that usually met in the drawing room, or salon, of an aristocrat's wife.

These ambitious and often intelligent women tried to attract the most brilliant literary lights of the day. The artists for their part came in search of patronage and reputation, taking advantage of various social forces: the emergence of Paris as the cultural center of France, the clustering of the nobility in the capital as the court grew in size and importance, and the pressures of a fiercely competitive society of women with money to spare. The would-be salon entrant had to make his mark rapidly, and wit, grace, and quick repartee were essential.

The salons stimulated the intimacy and elegance that were now preferred to the heroic ideals of the midcentury. They thus became the natural center and the perfect symbol of contemporary creative expression. An atmosphere of studied gentility was strongly apparent, even to outsiders, and it was well for a writer or painter not to offend the sensibilities of those who were the chief makers and breakers of reputations in the highly competitive world of letters and art.

The intellectual activities of most aristocrats revolved around both cultural centers, the court and the salon. At court they gathered in large, formal affairs to watch a play, a ballet, or an opera; in the salons they gathered in smaller, less formal groups, often including talented nonaristocrats, to discuss the latest gossip or cultural event. Even the enormous halls of a palace, hung with large canvases inherited from the past, contrasted with the frilly drawing rooms that served as salons, adorned with the small paintings that were the new fashion. In some ways the two were rival centers of activity, and a few prominent patronesses consciously sought to outdo a nearby prince.

Yet the contrasts should not be overdrawn. Most leading writers, musicians, and painters were equally at home in the two settings, for they needed the patronage of both; no artist could survive without nobles to commission works or pay salaries, and almost none were fortunate enough to have all their needs met by a single generous prince. Thus they turned to the multiple sources of support that the aristocracy, better educated than ever before and eager to outdo one another in patronage, were anxious to provide.

There was also a wider audience of course, because salons were urban institutions, and the city offered theaters, opera houses, and publishers. Thus it was occasionally possible for an artist to achieve popular success without gaining aristocratic approval. But this was a hazardous way of making a living, and for this reason the salon, despite its regulation of taste and expression, was a vastly preferable target for most artists. As a result the qualities of harmony and order that were so appealing to the aristocracy came to dominate the aesthetics of the age.

STYLE AND TASTE

Discussions of literature and art developed a new emphasis on lightness and grace during the late seventeenth century. The most influential literary critic of the period, Nicolas Boileau, wrote a manual of style, *Poetic Art* (1674), that exalted craftsmanship over feeling. He insisted that the perfectly shaped poem was the ultimate ideal, and he valued obedience to rule as opposed to emotion or an exuberant, disordered vision. Not surprisingly his own literary output consisted of light satires, flawlessly executed but ephemeral.

Boileau's prescriptions gained a large following in France and in other countries as well. The leading English poet of the era, for example, John Dryden, gave his energies to writing hundreds of lines of graceful verse that were often scathing but almost never profound. The sharp end of his wit could sting, as can be seen in the following lines about the duke of Buckingham, a prominent politician known for his inconsistencies and dilettantism:

A man so various, that he seem'd to be
Not one, but all mankind's epitome.
Stiff in opinions, always in the wrong;
Was everything by starts, and nothing long;
But, in the course of one revolving moon,
Was chemist, fiddler, statesman, and buffoon.
Absalom and Achitophel, ll. 545–550

Dryden was greatly admired for writing in this vein because it was a time when the elite prized sardonic aloofness.

Painters reflected these qualities only indirectly, but the change in their concerns was striking nonetheless. Gone were the vast canvases and towering themes of Rubens or Rembrandt. Instead, the leading figures of the decades around 1700 were flattering portraitists, like the Englishman Sir Peter Lely, or delicate genre painters, like the Frenchman Antoine Watteau. Their canvases were small, and their subject matter rarely departed from placid landscapes or melancholic and idealized aristocratic scenes. The art of these exquisite painters epitomizes the new interest in grace, elegance, and repose.

That is not to say that emotion was totally absent from the creative work of the age. Stark passions were expressed in the operas of Henry Purcell and the prose of John Bunyan, both writing in this period. But the characteristic of their work that distinguishes them from the previous generation of artists is precisely their discipline—their anguish pours out of a framework of monumental self-restraint. And thus we are brought back to the theme that runs through the life of the time: the emphasis on order and regularity. It is particularly apparent in the work of the greatest court writer of the epoch, the French playwright Jean Racine.

By its nature Racine's art was not for the multitude. His concern was with tragedy, and he used the Classical drama to create an intensity of emotion that had not been achieved since the days of its ancient practitioners, Euripides and Sophocles. Severely disciplined and yet overwhelming passion dominates his plays, which move to agonizing climaxes in superb, controlled language. Racine does not offer the appeal of recognizable human types; his characters are suffering men and women of unattainable nobility racked by impossible dilemmas that revolve around such perennial aristocratic preoccupations as honor and public duty. The heroine of *Phèdre* (1677) for example falls in love with her stepson and destroys him and herself as she wavers between love and honor. She wrestles with her dilemma in a series of solemn and carefully wrought but tormented speeches that give the play an almost unbearable emotional impact.

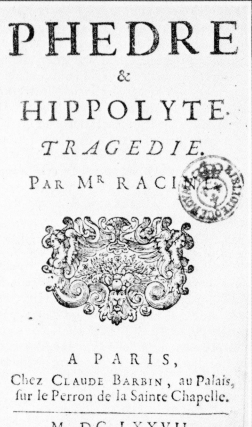

Jean Racine's plays appealed strongly to the aristocratic sensibilities of his age. He was regarded as the standard by which official taste could be measured and for many years was a major figure at the court of Louis XIV. The title page of Phèdre, *one of his most enduring contributions to the French theater, is taken from the original 1677 edition. (Photo: French Cultural Services)*

There is none of the dramatic excitement—the rapid action, changes of pace, and flexible verse forms—of a Shakespearean play; it is thus all the more remarkable that *Phèdre* conveys such gripping human feelings so powerfully.

Racine's appeal to the courtiers at Versailles was enormous. He explored the discipline and aristocratic bearing that, theoretically at least, the more thoughtful among them had adopted. They saw themselves on his stage, high-minded characters determined to act as social and political models. Racine thus portrayed an idealized court setting, guided by propriety and restraint, for all the world to see.

The tastes of the middle and lower strata of

Molière's plays displayed a trenchant wit that was often aimed at the nobility. For this reason his works had a rather uneasy reception at court but were extremely popular with the Parisian middle class. Shown here is the acting company founded by Molière, La Troupe Royale, which was the prototype for the Comedie Française. (Photo: French Cultural Services)

society are much harder to define, but there were a number of distinct ways in which they entertained themselves. Urban mercantile groups usually aped their superiors, though they were clearly more at home with the bawdiness of Restoration comedy or the scintillating wit of Molière than with Racine. They were also inclined to take part in creative activity themselves. Samuel Pepys for example remarked with satisfaction that his wife's painting efforts were coming along very nicely. And music, at least for the more educated urban dweller, was as much to be played

as heard. In this respect the middle classes blended with the lower rather than the upper social levels, for singing was one of the great recreations of the ordinary man. Ballads were a major form of communication, and printers were quick to run off thousands of copies of a new song that was likely to catch on. Churches moreover gave congregations an institutionalized focus both for creating and for listening to music.

Among reading publics the nobility tended to read the classics and philosophy while the middle class read popular literature such as tales of travel, descriptions of rarities and wonders, and religious writings. The few literate members of the lower classes probably read religious works only; the rest had the Bible or a book like John Bunyan's *Pilgrim's Progress* (1667) read to them. Singing and an occasional troupe of traveling players performing the antics of standard characters like Harlequin and Columbine would have been their main recreation apart from the celebrations they themselves put on—feast day processions, "rough music," and the like (see Chapter 16).

In these interests, however, there was little reflection of the underlying concern for order so noticeable in court circles. Most people looked to music or a play for uplift or for a good time. And nowhere did they find these qualities more brilliantly represented than in the plays of the Frenchman Molière.

Molière (born Jean Baptiste Poquelin) learned his art in the same school that had taught Shakespeare half a century before: the travelling theatrical company, in which he was actor, manager, and director. After many years of touring the provinces, he came to Paris a master of his profession and founded a company, known as the Comédie Française, which soon became a national institution.

Molière followed the formal Classical style of his day, modeling his verse on that of the ancients and observing the conventions of time and place laid down so strictly by the French Academy. But his objectives could not have been more different from those of a Racine. For he never lost sight of the old tradition of farce and burlesque, which in his youth had still been the chief attraction wherever plays were performed. He used Classical style to create comedies with a serious undertone, a sustained concern with the follies of mankind. He ridiculed such types as the pretentious ladies of the salons, hypochondriacs, and the ignorant but aspiring *nouveaux riches*—these captured forever in *The Bourgeois Gentleman* (1670), whose hero was delighted to discover that all his life he had been speaking prose.

The wit was unmatched, and soon Molière was winning highly favorable attention from Louis XIV himself. But occasionally the barbs came too close. The courtiers were offended when Molière had the nobles in one of his plays speak like ordinary people. And when in *Tartuffe* he ridiculed the hypocrisy that could lie behind ostentatiously displayed religious devotion, he roused powerful enemies in the Catholic Church. The play was banned, and a number of years passed before the playwright returned to the good graces of the monarch. But when *Tartuffe* reappeared in Paris, it was an instant success.

The contrast is revealing. Molière's sparkling dialogue and superb theatrical sense ensured his acceptance at court, but the welcome had its limits, set by standards of taste that the nobility considered unbreachable. In Paris he was always idolized, and for most Frenchmen he has remained unrivaled to this day. The difference, slight though it was, gave one of the first hints of the estrangement between court and country that was to build toward the explosion of the Revolution over the next century. The aristocrats may have set the style, but they were to become increasingly insulated from the rest of society, which eventually was to find its own cultural models and heroes in the eighteenth century.

SCIENCE AND THOUGHT

The fascination inspired by the scientist and the widespread efforts to imitate scientific method in other fields were closely connected with the interest in order so characteristic of the age. The approach and the findings of science offered perfect models of regularity, harmony, and discipline, and hence they could serve both as guides and as appropriate objects of patronage and interest. The second half of the seventeenth century thus became the great age of the virtuosos, the hundreds of noblemen who dabbed in experiments and sought friendships with scientists. But it was less as participants than as eager admirers that the elite embraced science. In the eighteenth century for the first time statues were erected to honor the great discoverers. They were a new kind of hero, and they became the most widely acclaimed men of their age.

The late seventeenth and early eighteenth centuries witnessed in addition a raging controversy known as the Battle of the Books, a long dispute over the relative merits of the so-called Ancients and Moderns. In the end there could be little doubt that the advocates of the Moderns had won the dispute, largely because of the unprecedented advances in the understanding of nature during the previous century. The achievements in astronomy, physics, mathematics, and anatomy were being seen ever more frequently as a measure of human capabilities. And the qualities that the scientist seemed to represent—order, reason, and logic—corresponded with the aristocrats' aesthetic preferences in this period: balance, uniformity, and decorousness. It was only natural that the supreme scientist of the late seventeenth century, Isaac Newton, should become the idol not only of his own generation but of generations to come.

Isaac Newton

The culmination of the scientific revolution was reached in the work of Isaac Newton, who made decisive contributions in the fields of mathematics, physics, astronomy, and optics and brought to a climax the progress that had been made by Copernicus, Kepler, Galileo, Descartes, and a host of other investigators. He united physics and astronomy in a single system to explain motion throughout the universe; he helped transform mathematics by the development of calculus; and he established some of the basic laws of modern physics.

Part of the explanation of his versatility lies in the workings of the scientific community at the time. Newton was a retiring man who got into fierce arguments with such prominent

This frontispiece from the 1710 edition of Jonathan Swift's long poem, The Battle of the Books, *satirizes the controversy that broke out in the late seventeenth century over the relative superiority of Ancient and Modern writers.*

contemporaries as the English physicist Robert Hooke, who was studying gravity, and the German "universal man," Liebniz, who was working on calculus. Had it not been for his active participation in the Royal Society of London and the effort that was needed to demonstrate his views to the membership, Newton might never have pursued his researches to their conclusion. He disliked the give-and-take but felt forced in self-justification to prepare some of his most important papers for meetings of the society. There could be no better indication of how important it was that science had created its own institutions and competitiveness.

It was to refute another rival, the Cartesian approach to science, which was then much admired, that Newton wrote his masterpiece, *The Mathematical Principles of Natural Philosophy* (1687), usually referred to by the first word of its Latin title, the *Principia*. This was the last widely influential book in European history to be written in Latin, still the international language of scholarship, and useful to Newton because he was determined to have as many experts as possible see his refutation of Descartes' methods. In contrast to the Frenchman, who had placed such emphasis on the powers of the mind, on pure reason, he felt that mere hypotheses, constructions of logic and words, were not the tools of a true scientist. As he put it in a celebrated phrase, "*Hypotheses non fingo*" ("I do not posit hypotheses"), because everything he said was proved by experiment or by mathematics.

The most dramatic of his findings was the solution to the ancient problem of motion. He stated his system in three laws: first, in the absence of force, motion continues in a straight line; second, the rate of change of the motion is determined by the forces acting on it (for example friction); and third, action and reaction between two bodies are equal and opposite. To arrive at these laws, he defined the concepts of mass, inertia, and force in relation to velocity and acceleration as we know them today.

Newton extended these principles to the entire universe by demonstrating that his laws govern the motions of the moon and planets too. Using the concept of gravity, he provided the explanation of the movement of objects in space that is the foundation for current space travel. There is a balance, he said, between the earth's pull on the moon and the forward motion of the satellite, which would continue in a straight line were it not for the earth's gravity. Consequently the moon moves in an elliptical orbit in which neither gravity nor inertia gains control. The same pattern is followed by the planets around the sun. In one of his most elegant insights, Newton described the attraction mathematically in what is known as the inverse square law: gravitational force varies inversely as the square of the distance between the two bodies.[5] The result has to be an ellipse, as Kepler had already discovered.

It was largely on the basis of the uniformity and the systematic impersonal forces Newton described that the view of the universe as a vast machine gained ground. According to this theory, all motion is a result of precise, unvarying, and demonstrable forces. There is a celestial mechanics just like the mechanics that operates on earth. It was not far from this view to the belief that God is a great watchmaker who started the marvelous mechanism going but intervenes only when something goes wrong and needs repair. Newton himself for example considered the creation of the force of gravity, which is not a *necessary* property of a body, as an indication of God's intervention in the assembling of the physical universe.

These general philosophical implications were as important as the specific discoveries in making Newton one of the idols of his own and the next centuries. Aristocrats, concerned with discipline and stability, could easily in-

---

[5] In other words, the attraction increases much more rapidly than the distance closes. Stated as an equation, where G is the gravitational pull and D the distance between the two bodies, the law is $G \propto 1/D^2$.

terpret the idea that a simple structure under-
lies all of nature as justification for the hierarchical patterns of government and society
that were emerging. The educated applauded
Newton's achievements, and the gentry made
him one of their own—he was the first scientist
to receive a knighthood in England. And only
a few decades after the appearance of the
Principia, Alexander Pope summed up the
public feeling in a famous couplet:

Nature and nature's laws lay hid in night;
God said, "Let Newton be!" and all was light.

Although he also devoted a great deal of
energy to mystical and numerological investigations (which he kept strictly separate from
his science), Newton still managed to find the
time to accomplish much else of immense scientific value. He was the main figure in late-
seventeenth-century mathematics, particularly
in the study of calculus, and his work on dynamics was a milestone in the subject. Another
striking achievement, the lunar explanation of
tidal action, was almost an aside in his masterpiece. The differences among various tides
allowed him to calculate the mass of the moon
—again almost in passing. Finally, his second
major work, the *Opticks* (1704), presented an
analysis that influenced the study of light for
more than a century.

But it was the work on motion and the
heavens that won Newton his reputation. So
overpowering was his stature that in these
fields the steady progress of 150 years came to
a halt for more than half a century after the
publication of the *Principia*. There was a general impression that somehow Newton had
done it all, that no important problems remained. In large areas of physics and astronomy, no significant advances were made again
until the late eighteenth century. There were
other reasons for the slowdown—changing

patterns in education, the influence of frivolous virtuosos, an inevitable lessening of momentum—but none was so powerful as the
reverence for Newton. The professional was
as overawed as the aristocrat in the presence
of a man who became the intellectual symbol
of his own and succeeding ages.

John Locke

The second idol of the late seventeenth and
eighteenth centuries, John Locke, was not
himself a scientist, but a major reason for his
fame was the belief that he had applied a scientific approach to all of knowledge.

Locke also wrote to refute Descartes, whose
dualism he rejected in favor of his own theory
of knowledge. He believed that at birth man's
mind is a *tabula rasa*, a clean slate; contrary to
Descartes, he asserted that nothing is inborn
or preordained. As a human being grows, he
observes and experiences the world. Once he
has gathered enough data through his senses,
his mind begins to work on them. Then, with
the help of his reason, he perceives patterns,
discovering the order and harmony that per-
meate the universe. Locke was convinced that
this underlying order exists and that every person, regardless of his individual experiences,
must reach the same conclusions about its
nature and structure.

This epistemology, elaborated in his *Essay
Concerning Human Understanding*, published
in 1690, was modeled directly on the example
of the scientists. The *tabula rasa* is the counterpart of the principle of doubt, experience
corresponds with experimentation, and reason
plays the role of the process of generalization.
Just as in science a single law appears again
and again whatever experiments are performed, so in all knowledge any true principle
is universal and will become apparent to every
person even though individual lives are different.

Locke's thinking thus included a reverence for scientific method, a reliance on material phenomena and empiricism, and a belief in order. In all these respects, his outlook captured the interest of cultivated readers in the late seventeenth and eighteenth centuries, for he provided them with a theoretical model, built on a rejection of emotion and an elevation of reason, that allowed them to regard their mental equipment and functioning as scientific.

When Locke turned his attention to political thought, he caught the feeling of the times even more directly, because he put into systematic form the views of the English gentry and of many aristocrats throughout Europe. The *Second Treatise of Civil Government*, also published in 1690, was deeply influenced by Hobbes. From his great predecessor Locke took the notion of the state of nature as a state of war and the need for a contract among men to end the anarchy that precedes the establishment of human society. But his conclusions were decidedly different.

Employing the principles of the *Essay Concerning Human Understanding*, Locke asserted that the application of reason to the evidence of politics demonstrates the inalienability of the three rights of an individual: life, liberty, and property. Like Hobbes, he believed that there must be a sovereign power, but he argued that it has no power over these three natural rights of its subjects without their consent. Moreover this consent—for levying taxes for example—must come from a representative assembly of men of property, such as the English Parliament.

The affirmation of property as one of the three natural rights (it was changed to "the pursuit of happiness" in the more egalitarian American Declaration of Independence) is significant. Here Locke revealed himself as the spokesman of the gentry. Only people with a tangible stake in their country have any right to control its destiny, and that stake must be protected as surely as their life and liberty. The concept of liberty remained vague, but it was taken to imply the sorts of freedom, such as freedom from arbitrary arrest, that were outlined in the English Bill of Rights. All Hobbes allowed a man to do was protect his life. Locke permitted the overthrow of the sovereign power if it infringed on the subjects' rights—a course the English followed with James II and the Americans with George III.

Locke's intentions were admirable—he had a higher opinion of human nature than Hobbes, he admitted that truth was hard to find, and he tried, as Hobbes had not, to curb the potential for tyranny in sovereign power. His prime concern was to defend the individual against the state, a concern that has remained essential to liberal thought ever since. But it is important to realize that Locke's views served the elite better than the mass of society because of his emphasis on property. With Locke to reassure them, the upper classes imposed their preferences and control on eighteenth-century European civilization.

The situation of Europe's aristocracy in 1715 was a far cry from its position in 1660. Then, in the wake of a series of grave political and intellectual crises, the ancient power of the nobles, based on their local independence, had seemed radically weakened in the face of the bureaucratic state. But as the political structures of the various European countries settled into new and stable forms, it became clear that their cooperation was essential for the running of a state, and they adapted to this new role with remarkable skill. Under the absolute monarchs they became the allies and indispensable agents of government; in other countries they dominated events. In either case they came out of the transition with their power intact and even enhanced.

Thus regardless of the relative levels of order and uniformity the various regimes achieved and regardless of their degrees of absolutism, they were alike in their reliance on aristocrats. No government, however centralized, could function without the participation of the upper classes, and in most states—Peter I's Russia excepted—they took up their transformed role willingly. And the new security of aristocratic power, both political and social, showed that the age-old conflict between princes and nobles had been resolved.

Moreover the qualities of order, discipline, and stability that the elite represented and that rulers sought were making themselves felt in culture as well as in society and politics. Changes in taste and even developments in science and philosophy were seen as reinforcing the aristocratic world view. The elaborately mannered life led by this newly invigorated ruling class reflected its confidence. And its remarkable society was to last for a glittering century until its frivolities and arrogance fell before a movement that demanded a better life not merely for the few but for all.

RECOMMENDED READING

Sources

* Locke, John. *An Essay Concerning Human Understanding.* A. D. Woozley (ed.). 1964. This study of the nature of the mind appeared at the same time as Locke's *Two Treatises of Government* and presents the philosophical basis of his political ideas.

Saint-Simon, Louis. *Historical Memoirs.* Lucy Norton (ed. and tr.). 2 vols. 1967 and 1968. Lively memoirs of the court at Versailles.

Studies

Adams, Antoine. *Grandeur and Illusion: French Literature and Society 1600–1715.* Herbert Tint (tr.). 1972. A clear and comprehensive survey of French literature and its social setting during the seventeenth century, with special attention to Classicism.

Baxter, S. B. *William III and the Defense of European Liberty, 1650–1702.* 1966. A solid and straightforward account of the career of the ruler of both England and the Netherlands.

* Carsten, F. L. *The Origins of Prussia.* 1954. The standard account of the background to the reign of the great elector, Frederick William, and the best short history of his accomplishments and the rise of the Junkers.

Chandler, David. *Marlborough as Military Commander.* 1973. A fluent and energetic narrative of military affairs, centered around the colorful career of a highly intelligent general.

Cranston, Maurice. *John Locke.* 1957. The best basic introduction to the man and his ideas. (See also Dunn and MacPherson.)

Dunn, John. *The Political Thought of John Locke: An Historical Account of the Argument of the Two Treatises of Government.* 1969. An interesting interpretation, taking a very different view from MacPherson (see below).

* Goubert, Pierre. *Louis XIV and Twenty Million Frenchmen.* Anne Carter (tr.). 1970. This is not so much a history of the king's reign as a study of the nature of French society and politics during Louis' rule.

Hatton, R. N. *Charles XII of Sweden.* 1698. A thorough and well-written biography that does justice to a dramatic life.

* ———. *Europe in the Age of Louis XIV.* 1969. A beautifully illustrated and vividly interpretive history of the period that Louis dominated.

* Hazard, Paul. *The European Mind, 1680–1715.* J. L. May (tr.). 1963. This stimulating interpretation of the intellectual change that took place around 1700 has become a classic work in the history of thought.

* Koyre, Alexandre. *Newtonian Studies.* 1965. These essays have come to be accepted as the basic introduction to Newton's ideas.

Lougee, Carolyn C. *Le Paradis des Femmes: Women, Salons, and Social Stratification in Seventeenth-Century France.* 1976. An interesting study of the place of women and the importance of salons in French high society.

* MacPherson, C. B. *The Political Theory of Possessive Individualism: Hobbes to Locke.* 1962. This provocative, Marxist-inspired study of the importance of property in English political thought views Locke's ideas in largely economic terms.

Manuel, Frank. *A Portrait of Isaac Newton.* 1968. Using psychoanalytic methods, this book shows Newton and the pressures he felt in a very different light from the usual analyses that pay tribute to genius.

* Plumb, J. H. *The Growth of Political Stability in England, 1675–1725.* 1969. A brief, lucid survey of the developments in English politics that helped create Britain's modern parliamentary democracy.

Stoye, John. *The Siege of Vienna.* 1964. An exciting account of the last great threat to Christian Europe from the Turkish empire.

* Sumner, B. H. *Peter the Great and the Emergence of Russia.* 1950. This short but comprehensive book is the best introduction to Russian history in this period.

* Wolf, J. B. *Louis XIV.* 1968. The standard biography, with particularly full discussions of political affairs.

* Available in paperback.

EIGHTEEN

ABSOLUTISM AND EMPIRE

The Eighteenth Century—generally understood as the period between the Peace of Utrecht in 1714 and the beginning of the French Revolution in 1789—is easier to visualize as a whole than the century of extraordinary turmoil that preceded it. It was a century of consolidation and maturation: of absolutism and empire; of demographic growth; of economic prosperity based on agriculture, trade, and traditional industries; of enlightenment and cultural brilliance. These various strands were of course interwoven, but any account must take them in some sequence. The growth of Europe's population—attributable in part to good harvests and the absence of famines—is a subject that historians have recently begun to explore, and it may one day be regarded as the logical starting point of discussion. In the meantime, it is the development of the state, long the focus of historical research, that is at present best understood.

Austria, Britain, France, Prussia, and Russia, the states that would dominate Europe and most of the world until World War I, can trace their emergence to great-power status, as well as their intense rivalry with each other, back to the eighteenth century. Russia and Britain now wielded enough power to play major roles in European affairs, while Prussia's rise to great-power status offers the most spectacular example of successful state building and territorial expansion. On the Atlantic seaboard, the maritime states of France and Britain dueled for trade and colonies in a rivalry that reflected the impact of middle-class commercial interests.

It sometimes seems as if international competition was the foremost preoccupation of eighteenth-century rulers. But in fact competition among states went hand in hand with internal state building—in most cases with efforts to consolidate royal absolutism. Conflict with rival powers compelled rulers to assert their sovereignty as forcefully as possible within their own borders in order to tap the revenues and manpower they required. The issue was power, and the model of absolutism created in Louis XIV's France showed them ways to that power.

With the exception of Britain, countries in which absolutism failed to develop—such as Sweden and the Netherlands—lost influence. Poland, once Russia's mighty rival, could not raise a large standing army or overcome the self-interest of its powerful aristocracy. By the end of the century it stood helpless before the onslaught of Russia, Austria, and Prussia. Three times Poland was partitioned among them, with the final partition in 1794 ending its existence as a sovereign state altogether.

In sum, the eighteenth century saw the maturation and consolidation of the modern state internally, and the testing of each state within the state system. In this process the basic map of modern Europe emerged and the centralized character of the major European states was confirmed.

I. THE STATE SYSTEM

The international rivalry embedded in the eighteenth-century state system was not as chaotic as it sometimes appears to have been. In practice there were limitations on the aggressiveness of states, and a phenomenon that can be called balance of power did exist. It is possible to indicate the sources of the conflicts that erupted and the kinds of appetites that sought satisfaction. Diplomacy and warfare had few ironclad rules, but they did have typical procedures and bounds. In combination these helped provide a context for the development of the European states.

PATTERNS OF INTERNATIONAL RIVALRY

Two terms may be used to describe the broad sweep of international relations, provided their meaning is not exaggerated. On the one hand were the periods of hegemony, or domination by one state; on the other were periods of equilibrium, or balance of power. For reasons that probably derive from Western ethnocentrism, we tend to assume that equilibrium among the several states is natural and that disturbances by overambitious powers are unnatural.[1] Be that as it may, it is true that the great aggressors of modern times, such as Louis XIV, Napoleon, and Hitler, have been resisted and ultimately defeated after stupendous struggles. Their designs on Europe varied considerably, but to their contemporaries they seem to have appeared equally dangerous.

In fact the essential meaning of "balance of power" is this limited or negative one: the situation after a bid for hegemony had been resisted and defeated. It was a genuine goal for Europeans only in the face of some inordinate threat to their accustomed pattern of rivalry. The state system did not have a built-in equilibrium. Apart from the way states concerted to resist the few rulers who sought to dominate the entire Continent, there was little agreement about what would be tolerated. Rarely did Europe's rulers cooperate simply to maintain peace or the status quo. On the contrary they acted in their own interests against the status quo with as much force as they could.

The Peace of Utrecht restored an enormous range of options and opportunities to European states that had been curtailed while Louis XIV seemed to threaten Europe with French domination. When the threat disappeared on Louis' death, in 1715, the more limited appetites and ambitions of Europe's other sovereigns could have freer rein. No country, however, was now necessarily more secure than it had been while Louis lived; nor was the likelihood of peace with justice for all Europe any greater.

For some eighty years—between Utrecht and Napoleon Bonaparte—no state threatened to dominate Europe. In this sense a balance of power prevailed. During the first twenty or so years, there was almost no war at all because of postwar exhaustion, but this respite came only from depleted resources and special dynastic considerations, not from lessons learned or from a revulsion against war. The ideal of peace had no place in diplomacy and had nothing to do with the eighteenth-century balance of power. For despite the absence of any bid for hegemony, between Utrecht and Napoleon the century saw two international

[1] Thus Leopold von Ranke, the great nineteenth-century German historian, emphasized "the primacy of foreign policy" in the development of Europe. To Ranke the essence of European civilization was a common Christian culture embodied in a diversity of national states whose very competition produced a metaphysical kind of harmony. See T. von Laue, *Leopold Ranke: The Formative Years* (1950), and Ranke's famous essay, "The Great Powers," reproduced as an appendix to that book. For a classic view emphasizing the anarchy of the state system see Albert Sorel, *Europe Under the Old Regime* (tr. 1968).

The series of treaties negotiated at the peace congress at Utrecht in 1713–1714 reaffirmed the balance of power in Europe and provided that the Bourbon thrones of France and Spain would never be united. England gained various colonial and commercial spoils, including Newfoundland and Gibraltar. Spain's overseas empire went to Philip V, while the Spanish Netherlands, Milan, Sardinia, and Naples went to the Austrian Hapsburgs. (Photo: The Bettmann Archive)

conflicts (the War of the Austrian Succession and the Seven Years' War), the loss of a substantial overseas empire by France, threats of extinction against the Hapsburg Empire and Prussia, and the disappearance of the sovereign state of Poland.

There was thus no absence of aggression and bellicosity in eighteenth-century Europe. But these wars did not mobilize entire societies; the atmosphere of the period can be suggested by such incidents as the English novelist Laurence Sterne's taking his famous *Sen-*

timental Journey to France while his country was at war with her. Moreover these contests lacked the fanaticism of the religious wars while not yet calling forth the kinds of commitment that came with later wars of revolution, national unification, or ideology. They were wars in which dynastic interests and territorial ambitions interacted with disputes over trade, colonies, and prestige. Eighteenth-century wars had limited, concrete objectives. They were not total wars.

Zones of Conflict

International relations focused on four geographical regions or spheres of interest: the North, Central Europe, Eastern Europe, and the New World across the seas.

The Baltic area in the North was of strategic interest to a number of states. Russia, Sweden, Prussia, and Poland all sought direct territorial control there, which could only be achieved at some other state's expense. Maritime powers like the British and Dutch were concerned both with the trading areas that fronted on the Baltic and the rich prize of naval stores that could be found there.

Most of Central Europe constituted a fragmented power vacuum over which the great powers and their allies vied. The Bourbon-Hapsburg rivalry revolved largely around who would have the most influence there. And even lesser dominions like Saxony and Bavaria could be pardoned for dreams of grandeur that were stimulated by the absence of sizable viable states. Moreover Great Britain's dynastic tie through George I with the principality of Hanover involved her in this vortex of Central European instability, which otherwise would have been unimportant to her. Farther south the power vacuum extended into Italy, which was like a colonial area for the satisfaction of dynastic ambitions.

"Eastern Europe" is admittedly an imprecise designation. Yet in regard to the eighteenth century, it conveys a firmer concept of region than the expression "Germany." The eastern boundary of the Holy Roman Empire had lost most of its significance, but it did generally set off the classic area of Europe from the vast reaches of the continent that lay to the east. Here the most important issue was the attempt to push back the Ottomans, a task shared—in a spirit of mutual distrust—by Hapsburgs and Russians (see Map 18.1). As questions of access to the Mediterranean were raised, the maritime powers were drawn in. This is the origin of the so-called "Eastern question" that bedeviled European diplomacy for the next 200 years. However, other complicating issues, such as the ethnic diversity and latent national aspirations of the region, had not yet arisen to complicate the picture.

The fourth theater of activity was the colonized New World. Spain, Great Britain, and France, secure within their own borders, had their most important interests here, though they were not fully aware of this. By 1739 a war had begun between England and Spain that was directly attributable to a dispute in the New World: British smuggling and its repression in the Spanish Empire. Henceforth colonial tensions would severely complicate European diplomatic relations.

There were thus many possible permutations in international affairs. The abler statesmen of the times were the ones who could see past traditional commitments or superficially attractive opportunities to the veritable interests of their states. Ultimately perhaps the most important development in the state system of the eighteenth century was the rise to prominence of Britain and Russia, the two great flanking powers of Europe. Previously both had really stood on the periphery of European power politics. After Utrecht their influence would be second to none.

DIPLOMACY AND WARFARE

Diplomacy in the eighteenth century reflected an increasingly complex range of considerations. Traditional dynastic interests were still important: princes and their ministers tried to exclude challenges to the reigning family's succession, to secure client states or new territory by dynastic claims, and to arrange marriages that would bring new titles or alliances.

Dynastic considerations could promote peace in certain circumstances and war in others. When a ruler felt insecure on his throne because of possible internal challenges to his title, he might seek to improve his relations with other states in order to avoid further complications. Coincidentally this was the situation in both France and Britain after Utrecht, and it helps explain the peace that prevailed between those inexorable rivals until 1740. An episode characteristic of the diplomacy of the time involved the Polish succession—the Polish kingship having been an elective office subject to influence by the great powers. Unable to agree over the matter, the powers fought a brief limited war; France's candidate then bowed out but was compensated with the duchy of Lorraine, which would eventually pass directly under French sovereignty by virtue of the new duke's marriage to a French princess.

On the whole, though, dynastic interests gave way to policies based on a more impersonal and abstract conception of the state. Men like Frederick II of Prussia, Count Wenzel Anton von Kaunitz of Austria, and William Pitt of Britain tried to shape their diplomacy to the specific needs of their states as they conceived them. "Reasons of state" centered on security, with the only guarantee of security understood to be the power to assure it by force. The search for defensible borders and the weakening of possible challengers were obvious principles. Eighteenth-century statesmen believed that the end (security and prosperity) justified the means (the maximal use of power). Until a country was completely invulnerable, its leaders felt justified in

MAP 18.1: THE EXPANSION OF RUSSIA AND THE PARTITION OF POLAND

Map legend:
- Russian Gains 1721-1795
- Boundary of Poland to 1772
- Poland 1793-1795
- Boundaries of the Three Powers at 1795
- Dates Indicate Acquisition of Territories

Scale: 0 — 100 — 200 miles

using the crudest and most amoral tactics in dealing with its neighbors.

Diplomats and armies shared the task of implementing "reasons of state." Emissaries were frequently put to work fabricating or embellishing claims to this province or that princely title. They were understood to be spies or at least snoopers by vocation. They offered the bribes that were a part of foreign policy and negotiated treaties sometimes knowing of their prince's intentions to violate them.

There was another, more conservative side to diplomacy: the eighteenth century marks its growth as a serious profession, parallel to the further rationalization of the state itself.

Foreign ministries or foreign offices were started and staffed with corps of experts, clerks, archives, and the like. The heads of the diplomatic machine were the ambassadors, stationed in permanent embassies abroad. This routinized management of foreign relations helped foster a sense of collective identity among the European states despite their interminable struggles. Linguistically and socially the diplomatic corps provided a veneer of sugar coating to international relations. French now reigned supreme as the common language of European diplomats; by 1774 even a treaty between Turks and Russians was drafted in that language. Socially the diplomatic corps was aristocratic and cosmopolitan. Whatever ruler they might be serving, noble ambassadors regarded themselves as members of the same fraternity.

In the wake of the exhaustion that followed the wars of Louis XIV's reign, diplomats began to play a more active role in the affairs of the Continent. Between 1715 and 1725 Europe actually saw a series of international congresses designed to settle differences in advance by means of covenants. This was only a superficial change, however, since the issues decided on were invariably minor.

Moreover the great powers dictated terms, dividing spoils and prestige at the expense of the smaller states. For example the territorial ambitions of Prussia, Austria, and Russia were reconciled at the bargaining table by their series of agreements to partition Poland's outer areas among themselves (see Map 18.1). The declaration they issued in 1772, at the time of the first partition, stated boldly that "Whatever the limitations of the respective claims may be, the acquisitions which result must be exactly equal." Rarely was such cynicism perpetrated on so grand a scale, but in its essence it was typical of the European state system. Settling disputes by negotiation could be as brutal and amoral as settling them by war.

Armies

Despite the settlement of many disputes by diplomacy, war was far from an alternative of last resort; it continued to be a commonplace instrument of statecraft. In the major Continental countries, the focus of bureaucratic innovation and monetary expenditure was the standing army, whose growth was enormous. France set the pace for this development. After 1680 the size of her forces never fell below 200,000. The growth of the Prussian army exemplifies what was happening all over Europe: between 1713 and 1786 its manpower increased from 39,000 to 200,000. But the cost, technology, and tactics of these armies served to limit the devastation and horror of eighteenth-century warfare despite the frequency of combat.

Costliness led rulers to husband their armies carefully. Princes were quick to declare war but slow to deploy their armies at full strength or commit them to battle. Observers of eighteenth-century warfare like the English writer Daniel Defoe therefore concluded that there was more money but less blood spent in war.

The techniques of building and besieging fortifications continued to preoccupy military planners. Looking back on those days from the vantage point of the French Revolution, one officer characterized eighteenth-century warfare not even as the art of defending strong places but of "surrendering them honorably after certain conventional formalities." The main body of troops—the infantry—was primarily trained for maneuvering and was taught to fire in carefully controlled line formations. A successful strategy equaled the ability to nudge an opposing army into abandoning its position in the face of superior maneuvering. Improved organization worked to counteract brutality. Better supplied by a system of magazines, more tightly disciplined by constant drilling, troops were less likely to desert or plunder than they had been during the Thirty Years' War.

Rarely was the annihilation of the opposing force the strategic objective of a battle. Some encounters were fought as if they were occurring on a parade ground, while pitched battles in open fields were usually avoided. Moreover important victories were frequently nullified when the winning army retreated toward its home bases to make winter camp. Finally, unconditional surrender was never required from an opponent. The same held true for naval battles. Commanders evinced great caution when engaging in combat and rarely followed up initial contacts by pursuing and destroying the bested squadron.

The officer corps of the military were generally the preserve of the European nobility, though they also served as channels of upward social mobility for wealthy sons of middle-class families who purchased commissions. In either case the officer ranks tended to be sinecures filled by men who lacked the professional outlook and requisite training for effective leadership. Officers were likely to be long on martial spirit and bravery but short on technical skills. The branches of service that showed the most progress were the artillery and the engineers, in which competent middle-class officers played an unusually large role.

A final element limiting the actual scale of war in the eighteenth century was the inherent weakness of coalitions of belligerents, which formed whenever a general war mushroomed. On paper these alliances looked formidable and seemed to promise vast deeds of destruction against their victims. On the battlefield, however, they were hampered by primitive communications and lack of mobility even at the peak of cooperation. Moreover the partnerships rarely lasted very long. The anarchy of the state system predictably bred distrust among supposed allies as well as enemies. Sudden abandonment of coalitions and the negotiation of separate peace treaties

mark the history of almost every major war fought under this arrangement.

II. ABSOLUTISM IN CENTRAL EUROPE

The relationship between international rivalry and internal modernization is dramatically illustrated in the examples of Prussia and Austria. Already in the mid-eighteenth century these two powers were vying for domination in Central Europe and they instituted reforms to better wage this struggle. Each experienced a period of vigorous state building under their absolute rulers, the essence of which was to increase the size of armies, collect larger revenues to support them, and develop bureaucracies to administer the provinces. It did not seem to matter whether the ruler was a modern-minded atheist like Frederick II of Prussia or a pious traditionalist like Maria Theresa of Austria. In their own way each understood their vocation as ruler and the demands of the state system.

THE RISE OF PRUSSIA

The fate of Bradenburg-Prussia was entirely different from Poland's. As Chapter 17 described, Frederick William the Great Elector had begun the creation of a standing army and bureaucracy in Brandenburg and had bargained the great magnates into yielding much of their political power. These policies had raised Brandenburg from virtual obscurity to a position of second rank in the state system. Frederick I had secured the prestige of a royal throne in Prussia for the Hohenzollern family, but while patronizing new cultural activities in Berlin, he had neglected to forge ahead with the state-building process. His successor, however, more than compensated for this laxness.

Frederick William I

Under the thoroughgoing absolutism of Frederick William I (1713–1740), Prussia began her climb toward great-power status. Strikingly different from his refined father, this spartan ruler approached affairs of state as all business and little pleasure. He disdained court life and considered theaters to be temples of Satan. His standards of frugality were exorbitant: he eliminated three-quarters of the court's expenses, dismissed numerous courtiers, and cut the salaries of those who remained. Uncluttered by royal ceremonies, his days were regulated in timetable fashion as he attempted to supervise everything himself.

This painting of the Battle of Fontenoy illustrates the typical battlefield stance adopted by eighteenth-century armies. The infantry was positioned in rigid line formation when firing, which limited its effectiveness. (Photo: National Army Museum)

It could be said that Frederick William I traded the costume of the courtier for the uniform of the soldier, since his purpose was to organize the state for military power. During his reign the army grew from 38,000 to 83,000, making it the fourth largest in Europe, behind France, Russia, and Austria. While still relying on foreign mercenaries for one-third of his troops, he also instituted a form of conscription known as the canton system. Nobles, bourgeois, and skilled artisans were exempted; the children of peasants were enrolled when very young and called up as needed, serving in peacetime for three months of the year and leaving to work on the land during the harvest period. The soldiers—whether foreign mercenaries, enlistees, or conscripts—were subjected to intensive drilling, wore standardized uniforms, and were maintained by an improved supply system that at least equaled the French.

The king went even farther in the reform of the officer corps. Determined to build an effective cadre of professionals, he forbade his subjects to serve in foreign armies and compelled the sons of nobles to attend cadet schools in which martial skills and attitudes were inculcated.

In this military state Frederick William I was the number one soldier. A colorful commander in chief, he maintained a personal regiment of enormous grenadiers and always wore a uniform, which he declared that he would be buried in.[2] He did not mean that he would die in battle, however. For all his involvement with military life, he studiously refrained from committing his army to battle prematurely or needlessly. Consequently he passed this force on intact to his son, Frederick II.

The process of centralization kept pace with the growth of the army. In 1723 a government superagency was created: called the General Directory of Finance, War, and Domains, it united under one roof the administration of all functions except justice, educa-

tion, and religion. Its main task was to coordinate the collection of revenue, expenditure (mostly on the army), and local administration. The king mobilized the state's resources in one activity that even French absolutism had not affected: education. Considering it a service to both God and country to give the population some basic instruction, he made education compulsory for all children where schools existed and instructed local communities and parents to set them up where they did not. Teachers held their jobs mainly as sidelines, most coming from the clergy. Uninterested in higher intellectual pursuits, however, the king allowed the universities to decline at the same time. They did not seem to fit in with his design of building state power.

Frederick William I's dour, puritanical attitude left an impact on his reforms that helped give them what would later be considered a peculiarly Prussian flavor. Distrustful of his bureaucrats, he granted them only a minimum of discretionary power, and while insisting on absolute obedience, he held them responsible for inefficiency. This treatment was capped by the operations of a network of inspectors called fiscals, who reported directly and secretly to the king on the behavior of officials. All these policies produced a rigid, rule-book mentality among the bureaucrats that became an oppressive force in Prussia by the end of the nineteenth century.

Frederick the Great

Frederick William I's most notable triumph was perhaps the grooming of his successor. This was no mean task. Frederick II (1740–1786) seemed diametrically opposite in temperament to his father and little inclined to follow in his footsteps. The father was a Teutonic philistine, a God-fearing Protestant, and a self-conscious Hohenzollern. The prince by contrast was a sentimental, artistically inclined youth who composed music and played on the flute, wrote poetry, and fer-

---

[2] Frederick William I's militarism is the subject of numerous anecdotes but also the graver charge that he inaugurated a style that helped produce Nazism. This view was particularly common during World War II. Thus an excellent study by Robert Ergang of this dynamic ruler, published in 1941, bore the astounding title, *The Potsdam Führer: Frederick William I.*

vently admired French culture. Later he would write philosophical treatises and histories and would correspond with Voltaire. Frederick II disdained German culture, had a low estimation of his Hohenzollern relatives, and was an atheist.

But the Prussian monarchy was mobilizing all its subjects for the tasks of state building, and the young prince was not exempted. On the contrary he was compelled to work at all levels of the state apparatus so as to experience them directly, from shoveling hay on a royal farm to marching with the troops. Relentlessly the father trained his son for kingship, forcibly reshaping his personality, inculcating him with a sense of duty, and toughening him to the grinding tasks of leadership. Despite Frederick's prolonged resistance, this hard apprenticeship succeeded. In the end, as a modern psychiatrist would put it, the prince identified with the aggressor.

When he assumed the throne, in 1740, Frederick II was prepared to lead Prussia in a ruthless struggle for power and territory. While his intellectual turn of mind caused him to agonize over moral issues and the nature of his role, he never flinched from actually exercising it. He did, however, attempt to justify absolutism at home and encroachment abroad. He claimed undivided power for the ruler not because some divine qualities inhered in the dynasty but because absolute rule was the only kind that could bring results. The monarch, he stated, was the first servant of the state. In the long run, he hoped, an enlightened monarch might be in a position to lead his people into a more rational and even moral existence. Certain objectives along this road could be attained immediately; in matters like religious toleration and judicial reform, Frederick was able to implement his ideals and gained a reputation as an "enlightened absolutist."

But these were relatively peripheral matters. The paramount issue was security, and the best justification of absolutism would be its effectiveness in ensuring it. Success for Prussia depended on her improving an extremely vulnerable geographic position by acquiring more territory and stronger borders and ultimately on attaining great enough power to make her truly independent (see Map 18.2). Until such a time Frederick would not undertake social innovations domestically that might disrupt the flow of taxes, conscripts, or officers into the army or provoke the nobility against him. "The fundamental rule of governments," he wrote, "is the principle of extending their territories." This summed up what was in fact his most singular contribution to the rise of Prussia and what earned him his title of Frederick the Great.

Frederick William I had carefully avoided squandering his impressive army in engagements that would not really benefit Prussia. By coincidence the year 1740, which saw Frederick II's accession to the throne, was also the moment when a suitable objective for this army presented itself. Frederick began his reign with a sudden attack on the Hapsburg Empire. His objective was to conquer the province of Silesia. Prussia had no claim to it; it was simply a wealthy and strategically located domain contiguous to Prussia that the Hapsburgs were temporarily unable to defend effectively, for reasons that will be discussed directly. The conquest of Silesia culminated a century of Prussian state building inaugurated by the great elector back in 1648. But this same act would have equal significance for the progress of absolutism in the Hapsburg Empire.

THE HAPSBURG EMPIRE UNDER STRESS

Even after the Hapsburg dynasty lost control of Spain and its lands overseas, its personal domains remained immense. Its ambitions and its problems were correspondingly large. The Hapsburgs' empire was the antithesis of a unified state; it was rather a dynastic holding company of diverse territories gathered under one crown through marriages, bargains, and conquests: the Archduchy of Austria, the Kingdom of Bohemia (which had included Silesia), the Kingdom of Hungary, and European "colonies" like the Austrian Netherlands, Lombardy, and Tuscany (see Map 18.2). The Hapsburgs had hoped to integrate Austria, Bohemia, and Hungary into a centralized, German-speaking, Catholic superstate. But centralization was resisted by the local diets in all provinces, and forced Germanization would be opposed by the Czechs, Magyars, and Slavs. Moreover the Hapsburgs' Catholicism clashed with the strong Protestant traditions of Bohemia and Hungary.

The War of the Austrian Succession

Under the reign of Charles VI, yet another problem complicated the destinies of his multinational empire. The long history of Hapsburg intermarriage had finally issued in a failure of the male line. Charles' only heir apparent was his daughter, Maria Theresa, an unprecedented situation for the dynasty. In 1713 Charles drafted a document known as the Pragmatic Sanction, declaring that all Hapsburg dominions would pass intact to the eldest heir, male or female. He thereby hoped to prevent a succession crisis and a division of the inheritance, which would dissipate Hapsburg power. Through the labyrinthine interests of the state system, Charles sought for the next twenty-five years to secure recognition and guarantees of the Pragmatic Sanction from the European powers. By making all kinds of concessions and promises, he won this recognition on paper. But when he died, in 1740, his daughter found that such paper commitments were worthless: the succession was challenged by force from several sides. Concentrating on diplomacy alone, Charles had neglected the work of state building, leaving an empty treasury, inadequately trained

army, and ineffective bureaucracy. The Pragmatic Sanction was scarcely pragmatic.

In contrast to Austria, Prussia's treasury was full, her army primed, and her ruler self-confident. For Frederick II the moment seemed right to grab off the Hapsburg province of Silesia, with its abundant resources and geographic proximity to Prussia. Without legal claims to it, Prussia's justification was simply her own "reasons of state" combined with the Hapsburgs' faltering fortunes. Frederick struck, assuming that other problems would keep Maria Theresa occupied. This in fact was the case. France's relatively pacific policy was just ending, as a clique of military aristocrats had gained the king's support and persuaded him to resume the traditional battle against the Hapsburgs. France's entering wedge was her ally Bavaria, whose duke, Charles Albert, now put forward a tenuous claim to the disputed Hapsburg succession. Spain entered the lists against Austria also, seeing a chance to walk away with Austria's Italian colonies. Worse yet, Maria Theresa faced a rebellion led by the surviving Czech nobility in Bohemia: in 1741 four hundred of them proclaimed Charles Albert of Bavaria king of Bohemia.

The young archduchess' fate would probably have been hopeless if Hungary's Magyar nobles had followed a similar course. Their grievances, however, were not so sharp, and they listened sympathetically to Maria Theresa's moving pleas for support. In exchange for her promise of autonomy within the Hapsburg Empire, the Magyars offered her loyalty and the troops necessary to resist the invaders.

Austria's principal ally was Great Britain, but Britain was interested only in combating France on the Continent. Therefore the British pressured Maria Theresa to concede Silesia and make peace with Prussia, in order to concentrate on the Franco-Bavarian invasion. With the help of Hungarian troops and Brit-

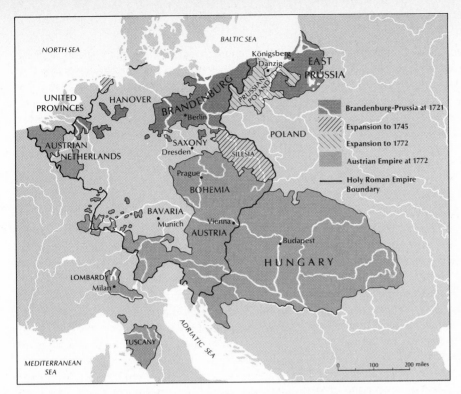

MAP 18.2: PRUSSIA 1721–1772 AND THE HAPSBURG EMPIRE

ish gold, Austria fought these opponents to a stalemate, and Frederick's conquest of Silesia proved to be the only major territorial change produced by this large-scale war. Apart from that, the Treaty of Aix-la-Chapelle in 1748 restored the status quo established by the Utrecht settlement. For England and France, who fought this war in their overseas colonies as well as in Europe, it was a stand-off. For Prussia it was a spectacular gain at Austria's expense. Austria regarded it as merely a temporary setback. The recovery of Silesia and the humiliation of Prussia became the primary objective of Austrian policy. This in turn required a major effort at state building within the Hapsburg domains.

Maria Theresa

The woman whose reign was assured not by her father's negotiations but by force of arms was a marked contrast to her archenemy, Frederick. The king of Prussia was practical and atheistic; the archduchess of Austria and Queen of Hungary was moralistic and pious. While Frederick barely tolerated a loveless marriage, the Hapsburg ruler enjoyed an unusually happy domestic life, bearing her husband numerous children and taking great personal interest in their upbringing. Her personality and her ruling style were traditional, but deceptively—under this exterior she was a shrewd innovator in the business of building and reasserting the power of her state.

Unlike Frederick, or for that matter her own son and successor, Joseph II, Maria Theresa still had a strong regard for her dynasty. She did not share the modern conception of the ruler's role as simply first servant of the state; she still believed in the divine mission of the Hapsburgs. Yet utilitarian considerations did increasingly enter into her planning, causing her to think more of her realm and less of the dynasty and the Almighty. Likewise this most pious of Catholic sovereigns—who disdained the permissive idea of religious toleration and who loathed atheists—found herself obliged to undertake stern reforms of the church. Particularly in its monastic wing, she found far too much wastefulness and self-interest; consequently she forbade the establishment of new monasteries or the taking of vows by anyone under twenty-four years of age. Moreover she abolished the clergy's exemptions from taxes, something her more easygoing French counterpart found impossible to do.

A new bureaucratic apparatus was constructed on the models of French and Prussian absolutism. At the center, in Vienna, reorganized and relatively streamlined central ministries recruited staffs of experts. For the arms and legs of this machine in the provinces, new agents were appointed, largely divorced from feudal and local interests, though in practice some concession had to be made to the enormous vested interests and regional traditions within the Hapsburg realm. The core domains (excluding Hungary and the Italian colonies) were reorganized into ten provinces, each subdivided into districts or circles that were in turn each directed by a royal official. With the help of these trusted agents, the central government could wrest new taxes from the increasingly weakened local diets. Meanwhile, by flattery and consideration, Maria Theresa lured important nobles from all corners of her domains

to Vienna to participate in its social and administrative life. It goes without saying that this was matched by military reforms, notably improvements in the training of troops and the establishment of academies to produce a more professional officer corps. By 1756 Austria was ready to face Prussia again.

III. THE MARITIME POWERS

The shift of the economic axis from the Mediterranean to the Atlantic seaboard began in the sixteenth century during the years of Spanish and Portuguese expansion. But it was left to the eighteenth century and to France and Great Britain to consolidate that shift and establish its full significance. Despite their great differences, both countries generated dynamic commercial activity, and both were beyond the state-building stage that other nations were now passing through. For the merchants and governments of France and England, colonial trade was an adjunct of state building—a question not only of profits but of power. In the process an almost global economy was created, whose mainspring was the system of plantation slavery.

THE ATLANTIC SEABOARD STATES

France After Louis XIV

Although France provided a model for absolutism, even under the Sun King centralization of power was never complete. Until the era of revolutions, the French aristocracy remained a strong group in the state that could create trouble for the monarchy.

Louis XIV's death, in 1715, released a great deal of such trouble. French absolutism was too firmly established to be swept away by an aristocratic reaction, but it could not prevent such attempts. For one thing Louis XIV's heir was still a child, and the duke of Orléans, who became regent in this interval, had no interest in the tradition of absolutism. On the contrary, to bolster his own delicate position, he supported key aristocrats in a grab for power. The regent restored the parlements to political power and replaced prominent royal bureaucrats with councils composed of France's most eminent aristocrats. The scheme quickly proved a complete failure since the councils were simply unable to govern effectively. The parlements, however, would never again surrender their power to veto royal legislation. Henceforth they became the rallying point of those who deplored the growth of centralized government and wished to restore the so-called unwritten constitution of France, which was supposed to limit the powers of the king and protect the prerogatives of various groups.

A second major problem facing France was of course her finances. The debt amassed by Louis' wartime expenditures was crushing. Since privileged groups like the nobility and clergy effectively escaped Louis' half-hearted attempts to tax them, other ways of improving the state's credit were sought. The brilliant Scottish financier John Law seemed to have the answer: a government-sponsored central bank that would issue paper notes, expand credit, and encourage investment in a new trading company for the French colonies. By tying the bank to his well-promoted East India Company, a venture promising its subscribers vast profits from the Louisiana territory, Law initiated an investment boom and a tremendous upsurge in available credit. But as was the case in England at the same time, the public's greed and credulity soon led to vast financial overextension as prices for East India Company stock rose to insanely high levels. A bust was inevitable, and when it came, in 1720, the entire scheme of bank notes and credit collapsed with it.

In different forms the same political and financial problems were to plague France through the eighteenth century until the Revolution opened up entirely new options for their solution. Meanwhile the uncertainties of regency government gave way to a long period of stability between 1720 and 1740, when Louis XV conferred almost unlimited authority on his aging tutor and adviser, Cardinal Fleury. Cautious, dedicated to the monarchy, and surrounded by talented subordinates, Cardinal Fleury made the apparatus of absolutism function quietly and with reasonable effectiveness. In these decades France turned the corner out of the low point of misfortunes that marked the end of Louis XIV's reign. Fleury's twenty-year tenure coincided with abundant harvests, slowly rising population, and commercial activity—in short with recovery.

Moreover Fleury was able to contain pressures and ambitions within the governing class. When he finally died at the age of ninety, these pressures exploded. War hawks immediately plunged France into the first of several protracted and unsuccessful wars that strained French credit to the breaking point. At home the situation likewise deteriorated. Having no one to replace Fleury as unofficial prime minister, Louis XV put his confidence in a succession of counselors, some capable and some mediocre. But he did not back any of them up when pressure from contending factions at court became uncomfortable. Lacking self-confidence and dedication to his task, the king avoided confrontations and neglected affairs of state, devoting his energy instead to the pleasures of the hunt and a succession of mistresses.

Although Louis XV clearly provided weak leadership for an extended period, France's difficulties must be seen not simply in personal but also in structural terms. The main problems—privilege, political power, and finances—posed intractable and perhaps impossible challenges to policy makers. Taxes have always been unpopular; governments that appear to levy new taxes arbitrarily seem despotic, even if the need for them is clear and the distribution equitable. One of France's soundest taxes was the *vingtième*, or twentieth, which was supposed to tap the income of all elements in French society with some measure of proportionality. The nobility and clergy, however, all but evaded the real brunt of the tax. Naturally the more aggressive royal ministers wished to remedy that situation. In the 1750s for example a plan was advanced for putting teeth into the *vingtième's* bite on the clergy's immense wealth. The plan proved to be the ruination of a capable royal official. With all its corporate might, the clergy attacked the plan; the parlements joined in the attack against the "despotism" of a crown that would arbitrarily tax its subjects. Thus not only did the privileged groups successfully block such useful reforms, but they made the monarchy's position more difficult by spreading a spirit of opposition and a fine-sounding rhetoric of liberty. In retrospect we see that the parlements were advancing their own special interests as they fought for a limitation on royal absolutism.

Another of Louis XV's ministers, René Maupeou, recognized that the parlements were an unbreachable obstacle to royal initiative, whether to do good or bad. Hence he prevailed on the king to use force as Louis XIV would have. In 1771 the parlements were dissolved and were replaced by magistrates loyal to the king. But the story could no longer end so simply as it might have a century before. Most of the articulate public now rallied to the parlements' support. The pressure of this elite "public opinion" was so great that it forced Louis XVI into restoring the parlements and dismissing Maupeou when he succeeded to the throne, wishing to begin his reign (1774–1792) with public confidence and popularity. Predictably the parlements repaid this kindness by persisting in opposing meaningful reform efforts attempted by Louis

XVI's ministers, leaving the monarchy in a hopeless impasse by the 1780s: virtually bankrupt, unpopular, and vacillating.

In the face of the structural weaknesses of the state and the special interests of the ruling classes, it is easy to forget the advances made in this most populous and wealthy European nation. Changes in population, rural economy, and the like, which will be discussed in Chapter 20, were clearly among the most important aspects of French history in the eighteenth century. So too was the commercial and maritime activity that went into the building of France's empire and the struggle to maintain it. No one knew at the time that the fate of royal ministers in the 1750s or 1770s foretold a stalemate that would help bring the Old Regime crashing down. The French peasantry at home and empire builders abroad continued to work at their callings, virtually unaffected by these storm signals.

The Growth of Stability in Great Britain

After the Peace of Utrecht, Great Britain too experienced a period of recovery. If the first half of the eighteenth century was an age of aristocratic reaction in France, it was a period of aristocratic dominance in Britain. The gentry and the wealthier freeholders, who elected the members of Parliament, represented a "political nation" of perhaps 100,000 in a population of 5 million in England and Wales in 1700. The distribution of the 558 seats in the House of Commons bore little resemblance to the relative size of the boroughs and shires. In 1793 fifty-one English and Welsh boroughs, counting less than 1,500 voters, elected 100 members of Parliament, nearly a fifth of the Commons. Many of these districts—such as Old Sarum, with an electorate of about six— were safely in the pocket of a prominent local family; little wonder that reformers would later call them "rotten." When a seat was disputed, the campaigns were seldom waged on principle but were competitions in bribery, influence, and intimidation. On a national scale loose party alignments did exist. The Whigs favored a strong Parliament and were somewhat more sensitive to commercial than to agricultural interests. The Tories usually supported the king and the policies that favored large landholders. In truth, however, the realities of politics were based on much smaller factions within these larger groups, and the principal political issue was the control of patronage and office.

But despite the oligarchic character of the social and political system, it is accurate to say that class lines remained considerably more fluid in Britain than on the Continent. The barriers separating the peerage, the gentry, and the commercial (and soon industrial) middle class were frequently pierced by marriage and by business or political associations. Some of the great Whig aristocrats in particular had substantial ties with the mercantile classes of London. Parliament, though scandalously unrepresentative of the population in the eighteenth century, at least was an institution that could be reformed and repaired. France had no similar functioning organism that could conveniently admit a larger part of the nation into participation in government.

A new dynasty, the Hanoverians, assumed the throne in 1714. Neither George I (1714–1727) nor George II (1727–1760) could speak English fluently, and while they showed some interest in their British realm, the language barrier and their concern for their Continental possessions limited royal influence and provided an opportunity for royal ministers and Parliament to grow in authority.

The dominant figure in British political history for the first half of the century was Sir Robert Walpole. He won his reputation for his skillful handling of government finances during a crisis of 1720, the collapse of the "South Sea Bubble." This panic involved shares of the South Seas Trading Company and was similar to the catastrophe that over-took John Law's scheme in France. From 1721 to 1742 Walpole largely controlled the British government and determined its policies. He maintained his power by dispensing patronage liberally and maintaining the friendship of the king. He probably did not pronounce the words attributed to him. "Every man has his price," but the slogan would well describe political life under Walpole. The other phrase that describes his policies at home and abroad is "*Quieta non movere*," "Do not disturb the peace"—or in the vernacular, "Let sleeping dogs lie."

Although Walpole was responsible for no great new ideas or grand policies, he did contribute both to his country's economic recovery and to the growth of its political institutions. Many historians have called Walpole the first prime minister, though the office still had no official existence and the name itself was first used by his enemies as a kind of insult. He insisted that all the royal ministers follow the same policies, which of course he set himself. He insisted too that the ministers inform and consult with the House of Commons as well as the king. He himself continued to sit in its sessions in order to recruit support for his decisions. Not until the following century would the Commons have the recognized power of forcing ministers it did not approve of to resign, but Walpole took a first step toward rendering the ministers responsible before Parliament. While he was not truly the first prime minister, he certainly helped shape the office.

In Great Britain as in France, the economic expansion from about 1730 on increased the wealth and the social and political weight of the commercial and financial middle class. Walpole's policy of peace pleased the large landlords but angered the merchants and businessmen of London, who viewed the growth of French commerce and colonial settlements with apprehension. They found their champion in William Pitt, later earl of Chatham,

William Pitt is shown here addressing the House of Commons. Pitt had an abiding confidence in England's role as an imperial power, and his oratory, presence, and discerning political intelligence kept him at the forefront of British politics during the midcentury crisis. (Photo: Radio Times Hulton Picture Library)

himself the grandson of a man who had made a fortune in India. Eloquent, supremely self-confident, infused with a great vision of Britain's imperial destiny, Pitt began his career in Parliament in 1738 by bitterly criticizing the timid policies of the government and demanding that France be driven from the seas. In 1758, when the Seven Years' War was going badly for England, he was called to the ministry, with what results we shall see.

The Decline of the Dutch

The United Provinces, or Dutch Netherlands, emerged from the wars of Louis XIV in an ambiguous position. The country had survived intact, and considering her military vulnerability this was no small accomplishment. On the other hand she suffered from demographic and political ossification. The population of 2.5 million failed to rise during the eighteenth century, thus setting the Dutch apart from their rivals, the French and the British, whose numbers grew rapidly. Likewise a centralized state apparatus failed to develop even during the stress of seventeenth-century warfare. The provinces remained loosely joined in a federation that was barely able to assure the common defense of the state. So self-interested were these seven separate oligarchies that they failed to concert even to repair the ports, which were vital to shipping.

The Dutch were bound to suffer economically when French and English merchants sought to eliminate their role as the middlemen of maritime commerce. Beside this was the failure of Dutch industry to compete effectively with its rivals. Onerous indirect taxes on manufactured goods and the high wages demanded by Dutch artisans forced up the price of Dutch products excessively. Moreover manufacturers proved unable to modernize their processes and technology. High costs and antiquated organization combined especially to set back the all-important cloth industry. Leiden and Haarlem virtually disappeared from the international market.

What kept the nation from slipping completely out of Europe's economic life was her financial institutions. Shrewdly Dutch merchants gradually shifted their activity away from the competition of actual trading ventures into the safer, lucrative areas of credit and finance. With their country the first to perfect the uses of paper currency and establish a stock market and a central bank, the Dutch now became financial instead of maritime middlemen. Amsterdam's merchant-bankers loaned great amounts of money to both private enterprises and governments abroad. One estimate places the Dutch holding of the British national debt in 1776 at three-sevenths of the total. Not only did the Dutch underwrite British credit, but Dutch bankers helped funnel British money to Britain's diplomatic allies. When relations between the Dutch and British were strained in the 1770s, Dutch investment easily found new homes in North America and France. The role of the United Provinces in the colonial struggles of the eighteenth century was thus indirect but considerable.

THE EIGHTEENTH-CENTURY EMPIRES

After 1715 a new era began in the saga of European colonial development (see Map 18.3).

Three pioneers in overseas expansion had by now assumed a generally passive role, content to defend the domains already acquired. Portugal, whose dominion over Brazil was recognized at the Peace of Utrecht, henceforth retired from active contention. Likewise the Dutch could scarcely compete for new footholds and now protected their interests through cautious policies of neutrality. Although Spain continued her efforts to exclude outsiders from her vast empire, she had to rely increasingly on the power of her kindred dynasty in France for any confrontation with Britain. The stage of active competition was in fact left to these two powers.

Mercantile and Naval Competition

Great Britain, a nation that had barely been able to hold her own in maritime competition against the Dutch in the seventeenth century, now began her rise to domination of the seas. The only serious rival of this island power was France.

Their rivalry was played out in four regions. The West Indies, where France and Britain each colonized several islands profitably, constituted the fulcrum of empire, for reasons that will be discussed shortly. Directly linked to the West Indian economy was the second colonial territory: slave-providing West Africa. The third area was the North American continent, where a significant difference between the two powers developed. Britain's colonies became populous centers of settlement, whereas New France remained primarily a trading area. Finally, both nations sponsored powerful companies for trade with India and other Asian lands. These ventures were supposed to struggle for markets and influence without establishing actual colonies.

There were obvious differences and important similarities between the two royal systems. French absolutism produced a centralized structure, with its colonies being run according to uniform standards. *Intendants* and military governors ruled across the seas as they did in the French provinces. The British North American colonies by contrast were and remained somewhat independent both from each other and from the home government, where crown and Parliament both claimed colonial jurisdiction. Each colony had a royal governor but also a locally oriented legislature and strong traditions of self-government. Nonetheless the French and British faced similar problems and achieved generally similar results. Most importantly both applied mercantilist principles to the regulation of trade, and both increased naval power to protect it.

Mercantilism was a Europe-wide phenomenon, not limited to the colonial powers. It involved the regulation of economic activity so as to increase the power of the state over that of its neighbors. In this sense Prussia was as mercantilist as Britain, for both regarded the economic activities of individuals as subordinate to government policy.

A key tenet of mercantilism was the need for a favorable balance of trade and an inflow of gold and silver, with the assumption that a nation's share of bullion could increase only at its neighbor's expense. Colonies could promote a favorable balance of trade by producing valuable raw materials or crops for the mother country and providing a market for the latter's manufactured goods. Foreign states had to be excluded from these benefits as much as possible. By discriminatory tariffs, elaborate regulations, bounties, and outright prohibitions, each government sought to channel trade with its colonies in the direction of itself. Mercantilism for the colonies boiled down to an elaborate system of protectionism for this trade.

The colonies were exploited for the benefit of the mother country and not solely for the profit of those who invested or settled in them. But enormous fortunes were made by the West Indies planters as well as by merchants, manufacturers, and ship owners at home. Moreover illicit trade brought comfortable profits to more than one colonial family. For example, French planters needed North America's beef, fish, and grain and were eager to exchange their own (cheaper) sugar or molasses for it. The Hancocks of Boston among others grew dependent on this kind of smuggling to the French West Indies.

"Empire" was another way of saying "trade," but this trade depended on naval power. Rivals had to be excluded and regulations enforced. Thus there was a reciprocal relationship between the expansion of trade and the deployment of naval forces, which added to the competitive nature of colonial expansion. The merchant traders and the war vessels that supported them needed numerous stopping places for reprovisioning and refitting. This meant that ports had to be secured for them in strategic locations and denied to rivals whenever possible in Africa, India, and the Caribbean.

The Profits of Empire

Colonial commerce provided new products like sugar and new consumer demand, which in turn created an impetus for manufacturing and capital accumulation at home. This cycle increased the opportunities for the English and French middle classes. It is estimated that French commerce quadrupled during the eighteenth century, the value of its trade being somewhere in the vicinity of 200 million livres in 1716 and reaching more than 1 billion livres in 1787. By the 1770s commerce with their colonies accounted for almost one-third the total volume of both Britain's and France's foreign trade. The West Indies trade (mainly in sugar) bulked largest, and its expansion was spectacular. The value of French imports from the West Indies increased more than tenfold between 1716 and 1788, from 16 million to 185 million livres.

The West Indies seemed to be ideal colo-

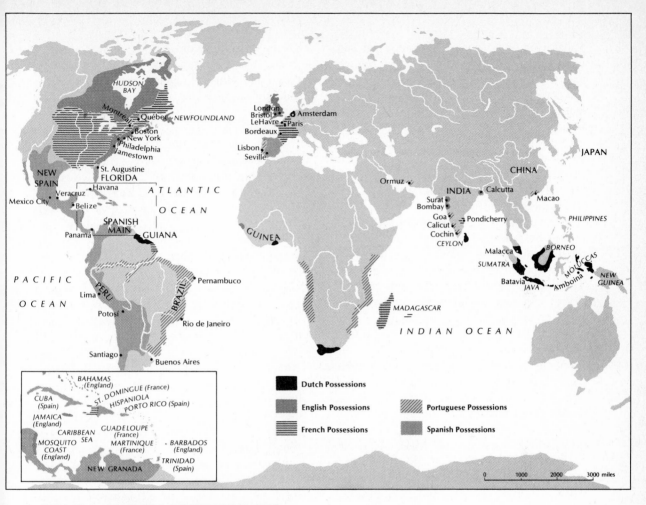

MAP 18.3: OVERSEAS POSSESSIONS 1713

Inset legend:

BAHAMAS (England)
CUBA (Spain)
ST. DOMINGUE (France)
HISPANIOLA
PORTO RICO (Spain)
JAMAICA (England)
CARIBBEAN SEA
GUADELOUPE (France)
MOSQUITO COAST (England)
MARTINIQUE (France)
BARBADOS (England)
TRINIDAD (Spain)
NEW GRANADA

- Dutch Possessions
- English Possessions
- French Possessions
- Portuguese Possessions
- Spanish Possessions

0   1000   2000   3000 miles

nies. By virtue of their tropical climate and the isolation from European society that made slavery possible, they produced abundant crops that were difficult to raise elsewhere: tobacco, cotton, and indigo in addition to sugar, a luxury that European custom turned into a necessity. Moreover the islands could produce little else. They could not raise an adequate supply of food animals or grain to feed the vast slave population; they could not cut enough lumber for building; and they certainly could not manufacture the luxury goods demanded by the planter class. In other words the islands yielded up valuable crops and were dependent markets for most other commodities.

Numerous variations of the famous triangular trade therefore revolved around the West Indies. One pattern began with a ship departing from a British port with a cargo of manufactured products—paper, knives, pots, blankets, and the like—destined for the shopkeepers of North America. Landing at Marblehead or Philadelphia, the ship might exchange its goods for New England fish oil, fish, beef, and timber. These would then be transported to

Jamaica or Barbardos to be traded for sugar that would be turned over to British refineries many months later.

Another variation might see a frigate set out from Providence, Rhode Island (the chief slaving port in North America), with a cargo of New England rum. Landing in Africa, it would acquire slaves in exchange for the rum and then sail to the Indies to sell the slaves— for bills of exchange and for molasses, from which more rum could be distilled.

The final step in the mercantilist colonial process was the reexport of refined and distilled products made of the sugar, indigo, or tobacco provided by the overseas possessions. These were most likely to bring gold into British or French hands since finished goods could command hard cash from customers all over the Western world. For colonial commerce was superimposed on a complex and profitable pattern of European trade in which the Atlantic states carried off the lion's share. The New World's sugar, furs, fish, and tobacco were added to Baltic grain and timber; Italian and Spanish wines, fruits, olives, and silks; and Levantine and Asian spices and fabrics. To all these regions the manufacturing centers of Western Europe continued providing products like nails and pots, glassware and crockery, and shirts and stockings as well as luxuries like carriages and tapestries.

Slavery, the Foundation of Empire

Slavery was the keystone of the eighteenth-century empires. The dynamic qualities of the global trade had slavery as a starting point. Vast, backbreaking labor was necessary to transform a favorable climate and the investment of speculators into harvested crops of staples. As one British merchant put it candidly, colonial trade "increases or diminishes in proportion to the numbers of Negroes imported there, who produce the commodities with which our ships are usually loaded, and enable planters to live well and purchase great quantities of British commodities." About the same time the chamber of commerce of Nantes, France's chief slaving port, publicly argued that without slavery there would be no French colonial commerce to speak of at all.

At the height of the slave traffic, probably about 88,000 Negroes were removed from Africa annually—half in British ships, a quarter in French, and the rest in Dutch, Portuguese, Danish, and American ships. Over 600,000 slaves were imported into Jamaica in the eighteenth century, while the population of Santo Domingo comprised about half a million slaves compared with 35,000 whites of all nationalities and 28,000 mulattoes and free Negroes at the time of the French Revolution.

Traffic in slaves was competitive and risky but highly profitable for those who succeeded. The demand for slaves in the Indies, Central America, and the Southern colonies in North America kept rising, pushing prices up. In both Britain and France, slaving was originally organized monopolistically, with chartered companies holding exclusive rights in the 1660s. There was no actual colonization or conquest in Africa, but the French and to a lesser extent the British attempted to establish forts, or "factories," on African soil for the coordination and defense of these companies. Gradually the monopolies were challenged by newcomers—groups of merchants and investors who combined to launch single ships on slaving voyages. The West Indian planters, who needed more and cheaper slaves, applauded this additional source. In port cities like Bristol and Liverpool, the independent traders clustered and prospered. By the 1730s the British government was opening membership in its company almost automatically to any subject engaged in the trade. This arrangement was a midway point between the older chartered joint-stock companies and the nineteenth-century pattern of direct government attempts at colonization to promote the

THE MAGNITUDE OF THE SLAVE TRADE

The following figures represent the best current estimate of the number of persons removed from Africa and transported as slaves to the New World during the entire period of the Atlantic slave trade.

British Caribbean	1,665,000
British North America (to 1790)	275,000
United States (after 1786)	124,000
French Caribbean	1,600,000
Dutch Caribbean	500,000
Brazil	3,646,800
Spanish America	1,552,000

Source: Philip D. Curtin, *The Atlantic Slave Trade: A Census* (1969).

interests of British merchants and investors.

Europeans alone did not condemn free blacks to slavery. The actual enslavement took place in the interior at the hands of aggressive tribes whose chiefs became the middlemen of this nefarious commerce. These black traders were shrewd and hard bargainers, and prices were set in goods rather than fixed currency. The competition among Europeans for the slaves tended to drive up the prices that the natives could command in hardware, cloth, liquor, and guns. In response some traders sought to open up new areas where the natives would be more eager to come to terms. This combination of competitiveness, increasing demand, and higher prices helped spread the trade and further darken the future of Africa.

Europeans in this period scarcely penetrated the interior of the continent; they were confined by the forbidding topography and the resoluteness of the natives to coastal areas. But the Europeans' intervention disoriented African life. It spurred on civil wars among the African tribes, diverting energies into military ventures and away from agricultural development; and it drained off a vast supply of labor that was needed in Africa itself.

The chief impact of course was on the slaves themselves. Many failed to survive the process of enslavement at all, perishing either on the forced marches from the interior to the coast or on the nightmarish middle passage across the Atlantic, which was comparable to the transit in cattle cars of Nazi prisoners to extermination camps in World War II. Since the risks of slaving ventures were high and the time lag between investment and return was usually a year and a half or two years, the traders sought to maximize profits by jamming in as many captives as possible. Small ships carried as many as 500 slaves on a voyage, packed below deck in only enough space for the individual to lie at full length, pressed against neighboring bodies, and enough headroom to crawl, not stand. The food and provi-

Slave traffic was the basis for empire building in the eighteenth century, and slave ships were a cruel and common sight on international waters. This print shows a method used to quell revolts on board ship and suggests the sheer violence underlying the trade. (Photo: New York Public Library, Rare Books)

sions were likewise held to a minimum. No accurate figures are available on the mortality rate that resulted from these odious conditions. It is no wonder then that agitation against slavery tended to focus initially on the trade rather than the institution itself. After the 1780s participation in slave trafficking diminished considerably both in England and France. A dark chapter in Europe's relations with the outside world dwindled to an end, though the formal suppression of slaving did not come for several more decades.

IV. THE MIDCENTURY CONFLAGRATION

The pressures created by the competition of states, dynasties, and empires in the eighteenth century exploded in midcentury in what was to be the last large-scale war of the prerevolutionary period. For the sake of clarity, it is helpful to consider the conflagration in two parts. One, the Continental phase, known as the Seven Years' War, had at its center Austro-Prussian rivalry and the growing ambitions of Russia. The other revolved around Anglo-French competition for empire in North America, the West Indies, and India. Colonial historians have called it the Great War for Empire, and it was this sector of conflict that had produced the more striking results when the smoke cleared.

THE SEVEN YEARS' WAR

In certain respects the Seven Years' War and its colonial corollaries anticipated what would happen in the European state system on the eve of World War I. Although it lacked the elements of domestic class conflict and popular nationalism that also contributed to the crisis in Europe in 1914, the war flowed from a tangled web of interlocking alliances, im-

perial competition abroad, and one state's desire to avenge a loss of territory—Austria's loss of Silesia in this case, France's loss of Alsace-Lorraine in World War I.

At midcentury a reconsideration of alliances began within the European state system under Austria's prodding. Previously the Bourbon-Hapsburg rivalry had been the cornerstone of European diplomacy. But by the 1750s at least two other sets of fundamental antagonisms had superseded it: France's competition with Great Britain in the New World and Austria's vendetta against Prussia over Silesia. For Austria the rivalry with Bourbon France was no longer important. Its position in the Holy Roman Empire depended now on humbling Prussia. France did not yet share a concern over Prussia, but her hostility to Austria had diminished. Austria was therefore free to pursue a turnabout in alliances—a veritable diplomatic revolution—in which an anti-Prussian coalition could be forged. Russia was the key to this coalition. Aside from her personal loathing of the atheistic Frederick II, Empress Elizabeth perceived Prussia as an obstacle to Russian ambitions in Eastern Europe. Moreover Prussia's geographical vulnerability made the kingdom an inviting target.

Prussia was understandably active on the diplomatic front in the hope of compensating for that vulnerability. Upset by the initiatives of Austria's brilliant foreign minister Kaunitz, Frederick's panicky countermoves only succeeded in alienating the other powers. Frederick sought to stay out of the Anglo-French rivalry by coming to terms with both these states. Having been France's ally in the past, he sought in addition to negotiate a treaty with England. England—seeking to protect her North German client state of Hanover—willingly signed a neutrality accord with Prussia (the Convention of Westminster) in January 1756. Frederick had no intention of repudiating his friendship with France, but to the

French—who had not been informed in advance of these negotiations—the Convention of Westminster appeared as an affront if not an actual betrayal. Such accords with France's mortal enemy England seemed an unscrupulous act by an untrustworthy ally. Hence France overreacted, turned against Prussia, and thus fell into Kaunitz's design. Russia too assumed a more militant anti-Prussian position since it considered the Convention of Westminster a betrayal by *its* supposed ally England. English bribes and diplomacy could no longer keep Russia from actively joining Austria to plan Prussia's dismemberment.

Fearing encirclement, Frederick gambled on launching a preventive war through Saxony in 1756 to break apart the coalition. Although he easily conquered the duchy—the gateway to Hapsburg Bohemia—his plan backfired, for it now activated the coalition that he dreaded. Both Russia and France met their commitments to Austria, and a grand offensive design against Prussia took final shape. Poorly led, France in effect put her army at Austria's disposal for Austrian objectives.

For a time Frederick showed his genius as a general and prevailed over the coalition. His forces achieved a spectacular victory at Rossbach, Saxony, in October 1757 over a much larger combined French-Austrian army. Skillful tactics and daring surprise movements would bring other victories, but strategically the Prussian position was shaky. Frederick had to dash in all directions across his provinces to repel a variety of invading armies whose combined strength far exceeded his own. Each successive year of the war, he faced the prospect of Russian attacks on Brandenburg in the north and Austrian thrusts from the south through Silesia and Saxony. Disaster was avoided mainly because of Russia's policy of evacuating for winter quarters back east regardless of her gains, but even so the Russians occupied Berlin. On the verge of exhaustion, Prussia at best seemed to face

a stalemate with a considerable loss of territory; at worst the war could continue and bring about a total Prussian collapse. But then again all the powers were war-weary, and his enemies were extremely distrustful of each other by now.

Frederick was plucked from the jaws of despair by one of those sudden changes of reign that commonly caused dramatic reversals of policy in Europe. In January 1762 his nemesis Empress Elizabeth died and was replaced temporarily by Tsar Peter III, a fanatic admirer of Frederick. He quickly pulled Russia out of the war and returned Frederick's conquered eastern domains of Prussia and Pomerania. Kaunitz's dream collapsed. At the same time the belligerent British minister Pitt was replaced by the more pacific John Stuart, earl of Bute, clearing the way for an Anglo-French settlement that did not insist on the punishment of Prussia.

The actual terms of the Peace of Hubertusburg (1763), settling the Continental phase of the midcentury conflagration, were therefore surprisingly favorable to Prussia in view of all that had happened. Saxony was returned to its elector, but no compensation was demanded from Prussia for the devastation she had inflicted on the duchy. Silesia was recognized as Prussian by the Austrians. In short the status quo was restored. Frederick could return to Berlin, his dominion preserved. He had marshaled all the state's resources to maintain his army in the field, and this army alone had assured the survival of his state.

MOUNTING COLONIAL CONFLICTS

In the New World, rival French and British colonies had been developing along complementary lines, and both groups were prospering. The thirteen British colonies on the North American continent were experiencing a remarkable growth because of continuous immigration and natural reproduction, reaching a population of about 1.5 million by midcentury. While some pushed the frontier westward and put the soil under cultivation, others clustered around the original settlements, a few of which could by then be called cities.[3] The extension of the frontier and the growth of towns helped impart a particular vitality to the British colonial world in contrast to which New France appeared less dynamic. Since there was little enthusiasm for emigration to Louisiana or Canada, the French remained thinly spread in their substantial territories. Yet their colonies were well organized, profitable, and vigorous in their own way. Indeed French West Indian planters were able to underprice the sugar of their British competitors, and the French trading company in India was initially more effective than its British rival in expanding operations.

While French fishermen and fur traders prospered in Canada, French soldiers established a series of strongholds to support them. These included Fort Louisburg—the greatest bastion of military strength in North America —at the entrance of the Gulf of St. Lawrence and a string of forts near the Great Lakes that served as bridgeheads for French fur traders and as a security buffer for the province of Quebec (see Map 18.4). At the other end of the continent, in Louisiana, New Orleans was established to open the far end of the Mississippi River to trade. During the War of the Austrian Succession, several skirmishes were fought in the New World, but both sides were agreeable to a restitution of captured territories at the peace table, which the Treaty of Aix-la-Chapelle arranged. Obviously this was a truce, not a peace.

On the contrary imperial rivalry intensified and military preparations increased. France reinforced Louisburg, and the British estab-

lished their first large military base in North America at nearby Halifax, Nova Scotia. The fishing grounds and waterways of the St. Lawrence gulf would be a major scene of contention in any future war. A second area that now loomed into prominence was the unsettled Ohio valley. Pushing south from their Great Lakes trading forts and north from their posts on the Mississippi, the French began to assume control over that wilderness. A new string of forts formed pivots for potential French domination of the whole area between the Appalachian Mountains and the Mississippi —territory claimed and coveted by British subjects in the thirteen colonies. The threat grew that the French could completely cut off the westward expansion of these colonies. Conversely the French feared that British domination in the Ohio valley would lead to encroachments on Canadian territory.

In this jockeying for position, the allegiance of the Indians was vital, and the French gradually gained the upper hand. Being traders only and not settlers, the French did not force the Indians from their native hunting grounds as the British had done repeatedly. Hence the Indians were willing to cooperate in sealing off the Ohio valley. A large land investment company called the Ohio Company of Virginia was most directly affected by this development, and in 1754 it attempted to break the French and Indian hold by sending an expedition against Fort Duquesne. Led by a young militiaman named George Washington, the expedition failed.

Thus, contrary to the British tradition of letting settled colonies pay for themselves, the home government was compelled to shoulder the burden of defense. An expedition of regulars was sent to do the job that George Washington could not. But it too met defeat in an ambush by experienced French and Indian skirmishers. Limited engagements were now giving way to a full-scale war. Each side began to reinforce its garrisons and naval squad-

[3] With a population of about 23,000 in 1760, for example, Philadelphia could scarcely be considered a colonial outpost. Commercially and socially (if not culturally) it was a city.

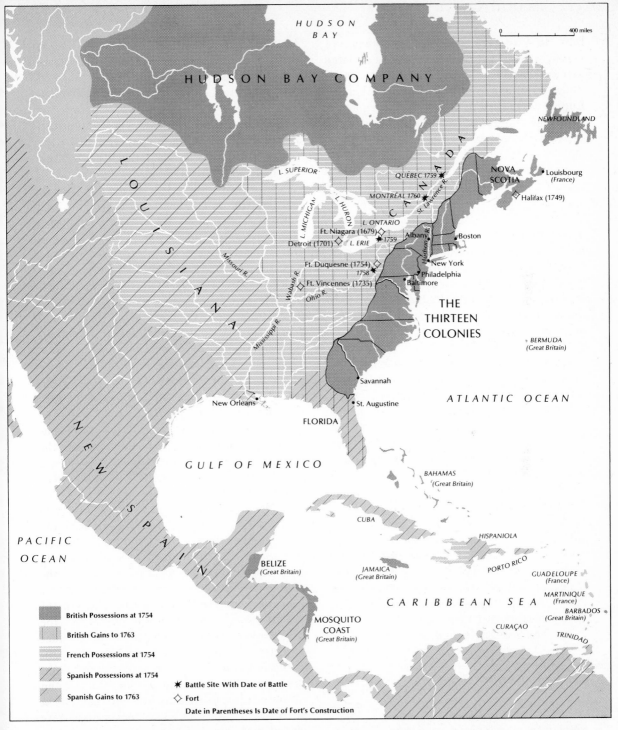

HUDSON BAY

HUDSON BAY COMPANY

0 ——— 400 miles

NEWFOUNDLAND

LOUISIANA

L. SUPERIOR

L. MICHIGAN

L. HURON

L. ONTARIO

Ft. Niagara (1679) ◇

Detroit (1701) ◇ L. ERIE ★ 1759

Missouri R.

Wabash R.

Ft. Duquesne (1754) ◇
1758 ★
Ft. Vincennes (1735) ◇

Ohio R.

Mississippi R.

QUÉBEC 1759 ★

MONTRÉAL 1760 ★

St. Lawrence R.

CANADA

NOVA SCOTIA

• Louisbourg (France)

◇ Halifax (1749)

Albany •

Hudson R.

• Boston

New York •

• Philadelphia

Baltimore •

THE THIRTEEN COLONIES

• BERMUDA (Great Britain)

NEW SPAIN

New Orleans •

• Savannah

• St. Augustine

FLORIDA

GULF OF MEXICO

ATLANTIC OCEAN

BAHAMAS (Great Britain)

CUBA

HISPANIOLA

PACIFIC OCEAN

BELIZE (Great Britain)

JAMAICA (Great Britain)

PORTO RICO

GUADELOUPE (France)

MARTINIQUE (France)

BARBADOS (Great Britain)

CURAÇAO

TRINIDAD

CARIBBEAN SEA

MOSQUITO COAST (Great Britain)

British Possessions at 1754

British Gains to 1763

French Possessions at 1754

Spanish Possessions at 1754

Spanish Gains to 1763

★ Battle Site With Date of Battle

◇ Fort

Date in Parentheses Is Date of Fort's Construction

MAP 18.4: ANGLO-FRENCH RIVALRY IN NORTH AMERICA AND THE CARIBBEAN 1754–1763

rons. In May 1756, after some two years of unofficial hostilities, war was formally declared between Britain and France. The French and Indian War, as this arc of the Great War for Empire was called in the colonies, originated as a contest to decide the balance of power in the New World, and it remained that throughout.[4]

THE GREAT WAR FOR EMPIRE

The midcentury conflagration was to be one of Britain's high moments in history, the stuff of patriotic legends and national self-glorification. The Great War for Empire started, however, in quite another fashion. Jumping to the initiative on several fronts, the better-coordinated French struck the first blows. Calcutta, the Mediterranean island of Minorca, and several key British forts on the Great Lakes all fell, while in Europe the British expeditionary force suffered defeat and humiliation. Yet the French had certain inherent disadvantages that were to show in the long run. Spread so thinly in North America, they would be hard put to follow early success in the French and Indian War with staying power. More important, France was dependent on naval support to reinforce, supply, and move her troops; unfortunately for her, what had been a fairly even match in the 1740s turned into clear British superiority in the 1750s, with British ships of the line outnumbering French almost two to one. When William Pitt became de facto prime minister in 1758, the tide was about to turn.

Pitt brought single-mindedness, clarity of

focus, and vigor to his task. Although honoring Britain's commitment to Prussia, he attached highest priority to defeating Bourbon France in the New World. His strategy for achieving this involved an immediate series of offensives and an imaginative use of the British navy. He assigned the largest segment of the British fleet to cover the French home fleet, and he waited.

The French hoped to invade the British Isles as the surest method of bringing the enemy to the peace table, and the French fleet was ordered to prepare the way. In 1759 major battles were joined between French squadrons from Brest and Toulon and the British ships assigned to cover them; the French fleet was decimated and the fate of empires decided. Henceforth the British had an almost free hand at sea. Not only were they now immune from French invasion, but they could prevent France from utilizing her superior military forces in the colonial world. Unable to transport men and supplies, she could no longer reinforce her garrisons. Unable to match the tactical assaults of British ships, she could not repel amphibious landings. In every theater of war, French colonial possessions were now falling thanks to British naval supremacy.

In the French and Indian War, for example, General James Wolfe defeated General Louis Joseph Montcalm in the battle of Quebec in September 1759. Had the French been able to reinforce Montreal, which they still held, they could have launched a counterattack against Wolfe's overextended lines. Here Pitt's strategy triumphed, since it was now precisely impossible for the French to reinforce overseas garrisons. By September 1760 this last outpost of French power in North America capitulated to the British, who had already ousted the French from the Ohio valley and the Great Lakes area. The same pattern unfolded in Africa and India. And in the West

[4] The classic treatment of Anglo-French rivalry in North America was written by the nineteenth-century American romantic historian Francis Parkman. See S. E. Morison (ed.), *The Parkman Reader* (1955), for a convenient selection of his writings.

THE
IMAGE
OF
MAN
IN 17TH AND 18TH CENTURY ART

The art of the time span that concerns us here—from about 1600 to the French Revolution—is designated by two awkward terms: Baroque and Rococo. They were coined at the end of the eighteenth century by advocates of the "Greek Revival" to mock the style of the previous two hundred years as bombastic, overblown, and artificial. A residue of their original negative flavor still clings to these terms today, and some scholars hesitate to use them on the ground that not all art of the seventeenth century is Baroque nor all of the eighteenth Rococo. We can sympathize with their dilemma; what does Caravaggio (Plate 33) have in common with Rubens (Plate 37), Frans Hals (Plate 39) with Poussin (Plate 43), or Tiepolo (Plate 36) with Watteau (Plate 44)? The contrasts are indeed astonishing. But earlier periods encompass a similar range of styles—compare, for example, Plates 9 and 10 or 21 and 23—yet this does not discourage us from calling them Medieval or Renaissance. The difficulty in the case of Baroque and Rococo is that, unlike Medieval and Renaissance, which refer to entire phases of Western civilization, these terms were invented specifically for art criticism and thus had a much narrower meaning from the start. In present-day use the meaning has broadened a good deal and its negative implication lessened, although we still do not speak of Baroque thought or Baroque society the way we do of Medieval thought or Renaissance society. Such terms, it seems, have a life of their own; once they have won general acceptance they are as difficult to replace as they are to do without. On the other hand, the very fact that we have no satisfactory name for the civilization of the seventeenth and eighteenth centuries tells us something about the character of this period, or at least about our perception of it: we see it, and its art, as no-longer-Renaissance and not-yet-Modern, rather than as a clear-cut entity in its own right.

It is no surprise, therefore, to encounter the same double aspect in the Baroque image of man. For the first time since recorded history began, the human form is no longer taken for granted as every artist's central concern; landscape and still life—where the presence of man is either incidental or merely implied—emerge as important subjects in painting. Man, if he (or she) happens to be an absolute sovereign claiming rule by divine right, may be glorified more than ever, but only at the risk of drowning in the allegorical apparatus (as does Marie de' Medici in Plate 37). Tiepolo (Plate 36) needs all the gods of Olympus to sing the praises of his patron, the Prince-Bishop, yet the ostensible center of all his splendid display is no more than a portrait medallion that has been pushed off to one side to make room for the soaring deities. At the other end of the scale, the image of man now includes the poor of this earth. They may be manifestations of the divine presence, as in Caravaggio (Plate 33), or they may be endowed with a dignity of suffering (as in Louis Le Nain's "Peasant Family," Plate 42) that seems to anticipate the social conscience of the nineteenth century (compare Plate 57). Whatever his station, man more often than not is shown as acted upon rather than acting, subject to forces beyond his control. The figures in Guercino's or Tiepolo's ceiling frescoes (Plates 34 and 36) are carried along by an overpowering stream of movement; Bernini's "St. Theresa" (Plate 35) is borne aloft semiconscious on a cloud as the angel of divine love prepares to pierce her heart. Even David's murdered "Marat" (Plate 46) must be understood as a secular successor of martyred Baroque saints, no less than Goya's Madrileños (Plate 48). Rembrandt, as seen by himself in old age (Plate 40), reflects a lifetime of troubled self-scrutiny. Watteau's "Gilles" (Plate 44) stands very still so that we may sense the pathos of his role as the universal butt of his fellow players' pranks. The fleeting form of Vermeer's "Girl with the Red Hat" (Plate 41) seems forever suspended in a beam of light, as does the assembled company in Velázquez's "Maids of Honor" (Plate 38). The spirited "Bathers" of Fragonard (Plate 45) share the weightlessness of the floating figures in Tiepolo's ceiling (Plate 36); they are buoyed up, and tossed back and forth, by the same irresistible currents we observe in Guercino's "Aurora" and Bernini's "St. Theresa" (Plates 34 and 35) although separated from them by more than a century.

Baroque art, then, in contrast to that of the Early and High Renaissance, no longer accepts the humanists' vision of man as the master of his own fate. Its image of man is contingent on three factors that govern man no less than they do the rest of the natural world—the flow of time, the flow of light, and the flow of motion. We sense them in Caravaggio's "Calling of St. Matthew" (Plate 33), at the very beginning of the period; light here is an active force that permits the artist to seize the most dramatic moment: Christ has just moved out of the shadows into the path of the beam illuminating his face and hand, and Matthew realizes he is being called but does not yet grasp the full meaning of the divine command. Thirty years later, in "The Jolly Toper" of Frans Hals (Plate 39), the subject is caught as he might have been by a modern camera, with the artist's dashing, open brush strokes recording a race against time. Vermeer's "Girl with the Red Hat" (Plate 41) has an equally casual pose, but we are now asked to observe not the movement of the figure but the movement of light, which settles on the surfaces in the picture like a rain of tiny droplets of color so that everything looks slightly "out of focus." Vermeer, fascinated by optical phenomena, may well have observed this effect by viewing his subject through a camera obscura, a device then in use that resembled a present-day camera but projected its images onto a translucent screen rather than a piece of light-sensitive film—one of the byproducts of the age that invented the telescope and microscope.

The use of the camera obscura by Vermeer and other painters makes us wonder how the image of man in Baroque art might be related to the scientific thought of the period. This, after all, was the first age to acknowledge that the earth was not the center of the universe but merely a planet revolving around the sun; could so shattering an insight have remained without effect on art? Was it coincidence that the great scientists of these two centuries, from Galileo to Newton, were concerned with problems of time, light, and motion (though surely not in the same way as the artists)? Having noted the parallel, we must confess that so far we are unable to establish any real links. In the Renaissance, an artist could be a humanist and a scientist as well, but now science and philosophy had become too complex, abstract, and systematic for artists to share; gravitation did not kindle their imagination any more than did calculus or Descartes's "I think, therefore I am." Still, artists and scientists (or "natural philosophers" as they were then called) could have expressed the same basic world view without necessarily being aware of each other.

Be that as it may, Baroque art had one thing in common with science: an internationalism that respected neither creeds nor national boundaries. Caravaggio had a greater impact in Catholic Spain and Protestant Holland than he did at home. Tiepolo, the Venetian, produced his largest works in Würzburg and Madrid. Poussin spent almost his entire adult life in Rome, yet his style became the acknowledged ideal of the French Royal Academy of Painting. Rubens worked in Italy for eight years and could have had as successful a career there as he did in Antwerp. Even Rembrandt, who never crossed the Alps, had admirers in Italy and in turn admired Italian art. It had taken the rest of Europe two centuries to absorb the achievements of Italian Renaissance art; the Baroque, in contrast, was an international style almost from the beginning. In this respect, too, it paved the way for the Modern era.

At the end of the sixteenth century Rome once again became the artistic capital of Europe. Now that the Catholic faith had weathered the storm of the Reformation, popes could resume the task their predecessors had set themselves a hundred years earlier: to make Rome the most beautiful city of the Christian world. The ambitious young artists they attracted soon replaced the waning tradition of Mannerism with a dynamic new style, the Baroque.

The greatest of these was Caravaggio, who coined a radically new image of man to fit the new era. In this respect, his *Calling of St. Matthew* is comparable to Michelangelo's *Creation of Adam* (Plate 24). Both are confrontations of Man and God, but the meeting now takes place in a common Roman tavern, and God has descended to man's everyday world. Matthew points questioningly at himself as two figures approach from the right. They are poor people, their bare feet and simple garments contrasting strongly with the colorful costumes of Matthew and his companions. What identifies one of the two as Christ? It is mainly his commanding gesture, borrowed from the Lord in Michelangelo's fresco and made even more emphatic by the strong beam of light that illuminates the Saviour's face and hand, thus carrying his call across to Matthew. Without this light, we would not be aware of the divine presence. Caravaggio here gives moving, direct form to an attitude no less appealing to Protestants than to Catholics—that the mysteries of faith are revealed not by intellectual speculation but spontaneously, through an inward experience open to all men.

Plate 33. Caravaggio
THE CALLING OF ST. MATTHEW
ca. 1597–1598, canvas, height 11'1"
S. Luigi dei Francesi, Rome

Plate 34. Guercino
AURORA *(ceiling)*
1621–1623, wall painting
Villa Ludovisi, Rome

Caravaggio's work, although acclaimed by artists and connoisseurs, never was widely popular in Italy. The simple people resented meeting their likes in his canvases, and the sophisticated objected to them as lacking propriety and reverence. They preferred the style exemplified in Plates 34 and 35: dynamic, illusionistic, rhetorical, spectacular in its appeal to the beholder's emotions. The *Aurora* of Guercino covers the ceiling of the main room in an aristocratic villa, but similar sweeping visions were soon to appear on the ceilings of countless churches. Through a cunning use of perspective, the walls of the room continue upward in the fresco, so that we cannot tell where the real architecture leaves off and the painted illusion begins. They leave an opening for the morning sky; Aurora, the personification of Dawn, rushes across it in her chariot drawn by dappled horses, driving the shadows of night before her. In another context, the scene might be a saint carried to heaven or a triumphant allegory of faith. If Guercino's invention strikes us as theatrical, we must keep in mind that this was the time that created the opera, a new, compound art form, and similar scenes were actually presented on the stage.

Bernini, the greatest Baroque sculptor, was also deeply involved with the world of the theater, both as a designer and a playwright. His *Ecstasy of St. Theresa* is "staged" with consummate skill. Housed in an architectural frame that has the function of a proscenium arch, the group occupies a space that is real but beyond our reach. Theresa of Avila, one of the important saints of the Counter-Reformation, had described how an angel pierced her heart with a flaming golden arrow: "The pain was so great that I screamed aloud, but at the same time I felt such infinite sweetness that I wished the pain to last forever. It was not physical but psychic pain, although it affected the body as well to some degree. It was the sweetest caressing of the soul by God." Bernini has made this visionary experience sensuously real—the angel is indistinguishable from Cupid, and the saint's ecstasy is palpably physical. Yet the two figures on their floating cloud are illuminated (from a hidden window above) in such a way that they seem almost dematerialized in their gleaming whiteness. Their visionary character is further reinforced by the stream of golden rays, which balances the heavenly wind that carries the figures heavenward, causing the turbulence of their drapery. It is hard to imagine a greater contrast than that between Bernini's group and another meeting of saint and angel, Donatello's *Annunciation* (Plate 17) carved two hundred years before, so gently human and the very opposite of theatrical. Yet it was the earlier master who ultimately made Bernini's achievement possible.

Plate 35. Gianlorenzo Bernini
THE ECSTASY OF ST. THERESA
1645–1652, marble, lifesize
Sta. Maria della Vittoria, Rome

Plate 36. Giovanni Battista Tiepolo
THE GODS OF OLYMPUS (*detail of ceiling, Grand Staircase*)
1750–1753, wall painting
Residenz, Würzburg

These two paintings, however different they may be in other respects, are linked by a common purpose—the glorification of a sovereign. In the age of absolutism, great kings as well as petty rulers insisted that they embodied the power of the state by the will of God, and their desire to see themselves depicted in this superhuman role provided the artists of the period with many splendid commissions, especially in the Catholic parts of Europe. Such a task fell to Rubens when the great Flemish master, at the height of his career, was asked to produce a cycle of large pictures for the Luxembourg Palace in Paris celebrating the life of Marie de' Medici, the widow of King Henry IV and mother of Louis XIII. Plate 37 shows the artist's oil sketch for one episode, the young queen arriving on French soil after a sea voyage from Italy. Hardly an exciting subject, yet Rubens has turned it into a spectacle of drama and splendor. As Marie walks down the gangplank, Fame flies overhead sounding a triumphant blast on two trumpets, and Neptune rises from the sea with his fish-tailed crew to steady the ship and to rejoice at the queen's safe arrival, while other classical deities welcome her ashore. Everything flows together here in swirling movement: heaven and earth, history and allegory—even drawing and painting, for Rubens used oil sketches such as this one to prepare his compositions, leaving the execution of the final version mostly to his assistants. Unlike earlier artists, he liked to design his pictures in terms of light and color from the very start (most of his drawings are figure studies or portrait sketches). This unified vision was Rubens's most precious legacy to later painters.

A century and a quarter after Rubens, the Venetian painter Tiepolo faced a similar assignment in the newly completed palace of the Prince-Bishop of Würzburg in Central Germany. Here we see the last and most refined stage of illusionistic ceiling decoration represented by its greatest master, whose grace and felicity of touch had made him famous far beyond his homeland. Tiepolo's ceiling fresco in the Grand Staircase is so huge that Plate 36 shows only about a quarter of the total area. Unlike Guercino (compare Plate 34), Tiepolo no longer depends on a foreshortened architectural framework to create the necessary sense of distance between the beholder and the heavenly vision above; his illusion is achieved mainly by contrasts of light and color. Solid clusters of figures along the edges of the ceiling, larger and more strongly modeled, served to make those soaring amid the blue sky and sunlit clouds in the center seem infinitely farther away. Who they all are and how they relate to the Prince-Bishop (who is present only as a portrait medallion, not visible in our plate) is a question we are not likely to ask as we admire this celestial pageant.

Plate 37. Peter Paul Rubens
MARIE DE' MEDICI LANDING IN MARSEILLES
1622–1623, wood panel, height 25"
Alte Pinakothek, Munich

Plate 38. Diego Velázquez
THE MAIDS OF HONOR
ca. 1656, canvas, height 10′5″
Prado Museum, Madrid

Although the bulk of his work consists of portraits—mostly of the Spanish royal family and members of the court—Velázquez began his career as a painter of scenes of everyday life under the strong influence of Caravaggio. He admired the Italian master's sympathy for the common people and his handling of light, but did not share his interest in dramatic action. When, still in his twenties, Velázquez moved from his native Seville to Madrid, he was befriended by Rubens, who may have helped him to see the beauty of the numerous paintings by Titian in the king's collection (compare Plate 25). He also traveled in Italy. All these experiences are reflected in *The Maids of Honor*, painted at the height of his career. A more suitable title might be "The Painter in His Studio," for Velázquez shows himself at work on a huge canvas that juts into the picture on the left; in the center is the little Princess Margarita, who has been posing for him, among her playmates and maids of honor, which include a large dog and a dwarf. This foreground group is caught in the bright light streaming into the room from an unseen window on the right. Two other figures, a bit farther back, are less clearly seen in the shadowy, high-ceilinged gallery; in the rear a courtier, brilliantly illuminated, is framed by an open door. Evidently, something has interrupted the painting session, and most of the figures are turning to look at the beholder: an unobtrusive but commanding presence makes itself felt. What could it be? The solution, it seems, is the bright rectangle above the head of the princess, which must be a mirror rather than a painting: in it, we see two heads, those of the King and Queen.

Have they just stepped into the room, to see the scene exactly as we do? Or does the mirror reflect part of the canvas—presumably a full-length group portrait of the royal family—on which the artist has been working? Be that as it may, the painting reveals Velázquez's fascination with the action of light, which seems infinitely more varied and dramatic than the action of the figures. His rich, fluid brushwork renders the full range of its effects on shape, color, and texture, from the sparkling highlights on the princess's hair and dress to the dimly perceived canvases in the background. For Velázquez, light *creates* the visible world. No wonder that the pioneers of Impressionism two hundred years later considered him the most "modern" of seventeenth-century painters.

Frans Hals, half a generation older than Velázquez, was born in Antwerp but as a young man moved to Haarlem in the newly independent northern part of the Netherlands, where he became a portrait painter as renowned as Velázquez was in Spain. He too divided his attention between portraiture and scenes of everyday life and owed an essential debt to the influence of Caravaggio. *The Jolly Toper* is surely a portrait, but Hals seems far less concerned with the sitter's individual personality than with the effect of the picture as an "action shot"—everything is tilted, from the huge hat that frames the face like a black halo to the wine glass in the sitter's left hand, thus conveying instability and transitory movement. The brushwork itself is open and lightning-quick, each stroke so clearly separate that we are tempted to count the total number. Caravaggio's sense of the "fruitful moment" here becomes a split-second race against time.

Plate 39. Frans Hals
THE JOLLY TOPER
1627, canvas, height 32"
Rijksmuseum, Amsterdam

Plate 40. Rembrandt
SELF-PORTRAIT WITH PALETTE
1660, canvas, height 44½"
Louvre Museum, Paris

Rembrandt, the greatest genius of Dutch art, is one of a small company of artists (Leonardo da Vinci, Michelangelo, and Van Gogh are others) whose popular fame as legendary figures distorts or obscures their true achievement. He has been the subject (or better perhaps, the victim) of many fictionalized biographies that present him as a "glorious failure," deserted in mid-career by a fickle public and plunged into poverty and neglect. Actually Rembrandt's fortunes during his later years declined far less catastrophically than his romantic admirers have claimed. He retained important patrons and received some major public commissions even toward the end of his life. It is true, however, that his work from the mid-1620s to the early 1640s, with its emphasis on dramatic display, differs markedly from that of the 1650s and 1660s, which is gently lyrical and introspective. The change reflects the maturing of a powerful personality. Nowhere is this process of growth recorded more completely than in the artist's numerous self-portraits (he produced more than sixty), culminating in the self-analytical frankness and simple dignity of those he did during his final years. In the example shown in Plate 40, we see him standing at his easel, palette and brushes in hand; he gazes at the beholder (or rather, at himself) with a look, sad and tender at the same time, that seems to convey an entire lifetime's experience of thought and feeling. What makes this revelation of character possible is the magic glow of Rembrandt's light, which filters into the picture space quietly from the upper left, endowing the artist's features with their strange mute eloquence. Unlike Velázquez, Rembrandt here explores the metaphysical and expressive rather than the optical aspects of the element that

Caravaggio had introduced into Western painting as an active force.

Rembrandt was unique among the Dutch painters of his time not only for his depth of human insight but for the wide range of his subjects, which included biblical and mythological themes, landscapes, scenes of daily life, portraiture, and still lifes. Most seventeenth-century painters tended to specialize, and more so in Holland than elsewhere because of the pressure of competition. Dutch artists had to rely on private collectors rather than state or church as their chief source of support. Many of them produced "for the market," and dealing in pictures became an important trade that followed the law of supply and demand. Since the market reflects the dominant, not the most discerning, taste of the time, it could happen that some artists whom we now regard as mediocre were over-priced while others, highly esteemed today, were undervalued. The most astonishing instance of this is Vermeer, whose genius seems to us second only to Rembrandt's but who was almost forgotten until a century ago. His specialty was domestic interiors, with one or two figures, usually women, engaged in quiet everyday tasks; he also did occasional outdoors views and portraits. Some pictures, such as *The Girl with the Red Hat,* leave us in doubt: is it a portrait or a figure study? The same question arises when we look at Hals's *Jolly Toper* (Plate 39). In every other respect, however, the two canvases offer a fascinating contrast. If Vermeer is akin to any other painter of his time, it is neither Hals nor Rembrandt but Velázquez; even more than the great Spaniard, he concentrates on the optical properties of light and color. Yet the jewel-like freshness of his vision suggests that his true progenitor is Jan van Eyck (see Plate 18).

Plate 41. Jan Vermeer
THE GIRL WITH THE RED HAT
ca. 1660, canvas, height 9"
National Gallery of Art
Andrew W. Mellon Collection
Washington, D.C.

Plate 42. Louis Le Nain
PEASANT FAMILY
ca. 1640, canvas, height 44½"
Louvre Museum, Paris

That the two pictures reproduced on these pages should both have been painted by Frenchmen born within a year of each other seems almost incredible. It attests not only the extraordinary diversity of Baroque art within a single country but the intermediate position of France between North and South. Louis Le Nain, although strongly indebted to Caravaggio, is even more closely linked with the Netherlandish tradition of realism stemming from Jan van Eyck and continued by Pieter Bruegel. Poussin, in contrast, is a classicist whose sources of inspiration are Titian (compare Plate 25), the Roman High Renaissance masters, and the world of antiquity. His style was formed in Rome, where he spent almost his entire adult life, yet his patrons and his influence were largely in France. He is the father of what was to become known as the "grand manner" in painting, based on firmly held theoretical ideas about the aim of art which he expounded in his voluminous correspondence. As his starting point he took the ancient dictum that "painting is mute poetry"; like the poet, the painter must strive to elevate the mind of his audience by dealing with noble and serious themes. He will reach his goal only if he suppresses the imperfections of nature-in-the-raw and depicts instead an ideal world of nature perfected. Nor must he give too much importance to color, lest he cater to sensuous pleasure instead of appealing to man's moral impulses. Logic and order, clarity of form and composition, are to be of primary importance. In Poussin's own work such as *The Inspiration of the Epic Poet,* this prescription could yield canvases of extraordinary beauty. Others, who fol-

lowed in his footsteps and took over his formula ready-made, were less successful. There were to be a great many of them, for Poussin's doctrines became the official program of the French Royal Academy of Painting and Sculpture, founded under Louis XIV to foster a single "approved" style. It, in turn, was the model for countless similar academies in the other countries of Europe, so that "Poussinism" survived until close to the end of the nineteenth century as the ideal of conservative, state-sponsored artists.

Plate 43. Nicolas Poussin
THE INSPIRATION OF THE EPIC POET
ca. 1628, canvas, height 6′
Louvre Museum, Paris

Plate 44. Antoine Watteau
GILLES
ca. 1717, canvas, height 6'
Louvre Museum, Paris

In France, the power of the Royal Academy to enforce "Poussinism" remained unchallenged for almost half a century. During the final years of Louis XIV's long reign, however, there appeared signs of an internal revolt, led by a faction that declared its allegiance to the style of Rubens (exemplified by such pictures as our Plate 37). These "Rubenists" advocated color rather than drawing as being more true to nature and appealing to everyone, while drawing can be appreciated only by the expert few. Their argument had revolutionary implications, for it made the layman the ultimate judge of artistic values ("I don't know anything about art, but I know what I like"). The final triumph of the "Rubenists" came in 1717 with the admission to the Academy of Antoine Watteau, whose pictures violated all official canons; instead of noble and elevating themes, they depicted, in a superbly elegant and sensuous style, scenes of refined society or of comedy actors in parklike settings. Often Watteau interweaves theater and real life so that no clear distinction can be made between the two. In his *Gilles* (Plate 44) the central figure is a stock character of the French comedy stage, a kind of "straight man" who invariably becomes the victim of pranks and comic misfortunes. In his awkward white satin costume, he stands isolated from the gay throng behind him, seemingly impassive yet suffering in silent agony. If Watteau's actors lack the robust vitality of Rubens, they play their roles so well that they touch us as if they were real-life characters.

Plate 45. Jean-Honoré Fragonard
BATHERS
ca. 1765, canvas, height 25"
Louvre Museum, Paris

The victory of the "Rubenists" signaled a shift in French art and French society. After the death of Louis XIV, the power of the absolute monarchy declined and with it the art patronage of the state, so that artists came to depend increasingly on private patrons. That the latter preferred Watteau to the disciples of Poussin is hardly surprising; it was they who sponsored what later was derisively termed the Rococo, an intimate, sensuous style uninhibited by classicistic doctrines. Watteau, who died at the early age of 37, had a great many followers, although none had the emotional depth that distinguishes his art.

The last, and finest, among these is Fragonard, who painted the *Bathers* (Plate 45): his brushwork has a fluid breadth and spontaneity reminiscent of Rubens's oil sketches (compare Plate 37), and his figures move with a floating grace that also links him with Tiepolo (see Plate 36), whose work he had admired in Italy. Fragonard had the misfortune to outlive his era. After the French Revolution, he was reduced to poverty and died forgotten, in the heyday of Napoleon, when classicism, and with it the doctrines of Poussin, had once more become the order of the day.

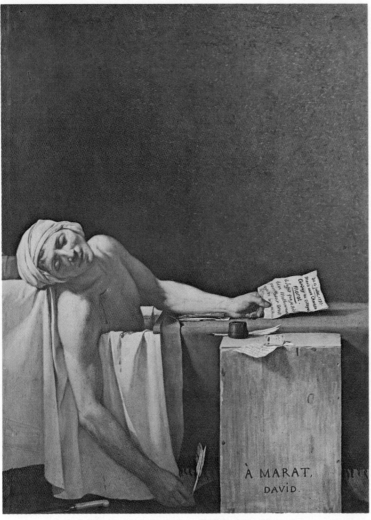

Plate 46. Jacques Louis David
THE DEATH OF MARAT
1792, canvas, height 65"
Royal Museums of Fine Arts, Brussels

The third quarter of the eighteenth century saw a gradual turning of the tide throughout European art. While Tiepolo and Fragonard were creating the last masterpieces of the Rococo, there was a growing reaction, in the name of Reason and Nature, against Baroque "artificiality." These two concepts had been proclaimed as supreme values by the thinkers of the Enlightenment; in art, they signaled a return to the doctrines of Poussin and a new admiration for the "noble simplicity and calm grandeur" of the Greeks (in the famous phrase of Johann Winckelmann, the influential German archaeologist and critic). Rome was the birthplace of this Neoclassic style, although its leading early protagonists were visitors from the north rather than Italians. It was there that Jacques Louis David, a highly gifted young French painter trained in the Rococo tradition, became a convert to the new style. After his return to Paris, David's artistic conversion became a political one as well: he passionately espoused the revolutionary ideas of the Enlightenment and, in 1789, the Revolution itself. At the height of the struggle, he painted his greatest picture, *The Death of Marat* (Plate 46). David's deep emotion has made a masterpiece from a subject that would have embarrassed any lesser artist; for Marat, one of the political leaders of the Revolution, had been murdered in his bathtub. A painful skin disease caused him to do his paperwork there, with a wooden board serving as his desk. One day a young woman named Charlotte Corday burst in with a petition and plunged a knife into him while he read it. David has composed the scene with awe-inspiring starkness as a public memorial to the martyred hero: it is Neoclassic in the clarity and simplicity of the forms and in the way the principal planes are arranged to parallel the picture surface, but the Neoclassic ideal of Nature Perfected is not in evidence. David must have realized that it could not help him achieve his purpose—to produce a historic account that was also a moving devotional image. For that he had to revert to the Caravaggio tradition of religious art, with its realism and dramatic lighting (compare Plate 33).

A few years later David became an ardent admirer of Napoleon. He was to produce several large pictures glorifying the emperor, but a favorite pupil, Antoine-Jean Gros, eclipsed him as the chief painter of the Napoleonic myth. Gros's first portrait of the great general shows him leading his troops at the battle of Arcole in northern Italy (Plate 47). It conveys Napoleon's magic as an irresistible "man of destiny" with an enthusiasm David could never match. Much as Gros respected his teacher's doctrines, his emotional nature impelled him toward the color and drama of the Baroque: hence the stormy sky, the spiral movement of the flag, the hero's disheveled, streaming hair, the violent turn of his body, the dynamic open brushwork—all of them devices of "visual rhetoric" that carry us back to Rubens (see Plate 37).

Plate 47. Antoine-Jean Gros
NAPOLEON AT ARCOLE
1796, canvas, height 29½"
Louvre Museum, Paris

Plate 48. Francisco Goya
THE THIRD OF MAY, 1808
1814–1815, canvas, height 8'9"
Prado Museum, Madrid

If Gros's *Napoleon at Arcole* may be termed Neo-Baroque, the same is true even more emphatically of Goya's *The Third of May, 1808* (Plate 48). But the great Spanish painter had never been a Neoclassicist. His early works are in a delightful late Rococo vein. During the 1780s he came to sympathize with the Enlightenment and the French Revolution. He now abandoned the Rococo for a Neo-Baroque style based on Veláz-quez and Rembrandt, the masters of the previous century he admired most. When Napoleon's armies occupied Spain in 1808, Goya and many of his countrymen hoped that the conquerors would bring the liberal reforms so badly needed, but the savage behavior of the French troops crushed these hopes and generated a popular resistance of equal savagery. *The Third of May, 1808,* commemorating the execution of a group of Madrid citizens, reflects this bitter experience. Its blazing color, fluid brushwork, and dramatic nocturnal light endow the picture with all the emotional intensity of religious art, yet these martyrs are dying for Liberty, not the Kingdom of Heaven; and their executioners are not the agents of Satan but of political tyranny—a formation of faceless automatons impervious to their victims' despair and defiance. With the clairvoyance of genius, Goya has created an image that was to be reenacted countless times in modern history.

Indies the long duel between the two powers turned into a rout. One by one the French islands were seized, and even Martinique—known as the jewel of the French Empire—had fallen by 1761.

Not all these conquests were preserved at the peace table, however. In exchange for an end to fighting, a war-weary Britain was prepared to return certain colonies in the Treaty of Paris in 1763. France was willing to surrender Canada, and Britain chose to retain the territory—perhaps mistakenly: this removed the threat of French power, which it turned out had been a major factor in the loyalty of the British colonists to the mother country. Since British West Indian planters feared added competition from the possible inclusion of the French islands in the British system, the British government decided to accede to French demands for the return of several of these. In the long run India proved to be Britain's most important colonial territory. Her domination of the subcontinent began with the Treaty of Paris, which excluded French troops from the region, permitting only British influence to have any force.

But there would be momentous repercussions from the Peace of Paris. First, it created a new situation for the thirteen North American colonies, and Britain's triumph turned into disaster twenty years later when they successfully broke away, with French assistance. In addition, though France's ill-fated efforts in the Seven Years' War had strained her finances substantially, she was unable to resist the opportunity to strike back at Britain during the war for independence. Partly for this reason she contracted further debts that could not be absorbed by the monarchy in its existing form. Finally, it is well to remember that supporting the entire state structure were the slaves in the colonies and the peasants in most states, whose labor ultimately produced the revenues that paid for the navies and armies. Their bill would eventually come due in one form or another.

During the eighteenth century the effectiveness of Europe's states in marshaling their power and resources within the state system was increasingly apparent. French and English merchants demonstrated an extraordinary capacity to capitalize on the commercial opportunities afforded by overseas colonies, plantation economy, and slavery. But these traders were backed by their states, especially in the form of naval power. The growth of the British and French empires and with them of the global maritime economy of the eighteenth century was in one sense an aspect of the competitive state system.

In Central Europe direct territorial aggrandizement was the issue. Prussia, Austria, and Russia faced each other directly at war and at the negotiating table. Here helpless lesser states were sacrificed to the "reasons of state" of the great powers; most notable was Poland, whose disappearance from the map in three successive partitions must be accounted as one of the century's most important events.

All these interests clashed in the midcentury conflagration, a classic episode of competition in the European state system. The scale of fighting in the Seven Years' War was enormous. Yet the system was able to contain the massive aggression and survive the convulsion almost intact. Although Prussia had been driven to the brink of extinction, she actually lost little in the peace settlement; in the end Frederick II even retained Silesia. All in all, however, the Continental powers had proved to be well matched. The colonial phase of the hostilities, the great War for Empire, was more decisive, though here too a degree of balance was restored by Britain's concessions to France at the peace table. The significance of these outcomes will be best appreciated when contrasted later with the resulting upheaval of World War l.

RECOMMENDED READING

Sources

Edwards, Bryan. *The History, Civil and Commercial, of the British Colonies in the West Indies.* 2 vols. 1793. A contemporary account of Empire and slavery.

Luvvas, J. (ed.). *Frederick the Great on the Art of War.* 1966.

* Macartney, C. A. (ed.). *The Evolution of the Hapsburg & Hohenzollern Dynasties.* 1969. An excellent collection of documents.

Studies

* Anderson, M. S. *Europe in the Eighteenth Century, 1713–1789.* 1977. The best general survey of the period.

Barker, Ernest. *The Development of Public Services in Western Europe.* 1966.

* Beloff, Max. *The Age of Absolutism, 1660–1815.* 1966. An overview of state building and the state system.

* Cobban, Alfred. *A History of Modern France: Vol. I, 1715–1799.* 1966.

* Craton, Michael. *Sinews of Empire: A Short History of British Slavery.* 1974.

Dakin, Douglas. *Turgot and the Ancien Régime in France.* 1939. An insider's view of the problems and achievements of enlightened administration in France.

* Dehio, L. *The Precarious Balance: Four Centuries of the European Power Struggle.* 1965. An essay in the Germanic tradition of diplomatic history.

Dorn, Walter. *The Competition for Empire, 1740–63.* 1940. Despite its title, a good if old-fashioned general history.

* Genovese, Eugene. *The World the Slaveholders Made.* 1969. A Marxist analysis.

* Goodwin, A. (ed.). *The European Nobility in the 18th Century.* 1967.

Owen, John B. *The Eighteenth Century, 1714–1815.* 1974. A dry, detailed history of England.

Pares, Richard. *Yankees and Creoles: The Trade Between North America and the West Indies Before the American Revolution.* 1968.

* Parry, J. H. *Trade and Dominion: The European Overseas Empires in the Eighteenth Century.* 1971.

Pick, Robert. *Empress Maria Theresa: The Early Years.* 1966.

* Plumb, J. H. *England in the Eighteenth Century, 1714–1815.* 1950. Brief but informative.

* Ritter, Gerhard. *Frederick the Great.* 1968.

* Rosenburg, Hans. *Bureaucracy, Aristocracy, and Autocracy: The Prussian Experience, 1660–1815.* 1958. Difficult, highly conceptualized, important history.

Thompson, Gladys. *Catherine the Great and the Expansion of Russia.* 1962.

* Wangermann, E. *The Austrian Achievement, 1700–1800.* 1973. A concise, suggestive synthesis with an imaginatively integrated profusion of illustrations.

---

* Available in paperback.

NINETEEN

THE AGE OF
ENLIGHTENMENT

Sharp breaks in the intellectual and cultural life of Europe have been rare. Nonetheless, taken broadly rather than as literal chronological periods, the seventeenth, eighteenth, and nineteenth centuries represent three distinct phases of Western cultural development. The seventeenth century was the towering age of genius in European thought—a period of great scientific and philosophical innovation. It was also an elitist age in terms of the audience for cultural activity and the system of aristocratic patronage. If we jump ahead to the nineteenth century we encounter a decidedly middle-class intellectual and artistic milieu as well as the beginnings of mass literacy and mass culture toward the end of the century.

Obviously then the eighteenth century is transitional. In the domain of thought it was a time when the impact of science and the growth of religious skepticism matured into a naturalistic world view. Philosophy became less metaphysical and more critically concerned with practical matters, with "enlightenment." The most important eighteenth-century thinkers were not seeking to extirpate Christianity from Western civilization, but they no longer believed in it themselves and wished to counter what they took to be its spirit of complacency and to reduce its influence in temporal affairs drastically. Intellectuals developed a strong sense of their own power to enlighten their society and point it toward change. They were reformers who—contrary to Christian belief and unlike reformers within the church—believed that there was no reality beyond human society, no afterlife to divert the spirit of man from worldly concerns. In this spirit they provided an arsenal of critical ideas, particularly the notion of social utility as a standard of value, and a preoccupation with the issue of freedom.

While they were thus critics of their society, eighteenth-century intellectuals were very much at home in and proud of European culture. Theirs was an age in which publishing activity increased explosively, in which major new literary and musical genres were developed, and in which a number of cultural trends reflected the presence of an expanding middle class in a still-aristocratic age.

I. THE ENLIGHTENMENT

The eighteenth century reworked and diffused the ideas of the seventeenth. Building on seventeenth-century science, on skepticism in matters of religion, and on a heightened appreciation of Classical antiquity, intellectuals redefined the function of philosophy. They believed that human behavior and institutions could be studied rationally, like Newton's universe, and their faults corrected. They saw themselves as participants in a movement—the Enlightenment—that was making men and women more understanding, more tolerant, and more virtuous.

THE BROADENING REVERBERATIONS OF SCIENCE

It is hard to think of two men less revolutionary in temperament than René Descartes and Sir Isaac Newton. Writing for a small, learned audience, each was conservative on matters outside the confines of science, had relatively little concern for social relations or institutions, and was a practicing Christian. Yet their legacy to succeeding generations produced what has been described as "a permanent intellectual insurrection." Their conceptual systems—along with those of John Locke and the Dutch philosopher Baruch Spinoza—were transformed and propagated in directions and in a spirit undreamed of by their authors.

While eighteenth-century scientists pondered the details of the diverging cosmologies of Descartes and Newton, nonscientists continued the process, begun in the previous century, of applying their basic methodology to all realms of human thought. Experimentation, methodical doubt, and naturalistic explanations of phenomena were fused into a "scientific" or "mathematical spirit," which at bottom meant simply confidence in reason and a skeptical attitude toward accepted dogmas. Its advocates took upon themselves the task of popularizing science, with the aim of transforming the values of Western civilization. As part of this effort men like Bernard de Fontenelle, secretary of the French Academy of Sciences from 1699 to 1741, translated the discoveries of scientists into clear and even amusing general reading. The literary talents of these enthusiasts helped make household words out of Newton and Descartes among the educated laymen of Europe.

A more calculating and ambitious propagandist of the scientific spirit was Voltaire, the Frenchman who is virtually synonymous with the Enlightenment in all its aspects. While his chief talents lay in the realm of literature and criticism, Voltaire also spent several years studying Newton's work, and in 1738 he published a widely read popularization called *Elements of the Philosophy of Newton*. However dry the study of physics, Voltaire argued, it frees the mind from dogma, and its experimental methods provide

a model for the liberation of human thought. Moreover Voltaire situated Newton's achievement in the context of the liberal England that also produced Bacon and Locke, the three of whom Voltaire adopted as his personal Trinity. In his *Philosophical Letters on the English* (1734), a celebration of English toleration and an indirect attack on what he considered French bigotry, censorship, and social snobbery, Voltaire had already noted the popularity and respect enjoyed by British literary figures and scientists. He saw this recognition of talent and distinction as a crucial component of a free society and as necessarily related to the achievements of a man like Newton.

Popularizations of scientific method stimulated public interest in science as well as public and private support for research projects. Mathematicians, cartographers, and astronomers were direct beneficiaries of the support and made notable advances in their fields. But progress was far from linear or automatic. In chemistry for example the traditions of alchemy persisted, and such phenomena as combustion long resisted objective analysis. At the end of the century, however, a major breakthrough occurred when the Englishman Joseph Priestley isolated oxygen and the Frenchman Antoine Laurent Lavoisier analyzed the components of air and water. Lavoisier also came close to explaining the process of combustion.

The more dubious side of the vogue for science could be observed in the great popularity of mesmerism. This pseudoscience of magnetic fields purported to offer its wealthy devotees relief from a variety of ailments by the use of special "electrical" baths and treatments. Although repeatedly condemned by the authoritative studies of the Academy of Sciences in Paris, mesmerism continued to attract both the educated and the credulous.

The scientific enterprise most representative of eighteenth-century attitudes was natural history, the science of the earth's development—a combination of geology, zoology, botany, and historical geography. This field of study was easy for the layman to appreciate, which made its foremost practitioner probably the most widely acclaimed scientist of the century. He was G. L. Buffon, keeper of the French Botanical Gardens—a patronage position that allowed him to produce a multivolume *Natural History of the Earth* between 1749 and 1778. Drawing on a vast knowledge of phenomena such as fossils, Buffon went beyond previous attempts to classify the data of nature, seeking to relate and generalize from them in order to provide both a theory and a description of the earth's development. A nonbeliever himself, Buffon did not explicitly attack religious versions of such events as the Creation. He simply ignored them, an omission whose significance was obvious enough to his many readers. Similarly, while he did not specifically contend that man had evolved from beasts, he implied this, writing for example, "It is possible to descend by almost insensible degrees from the most perfect creature to the most formless matter." Buffon's earth did not derive from a singular act of divine creation that would explain the origins of man. The readers of his *History* or its numerous popularizations in several languages were thus introduced to a demystified universe that had developed through evolution. Buffon's work sharpened the thrusts of science and secularism.

THE RISE OF SECULARISM

The erosion of revealed religion as a source of authority is the hallmark of the Enlightenment. The viewpoint it engendered, secularism, derived some of its impetus from seventeenth-century scientists and liberal theologians who were themselves dedicated Christians. They had hoped to accommodate religion to new philosophical standards and scientific formulations and to eliminate the superstitious imagery that could make religion seem ridiculous. They regarded the devil for example as a category of moral evil rather than a specific horned creature with a pitchfork, and they endowed the world of nature with religious significance, perceiving it as a form of revelation in which God's majesty could be discerned. Deemphasizing miracles and focusing on reverence for the Creator and on the moral teachings of the Bible would bolster religion, they hoped. And indeed their modifications retained the adherence of many educated people to Christianity during the eighteenth century. Yet in the final analysis, this kind of thinking served to diminish the force of religion and its authority in society.

A more important source of the secular outlook was the idea of toleration as propounded by the highly respected critic Pierre Bayle. Consciously applying methodical doubt to subjects that Descartes himself had excluded from such treatment, Bayle's *Critical and Historical Dictionary* (1697) put the claims of religion to the test of critical reason. Certain Christian traditions emerged as myth and fairy tale, and historical Christianity was seen as a record of fanaticism and inhumanity. Bayle's chief target was Christianity's sectarianism and attempts (like Louis XIV's revocation of the Edict of Nantes) to impose orthodoxy at any cost. Though himself a devout Calvinist, Bayle argued for complete toleration, which would allow human beings to practice any religion or none at all. A man's moral behavior rather than his creed is what should count. Ethics do not depend on Christian revelation; a Muslim, a Confucian, a Jew, even an atheist can be a moral man.

Christianity had more vehement critics than Bayle. Atheistic and blasphemous attacks were to be found in privately circulated writings rather than published books in the first half of the century. These clandestine tracts treated revealed religion as a form of hysteria that had resulted in centuries of bloodshed. Their titles tell their messages: *Critical Examination of the Apologists of the Christian Religion, Mortal Souls, The Divinity of Jesus Christ Destroyed, Faith Destroyed.* Faith was indeed destroyed here, along with such props as miracles, priests, and divine prophets.

The Enlightenment's most unstinting antireligious polemicist was Voltaire, which was the pen name of François Marie Arouet. This prolific writer was one of the century's most brilliant literary stylists, historians, and poets. Had he been satisfied with merely exploiting these talents, his fame would still have been considerable. But he was also a profoundly sincere antagonist of Christianity who was determined to bring the spirit of the clandestine literature out into the open. For tactical reasons much of his attack against "*l'infâme* ("the infamous thing"), as he called Christianity, was directed against its more vulnerable practices, such as monasticism. But his ultimate target was Christianity, which, he declared, "every sensible man, every honorable man must hold in horror."

Voltaire's masterpiece was his *Philosophical Dictionary* (1764), a best seller in its day that he was obliged to publish anonymously and that was burned by the authorities in Switzerland, France, and the Netherlands. Modeled after Bayle's dictionary, it was far blunter. In theology, he wrote, "we find man's insanity in all its plenitude." Organized religion is not simply false but pernicious, he argued. Superstition inevitably breeds fanaticism; crimes of organized religion like the St. Bartholomew's Day Massacre are not incidental but are the essence of its irrationality.

Voltaire hoped that educated Europeans would abandon Christianity in favor of deism, a naturalistic belief that accorded God recognition only as the Creator and held that the world, once created, functions according to natural laws that God cannot interfere

with. Man is now left to live in an ordered universe essentially on his own, without hope or fear of divine intervention and without the threat of damnation or the expectation of eternal salvation. Religion should be a matter of private contemplation rather than public worship and mythic creeds. Certain figures in the Enlightenment went beyond this to philosophical atheism, but on the whole Voltaire's mild and undemanding deism remained the characteristic view of eighteenth-century nonbelievers. Despite its innocuousness, however, this form of spirituality was wholly secular, and progressive churchmen who could accept many arguments of eighteenth-century science and philosophy could not accept this.

THE PHILOSOPHES

Science and secularism were the rallying points of a group of French intellectuals known as the philosophes, or philosophers. This term was employed by their traditionalist enemies to mock their pretensions, but they used it themselves with a sense of pride. For they were the avant-garde, the men who raised the Enlightenment to the status of a self-conscious movement.

The leaders of this influential coterie of writers were Voltaire (whom one meets at every turn in eighteenth-century intellectual life) and Denis Diderot (whom we will meet shortly). Its ranks included the mathematicians Jean d'Alembert and the marquis de Condorcet, the jurist baron de Montesquieu, the statesman Jacques Turgot, and the social scientists and philosophers Claude Adrien Helvétius and baron d'Holbach. Outside of France their kinship extended to a clustering of brilliant Scottish philosophers and thinkers, among them David Hume and Adam Smith; to the German playwright and critic Gotthold Ephraim Lessing and the philosopher Immanuel Kant; to such founders of the American Philosophical Society as Benjamin Franklin and Thomas Jefferson; and to the Italian economist and penal reformer the marquis of Beccaria.

The philosophes and their foreign confreres have been well described by a sympathetic historian as a close family with many distant relatives.[1] The family was troubled by a good deal of internal bickering, but its members always enjoyed a sense of common identity. What they shared above all was a critical spirit, the desire to reexamine the assumptions and institutions of society, to expose them to the tests of reason, experience, and utility. Today this sounds banal, but it was not so at a time when almost everywhere religion still dominated society. To assert the primacy of reason meant to turn away from the essence of religion: faith. It meant a decisive break with the Christian world view, which placed doctrine at the center of intellectual activity. For centuries the intellectual mentors of Western civilization had been urging man to submit to what he could know least—the divine. The philosophes hoped to change this completely. They invoked the paganism of ancient Greece and Rome, where the spirit of rational inquiry prevailed among educated men. They ridiculed the Middle Ages as the "Dark Ages," using the attitudes of that period as a contrast with their own sense of liberation and modernity. In *The Decline and Fall of the Roman Empire* (1776–1788), Edward Gibbon passed the verdict that Christianity had eclipsed a Roman civilization that had sought to live according to reason rather than myths.

The inspiration of antiquity was matched by the stimulus of modern science and philosophy. The philosophes laid claim to Newton, who made the universe intelligible without the aid of revelation, and Locke, who uncovered the workings of the human mind.

From Locke they argued that human personality is malleable—its nature is not immutably fixed, let alone corrupted by original sin. Men are therefore ultimately responsible to themselves for what they do with their lives. Inherited arrangements are no more nor less sacred than experience has proved them to be. The philosophes acclaimed the role of the enlightened intellectual in society. As the humanists had several centuries before, they placed man at the center of thought. What distinguished them from the humanists was that they placed thought in the service of change. This at any rate was their hope, and in pursuing it the philosophes launched a noisy public movement.

They appeared clamorous to their contemporaries because they had to battle entrenched authority. Intellectual freedom was absolutely essential to them, and in most places they had to fight for it against not only the church and traditionalists but also the state and its apparatus of censorship. They were often obliged to publish their works abroad and anonymously. Sometimes they were pressured into withholding manuscripts from publication altogether or into making humiliating public recantations of controversial books. Even with such cautionary measures, almost all philosophes saw some of their publications confiscated and burned; and a few were forced into exile—Voltaire himself spent several decades across the French border in Switzerland—or sent to jail: Voltaire and Diderot both spent time in the Bastille. True, the very notoriety produced by these repressions often stimulated the sale of their works, but the anxiety outweighed the advantages. Allies of the philosophes in Italy and Spain labored under even greater constraints since the Inquisition still existed in the eighteenth century to suppress heresy with surprising ruthlessness.

By the 1770s, however, the philosophes had survived their running war with the au-

---

[1] Peter Gay, *The Enlightenment: An Interpretation.* (1966).

thorities. Some of them lived to see their ideas widely accepted and their works acclaimed. Thus, even if they had contributed little else to the Western experience, their struggle for freedom of expression would merit them a significant place in its history.

But they contributed far more than that. In their scholarly and polemical writings, they investigated a wide range of subjects and pioneered in several new disciplines. Some philosophes—Voltaire for example—were path-breaking historians. Moving beyond traditional historiography, which chronicled battles and rulers' biographies, they studied culture, social institutions, and government structures in an effort to understand as well as describe the past. Practically inventing social science, they dissected on a theoretical level the basis of social organization (sociology) and the human mind (psychology) and on a more practical level such matters as penology and education. These studies were in turn related to the issues of morality and the study of ethics. Their characteristic approach to ethics was utilitarian. With David Hume they tried to define value judgments about good and evil in more pragmatic terms than was common, and they concluded that social utility should become the standard for public morality. This approach to moral philosophy, however, raised the question of whether any human values were absolute and eternal. Responding to this challenge affirmatively, Kant tried to harmonize the tradition of philosophical idealism with the Enlightenment.

A major branch of Enlightenment social science was the physiocratic school. Its adherents believed that economic progress depended on freeing agriculture and trade from mercantilist restrictions and on reforming the tax structure by levying a uniform and equitable land tax. To stimulate agricultural productivity they advocated allowing the grain trade to operate according to the laws of supply and demand, which, they reasoned, would en-

courage growers to expand productivity and transport their harvest to where it was most needed. In this way the chronic grain shortages that plagued France could be eliminated.

In Britain Adam Smith made a parallel attack on mercantilist restrictions in *The Wealth of Nations* (1776). Like the physiocrats, Smith believed that economic progress required that each individual be allowed to pursue his own self-interest freely rather than regimented by the state, the guild, or tradition. Smith argued that on all levels of economic activity—from the manufacturing process to the flow of international trade—a natural division of labor should be encouraged. High tariffs, guild restrictions, and the like artificially obstructed this. Both Smith and the French physiocrats were thus early proponents of the economic doctrine of "laissez faire la nature," meaning simply "let nature take its course," which would be taken up by manufacturing interests during the Industrial Revolution.

By contrast other Enlightenment figures, analyzing the origin and role of private property, concluded, on the level of theory at least, that it was a form of primitive usurpation that should be replaced by some collective principle. Men like the French philosopher and historian Gabriel Bonnet de Mably were accordingly the forerunners of a utopian socialism that would be an alternative response to the early Industrial Revolution.

All in all the Enlightenment produced not only a characteristic intellectual spirit but also a wide range of critical writings on many aspects of human society. In addition the philosophes collectively generated a single work that exemplified and fulfilled their notion of how knowledge could be useful: Diderot's *Encyclopedia*.

Diderot and the Encyclopedia

Denis Diderot never achieved the celebrity of his friend Voltaire, but his career was equally central to the concerns and achievements of the philosophes. The son of a provincial cutler, he was educated in Jesuit schools as were many other young Frenchmen but at the first opportunity headed for Paris. Continuing to educate himself while living a bohemian existence, Diderot soon developed an unshakable sense of purpose: to make himself into an independent and successful intellectual.

Within a few short years, he had published a remarkable succession of writings—novels and plays, mathematical treatises, some notable pieces of muckraking (including a devastating attack on inept medical practices), and several works dealing with religion and moral philosophy. The most original aspect of his philosophical writings is his examination of the role of passion in human personality and in any system of values derived from an understanding of human nature. In particular he affirmed the role of sexuality, arguing against artificial taboos and restrictions. As an advocate of what was sometimes called "the natural man," Diderot belies the charge leveled against the philosophes that they overemphasized reason and neglected emotion. The thread of religious criticism in these works is likewise notable. Starting from a position of mild skepticism, he soon passed to deism but ended beyond that in a position of atheism.

Diderot's unusual boldness in getting his works published brought him a considerable reputation but also some real trouble. Two of his books were condemned by the authorities as contrary to religion, the state, and morals. And in 1749 he spent 100 days in prison, being released only after making a humiliating apology.

At about that time Diderot was approached by a bookseller (roughly today's publisher) to translate a British encyclopedic reference work into French. After a number of false starts, Diderot persuaded the bookseller to sponsor instead an entirely new work that would be more comprehensive and up-to-date and would reflect the attitudes of the

philosophes. The *Encyclopedia, or Classified Dictionary of the Sciences, Arts, and Occupations* would inventory all important fields of knowledge from the most theoretical to the most mundane and would constitute an arsenal of critical concepts. As the preface stated: "Our Encyclopedia is a work that could only be carried out in a philosophic century. . . . All things must be examined without sparing anyone's sensibilities. . . . The arts and sciences must regain the freedom that is so precious to them." More importantly the ultimate purpose of the encyclopedia according to the editors was "to change the general way of thinking." Or as Diderot put it in a letter to a friend, they were promoting "a revolution in the minds of men to free them from prejudice." Written in this spirit by an array of talented collaborators, the twenty-eight-volume *Encyclopedia* (1751–1772) fulfilled the fondest hopes of its editors and 4,000 initial subscribers.

In such a work religion could scarcely be ignored; nor could it be attacked frontally. Instead it was treated with artful satire or else relegated to a merely philosophical or historical plane. Demystified and subordinated, it was probed and questioned as was any other subject, much to the discomfort of learned but orthodox men.

If the *Encyclopedia* had a core, it was science. But the editors' preferences ran toward the utilitarian and technological side of science. Great attention was lavished for example on articles and plates illustrating various manufacturing processes and tools, and the roles of the mechanic, engineer, and artisan were elevated in the *Encyclopedia's* scheme of values. The implication was that theoretical scientists could profit from closer attention to technological problems and closer collaboration with technicians. This suggested that the handicrafts and applied technology constituted a realm of knowledge comparable to pure sciences, such as physics and mathematics. At the same time it emphasized an important social perspective: the social utility of the artisan and the benefits of efficient production, as distinct from the role of the elite classes, in the advance of civilization.

Social science also figured prominently in the *Encyclopedia*. Learned articles summarized many theories about social organization and human nature, and again the emphasis was placed on the notion of social utility. On economic topics the encyclopedists tended to echo the physiocratic crusade against mercantilist restrictions on trade and agriculture. But no articles reflected the preoccupations and opinions of the popular masses on such issues as wages or social organization. While the *Encyclopedia*'s bent was not specifically middle-class, it did echo many aspirations of the bourgeoisie while threatening none of its existing prerogatives, especially in matters of property. And on political issues the *Encyclopedia* did not take a particularly controversial line on the central question of authority and sovereignty. It tended to accept absolute monarchy with equanimity, provided it was reasonably efficient and just. The major concerns of the editors were civil rights, freedom of expression, and the rule of law.

Measured from the perspective of the French Revolution—that is, with hindsight—the *Encyclopedia* thus does not seem revolutionary. Yet in the context of the times, it was. The revolution that Diderot sought was in intellectual orientation: his purpose was to spread the "critical spirit" from the precincts of the philosophes to the educated elites in general. Judging by the reaction of religious and government authorities, he was eminently successful. "Up till now," commented one French bishop, "hell has vomited its venom drop by drop." Now, he continued, it could be found assembled between the *Encyclopedia*'s covers. And the attorney general of France declared in 1758, "There is a project formed, a society organized to propagate ma-

Diderot's Encyclopedia *focused much of its attention on technology. Plates illustrating the mechanical process, such as the one shown here for casting sculpture, were provided in separate volumes.* (Photo: The Bettmann Archive)

terialism, to destroy religion, to inspire a spirit of independence, and to nourish the corruption of morals."

The *Encyclopedia* was accordingly banned, and its bookseller's license to issue the remaining volumes was revoked. Most of the contributors prudently withdrew, but Diderot was too committed. Retreating underground, he continued the herculean task until the subscribers received every promised volume, including eleven magnificent folios of illustrations. By the time these appeared, the persecutions had receded, and indeed the *Encyclopedia* was reprinted in several cheaper editions that sold out rapidly, making a fortune for their publishers. More importantly this turn of events ensured the renown of the philosophes' most impressive achievement—a work recognized both in its own time and thereafter as the landmark of an age.

II. EIGHTEENTH-CENTURY CULTURES

The Enlightenment was merely one dimension of Europe's proliferating cultural life. The economic expansion and prosperity, which will be discussed in the next chapter, were matched by a marked increase in literary output serving increasingly diverse audiences. Although the aristocracy still dominated society, people of lesser origins were prominently participating in and supporting culture. Eighteenth-century high culture was distinctly cosmopolitan, that is, spilling across national borders as well as social class lines. Its trends included an increase in travel within Europe, a dramatic expansion of publishing activity, the creation of new literary and scientific academies, and the development of new genres in fields like fiction and music. Popular culture, on the other hand, remained extremely traditional and localized.

HIGH CULTURE

As the expansive, cosmopolitan aspects of European high culture are described here, it must be remembered that the mass of Europe's population remained entirely parochial and virtually untouched by these developments. Most peasants and urban laborers continued to live within the culturally hermetic boundaries of their parish, their family, their job. But for the educated and wealthy, the numerically small but extremely influential elites,

there was a sense of belonging to an international European civilization. It was a civilization dominated by France and by the French language, which had now displaced Latin and Italian as the language of the educated. Even Frederick II of Prussia favored French over German. Whatever deleterious effects such an attitude might have—and the German dramatist Lessing considered it a disastrous prejudice—this meant that ideas and literature circulated without language barriers among Europe's elites.

Travel

Europeans' sense of their common identity was sharpened by a flood of travel literature and by their appetite for visiting foreign parts. Although transportation was slow and uncomfortable, many embarked on a "grand tour" of the Continent and Great Britain. The highlights of such a trip were visits to large cities and to the ruins of antiquity—to the glories, that is, of both the modern and the ancient world.

London, Paris, Rome, and Vienna were already large, bustling, and impressive metropolises. These and smaller cities in Germany, Italy, and the United Provinces were undertaking considerable urban improvement. With generally excellent taste, rulers and municipal authorities were continuing to embellish their cities with large plazas, public gardens, airy boulevards, theaters, and opera houses. Toward the end of the century, amenities such as street lighting and public transportation began to appear in cities, with London leading the way. From the private sector came two notable additions to the urban scene: the coffee shop and the storefront window display. Coffeehouses, where customers could chat or read, and enticing shop windows, which added to the pleasures of city walking (while also stimulating consumer demand), enhanced the rhythms of urban life for tourists and natives alike. Sophisticated

Europeans took great pleasure in their cities. When a man is tired of London, Samuel Johnson remarked, he is tired of life.

Travelers on tour invariably passed from the attractions of bustling city life to the monuments of antiquity. The philosophes called attention to pagan philosophers like Cicero; paralleling this, interest heightened in the remnants of Greek and Roman architecture and sculpture. Europeans endorsed the view of the German art historian Johann Winckelmann that Greek sculpture was the most worthy standard of aesthetic beauty. A lasting result of this fascination with antique ruins was Edward Gibbon's decision, on visiting the awesome remains of ancient Rome, to undertake *The Decline and Fall of the Roman Empire*.

The Republic of Letters

Among writers, intellectuals, and scientists, the sense of a cosmopolitan European culture devolved into the concept of a republic of letters. The phrase, introduced by sixteenth-century French humanists, was popularized by Pierre Bayle, a great progenitor of the Enlightenment, who published a critical journal that he called *News of the Republic of Letters*. The obvious import of the rubric is that the realm of culture and ideas is an intellectual homeland that cuts across all political and geographical borders. In one sense it is an exclusive republic, limited to the educated; but it is also an open society in that people may belong regardless of their social origins. For this reason European intellectuals felt that their republic of letters was a model for general social values.

Aside from the medium of the printed word, the republic of letters was organized around two institutions; the salons and the academies. Each advanced the process of social interchange, gathering together people from various countries distinguished by either status or talent. The philosophes themselves exemplified this social mix, for their "family" was composed in almost equal measure of nobles (Montesquieu, Holbach, Condorcet) and commoners (Voltaire, Diderot, d'Alembert). Voltaire insisted that he was as good as any aristocrat but had no intention of trying to topple the aristocracy from its position; rather he sought amalgamation. As d'Alembert put it, talent on the one hand and birth and eminence on the other both deserve recognition and deference.

The salons, conducted mainly by wives of wealthy bourgeois or noble families, sought to bring together important writers with the influential aristocrats they needed for favors and funds. The marquise de Pompadour, Louis XV's mistress, was the most notable personage to run such an assembly. Since a premium was placed on style and elegance in the salons, the intellectual was required to make his ideas lucid and comprehensible to the layman, which in turn increased the likelihood that his thought would have some influence. The salons helped particularly to enlarge the audience and contacts of the philosophes and served to introduce them to a flow of foreign visitors ranging from German princes to Benjamin Franklin. Private newsletters to which interested foreigners subscribed kept them abreast of activities in the Parisian salons when they could not attend personally.

Throughout Europe freemasonry played a similar role of cultural diffusion, promoting interchange across both national and social lines and creating another cosmopolitan dimension to European intellectual life. Operating in an aura of secretiveness and symbolism, the masonic lodges fostered a curious mixture of medieval mysticism and modern rationalism. They had begun really as clubs or fraternities dedicated to humane values; thus they attracted a wide range of enlightened nobles and distinguished commoners. But toward the end of the century, they were rent by sectarian controversies, and their initial sense of universalism eroded.

Far more important for the dissemination of ideas in the eighteenth century were the learned academies. These ranged from the Lunar Society in Birmingham, a forum for the most progressive British industrialists and technologists, to state-sponsored academies in almost every capital of Southern and Central Europe, which served as conduits for advanced scientific and philosophical ideas coming from the West. In France moreover academies were established in more than thirty provincial cities—a vital development in that it promoted widespread intellectual activity and created strongholds of advanced thinking in almost every region of that large country.

These provincial academies were founded after the death of Louis XIV, as if in testimony to the liberating effect of his disappear-

A lecture at a learned gathering. (Photo: Lauros-Giraudon)

ance. They began as literary institutes, concerned with upholding traditional values like purity of style. A few remained conservative adherents to the status quo into midcentury: the motto of the Cherbourg Academy in 1755 was "Religion and Honor." But most of them gradually shifted their interests from conventional literary matters to scientific and utilitarian questions in such domains as commerce, agriculture, and local administration. They became offshoots so to speak of the *Encyclopedia*. Indeed when a Jesuit read a harangue against the *Encyclopedia* in the Lyons Academy many members threatened to resign unless he retracted his remarks. By the 1770s and 1780s, the essay contests sponsored by the provincial academies and the papers published by their members had turned to such topics as population growth, capital punishment and penology, education, poverty and welfare, the grain trade, highways, guilds, and the origins of sovereignty.

There was a parallel shift in membership. The local academies began as privileged corporations, dominated by the nobility of the region. Corresponding or associate membership was extended to commoners from the ranks of civil servants, doctors, and professionals. Gradually the distinction between regular and associate participants crumbled. More commoners were admitted to full membership, and a social fusion took place, though it remained fragile and untested until 1789. Nobles and commoners alike were eager to discuss reforms and work for the betterment of local conditions. The scientific spirit had spread to them, making them receptive to the cause of practical reform and utilitarian ideas.

Publishing and Reading
The printed word was of course the chief medium of cultural diffusion. To be sure, the eighteenth century was not an age of mass education or literacy. Rudimentary public schools in Prussia, charity schools for the poor

in Britain, and parish schools run by local priests in France did not produce literacy among the majority of the lower classes. Nonetheless the proportions of those who could read were advancing slowly, and population increases caused a substantial overall gain in literacy. Both factors help explain the tremendous rise in publishing activity geared to several different reading publics.

Untapped markets for reading material were opened up by itinerant circulating libraries, which originated in England around 1740; by the end of the century, almost 1,000 had been established. Recognizing a specialized demand among women readers, publishers also began to increase the output of new kinds of fiction and "ladies' magazines." Moreover they were more receptive to women writers of fiction and poetry, especially the so-called blue-stockings of the salons, who were early literary feminists.

The most notable development in publishing during the eighteenth century was the proliferation of journals and newspapers. In England, which pioneered in this domain, the number of periodicals increased from 25 to 158 between 1700 and 1780. There were several kinds. Single-essay periodicals, whose objective was moral and aesthetic uplift and whose model was Joseph Addison and Richard Steele's *Spectator*, continued to be popular. By contrast, the miscellany contained extracts and summaries of books and covered current events and entertainment; one such, the *Gentleman's Magazine*, had the astonishing circulation of 15,000 in 1740. More sophisticated periodicals, like the *Monthly Review* and the *Journal des Savants*, specialized in critical book reviews and serious articles on science and philosophy, and they served the important function of extending the republic of letters beyond the scholar's study into the public domain. Most important for the future of reading habits in Europe was the daily newspaper, originated in England. Papers like

England broke new ground in publishing by introducing the daily newspaper. The page shown here is from a 1760 issue of "The Public Ledger," a London paper. (Photo: Radio Times Hulton Picture Library)

the *London Chronicle* were originally intended for family reading and entertainment. Gradually they assumed other functions: they took classified advertisements, they began to report news, and finally—after considerable battling—they began to cover politics and report parliamentary debates. Under France's censorship regime, newspapers did not become politically oriented until the French Revolution, at which time a politically aroused France probably surpassed England as the country of newspaper reading.

In the field of general publishing, booksellers now assumed strategic prominence. They were the intermediary between reader and author—they combined the functions of editor, printer, salesman, and (if need be) smuggler. Their judgment and marketing techniques helped create as well as fill the demand for books since they conceived, commissioned, and financed a variety of works. The system had varying results. We have seen the *Encyclopedia* originate as a bookseller's project. So too did such enduring masterpieces as Samuel Johnson's *Dictionary*, a monumental lexicon that helped purify and standardize English usage. Many respectable popularizations of scientific, historical, and philosophical treatises were likewise brought into print by publishers, who commissioned skillful stylists like Oliver Goldsmith to write them. But there was a demeaning side to this system, for booksellers also employed hack writers to turn out potboilers, romances, and other works that pandered to low tastes, paying them for quantity and speed rather than quality. These drudges led a precarious and struggling existence along with marginal theatrical people in the milieu known as Grub Street. And Grub Street had even lower depths: for the more unscrupulous booksellers and desperate writers, there was money to be made in scurrilous political pamphlets committing character assassination and of course in pornography. Sometimes the two were combined in pamphlets dwelling on the alleged perversions of kings and queens.

With the growth of publishing, the vocation of writer was taking on a variety of forms. To be sure, practically all writers aspired to hold some lucrative sinecure or to be supported by important aristocrats. But authors valued their independence as much as patronage and security; the most successful could now live off their own work without patrons. On the other hand the number of would-be writers increased enormously, and many were decidedly unsuccessful and frustrated. The explosion of the printed word therefore raised troubling questions. Would refinement and moral sensitivity be overwhelmed by vulgarity and commercialism? This is a problem gripping today's media, and it was born in the eighteenth century. On balance it seems reasonable to conclude that the new demand for books and the new economics of publishing created significant opportunity for professional writers to express

and fulfill their own talents and for literate citizens to expose themselves to a variety of ideas, new and old. The entertainment and instruction of a middle-class audience became a principal focus of writing.

POPULAR CULTURE

While the culture of aristocratic and middle-class elites has been extensively studied, the cultures of artisans, peasants, and the urban poor are only dimly known. In those sectors of society culture primarily meant recreation and was essentially public and collective. Moreover, while there was a written form of popular culture that we shall discuss, it was minor compared to the prevalent oral culture, which has left few traces in the historical record. Nonetheless it is possible to suggest some of the rich variety of cultural materials and recreations of the common people.

Popular Literature

Far removed from the markets for Voltaire and the *Gentleman's Magazine*, there existed a distinct world of popular literature—the reading matter consumed by artisans and peasants, the poor and the almost poor, those who could barely read and even those who could not read at all. From the seventeenth through the early nineteenth century but particularly in eighteenth-century France, a type of literature was specially produced for this audience. It consisted of small booklets and brochures written anonymously, printed on cheap paper, and costing only a few pennies. They were sold by colporteurs—itinerant hawkers—who knew the tastes of these customers and saw to it that they were satisfied. The booklets were often read aloud by those who could read to those who could not; but even the illiterate bought them, apparently somewhat in awe of the printed word and valuing its possession.

There were three major varieties of popular literature. The first was explicitly religious: devotional tracts, saints' lives, catechisms, manuals of penitence, and Bible stories, all written simply and vividly and generously laced with miracles. Preoccupied with fears of death and damnation, the readers sought reassurance here that a virtuous, sensible life would end in salvation. A second kind of popular literature was the almanac, which corresponded with a concern for getting along in this life as well. Almanacs and how-to-live-successfully pamphlets (forerunners of the *Reader's Digest* and Norman Vincent Peale) discussed things like cleanliness, nourishment, and the kinds of potions to take for illnesses. They also featured astrology—how to read the stars and other signs for clues about what the future might bring. The third type was entertainment literature: tales and fables, burlesques and crude satires, mixtures of fiction and history in which miraculous events frequently helped bring the story to a satisfactory conclusion.[2]

Although important information may have trickled down through these booklets, most of them were blatantly escapist. The pervasive religiosity and superstition of popular literature marks it off decisively from the growing rationalism and secularism of middle-class and avant-garde culture. Moreover it could be argued that by ignoring the real problems of famine, taxes, and material insecurity, these writings fostered submissiveness, a fatalistic acceptance of a dismal status quo. Seeing the nature of popular literature helps us understand why Voltaire had no hope of extending his ideas on religion to the masses and indeed even feared to discuss them in front of his servants.

Almanacs and pamphlets were produced for the lower classes by outsiders, printers and

writers who were themselves educated. A more common and authentic form of popular culture was oral: folk tales told at the fireside on long winter nights and songs that expressed bawdiness or violence far more directly and meaningfully than the written word. Themes relating to hunger or sex or oppression were more likely to turn up in songs, often sung in local dialects that would have been incomprehensible to an educated Parisian, Londoner, or Viennese.

Groups and Recreations

If the educated had their freemasons' lodges and learned societies, the people also had organized groups. Many journeymen artisans, for example, belonged to secret societies that combined fraternal and trade-union functions. These young artisans usually toured their country, stopping periodically to work with comrades in other towns in order to improve their own skills. But the main emphasis of their associations was on camaraderie and ritual celebration. Rivalries were common between federations of such associations and occasionally degenerated into pitched battles —a far cry from the nineteenth-century ideal of labor solidarity.

Corresponding to the coffee shop and salon of the urban middle classes were the public house or "pub," the cafe in local urban neighborhoods, and the *guinguette* in the suburbs of the common people. These "dives" (as they would doubtless be called today) catered to a large, poor clientele, especially on Sunday and Monday, which working people often took as a day off. The *guinguettes* were located outside the city walls so that the wine they sold would not be subject to urban excise taxes. Wine was just beginning to be consumed by the common people in the eighteenth century. And even then it was something of a luxury except in its cheapest form, which was always adulterated or watered. In

---

[2] See Geneviève Bollème, *La Bibliothèque bleue.* (1971).

England, however, gin was the poor person's drink—cheap and plentiful until a hefty excise tax was levied following the government's realization that too many people were drinking themselves into disability and death.

More commonly drinking was not done in that morbid fashion but as part of a healthy and vibrant outdoor life. A recent study of popular pastimes in England suggests the outlines of a traditional popular culture that flourished before the Industrial Revolution. It was marked by a full calendar of holidays that provided numerous occasions for group merrymaking, eating, drinking, dressing-up, contests, and games. This was a particularly beneficial setting for boys and girls in their teens and twenties to meet each other. The highlight of a country year usually came either between spring sowing and the summer harvest or in the early autumn after the summer harvest was in, when most villages held a public feast lasting several days. In Catholic countries similar festivities were often linked with church rituals, with the most popular observances including the commemoration of saints and pilgrimages to holy places.

Popular culture involved "relaxation in noise and tumultuous merriment," preferably in public and out in the open. Football matches, for example, were a popular form of recreation in England, both for participants and observers. At times the high spirits generated on these occasions turned into good-natured riots. In August 1765 the *Northampton Mercury* reported: "We hear from West-Hadden, in this county, that on Thursday and Friday a great number of people being assembled there, in order to play a Foot-Ball Match, soon after meeting formed themselves into a tumultuous mob, and pulled up and burnt the fences designed for the inclosure of that field, and did other considerable damage."

Blood sports were another type of popular recreation in the preindustrial era. Bullbait-ing, for example, involved setting loose a pack of dogs on a tied-up steer, and was often arranged by the collaboration of a butcher (who provided the steer that would subsequently be slaughtered and dispensed as meat) and a publican (who provided the yard of his inn as the arena and sold refreshments to the spectators). Cockfighting was similar in its gory results and was popular with gentlemen and commoners alike, who enjoyed wagering on the outcome. These so-called sports appear repulsive today, and by the end of the eighteenth century such cruelties to animals were being denounced by reformers and moralists. It is notable, however, that no similar attack was leveled against the gentry's organized bloodletting in the form of fox hunting.

LITERATURE, MUSIC, AND ART

Unlike the seventeenth century, sometimes classified as Baroque, the eighteenth can be given no comprehensive stylistic label. Literary styles varied, ranging from Neoclassicism in poetry to major innovation in fiction. The nature of the audience and the sources of a writer's support varied considerably. The same was true for composers. But if any trends may be singled out for attention, they are the rise of the novel and the development of the symphony.

The Novel and Poetry

For all practical purposes the novel may be said to have originated in England, where writers and booksellers were particularly aware of a growing middle-class reading public. The acknowledged pioneer of this new genre was Samuel Richardson, himself a bookseller. Epistolary in form—a series of letters telling the story—*Pamela, or Virtue Rewarded* (1740) was a melodrama of the trials and tribulations of an honest if somewhat hypo-

In this famous "Gin Lane" etching of 1750 by Hogarth, the results of excessive gin drinking by the common people are depicted as death, apathy, and decay. A cheerful and orderly companion piece called "Beer Street," however, made it clear that drinking in moderation was a perfectly acceptable habit. (Photo: Metropolitan Museum of Art, Harris Brisbane Dick Fund, 1932)

critical servant girl whose sexual virtue is repeatedly challenged but never conquered and whose wealthy employer finally agrees to marry her. *Pamela* was an instant success. Breaking away from the standard forms and heroic subjects of most previous narrative fiction, Richardson dealt with the qualities of recognizable types of people. Pamela's earnest hypocrisy, however, prompted a playwright and lawyer named Henry Fielding to pen a short satire called *Shamela*, which he followed with his own novel *Joseph Andrews*. Here comedy and adventure replaced melodrama; indeed Fielding prefaced the book with a remarkable manifesto claiming that the novel was to be a comic epic in prose. Fielding realized the full potential of this bold innovation in *Tom Jones* (1749), a colorful, robust comic panorama of English society featuring a gallery of brilliantly developed characters. Fielding was providing a literary counterpart to the world that William Hogarth was creating in his etchings—vivid exaggerations of the various social milieus, particularly the period's low life.

In general the novel was emerging as a form of fiction that told its story and treated the development of personality in a realistic social context, and in some ways it mirrored its times better than any other form of fiction. Novelists could use broad comedy, as did Laurence Sterne, or they could be totally serious, as was Johann Wolfgang von Goethe in *The Sorrows of Werther* (1774), a *Bildungsroman* (novel of development) telling the tragic story of the coming of age of a melancholy youth. In either case the writer freed himself from classic aesthetic norms and specified rules of composition. Authors could now experiment endlessly with forms and techniques and could deal with a wide range of social settings. Consequently they drew less and less on the life styles of aristocrats for their social ideals, and much of the century's fiction, in the drama as well as the novel,

focused on middle-class family life and its everyday problems of morality, love, and social relations. This reflected actual changes in middle-class values, which were increasingly emphasizing close family relations.[3]

Meanwhile a genre called the philosophical tale was being perfected by writers with more didactic objectives. The chief progenitor of the form was the great Irish satirist Jonathan Swift, notably in his well-known *Gulliver's Travels* (1726). The French philosophes naturally gravitated toward this genre of satire since it allowed them to criticize their society covertly and hence to avoid open clashes with the censors. Thus Montesquieu created a range of mythical foreign settings, exotic backgrounds, and travelers from the Levant to ridicule contemporary mores in *The Persian Letters* (1721). Likewise Voltaire achieved great success in his tale *Candide* (1759), a critique of the notion that this was the best of all possible worlds. His wholly fictional characters and incidents disguised an Enlightenment sermon against the idiocy and cruelty that he saw in European society. Voltaire and Fielding met on this ground, for both were concerned with imparting a commonsensical notion of morality and humanity.

During most of the century, the innovation that was occurring in prose fiction contrasted with the traditionalism of poetry, still the most prized form of literary expression. Here unchanged rules on what made "good literature" still prevailed. Each type of poem had its particular essence and rules; diction was supposed to be elegant and sentiments refined and elevated. The raw materials of emotion were to be muted and transformed into language and

---

[3] In his *Centuries of Childhood* (1962), Pt. 3, Philippe Ariès points out how parents were becoming much closer to their children in the eighteenth century. Instead of sending them to boarding school, they more frequently placed them in schools near home. Families also now insisted on more privacy for themselves in household architecture.

634 / THE AGE OF ENLIGHTENMENT

allusions that only the highly educated could appreciate. Art was viewed in this Neoclassical tradition as imitative of eternal standards of truth and beauty. It was not permissible for the poet to unburden his soul or hold forth on his own experience. The audience for poetry was the narrowest and most elitist segment of the reading public—"the wealthy few," in the phrase of William Wordsworth, who criticized eighteenth-century poets for pandering exclusively to that group.

By the end of the century, the restraints of Neoclassicism finally provoked rebellion in the ranks of English and German poets. Men like Friedrich von Schiller and Wordsworth defiantly raised the celebration of individual feeling and inner passion to the level of a creed, which eventually became known as Romanticism. Hoping to appeal to a much broader audience, these writers decisively changed the nature of poetic composition and made this literary form, like the novel, a far more flexible vehicle of expression.

Music and Art

The rise of the novel in literature was paralleled by the development of the symphony in music. But it must be noted at once that a great deal of eighteenth-century music was routine and undistinguished. For much of the century, composers were still obliged to serve under royal, ecclesiastical, or aristocratic patronage. They were bound by rigid formulas of composition and by a public taste tyrannically insistent on conventions. A pleasant melody in a predictable form was what the listener wanted from his composers. Much instrumental music was commissioned as background fare for dancing or other social occasions. Likewise Italian opera was popular and quantitatively impressive—Alessandro Scarlatti, for example, composed 115 operas. But very few of these repetitive compositions have survived the test of time; their sheer number

is an obvious clue to the casual circumstances of their composition and their likely fate.

The heartland of Europe's music tradition was Austria. Here a trio of geniuses transformed the routines of eighteenth-century composition into vibrant, original, and enduring masterpieces. The early symphonies of Franz Joseph Haydn and the young prodigy Wolfgang Amadeus Mozart were conventional exercises in Rococo decorativeness. The music was light and as tuneful as its audience could wish, but it had little emotional impact. By the end of their careers, Haydn had written 104 symphonies and Mozart 41. They had stabilized the form into its familiar four movements (fast, slow, minuet, fast); they had each developed extraordinary harmonic virtuosity; but more than these accomplishments, they had infused the form with a lyricism that often crossed the border into the realm of passion. In short, the symphony had changed radically from the elegant trifles of earlier years.

The German composer Ludwig van Beethoven consummated this development and assured that the symphony, like the novel, would be adaptable and ever-malleable. In each of his nine symphonies as well as his five piano concertos, he progressively modified the standard formulas. The orchestra was much enlarged, and the movements were made far more intricate and longer. His last symphony burst the bonds of the form. Striving to make a Promethean musical statement, Beethoven introduced a large chorus singing one of Schiller's odes to conclude the composition, making it an explicit celebration in music of freedom and brotherhood. Laden with emotion and programmatic content, the music is yet recognizable as an advanced form of the eighteenth-century symphony. Thus it provides a bridge between the culture of two periods: eighteenth-century Classicism and nineteenth-century Romanticism.

The ornate interiors of eighteenth-century opera houses began filling to capacity as music grew in popularity. Italy was a focal point of the musical world, with four opera houses in Rome and three in Naples. (Photo: Librairie Larousse)

Beethoven also progressed farther than most of his predecessors in freeing himself from subordination to a powerful single patron. Haydn had pioneered in this direction by signing a lucrative contract with a London music publisher and impresario that underwrote the composition and performance of his last twelve symphonies. Beethoven relied even more on public concerts and specific commissions instead of tying himself to a particular patron.[4]

---

[4] Johann Sebastian Bach (1685–1750) is considered by many music lovers a genius on a par with Mozart and Beethoven. But in his own day, as the organist and resident composer for a number of obscure German churches, Bach was little known to the outside world. Ironically, whereas today he is admired only by "highbrows," in his time he provided what was in effect popular music for the people—organ music, hymns, and cantatas for religious worship.

Unlike fiction and music, painting did not experience notable innovations in the eighteenth century, and with the exception of Jacques Louis David (see plate 46) eighteenth-century painters were overshadowed by their predecessors as well as by their successors of the Romantic and post-Romantic schools of nineteenth-century art. Neoclassicism was a dominant style in the late eighteenth century, with its themes inspired by antiquity and its timeless conceptions of truth and beauty, similar to those of Neoclassical poetry. There were, however, at least two developments which paralleled the widening social context of the other arts. In the first place, just as composers and musicians began to perform in public concerts, so did painters begin to exhibit regularly in public, especially in the annual salons sponsored by the royal academies of art in London and in Paris. The head of London's Royal Academy, founded by George III in 1768, was Sir Joshua Reynolds. A notable portrait painter, Reynolds—solely by virtue of his talent—rose to a position of wealth and eminence, thus exemplifying the Enlightenment ideal of opportunity. Moreover, his success brought him the independence from a patron that writers, composers, and artists all aspired to.

A second development in the social history of eighteenth-century art lay in the new kinds of subject matter and themes taken up by certain artists, which paralleled what novelists and playwrights were doing. Jean Baptiste Greuze, for example, made a hit in the Parisian exhibitions of the 1770s with his sentimentalized paintings of common people in family settings caught in a dramatic situation, such as the death of a father. William Hogarth was not primarily a painter at all but an engraver working through the medium of prints and book illustrations. His art therefore had a much wider circulation than the work of any painter. And his choice of subjects ranged far and wide through the ranks of society—especially in scenes of low life among the poor and the working classes (see illustration, p. 632). Hogarth's art was not only technically brilliant, it remains a basic source for the study of English social history.

III. THE ENLIGHTENMENT AND THE STATE

On the whole the Enlightenment was not highly critical of existing forms of government, though specific policies of rulers and ministers were often criticized. In Central Europe monarchy was the starting point of most political theory or reform programs. In France the monarchy and the aristocracy were more evenly matched, and the contrasting political views of Montesquieu and Voltaire reflected this fact. With Jean Jacques Rousseau, however, we come to the century's most original political theorist—a man less concerned with actual political arrangements than with the inherent possibilities for individual and political freedom.

GERMAN ABSOLUTISM AND THE PROBLEM OF REFORM

During the late nineteenth century, German historians invented the concept of "enlightened absolutism" to describe the Prussian and Hapsburg monarchies of the eighteenth century. Apologists for German development and critics of the liberal and revolutionary traditions associated with France, they argued that the strength of an enlightened ruler was the surest basis for progress in early modern Europe. A king who ruled in the interest of his subjects, they implied, precluded violent divisions like those of the French Revolution. Heads of state came to govern in this manner only after a long evolution, for according to these historians, absolutism had evolved through three phases. First came the period of "confessional absolutism," when kings were preoccupied with religious uniformity; it was exemplified by Philip II of Spain and the notion that the prince's religion is the religion of the state. This phase was followed by a more secular and dynastic stage, "courtly absolutism," exemplified of course by Louis XIV and his famous epigram, "I am the state." In contrast to Louis' extravagant style and goals, Frederick II of Prussia marked the "enlightened" phase of absolutism, as evidenced by his dictum that the ruler is the first servant of the state.

This three-phase scheme is a distortion of history. Earlier chapters have amply demonstrated that fundamental issues differed little in these supposed stages of absolutism. Absolute monarchs strove at all times to assert their authority over the constituent elements of society and to maximize the power of their state in relation to other realms, principally by means of territorial expansion. Any notion that the Enlightenment caused the monarchs to alter this is erroneous. Still, there were visible modifications of specific practices and style in the way that absolute monarchy conducted its business. And in this the role of culture and ideas was not entirely absent.

Conceptions of "Enlightened" Rule
Some of the modifications observable in eighteenth-century absolutism may well have been prompted by prominent philosophes, with whom sovereigns like Frederick II and Catherine II of Russia (1762–1796) maintained significant contacts. Voltaire for example spent a long sojourn at Frederick's palace, while Catherine offered to buy Diderot's library to help him out of financial troubles and delay taking possession of it until his death. At various times monarchs and philosophes lavished saccharine praise on each other. How significant was this mutual admiration? For the monarchs it was probably primarily a question of public relations, of image making. Yet the fact that they should even find it desirable to be supportive of men like Voltaire and Diderot is suggestive. They may have felt the need to justify themselves publicly and even to coopt the prestige of Europe's leading intellectuals.

Catherine the Great played this game to its limit, promising at one point in her reign to begin moving gradually toward representative government and constitutionalism—a policy that was hailed as a historic landmark by philosophe admirers who were too remote from St. Petersburg to see its falsity. In 1767 she convened the Legislative Commission, a quasi-representative body of delegates from various strata of Russian society. They were invited to present grievances, propose reforms, and debate such proposals. In the end nothing came of this except some good publicity for Catherine. She soon dissolved the commission under the pretext of having to turn her attention to a new Turkish war. Some time later she promulgated a Charter of the Nobility, which, instead of limiting the nobility's privileges, strengthened its corporate status and increased its control over the serfs in exchange for a pledge of loyalty to the throne.

No such experiment in representation was even tried in Central Europe, where other conceptions of enlightened rule and reform prevailed. German writers were particularly adept at finding theoretical justifications for the powers of an autocrat. They viewed the state as a machine and the ruler as its necessary mainspring. Progress came from sound administration, whose instrumentalities were an enlightened monarch and well-trained bureaucrats. In keeping with this notion, German universities began to train civil servants, and the rudiments of a merit system of civil service recruitment were introduced in Prussia and other states.

The orders for the bureaucracy were to come from the ruler, who was expected to dedicate himself to the welfare of his subjects in return for their obedience. The vehicle for the command-obedience chain was to be a coherent and explicit body of public law, fairly administered by the above-mentioned bureaucrats. According to its advocates, this system would produce the rule of law, the *Rechtsstaat*. A society thus based on "right" did not require a written constitution or public representation; the monarch and the bureaucrats together, following their sense of public responsibility, ensured the citizen's rights.

Many German intellectuals subscribed to this view and accordingly believed that they were living in a free and progressive society—free from arbitrary injustice, and progressive because rationality was exercised in government. Although many would sympathize with the French Revolution of 1789, they were inclined to regard the turmoil of a revolution as unnecessary for their own situation.

Joseph II and the Limits of Absolutism

The most notable sponsor of reforms from above was Joseph II, Hapsburg ruler from 1765 to 1790. Although he did not identify with the philosophes and maintained his own Catholic faith, he was actually the most "enlightened" of the major monarchs of the eighteenth century—as well as one of the most autocratic personalities. It was a difficult combination.

Joseph believed that the primary right of the people was to be governed well. But for him this entailed far more than the customary administrative and financial modernization necessary for survival in the state system. The emperor began by implementing several reforms long advocated by Enlightenment thinkers: freedom of expression, religious toleration, state control over organized religion, and legal reform. By greatly reducing royal censorship, Joseph opened the way for Vienna to become a major center of literary activity. In an edict of toleration in 1781, he emancipated Protestants and Jews, granting them the right to worship publicly and to hold property and public office; he went so far as to ennoble some Jews. On the other hand he worked to reduce the influence of the Catholic Church by ordering the dissolution of numerous monasteries on the grounds that they were useless and corrupt. Part of their confiscated wealth was used to support the medical school at the University of Vienna. In an attempt to force the church to serve its parishioners better, he eliminated much of Rome's authority and forced the clergy to modernize rituals and services. It should come as no surprise, however, that most of his Catholic subjects preferred their traditional ways to this nationalized brand of Catholicism.

When Joseph ordered the drafting of a new criminal code, he substantiated the Enlightenment's belief in legal reform as an instrument of social progress. Certain categories of crimes, such as witchcraft, were abolished altogether. The death penalty and various brutal punishments were eliminated for most crimes; the use of torture in criminal proceedings was forbidden; motive was recognized as a factor in determining guilt. Most strikingly the code recognized no class difference in the application of criminal law. Noble offenders were subject to the same laws as were commoners and could be sentenced to the same punishments.

These significant departures from the status quo were preliminaries to the most important of Joseph's efforts at social reform: to improve the lot of the peasants. In this respect the emperor was far bolder not only than any other eighteenth-century sovereign but than most philosophes and civil servants. The question of social justice for the rural lower classes was a weak point of "enlightened absolutism" elsewhere. Catherine II not only failed to improve conditions among the serfs but allowed their status to deteriorate even further, to the point where those on royal lands, who could be bought and sold at will, were being treated almost as slaves. Frederick II had better intentions but accomplished little. He attempted to stop corporal punishment of serfs by their masters, but even this modest reform was not forced on the nobles and was carried out only on royal lands. As for the more basic issues, land ownership and labor services, nothing was done to place limits on the lords' prerogatives. While most Prussian peasants could not be sold, they could not move of their own volition or lay claim to the land they tilled, and they spent much of their time performing services directly for their lord.

Faced with a roughly comparable situation in the Hapsburg domains, Joseph attacked all aspects of the problem. He set out to eradicate the system of serfdom and transform the peasant into a free citizen in command of his person and of the land he cultivated. To begin with, Joseph abolished personal servitude and gave peasants the right to move, marry, and enter any trade they wished. He then promulgated various laws to help secure their control over the land they worked. Finally and most dramatically, he made a decisive attempt to ensure the income and limit the obligations of the peasant tenant. All land was to be surveyed and subject to a uniform tax. Twelve percent of its annual yield would go to the state, and beyond this the peasant would be obliged to pay a maximum of 18 percent of his income to the lord in lieu of his former feudal obligations. No longer would he owe the labor service to his lord that sometimes consumed more than 100 days each year.

These reforms were ordered in a purely authoritarian fashion, with no regard for public opinion and no notion of consent from any quarter. They provoked a predictably vigorous opposition from the landowning classes. But they also won scant visible support from the peasant masses, who were deeply distrustful of anything the central government did because of its religious policies. No effort was made to build support among the peasants by explaining the reforms in the hope of offsetting the nobility's reaction. As a sympathetic chronicler of Joseph's reign sadly observed, "He brought in his beneficial measures in an arbitrary manner."

The arbitrariness was not incidental to Joseph's methods. He acknowledged no other way of doing things, no limitation on his own sovereignty. His reaction to the opposition that his reforms aroused illustrates this: he moved to suppress the unexpected dissent in the firmest possible way. Not only did he restore censorship in his last years, but he elevated the police department to the status of an imperial ministry, granting it unprecedented powers. By the time he died, in 1790, he was a disillusioned man. His realm resembled less a *Rechtsstaat* than a police state.

Contrasting the century's two most notable monarchs points up the limits of "enlightened absolutism." On basic social issues like the status of the rural masses, who made up about 90 percent of the population, absolutism displayed little capacity to initiate change regardless of the ruler's intentions. Frederick II resigned himself to the impossibility of improving established practice and attempted to do little in the peasants' behalf. Joseph II tried to do a great deal in their behalf—for them, not with them—only to find that autocracy could not accomplish his objectives without provoking major upheaval.

FRENCH LIBERAL THOUGHT

Like "nature" and "reason," the word "freedom" was central to the Enlightenment. Its most important meaning to the philosophes was the freedom of the human mind to throw off centuries of what they considered ignorance and tyranny. Their foremost practical concerns were freedom of expression and of religion, which they viewed as the necessary preconditions for other kinds of liberty. If human beings were able to confront the world without bowing to the supernatural and subordinating thought to any arbitrary authority, then society's problems could be progressively dealt with. It is to the great credit of eighteenth-century intellectuals that they fought for this cause so relentlessly that freedom of thought has become a hallmark of the Western liberal tradition.

Modern standards of social and political consciousness, however, tend to set the philosophes apart from today. For in the eighteenth century, they had relatively little awareness of and concern for the potentiality of the mass of the people. Few philosophes can be considered precursors of egalitarianism. Toward the mass of impoverished peasants and laborers, the educated had two attitudes: pity and fear. Pity took the form of organized, inadequate philanthropy, sponsored by church and state and doled out condescendingly. Fear of the mob—the *canaille* ("rabble"), Voltaire called it—was axiomatic. Even in Great Britain the disfranchisement of the poor and the need for instruments of social control like the poor law were taken for granted. By today's standards, then, the perimeters of controversy in political and social thought were extremely narrow. For most writers the issue of political freedom was relevant to only a small segment of the population—the classes at the top of the social pyramid.

The Balance of Powers Versus the Royal Thesis

In France, still under the shadow of Louis XIV's stifling centralism, many people were intrigued by Britain's political institutions, as idealized in the writings of John Locke. Obvious defects like the Corporation and Test acts, which denied civil rights to dissenters and Catholics, or the corruption in the parliamentary borough system were either unknown to Frenchmen or overlooked in favor of liberties like the requirement of a writ of habeas corpus. The Continent was particularly impressed by the Glorious Revolution of 1688, and by the House of Commons, which stood up to both crown and Lords.

This inspiration is echoed in *The Spirit of Laws* (1748) by the great French jurist Montesquieu. His book was a pioneering effort in political sociology, the comparative study of governments and societies. Montesquieu was not proposing that Britain serve as a model for other countries, for he was arguing precisely that there is no absolute or universal standard of good government. The subtitle of this long and rambling discourse conveys this: *The Relation that the Laws Should Have to the Constitution of Each Government, the Customs, Climate, Religion, Commerce, etc.* Yet Montesquieu sought to display the virtues of the idealized British system, feeling that all societies could learn from it about liberty.

The sections on liberty won a wide readership in Europe and in America, where the book was influential among the drafters of the United States Constitution. Political liberty, said Montesquieu, is the absence of one dominating power in the state, whatever its kind: the king, the aristocrats, the people. The conservation of liberty depends on the separation and balance of powers, such as the executive, the legislative, and the judicial. If a single leader or group controls all functions, the country lives under despotism.

The only power in most states that can effectively check the possibility of royal despotism without itself degenerating into the despotism of the mob, he felt, is the aristocracy, the upper classes. In effect Montesquieu was arguing that "privilege was the ancestor of liberty," as one historian put it recently. This might seem paradoxical since privilege appears to be the opposite of liberty. But this was not the view of the eighteenth century, which commonly considered strong privileged groups—noblemen, corporations, chartered towns—the only effective bulwarks against encroachments of royal power. Only such intermediary bodies, independent of both the masses and the crown, could prevent tyranny. To put it another way, the price of a society free from despotism is privilege for some of its members. For Montesquieu the pivotal privileged group in France was the magistrates of the parlements (he himself was a magistrate in Bordeaux), for they were the guardians of the law. Protected by the ownership of their own offices, these men were for Montesquieu the most likely champions of French liberty.

Montesquieu thus hoped to limit the central government's power by balancing it with other power centers. Precisely the opposite argument was put forward by other thinkers: to maximize the central government's strength and thus its capacity to accomplish reforms. The separation of powers could guarantee certain kinds of freedom, but it could also perpetuate inequities and inefficiency. Executive authority could be a source of tyranny, but it could also be a stimulus to social and economic reform. Therefore Voltaire for one tended to regard an independent aristocracy not as a bulwark of freedom but on the contrary as an obstacle to change. While Montesquieu justified the power of the parlements to prevent arbitrary decrees, Voltaire argued that they were bastions of special interest that themselves exercised a heavy hand in society and repeatedly prevented necessary reforms.

Men who like Voltaire considered the monarchy as the likeliest agent for reform in France—as the best of several weak alternatives —were proponents of what was called the royal thesis. They hoped that a new power elite of enlightened administrators would cluster around the monarchy to replace the age-old power elite of nobles and priests. Voltaire did not advocate any kind of despotism, enlightened or otherwise. He merely felt that for all its dangers a strong monarchy was preferable to a strong corporate nobility.

The royal thesis seemed particularly justified when Louis XVI ascended the throne in

1774 and appointed Jacques Turgot, a contributor to the *Encyclopedia* and one of France's most progressive thinkers and talented administrators, as his finance minister. The philosophes unanimously applauded this appointment and looked forward to a truly reformist administration. The policies that Turgot initiated for tax reform and economic opportunity were relatively modest moves toward a more open society and increased initiative for private citizens. Modest though they were, however, they encroached on a number of special preserves. Turgot was therefore attacked by the entrenched interest groups, including the parlements. Within two years he was dismissed by a king who disliked agitation and controversy. The flaws in the royal thesis were numerous, but the most obvious was the disinclination of the Bourbon king himself to support it vigorously.

Rousseau

Only one major political theorist advanced well beyond the two classic eighteenth-century positions associated with Montesquieu and Voltaire. But to understand the profound originality of his thought, one must first appreciate his unique position in the republic of letters. For Jean Jacques Rousseau provided in his life and writing a critique of the Enlightenment as well as of the status quo. Obsessed with the issue of moral freedom and individual autonomy, he found society far more oppressive than most philosophes allowed.

Young Rousseau won instant fame when he submitted a prize-winning essay in a contest sponsored by a provincial academy on the topic, "Has the restoration of the arts and sciences had a purifying effect upon morals?" Unlike most respondents, Rousseau answered that it had not. He argued that the lustrous cultural and scientific achievements of recent decades were producing pretentiousness, conformity, and useless luxury. Most scientific pursuits, he wrote, "are the effect of idleness which generate idleness in their turn." The system of rewards in the arts produces "a servile and deceptive conformity . . . the dissolution of morals . . . and the corruption of taste." Against the decadence of high culture he advocated a return to "the simplicity which prevailed in earliest times"—manly physical pastimes, self-reliance, citizens instead of courtiers.

These strictures against his own society led commentators to think of Rousseau as a "primitivist," extolling the virtues of the state of nature and the "noble savage." But this was not the case. Rousseau regarded the state of nature as a state of anarchy where force ruled and men were slaves of appetite. Yet this opinion made him no less contemptuous of eighteenth-century salon society, whose artificial rituals prevented the display of genuine emotion, and valued style over substance. Worse yet, he said, the educated and refined elite nurtured a sense of superiority that undermined common sense moral standards.

For Rousseau the basis of morality was conscience, not reason. "Virtue: sublime science of simple minds," he wrote, "are not your principles graven on every heart?" This theme he returned to in his two popular works of didactic fiction, *Julie, or the New Heloise* (1761), and *Emile, or Treatise on Education* (1762). In the novel *Julie* the hero is repeatedly tempted into immoral acts by passions and appetites but triumphs over them in the end. *Emile* recounts the story of a young child raised to be a moral adult by a tutor who emphasizes experience rather than book learning and who considers education as a process of individual self-development. Both books attack the complacent secularism or deism that prevailed among intellectuals of the time, arguing for a more profound, personal religiosity. For these reasons Rousseau's fiction was highly prized by young poets, who were themselves seeking a more personal idiom of expression and who valued the force of the emotions that classical rules of composition discouraged. Thus Rousseau was both a pioneer of progressive education and a precursor of literary romanticism.

Rousseau himself was by no means a saint. On the contrary his struggle against his own passions—illustrated by the illegitimate child whom he fathered and abandoned—doubtless contributed to his preoccupation with morality and conscience. Nonetheless his life as well as his writings influenced the generation of intellectuals coming of age in the 1770s and 1780s. He was a true rebel among his contemporaries, rejecting much of the celebrity that his pen brought him. Not only did he quarrel with the repressive authorities of church and state—who repeatedly banned and burned his books—but he attacked the pretensions of his fellow philosophes, whom he considered arrogant and cynical. By the 1770s heroes of the Enlightenment like Voltaire and Diderot had won their battles and had become almost too successful to serve any longer as critics of society. They were masters of the most important academies by then, and in a sense they had themselves become the establishment. For younger writers and thinkers who were critical of the existing distribution of power and patronage, Rousseau remained an inspiration. He was a cultural hero for frustrated intellectuals and reformers, some of whom became revolutionaries in 1789.

What proved to be Rousseau's most famous work, *The Social Contract* (1762), became so only after the French Revolution, which dramatized many of the issues that it raised. The Revolution did more for the book than Rousseau did for the Revolution, which he neither prophesied nor advocated. *The Social Contract* was not meant as a blueprint for revolution but rather as an ideal standard against which the reader might measure his own society. Rousseau did not expect that this standard could be achieved in practice since existing states were too large and complex to allow the kind of participation that was the essence of his vision.

A free society in Rousseau's conception is one in which authority and sovereignty derive from the individual himself. A government that is entirely distinct from the individuals over whom it claims to exercise authority has no validity. In short Rousseau denied the almost universal idea that some men are meant to govern and others to obey. In the ideal polity, an individual has had a role in making the law to which he submits. By obeying it he is thus obeying himself as well as all his fellow citizens. For this reason he is free.

The foundation for a society of this kind lies in a primal act of sovereignty in which each citizen voluntarily subscribes to a social contract that establishes the society's ground rules. The government that is erected under such a contract is a revocable trust. To the perceptive reader *The Social Contract* suggested a community based on the voluntary participation of its members rather than the chance destiny of history or inheritance. The only legitimate "sovereign," then, is the people. This sovereign in turn creates a government that will carry on the day-to-day business of applying the laws.

Rousseau was not advocating majority rule but rather consensus as to the best interest of all citizens, even if it *appears* contrary to the welfare of some. For in fact the best interest of the community must be their best interest too since they are voluntary members of the community. This concept, which Rousseau called the general will, is paradoxical and difficult to grasp. Acceptance of the general will is an act of moral freedom, a very demanding principle. Freedom for the citizen means doing what one *ought*, not what one *wants*. It derives from conscience, which must do battle within the individual against passion, appetite, and self-interest. Thus, to use Rousseau's most striking phrase, the government must occasionally "force its citizens to be free." Freedom cannot exist in a state of nature or in any arrangement dictated by force. It is a tenuous social arrangement involving consent, participation, and subordination of individual self-interest to the commonweal.

More than any of the philosophes, Rousseau understood that the issue of freedom—one of the Enlightenment's central concerns—cannot be dealt with simply in terms of individual autonomy and well-being. The moral freedom of a man depends on the arrangements governing the collectivity of men.

Shortly after the French Revolution began in 1789, conservatives such as the Irish statesman Edmund Burke charged the philosophes with causing it. Burke thought the philosophes had subverted their society by consciously undermining all authority, particularly that of the monarchy and the church. As if substantiating Burke's claim, but in an opposite spirit, many revolutionaries made a cult of the memory of Voltaire and Rousseau. All this has confused the issue of the actual nature and impact of the Enlightenment.

The philosophes, most of whom had died by the 1770s, were far from being incipient revolutionaries. Members of Europe's cultural elite, they intended only that their society gradually reform itself. Distrustful of the uneducated masses, afraid of sedition and popular anarchy, they had everything to fear from a revolutionary upheaval. They were critics of their society but not its subverters.

Nonetheless the Enlightenment did challenge the traditional values of European society. From Voltaire's early polemics against Christianity through the sober social science of the Encyclopedia *and the impassioned writings of Rousseau, new ideas and new modes of thought were diffused among important elements of Europe's educated classes. The philosophes did not offer new doctrines such as Socialism for men to implement. Rather they challenged the automatic respect for convention and authority, promoting the habit of independent-minded reflection and the conviction that change was both necessary and possible.*

In and of themselves the crusades of the philosophes against religion and against glaring contemporary abuses were by no means revolutionary. But they promoted a climate in which the status quo was gradually put on the defensive and in which revolution—when provoked under other circumstances—was not unthinkable.

RECOMMENDED READING

Sources

* Crocker, L. G. (ed.). *The Age of Enlightenment.* 1969.
* Gendzier, Stephen J. (ed.). *Denis Diderot: The Encyclopedia: Selections.* 1967.
* Manuel, Frank E. (ed.). *The Enlightenment.* 1965.
Rousseau, Jean Jacques. *The Social Contract and Discourses.* 1950.
* Voltaire. *The Portable Voltaire.* 1949, 1977.

Studies

* Behrens, C. B. *The Ancien Régime.* 1967. A long essay tying together society, culture, and government. Abundantly illustrated.
Bruford, W. H. *Germany in the Eighteenth Century: The Social Background of the Literary Revival.* 1952.
* Cassirer, Ernst. *The Question of Jean-Jacques Rousseau.* 1963.
Cobban, Alfred. *In Search of Humanity.* 1960. A dry but useful discussion of the major philosophes.
* Cragg, G. R. *The Church and the Age of Reason, 1648–1789.* 1966.
* Ford, Franklin. *Robe and Sword: The Regrouping of the French Aristocracy After Louis XIV.* 1953. Should be read in conjunction with Montesquieu's ideas.
* Gay, Peter. *Voltaire's Politics: The Poet as Realist.* 1959. A lively and sympathetic portrait.

Hampson, Norman. *A Cultural History of the Enlightenment.* 1969. Possibly too interpretive to serve as an introduction, it nonetheless presents the subject most interestingly. (For a more advanced study see Peter Gay's two-volume work, *The Enlightenment: An Interpretation,* 1966 & 1969.)
Herr, Richard. *The Eighteenth-Century Revolution in Spain.* 1958. Absolutism and Enlightenment in Spain—a case study not discussed in the present text.
Kors, Alan. *D'Holbach's Coterie: An Enlightenment in Paris.* 1976.
Korshin, P. J. (ed.). *The Widening Circle: Essays on the Circulation of Literature in Eighteenth-Century Europe.* 1976.
* Krieger, Leonard. *Kings and Philosophers, 1689–1789.* 1970. A good introduction to eighteenth-century thought and government.
Malcolmson, R. W. *Popular Recreations in English Society, 1700–1850.* 1973.
* Paulson, Ronald. *Hogarth: His Life, Art, and Times* (abridged ed.). 1974.
Schackleton, R. *Montesquieu.* 1961.
Venturi, Franco. *Italy and the Enlightenment.* 1972. Essays on important Italian philosophes by a leading historian.
* Watt, Ian. *The Rise of the Novel: Studies of Defoe, Richardson, and Fielding.* 1957.
Wilson, Arthur. *Diderot.* 1972. An exhaustive, masterful biography.

---

* Available in paperback.

TWENTY

REVOLUTIONS OF THE EIGHTEENTH CENTURY

The eighteenth century forms a bridge in Western history between two fundamentally distinct epochs. Europe in 1700—the Europe of the "old regime"—largely preserved the institutions and the way of life that it had acquired over the long centuries of the past. In 1700 the economy remained based predominantly upon agriculture. People were aided in their labors by animals, wind, and water, but their technology offered them comparatively little help. In social and political life, inequality was the rule. Kings and emperors, who claimed to hold their authority directly from God, presided over realms which were composed of distinct orders or estates, each with its own obligations and privileges.

In contrast, the European society of 1800 was witnessing violent upheavals at every level. Western man had begun a radical transformation of his methods of raising food and producing goods. This Industrial Revolution, which continues in our day, achieved a stunning conquest of the material world, restructured society, changed all aspects of Western life in its early phases, and now offers similar promises and poses similar problems to all the peoples of the earth.

Concurrently with the inauguration of the Industrial Revolution, profound changes were undermining the peace of Western society. As we have seen, the leaders of the Enlightenment broke with traditional religious assumptions; they denied that morality and social order had to be based on divine revelation and supernatural grace. Human reason could replace or was equivalent to the word of God. In a larger context growing numbers of men—not only from the middle classes but from the older privileged orders as well—had come to believe that society was ill-served by traditional institutions, and they agitated powerfully to reform them. The demand for reform bore as its principal fruit the great revolutions that swept across wide areas of both Europe and North America in the late eighteenth century.

The latter 1700s thus initiate the great age of revolutions in the West. Of course all periods of the Western past have experienced change, and all have contributed to the making of our present society. But the economic changes and popular revolts begun toward the end of the century hold a pivotal position in the growth and transformation of Western civilization. Perhaps no other movements have left such visible marks on the character of our modern life —our government, our economy, and our social ideals.

I. THE INDUSTRIAL SYSTEM

Since the eighteenth century, the economy of the Western world has been in nearly continuous transformation. Humankind has achieved spectacular efficiency in raising food, producing goods, amassing wealth, multiplying itself, and changing the face of the earth. While no one can be certain, it is probable that more human beings are alive today than inhabited the earth over all the millennia before 1700. In a series of lectures given in 1880–1881, a young sociologist and economist at Oxford University named Arnold Toynbee chose (though he did not coin) the phrase "Industrial Revolution" to describe this metamorphosis.[1]

CHARACTERISTICS OF AN INDUSTRIAL ECONOMY

With a fund of information unavailable to Toynbee, it is easy to criticize the term that he more than anyone made part of the historical vocabulary. It does not for example encompass changes in agriculture or transportation, without which the Industrial Revolution properly speaking would not have occurred. The traditional dates for it in Great Britain, 1760 to 1815 or 1830, are much too confined. If great factories are the mark of an industrial society, Britain and even more the Continent would have to be considered still underdeveloped by 1830. The revolution did not end in 1830. Indeed the great advances based on the spread of the railroads, the application of chemistry to manufacturing, and the development of electrical power and the internal combustion engine did not affect the economy until the middle and late nineteenth century; moreover computers, atomic power, and automation carry the changes forward into our own future.

There are then many industrial revolutions, and they cannot be considered as marked off by precise dates. Nor was the initial transformation confined to manufacturing. But most historians would be reluctant to deny

that there was a period beginning in the late eighteenth century, initially in Great Britain, when profound changes occurred in the production of goods and food that eventually equipped a significant part of the Western world with a kind of economy unknown in all prior historical ages. This is the period of what is conventionally called the Industrial Revolution.

What essentially distinguishes an industrial, or modern, economy from the traditional economies of previous epochs? Arnold Toynbee and many later writers equated the Industrial Revolution with the application of steam power to manufacturing, which brought about the factory system. The steam engine, used to drive mills from the 1780s on, destroyed the putting-out system of domestic industry, in which artisans worked at home with their own tools on materials delivered to them by merchants or entrepreneurs. The use of steam power required that the workers congregate in great mills or factories, and they thus came to form a new social unit. But the emergence of the factory system does not seem today an adequate explanation of this economic transformation. In agriculture and transportation there were no factories; yet the progress in these economic sectors was an essential component of the Industrial Revolution, as noted before.

Perhaps the most distinctive feature of an industrial economy is its capacity for sustained growth. Its productivity is so great that it is able not only to meet its current consumption needs and replace its worn tools but also to invest in new capital equipment, which expands its means of producing. In short the wealth produced, the capital equipment, and the economy will not be the same at the end of a given period as they were at the beginning. The essential feature of an industrial economy —we might say of a modern society, in contrast to all societies we have studied so far—is that it never stays the same. Far more than in

---

[1] Arnold Toynbee was the uncle of Arnold J. Toynbee, the distinguished author of *A Study of History*, perhaps the most ambitious effort at developing a philosophy of history to appear in recent years. His own lectures on the Industrial Revolution were compiled and edited by friends after his death in 1883, at the age of thirty.

any other age, continuous, rapid, and all-pervasive change has been the law of Western life since the eighteenth century.

Of course the whole of European economic history before the Industrial Revolution cannot be described as stable and changeless. It would clearly be misleading to link together the Europe of Charlemagne and the Europe of the sixteenth and seventeenth centuries as if they were equally representative of a preindustrial, or traditional, economy. Preindustrial societies can experience profound changes; witness the agricultural and commercial expansion of the Central Middle Ages and the commercial boom of the sixteenth century. The economy advances, but after a spurt of growth it tends to stabilize, though on a higher plateau of productivity. The reason for this is that changes in the capacity to produce set in motion changes in levels of consumption, which absorb the new output and limit further capital investments. A society that attains some new wealth may elect to spend it on supporting a larger population or on raising the standard of living. A balance is reestablished between production and consumption, and investment is reduced. The economy has not achieved the capacity of self-sustaining growth. It is not industrial or modern.

Preconditions of Industrialization

To achieve self-sustaining growth, a society must first satisfy what many economists today call preconditions. A major obstacle to industrialization is a highly skewed distribution of wealth, which distorts the structure of demand. If a narrow aristocracy absorbs nearly all the disposable income, the economy, beyond meeting the subsistence needs of the people, will organize itself largely to serve the wealthy few. Catering to the desires of the rich, the economy will produce expensive goods, often exquisite in quality and workmanship, but always in small quantities. This structure of demand, which was widely char-

acteristic of European states in the old regime, will not easily support a change in the mode of production, which, at least initially, will tend to sacrifice quality of product to quantity of output. A powerful demand for cheap goods, mass-produced, is a prerequisite for the beginnings of industrialism.

The society which seeks to industrialize must also possess certain substantial, uncommitted resources. Poor utilization of resources is a mark of preindustrial economies. It must also contain a large and mobile population, with a high percentage of skilled and productive workers. It must further have adequate facilities for transporting raw materials to factories, products to market, and people to wherever they are needed. Efficient means of recruiting or forming capital are also essential, as continued economic growth is critically dependent upon a high rate of reinvestment. And leaders are needed who place a high premium on industrial growth, who can influence the decisions of government in its favor, and who have the freedom to introduce radical changes into established modes of production.

In broadest terms, industrialization requires a social milieu favorable to change and innovation. In the Europe of the old regime, many institutions, practices, and attitudes tended to dampen incentive, fix individuals to their station in life, and obstruct entrepreneurial freedom. The existence, widespread across Europe, of feudal or seigneurial rents and tolls—forced payments to lords for which they gave no compensation and rendered no service in return—hampered economic improvements, as increased production would largely benefit these parasitic groups. In the opinion of some economists, a set of property rights which rewards primarily those individuals who are engaged in socially beneficial activities is a precondition for industrialization. In the typical village of northern Europe, under the open-field system (see pp. 173–174), each cultivator had to follow the same routines of working the soil; he was not free to change his methods of farming without the concurrence of his neighbors. In the towns, the guilds presented a major obstacle to economic innovation. Guild regulations, which in the eighteenth century were more exactly government regulations enforced by the guilds, prescribed the techniques to be used in production and often dictated the terms and conditions under which goods could be sold, apprentices taken on, or workers hired. In sum, the guilds in the towns, like the villages in the countryside, exerted a kind of collective management over production. By restricting competition they tended to help weak members at the expense of the strong. On the other hand, the town guild, again like the rural village, blocked innovation, froze technology, and discouraged effort.

Another policy of the old regime which obstructed innovation was the licensing of monopoly companies, with exclusive rights to trade in certain regions, such as the East Indies, or to manufacture certain products. With assured markets and profits, these companies were not likely to assume the risks of new ventures, and they blocked others from doing so. Entrepreneurial effort may also have been discouraged by a cultural attitude, which still lingered in European society, that money made in trade or manufacture was somehow tainted. Particularly on the Continent, the highest aspiration of the successful businessman seems often to have been the purchase of a noble title.

The preconditions of industrialization are, in other words, political and cultural, as well as economic. From the mid-eighteenth century on, Enlightenment reformers—the physiocrats in France, Adam Smith and the liberal economists in England—launched concentrated attacks against communal management of land in the countryside, the guild control of industry in the towns, and privilege and monopoly

in all forms. In the name of economic rationalism, they denounced both the special advantages held by a favored few and special consideration extended to the poor and weak; enlightened society should countenance no privilege and no pity. Their hard but telling logic slowly affected policy. Guilds were already weak in the countryside and in towns of recent growth, like Manchester and Birmingham in England. Also, new industries, such as cotton manufacturing, largely escaped their supervision. The government of revolutionary France, in the Le Chapelier law of 1791, permanently outlawed guilds and trade associations. In the Corporation Act of 1835, the British Parliament similarly abolished the guilds, but they had long since become ineffective in their function of regulating the economy. The government policy of chartering monopolies was gradually abandoned (the English East India Company, for example, lost its exclusive trading rights in India in 1813). Legally and socially, the entrepreneur was winning unprecedented freedom.

Finally, the degree of effort made to industrialize is also decisive. Small increments in production will likely be offset by equal increases in consumption to support more babies or allow the population an improved standard of living. To sustain a high rate of reinvestment in the face of these demands, the effort must exceed a certain critical minimum.[2] Industrialization cannot be achieved slowly, by small or leisurely steps over time. It requires a strong drive—as Toynbee called it, a revolution.

THE FRONT RUNNERS: GREAT BRITAIN AND FRANCE

Of all the countries of Europe, Great Britain best satisfied the preconditions of industriali-

[2] Cf. Harvey Leibenstein, *Economic Backwardness and Economic Growth: Studies in the Theory of Economic Development.* 1967.

zation. The community was large enough to achieve significant economies of scale with relatively minor improvements in production; that is, it could reduce costs and thus save capital outlay per unit by increasing the volume of production. A contributory factor was the excellent balance of resources within the modest dimensions of the English realm. The plain to the south and east, which contained the traditional centers of English settlement, was fertile and productive. The uplands to the west and north contained rich deposits of coal and iron, and their streams had given power to mills since the Late Middle Ages.

The sea too was a major resource, for no part of the island kingdom was distant from it. At a time when water transport offered the sole economical means for moving bulky commodities, the sea brought coal close to iron, raw materials close to factories, and products close to markets. Equally important, it provided contact with distant shores. Foreign trade stimulated the economy with new or better products, such as cottons from India, that industries at home attempted to imitate.

Moreover, in the late eighteenth century, Britain witnessed a considerable expansion of canals and turnpikes. Usually short in this compact land, they were cheap to build and profitable to operate. By 1815 the country possessed some 2,600 miles of canals. In addition there were few institutional obstructions to the movement of goods. United under a strong central government since the Middle Ages, Britain was free of internal tariff barriers. Merchants everywhere counted in the same money, measured their goods by the same standards, and conducted their affairs under the protection of common law. In France, according to Voltaire's sarcastic comment, one changed laws as frequently as horses when traveling by stagecoach across it.

Other characteristics of Britain's society made her ripe for the broadcast changes of the Industrial Revolution. The population had a long tradition of skill and could adapt rather easily to the personal and collective discipline required by the factory system. In about 1700, the standard of living of the English masses was probably the highest in Europe. English society was also considerably less stratified than that on the Continent, and the propertied classes tended to be oriented toward innovation. Primogeniture was the rule among both the peers (the titled members of the House of Lords) and the country gentlemen or squires, and the need to provide for their frequently large families encouraged them to increase their estates and revenues. From their ranks came the so-called "improving landlords." Their younger sons, left without lands, had to seek careers in other walks of life, many of them in commerce and manufacturing. They frequently recruited capital for their ventures from their landed (and sometimes titled) fathers and elder brothers. Capital, therefore, like people, frequently crossed class lines in England. Another important pool of entrepreneurs was the considerable number of English religious dissenters, chiefly Calvinists and Quakers, who concentrated their energies on business enterprises because they were denied careers in government or the church.

The responsiveness of the propertied elements to investment opportunities was a remarkable feature of English society in the eighteenth century and one of the chief reasons why Britain was the home of the Industrial Revolution. These entrepreneurs and investors had a relatively greater influence on government than comparable groups on the Continent. Since the revolution of 1688, the government had been particularly sensitive to the interests of the propertied classes. They in turn had confidence in the government. The close ties between property and power facilitated the economic growth of the realm and was one important reason for the relative stability of the British regime in this age of revolutions.

Historians are not sure exactly what precipitated the takeoff of the eighteenth-century British economy or even what sectors led others in the industrializing effort. At one time scholars stressed the work of individual leaders, the improving landlords in agriculture or inventors and entrepreneurs in the cotton industry. Today it is generally recognized that agricultural changes came only slowly and that the growth of the cotton industry, however rapid, still accounted for only a small part of England's gross national product. Historians are thus inclined to lay greater emphasis on broad economic stimuli felt in several sectors simultaneously. One recently formulated theory, partially Marxist in inspiration, stresses the economic and political exploitation of overseas colonies as the critical stimulus in early industrialization. Colonies offered a huge market for inexpensive goods, especially cotton fabrics, which the new machines produced most efficiently. They provided cheap raw materials, and the large profits of the colonial trade promoted the formation of industrial capital.

Overseas trade was certainly booming in the eighteenth century, and certainly gave a powerful thrust to industrialization. Still the possession and exploitation of a colonial empire could not of itself assure early industrialization—witness Spain, Portugal, or Holland. Probably no less important was the growth of home population, which assured an enlarged domestic market and an abundance of cheap labor. Cultural changes may also have had an effect in that many men were willing to risk replacing old methods by new, and on other planes people were questioning and transforming traditional ways of thought and behavior. Then too the industrial growth itself, once initiated, seems to have exerted a reciprocal influence on trade, population, and attitudes.

The processes of this first industrialization

THE GROWTH OF ENGLAND'S FOREIGN TRADE IN THE EIGHTEENTH CENTURY

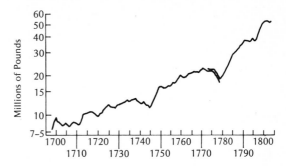

Three-year moving averages of combined imports and exports. (Adapted from Dean, Phyllis, and Cole, W. A., *British Economic Growth, 1688–1959*, Cambridge, 1964, p. 49.)

are thus highly complex and still not entirely understood. What seems certain is that a strong demand for cheap goods was growing at home and abroad in the eighteenth century, that important segments of the British community perceived this opportunity and responded to it, and that resources in England were abundant enough to support fundamental changes in traditional methods of production.

In Continental Europe France came closest to Britain in meeting the preconditions of industrialization in the eighteenth century. But the French economy labored under handicaps. France was larger, and the expense of transportation grew rapidly with distance. Waterways were not so conveniently distributed, and roads were miserable even in the age of Louis XIV's minister Colbert. Internal tariffs at provincial borders continued to restrain trade. In 1664 Colbert had created an area of free trade that embraced the older central provinces of the monarchy, but beyond it tariffs, tolls, and seigneurial dues burdened commerce. Merchants in the northeastern provinces of the Franche-Comté and Alsace for example found it easier to trade with the imperial cities of the Rhineland than with

Paris. Contrasts in legal systems and in weights and measures further complicated and slowed exchange.

After 1715 France enjoyed some seventy-five years nearly free from foreign invasions and internal uprisings; this was the calm before the terrible storms of the Revolution. The period of peace saw a remarkable proliferation of communications arteries. By 1738 the Picardy Canal linked the Somme and Oise rivers in the north. The Central Canal, built between 1783 and 1793, joined the Loire and Saône. Work was begun in 1777 on the Burgundy Canal, which enabled barges to move from the English Channel to the Mediterranean. The improvement of French roads, given major attention by Philibert Orry, a chief financial officer under Louis XV, was perhaps even more impressive. In 1738, he imposed a heavy corvée on the parishes, requiring from them contributions in labor for the construction and maintenance of roads. About a decade later the government founded the Ecole des Ponts et Chaussées ("School of Bridges and Roads"), which soon became probably the best engineering school in Europe and which still functions today. By the late eighteenth century, France had acquired a magnificent system of royal highways that many contemporaries considered unsurpassed in Europe.

Foreign trade expanded too, especially with the West Indies and the Levant, despite the military reversals in North America and India. The number of French ships engaged in foreign commerce increased about fourfold between 1716 and 1789; on the eve of the Revolution, some 1,800 vessels showed the French flag. In the same period exports of manufactured products rose by 221 percent and all other commodities by 298 percent. The great ports of Bordeaux and Marseilles enjoyed a period of prosperity unequaled since the Middle Ages.

Stable coinage aided the financing of enterprises. In 1726 the government fixed the value of the principal gold coin, the louis, and kept it stable for the remaining years of the old regime—a remarkable feat in the light of the monarchy's desperate financial needs. The collapse of John Law's investment scheme in 1720 had a regressive effect on French banking, to be sure. French investors developed a lasting suspicion of banks, paper money, and joint-stock companies. Businessmen tended to rely on resources that they or their close relatives could muster and preferred to deal in hard cash rather than commercial paper. Small size, small capital, and conservative management worked to hold back French business enterprises. But this only dampened, not suppressed, the boom of the eighteenth century.

II. ECONOMICS AND DEMOGRAPHY

The birth of the new economic system required the development of effective ways of recruiting, managing, and channeling capital into those enterprises with the greatest potential for profit. The commercial capitalism of the previous centuries was thus gradually being transformed into industrial capitalism. Changes in monetary practices affected trade and prices, and price movements had a major impact not only upon the economy but upon government as well. At a still more fundamental level, these economic changes influenced the patterns of marriages, births, and deaths in European society. In fact, they helped stimulate a population explosion, which in turn had a powerful repercussion on European life.

FINANCIAL MANAGEMENT

Critical to the takeoff of the industrialization process is a high rate of reinvestment, which in turn depends on the skillful management of money by both individuals and public institutions. Here again Great Britain was the most advanced country of Europe. From the sixteenth century on, the demands of overseas trade promoted the formation of joint-stock companies. By the seventeenth century, great concerns controlling trade with India, the South Seas, Africa, and the Levant were dominating England's overseas commerce. The financial panic in 1720 caused by the collapse of the South Sea Bubble prompted Parliament to pass the so-called Bubble Act, which required that all joint-stock ventures secure a royal charter. This limited the formation of stock companies, for a charter was difficult and expensive to obtain. Eventually, however, the joint-stock company was to become as much the child of modern capitalism as the factory.

The early industrial enterprises, chiefly partnerships, could rely on a growing banking system to meet their capital needs. In the seventeenth century the goldsmiths of London had assumed the functions of bankers. They accepted and guarded deposits, extended loans, transferred upon request credits from one account to another, and changed money. In the eighteenth century banking services became available beyond London; country banks, of which there were 300 in 1780, numbered more than 700 in 1810. The English businessman was familiar with bank notes and other forms of commercial papers, and his confidence in paper facilitated the recruitment and flow of capital.

The founding of the Bank of England in 1694 itself marked an epoch in the history of European finance. It enjoyed a phenomenal success in the eighteenth century as it has since. It assumed responsibility for managing the public debt and sold shares in the debt (equivalent to shares in the bank) to the public. It faithfully met the interest payments due to the shareholders, with the help of government revenues it was given to administer, and simultaneously placed at the disposal of the

government financial resources unavailable to any Continental state. The bank was so well run that it may have attracted investments away from the private sector of the economy. But stability in government finance also assured stability in the entire money market. Moreover the system also enlisted the tax powers of the government in the cause of industrialization. Taxes and interest payments took money from the mass of the people, who were likely to consume it, and gave it to the wealthy, who were likely to invest it. Some kind of forced savings was probably essential in preserving the high rate of reinvestment essential for industrialization.

PRICES

The eighteenth century in Britain and in France and other regions of the West as well was thus an age of increasing wealth, but the economy did not expand steadily. Rather it experienced periods of sharp fluctuation, of rapid growth and severe decline, of boom and bust. French scholars have made particularly rigorous studies of the economic cycles of the period in France as revealed primarily through the history of prices. Their analyses have provided a new and powerful if sometimes controversial tool for investigating social change in eighteenth-century France and for interpreting the French Revolution itself.[3] We are less well informed concerning price movements and business cycles in other parts of Europe and in North America, but the available information suggests that the economy in these societies was behaving comparably to France's.

For the first thirty years of the eighteenth century, prices in France and apparently in

---

[3] The French historian E. Labrousse has written the fundamental studies on price movements in eighteenth-century France; see especially his *La crise de l'économie française à la fin de l'Ancien Régime et au debut de la Révolution.* 1944.

England too remained stable. The economy similarly remained relatively stagnant, one reason being the exhaustion of the European states during the War of the Spanish Succession and the difficult decade and a half of readjustment following it. The economic eighteenth century, as some French scholars call it, began about 1730 and lasted until about 1817, the time of the peace settlements following the Napoleonic wars. Inflation in prices dominated the era. Since French money was kept stable after 1726, the strong upward movement must be attributed to other causes. The great increase in foreign trade brought a new abundance of precious metals to Europe, especially gold from Brazil. But primarily, as we shall see further, the price rise reflected the pressures of a growing population and a growing demand for food, land, goods, and employment.

The present-day reconstruction of price movements in the eighteenth century distinguishes four periods:

1. Phase A: inflation. After 1730 prices moved slowly upward. The movement accelerated between 1758 and 1770, bringing prosperity to some segments at least of French society and making these years the "splendor of Louis XV."
2. Phase B: depression. Prices leveled off about 1770 and began to move downward after 1778. The next decade was one of hard times, which aggravated the financial difficulties of the government.
3. The Revolution cycle. From 1787 to 1791 a series of bad harvests raised the prices of grain. Striking after a protracted period of hard times, these shocks helped precipitate the social and political crisis that ended France's "*ancien régime*," the Old Regime.
4. Continuation of phase A, inflation and prosperity, after 1791.

Over the long term the inflation did not affect all products, all sectors of the economy, and all segments of society equally. Prices in France between 1726 and 1789 increased by an average of about 65 percent. The cost of cereals, the basic food for the poor, rose slightly more than the average and considerably more than other agricultural products, such as wine and meat. Rents rose sharply, suggesting a shortage of available land; in relation to averages for the decade of the 1730s, rents paid in money had grown by 98 percent in the years 1786–1790. Wages on the other hand increased by a meager 22 percent in the same period, which would point to a glut of workers competing for employment.

These differentials had important social and economic effects. High rents in the countryside and low wages in the city took wealth from the poor and delivered it to the landlord and employer. This movement of money particularly benefited the entrepreneurial groups. Inflation helped drive many of the poor from the soil, to the advantage of their better-off neighbors, who were eager to expand their holdings; it was thus a principal cause of acute rural unrest. In the city it enabled the industrial entrepreneur to sell his goods for more and pay his workers less. Burdening the poor, it also worked against the economically inactive members of society—the nobles, for example, who lived from fixed rents or dues set in money. Inflation hurt the government too, for its revenues did not grow so fast as its expenditures. A large portion of French lands, owned by the aristocracy or the clergy, was tax-exempt. The government therefore relied primarily on indirect taxation that weighed on the lower classes, and they controlled less and less of the national wealth. Inflation was thus shrinking the traditional tax base of the French monarchy and paving the way for financial crisis.

These price changes were in turn influenced

by another factor, which also helped make the eighteenth century an age of revolutions—an enormous increase in the numbers of Europeans.

POPULATION

What some French historians now call the demographic eighteenth century began about 1730. Reasonable estimates put the population growth of Europe at between 60 and 80 percent over the following 100 years. Probably never before had Western Europe experienced so rapid and substantial an increase in its people, and never has it since. (In Eastern Europe, especially the lands of the Russian Empire, a comparable population explosion occurred after 1860.) The growth was particularly marked in Great Britain and France. England grew from an estimated 5 million people in 1700 to more than 9 million in 1801, the date of the first British census. Swelled by continuous immigration and a high birth rate, the population of England's North American colonies grew at probably twice the English rate —from an estimated 275,000 in 1700 to 3.93 million in 1790. The French, according to various estimates, numbered 16 to 19 million at the death of Louis XIV, in 1715, and probably 26 million or more in 1789. With an estimated 18 percent of the total population in Europe about 1750, France was by far the most populous nation in the West; the Russian Empire alone surpassed her, and only by a few million. Her proportion of Europe's inhabitants reached its peak in the age of the Revolution and Napoleon, after which it fell continuously until the present generation. The country's military and political dominance of Europe under Napoleon was in no small measure founded on this demographic preponderance.

Spain increased from perhaps 7 to 10 million and the Italian states from 9 to 13 million. Prussia was growing more rapidly, from perhaps 1.7 to 3.1 million. But all these countries remained thinly populated in comparison with France, and they were not to feel the full pressures emanating from population growth until the following century.

Much mystery surrounds the reasons for this population explosion. Historians once spoke with confidence of a "demographic transition." According to this simple and appealing theory, the population in traditional societies reproduces itself at a rate close to the biological maximum, but its growth is impeded by an equivalently high death rate. The immediate impact of industrialization is a reduction of the death rate, principally through improved measures of public health. The yawning gap between the steady birth rate, which continues high, and the dropping death rate results in substantial expansion of total numbers. Eventually, however, in the later stages of industrialization, the birth rate declines, settles to equilibrium with the death rate, and this slows to a halt the further growth of population.

The most recent research in historical demography has questioned and modified, without entirely rejecting, this classical model. The system of reproduction prevailing in traditional European society seems to have been homeostatic or self-adjusting: that is, birth rates rarely attained the biological maximum, but tended to vary in exact correspondence with death rates. This assured a stable population, which lived well within its available resources. The initial break with this homeostatic system involved births rather than deaths. In England, for example, according to rough but reliable estimates, the birth rate rose from 33.6 per thousand population in the first half of the eighteenth century to 39.7 in the latter half, a peak never since attained. Thereafter the English birth rate entered upon a path of slow, irregular but eventually substantial decline.

TABLE 20.1
THE VITAL REVOLUTION IN IRELAND

YEAR	MILLIONS OF PERSONS	YEAR	MILLIONS OF PERSONS
1712	2.8	1781	4.0
1718	2.9	1785	4.0
1725	3.0	1788	4.4
1732	3.0	1791	4.8
1754	3.2	1821	6.8
1757	3.5	1831	7.8
1772	3.6	1841	8.2
1777	3.7		

Ireland, thinly settled in the seventeenth century, experienced one of the highest rates of population growth in western Europe from c. 1700 until 1841. The increase was closely associated with the spread of potato cultivation, but it cannot be determined whether the potato removed previous limits on population size, or whether the population, growing for other reasons, turned more and more to that easily cultivated plant. The figures to 1791 are adopted from K. H. Connell, *The Population of Ireland* (Oxford, 1950), p. 25. The later figures are from official censuses.

Why did births initially increase? A likely explanation is that the booming commerce and new industries created jobs. Jobs in turn enabled young persons to depart early from the homes in which they grew up, to marry, and to begin families sooner than would otherwise have been possible. Ready employment also favored procreation; children could earn wages at early ages and were more an asset than a burden to their families. Still, this spurt in births may have occurred in advance of significant economic expansion. Did incremented births stimulate the economy, or did a stimulated economy encourage births? Historians can only affirm that the two were intimately connected.

The impact of industrialization upon deaths was slow in appearing and equally complex. In many ways, the industrial system aided people to longer lives. Established trading networks and cheap transport allowed food to be carried efficiently over great distances, and took the edge off most years of famine and dearth. Living standards, fluctuating but slowly improving, led to better care for children and the sick and better nutrition and hygiene for all. Cheap, plentiful, and washable cotton garments allowed new levels of personal cleanliness. Soon, cheap iron pipes brought clean water into households and carried sewage away, both moved by the cheap power of steam. Medical advances such as the development of the vaccination helped protect the population. On the other hand, the growth of large cities introduced millions into a biologically unfavorable environment. In many great European cities, death rates did not sink below birth rates until the second half of the nineteenth century. In most great European cities, infant mortality remained stubbornly high for well into the twentieth century.

Still, over the long term, the death rate was declining, and it fell more rapidly than the relative number of births. The theory of a demographic transition retains a certain crude validity. But it is not at all a full description of the behavior of the population in the period of industrialization. As research continues we may hope to learn more concerning this basic change in the terms of human life, one of the great turning points in Western history.

III. AGRICULTURE

The term "Industrial Revolution" misleadingly conveys that the economic changes of the time were confined to the cities, but in fact the countryside too was necessarily affected. In England in 1700, an estimated 80 percent of the population lived directly from agriculture; by about 1800 that portion had fallen to approximately 40 percent. This massive shift of labor and resources from agriculture to industry would have been inconceivable had the countryside not been able to supply a greater abundance of food with a reduced amount of labor. To be sure, change came only slowly to rural areas, especially on the Continent; the peasant cultivators clung tenaciously to traditional ways. But significant improvements were still achieved in agricultural methods, and these in turn enabled the countryside to supply the industrial towns with food, labor, capital, and markets.

THE ENCLOSURE MOVEMENT IN GREAT BRITAIN

The considerable improvement that Britain experienced in agricultural technology in the eighteenth century contributed greatly to her industrialization. In any agricultural system the central problem is the restoration of fertility to the soil, especially after repeated harvests. Since the Early Middle Ages, farmers in Europe had relied principally on resting their lands periodically under the two- and three-field system of crop rotation (see Chapter 6). This allowed bacteria in the soil to take needed nitrogen from the air. A quicker method, heavy manuring, could not be used widely because the poorly productive farms could not support sufficient animals.

The secret of improving agricultural productivity lay in suppressing the fallow periods. This required that more animals be produced to provide the necessary fertilizer. One of the first of the British landlords to seek a solution was Jethro Tull, an agriculturist and inventor. Much of his work was impeded by false assumptions prevalent in the first half of the eighteenth century—for example that plants actually devour the soil and that animal fertilizer is bad for them. But the zeal with which he conducted his experiments proved infectious. He also designed a horse-drawn hoe and a mechanical seeder, early steps in the mechanization of agriculture.

By the late eighteenth century, Norfolk, in the east of England, had achieved particular prominence for its techniques of "high farming." In the 1730s Tull's contemporary Charles "Turnip" Townshend stressed, as his nickname suggests, the value of using turnips and other field crops in a rotation system of planting instead of letting the land lie fallow. Some five decades later Thomas William Coke wrote extensively on field grasses, new fertilizers such as oil-cake and bone manure, and the principles of efficient estate management. The eighteenth-century high farmers also experimented with the selective breeding of animals. Coke improved the Suffolk breed of pigs, adding to the advances made by Robert Bakewell, a generation his senior, who had developed the Leicestershire breed of sheep and dramatically increased the weight of marketed cattle.

To make use of the new methods, the improving farmers had to be free to manage the land as they saw fit. This was all but impossible under the open-field system, which had dominated the countryside since the Middle Ages. Characteristically even the largest landlords held their property in numerous elongated strips that were open to the land of their neighbors. Owners of contiguous strips had to follow the same routines of cultivation. One could not raise grasses to graze cattle when another was raising wheat. The village as a whole determined what routines should be followed and was thus the effective manager of each holding. The village also decided such matters as how many cattle each member could graze on common meadows and how much wood he could take from the forest. The open-field system froze the technology of cultivation at the levels attained in the Middle Ages. The landlord who wished to form a compact farm and apply new methods could not function within this framework. He needed the freedom to innovate.

He could gain that freedom only by enclosing his property. But both common law and cost considerations ruled out fencing the long, narrow strips. The entire village had to be enclosed, and this required the agreement of all its members, even the poorest. Voluntary enclosures were thus nigh-on impossible to arrange. There was an alternative, however: an act of Parliament, usually passed in response to a petition, allowing the enclosure of a village even against the opposition of some of its members. The procedure was difficult and expensive. The lands of the village had to be surveyed and redistributed in compact blocks among the members in proportion to their former holdings. Frequently too roads had to be constructed to ensure access to the fields. But over the course of the eighteenth century, the high rents and returns to be earned thanks to the new methods were making enclosures very desirable investments.

The first parliamentary act authorizing the enclosure of a village was registered in 1710, but this recourse was not exercised often until after the 1750s. Then the number of acts soared: 156 passed in 1750–1760 but 906 in 1800–1810. This sweeping change all but eradicated the traditional village and the open-field system from the British countryside.

While the enclosure movement was clearly rational from an economic standpoint, it brought much human misery in its wake. The redistribution of the land deprived the poor of their precious rights in the commons and often left them with tiny, unprofitable plots. Frequently they were forced to sell their holdings to their richer neighbors and seek employment as landless laborers or urban workers.

Historians have interpreted the importance of enclosures in English economic and social history variously. They have viewed the system as a counterpart or even a precondition of industrialization in the cities. The peasant cultivator, thrown off the soil, provided the factories with cheap labor; the productive fields yielded the needed food; the prosperous gentry and its tenants purchased the manufactured products and helped provide industrial capital.

Today research is showing that enclosures did not perhaps mesh quite so neatly with industrialization. There was no massive rural depopulation in their wake; the industrial labor force seems to have recruited its members as much from artisans already established in the towns as from the dislodged rural poor.

On the other hand it would be unwise to discount the importance of this movement. It transformed the English countryside even in a physical sense, giving it the appearance it retains today: the large, verdant fields, neatly defined by hedges and walls. It resulted in the near-disappearance of the peasant cultivator, working his own land in the village of his ancestors. If enclosures did not violently push people to the towns, neither did they encourage growth in rural settlements. They were therefore a major factor in the steady shift of population from countryside to city and in the emergence of the first truly urban, truly industrial society in the modern world.

AGRICULTURE ON THE CONTINENT

Change came more slowly to the countryside in Continental regions. The centers that witnessed the most active development were the Netherlands, the Paris basin and the northeast of France, the Rhineland, and the Po valley—all areas of dense settlement where high prices for food encouraged investments in agricultural improvements. Many great landlords emulated the British in improving methods of cultivation.

Continental farmers also waged a battle for managerial freedom, though it was by no means so sweeping as the English enclosure movement. For example many French villages worked the land under a system similar to the open-field arrangement known as *vaine pâture* ("empty pasture," or fallow). This too required owners to follow the same routines of cultivation as their neighbors, with the village determining the rights of its members on common lands. From the middle of the century on, the representative assemblies of several provinces outlawed obligatory *vaine pâture* and allowed individual owners to enclose their land, and some authorized the division of communal properties. But the French monarchy did not adopt enclosures as national policy, and after 1771 even the provincial governments no longer seem to have authorized or required them. Traces of the medieval village and the medieval countryside thus lasted longer in France and other Continental regions than in England.

There is a further contrast between Great Britain and the Continent that is of considerable interest in social history. Enclosures in Britain led to the domination of rural society by great landlords and prosperous tenant farmers, who usually held the land under long leases. In France on the eve of the Revolution, probably 35 percent of the land was owned by the peasants who worked it. In this regard the French peasants were more favored than those of any other European country, Britain included.

If the soil had been worked efficiently and if the population had remained stable, the distribution of the land would clearly have been socially advantageous. But in fact small peasant proprietors rarely had the resources to adopt new techniques, and their very numbers, apparently growing rapidly, obstructed their efforts. The society of small farmers was therefore vulnerable to population pressures and was easily disturbed by violent movements in prices—two major characteristics of eighteenth-century economic history, as we have seen. Because of poor transportation one region could easily suffer a food shortage or even famine while neighboring areas were enjoying relative plenty. The pattern of land distribution in France and the character of rural society, superficially so favorable to the peasant, was thus also a source of acute unrest in the countryside.

In the regions close to the Mediterranean Sea, difficult geographical and climatic conditions—the often rugged terrain, thin soil, and a dearth of summer rain—did not readily allow the introduction of new techniques. The peasants continued to work their lands much as they had in the Late Middle Ages and for the same poor reward. The eastern regions of the Holy Roman Empire, Poland, and Russia had participated hardly at all in the commercial expansion of the early modern period; capital remained scarce and interest rates high. The political fragmentation of the empire and a paucity of transportation in Poland and Russia limited the size of the markets and the incentives to higher production. Areas close to the Baltic Sea, such as east Prussia, benefited from the growing demand for cereals in Western countries, but on the whole Eastern Europe was not to experience the full force of agricultural change until the next century.

IV. THE NEW SHAPE OF INDUSTRY

In manufacturing, the essential achievement of the Industrial Revolution was an enormous increase in the productivity of labor. This was attributable to two innovations: the development of more efficient tools and machines, and the exploitation of new sources of energy. Economists would call this process "factor substitution," whereby capital, represented by the new tools and machines, was substituted for the skills and energy of men. Initially the new tools were cheap and simple enough to be used by artisans in the home or in small workshops. But the growing complexity of machinery, in particular the application of steam, called into being a new social unit—the factory. The new system of production changed the face of the great European cities and brought in its wake acute new social and political problems.

COAL AND IRON

The most successful innovations of the Industrial Revolution were dependent upon efficient utilization of raw materials, particularly cheap metals such as iron, which could be formed into machines, and cheap fuel such as coal. Countries poorly endowed with these resources (as, for example, the Mediterranean lands of Europe) faced formidable obstacles in their industrial growth. England, on the other hand, was well supplied, and her deposits of coal were found in convenient proximity to her iron ore.

Since the Late Middle Ages, the English economy was handicapped by a shortage of wood, as the once great forests had been progressively cut down. Consequently England turned in ever greater measure to the use of coal as fuel, to heat homes, brew beer and ale, heat the vats for dyeing cloth, or fire the furnaces for making glass, pottery, or bricks. As miners began taking coal from deeper veins, they often penetrated beneath the water table and faced the critical task of pumping out the water. The need for powerful pumps stimulated experiments to harness steam in the late seventeenth century. A successful solution came with the development of the Savery and Watt engines. In the nineteenth century when steam was used to propel ships and trains, coal could be transported cheaply from mine to furnace. This allowed the price of coal to plummet.

In one process, however, coal was not satisfactory: the smelting of iron. Here the fuel had to be burned in direct contact with the iron ore, and mineral impurities in the coal combined with the iron to make an unsatisfactory product. Ironmasters traditionally used charcoal in the making of high-quality, malleable or wrought iron, but charcoal was expensive and the output of wrought iron consequently limited. In 1709 Alexander Darby succeeded in smelting ore with coke prepared from coal, but his invention had little immediate impact on the industry. Ironmasters used coke for smelting pig iron, which could be cast but not worked or machined. To refine the metal into wrought iron or steel they continued to use charcoal.

But the demand for and price of iron rose after 1760, and this stimulated the development of new techniques. In the early 1780s Henry Cort devised the puddling process, the first commercially feasible effort to purify iron using coke alone. This invention freed ironmaking from dependence on forests. Ironmasters were simultaneously growing more adept at utilizing the metal. Perhaps the most skilled of them was John Wilkinson, a man with boundless faith that iron would become the basic building material of the new age. His improved techniques for boring cylinders made both better steam engines and better cannons possible. He built the first iron bridge in the world over the Severn River in 1779, experimented with iron rails, launched an iron boat, and at his death was buried in an iron coffin.

Low-cost metal, which could be precisely machined, and low-cost fuel in turn removed the chief obstacles to major and continuing improvements in the techniques of making goods.

INVENTIONS IN TEXTILE PRODUCTION

In Great Britain the industry that led all others in growth and technological improvements was the manufacture of cotton cloth. Its beginnings were modest; wool had been the traditional basis of urban industry everywhere in Europe. Spinners could not produce a sturdy thread from cotton fiber, so that weavers used it principally in combination with other threads, such as linen or wool.

In the early eighteenth century, several factors gave a powerful stimulus to both techno-

logical development and investment in cotton manufacturing. Trade with India had brought large quantities of muslin, calico, madras, and other fine cottons to England and built a healthy market. Wool could not be painted or printed, and cotton fabrics with bright designs appealed to the tastes of the age. To

In this design of a blast furnace, taken from a French copper engraving of the eighteenth century, the large water wheel powers the bellows, which in turn supply the needed jets of air to raise the temperature of the furnace. The continued importance of water power was a principal reason why many early factories were built in rustic settings. (Photo: The Granger Collection)

limit the competition that Indian cottons offered to domestically produced wool, in 1700 Parliament prohibited the importation of printed calicoes from India, Persia, and China and in 1721 even tried to prohibit the wearing of certain kinds of cotton cloth. By obstructing imports the government unwittingly provided a marvelous opportunity for the domestic entrepreneur. Fortune awaited those who could market cottons comparable in quality and price to those once imported from the East.

The industry thus had a double task: to speed its production processes and to improve the quality of the finished cloth. Spinning could be done by women in conjunction with their daily chores, but weaving was slow and difficult work, almost always done by men. In 1738 John Kay of Lancashire, by profession a clockmaker, invented a flying shuttle, propelled by hammers instead of passed by hand. It accelerated the weaving process, removed restrictions on the width of the cloth, and reduced the number of workers needed on a broadcloth loom.

Now the weavers could work more quickly and efficiently than the spinners. To speed the production of thread and restore equilibrium among the processes of manufacture, James Hargreaves devised his spinning jenny in the mid-1760s. The jenny, like the flying shuttle, required no source of power beyond the worker's muscle, and it could spin between six and eight threads simultaneously; later models could make as many as eighty. About the same time Richard Arkwright produced a spinner called the water frame that drew cotton fibers through rollers and twisted them into thread. Much dispute surrounds Arkwright's claim to this invention; it is likely that he pirated its basic design. But if his originality is questionable, he did possess qualities of imagination, daring, and drive. He was an entrepreneur, one of the first self-made men to lead the Industrial Revolution.

The water frame, as its name suggests, was too large to be driven by human exertion. Arkwright first used horses, but within a few years he built a factory driven by a water mill. In 1785 he adopted the steam engine as his source of power, and the modern factory was born. Technical advances kept apace. A weaver named Samuel Crompton combined the features of the jenny and the water frame into a spinning mule—so called because it was a hybrid—which spun a fine and strong thread, excelling in quality the best Indian product. Once more the equilibrium of the productive processes was disrupted, and the now-slower work of weaving restricted output. In 1784 Edmund Cartwright designed a power loom, though technical difficulties and the violent opposition of weavers limited its use until after the Napoleonic wars.

Other inventions accelerated other processes in cotton manufacturing during the last two decades of the century. An American, Eli Whitney, produced the cotton gin, which mechanized and enormously accelerated the separation of seed from fiber in the raw cotton. Sir Thomas Bell developed a method for printing the cotton cloth on cylindrical copper presses, and British and Continental inventors improved the chemical processes of bleaching and tinting the cloth.

Cotton production soared. Lancashire, with its great city of Manchester, and the neighboring counties became the great centers of cotton manufacture, soon serving the entire world. These were thinly settled areas before the eighteenth century, with few incorporated towns and no established guild systems to obstruct innovation. Lancashire offered the further advantages of water power, coal, and a good harbor, Liverpool. In 1743 England had imported about 1 million pounds of raw cotton; the figure was over 60 million by the turn of the century. And by the early 1820s cotton exports made up 46 percent of Britain's export trade.

HARNESSING STEAM

Arkwright's water frame, Crompton's spinning mule, and Cartwright's power loom all required energy beyond the ability of men or horses to provide. Even earlier, as we have seen, the mining industry had developed a critical need for cheap power. Since ancient times men had noticed that steam exerts strong pressure. The third-century Greek scientist Hero of Alexandria had employed a jet of steam to spin a small wheel; the account of his experiments, translated into English in 1575, helped alert scholars to a simple means by which heat could be converted into motion. However, the first experiments with engines powered by fire were based on another principle: the pressure the atmosphere exerts against a vacuum.

In the seventeenth century several scientists —among them Pascal in France and Otto von Guericke in Germany—proved that the atmosphere has weight. Guericke used atmospheric pressure to push a piston through a cylinder, overcoming the efforts of twenty men to restrain it. Sensational experiments like this one led directly to efforts to construct an "atmospheric engine." To create the vacuum some inventors tried gunpowder, but the fuel was too unstable to control. Steam was more manageable, and before the end of the century, atmospheric machines were being designed both in England and on the Continent that utilized the condensation of steam to create the needed vacuum.

The inventor of what must be considered the first commercially successful atmospheric engine was an Englishman, Thomas Savery, who described it to the public in a book published in 1702 and significantly entitled *The Miner's Friend*. Working as a pump, Savery's invention allowed the steam to come into direct contact with the water it was moving; this condensed the steam, dissipated heat, and rendered the pump woefully inefficient. How-

ever, Savery's engine at least proved that a fire pump was a practical possibility. A decade later another Englishman, Thomas Newcomen, returned to the piston and cylinder design and completely separated the engine from the pump. Although it still wasted a great deal of power, its reintroduction of the piston made it more efficient than Savery's by a third, and Newcomen engines were soon being used not only in Great Britain but in Hungary, Austria, France, and Denmark.

In the 1760s a young mechanic and instrument maker working at the University of Glasgow, James Watt, was given the task of repairing a small Newcomen engine used in scientific lectures. He recognized its two major inefficiencies: its great weight in relation to its power output and the quantities of fuel it required. Fascinated by the problem, he redesigned the machine and made the fundamental change of providing a separate chamber for the spent steam to condense in. His first engine, patented in 1769, was essentially an improved Newcomen engine, still relying on atmospheric pressure for its principal motive force.

But Watt had also recognized the advantage of using the pressure of expanding steam directly. The implementation of this idea took many years and required new levels of precision in machining cylinders and pistons, new designs for valves, and new knowledge of lubricants and the properties of steam itself. Watt's first practical model incorporating this principle, patented in 1782, was nearly three times more efficient than the Newcomen engine, its distant parent. He also devised a system of gears, called the sun and planet, for converting the reciprocating motion of the piston to the rotary motion needed to drive most machines. A still more important invention was the governor, or flywheel, which smoothed the movements of the engine.

Watt's partner, the industrialist Matthew Boulton, shared the merit of placing the inventions at the service of the economy. The site of Boulton's plant was Birmingham, which became the first great center for the manufacture of these new and powerful machines. From the 1780s on the steam engine was giving power to factories as well as pumps; some 500 were built before 1800.

Even these early machines represented a remarkable improvement over traditional sources of power, ranging as they did between 6 and 20 horsepower. The average man working hard can muster about one-tenth horsepower, or about 75 watts. This would not be enough to drive most of the major appliances in American homes today, such as washers, vacuum cleaners, dryers, even beaters and blenders. The horse itself works continuously at a power output of only one-half horsepower. James Watt himself first defined the unit of horsepower as 33,000 foot-pounds per minute, but this could be achieved only by the strongest horses and only for short periods. So poor in power output are animals—men and horses—that even before the advent of the steam engine they were far surpassed by windmills and water mills.

The largest windmills in the eighteenth century could develop probably as much as 50 horsepower, but perhaps two-thirds of this was lost in friction as the power was transmitted from the rotors to the pump or mill. The best water mills of the period seem to have produced 10 horsepower, but most of them rarely surpassed 5. Still, this would replace 10 or more horses and save the miller the expense of feeding and caring for so many animals. With such advantages the construction of water mills rapidly quickened over the course of the eighteenth century; flowing water rather than steam powered the early phases of the Industrial Revolution. But then too sometimes winds ceased and streams froze, and water and wind power could not be transmitted from where it was harnessed to where it was needed. Steam engines could both produce more power more reliably and be placed where they were needed. To the traditional power-starved economy of Great Britain as of the world, the steam engine offered an enormous increment in its capacity to do work. More than any other invention, its appearance marks the advent of a new era.

INDUSTRY ON THE CONTINENT

Industrial growth was much slower on the Continent than in England. The numerous political divisions, tolls and tariffs, and the difficulties of transport restricted the size of markets. Continental society was more stratified than the English and did not develop effective mechanisms for recruiting the sons of nobles and gentry for business careers. It was also apparently less wealthy and could not initially generate a strong demand for industrial products. Business enterprises tended to be small, largely restricted to members of the same family, and cautious in policy. Cultural attitudes still placed high prestige on the life of the country gentleman, and this blocked the flow of men and capital from agriculture to manufactures.

Yet the Continental countries were experiencing important industrial changes, if not a revolution, in the eighteenth century. In France, cotton industries were taking root in Alsace, Normandy, and the region of Lille on the borders of the Austrian Netherlands. At Rouen, in Normandy, the largest center of cotton manufacture, production grew by 107 percent between 1732 and 1766. John Kay introduced his flying shuttle at Rouen in that period, and toward the end of the century the industry, while still comparatively backward, was adopting English-model mechanical spinners. The silk cloth industry, first promoted by Colbert, enjoyed a comparable boom, benefiting from the growing affluence of eighteenth-century fashionable society. At Lyons, the center of silk manufacture with a population of perhaps 143,000, the silk shops alone came to employ some 30,000 workers.

Coal production was also expanding. At Anzin, in northeastern France, one of the earliest centers of large-scale coal mining, output grew by 681 percent between 1744 and 1789. Iron manufacture at first lagged behind. The first foundry utilizing coke rather than charcoal went into operation only in 1769, and the industry's total output increased by only 72 percent in the half-century preceding 1789. Nonetheless, the iron as well as the coal works furnished France early if still restricted examples of the factory system; they also equipped her with an armaments industry destined to serve her well during the wars of the French Revolution.

Switzerland too was a region of early industrial growth. Her ancient mercantile traditions, abundant resources in water power, and strategic position on the passes linking northern and southern Europe gave her distinct advantages in developing cotton manufactures and other forms of light industry. French Flanders (the southern half of the Austrian Netherlands), the valley of the lower Rhine, Silesia (acquired by Prussia in 1741), and Bohemia-Moravia were other centers of modest but real industrial growth, especially in textiles. In Germany and Central Europe the wars and reforms of the French revolutionary period, while frequently disruptive, also served to eradicate many of the institutional obstacles to trade. Growth still came slowly, and no continental region could challenge the industrial supremacy of England before 1850. But well in advance of that date, these areas were laying the basis for a strong leap forward.

While changing its basic methods of raising food and producing goods, European society was also engaged in reforming its fundamental institutions and principles of government.

V. CONSTITUTIONAL CONFLICTS

The great expansion in population, the growth of the economy, and changes visible in almost every other aspect of eighteenth-century life inevitably disturbed the political equilibrium of the European states. Groups within the various societies believed, often with good reason, that these transformations were hurting their interests and that their governments were unresponsive to their legitimate needs. They therefore sought to reform the constitutional structure of the state. The latter half of the century particularly was a period of high social tension, constitutional crises, and spirited debate over the nature and function of government.

THE ESTATES

To understand the nature of the constitutional crises, we must first recall a salient characteristic of government under the old regimes. In virtually all the governments of Europe, a role of major importance was assigned to the corporations of citizens known as estates. By definition an estate was a functional group within society—clerics, who prayed; nobles, who fought and counseled; merchants, who traded; and artisans and peasants, who labored. Birth or appointment gave people admission to the various estates, and membership conferred certain distinctive rights and obligations. Through parliaments or assemblies the estates were also supposed to play a role in making government decisions.

Traditionally the clergy constituted the first estate and the nobles the second, but usually these two groups maintained a common aristocratic viewpoint. The ruler was also an estate, considered a corporation of one in his person —or rather his office; he had, in the political imagery of the day, another body that never died. This is implied in the usual acclamation of subjects at the death of their sovereign: "The king is dead. Long live the king!" Beneath these privileged orders was the estate of the people, the third estate in France or the commons in England. In most European domains this was the most amorphous and the least influential of the constituent bodies of society.

The estates were developing self-awareness and political ambition in the eighteenth century, and most remarkable, in the latter half even the third estate came to exert its latent power. In 1788 a French priest, Emmanuel Joseph Sieyès, posed the question in a pamphlet, "What is the third estate?" He replied simply that it was everything—the entire nation, the people. He noted further that in the past it had been nothing, but now its ambition was to become a force in the state. His assessment of both the past and the future was accurate. The rise to prominence and power of the people at the expense of the hitherto dominant aristocratic orders make this period, as one historian calls it, the "age of the democratic revolution."[4]

MONARCHICAL REFORMS

In the great eighteenth-century struggle over the exercise of power, the ruler was often the first to seek and effect constitutional change. The rights and immunities of the separate estates, primarily the aristocratic orders, reduced his fiscal resources and often deprived him of authority in conducting foreign affairs and pursuing internal reform. The privileges and monopolies enjoyed by provinces, towns, and guilds further restrained trade, hampered economic growth, and militated against the common welfare, of which eighteenth-century heads of state increasingly believed themselves the chief defenders.

The enlightened despots of the period made

[4] See especially R. R. Palmer, *The Age of the Democratic Revolution.* 1959-1964.

an attack on obstructive privilege a usual part of their policy, and many of them may be considered crowned constitutional reformers. Sweden offers perhaps the best example. Her estates, meeting in a four-house Diet (or Riksdag), long held the king in trammels, as he could not tax, change the laws, or make war, peace, or alliances without their agreement. The Diet itself offered no effective leadership because it was divided into hostile factions, especially among the nobles, that spent their energies in ceaseless battles for office and patronage and readily sold their support to foreign powers eager to influence Swedish policy, notably France or Russia.

In 1771 a new king trained in France and imbued with liberal ideas, Gustavus III, ascended the throne. The following year, with the aid of the army and French support, he mounted a coup d'état against the Diet. At the point of bayonets, he forced a constitution on the houses—the first comprehensive, written document of its kind adopted by a European state. It gave the king broader if still limited powers: the Diet could assemble only on royal summons and could discuss only what the king proposed, though its agreement was still necessary for new taxes and laws.

Gustavus then proceeded to remake Swedish institutions, almost without the Diet's participation. He changed the laws governing ownership and inheritance of land, opened offices to all classes, reformed the courts, tried to suppress corruption, established freedom of the press and of religion, and lifted restrictions on trade in grain. Stung by the reforms, which often touched their privileges, the nobles grew ever more disgruntled and from 1786 on openly challenged the king's authority. In 1788 they refused to support him in a war he had declared against Russia. In response, through the Act of Union and Security the next year, Gustavus once more altered the constitution, allocating to the king sole authority in foreign affairs and still further diminishing the role of the aristocracy in the Swedish state. Deprived of constitutional means of expressing their dissent, the dissatisfied nobles conspired against the king, who was shot dead at a masquerade in 1792. This dramatic incident later inspired Giuseppe Verdi's opera *The Masked Ball*, first produced in Rome in 1859. To sooth the censors, who looked askance at successful conspiracies, Verdi changed the locale to Boston, Massachusetts; he made Gustavus himself an English governor, who presumably could die on stage without undermining the public order.

If Gustavus' career offers an excellent example of fundamental reforms imposed from above, it also shows the violent opposition such policies could evoke from the aristocracy. In many European states the aristocracy was not content simply to defend its traditional privileges but agitated for a still larger share in the exercise of power.

ARISTOCRATIC RESURGENCE

Europe's aristocracies had understandable cause for discontent with the changes occurring in the eighteenth century. The growth of trade, the expansion of capital, and pervasive inflation left many nobles hard-pressed economically, and as a countermeasure many of them tried to reactivate their ancient and half-forgotten feudal prerogatives over the peasants. In the political sphere as well, monarchs were allocating a progressively smaller place to the nobles in the business of government.

Aristocracies all over Europe thus sought to advance their fortunes and consolidate what they took to be their rightful place under their countries' constitutions. Armed with the ideas of Montesquieu, they claimed that nobles had the exclusive right to serve as the chief counselors of the king as well as the obligation of leading the community in the conduct of its important affairs. By the last decades of the century, the aristocracy had in fact secured a

near-monopoly over high offices in both the state and the church. In 1781 for example the rank of commissioned officer in the French army was limited almost exclusively to those who could show four generations of nobility. And on the eve of the Revolution, the 18 archbishops, 118 bishops, and 8,000 canons (high ecclesiastics) in the French Church were all of noble extraction; in contrast half this group had come from bourgeois stock in 1730. Simultaneously aristocrats demanded that the assemblies of estates, which they dominated or hoped to dominate, be granted a larger share of political power.

Perhaps the best example of a revolution led by the aristocracy in support of such claims arose in the Austrian Netherlands. The ten provinces were governed under charters granted by the Hapsburgs and other rulers that dated back to the Middle Ages. Representative assemblies, which controlled the government in all the provinces, largely determined the laws and imposed the taxes, apparently the lightest in the whole of Europe. Guilds, whose privileges similarly dated from the Middle Ages, were particularly strong in the Flemish towns and tightly regulated the economy.

In the 1780s Holy Roman Emperor Joseph II of Austria as part of a general reform of his realm sought to centralize and modernize Hapsburg administration of the southern Netherlands. He tried to abolish the special privileges enjoyed by the ten provinces, and in the interest of freeing the economy, he also sought to break the guild monopolies. Much to the alarm of the United Provinces and Britain, he tried as well to reopen the port of Antwerp, which had been closed to international trade since 1648. These changes were coupled with other liberal reforms—the abolition of torture, the introduction of religious toleration, the suppression of some few monasteries, and the important social reforms for the rural population that were discussed in Chapter 19. Finally, in 1787 he overhauled

In this engraving by a contemporary artist, Jean-Paul Laurens, Louis XVI is greeted upon his arrival at the opening session of the Estates General. The convocation of the Estates was the first in a sequence of events that would ultimately lead to the abolition of the monarchy and the king's execution. (Photo: New York Public Library, Picture Collection)

the court system, under which the estates had exercised their chief judicial and administrative prerogatives.

The patricians protested these reforms. In late 1788 the representative assemblies of two provinces refused to grant Joseph money, and the emperor retaliated by revoking their ancient charters, with the aim of bringing them under the direct and unlimited powers of the crown. The frightened aristocrats organized secret societies, called Pro Aris et Focis ("For Altars and Hearths"), the name implying an objection to Joseph's treatment of the Catholic Church. The following year, doubtless encouraged by the defiance of the Estates General in France, the provinces declared their independence. In the face of concerted

opposition, Austrian rule collapsed. But the revolutionaries now found themselves divided. One party, led by a Brussels lawyer, held that independence from Austria sufficed and no further changes were required. The provinces should be ruled by their assemblies, which meant by their traditional aristocracies. But a second party, led by another lawyer, sought to limit the privileges of the provinces, guilds, and assemblies. These democrats, as they were called, now faced the aristocrats in a struggle over the constitution of the land. In 1790, with the support of the church and most of the peasants, the conservatives prevailed, and the leaders of the democratic faction were forced into exile.

The death of Joseph II the same year and the succession of his brother Leopold II further complicated the picture. Leopold was about as sympathetic to reform as a monarch could be in the eighteenth century, and he energetically sought to make a common front with the democrats against the aristocrats. The coalition was successful, and Austrian rule was restored in the provinces in December. The democrats flocked back, but the coalition between the monarch and the people never had the opportunity to reform the government freely. The increasing radicalism of the Revolution in France made Leopold progressively suspicious of the intentions of his own democratic allies. Finally, in 1792 French revolutionary armies poured into the Austrian Netherlands and ended all possibility of peacefully wrought change.

POPULAR MOVEMENTS

In their competition for power, both monarchs and aristocrats were likely to seek an ally in the politically inert but potentially powerful third estate, the people. The small Swiss city of Geneva offers an early example of popular participation in movements for reform. In England too, by the late eighteenth century, popular reform movements were assuming major importance in politics.

Geneva
Socially and juridically, the population of Geneva was divided into three groups. The patricians held the highest offices and dominated the Small Council, the executive body or board of governors of the city. The burghers, representing about a fourth of the population, elected the Great Council, which could approve but not propose legislation and which chose the chief officers from lists prepared by the Small Council. The majority of the population, called natives, had no political rights and were also excluded from certain professions.

In the 1760s the patricians and burghers entered into a protracted argument over the exercise of power in the government. The Small Council for example tried to suppress certain writings of Jean Jacques Rousseau, himself born in Geneva and an honorary citizen; the burghers protested. In addition they claimed the right to initiate legislation and present it to the Small Council. Because they

realized that this violated traditional constitutional procedure, the burghers took the step of appealing to theories of popular sovereignty—a fateful decision, for the same theories could be used against their own privileged status. They also cultivated the support of the totally disfranchised natives. In the face of violent agitation, the Small Council accepted a reform edict that enlarged the role of the Great Council in the government and extended certain minor concessions to the natives. The natives, now politically aroused, demanded that they be allowed to participate in political life. Riots broke out in 1770, and the government responded by suppressing the natives' political clubs and even threatening their leaders with death. In 1782, with the support of France, the government rescinded the reform edict. Fear of the people had brought a counterrevolution.

Great Britain
In Great Britain too a tripartite conflict arose involving the king, the aristocracy, and the people in the late eighteenth century. As elsewhere a major role in initiating a popular movement was played by a reforming monarch, George III (1760–1820). Unlike his namesake grandfather and great-grandfather, George had been born in England and knew the land, its language, and its political system well. He was also intent on advancing royal authority. He did not seek to by-pass Parliament but rather tried, much as the Whig ministers had before him, to control its members through patronage and influence. The Whigs saw the royal ambitions and the system through which it worked as a threat to their own traditional hegemony. Not only did they oppose the king and his ministers in Parliament, but they enlisted the support of reform elements originating outside of Parliament itself.

One such group, known as the Radical Dissenters, was led by such men as the clergyman Richard Price and the scientist Joseph Priestley. The appearance of daily newspapers (the *Morning Post* was founded in 1772 and the *Times* in 1785) gave them a marvelous means of spreading their views, and they leveled destructive criticism against the defects of the British political system. Characteristically they called for representation proportionate to population, stricter laws against corruption, exclusion from the Commons of royal officeholders, and freedom of the press.

The most notorious of popular agitators was a journalist by the name of John Wilkes. Ambitious, eloquent, and ruthless, Wilkes purchased a seat in Parliament with the aid of an opportune marriage. But success through traditional channels came too slowly, and he assumed the risky but promising role of a popular champion for reform. He viciously attacked in print the king's prime minister, and indirectly the king himself over the terms of the Treaty of Paris in 1763, which he considered unfavorable to Britain's imperial interests. The government arrested him for sedition and libel on a general warrant—that is, with the name of the accused omitted. During his trial crowds in London marched in his support shouting "Wilkes and liberty," and the courts quashed the indictment. The government then accused him of having authored a pornographic poem, called "An Essay on Women," and this time Wilkes fled to France. There he stayed for four years, but in 1768, still under indictment, he returned to stand once more for Parliament. At his second attempt he was elected. Three times the Commons refused to seat him, and three times he was returned. With the ardent support of radicals and to the acclaim of the London crowds, Wilkes finally won his seat.

The agitation for parliamentary reform in Great Britain was soon swept up in the larger issues raised by the outbreak of the French Revolution. The events of 1789 across the Channel naturally frightened certain social groups, but the Revolution's opponents were initially drowned out in a chorus of enthusiasm that swept the literate classes in Britain as on the Continent. It was hard after all to defend what was taken to be the traditional despotism of the French monarchy. But the increasing radicalism of the Revolution generated disenchantment and hostility.

The Wilkes affair, the agitation for parliamentary reform, and the reactions to the uprisings in France characterized the reform movements in a British context; revolutionary action did not. Wilkes and other radicals appealed not only to the London crowds but also to many underprivileged groups—traders, craftsmen, and the like—who did have the franchise and were thus able to express their political dissatisfaction by voting Wilkes and other men displeasing to the government into Parliament. This added to the effectiveness of the reform movement, but it also diluted its revolutionary thrust. Most radicals called only for the reform, not the replacement, of the British political system. They still retained some measure of respect for the nation's political traditions.

Ireland and North America

Great Britain did face revolutionary agitation in her overseas possessions, notably Ireland and North America. In Ireland a largely Protestant gentry was demanding autonomy for the country's Parliament under the British king and reform in the trade laws, which injured the Irish economy. But the religious and cultural gulf that divided the Protestant gentry from the Catholic people prevented an effective alliance between them, and the throne was usually able to purchase the loyalty of the upper classes with relatively minor concessions. In 1782 for example, in response to agitation led by the Protestant patriots Henry Flood and Henry Grattan, Britain gave the Irish Parliament the sought-for autonomy. This assured the loyalty of Irish gentry during the final phase of the American Revolution and the more difficult struggle with revolutionary France.

In her thirteen North American colonies, Britain faced a much different situation. George III and his prime minister, Lord North, attempted to force the colonies to pay the costs, past and present, of their own defense. The policy would have meant a pronounced centralization of authority within the government of the British Empire.

The prominent landlords and merchants of the Eastern seaboard took the leadership in opposing the fiscal measures and the constitutional changes they implied. Like the upper classes in many European lands, they too applied to the third constituent division of society—the people. But the resistance in North America otherwise differed profoundly from comparable movements in Europe. The American social leaders could not appeal to a body of corporate privileges that the actions of the king were allegedly violating. They therefore appealed to the traditional rights enjoyed by all British subjects, regardless of rank, and to theories of popular sovereignty as advanced particularly by John Locke; the Declaration of Independence was to give eloquent expression to these broad concepts. The same lack of a true estate system in colonial American society, the amorphous and fluid margins separating the social strata, further prevented the development of conflicts between patricians and the lower social orders, which so often occurred in Europe.

These differences partially explain the unique character of the American Revolution. Its effects on society were limited. But in the theory that supported it and in the close and continuing alliance between the upper and lower classes, it was perhaps the most democratic of the revolutions of the eighteenth century. It created the first state and government in which the exercise of power was explicitly declared to be based not on divine right or inherited privilege but on the consent of the governed. It also represented the first successful rebellion of an overseas colony against a European country. The example and effects of the American Revolution were thus of major importance in the dissolution of Europe's old regimes.

VI. THE FRENCH REVOLUTION

The pivotal event of European history in the eighteenth century—some would say in the modern epoch—was the French Revolution, which broke out in 1789. It conquered much of Europe with its arms and, slowly, all of Europe with its ideals. Those ideals essentially defined the contours of a modern, liberal society. In place of the traditional toleration of involuntary service (feudal charges on the land, vestiges of personal serfdom, slavery overseas), the Revolution preached liberty. In place of hierarchy and inherited social status, the Revolution demanded equality. In place of privileged and exclusive estates and corporations and established religions, the Revolution proclaimed fraternity. Liberty, equality, fraternity: this grand revolutionary slogan still represents a social ideal, to which most modern Europeans and Americans would subscribe.

ORIGINS

Historians have long studied and discussed the origins of this tremendous upheaval, and the explanations they have offered for it are many. The incompetence and indecisiveness of Louis XVI, and the frivolous character of his Austrian queen, Marie Antoinette, certainly affected the course of events, but could hardly have incited a national uprising. The ideas of the philosophes were surely corrosive of inherited values and institutions, and powerfully shaped revolutionary policies. But the philosophes themselves never advocated violent change, and most entertained deep suspicions of the restless, ignorant masses.

The interpretation which today most sharply divides historians holds that the revolution was rooted in class struggle. In the words of a prominent French historian, Albert Soboul, who writes from within a Marxist tradition, the uprising forms "the classical model of a bourgeois revolution." In this view, the French middle classes, gaining in wealth across the eighteenth century, resented the privileges of the nobility and the obstacles which the old regime placed in the path of capitalistic development. They fought to change social institutions in their own interest and claimed the seats of power in their own name. The Revolution, in sum, placed a bourgeois regime atop an already bourgeois economy.

This forceful theory has, however, evoked an equally vigorous rebuttal. Its critics question the coherence, some even the existence, of a capitalistic bourgeoisie in eighteenth-century France. Intense research has shown that the barrier between the second and third estates was porous and often passed, and the lines of social division frequently blurred. The gap between the nobles and the upper bourgeoisie was as nothing compared with the gulf which separated these orders, both privileged, from the common people. Perhaps most cogently, these critics point out that the revolutionary leaders were lawyers and administrators, rarely merchants or industrialists. The leaders of the new economy looked with doubt and fear upon the revolutionary course, supposedly (according to Soboul) flowing in their favor. The bourgeoisie, it is argued, did not make the Revolution. Rather, the Revolution made the bourgeoisie, in the sense that the reforms it achieved stimulated decisive growth in the capitalistic economy.

This ingenious revision of the Marxist argument still fails to answer the question: Who made the revolution? A recent explanation stresses the failure of French society to accommodate the growing numbers of its young. In an age of rapid demographic expansion, the young outnumbered their elders and were too numerous for the available places and careers which society could offer. Those who aspired to careers in the professions, as lawyers, doctors, clerics, officers, or administrators, faced exceptionally bitter competition and frequent frustration. Understandably they resented the advantage which a noble title or high connections might confer upon a rival. Numerous leaders of the epoch—Maximilien Robespierre, for example (see pp. 691–692)—were young lawyers from small towns whom the Revolution nurtured and frequently devoured. In this view, the French Revolution was at least in part a fronde of the frustrated and an upheaval of the young.

In the late eighteenth century, powerful forces, rooted in larger numbers of people, new forms of economic organization, and new values and ideas, strained French society. The monarchy sought to contain those forces within the established social and political system. Its effort to accomplish this, its abject failure, the reconstruction of a new social and political order are the great themes of French revolutionary history.

FISCAL CRISIS

Whatever the deep sources of the outbreak, this much at least is certain: the Revolution was precipitated by the impending bankruptcy of the French monarchy in 1789. The crisis struck France at a particularly difficult point—during a sharp downturn in the economy aggravated by two years of bad harvests. Unemployment and hunger stirred up the people. Why was the country facing bankruptcy in 1789? And why had reform been so drastically delayed?

In the 1730s France's economy had entered a period of expansion, and the growing resources it developed should have provided the monarchy with adequate revenues. Despite this the government faced nearly continuous fiscal straits. The chief reason for its poverty in the midst of plenty was the narrow tax base of its finances. The system of privilege largely exempted ecclesiastical and noble lands from a proportionate contribution to fiscal needs.

The last years of the reign of Louis XV witnessed both bad economic times and deepening fiscal distress. In 1771 the chancellor, René Nicolas de Maupeou, tried to force reform decrees through the Parlement of Paris, and when he met with concerted opposition, he dissolved the Parlement and exiled more than 100 aristocrats from the capital. His action almost exactly parallels Gustavus III's attack on the Swedish Diet. Maupeou abolished the sale of offices and created a new system of courts in which the judges held their positions by royal appointment, not by inheritance or purchase. While still not touching tax exemptions, Maupeou's policies seemed a first, bold step in reducing privilege in French government and society.

However, the monarchy was ill-served by the man who guided it. The aging Louis XV gave himself to his pleasures, and the extravagance of the court spread resentment against him. He died in 1774, and the court felt it advisable to carry the king once hailed as the Beloved to his final resting place at night, almost without ceremony, almost in secret. But many people in France still expected great things from the monarchy in the person of his grandson and heir, a young man who showed authentic concern for his people.

LOUIS XVI AND HIS FINANCE MINISTERS

Louis XVI was nineteen years old when he succeeded his grandfather as king of France in 1774. A man of blameless private life, he was nonetheless critically lacking in confidence in himself and was psychologically incapable of either conceiving or pursuing a firm course of action. His still younger queen, Marie Antoinette, daughter of Maria Theresa, was prone to intervening in her husband's decisions, which earned her the resentment of the court and the people.

Louis at once tried to conciliate the nobles, whose position in government had been gravely threatened by Maupeou's reforms. He restored to the parlements their former prerogatives. This was a popular gesture as it seemed to mark a move away from royal absolutism toward a limited and responsible monarchy. But it proved to be a major tactical error, for it gave a voice and a constitutional position to the nobles, the chief defenders of privilege. Louis was better served by his choice of ministers—in particular Jacques Turgot, a former *intendant* and a man of high talents steeped in the thought of the physiocrats, who assumed the office of controller general of finance.

Turgot imposed a policy of austerity to put France's house in order—no new taxes, no new loans, and no new expenses. He sought reform too; in 1774 he removed all restrictions on commerce in grain, and in 1776 he abolished the guilds. As a good physiocrat he contemplated replacing all indirect taxes that hampered trade with a single tax on land—all land—which he called the territorial subsidy and which would have represented the end of all noble privileges. Privately, he favored a system of advisory assemblies to replace the parlements, culminating in a national congress called the Great Municipality of the realm. Turgot in sum desired a constitution for France.

The king refused to support him. His economic policies aggravated the court, his philosophical ideas and support of tolerance offended the clergy, and his schemes for tax reform frightened the nobles. Above all his austerity and refusal to make certain appointments angered the queen. Louis, worn down by complaints against the minister, dismissed him in 1776. With him went the last hope for reform in France under royal leadership.

The king then turned to a Protestant banker from Geneva with a reputation for financial wizardry, Jacques Necker. A shrewd man with a strong sense of public relations, Necker abolished the last vestiges of serfdom on the royal lands, ended torture in judicial proceedings, and reorganized hospitals and prisons. He thus earned an enormous and largely unmerited popularity. His solution for the financial crisis, which was greatly aggravated when war broke out with England in 1778, was more loans, for was not France after all a rich nation? His policy of borrowing and spending helped several bankers on to fortune and raised his popularity among the financial bourgeoisie. But new loans only delayed and in delaying worsened the eventual reckoning. With bankruptcy ever closer and support decaying around him, Necker adroitly maneuvered the king into asking for his resignation. He left the government in 1781 with his reputation as a financial reformer still intact.

After a further shuffle of ministers, in 1783 Louis turned to another experienced administrator and former *intendant*, Charles Alexandre de Calonne. He first proceeded on the principle that the government's credit was based on confidence and that confidence was best assured by the court's carefree spending. Never had the fetes at Versailles been so splendid since the days of the Sun King. But fear of bankruptcy steadily mounted. Then in 1786 Calonne reversed his casual policies and proposed a single tax on all lands without exception—Turgot's territorial subsidy. Rather than submitting the reform to the Parlement of Paris, which would be certain to reject it, the king at Calonne's bidding summoned an Assembly of Notables, which met in February 1787. To Calonne's shock the 147 notables

refused to accept the decrees, and after several stormy sessions he was dismissed by the king. His successor, Loménie de Brienne, the former archbishop of Toulouse, brought the proposal for a land tax before the Parlement of Paris, which as predicted rejected it. The full dimensions of the king's mistake in restoring rights to the Parlement were now revealed. Louis dissolved it and exiled its members to the small provincial town of Troyes, but they continued to defy the government, asserting that only the Estates General could authorize new taxes.

The government now faced the mass defiance by the nobility that many historians call the prerevolution. The provincial parlements issued declarations of support for their counterparts of Paris. Riots broke out in several cities and provinces. The civil administration seemed on the verge of breakdown, and the loyalty of the army itself was uncertain. Louis was forced to retreat before the uprising of the privileged. He summoned the Estates General to convene in May 1789 and recalled Necker. The summoning of the national assembly was the critical first step in the Revolution, for it represented the failure of royal absolutism to achieve reform; it meant too entry onto the scene of the middle classes and beyond them the people.

THE ESTATES GENERAL AND THE CONSTITUENT ASSEMBLY

From February to May 1789, a period of growing scarcity of grain, the three traditional orders of France elected their representatives to the Estates General, which had last been convened in 1614. By a special royal concession, the third estate was accorded twice as many delegates as the two higher orders. The delegates also drew up lists of grievances (*cahiers de doléances*). Recent analyses of their content, pursued in France and America, have shown that the great majority were conservative in tone: they refer only to local ills and express confidence that the royal government would recognize and redress them. Only a few delegates from large cities, Paris especially, allude to the general principles of social order and of justice elaborated by the philosophes. It is impossible, in other words, to read in the *cahiers* the future course of the Revolution. Still they promoted widespread reflection on France's failings; their preparation was a stage in the raising of a revolutionary consciousness.

The popular expectation that the monarchy would provide leadership in reform proved to be ill-founded. When the representatives met on May 5, Louis proposed nothing. He even left unsettled the critical question of whether the assembly would vote by order, which would assure control by the privileged, or by head, which would give the dominant voice to the third estate, since many nobles and ecclesiastics sympathized with its cause.

In the absence of royal direction, the third estate seized the initiative and demanded that the privileged orders meet with it to constitute a national assembly. The king, who finally decided to cast his lot with the nobility and clergy, locked the third estate's delegates out of their meeting room until a session could be arranged in which he would state his will. Unable to sit in their usual hall, they retired to a tennis court, and there all but one swore that they would not bow to force. The king, in the face of this defiance, once more conceded and on June 24 allowed the three estates to form together the National Assembly, which changed its name shortly to the Constituent Assembly, empowered to give France a constitution.

Meanwhile unrest was growing daily in this year of hunger, and Louis' own ill-considered actions added to the turmoil. He gathered 20,000 soldiers around Paris and on July 11 dismissed the popular Necker. The dismissal provoked open insurrection in Paris. On July 14, in search of arms, the insurgents first attacked the military hospital of the Invalides and then the Bastille, an old fortress used as a prison. The latter was only one of several violent incidents in these troubled days, but the fall of the Bastille seemed to represent a victory of the people in the name of liberty over traditional despotism. Again the king capitulated. He removed the troops around Paris and recalled Necker. On July 17, to please the populace, he donned a cockade bearing the colors of white for the monarchy and blue and red for the city of Paris. This tricolor was to become the flag of the new France.

But these gestures hardly pacified the hungry masses. Rather, unrest reached the provincial towns, which rallied to declare their solidarity with the third estate, and then spread fully into the countryside. The sources of peasant dissatisfaction were many and long standing. Population growth and the parceling of holdings had sown widespread rural impoverishment. It has been estimated that one-tenth of the country population lived solely by begging; still larger proportions were reduced to mendicancy during years of dearth. Feudal dues and the ecclesiastical tithe weighed heavy upon those struggling to survive on the margins of subsistence. Suspicions, too, were rampant that the nobles were hoarding grain and pursuing a policy of fomenting famine in order to block reform. In July, peasants of Normandy, Franche-Comté, Alsace, the Mâconnais, and elsewhere sacked the castles and homes of the nobles and burned the documents that recorded their feudal obligations. From about July 20, this peasant insurgency blended imperceptibly into a popular panic, known as the Great Fear. Rumors flew through the countryside that "brigands" of unknown origin and loyalties—perhaps hirelings of the nobles—were marching on the villages, intent on destroying the new harvest upon which depended all hope of relieving the famine. The fear was baseless, but it prompted a mass recourse to arms in the provincial towns and villages, stirred up hatred and suspicion of the nobles, and destroyed what confidence remained in the traditional social and constitutional order. Peasant insurgency and the Great Fear showed that the royal government faced something far more ominous than bread riots in the capital; it was confronting a national and popular revolution.

Peasant unrest also frightened the delegates of the Constituent Assembly. On the night of August 4, the representatives of the nobility and clergy vied with one another in dramatically renouncing their ancient privileges, and the Assembly solemnly decreed that the feudal regime was forever abolished in France. The delegates showed a high regard for the rights of property, however, in insisting that the nobles be compensated for the feudal rents they were losing. But the peasants seem to have been satisfied with the concessions they attained. Strongly religious, traditionally suspicious of the motives of townsmen, rural France thereafter became a largely conservative presence in the further unfolding of the Revolution.

On August 26 the Assembly drew up the Declaration of the Rights of Man and of the Citizen. In phrases reminiscent of the American Declaration of Independence, the document affirmed the rights of men to practice what religion they chose, to receive quick and fair justice, to assemble, to own property, and to be represented in government. So also all citizens were obligated to assume a fair share of the tax burden.

But still the hunger continued, and social tensions remained high. On October 5 crowds of women demanding bread besieged Versailles and forced the king and the royal family to come to Paris. The Assembly followed within a few days. Versailles, Louis XIV's great palace, symbolized not only royal absolutism but the detachment of the government from the people. The government's return to Paris thus indicated the new power of the popular forces in France.

The Restructuring of France

From 1789 to 1791, the Constituent Assembly labored hard and productively on a constitution for the new France. While recognizing the rights of all French citizens, the constitution effectively transferred power from the privileged estates to the general body of the rich and the educated, in which the nobility remained as individuals without titles or privileges. In reshaping institutions, the Assembly sought to implement principles of rationality, efficiency, and humanity, much as the philosophes advocated. Especially as they touched local administration, justice, and the courts, the reforms proved remarkably durable; even today, the work of the Assembly is visible in France.

At the center, the constitution created a limited monarchy with a clear separation of powers. The king was to name and dismiss his ministers at will, but he would be required to secure their approval for his major decisions. The legislative branch would consist of a single house, the Legislative Assembly, with members elected for two years by a complex system of indirect voting. The king would exercise a suspensive veto over their enactments, but if the bill was passed by three Assemblies, it would become law even without royal approval. The franchise was to be limited to "active" citizens who paid a certain sum in taxes, and the property qualification would be even higher for those who wished to stand for public office. But some two-thirds of the adult male population attained the right to choose the electors, who in turn would choose the delegates. Although the system favored the rich, it was considerably more liberal than the political structure in for example contemporary Britain.

With regard to local government, the Con-

In October 1789, the hungry women of Paris marched to Versailles and forced the king and the royal family to return to Paris with them. With the government now located in the city, the Parisian populace was able to exert a much stronger influence upon it. (Photo: New York Public Library, Picture Collection)

stituent Assembly abolished the parlements and provided a standardized provincial administration in France. The land was divided into eighty-three departments, each allowed considerable autonomy—something not characteristic of later French constitutions. Offices were no longer to be sold, and torture and unusual punishments in judicial procedures were prohibited. The Assembly called for a new codification of French law, but this desideratum was to be achieved only by Napoleon. In economic affairs the principle of laissez faire inspired the Assembly's decisions. It lifted all internal tariffs and did away with all chartered trading companies and monopolies. The law also forbade the formation of associations of workers since they too were considered hindrances to freedom of trade and contract.

In finance the Constituent Assembly decided to honor the royal debt, which it considered, as it did all forms of commitment involving property, an inviolable obligation. To find new revenue it confiscated all ecclesiastical property in November 1789, placing it "at the disposition of the nation" and simultaneously making the government responsible for the costs of religious services. On the basis of this fund of church lands (to which the property of émigré nobles and the crown would subsequently be added), the Assembly issued paper bills known as assignats, which circulated as money. The secularization of ecclesiastical holdings had one important social result. Those bourgeois and rich peasants who acquired them acquired too a vested interest in the work of the Revolution. They

MAP 20.1: FRANCE: PROVINCES AND REGIONS BEFORE 1789

Within the map:
ENGLAND
ENGLISH CHANNEL
FLANDRE ET HAINAUT
ARTOIS
HOLY ROMAN EMPIRE
Rhine R.
PICARDY
METZ ET VERDUN
Seine R.
ÎLE DE FRANCE
Varennes
NORMANDIE
Paris
Versailles
CHAMPAGNE ET BRIE
LORRAINE
ALSACE
BRETAGNE
MAINE
ORLÉANAIS
Loire R.
Orléans
ANJOU
TOURAINE
NIVERNAIS
BOURGOGNE
FRANCHE COMTÉ
SWISS CONFEDERATION
SAUMUROIS
BERRY
POITOU
BOURBONNAIS
AUNIS
MARCHE
LYONNAIS
SAVOY
ANGOUMOIS
Lyons
ATLANTIC OCEAN
SAINTONGE
LIMOUSIN
AUVERGNE
KINGDOM OF SARDINIA
Bordeaux
Caronne R.
Rhône R.
DAUPHINÉ
GUYENNE ET GASCOGNE
PAPAL LANDS
PROVENCE
BÉARN
LANGUEDOC
FOIX
Marseilles
ROUSSILLON
SPAIN
CORSICA
MEDITERRANEAN SEA
0   100 miles

(From Breunig, Charles, *The Age of Revolution and Reaction, 1789–1850*, New York: Norton, 1970, p. 18.)

were numerous and strong enough to assure that the achievements of the Constituent Assembly would never be undone.

The following July the Assembly reformed the Catholic Church in France through the Civil Constitution of the Clergy. The law reduced the number of bishops to eighty-three, reshaping diocesan boundaries to conform with those of the departments; required that both bishops and parish priests, like civil officials, be elected by those they served; and when resistance became manifest to these enactments, the Assembly demanded that all

MAP 20.2: FRANCE: REVOLUTIONARY DEPARTMENTS AFTER 1789

(From Breunig, Charles, *The Age of Revolution and Reaction, 1789–1850*, New York: Norton, 1970, p. 18.)

clerics swear to uphold the new legislation. The Civil Constitution ignored the traditional canon law and would have suppressed the autonomy of the church or for that matter the authority of the pope in France had it been able.

The Civil Constitution raised a storm of protest among both the clergy and the Catholic faithful. All but seven bishops and half the parochial priests refused to take the required oath. These were called the refractory clergy. Reforms in the French Church were a recognized need, and many of the provisions corresponded with the wishes of informed and pious Catholics. But the effort to impose reforms without consideration of traditional procedures in the church was a grave tactical error. The Revolution had hitherto found much sympathy among the lower clergy especially. But the Civil Constitution linked the cause of reform with anticlericalism and impiety. It made enemies for the Revolution when it desperately needed friends.

COUNTERREVOLUTION

The Constituent Assembly permanently changed France, but it failed to find broad social support for its reforms. The radical left denounced its deference to the monarchy, its favoring of the rich, and the restricted suffrage granted under the new constitution. The radicals organized themselves into clubs and associations of clubs to discuss, develop, and disseminate their views. One of the most powerful of the clubs was the Jacobin, so called because its members met in the former Dominican convent of St. Jacques in Paris. On the right the nobles resented the fact that the Revolution they had hoped to lead had turned against their interests. The king himself, who might have given stability to the new regime, again hesitated, now favoring and now opposing the reforms.

In June 1791 Louis and his family secretly fled from Paris. He hoped to reach the city of Metz, near the Rhine frontier, where he expected to find a garrison of troops favorable to him and where help from Austria would be close if needed. But he was recognized at the small post station of Varennes near Reims and brought back to Paris. The Assembly, which saw the critical need for royal support, pretended that the flight had been forced on him and reaffirmed his status as king. But the nearly traitorous act lent strength to the radical agitation.

The Constituent Assembly itself adopted a measure that would withdraw power from those most committed to enforcing its reforms: its own members. Still seeking popular support, it decreed that no present delegates could stand for election to the new legislature. This self-denying ordinance assured that the Legislative Assembly would be composed of men younger, less experienced, and probably more daring than their predecessors.

The new national body was elected as provided by the constitution, and it convened for the first time on October 1, 1791. Almost from the first the question of war dominated its mood and work. By an odd coincidence both the right and the left in France saw advantage in a war between France and Austria. The king and the court hoped that military defeat would discredit the new regime and restore full power to the monarchy, and many Jacobins were eager to strike down the foreign supporters of counterrevolutionaries at home and émigrés abroad. When Francis II took the throne of the Hapsburg dominions in March 1792, the other half of the stage was set. Unlike his father Leopold, who strongly rejected intervention, Francis fell under the influence of vengeful émigrés and shortsighted advisers. He determined to assist the French queen, his aunt, and he hoped to achieve territorial gains for Austria at the expense of France. With both sides geared for battle, France went to war against the Austro-Prussian coalition in April.

Each camp expected rapid victory, but both were deceived. The French offensive was quickly driven back, and soon invading armies were crossing French borders. The Legislative Assembly ordered the exile of refractory clergy and the establishment of a special corps of 20,000 national guardsmen to protect Paris. Louis vetoed both measures and held to his decision in spite of demonstrations in the capital. This was for all practical

This contemporary text and music of the Marseillaise carries a sketch of the "sons of the revolution" marching and singing. The anthem's original title was War Song for the Army of the Rhine. (Photo: The Mansell Collection)

purposes his last act as king. Meanwhile the Assembly declared the mother country to be in danger and called for volunteers from the provinces to defend the frontiers. As France mobilized for war an officer named Rouget de Lisle composed a marching song for his volunteer battalion—a song eventually known as the *Marseillaise*. Now the national anthem of France, it ranks among history's most stirring summons to patriotic war.

The *Marseillaise* accurately reflected the spirit of resistance that was developing in France. As Prussian forces began a drive toward Paris, their commander, the duke of Brunswick, recklessly demanded that Paris disarm itself and threatened to level the city if it resisted or if it harmed the royal family. This seemed the final proof that Louis was in league with the enemy. Far from intimidating the revolutionaries, the threat drove them into action. Since the Legislative Assembly had refused to act decisively in the face of royal obstructionism, the Parisians organized an insurrection. On August 10, 1792, a crowd of armed Parisians stormed the royal palace at the Tuileries, literally driving the king from the throne. The Assembly then had no choice but to declare him suspended. That night more than half its members themselves fled Paris, making it clear that the Assembly too had lost its legitimacy. Recognizing this, the representatives who remained prepared to dissolve the Assembly permanently and ordered elections for a new body, the National Convention. They left to the Convention the responsibility of declaring a republic in France and of judging her former king. More even than the storming of the Bastille in July 1789, the events of August 10, 1792, marked the passing of the old regime in France.

In the eighteenth century major transformations began in all aspects of Western life. The inhabitants of Europe and North America expanded at an extraordinary rate to unprecedented numbers, initiating a population explosion that has continued into modern times and now affects the entire world. The demographic revolution was closely related in both effect and cause to a revolution in manufacturing. The new industrial economy, if still of small size, created a new organization of production based on steam power and high engineering skill, factors that would sustain the economic growth of the following century. And the overall economic system took on a configuration that differed from the patterns of all prior periods in its capacity to transform itself ceaselessly and thus to lend a new dynamic quality to the society living from it.

These profound changes were accompanied by a crisis in social and political institutions. A tripartite struggle developed involving the ruler, the aristocracy, and the people over the proper allocation of power in the state. Several European monarchs sought to impose reform from above. The aristocracies on the other hand bitterly resented encroachments on their privileges, and some were willing to pursue the defense of their interests to the point of revolution. Both rulers and patricians appealed to the third estate, the people, often with unexpected results. The emerging claim to power of the unprivileged classes is the greatest change effected by the revolutions of the eighteenth century. No longer would the political history of the Western world focus exclusively on the elite.

The peoples of the West thus faced the task of building a new economic, social, and political order. What should its character be? How should power be managed, and how should wealth be distributed? What values should now govern human lives? These were the issues destined to occupy the Western nations as they entered the industrial and democratic age.

RECOMMENDED READING

Sources

Aspinall, Arthur, and E. Anthony Smith (eds.). *English Historical Documents, Vol. XI: 1783–1832.* 1959.

* Burke, Edmund. *Reflections on the Revolution in France.* 1969.

Higgins, E. L. (ed.). *The French Revolution as Told by Contemporaries.* 1939.

Horn, D. B., and Mary Ransome. *English Historical Documents, Vol. X: 1714–1783.* 1957.

* Kaplow, J. (ed.). *France on the Eve of the Revolution.* 1971.

* Smith, Adam. *Enquiry into the Nature and Causes of the Wealth of Nations.* 1961.

Stewart, John H. (ed.). *A Documentary Survey of the French Revolution.* 1951.

* Young, Arthur. *Travels in France During the Years 1787, 1788, 1789.* 1972.

Studies

* Ashton, T. S. *The Industrial Revolution, 1760–1830.* 1968.

* Cobban, A. *The Social Interpretation of the French Revolution.* 1968. Lively critique of the theory that the Revolution was engendered by class conflict.

* Deane, Phyllis. *The First Industrial Revolution.* 1975. Based on lectures, covering the years 1750–1850.

* De Tocqueville, Alexis. *The Old Regime and the French Revolution.* Stuart Gilbert (tr.). 1955.

Godechot, Jacques. *France and the Atlantic Revolutions of the Eighteenth Century.* 1965. Good comparative study of revolutions, by a French scholar.

* Hampson, Norman. *A Social History of the French Revolution.* 1963. Institutional rather than social; clearly organized and written.

Landes, David S. *The Unbound Prometheus. Technological Change and Industrial Development in Western Europe from 1750 to the Present.* 1969. Broad survey, effectively written, with an emphasis on technology.

* Lefebvre, Georges. *The Coming of the French Revolution.* R. R. Palmer (tr.). 1957. Short, clear, classical analysis by a prominent French historian.

* Mantoux, Paul. *The Industrial Revolution in the Eighteenth Century.* 1962. Basic introduction, with stress on inventions and factories.

Palmer, Robert R. *The Age of the Democratic Revolution. A Political History of Europe and America, 1760–1800.* 1959–1962.

Population Patterns in the Past. R. D. Lee (ed.). 1977. Collection of advanced studies.

Rudé, George F. *Paris and London in the Eighteenth Century. Studies in Popular Protest.* 1975.

* Soboul, Albert. *The French Revolution, 1787–1799.* 1975. The Revolution seen as an uprising of the bourgeoisie.

_____

* Available in paperback.

TWENTY-ONE

THE TERROR
AND NAPOLEON

The end of the eighteenth century is often called the age of the dual revolution—the industrial revolution beginning in England and the social and political revolution centering in France. But where the former unfolded gradually, the latter exploded. By 1791—just two years after the fall of the Bastille—the foundations of government and society in France had been profoundly altered. The estate structure, dominated by the monarch and the nobles had been destroyed; middle-class values and leaders were in the ascendant; the peasantry had been freed from most remnants of the seigneurial system; absolutism had been replaced by constitutional monarchy, legislative representation, and local self-government; freedom of religion and expression had been inaugurated.

Yet the Revolution was far from over, and in the short view one might say that it was only just beginning. True, the gains just enumerated ultimately proved to be the most enduring and doubtless the most important. But they had been won at the price of great opposition, and the old order was far from admitting defeat. Priests, émigrés, and royalists in France were seconded by Old Regime monarchs, aristocrats, and armies elsewhere in Europe in their resistance to the Revolution. Moreover within France itself vast sections of the population were disaffected from the "patriots" of 1789 for a variety of reasons.

Challenged in 1792 by war and counterrevolution, the patriots themselves were divided. Some were alienated by the leaders of the Revolution and ultimately joined its opponents. Others were radicalized and gave their allegiance to the Jacobins. These in turn were seeking allies among the urban popular classes—the sans-culottes. Building on the momentum of August 1792, when Louis XVI had been driven from the throne, the Jacobins forged a coalition with the sans-culottes, who wanted to revolutionize the Revolution. The goals of this second revolution were more advanced than those of 1789: a democratic republic based on an ever-widening definition of social equality. Its hallmark was a posture of relentless militancy.

Each increment of revolution produced new opponents at home and abroad, but each increment of opposition stiffened the determination of the Revolution's supporters. An epochal confrontation was in the making that would engulf Europe. It began with a power struggle between revolutionary factions, a conflict of personalities as much as of political orientations; it ended in a coup that led France into a dictatorship under Napoleon Bonaparte.

I. THE SECOND REVOLUTION

The National Convention elected after the fall of the monarchy had a challenging mandate. It was supposed to consolidate the achievements of the first revolution but also establish a democratic republic, in effect moving the Revolution into a second stage. It is impossible to say how this would have proceeded had the times been calm, but of course they

THE TERROR AND NAPOLEON / 687

were not. France was immediately beset by an emergency situation—a convergence of invasion, civil war, and economic crisis. This situation demanded new initiatives which affected the course of the second revolution. To save and expand freedom, it was argued, force and terrorism were necessary. Thus the ideals of democracy and social equality were confused with problems of national defense and with the brutal dilemma of means versus ends. Although the second revolution lasted for little more than two years (1792–1794), it challenged the very foundations upon which government and society had always been organized.

THE NATIONAL CONVENTION
(1792–1794)

By late 1792 revolutionary France had the makings of a new government. The Revolution had been saved from defeat by the belated success of the French army. Bolstered by units of citizen volunteers, the army halted the invading coalition at the Battle of Valmy in September, and two months later inflicted decisive defeat on the armies of the old order at Jemappes in the Austrian Netherlands, which were now occupied by the French. Meanwhile, in France a National Convention elected under universal male suffrage convened to declare the birth of a republic, to govern the country until a new democratic-republican constitution could be implemented, and to try the ex-king for treason.

Louis XVI's fate was the Convention's first major business and it proved an extremely divisive issue. While the king was found guilty of treason unanimously, there was a sharp and prolonged debate over his punishment. Some argued for clemency, while others insisted on his execution as a symbolic break with the old order as well as a fitting punishment for his betrayal. Finally, by a vote of 387 to 334, Louis was sentenced to death,

and efforts to reprieve this sentence or delay it for a popular referendum were defeated. On January 21, 1793, Louis was beheaded, put to death like an ordinary citizen. The French in general and the Convention in particular had become regicides—king-killers. This decision made compromise with the counter-revolution unlikely and total victory imperative. The Revolution would have to move forward.

France was now a republic, a country in which the influence of kings, priests, and nobles was to be eliminated, in which regionalism was supposed to give way to unity, in which social justice and reform could advance. Yet in a few months everything began to go wrong, and the Revolution faced a new and more serious crisis. By the early spring of 1793 the republic was under siege, internally divided and foundering. At least five problems faced the Convention: factionalism and conflict within its own ranks; a new invasion by a coalition of anti-French states; peasant dissatisfaction and internal civil war; economic dislocation including inflation and scarcity of bread; and growing militancy among Parisian radicals.

From the Convention's opening day two groups of deputies vied for leadership. The bitterness of their rivalry proved to be extremely divisive and threatened to paralyze the republic altogether. Yet this conflict reflected a painful reality: opinion *was* divided by what had already happened, and a consensus or stable majority was extremely difficult to find. The factional conflict originated in 1791–1792 as a quarrel within the Paris Jacobin Club and intensified after the insurrection of August 10. A group of deputies and journalists centering on Jacques Brissot had helped lead the country into war, but had then shrunk back from the vigorous measures necessary to pursue it. (This group later would be labeled the "Girondists" since several of its spokesmen were elected deputies to the Con-

Tried and sentenced by the National Convention for treason, Louis Capet (formerly Louis XVI) stoically mounted the guillotine on January 21, 1793. His execution made it clear that the Revolution had taken a sharp turn and that it would deal implacably with its enemies. (Photo: The Granger Collection)

vention from the department of Gironde.) Advocates of provincial middle-class interests, fiery orators, and ambitious politicians, they gradually fell out of step with the growing radicalization of the Parisian populace. The Girondists continued to hope that they could gain political power through the king and therefore did not cooperate in the overthrow of the monarchy.

Subsequently they blamed the violence of the September prison massacres on their Jacobin rivals. That episode—one of the bloodiest events of the French Revolution—erupted in the wake of the August 10 insurrection. As able-bodied volunteers were leaving for the war, Parisians nervously eyed the jails, which were jammed with political prisoners and common criminals. Seeing these prisoners as a potential counterrevolutionary striking force and fearing a plot to open the prisons, popular leaders like the journalist Jean Paul Marat warned of the threat. This growing sense of alarm finally exploded early in September. For three successive days groups of Parisians invaded the prisons, set up popular tribunals, and executed more than 1000 prisoners. No official dared intervene to stop the slaughter. But Brissot and his friends later blamed this spontaneous violence on their political rivals.

Brissotins or Girondists denounced the leading Parisian Jacobins—Robespierre, Marat, and Danton—as demagogues. By this time Brissot and his friends had been forced out of the Jacobin Club, and the Parisian electors sent a deputation to the Convention without a single "Brissotin," but which did include Danton, Robespierre, and Marat. This Parisian deputation became the nucleus of a group called "the Mountain," since it occupied the upper benches of the Convention's hall. The Mountain now dominated the Jacobin Club and attracted to its ranks the more democratically oriented provincial deputies. The Mountain attacked the Girondists as compromisers, as men unattuned to the new demands of the French people. The Girondists in turn denounced the Mountain as would-be tyrants who were captives of Parisian opinion to the detriment of the provinces and the propertied classes.

Between these two factions stood several hundred deputies in the center (called the Plain, in contrast to the Mountain). Committed to the Revolution, they were uncertain whom to trust and would support those men or policies that promised success in consolidating the Revolution. They disliked and feared popular agitation, but they were reluctant to turn against the popular movement, agreeing with the Mountain that the Revolution depended on it. In the debate on the king the center was split, but a majority finally embraced the Jacobins' demand for execution, whereas a few prominent Girondists had argued for clemency. Military and economic problems were eventually to propel the majority to disavow the Girondists and support the Mountain.

The Revolutionary Crisis

Within a few months the Convention faced a perilous convergence of invasion, civil war, and economic crisis which demanded new policies and imaginative responses. The military victories of 1792 were quickly forgotten when Austria and Prussia mounted a new offensive in 1793, an alliance soon strengthened by the addition of Spain, Piedmont, and England. Between March and September reversals occurred on every front, while the regular army was weakened by the emigration of officers and by poor leadership. In fact the French commander, General Dumouriez, the Revolution's first military hero the year before, sought—unsuccessfully—to bring his army back to Paris in order to topple the Convention.

The Convention's first response to the deteriorating military situation was to introduce a system of conscription. But this in turn touched off a peasant rebellion in western France. Long-simmering resentments by a traditional peasantry, who hated the small patriot middle class in the cities for monopolizing political power and who resented the Revolution's persecution of their priests, finally ignited when the republic tried to conscript them. Peasants and weavers in the Vendée region south of the Loire River began to attack the government's supporters in the region's isolated towns. Gradually this insurrection was influenced by priests and émigrés who organized the rebels into guerrilla bands and finally into what called itself the Catholic and Royalist Army. Wherever it triumphed, the Bourbons were proclaimed kings again and patriots were massacred. Several major cities were occupied briefly and for a while the rebels threatened the port city of Nantes, which could have been used for a landing of British troops if it fell from the government's control.

The bitter factionalism in the Convention had meanwhile generated conflict elsewhere in the country. Various provincial centers that sympathized with the Girondists hovered on the brink of rebellion against the Convention's leadership and against Parisian radicalism. In Normandy and Brittany forces were raised to threaten Paris, while in the south local Jacobins lost control of Marseilles, Bordeaux, and France's second largest city, Lyons. Like the Vendée rebellion, the Lyons resistance to Paris was eventually taken over by royalists who hoped to ignite the entire south of France against Paris. This was an intolerable challenge to the Convention. Labeling the anti-Jacobins in Lyons and elsewhere "federalists," the Convention sent out armed forces to suppress them. Ironically, in the United States at this time the word "federalist" referred to those who advocated a strong central government. In France it was used in the opposite sense, meaning those who sought to undermine the republic's unity. As such, the federalists were considered counterrevolutionary, for to disavow Paris meant to disavow the Revolution itself.

Parisian radicalism—against which the federalists were reacting—was in large measure provoked by severe economic troubles that were engulfing the infant republic. By February 1793 the Revolution's paper money, the assignats, had declined to 50 percent of its face value in the marketplace, and it continued steadily downward after that, to as low as one-third. This disastrous devaluation was compounded by a poor harvest. Panic over the scarcity of grain and flour swept across France, especially in the cities. Municipal leaders attempted to fix the price of bread so as to make it available to the masses, but they simply could not secure adequate supplies. Likewise the central government could not supply its armies under these conditions. Human cupidity of course made matters worse; uncivic-minded Frenchmen attempted to profit from the situation by hoarding scarce commodities or by speculating in assignats.

The strongest impetus for taking vigorous measures against all these problems, military, political, and economic, came from the urban populace in Paris and other cities. But the vehemence of certain Parisian sans-culottes posed yet another threat to the Convention: the threat of excessive radicalism and anarchy. The ultraradicals, like their enemies the federalists, were unwilling to defer to the Convention. Sans-culotte spokesmen who emerged in these months communicated the view that the Convention, the Jacobin Club, and even the Paris city government were not sufficiently responsive to popular demands. They therefore demanded a purge of the Convention to rid it of its moderates, a program of revolutionary public safety, and radical economic intervention to break through the laissez-faire immobility of the government: (1) price control (called a law of the Maximum) for all necessary commodities, (2) severe laws against hoarding and speculation, and (3) forced requisitions on the peasantry, to be carried out with the assistance of an armed force or revolutionary army of the interior.

Behind these demands lay the threat of armed insurrection. Many Parisians were sympathetic to this platform, aimed at revolutionizing the Revolution. For the Jacobins the pressure from the sans-culottes was a volatile mixture: it provided aid in their struggle against the Girondists and federalists, but it posed the danger of spilling over into anarchy.

In a sense all elements of the revolutionary crisis hinged on one problem: the lack of a strong, effective government that would not simply respond to popular pressure but organize and channel it into constructive action. The first step in the creation of such a government seemed to be the purge demanded by the radicals. On May 31 the sans-culottes launched a demonstration to force home their demands, and the Plain at this point decided that the Mountain must be supported against the Girondists, who were thundering against sans-culotte "tyranny." On June 2 twenty-three Girondists were expelled by the Convention and placed under house arrest; they would subsequently be tried for treason. A turning point had come, but the future course of the Revolution was still in question.

THE JACOBIN DICTATORSHIP

The sans-culotte movement in Paris had hoisted the Mountain to power in the Convention. The question now was which side of the coalition would dominate. Popular demands swelled for terrorism against counter-revolution and for vigorous provisioning policies. The conviction was spreading among the urban masses that the sovereign people could dictate its will to the Convention by demonstrations and the threat of insurrection. At the same time federalism exploded in the provinces in response to the purge of the Girondists; Lyons and Marseilles were now in full-scale rebellion.

The high point of popular agitation came on September 5, when a massive demonstration placed demands for drastic measures before the Convention. The Convention now depended on the support of the sans-culottes; moreover certain of the measures would strengthen the government's control over the country. The demonstrators' main slogans were "Food—and to have it, force for the law" and "Let terror be placed on the order of the day." Concretely they won the passage of laws imposing general price control, forbid-

ding hoarding, creating revolutionary armies of the interior, and empowering local revolutionary committees to incarcerate citizens whose loyalty was suspect or who seemed to threaten the public safety—the so-called law of suspects.

The Revolutionary Government
Back in June the triumphant Jacobins had drafted a democratic constitution, one of the original purposes for which the National Convention had been called. It had been submitted to a referendum and overwhelmingly approved by 3 million voters; thus it provided the cornerstone for a new legitimate government. But the constitution could not be implemented in the throes of such a crisis as now faced the nation, particularly in view of her internal divisions. In October the Convention acknowledged this, formally placed the constitution aside, and proclaimed the government "revolutionary until the peace." Such luxuries of citizenship as the elections, local self-government, and guarantees of individual liberty promised in the constitution would be enjoyed only after the republic was secure from its enemies within and without.

An array of revolutionary laws and institutions now existed; it remained for a group of determined and skillful political leaders to take the reins and make them effective. Such men were to be found on the Committee of Public Safety, appointed by the Convention to supervise military, economic, and political affairs.

The committee's leading personality and tactician was Maximilien Robespierre. An austere bachelor in his mid-thirties and a provincial lawyer before the Revolution, Robespierre had been a prominent spokesman for the left in the Constituent Assembly where he had advocated the rights of women, Jews, and free Negroes, and had crusaded for the democratization of the regime. In 1792 he was an official of the Paris city government and a newspaper editor. But his principal political forum was the capital's Jacobin Club, which by 1793 he more or less dominated. Elected to the Convention from Paris, he was selfless and self-righteous in his total dedication to revolutionary causes. He sought to guide the sans-culottes and serve their interests as much as possible, but at all times he placed the survival of the Revolution above their particular grievances. Thus in his leadership he struck a delicate balance between his sense of responsibility and his sympathy for popular aspirations. The two were not always compatible. His main object was to bring the republic through the emergency by creating confidence and efficiency in the revolutionary government, and in this he succeeded. His hope of reconciling class interests in the cause of democracy was ultimately frustrated.

The legislation for creating a centralized revolutionary government was passed in December 1793, at last filling the vacuum left by the fall of the monarchy. Under a law enacted December 4—or 14 Frimaire, year II, according to the new French calendar—revolutionary committees in towns and villages were made responsible to the Committee of Public Safety, which could purge them. Local officials were redesignated national agents, their initiative was curbed, and they too were subject to removal by the Committee. Revolutionary tribunals, representatives on mission (deputies sent to the provinces as commissars), and revolutionary armies of the interior were all placed under the Committee's scrutiny and control.

Crucial links in this chain of revolutionary dictatorship were the Jacobin clubs. They too were organized into a centralized network, led by the Paris Jacobin Club. They nominated citizens for posts on revolutionary committees and exercised surveillance over them. The clubs were to be "arsenals of public opinion," to support the war effort in every way

possible, and to denounce uncivic behavior among their fellow citizens.

No serious dissent was tolerated under the Jacobin reign. Freedom of expression was limited by the government's sense of the need for unity during the emergency, and the politically outspoken were purged. The first to fall were a group of ultraleftists led by Jacques René Hébert, a radical journalist and Paris official. They were accused of a plot against the republic. In reality they had questioned what they considered the Convention's leniency toward "enemies" of the people. Next came the turn of the so-called indulgents, among them Danton. They had argued—prematurely, in the government's view—for a relaxation of terrorism and centralization. They were arrested, indicted on trumped-up charges of treason, and sentenced to death by the revolutionary tribunal. This succession of purges, starting with the Girondists and ultimately ending with Robespierre himself, seemed to suggest, as one contemporary put it, that revolutions devour their own children.

The Reign of Terror

Most of those devoured by the French Revolution, however, were not its own children. They were rather an assortment of armed rebels, counterrevolutionaries, and unfortunate citizens swept into the vortex of war and internal strife. The Reign of Terror developed in response to the multifaceted crisis described on the previous pages. On the level of attitude, the Terror reflected a revolutionary mentality that saw threats and plots all around (some real, some imagined). The laws of the Terror were designed to intimidate a wide range of people perceived as enemies of the Revolution. They included the law of suspects, which led to the incarceration of 400,000 to 500,000 prisoners, and laws against the life and property of refractory priests and émigrés. They included also the price-control regulations and other legislation aimed at preventing the collapse of the Revolution from economic chaos or food shortages.

The Terror was the force behind the law—the determination and techniques to make these laws work. Its purpose was to coerce Frenchmen into abiding by the Revolution in some minimal fashion and into accepting certain sacrifices of self-interest to permit the republic and the Revolution to survive. By the same token the emphasis on organizing the Terror, on supervising it from some central point of authority, was designed to prevent anarchic violence like the prison massacres of September 1792 and the infamous *noyades* (drownings) of Nantes, in which hundreds of Vendée rebels and priests were brutally drowned in the Loire River. Wholesale slaughter was disavowed by the Committee of Public Safety, which for example prevented the indiscriminate condemnation of federalists and put a stop to violent de-Christianization. The Terror was meant to impress by the severity of examples, not by the liquidation of whole groups.

Statistical analysis of the death sentences during the Terror suggests that there was a relationship between executions and clear-and-present danger. A total of 17,000 death sentences were handed down by the various revolutionary tribunals and commissions, and an estimated 10,000 additional armed rebels were executed without trial. Over 70 percent of the sentences were passed in the two zones of intense civil war: 19 percent in the southeast (the Lyons region) and 52 percent in the west (the Vendée region). Moreover 72 percent of these were for armed rebellion. Conversely one-third of the departments had fewer than ten death sentences each and were relatively tranquil. While much of the revolutionary rhetoric and some of its legislation were aimed at the upper classes, the death sentences of the Terror hit hardest at the largest groups in the population: urban and rural common people who actively participated in the rebellions.[1]

The Paris Jacobin Club was founded by a group of progressive deputies to the Constituent Assembly of 1789. After August 1792 and the elections to the Convention, it became a forum for democratic deputies and middle-class Parisian radicals, as well as a "mother club" with which popular societies in the provinces affiliated themselves. As such, it was the closest thing the French revolutionaries had to a party apparatus. (Photo: New York Public Library, Picture Collection)

Apart from the repression of the Vendée revolt, the Terror's bloodiest episode took place in Lyons. The Convention laid siege to the city until it capitulated in October 1793. Implacable in its hostility, the Convention declared that "Lyons has made war against liberty and thus Lyons no longer exists." The entire population was disarmed, and the houses

---

[1] These statistics are drawn from Donald Greer, *The Incidence of the Terror.* 1935.

TURNING POINTS IN THE REVOLUTION

July 14, 1789:	Storming of the Bastille and triumph of the third estate.
August 10, 1792:	Storming of the Tuileries and end of the constitutional monarchy.
September 2–5, 1792:	Paris prison massacres.
May 31–June 2, 1793:	Sans-culotte march on the Convention and purge of the Girondists.
September 5, 1793:	Demonstration before the Convention and enactment of terroristic legislation and economic controls.
9 Thermidor, year II (July 27, 1794):	Fall of Robespierre.
1–2 Prairial, year III (May 20–21, 1795):	Unsuccessful insurrection by the Parisian sans-culottes for "Bread and the constitution of 1793."
18 Brumaire, year VIII (November 9, 1799):	Coup d'état by Napoleon Bonaparte and the revisionists.

of many wealthy citizens were burned. On-the-spot courts-martial were held and executions followed immediately. Some were carried out gruesomely, with the encouragement of irresponsible commissars. Almost 2,000 people were put to death, two-thirds of them from the upper classes. The fanaticism of the Parisian sans-culottes sent against Lyons reflected both their class consciousness and their revolutionary fervor during the dark days of crisis.

THE SANS-CULOTTES AND THE POPULAR REVOLUTION

After their massive revolt against the old order in 1789, the peasants were generally passive or overtly hostile to the Revolution's further progress. They contributed little as a group to the second revolution. The urban common people or sans-culottes, however, not only propelled the insurrectionary movements in the cities in 1789, but became ardent proponents of further revolutionizing in the social, political, and economic spheres. Their participation in the second revolution was essential to its success.

The role of the people in the Revolution has always been noted but until recently they have not been studied directly and in their own right. Instead their actions and concerns have been refracted through the eyes of their enemies or their spokesmen, themselves middle or upper class and far removed in their own life style from the common people. Inspired by Georges Lefebvre's classic studies of the peasants, historians have recently been writing about the French Revolution "from below"—about specific groups of common people. These studies convey their social identity, their aspirations, attitudes, and revolutionary activity as they tried to place their collective stamp on what they regarded as their Revolution.

The most dramatic impact made by the sans-culottes on the Revolution came during the famous insurrectionary *journées*, or "days" of crowd actions, demonstrations, and uprisings, that marked turning points in the Revolution's course (see list). We now know that the participants in these crowds and striking forces were not criminals and drifters, as antirevolutionary writers have claimed. They were Parisian workingmen—carpenters, cobblers, wine sellers, clerks, tailors, cafe keepers, stonemasons—mainly small-scale artisans, shopkeepers, and journeymen. The sans-culottes were not a class in the Marxist sense, for they varied in their relationship to the means of production: some, such as small workshop proprietors, owned them; others provided only their labor. But all shared the life style of Paris' popular neighborhoods and had a strong sense of community.

Popular Attitudes

The long hours of hard work that characterized the sans-culottes' existence generally yielded a modest livelihood that was painfully reduced by rises in the cost of living. Accordingly they were extremely concerned over the availability and prices of basic commodities like bread, candles, meat, and fuel. As consumers they faced the economic crisis of the revolutionary period with distress and anger. Their most basic demand was for government intervention to assure them the basic necessities of life. This incidentally is one reason that women were prominent among revolutionary activists: they were most directly concerned with putting food on their family's table. This concern was summarized by the call for "Food—and to have it, force for the law." By 1793 the Revolution's leaders were compelled to recognize this, and the right to subsistence was prominently proclaimed in the Jacobin constitution of 1793. Concretely it meant a combination of government price control, requisitioning, and a public works program to provide employment. Most of this violated the middle-class laissez-faire view of how the economy should work.

The sans-culottes, while firm believers in property rights, insisted that they must be limited by considerations of social utility. The right of an individual to a modest amount of property, like one small workshop or one store, was considered inviolate, but the sans-culottes denied that anyone had the right to "misuse" property by hoarding, speculating, or accumulating far more than he needed. Concepts of freedom and equality had a practical economic side in their opinion. As one petition put it, "What is the meaning of freedom, when one class of men can starve another? What is the meaning of equality, when the rich, by their monopolies, can exercise the right of life and death over their equals?"

Under the stress of soaring inflation and economic dislocation, the sans-culotte call for the right to subsistence and the middle-class call for laissez faire clashed dramatically. The willingness of the Mountain and the Jacobin Club to acknowledge the right to subsistence and to regulate the economy, at least during the war emergency, won them support among the people.

Bitterly antiaristocratic, the sans-culottes feared that the middle class might replace the nobility as a new kind of elite. The social attitude was reflected in everyday behavior. Extolling simplicity in dress and manners, they attacked opulence and pretension wherever they found or imagined them to be. Under their disapproving eye, high society and fancy dress generally disappeared from view. There was a revolution too in manners and morals. Vices like prostitution, pornography, and gambling were attributed to aristocrats and were denounced in the virtuous and austere society of the Revolution; drinking was the common man's vice and was tolerated.

The sans-culottes symbolized their break with the past by changing the names of their streets, cities, and public places to eliminate signs of royalism and aristocracy. The Palais Royal became the Palais d'Égalité ("Equality Palace"). Many people underwent debaptizing, exchanging their Christian names for the names of secular heroes like Gracchus, the ancient Roman reformer, or names derived from trees and plants. The Gregorian calendar was replaced with a more geometric revo-

lutionary calendar, computed from September 22, 1792, forward, in which weeks were replaced by units of ten days. Titles like "monsieur" and "madame" were dropped in favor of the simple, uniform designation of "citizen"—just as revolutionaries of a later generation would call each other "comrade."

Participatory Democracy

The Convention believed in a system of parliamentary or representative democracy, with an active political life at the grass roots but with power delegated to elected officials. And as we saw, during the emergency the Jacobins were willing to impose a virtual dictatorship in the form of the highly centralized revolutionary government. The sans-culottes, on the other hand, favored a popular scheme of participatory democracy. They believed that the local voters or in larger cities the local section assembly of citizens was the ultimate sovereign body; it could never permanently delegate its authority, even to the popularly elected Convention. In short they wanted the decision-making power actively lodged with the people rather than their deputies. To Robespierre this ideal of unrestrained direct democracy appeared unworkable and akin to anarchy.

At the beginning of the revolutionary year II (1793–1794), the forty-eight sections in Paris functioned almost as tiny autonomous republics in which the people ran their own affairs directly in the general assembly, a system an American would call town-meeting democracy. When necessary the sections co-

The Parisian citizen-soldiers were the most adamant revolutionaries of the era. Aristocrats called them sans-culottes (meaning "without knee-breeches") by way of insult, but the bitterly antiaristocratic militants proudly adopted it as their popular name. (Photo: The Mansell Collection)

operated with each other to exert collective pressure on the government. On the various *journées* the sans-culottes demonstrated their conviction that the people, if necessary in a state of armed insurrection, ought to be the ultimate arbiter of the republic. Political life in those months, especially but not exclusively in Paris, had a naive, breathless quality, generating high enthusiasm among thousands of sans-culottes, making them feel that for the first time the power of self-government was theirs.

The Convention looked on with mixed feelings. On the one hand they were uneasy allies, committed to the ideals of democracy and equality. On the other hand they were pragmatists who feared the anarchic force of this popular movement—its unpredictability, its disorder, and its inefficiency. The Mountain attempted to steer a difficult course between encouraging this civic participation and controlling it. The sans-culotte militants did a great deal for the war effort: they rooted out counterrevolutionaries, spread revolutionary usages, recruited soldiers, and formed committees for public relief. Like the Jacobin clubs in the provinces, the Parisian sans-culottes promoted the ideal of self-help.

From the sections, however, there came an endless stream of exhortations, petitions, denunciations, and veiled threats to the government. In the end the Convention decided that politically and administratively the direct democracy of the sections had to be disciplined. In the spring of 1794, it passed a series of measures restricting the meeting times, activities, and rights of the sections that removed most of their effective powers. What the government failed to realize was that once the ardor of the sans-culottes was forcibly cooled off, their support of the Convention, and their willingness to sacrifice, would also diminish. The results would leave these leaders vulnerable to reaction.

THE VICTORIES OF THE YEAR II

Even while the Mountain was curtailing the powers of the sans-culottes, however, it continued to bank on their support for the military defense of the nation. For the Revolution's more far-sighted leaders knew that France's ultimate fate rested in the hands of her armies. Drawing on the citizenry at large, the Convention forged a new armed force that overcame the coalition of hostile states arrayed against France.

Revolutionary Foreign Policy

As initially formulated in 1789, revolutionary ideology had offered no direct threat to the status quo of the European state system. It had perceived its influence as consisting only in the force of example. French power was not to be felt across the country's borders except as persuasion. Indeed the orators of the National Assembly had argued that the best foreign policy for a progressive and free society was peace, neutrality, and isolation from the diplomatic intrigues of monarchs.

But peace did not imply pacifism. When counterrevolution at home coalesced with threats from abroad, the revolutionaries were eager to resort to war against both. The hostilities that broke out in 1792 were for the most part defensive in origin as far as the French were concerned. But as in all major wars the initial objectives were rapidly forgotten, and as the conflict spilled over large parts of Europe, it disrupted the political organization and boundaries of many Continental states.

The revolutionary wars involved considerations that were perennial in international conflicts as well as certain new and explosive purposes. On the one hand the French adopted traditional objectives such as rounding off and extending their frontiers and exacting agreements from adjoining states aimed at protecting those frontiers. At the same time they pursued revolutionary principles such as the right of a people to self-determination. As early as September 1791, the National Assembly had declared that "the rights of peoples are not determined by the treaties of princes."

As we have seen in the previous chapter, there were people in many areas of Western Europe who were eager to challenge the ancient arrangements—"the treaties of princes" —that determined their political destiny. Particularly in the zone of Europe lying west of the Elbe River, several internal conflicts had already arisen before 1789, and the success of the French could not help but renew liberal and revolutionary sentiment. Patriots in Geneva, the United Provinces, and the Austrian Netherlands had already tasted repression. They were eager for another round in their various struggles and looked to France for assistance.

Refugees from these regions had fled to France and formed pressure groups that lobbied with French leaders and corresponded with rebels back home. Their fondest hopes rested on the chance that in fighting against the coalition, the French might liberate their own lands. If they were contiguous to France (as were the Austrian Netherlands, Savoy, and the Rhineland), France might then annex them to her own republic; elsewhere (in Holland, Lombardy, Ireland, and the Swiss Confederation) she might help set up independent republics by overthrowing the ruling princes or oligarchies. In the wake of war and revolutionary enthusiasm, the foreign patriots induced the Convention to declare in November 1792 that it "accords fraternity and aid to [foreign] people who wish to recover their liberty," though the French had in mind only those whose governments were actively leagued against France.

While there had been some talk of mounting a universal crusade to bring freedom to oppressed peoples, French leaders were in reality committed to a pragmatic policy. As the war spilled over into the Austrian Netherlands and Germany, they had to organize their forces and ensure a base of support abroad. This in turn required that the primary aims of war embody the spirit and stated objectives of the revolutionary society, not the age-old motive of aggrandizement through occupation and domination. Thus in December of 1792 the government proclaimed further that it would establish the freedom of those to whom it had brought or would bring armed assistance. This meant that in each land where the French prevailed, feudal practices, hereditary privileges, and repressive institutions would be abolished. A provisional government would be established to cooperate with the French forces in supervising and paying for the liberation. Full independence was a long-term promise; more immediately the occupied territory would be obliged to underwrite the expenses of French troops.

These intentions were greeted enthusiastically by progressive elements in the middle and noble classes and in some instances by artisans. But most nobles, priests, and peasants and large sections of the middle class were hostile or indifferent to them, resenting the requisitions and special taxes, though they did not necessarily wish a restoration of the old order.

By 1794 France had a permanent foothold in the Austrian Netherlands, which was shortly to be annexed to the Great Nation, as France now called herself. Apart from this, however, Robespierre proved to be relatively isolationist. Arguing that freedom had to be secured at home before it could be exported abroad, the Committee of Public Safety declined to intervene in behalf of a Polish revolutionary movement, refused to invade Holland, and designed a strategy that precluded any involvement in Italy. In short, while occupying the Austrian Netherlands and hoping to annex the left bank of the Rhine, the Convention renounced any drive for the establishment of new "sister republics."

The Revolutionary Armies

The fighting men who carried the Revolution abroad were a very different body from the corps inherited from Louis XVI. The royal army had undergone major reforms since 1789 that opened military service as a decent career to all kinds of Frenchmen. At the same time the organization of militias and national guards, with their elected officers, introduced a new concept of the citizen-soldier as against a professional army apart from civil society.

The army's chief problem came after the war began, when large numbers of royalist officers either deserted altogether or behaved disloyally. At the crucial Battle of Valmy, a remnant of the old army showed that it could fight effectively, but its numbers were too reduced by desertion and neglect to offer continued resistance. A hasty call-up of volunteers proved inadequate both in numbers and effectiveness.

The coalition launched its second major assault in 1793, and the poor performance of the French troops made it clear that drastic innovations were required. The Convention initiated far-reaching conscription and mobilization, the so-called mass levy of August 1793 (levée en masse). All unmarried men between the ages of eighteen and twenty-five were drafted for combat service, while older and married men were assigned convoy and guard duty or similar tasks. All social classes were affected, and in a short time almost half a million French citizens were placed under arms. With elected officers at their head, the citizen-soldiers marched off to the front under banners reading, "The French People, risen against the tyrants."

The Convention had already decided to combine these blue-uniformed recruits with their white-uniformed counterparts from the old professional army in units called demibrigades. In the future noncommissioned officers would be elected by all troops, but higher ranks would be chosen by superior officers according to merit and seniority. The expectation was that discipline would be taught to the new troops by the professionals, who in turn would absorb a spirit of patriotism from the recruits. Although the actual amalgam took several years to complete, its spirit proved immediately successful.

One reason for this success was the Convention's attitude toward military discipline in a revolutionary society. Civilian control over the military was firmly established, and discipline now applied to officers as well as men. The government insisted that generals show the will to win, confidence in the republic, and talent. A large number of young men were raised quickly through the ranks to command positions. Lazare Hoche, perhaps the most spectacular case, led an entire army at the age of twenty-five and died a military hero at twenty-seven. Other generals were less fortunate. The commander of the ill-fated Rhine army in early 1793 was branded a traitor, tried, and guillotined. The revolutionary slogan "Win or die" was a serious matter.

A dramatically new approach to military life was thus taking shape: citizen-soldiers recruited through conscription, concern for their needs and morale, generous veterans' benefits if they were wounded, quick promotions for loyal and capable men, exemplary discipline for officers who wavered in spirit or on the battlefield. The question still remained of how the new army would be used in the field, and the answer reflected the combination of revolutionary spirit and hardheaded practicality that prevailed in the republic.

The mass of soldiers in the new demibrigades did not have the necessary training to be deployed according to the traditional tactics of Old Regime armies. Conversely they were infused with a sense of patriotism that it would be well to utilize. Hence strategists perfected the new battle formation of massive columns that could move quickly without much practice in drilling. Mass and mobility characterized the armies of the French Revolution. As General Hoche put it, "No maneuvers, no art; only fire and patriotism," and the Committee of Public Safety advised its commanders, "Act offensively and in masses. Use the bayonet at every opportunity. Fight great battles and pursue the enemy until he is utterly destroyed." In this spirit the Jacobins and sans-culottes sought all-out war, and strategy was shaped to achieve it.

The Jacobins did not neglect the home front, whose contributions to the war effort were obviously crucial for victory. Economic mobilization, directed by the Convention and the Jacobin clubs, produced the necessary material support for the armies. Weapons, ammunition, clothing, and food were all produced or requisitioned in extraordinary quantities by herculean effort. Without them the military reforms would have achieved no purpose.

In late 1793 and early 1794, the armies won a series of decisive battles. They culminated in the Battle of Fleurus in June 1794, when the Austrian Netherlands was once again occupied; the annexation, officially conceded by the Hapsburgs in 1797, would last until 1814. At the Pyrenees and the Rhine, French armies were victorious, forcing their enemies one by one to come to the peace table—first Spain

and Prussia, then Piedmont, and finally Austria. An army crippled at the outset by treason and desertion, defeat, lack of training and discipline, and collapsing morale had been forged into a potent force in less than two years. Militarily the second revolution was a brilliant success.

II. FROM ROBESPIERRE TO BONAPARTE

To its most dedicated supporters, the revolutionary government had two major purposes: first, to surmount a crisis and steer the republic to victory; second, to democratize France's social fabric. Only the first objective won the widespread adherence of middle-class republicans. It is not surprising, therefore, that after the victories of the year II, the revolutionary government was overthrown and the second revolution dismantled. Jacobinism and democracy, however, had become a permanent part of the French experience, as had royalism and reaction. The political spectrum of modern Europe had been created. Within this spectrum the men of 1789 attempted to command an elusive centrist or moderate position, but they proved inadequate to the task. During the four unsteady years of the Directory regime, however, revolutionary expansion outside of France proceeded aggressively. It triumphed briefly but soon precipitated a second anti-French coalition. This challenge brought the weaknesses of the Directory regime to a head and opened the way to the ascendancy of Napoleon Bonaparte.

THE THERMIDORIAN REACTION
(1794–1796)

The National Convention held a polarized nation together, consolidated the republic, and defeated the Revolution's foreign enemies. But in achieving these successes, the ruling Jacobins increasingly isolated themselves, making enemies on every side. Moderates and ultrarevolutionaries alike resented the rule that they imposed. Wealthy peasants and businessmen chafed under the economic regimentation. Moreover the pressure of events and the relentless necessity to make hard and unpopular decisions wore out the Revolution's most prominent leaders.

After the decisive victories of the year II, the Convention's unity disintegrated. As the fifth anniversary of the Bastille's fall approached, Robespierre's enemies were emboldened to rise against him. Longstanding rivalries, differences over policy, and clashes of temperament now exploded. Robespierre girded himself to denounce yet another group of unspecified intriguers, presumably to send them to the fate of Danton and Hébert. But his rivals both left and right formed a hasty coalition and struck back, denouncing Robespierre to the Convention as a tyrant and would-be dictator.

The plotting of these individuals was crucial, but Robespierre's downfall is attributable also to the fact that he was no longer needed by the Convention. Having supported him with reluctance during the emergency, the moderate deputies were now willing to abandon him. The Parisian sans-culottes might have maintained Robespierre in power despite this desertion, but as we have seen, the Jacobins had alienated them by curbing the autonomy of the sections. Many sans-culottes were therefore indifferent to the struggle of personalities that took place in the Convention that July.

On the twenty-seventh — 9 Thermidor — Robespierre was declared an outlaw by the Convention. Efforts to rally a popular force in his defense that night proved ineffective; and on the following day he and several loyal associates were seized and guillotined. French-

men perhaps did not realize it at the time, but 9 Thermidor thus became one of those crucial *journées* on which the Revolution's course was decisively altered.[2]

After Robespierre's fall the Revolution's momentum was broken, and the apparatus of the Terror was dismantled. Soon the anti-Jacobins began to attack the revolutionaries in turn. Their strident calls for retribution against the terrorists eventually produced a terrorism of their own—a "white terror" aimed against Jacobins and sans-culottes that resulted in street fighting, assassinations, and in the south of France massacres.

To survey the unfolding of the Thermidorian reaction is equivalent to viewing a film of the preceding half-decade run backward through the projector. Suspects were released, the revolutionary committees abolished, defendants before the revolutionary tribunals acquitted, and their former accusers indicted in their place. The Paris Jacobin Club was closed, while in the provinces the affiliated clubs gradually withered away under harassment and restrictive legislation. Amnesty was extended to the Girondists and to the Vendée rebels; Mountain deputies were now denounced. Paris underwent "de-sans-culottization"—the section leaders of the year II were driven out of political life and threatened with retribution. At all levels those who had borne the burden of responsibility and action in the year II suddenly found themselves attacked.

Paralleling these political reversals was a marked change in the state of public morals and social behavior. The upper classes now set

---

[2] "Thermidor" has become a generic term to denote the phase in a revolution when the pendulum swings back toward moderation or reaction. It has been argued that the drafting of the United States Constitution in 1787 was the Thermidor of the American Revolution and that Stalin's reign was the Thermidor of the Bolshevik Revolution.

the tone. For those who sought a life of pleasure and luxury, Thermidor was a reprieve from the austerity and restraint of the year II. Public virtue gave way before indulgence and license. Luxury not only reappeared but by all contemporary accounts was flaunted with scandalous vulgarity. High society, with its balls, salons, and fancy dress, was reestablished. The titles "monsieur" and "madame" replaced the republican designation "citizen." Most important, this high society of the rich showed itself bored by the spectacle of popular misery.

Unfortunately this social reaction occurred at a time of extensive mass suffering. In keeping with free-trade ideology, the Thermidorians abandoned the legislation regulating the economy. The marketplace was again permitted to operate by its "natural laws" of supply and demand, producing a skyrocketing inflation. Worse yet, France experienced a harvest in 1795 more meager than in the crisis years of 1788–1789 and 1793. But despite such ill luck, the Thermidorians declined to intervene to protect small consumers from economic ravages. They refused to try to provide a minimum supply of bread at an affordable price, a relief effort that the revolutionary government and even the Old Regime monarchs had made. In the face of near-famine, every index of social welfare now revealed disaster. Suicide and mortality rates rose markedly; police reports spoke of little else besides popular misery, discontent, and destitute people collapsing in the streets from undernourishment.

Since the government would not help, the former militants attempted to spark a political reversal to halt the reaction and force the authorities to act. Their hopes centered on the constitution of 1793, whose prompt and full implementation they now demanded. The slogan of sans-culottes in the sections during the spring of 1795 was simply "Bread and the constitution of 1793." The Thermidorians, however, were moving in precisely the opposite direction. Viewing that constitution as far too democratic, they were looking for an excuse to scrap it altogether.

The militants began demonstrating in April, and the government countered by ordering local authorities to disarm them. The only recourse left was insurrection, and it began on 1 Prairial, year III (May 20, 1795). It was a grim, mournful uprising, a rear-guard action against disaster. The sans-culottes took over the Convention briefly in cooperation with a handful of sympathetic deputies. But their hours were numbered, for the Thermidorians had retreated merely to organize their armed forces. In two days of street fighting, the sans-culottes were driven back, cut off, and defeated. Severe repression followed: 36 people were executed, some 1,200 imprisoned, and an additional 1,700 interrogated and disarmed. Probably the majority of these had not even taken part in the insurrection but were being singled out in retribution for the role of the sans-culottes during the Terror.

These *journées* were the end of the popular movement, the last time that the Parisian revolutionary crowd would be mobilized. It was now clear just how much the sans-culottes and the Jacobins had needed each other. Isolated from each other, they had both been defeated. In the process the democratic republic of the year II was lost. Whatever the possibilities had been for achieving some form of social democracy (and the issue remains ambiguous), they were now severely reduced.[3] The Thermidorian reaction seemed to

[3] The Convention's measures to promote social democracy included the abolition of slavery, the final abolition of seigneurial rights without compensation to the lords, and equal division of estates among heirs. Legislation for a system of free public education, a progressive income tax, a war veterans' bonus, and the distribution of the property of convicted suspects to indigent patriots was never implemented.

guarantee that the middle class would maintain control of France.

THE DIRECTORY (1796–1799)

By the end of 1795, the remaining members of the Convention assumed that the Revolution was over. The extremes had been vanquished, and the time for the "peaceable enjoyment of liberty" was at hand. They had drafted a new constitution—the constitution of the year III—and proclaimed a general amnesty, and they were prepared to turn a new page. The revolutionary government, which had replaced the fallen constitutional monarchy, had in turn been replaced by a middle-class constitutional republic. It was known as the Directory, after its five-man executive body.

The Directory's proponents, concerned above all with retaining power, openly declared that the republic would "be governed by the best citizens, who are found among the property-owning class." Accordingly the constitution abandoned the universal suffrage of 1793 and restored the propertied franchise of 1791 and the multilayered system of indirect elections. It called for a cumbersome separation of powers, designed to moderate the political process, while it guarded against the rise of a potential dictator by installing the five-man Directory. Equally important, it omitted devices to facilitate active democracy, such as referendums, and said nothing of popular rights, like the right to free education and to subsistence, all of which were specified in the 1793 constitution. The concern with eliminating the popular democracy of the year II was balanced by measures to prevent a royalist resurgence. Fearing that free elections at this point might swing the republic too far to the right, the Convention decided to coopt two-thirds of its membership into the new legislature established by the constitution. A royalist attempt to oppose this with an armed protest was crushed.

The government thus repudiated both the royalist movement and the second revolution. As regicides the directors necessarily opposed royalism; on the other hand they were determined that popular democracy and terrorism would not recur. Apart from these considerations they were inclined to forgive and forget. They attempted to command a position somewhere near the hypothetical center of the political spectrum, a stance that one historian has aptly called the mirage of the moderates.

To maintain themselves in power, the Directory politicians were obliged to remove with one hand freedoms that they had granted with the other. They repeatedly purged locally elected officials; they periodically undermined freedom of the press and of association, ostensibly guaranteed in the new constitution, by suppressing new Jacobin clubs and hostile newspapers. Above all they refused to acknowledge the legitimacy of organized opposition, whether rightist or leftist. This explains the succession of coups and purges that marked the Directory's four years. Although the repressive measures were mild compared with those of the second revolution —deportation was generally the harshest punishment meted out for dissent—their net effect was to make the regime dysfunctional. In the end a significant number of Thermidorians were obliged to abandon their own creation altogether.

The Political Spectrum

For all its dictatorial qualities, however, the Directory regime was free enough to allow most shades of the political spectrum some visibility. Obliterated previously by the Jacobin commonwealth and later by the Napoleonic dictatorship, the full range of opinions and divisions in France was clearly revealed during the years of the Directory and would persist with certain modifications down to the fall of the Third Republic, in 1940.

The most important legacy of all was probably apathy, born of exhaustion or cynicism. Most citizens, especially peasants, were weary of controversy, distrustful of politicians, and hostile to administrators and tax collectors, whatever government they served. As a result participation in the Directory regime's annual elections was extremely low.

Within this context of massive apathy, politically conscious Frenchmen were deeply divided. The ultraroyalists were uncompromising enemies of the Directory, dedicated to overthrowing it. They included émigrés, armed rebels, and refractory priests, along with their peasant followers, and many of them cooperated with the exiled Bourbons and English spies. Shading off from the ultraroyalists were the monarchists, mainly from the middle and peasant classes. They hoped to alter the republic's foundations and to drift gradually back toward royalism without necessarily overthrowing the republic by force. Their goals included allowing the émigrés to return, restoring the position of the refractory clergy, and stamping out entirely the last vestiges of Jacobinism. Since Napoleon largely acquiesced in these changes, they formed a major base of his support.

On the left of the spectrum stood the Jacobins, or democrats. They were committed not only to preserving the Revolution of 1789 and the republic but to identifying positively with the second revolution as well. They did not advocate a return to the Terror, hoping rather, like the constitutional royalists, to work legally within the new institutions of the Directory to regain power. The Jacobin policy was to promote grass-roots activism through local political clubs, petitions, peaceful demonstrations, newspapers, and electoral campaigns. The clubs attracted a small cross section of middle-class revolutionaries and sans-culotte militants, thus keeping alive the egalitarian social ideals of the year II. In addition to calling for the implementation of existing laws against counterrevolutionaries, the Jacobins advocated free public education, a veterans' bonus for soldiers, the right to subsistence, and progressive taxation.

At the far end of the spectrum emerged a tiny group of collectivists whose significance would loom much larger in the nineteenth century than it did in 1796. This was the circle of Gracchus Babeuf. They viewed the year II as simply a stage in the revolutionary process that now had to be followed by a final revolution against the middle-class republic in the name of the masses. Their objectives were a vaguely defined "real equality" and a "community of goods," a distributive type of communism. Believing that the middle-class republic was simply a new form of tyranny, they plotted its overthrow by means of a highly centralized secret conspiracy. When Filippo Buonarroti published a firsthand account of the plot in the 1820s, it became a handbook of revolution, influencing Karl Marx and ultimately Lenin.

The Directory's adherents stood somewhere in the center of this broad spectrum, shifting their ground uncertainly and unsuccessfully to find a solid position. They were hostile to the royalists, but possibly even more antagonistic to the Jacobins. Thus they sometimes collaborated with the reactionaries, as when they used the Babeuf plot as a pretext for repressing the entire left, though most democrats had deplored Babeuf's calls for insurrection and did not take his communism seriously. This propelled the Directory into a tentative alliance with the right, and the climate of public opinion became increasingly reactionary. However, when the first regular elections held in the year V (1797) produced a royalist victory, the moderates reversed themselves. Backed by General Bonaparte's army of Italy, they purged the legislature of the most notorious royalists, annulled numerous elections, suppressed about forty royalist newspapers, restored the sanctions against priests and émigrés, and allowed the Jacobins to open new clubs.

But after a few months, as the clubs began to revive a democratic spirit, the Directory grew fearful. During the elections of the year VI, democratic and conservative republicans began to campaign against each other in what almost amounted to party rivalry. The Directory again intervened, closing the clubs, manipulating the electoral assemblies, and where this failed, purging the democrats elected. It is revealing to note that almost at the same time the American republic was going through a similar process, but there the rival parties finally agreed to disagree, and organized opposition was accepted as part of the legitimate political system. In France organized opposition was not tolerated, and that crucial decision contributed to the republic's demise.

THE RISE OF BONAPARTE

While France was retreating from her Revolution internally, however, she supported and spread it more forcefully than ever abroad. For the Revolution in Europe, the Directory years marked a high point of success. Under the Directory she gradually turned to a policy of encouraging wars of liberation and the establishment of sister republics (see Map 21.1). This eventually led to the creation of progressive representative governments in the United Provinces and the Swiss Confederation, which became known respectively as the Batavian and Helvetic republics. It led also,

despite the Directory's attempt to prevent it, to the spread of war and liberation to the entire Italian peninsula. This in turn came about because certain commanders in the field began to create their own diplomacy. Among them was a young brigadier general, Napoleon Bonaparte.

The Making of a Hero

Bonaparte personifies the world-historical figure—the rare person whose life decisively affects the mainstream of human events. Born in 1769 of an impoverished but well-connected family on the French-controlled island of Corsica, he scarcely seemed destined to play such a role. His youthful ambitions were limited to Corsica itself, and most of his adolescent fantasies seem to have involved leading the island to independence from France. He was sent to French military academies, where he proved a diligent student, very adept at mathematics, and an eager reader of history. Aloof from his aristocratic classmates, whose pretensions he resented, young Bonaparte was extraordinarily self-reliant and energetic. Imagination and energy would remain among his chief personality traits, but before the Revolution he lacked any notable objective. Meanwhile he became an expert in artillery.

The Revolution saw him return to Corsica, but his ambitions ran afoul of more conservative elements on the island, and eventually the heat of provincial factionalism drove him and his family off Corsica altogether. At that juncture Napoleon moved onto a far larger stage of action. His rise as a military officer was steady and rapid; it was based in part on the luck of successive opportunities but equally on his ability to make fast, bold decisions and carry them out with remarkable efficiency. On leave in Paris in 1795, he made important contacts among the leaders of the Directory and was assigned to the planning

MAP 21.1: THE REVOLUTIONARY REPUBLICS 1792–1799

bureau of the war ministry. This put him in a position to advocate a new strategy—the opening of a major front in Italy for a French strike at the Hapsburg forces from the south, pushing northward into Germany while armies on the Rhine drove in from the west. The strategy approved, he was given command of the Army of Italy in 1797.

The total number of opposing Austrians outnumbered the French, but Bonaparte moved his troops rapidly and skillfully to achieve surprise and numerical superiority in specific encounters. The end result was a major victory that brought the French the Hapsburg province of Lombardy with its capital, Milan. Bonaparte's overall plan almost miscarried since the army of the Rhine was unsuccessful in its part of the offensive. But this fact made his own victories all the more important to the Directory. Moreover Napoleon ensured his popularity with the Paris government by making his campaign self-supporting through organized levies on the Italians instead of allowing his troops the customary prerogative of looting.

On the scene in Italy, Bonaparte brought a great new sense of excitement and showmanship to the French occupation. His personal magnetism, his theatrical skill, and his ability to manipulate men and policies all won him tremendous popularity among the Italians. He encouraged them to organize their own revolutionary movement, seeing the liberation of Italy as a means of both solidifying support for his army among them and ultimately enhancing his own reputation. This distressed the Directory since its own objective was to trade off conquests in Italy for security on the Rhine frontier, but in the end the government had to accept the fruits of the young general's victories over Austria and the Treaty of Campo Formio, which he personally negotiated in October 1797. Austria recognized a new and independent state in northern Italy, the Cisalpine Republic, and made peace with France, though leaving the Rhine question to future negotiations.

Patriotic aspiration in France now focused on defeating the last member of the coalition—the hated British enemy. Bonaparte naturally yearned for the glory of accomplishing this, and he was authorized to prepare an invasion force. Previous seaborne landings directed at Ireland had failed, and Napoleon too was finally obliged to abandon the scheme because of insufficient naval capability.

In February 1798 Napoleon instead proceeded southward to launch an expedition to Egypt. The objective was to strike at Britain's colonial interests, ultimately including the approaches to India. But British naval superiority, in the form of Admiral Horatio Nelson's fleet, turned the mission into a debacle. At the Battle of the Nile, the French fleet was decimated, and the army was marooned without support in North Africa. In addition Napoleon suffered reversals in engagements with Turkish forces. Only skillful news management prevented the full dimensions of the defeat from being known in France; the expedition's exotic details—including the much-publicized element of scientific exploration—dominated the version of the events that most Frenchmen learned. Ultimately Napoleon extricated himself from this morass by slipping off through the blockade alone, to all intents and purposes abandoning his army. Since important things were happening in France, he was confident that this would be overlooked.

The Brumaire Coup

While Bonaparte was in Egypt, the Directory was faltering under the political pressures discussed earlier. Charges of tyranny and ineffectiveness accumulated against the executive. Its diplomacy had proved a failure; further expansion in Italy, which had produced several new sister republics on the peninsula, had precipitated a new coalition against France—Great Britain, Russia, Austria, Naples, and Turkey. Facing a new war in the spring of 1799, the government was denounced for tolerating corruption by war contractors and for harassing patriotic generals.

In the elections of that spring, the widespread discontent was manifested in the defeat of many government-sponsored candidates. Shortly thereafter the legislature was able to oust four of the five directors and replace them with an ill-fated consortium of Jacobins and conservatives led by Sieyès. The pretext for toppling the incumbents came from military reversals in June, when ill-supplied French forces were compelled to evacuate most of Italy and were yielding in the Helvetic Republic. Sieyès' supporters were secretly eager to alter the constitution itself. They had lost confidence in the seemingly ineffectual institutions of the Directory regime and the instability that they felt in its annual elections. They were "revisionists," hoping to redesign the republic along more oligarchic lines. The Jacobins were their main enemies, for they wished conversely to democratize the Directory gradually. The moderate or centrist position had virtually disappeared.

The military crisis briefly favored the Jacobins, who responded with a battery of emergency measures to rally the country. Simultaneously they urged legislation to guarantee freedom for newspapers, political clubs, and other forms of organized dissent. The revisionists opposed these proposals, stalled, and ultimately succeeded in having them rejected. Meanwhile the autumn brought success for the French forces in the Helvetic state and in the Batavian Republic, where they repulsed an Anglo-Russian invasion. Most of Italy was lost, but the real threat to France herself had passed. At this point the revisionists began a concerted offensive at home against the democrats, closing down their clubs and newspapers and preparing for a coup d'état against the constitution, whose main supporters were now the powerless Jacobins.

Bonaparte's return to France seemed fortuitous at this time of uncertainty. No dire military threat remained to propel the country into the arms of a general; the revisionists were primarily concerned with scrapping a relatively open-ended regime that might evolve in a democratic direction and establishing a more rigid, oligarchic republic. But they did need a general's cooperation, for generals were the only national heroes in this demoralized period, and a general would come in handy to organize whatever force might be necessary to ensure the success of the coup. Bonaparte was not the revisionists' first choice, but he proved to be the only one available. In addition his trip up from the Mediterranean was greeted with a hero's welcome; the people had only a dim knowledge of the Egyptian fiasco and saw him in his well-earned role of victor in the Italian campaign.

Contrary to the intentions of Sieyès and his coconspirators, Bonaparte proved to be the tail that wagged the dog. As the plans were prepared, he thrust himself into an increasingly prominent position, emerging as the most ambitious and boldest of those involved. It was he who addressed the legislature to denounce a mythical Jacobin plot and to demand emergency powers to set up a new provisional government. These powers were granted, and Bonaparte joined with the two remaining directors to form a new executive, charged with bringing in a new constitutional draft. Soldiers were present to prevent any resistance. The legislature was then purged, with a cooperative rump left to ratify the new arrangements. This was how the *journée* of 18 Brumaire, year VIII (November 9, 1799), unfolded.

The Brumaire coup had not been designed to create a dictatorship, let alone a military dictatorship, but that was precisely its eventual result. In the ensuing maneuvering among the revisionists, Bonaparte's ideas and personality prevailed. The general came out of the coup as the strong man in a triumvirate of consuls, and Sieyès' elaborate plans for a republican oligarchy ended in the wastebasket, he himself accepting a pension and retiring to the country.

In other respects the plotters' plans succeeded. Elections and legislative power were meant to be limited, and they were; the middle-class elite was meant to erect barriers against the advance of democracy, and it did. The social changes propounded in the revolution of the year II were permanently blocked, while those of 1789 were consummated and protected. The price was a surrender of popular sovereignty and parliamentary liberalism.

On one final point the revisionists were to be particularly deceived. With Bonaparte's cooperation they had implicitly held out the promise of obtaining a durable peace through victory. Instead, the new regime promoted expansion and continuous war of unparalleled dimensions.

III. THE NAPOLEONIC IMPERIUM

Bonaparte rapidly became a forceful and skillful dictator. Certain of his institutional and social reforms proved so durable that they survived his downfall by well over a century. At the time, however, it was his success on the battlefield against France's foes that gave him a free hand domestically. And it was again on the battlefield that his enigmatic ambitions began to grow, transforming him from a general of the Revolution to an imperial conqueror of the Continent. Bonaparte's occupation of Italy, Germany, Spain, and other lands set contradictory forces of change in motion, for nationalism, liberalism, and reaction alike were sparked by his presence.

THE NAPOLEONIC SETTLEMENT IN FRANCE

Napoleon's prime asset in his rapid takeover of France was the resignation of its citizens. Most Frenchmen were so weary politically that they were inclined to see in Napoleon what they wished to see. The Committee of Public Safety had won grudging submission only through its terroristic policies; Napoleon achieved the same result almost by default. The fact that he was highly eclectic, an effective propagandist for himself, and a man of great personal magnetism helped placate a divided France. Ultraroyalists and dedicated Jacobins were never reconciled to his regime, but most citizens fell between those extremes and were able to find something to cheer about in the general's accomplishments.

Napoleon's attitudes are not easily classified: he was not a reactionary or a Jacobin, not a conservative or a liberal, though his opinions were flavored by a touch of each persuasion. The things he was most concerned with were authority and justification of his actions through results. The men of 1789 could find in him an heir of the Revolution because of his hostility toward the Old Regime. The corporate system, the creaking institutions of absolutism, and the congealed structures of aristocratic hierarchy were all immensely distasteful to him; he considered them unjust and ineffective. Apart from these negative perspectives, Napoleon valued the Revolution's positive commitment to equality of opportunity. This was the major liberal concept of 1789 that he continued to defend. Other rights and liberties he apparently felt could be curtailed or ignored.

Ten years of upheavals had presented a grim paradox: the Revolution had proceeded in the name of freedom, and yet successive forms of repression had been mounted to defend it. Napoleon fitted comfortably into this mold; unlike the Directory, he made no pretense about it. The social gains of the Revolution would be preserved through the exercise of strong control. His field of action was far greater than that of the most powerful eighteenth-century monarch, for no entrenched aristocracy existed to resist him. Benefiting from the clearing operations of the Revolution, he could reconstruct far more than any previous ruler and thus could show more results in justification of his authority.

Tragically, however, Napoleon drifted away from his own ideal of rationalization. Increasingly absorbed in his personal power, he began to force domestic and foreign policies on France that were geared to his imperial ambitions. As a result he increasingly directed his government toward raising men and money for the military machine, abandoning the fragile revolutionary legacy in the process.

Political and Religious Settlements

Bonaparte imposed a constitution on France that placed almost unchecked power in the hands of a single man, the first consul, for ten years. It also called for his own appointment to that position. Two later constitutional revisions, which were approved in plebiscites, further increased executive authority while diminishing the legislative branch until it disappeared altogether. The first, in 1802, converted the consulship into a lifetime post; the second, in 1804, did away with the republic by proclaiming Napoleon emperor of the French with hereditary title. The task of drafting legislation was transferred from elected representatives to appointed administrators in the Council of State. This new body was charged with advising the emperor, drafting legislation under his orders, and supervising local authorities and public institutions. This marked the birth of government by experts that remained an alternative to parliamentary government throughout subsequent French history.

The system of local government established in 1800 came ironically close to restoring the centralized bureaucracy of the Old Regime, which had been unanimously condemned in 1789. Under Bonaparte local elections, which the Revolution had emphasized, were virtually eliminated. Each department was now administered by a prefect appointed by Paris. The 400-odd subprefects on the district level as well as the 40,000 mayors of France's communes were likewise chosen in Paris. With minor changes the prefect system survives in France to this day, severely limiting local autonomy and self-government.

Police-state methods finished what constitutional change began: the suppression of genuine political activity in French life. Inheriting a large police ministry from the Directory, Napoleon placed it under the control of a former terrorist, Joseph Fouché, directing him to eliminate organized opposition and dissent. Newspapers were reduced in number and drastically censored;[4] the free journalism born in 1789 was replaced by government press releases and news management—the propaganda techniques Napoleon had adopted in Italy and Egypt became standard procedure for the consulate and empire. Clubs were prohibited, certain dissidents deported, and other presumed opponents placed under surveillance by police spies. All this wrested submission from the whole range of political activists—royalist die-hards, sans-culotte militants, and liberal intellectuals. Opposition

---

[4] Before the Brumaire coup Paris had had seventy-three newspapers; by 1811 it had only four, all hewing to the official government line.

was reduced to clandestine plotting or passive resistance in such forms as desertion from the army.

Napoleon's actions in the religious sphere were designed to promote stability at home and popularity abroad. By 1800 revolutionary policy amounted to half-hearted secularism, with Catholicism tolerated but barred from a voice in public activity. Continuing proscription of the refractory clergy made the free exercise of the religion difficult, and the orthodox Catholic world continued to stigmatize the entire Revolution as antichurch.

Napoleon judged that major concessions to Catholic sentiment were in order, provided they could be carefully controlled by the state. He proceeded to negotiate an agreement with Pope Pius VII, the Concordat of 1801, acknowledging Catholicism as the "preferred" religion of France but explicitly protecting freedom of conscience and worship for other cults. The church was now permitted to operate in full public view; indeed primary education would be more or less turned over to the clergy, and clerical salaries would be paid by the state. Bishops would again be consecrated by the pope, but they would be nominated by the consul. Most important, the concordat reserved to the state the power to regulate the place of the church within French society. One major revolutionary change was sustained: lands confiscated from the church and sold during the Revolution were to be retained by their purchasers. Another major change was abandoned: the ten-day week was dropped and the Gregorian calendar restored.

The balance of church-state relations was firmly fixed in the state's favor, for it was Napoleon's intention to use the clergy as a major prop of the new regime. With priests now responsible to the government, the pulpit and the primary school became instruments of social control, to be used, as the imperial catechism put it, "to bind the religious conscience of the people to the August person of the Emperor." Napoleon summarized his approach to religion in his statement that the clergy would be his moral prefects. Eventually devout Catholics came to fear that this highly national version of church organization would be detrimental to true Catholicism, and Pius renounced the concordat—to which Napoleon responded by removing the pontiff to France and placing him under house arrest.

The Social System

With Old Regime obstacles to civil equality removed, Napoleon believed that the Revolution was complete. It remained now to erect an orderly, hierarchical society to counteract what he regarded as the excessive individualism of revolutionary social reforms. The foundation stones of social change—the transfer of church lands, the end of the guild system, the abolition of feudalism—would be consolidated. At the same time the authority of state and family would be reasserted and the social dominance of the middle class reaffirmed.

In the absence of electoral politics, Napoleon used the state's vast appointive powers to confer status on prominent local figures, thus associating them with his regime. These regional dignitaries were chosen from among the prosperous landowners and middle class, while the common people were definitively returned to their supposedly rightful place of deferential passivity. A new source of status was added to enhance the prestige of those who served the regime well: the Order of the Legion of Honor, nine-tenths of whose members were military men. "It is with trinkets that mankind is governed," Napoleon is supposed to have said. Legion of Honor awards and local appointments under the patronage

system were precisely such trinkets, and they endured long after their creator was gone.

Napoleon helped consolidate middle-class dominance in more practical ways. A system of compulsory labor "passports" gave employers control over their workers' movements; trade unions and strikes were strictly prohibited. Leading bankers realized their long-standing ambition to have a national bank chartered that they themselves fully controlled and that enjoyed the credit power derived from official ties to the state. In education Napoleon created elite secondary schools, or lycées, designed in part to produce high civil servants and officers. They were joined to a rigidly centralized academic system that survived intact into the twentieth

Legion of Honor decorations—distributed initially at the Hôtel des Invalides in 1802—were Napoleon's way of recognizing talent, especially in the form of military service to the state. Whereas in one sense they represented the principle of equality of opportunity, they also reflected the regime's growing militarism. (Photo: The Bettmann Archive)

This etching of the Battle of Austerlitz (December 1805) dramatically captures the two faces of Napoleonic warfare: the glory and the gore. In the background an Austrian flag is being presented to the Emperor—the mark of his brilliant victory in that engagement. But in the foreground the mangled corpses of the casualties are plainly evident. As the years went on, the glory became more and more dubious, while the dead and disabled grew too numerous to contemplate. (Photo: Culver Pictures, Inc.)

century, dominating the pattern of French education and some would say retarding it. Teachers and professors were certified and assigned by Paris; an enormous bureaucracy regulated educational affairs down to the smallest detail of curriculum and maintenance.

An equally durable legal codification covered social relations and property rights. The Civil Code, renamed the Napoleonic Code in 1807, guaranteed fundamental departures from Old Regime practices, and as such it was a revolutionary document that progressives were pleased to see exported throughout Europe. Feudal aristocracy and the property relations deriving from it were obliterated.

Instead all citizens could now exercise unambiguous contractual ownership. The code established the right to choose one's occupation, to receive equal treatment under the law, and to enjoy religious freedom. At the same time it confirmed the Thermidorian and Directory retreat from the social policies of the second revolution. Property rights for example were not matched by anything resembling a right to subsistence.

Revolutionary legislation had emancipated women and children by establishing their civil liberties. Napoleon undid most of this progress by restoring the father's absolute authority in the family. A wife owes obedience to her husband, said the code, which proceeded to deprive her of property and juridical rights that had been granted during the Revolution. The rights of illegitimate children were also eliminated, and the husband's options in disposing of his estate were enlarged, though each son was still guaranteed a portion. Napoleon insisted on relatively liberal provisions for divorce—but only as far as the husband was concerned. Penal codes and criminal procedures also rolled back revolutionary libertarianism. Defendants' rights and the role of juries were both curtailed.

The Napoleonic Code, the concordat, the education system, and the patronage structure all proved extremely durable institutions. They fulfilled Napoleon's desire to create a series of "granite masses" on which French society could be permanently reconstructed. His admirers emphasize that these achievements contributed to social stability despite France's chronic lack of stable governments. One can argue that they were skillful compromises between revolutionary equality and libertarianism on the one hand and a sense of hierarchy and authority on the other. Detractors point out first that they were class-oriented, withdrawing from the mass of Frenchmen promises held out by the second revolution; and second that they created an overcentralized, rigid institutional structure that sapped French vitality in succeeding generations. Whatever their merits or defects, these institutions did take root. They did not prove ephemeral reflections of the luster of the imperial throne, as did other aspects of Napoleon's reign—notably his attempt to create a hereditary empire and a French-dominated Europe.

NAPOLEONIC HEGEMONY

Although Bonaparte was not needed to repel an imminent invasion at the time of the Brumaire coup, he was expected to provide strategy and command for a successful conclusion of the war against the second coalition. Accordingly the first consul left France at the earliest opportunity in late 1799 with an army prepared to engage Hapsburg forces in northern Italy. The outcome of this campaign would confirm or destroy the settlement he had imposed on the revisionists. A decisive victory would make him impregnable; a rout would obviously destroy his political future.

Napoleon's strategy called for a repeat of the 1797 campaign: he would strike through Italy while the army of the Rhine pushed eastward against Vienna. This time it worked. Following French victories at Marengo, in Lombardy, and Hohenlinden, in Germany, Austria sued for peace. The Treaty of Lunéville, in February 1801, essentially restored France to the position she had held after Napoleon's triumphs in 1797.

In the British Isles a war-weary government, now standing alone against Napoleon, decided to negotiate a treaty also. The Peace of Amiens, March 1801, ended hostilities and reshuffled territorial holdings outside Europe. But it was a precarious truce because it did not settle the future of French influence and expansion or commercial relations between the two nations. Napoleon soon showed that he was willing to violate the spirit of the treaty while abiding by its letter. The British and Austrians alike were dismayed by the continued expansion of French influence in Italy, the Helvetic Republic, and North America. Most important perhaps, France made it clear that she would exclude British trade rather than restore normal trading relations. Historians generally agree that the Peace of Amiens failed because neither side was strongly interested in making it last. Their century-long struggle for preeminence had yet to be decided.

A third coalition, a replay of its predecessors, formed as the treaties broke down. France's ostensible war aims were still the preservation of the regime at home and the sister republics abroad. The coalition had the ideological and diplomatic objectives of restoring the Batavian Republic and Italy to "independence," dissolving French influence elsewhere, and if possible reducing France to her original borders. But like most alliances of its sort, the third coalition was to be dismembered piecemeal.

French hopes of settling the issue directly by invading England proved unrealizable. At the Battle of Trafalgar, in October 1805, an already outnumbered and outmanned French navy was crushed by Admiral Nelson's fleet. An innovative tactician who broke rule-book procedures on the high seas as French generals had been doing on land, Nelson ensured the security of the British Isles for the remainder of the Napoleonic era.

Napoleon turned now against the Austro-Russian forces. Moving 200,000 French soldiers with unprecedented speed across the Continent, he took his enemies by surprise and won a succession of startling victories.

After occupying Vienna he proceeded against the coalition's main army in December. Feigning weakness and retreat at the moment of battle, he drew his now numerically superior opponents into an exposed position, crushed the center of their lines, and inflicted a decisive defeat. The Battle of Austerlitz was Napoleon's most brilliant tactical achievement, and the Hapsburgs were compelled to jump for the peace table. The resulting Treaty of Pressburg was extremely harsh and humiliating for Austria. Not only was a large indemnity imposed on her, but she was required to cede her Venetian provinces.

The Conquest and Reorganization of Europe
By this time Napoleon had far surpassed his role of general of the Revolution and was beginning his imperial march toward the conquest of Europe. The French sphere of influence had increased dramatically to include most of southern Germany, which was organized into the Confederation of the Rhine, a client realm of France. At the moment only Prussia stood outside this sphere. Her neutrality during the war with Austria had been effected by skillful French diplomacy and Prussian miscalculation. Only after Austria had been forced to the peace table did Prussia recognize the threat she had allowed to rise against her interests by missing her chance to combine effectively with her neighbor to the south. Belatedly she mobilized her famous but antiquated army; it was rewarded with stinging defeat by France in a number of encounters culminating in the Battle of Jena in October 1806. With Prussian military power proved a paper tiger and the conqueror ensconced in Berlin, the prestige of the ruling class disintegrated, and the masses docilely accepted the occupation that followed. Napoleon was now master of the northern Ger-

man lands as well as the south. For a while it appeared that he would obliterate Prussia entirely, but in the end he restored her sovereignty after amputating part of her territory and imposing a crushing indemnity.

The subsequent reorganization of Central Europe brought Napoleon considerable gratification and prestige. He formally proclaimed the end of the moribund Holy Roman Empire in 1806—Francis II had already changed his own title to Emperor Francis I of Austria two years earlier—and proceeded to liquidate numerous small German principalities whose profusion had created such chaos. In their place he erected two new states: the Kingdom of Westphalia, on whose throne he placed his brother Jérôme; and the grand duchy of Berg, to be ruled by Joachim Murat, his brother-in-law. His ally Saxony was proclaimed a full-scale kingdom, while a new duchy of Warsaw was created out of Prussian Poland. This "restoration" of Poland had major propaganda value; it made the emperor appear a champion of Polish national aspirations in view of the fact that the rulers of Prussia, Russia, and Austria had dismembered Poland in a series of partitions ending in 1794. Moreover Napoleon could now enlist a Polish army and use Polish territory as a base of operations against the last Continental member of the coalition, Russia.

In February 1807 Napoleon confronted the colossus of the East in the Battle of Eylau; the resulting carnage was horrifying but inconclusive. When spring came Napoleon was in a desperate position. Only a dramatic victory could preserve his conquests in Central Europe and vindicate the extraordinary decisions of the past two years. Fortunately for the Emperor the Battle of Friedland in June was a French victory that demoralized Tsar Alexander I and persuaded him to negotiate. Meeting at Tilsit, the two emperors buried

their differences and proceeded to create a mighty alliance of two superstates that would dominate Europe, essentially partitioning it into Eastern and Western spheres of influence. Each would support the other's conquests and mediate in behalf of the other's interests. The Treaty of Tilsit of July 7 sanctioned Napoleon's reorganization of Europe as well as the dramatic expansion of French territory eastward. Apart from outright annexations the chief vehicle for Napoleon's rearrangements was the creation of satellite kingdoms. The old sister republics were now induced to evolve into kingdoms just as France herself had. And it happened that Napoleon had a whole family of brothers ready to assume royal crowns.

The distorted shape of Napoleonic Europe at its high point, around 1810, is best appreciated on a map (see Map 21.2). His chief satellites included the Kingdom of Holland, comprising the Batavian Republic, with brother Louis on the throne; the Kingdom of Italy, with Napoleon himself as king and stepson Eugène de Beauharnais as viceroy; the Confederation of the Rhine, including brother Jérôme's Kingdom of Westphalia; the Kingdom of Naples, covering southern Italy, with brother Joseph wearing the crown until he was transferred to Spain and passed it to brother-in-law Murat; and the duchy of Warsaw. The old Austrian Netherlands, the Rhineland, Tuscany, Piedmont, Genoa, the Illyrian provinces, and the Ionian Islands had been directly annexed to France. Switzerland persisted as the Helvetic Republic but under a new constitution dictated by France. In 1810, after yet another war with Austria, imperial policy was consummated by a marriage between the house of Bonaparte and the house of Hapsburg: Napoleon, having divorced Joséphine de Beauharnais, married Marie Louise, daughter of Francis I.

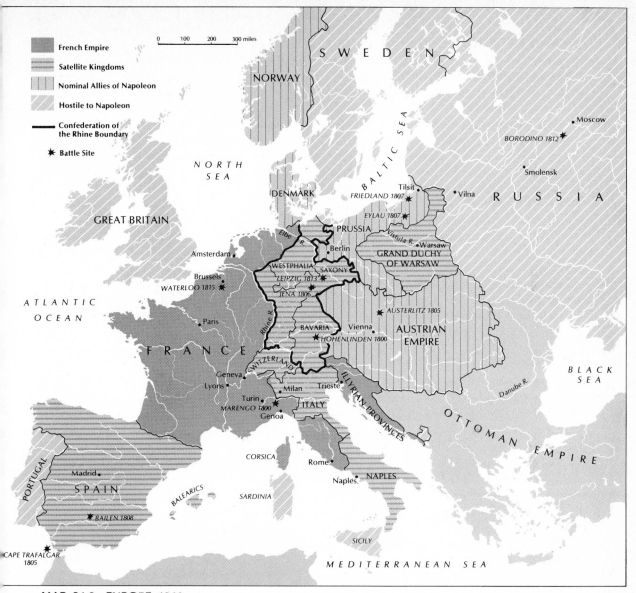

Legend:
- French Empire
- Satellite Kingdoms
- Nominal Allies of Napoleon
- Hostile to Napoleon
- Confederation of the Rhine Boundary
- ✱ Battle Site

Scale: 0 100 200 300 miles

SWEDEN

NORWAY

NORTH SEA

BALTIC SEA

• Moscow

BORODINO 1812 ✱

• Smolensk

DENMARK

Tilsit
FRIEDLAND 1807 ✱
EYLAU 1807 ✱

• Vilna

RUSSIA

GREAT BRITAIN

Elbe R.

PRUSSIA

Berlin

Amsterdam •

WESTPHALIA

SAXONY

Vistula R.
• Warsaw

GRAND DUCHY OF WARSAW

ATLANTIC OCEAN

Brussels •
WATERLOO 1815 ✱
LEIPZIG 1813 ✱
JENA 1806

Rhine R.

Paris •

BAVARIA
Vienna •
AUSTERLITZ 1805 ✱

FRANCE

✱ *HOHENLINDEN 1800*

AUSTRIAN EMPIRE

BLACK SEA

SWITZERLAND

Geneva •
Lyons •

Milan •

Trieste •

ILLYRIAN PROVINCES

Danube R.

Turin •
MARENGO 1800 ✱

ITALY

Genoa •

OTTOMAN EMPIRE

CORSICA

Rome •

PORTUGAL

Madrid •

SPAIN

BALEARICS

SARDINIA

NAPLES

Naples •

✱ *BAILEN 1808*

SICILY

CAPE TRAFALGAR 1805 ✱

MEDITERRANEAN SEA

MAP 21.2: EUROPE 1810

The Continental System

Only Britain remained to be vanquished; meanwhile she stood between Napoleon and his dream of complete hegemony over Europe, not to mention the world beyond. Since Britain was invulnerable to invasion, Napoleon's objective was to destroy her influence by means of economic warfare.

Unable to blockade British ports directly, the emperor sought to close the Continent—

to blockade Britain from her markets, stop her exports, and thus ruin her trade and credit. In mercantilist fashion he reasoned that if she had nowhere to sell her manufactured goods, no gold would come into the country, which would eventually bankrupt her. At the same time overproduction would cause unemployment, and the ensuing labor unrest might turn the British people against the government and force it to make peace with France. On the other hand French advantages in Continental markets would naturally increase with the elimination of British competition.

Accordingly Napoleon mounted his so-called Continental system: he would prohibit British trade with all French allies and all commerce by neutrals carrying British products, prevent all ships coming from British ports from landing in Europe, and have any goods coming from or belonging to the British Isles impounded.

The British responded in 1807 with the Orders in Council that in effect reversed the blockade: they *required* all neutral ships to stop at British ports to procure trading licenses and pay tariffs. In other words they intervened in all trade between neutrals and most European ports. Violators became lawful prizes to seize. Napoleon's angry answer to this was the threat simply to commandeer any neutral ship that obeyed the Orders in Council by stopping at British ports.

Thus a total naval war involving neutrals grew out of the Continental system. Indeed there scarcely remained such a thing as neutral immunity since every ship was obliged to violate one system or the other and thus run afoul of naval patrols or privateers. While the British took only about 40 French ships a year after 1807 (for few were left to sail the seas), they seized almost 3,000 neutrals a year, including many American ships.

Britain was hurt by the Continental system. Her gold reserves dwindled, and internal strife did erupt in 1811, a year of widespread unemployment and rioting. France was affected adversely by the counterblockade, which cut her off from the raw materials necessary for industrial production as well as from British finished goods, extremely popular on the Continent. But the satellite states probably suffered the most, becoming economic vassals of France. In Amsterdam for example shipping volume declined from 1,350 ships entering the port in 1806 to 310 in 1809; as a result commercial revenues dropped calamitously. Out of loyalty to the people whom he ruled, King Louis Bonaparte tolerated smuggling. This so infuriated Napoleon that he ousted his brother from the throne and annexed the Kingdom of Holland to France. Smuggling was in fact the weak link in the system, creating holes in Napoleon's dike of economic sanctions that constantly needed plugging. This in turn drove Napoleon to more drastic policies.

RESISTANCE TO NAPOLEON

Having vanquished every major European power on the battlefield except Britain, Napoleon now felt that nothing stood in his way. Since Spain and Russia did not seem responsive enough to his will, the emperor chose to deal with each of them by force, assuming that his plans against Britain could then be pursued to their conclusion. On all counts he was mistaken. Napoleon's confrontations with Britain, Spain, and Russia proved in various ways that his reach had exceeded his grasp.

The Spanish Ulcer
Spain and France had a common interest in weakening British power in Europe and the colonial world. But their alliance after 1795 brought only reversals for Spain, including

the loss of her Louisiana Territory and (at the Battle of Trafalgar) most of her fleet. Domestically things were no better. The royal household had been the scene of scandalous and bitter controversy for some time. A lover of Queen Maria Louisa's, Manual de Godoy, had achieved astonishing ascendancy as prime minister and proved to be a corrupt opportunist who was extremely unpopular with the people. He was despised by Crown Prince Ferdinand, who was equally hostile to Godoy's protectors, the king and queen.

Napoleon looked on the resultant turbulence with extreme irritation. At the zenith of his power, he easily drifted toward the solution of reorganizing Spain himself. As a pretext for military intervention, he put in motion a plan to invade Portugal, supposedly to partition her with Spain. Once the French army was well inside Spain, it could impose the political solution to Spain's instability that Napoleon desired.

The squabbling King Charles IV and his son were tricked, threatened, and bribed into abdicating, one after the other; a group of Spanish notables was gathered to petition Napoleon to provide a new sovereign, preferably his brother Joseph; and Joseph was duly proclaimed king of Spain. With French troops already settled around Madrid, Joseph prepared to assume his new throne, sincerely eager to rule well under a liberal constitution that was drawn up. But as he took up the crown, an unanticipated drama unfolded.

Faced with military occupation, the disappearance of their royal family, and the crowning of a Frenchman, the Spanish people rose in rebellion. It began on May 2, 1808, when an angry crowd rioted against French troops, who responded with brutal reprisals. This bloody incident, known as the Dos de Mayo and captured in Goya's famous paintings (see Plate 48), has been preserved in Spanish leg-

end. The kidnapping of Prince Ferdinand a short time later galvanized the uprising into a sustained offensive against the French and pro-French Spaniards. Local notables created juntas to organize the rebels, mainly peasants, priests, and monks, and coordinate them with regular Spanish troops.

The troops were generally ineffective against the French but did produce one telling victory: two French divisions were forced to surrender at Bailén in July, an episode that broke the aura of Napoleonic invincibility. The main brunt of professional military operations in what had now become the Peninsular War was borne by the British, whose expeditionary force first drove the French out of Portugal and eventually rolled them back across Spain under the inspired command of Arthur Wellesley, later duke of Wellington. All the while as many as 30,000 Spanish guerrilla fighters were providing another dimension to the conflict and contributing to its brutality. Their atrocities and harassment of the French kept the foreign invaders in a constant state of anxiety and led to reprisals that in turn escalated the war's bitterness.

All told the juntas, the guerrillas, and the British held a massive French army of up to 300,000 men pinned down in Spain and made it impossible for Napoleon to mobilize fully elsewhere on the Continent. He referred to the war as the "Spanish ulcer." In addition, though Napoleon had contempt for the rebel monks and peasants, other Europeans were inspired by their example that resistance to the French emperor was possible.

Meanwhile the war proved a disaster for Spanish liberals. Torn between Joseph, who would have been a liberal ruler, and the nationalist rebels, they ended by falling into an unviable position between the two. Those who supported Joseph found that he was never able to rule independently. It was Napoleon who gave the orders in Spain, relying on his generals to carry them out. Those who stood behind the rebels were able to organize a provisional government in 1812 by convening the ancient parliament, the Cortes, in the town of Cádiz. There they drafted a liberal and nationalist constitution, which pleased the British and therefore was tolerated by the local juntas. But in reality the priests, peasants, and nobles who made up the bulk of rebel sympathizers disdained the liberals and were fighting rather for the Catholic Church and the Spanish Bourbons. When in 1814 the French were finally expelled and Ferdinand VII took the throne, the liberals' joy was short-lived. Ferdinand tore up the constitution of 1812, restored the monasteries and the Inquisition, closed down the universities, revived censorship, and arrested the leading liberals. The main beneficiaries of the Spanish rebellion and the Peninsular War were thus Spanish reactionaries and the British expeditionary force.

The Russian Debacle

In 1811 Napoleon did not yet realize how his entanglement in Spain would drain French military power and encourage intellectuals and statesmen in Central Europe to contemplate nationalist uprisings against him. On the contrary never were Napoleon's schemes more grandiose than in that year. Surveying the crumbling state system of Europe, he imagined that it could be replaced with a supranational empire, ruled from Paris and Rome and based on the Napoleonic Code. He believed that the era of the balance of power was over and that nationalist strivings would not stand in his way. On both counts he was mistaken.

The key obstacle to imperial reorganization and French domination was Russia. Wishing to retain her sphere of interest in Eastern Europe and the Baltic region and increasingly discontented with the restrictions of the Continental system, Russia was a restive ally. Alexander was being pressured on the one hand to resist France by British diplomats, French émigrés, anti-Napoleonic exiles such as Baron Stein of Prussia, and nationalist reactionaries. On the other hand Russian court liberals, more concerned with domestic reforms, were eager for him to maintain peace with France; but by 1812 their influence on Alexander had waned. On his side Napoleon wanted to enforce the Continental system and reduce Russia's capacity to interfere with Europe's destiny. As he put it with characteristic bluntness, "Let Alexander defeat the Persians, but don't let him meddle in the affairs of Europe." Once again two major powers were facing each other with progressively less interest in maintaining peace.

Napoleon decided to strike, and he embarked on his most ambitious military campaign. His objective was to annihilate the Russian forces or barring that to conquer Moscow and chase the army to the point of disarray. Almost 600,000 men (many drawn from the satellite states), long supply lines, and repeated forced marches were his principal weapons. The Russian response was to retreat in collected fashion and avoid a fight until a propitious moment. Meanwhile many nobles abandoned their estates and burned their crops to the ground. At Borodino, however, the Russians turned and took a stand. In the enormous battle that ensued, they sustained 45,000 casualties but managed to withdraw in order. The French lost 35,000. At this price they were able to enter Moscow on September 14, 1812, but the Russian army was still intact and far from demoralized.

On the contrary Moscow demoralized the French. They found the city deserted, bereft of badly needed supplies. The next night it was mysteriously set ablaze, causing such extensive damage as to make it unfit for winter quarters. Realistic advisers warned the emperor that his situation was untenable, while others told him what he wished to hear—that Russian resistance was weakening. Napoleon indulged in a reverie of false optimism and indecision. Militarily it was imperative that the French begin to retreat immediately, but that would constitute a political defeat. On October 19 Napoleon finally ordered a retreat, but it was too late.

The delay forced an unrealistic pace on the army that it was in no condition to sustain. Supplies had been outrun, medical care for the thousands of wounded was nonexistent, horses were lacking. The French officers were poorly organized for the march, and the soldiers were growing insubordinate. Food shortages compelled foraging parties to sweep some distance from the main body of troops, but these men fell prey to Russian irregulars, who operated with increasing effectiveness. And there was the weather—just a normal Russian winter in which no commander would wish to find himself on a march of several hundred miles, laden with wounded and loot but without supplies, horses, and food.[5] Napoleon's poor planning, the harsh weather, and the operation of guerrilla bands made the long retreat a nightmare of suffering for the Grand Army. It is estimated that no more than 100,000 troops survived the ordeal. Worse yet, the Prussian contingent took the occasion to desert Napoleon. This opened up the possibility of mass defections from the empire and with them the formation of a new coalition.

---

[5] Whether he had planned it that way or not, the Russian commander Kutuzov drew Napoleon deep into Russia, trapped him far from his lines of supply, and then launched a counteroffensive. During World War II the Russians dealt with Germany's invasion similarly, and it has been claimed that Stalin was following Kutuzov's classic strategy. The parallel included the use of guerrilla warfare and scorched-earth tactics to harass the enemy.

German Resistance and the Last Coalition

It is testimony to Napoleon's fortitude—if also to his imperviousness to the horror around him—that he was unshaken by all this. On the lonely sleigh ride back to his main lines, he was already planning how to recoup his losses, raise new armies, and set things aright. Other statesmen were equally determined to capitalize on his defeat and destroy the empire once and for all.

Napoleon's credibility with liberal reformers in Central and Eastern Europe still stood, but it was now challenged by ringing cries for a nationalist revival in the Confederation of the Rhine that would throw off the tyrant's yoke. This type of thinking reinforced the continuing efforts of statesmen like the Prussian Stein and the Austrian Prince Klemens von Metternich to revive the struggle against Napoleon. Less spectacularly military reformers in Prussia had adopted French methods of conscription and organization, the better to oppose France. On the level of propaganda and the symbolic gesture, German publicists talked of a popular war of liberation—the ultimate tribute to the French Revolution.

Against this background of growing nationalist sentiment and military reform, the diplomats worked and waited. Finally, in March 1813, Frederick William III of Prussia signed a treaty with Russia, forming the nucleus of an offensive coalition against Napoleon. A great struggle for Germany ensued between the Russo-Prussian forces and Napoleon and his allies. Austria continued to claim neutrality and offered to mediate the dispute. At a conference in Prague, Napoleon was invited to restore all conquests made after 1802. Napoleon rejected this, and the allies sighed with relief, since the proposal was merely a stalling tactic until Austria could be persuaded to enter the war.

In August Emperor Francis I finally declared war on his son-in-law, while Napoleon learned of new defeats in Spain. Calling up underage conscripts, Napoleon was able to field one last army, but he found that his major southern German ally, Bavaria, had finally been induced to change sides. At Leipzig a major batttle raged for three days in October, at the end of which Napoleon was defeated. His last confederation allies deserted him.

With Napoleon driven back into France, the British reinforced the coalition to assure that it would not disintegrate now that Central Europe had been liberated. Final terms were offered to the emperor: he could retain his throne, but France would be reduced to her "normal frontiers." (The precise meaning of this was purposely left unclear.) Again Napoleon counted on a dramatic reversal and chose to fight. With some reluctance the allies invaded France. Napoleon led the remnants of his army skillfully but to no avail; Frenchmen had lost confidence in him, and no civilian spirit of resistance to invasion developed as it had in 1793. Paris fell in March 1814. The price for this last defeat was the demand for unconditional surrender and the emperor's abdication. Napoleon was removed to the island of Elba, between Corsica and Italy, and was granted sovereignty over it. After twenty-two years of exile, the Bourbons returned to France.

The second revolution, guided by the Jacobin dictatorship and propelled by the sans-culottes, lasted little more than two years in 1792–1794. When the crisis had been surmounted and counter-revolution vanquished, France disavowed the Jacobin leaders. The National Convention put an end to the Terror and also to the promise of social democracy. It attempted to install a moderate republican government, in essence by recreating the middle-class regime of 1791 without a king. This proved impossible. While France exported revolution to receptive states in the years of the Directory, the revolution at home foundered.

In supporting a coup whose leadership was taken over by General Bonaparte, conservatives did not foresee that his solution to the problem would be a dictatorship. But France soon succumbed to Bonaparte's one-man rule as his prestige grew thanks to his feats on the battlefield. Before long the republic disappeared, replaced by the Napoleonic Empire.

Under the empire confrontation of France with Old Regime Europe engulfed the entire Continent. France still embodied the specter of revolution, but by this time it amounted to little more than Napoleon's contempt for the inefficiency and irrationality of the old order. Even so this was a powerful challenge to the status quo. Napoleon believed that the state system was dead, that Europe must be reorganized under French hegemony, and that administrative reform and the Napoleonic Code should be spread to the new realms.

His conquests eventually overreached his ability to maintain them except by increasingly tyrannical measures, which in turn provoked a whole range of responses in Europe. Resistance coalesced, the empire came crashing down, and the Bourbons returned to France. But the clock could not really be set back from Europe's experience of revolution and Napoleonic transformation. The era of modern political and social conflicts had begun.

RECOMMENDED READING

See also titles listed for Chapter 20.

Sources

* Beik, Paul H. (ed.). *The French Revolution.* 1970.
* De Caulaincourt, Armand. *With Napoleon in Russia.* 1935.
* Herold, J. C. (ed.). *The Mind of Napoleon.* 1961.
Stewart, J. H. *A Documentary Survey of the French Revolution.* 1951.
Thompson, J. M. (ed.). *Napoleon Self-Revealed.* 1934.

Studies

The best general history of this period is a series of volumes by the great French historian Georges Lefebvre: *The French Revolution* (2 vols.) and *Napoleon* (2 vols.), all published in translation by the Columbia University Press, with full bibliographies.

Anderson, Eugene. *Nationalism and the Cultural Crisis in Prussia, 1806–1815.* 1939.
Chandler, David. *The Campaigns of Napoleon.* 1966. For military history buffs.
* Cobb, R. C. *The Police and the People: French Popular Protest.* 1970. A discussion of peasants and sans-culottes that should be compared to Soboul's.
* Connelly, Owen. *Napoleon's Satellite Kingdoms.* 1965.
Furet, F., and D. Richet. *The French Revolution.* 1970. An attempt to break with Marxist traditions in French historiography.

Gershoy, Leo. *Bertrand Barère, a Reluctant Terrorist.* 1962. Perhaps the best English-language biography of a revolutionary figure.
* Geyl, P. *Napoleon, For and Against.* 1949. Napoleon and the historians—as interpreted by a leading Dutch historian.
Godechot, Jacques. *The Napoleonic Era in Europe.* 1971. A recent textbook.
* Herold, J. C. *The Age of Napoleon.* 1963. A brilliant example of "popular" history.
* Holtman, Robert. *The Napoleonic Revolution.* 1967. More favorable to Napoleon than Herold.
Kennedy, Michael. *The Jacobin Club of Marseilles.* 1973.
* Lyons, M. *France Under the Directory.* 1975.
* Markham, Felix. *Napoleon.* 1966. Perhaps the best biography in English.
* Palmer, Robert R. *Twelve Who Ruled: The Year of the Terror in the French Revolution.* 1941. A modern classic.
* Rudé, George. *The Crowd in the French Revolution.* 1959.
———. *Robespierre: Portrait of a Revolutionary Democrat.* 1975.
Soboul, Albert. *The Parisian Sans-Culottes and the French Revolution.* 1964. An abridgment of a landmark French thesis; should be compared to Cobb's discussion.

---

* Available in paperback.

Absolute monarchies (absolutism), 548–565, 592–598; enlightened absolutism, 636–639
Academies, 626–627; French, 573–574, 625–627
Academies of art: Académie Royal (Académie des Beaux Arts), French, 636; Royal Academy of Arts, British, 636
Academies of sciences: Berlin, 522, 562; British, *see* Royal Society (London); French Royal, 522; Naples, 522; St. Petersburg, 564
Addison, Joseph, 627
Africa: trade routes around, 399; slave trade in, 603, 605–608; British in, 613
Agincourt, Battle of, 354, 380
Agriculture: in fifteenth century, 338; in Industrial Revolution, 647, 651, 656–659; in eighteenth century, 658–659
Alberti, Leon Battista, 371
Albertus Magnus, 394
Albuquerque, Affonso de, 400
Alcalà, University of, 457
Alchemy, 394, 507, 617
Alembert, Jean Le Rond d', 619, 625
Alexander I, Tsar, 716, 720
Alexis I, Tsar, 502, 503
Alfonso V, King of Aragon (Alfonso I, King of Naples and Sicily), 359
Alfonso X, King of Castile, 343
Almanacs, 630
Alsace, 477, 651, 664, 675
Alsace-Lorraine, 608
Alva, Duke of, 467
America: discovery of, 400–401; Spanish conquest and colonization, 401–403, 421, 423. *See also* Canada; Latin America; United States
American colonies: British, early, 480, 536, 569; British and Spanish, rivalry, 589; British and French, rivalry, 603–604, 610–612; British, growth, 610, 655; French and Indian War, 610, 612–613
American Revolution, 671
Amsterdam, 496, 497, 718
Anabaptists, 450, 451
Anagni, 359
Anatomy, 508–509, 514, 518, 523
Angevin dynasty, 359
Anglican Church, *see* Church of England
Anjou, 413
Anne, Queen of Great Britain, 569
Antwerp, 391, 468, 493, 496, 667
Anzin, 665

Aquinas, St. Thomas, 383, 386, 394, 446, 455
Aquitaine, 350, 352
Arabs, in African trade, conflict with Portugal, 399–400
Aragon, 339, 359, 416, 419, 422, 423, 494
Archimedes, 507, 508
Aristocracy: Spanish, 417, 559; English (gentry), 479, 480, 565–567, 570; Russian, 564–565; in Netherlands, 570–571; in Sweden, 571–573; in Poland, 573; in eighteenth century, 667–669
Aristotle, 513; scientific writings questioned, 394, 507
Arkwright, Richard, 662, 663
Armagnacs, 356
Armies: conscription, 464, 594; in sixteenth century, 464, 466; in seventeenth century, 536; in eighteenth century, 591–594; purchase of officers' commissions, 592; in French Revolution, 699–700
Arras, 382
Art: patrons of, 364–365, 388–389; in Renaissance, 388–393; religious themes, 438–440; in late seventeenth century, 523–524, 526, 529, 531–532, 575; academies, 636; in eighteenth century, 636
Asia: trade with, 404–405, 479; search for routes to, 398–399
Assisi, 358
Astrology, 394, 507, 630
Astronomy: of Copernicus, 509–512; Kepler's laws, 511–512; Galileo's theories, 512–514; Descartes' theory, 518; Newton's laws, 580, 581
Atomism, 507
Augsburg, Diet of (1555), 449
Augsburg Confession, 447, 448
Augustine, St. (of Hippo), 374, 375, 435, 436
Austerlitz, Battle of, 715
Austria, 403, 425; in Holy Roman Empire, 424, 557
Austrian Empire (Austria-Hungary), 477, 558; War of the Austrian Succession, 588, 596–597, 610; in eighteenth century, 591, 592, 596; Seven Years' War, 608–609; music in eighteenth century, 634; under Joseph II, 638–639, 667–668; laws, 638, 639; and revolt of Netherlands, 667–669; with Prussia in war against France, 680, 682, 687; and allies, war against France, 689, 700; Napoleon's first victory over, in Italy, 706–707; in coalition against Napoleon, 707, 714–716, 721–722
Averroës (ibn Rushd), 394
Avignon: popes in, 358–359, 361–362, 387, 435; plague in, 336–337
Azpilcueta, Professor, 403
Aztecs, 402

INDEX

Babeuf, Gracchus, 704
Bach, Johann Sebastian, 635 *n.*
Bacon, Francis, 482, 508, 516, 518, 519, 522, 617
Bahamas, 401
Bailén, 719
Bakewell, Robert, 657
Balboa, Vasco Nuñez de, 401
Balkan Peninsula, 558
Baltic area, 559, 565, 588, 659; wars in seventeenth century, 571–572
Baltic Sea, trade, 339, 404, 479
Banking: in fourteenth century, 344; in sixteenth century, 404, 415; German and Italian loans to Spain, 493; in Netherlands, 496, 603; in Great Britain, 653; under Napoleon, 713
Bank of Amsterdam, 496
Bank of England, 569, 653
Barcelona, 416, 493, 495; famine and plague, 336
Baroque art, 456, 523, 527, 529, 531, 562
Basel, Council of (1431–1443), 364
Battle of the Books, 579
Bavaria, 474, 596, 597, 722; dukes of, 456
Bayle, Pierre, 618, 619, 625
Bayonne, 354
Beauharnais, Eugène de, 716
Beauharnais, Joséphine de, 716
Beccaria, Cesare Bonesana, Marquis de, 620
Beethoven, Ludwig van, 634–635
Bell, Sir Thomas, 662
Berg, grand duchy of, 716
Berlin, 522, 609, 715; under Frederick I, 561–563
Bermuda, 480
Bern, 452
Bernardine of Siena, St., 370
Bernini, Giovanni Lorenzo, 529
Bible: Vulgate, 442, 455; Gutenberg, 342; in vernacular languages, 386–388, 436–437; in Protestantism, 446, 448–452; Luther's translation, 447; Catholic view of, 455
Birmingham, 664
Birth rate and population, 655–656
Black Death, 335–337, 352, 371, 375
Boccaccio, Giovanni, 370, 375, 389
Bodin, Jean, 472
Bohemia, 340, 425, 557, 559, 596, 665; Hussites, 388; in Thirty Years' War, 472, 474
Boileau, Nicolas, 575
Boleyn, Anne, 410
Bologna, 358, 369, 373
Bonaparte, Jérôme, 716
Bonaparte, Joseph, 716, 719
Bonaparte, Louis, 716, 718
Bordeaux, 354, 488, 491, 652, 690
Boris Godunov, Tsar, 501

Borodino, Battle of, 720
Bosch, Hieronymus, 438
Bosworth Field, Battle of, 356
Botticelli, Sandro, 365, 378
Boulton, Matthew, 663–664
Bourbon dynasty, 469, 588, 608, 704; return to France, 722
Bourgeoisie and French Revolution, 672. *See also* Middle class
Boyle, Robert, 522
Brahe, Tycho, 511, 512
Bramante, Donato d'Agnolo, 365
Brandenburg, 609; Diet of, 559–560
Brandenburg-Prussia, 477, 559–562, 592
Brandt, Sebastian, *Ship of Fools*, 437–438, 442
Brazil, 399, 536, 603
Breitenfeld, Battle of, 474
Bremen, 339, 477
Brethren of the Common Life, 386
Brill, 467
Brissot, Jacques, 687
Brittany, 410, 413, 690
Brotherhood of the Ten Thousand Virgins, 437
Brotherhoods (religious groups), 386, 436
Brueghel, Pieter, the Elder, *Massacre of the Innocents*, 467, 468
Bruges, 391
Bruni, Leonardo, 370, 375–376
Brunswick, Karl Wilhelm Ferdinand, Duke of, 682
Brussels, 529
Bucer, Martin, 411
Buffon, Georges Louis Leclerc de, 618
Bullinger, Heinrich, 451
Bunyan, John, 575, 578
Buonarroti, Filippo, 704
Burckhardt, Jacob, 368
Burgundy, 356; annexed by France, 413
Buridan, Jean, 394
Burke, Edmund, 643
Business: in fourteenth and fifteenth centuries, 344; in sixteenth century, 407

Cabala, 508
Cabot, John, 410
Cádiz, 720
Calais, 352, 354
Calcutta, 612
Calendar: 510–511; Julian, 510
Calonne, Charles Alexandre de, 674
Calvin, John, 451–454, 456, 457; *Institutes of the Christian Religion*, 451, 453
Calvinism, 451–454; Lutheranism and Zwinglianism compared with, 452–453; in religious wars, 468–470, 472; in Scotland, 482; in France, *see* Huguenots

Cambrai, 391

Canada, 480; French colony, 536, 610; New France, 603, 610; British possession, 613

Canals, 650, 652

Cannons, invention of, 340

Cape of Good Hope, 399

Capet dynasty, 348, 350, 354

Capitalism, industrial, 650, 652

Cardinals, College of, 359, 362, 363, 454–455

Carolinas, 569

Carolingian minuscule writing, 343

Cartier, Jacques, 415–416

Cartwright, Edmund, 662, 663

Cassel, 352

Castiglione, Baldassare, *Book of the Courtier*, 371

Castile, 416, 417, 419, 422, 423, 494, 495

Catalonia, 336, 346, 416, 559; rebellion against Spain, 494, 495

Catherine II (the Great), Empress of Russia, 637, 638

Catherine de Médicis, Queen of France, 469

Catherine of Aragon, 410

Catholic Church: in sixteenth century, 454–459; in religious wars, 466–470, 472, 474; and Eastern Orthodox (Uniate Church), 500–501; in Poland, 500, 501; and Galileo, 514; and Jansenism, 520, 555; in France, 520, 555, 556, 667; and Baroque art, 526, 529; in England under James II, 567, 569; in Austria, 596, 598, 638; in France, revolutionary reforms, 677–680; Napoleon and, 711

Catholic League (France), 469–470

Catholic Reformation (Counter Reformation), 454–459, 543; and Baroque art, 526, 529

Cecil, Robert, Earl of Salisbury, 478–479

Cervantes Saavedra, Miguel de, 523–525

Cesi, Prince Federigo, 523

Ceuta, 399

Charles I, King of England, 482–485; execution, 485

Charles I (of Anjou), King of Naples and Sicily, 359

Charles II, King of England, 485, 486, 522, 565, 567–569; restoration, 487

Charles II, King of Spain, 554

Charles IV, King of France, 350

Charles IV, King of Spain, 719

Charles V, Holy Roman Emperor, 404, 410, 413, 419, 421–423, 425, 426, 428; and Lutheranism, 444–445, 448–449

Charles V, King of France, 354

Charles VI, Holy Roman Emperor, 596

Charles VI, King of France, 354, 380

Charles VII, King of France, 354, 355

Charles VIII, King of France, 410, 413–414, 419, 426

Charles X Gustavus, King of Sweden, 499, 500

Charles XI, King of Sweden, 571

Charles XII, King of Sweden, 571–572

Charles, Duke of Lorraine, 557

Charles Albert, Duke of Bavaria, 596

Charles the Bold, Duke of Burgundy, 413

Chaucer, Geoffrey, *Canterbury Tales*, 382–383

Chemistry, in eighteenth century, 617

Cherbourg Academy, 627

Chivalry, 379–380

Christianity: in Renaissance, 378, 383–388; Enlightenment questions beliefs, 618–620. *See also* Catholic Church; Church; Protestantism

Christina, Queen of Sweden, 499–500, 571

Chrysoloras, Manuel, 376

Church: music, 388, 389; heresy suppressed by, 387–388 (*see also* Inquisition); Great Schism, 362–364, 435; conciliar movement, 363–364; in Spain, 364, 417, 419, 436; art promoted by, 388–389; Church of England separated from, 410–411; in France, 415; dissatisfaction with, 434–436. *See also* Catholic Church; Catholic Reformation; Eastern Orthodox Church; Protestantism

Church of England (Anglican Church), 568; foundation of, 410–411; Puritans and, 480–481; in Civil War, 482–484

Cicero, Marcus Tullius, 374, 625

Ciompi revolt, 346–347

Cisalpine Republic, 707

Cities: revolts in fourteenth century, 346–347; Italian, 368–369; growth in sixteenth century, 404, 407; in eighteenth century, 624–625

City-states, Italian, 357–358, 426–428

Classes, *see* Social classes

Classicism: in Renaissance art, 391; in sixteenth century, 523, 526, 531–533, 564; in French literature, 532–533, 575, 578

Clement V, Pope, 359, 361

Cleves, 559, 560

Coal, in Industrial Revolution, 660, 665

Cobos, Francisco de los, 421

Coins, French, 652

Coke, Thomas William, 657

Colbert, Jean Baptiste, 551, 556, 651, 664

College of Cardinals, *see* Cardinals, College of

Cologne, 339, 436

Colonialism, and exploitation, 651

Columbus, Christopher, 399–401

Comédie Française, 578

Common Law, 409, 482

Communes, in Spain, 421

Companies (commercial): chartered, 480, 649, 653; joint-stock, 653

Condé, Henry II, Prince de, 489

Condé, Louis II de Bourbon, Prince de, 491

Condorcet, Marie Jean de Caritat, Marquis de, 619, 625

Confederation of the Rhine, 715, 716, 721

Confraternities, 386

Constance, Council of (1414–1418), 364, 435

Constantine I (the Great), Donation of, 377
Continental system, 717–718
Convention of Westminster (1756), 609
Copernicus, Nicolaus, 393, 425, 509–513, 579
Corneille, Pierre, 532–533
Corsica, Napoleon in, 705
Cort, Henry, 660
Cortés, Hernando, 402
Cossacks, 501
Cotton gin, 662
Cotton industry, 650, 651, 660–662, 665
Counter Reformation, *see* Catholic Reformation
Crécy, Battle of, 352
Crompton, Samuel, 662, 663
Cromwell, Oliver, 483, 485–487
Cromwell, Richard, 487
Cromwell, Thomas, 410–411
Cuba, Columbus, explores, 401
Culture, popular, *see* Popular culture
Czechs, 596

Danton, Georges Jacques, 689, 692, 701
Danube River (valley), 477
Darby, Alexander, 660
David, Jacques Louis, 636
Death, cult of, 380–381
Declaration of Independence (American), 582, 671, 676
Declaration of the Rights of Man (French), 676
Defoe, Daniel, 591
Demography, *see* Population of Europe
Denmark, 498, 499; Lutheranism in, 447, 448
Descartes, René, 516, 518–519, 522, 524, 579–581, 616–618; portrait by Hals, 517
Des Prés, Josquin, 392
Devotio moderna, 386–387, 391
Dias, Bartholomeu, 399
Diderot, Denis, 619, 620, 625, 627, 637, 642; *Encyclopedia*, 621–624, 627, 628, 644
Diggers, 486
Dijon, 413
Dominican Order, 385, 444, 514
Dominici, Giovanni, 370
Donatello, *Annunciation*, 391
Donation of Constantine, 377
Dryden, John, 575
Dufay, Guillaume, 392
Dumouriez, Gen. Charles François, 689
Dunkirk, 487
Duns Scotus, John, 383
Dürer, Albrecht, 440

Eastern Orthodox Church: in Russia, 502, 562; and Catholic (Uniate Church), 500–501
East India Company: Dutch, 496, French, 599; British, 649

Eckhart, Meister, 386
Ecôle des Ponts et Chaussées, 652
Economics, Adam Smith and physiocrats, 621
Edict of Nantes (1598), 470, 490; revocation of, 555–618
Edict of Restitution (1629), 474, 475
Education: in Renaissance, 369, 373–374, 376–377, 379; and social class in seventeenth century, 535; schools in eighteenth century, 627; under Napoleon, 713
Edward, Prince of Wales (the Black Prince), 352
Edward III, King of England, 350, 352
Edward VI, King of England, 411
Elba, Napoleon in, 722
Elizabeth, Empress of Russia, 608, 609
Elizabeth I, Queen of England, 412, 466, 467, 478–480
Encyclopedia (Diderot), 621–624, 627, 628, 644
England: judicial system, 409, 482; justices of the peace, 408, 409; Exchequer, 409; Church (medieval), 364, 387–388; laws, 409, 482; taxes, 346, 354–355; population decline, 335; prices and wages in fourteenth century, 339, 346; Peasants' War and revolt, 346, 347; Hundred Years' War, *see* Hundred Years' War; War of the Roses, 348, 355–356, 409; urban population, 369, 404; in sixteenth century, economic conditions, 403, 404, 407; land enclosures, 404, 657–658; king's power, 408–409, 482–483, 487, 565, 567, 569; Tudor monarchs, 408–412; Star Chamber, 409 *n.*, 410, 482, 483, 565; French treaty with (1492), 410; break with Church of Rome, 410–411 ((*see also* Church of England); monasteries dissolved, 411, 479; Calvinism in, 454; Spanish war with, 466–467; economic leadership, 477, 479–480; in seventeenth century, 548–584; 565–571; gentry (aristocracy), 479, 480, 565–567, 570; colonies, early, 480, 535–536, 569; industrial expansion, 480; Civil War, 482–485; under Cromwell, 485–487; population changes in seventeenth century, 536, 538; cottage industries, 541; succession from Stuarts to Hanoverians, 567–569; Exclusion Crisis, 567, 568; under William III (Glorious Revolution), 568, 640; Act of Toleration, 568; Bill of Rights, 568, 582; voting qualifications, 568–569; union with Scotland, 569. *See also* Parliament; Tories; Whigs; after 1707, *see* Great Britain
English literature: fourteenth century, 382–383; Shakespeare, 523, 525–526; seventeenth century, 575, 577; eighteenth century, 627, 629, 631, 633–634
Enlightenment, Age of, 616–644; science, 616–618; Christianity and atheism, 618–620; philosophes, *see* Philosphes; republic of letters, 625–627; publishing, 627–630; in government, 636–639; French liberal political thought, 639–643; and industrialization, 649
Erasmus, Desiderius, 386, 387, 440–442, 449; *The Praise of Folly*, 442
Essex, Robert Devereux, Earl of, 478
Estates, three, 665–666
Estates General (France), 349, 350, 355, 412, 489 Louis XVI and, 668, 674–675; third estate in, 674–675

Estonia, 565

Eugène, Prince of Savoy, 555, 557–558

Euripides, 575

Europe, Western: in fourteenth and fifteenth centuries, 334–366, 371–372; famine in fourteenth century, 337–338; revolts and social disturbances (1300–1450), 345–348; governments, fiscal and factional problems, 348–350; late fifteenth to mid-sixteenth centuries, 398–431; economic growth in sixteenth century, 403–408; "new monarchs," 408–424, 427–428; international relations, development of, 427–429; wars in seventeenth century, 462–478; culture and society in seventeenth century, 506–545, 573–582; governments in seventeenth century, 548–573; in eighteenth century, international relations and absolutism, 586–614; eighteenth-century cultures, 624–636 ((*see also* Enlightenment); in eighteenth century, constitutional conflicts, 665–671; revolutionary republics (1792–1799), 705, 706. *See also* Population of Europe

Exploration, 398–403, 410, 415–416; economic effects of, 403–407

Eyck, Jan van, 391

Eylau, Battle of, 716

Factory system, 647, 650

Factory workers, *see* Labor

Family: in Italy, size and structure, 369–371; in seventeenth century, demographic patterns, 536–537

Felix V, Pope, 364

Feodor I, Tsar, 501

Ferdinand II, Holy Roman Emperor, 472, 474–475

Ferdinand V, King of Spain, 400, 416–417, 419, 456; King of Naples and Sicily, 426

Ferdinand VII, King of Spain, 719, 720

Feudalism, in Russia, 501; government systems, 348–349, 356; in Hundred Years' War, 352; in France, abolished, 676

Ficino, Marsilio, 378

Fielding, Henry, 633

Fifth Monarchists, 486

Firearms, invention and development of, 340, 413, 462–463

Flanders: textiles, 352; in Hundred Years' War, 352; in Renaissance, art and music, 391–392; industries, 665

Fleurus, Battle of, 700

Fleury, André Hercule de, Cardinal, 599

Flodden Field, Battle of, 410

Florence, 373; banks, 344; Ciompi revolt, 346–347; in Renaissance, 358, 369, 376, 378; Sta. Maria Novella convent, 372; Platonic Academy, 378, 389

Florence, republic, 358, 359, 376–377, 426

Fontenelle, Bernard de, 617

Fort Duquesne, 610

Fouché, Joseph, 710

France: population decline, 335; in fourteenth and fifteenth centuries, 339, 348, 354–356, 364; Hundred Years' War, *see* Hundred Years' War; taxes, 349, 355, 412, 490, 556, 600, 673, 674; *gabelle*, salt tax, 349, 355, 412, 415; *taille*, hearth tax, 355, 415; English war with (1514), 410; in fifteenth and sixteenth centuries, 412–416, 454, 456; government structure, 412–413, 415 (*see also* Estates General, Parlement of Paris); army in fifteenth century, 412–413; wars with Italy, 413, 415, 416, 419, 426; sale of offices, 415, 490; Church in, 415, 454, 456, 667; Calvinists, *see* Huguenots; civil war (religious), 469–470, 472, 493; in Thirty Years' War, 474, 475, 477; in seventeenth century, 487–492; Spanish invasion of, 490; in Spanish revolt, 494, 495; colonies in seventeenth century, 535; population in seventeenth century, 536, 538; under Louis XIV, 549–557; war with Netherlands in 1670s, 551, 570–571; famines in seventeenth century, 555, 556; cultural and intellectual life in seventeenth century, 573–578; in eighteenth century, international relations, 588, 596–601, 608, 609; army in eighteenth century, 591; rivalry with Britain in colonial development, 603–608, 610–612; French and Indian War, 610, 612–613; naval battles with Britain (1759), 612; eighteenth-century culture, 624–627, 629–630, 633, 636; Enlightenment, *see* Enlightenment, Age of; guilds abolished, 649; preconditions of industrialization, 651–652; canals and roads, 652; currency and finance, 652; foreign trade, 652; prices in eighteenth century, 653–654; population in eighteenth century, 655; agriculture, 658–659; Industrial Revolution, 664–665; Church before Revolution, 667; fiscal crisis before Revolution, 672–674; Revolution, *see* French Revolution; British war with (1778), 674; Assembly of Notables, 674; National Assembly, 675, 697; Constituent Assembly, 675–678, 680, 691; constitutional reforms, 676–680, 691, 695, 702, 703; Legislative Assembly, 676, 680, 682; provinces and departments before and after 1789, 678–679; war with Austria and its allies, 680, 682, 687, 689; Directory, 703–705, 707–709; Napoleon's empire, 709–722 (*see also* Napoleon); education, 713. *See also* French language; French literature

Franche-Comté, 424, 651, 675

Francis I, King of France, 415–416, 428, 454

Francis II, Holy Roman Emperor (Francis I of Austria), 680, 716, 721

Francis of Assisi, St., 381

Francis Xavier, St., 459

Franciscan Order, 385

Franklin, Benjamin, 620, 625

Frederick I, King of Prussia (Frederick III, Elector of Brandenburg), 560–562, 592–593

Frederick II, Elector of the Palatinate, 474, 475

Frederick II (the Great), King of Prussia, 571, 589, 592, 594–597, 624; in Seven Years' War, 608–609; enlightened absolutism, 637, 639

Frederick II (Hohenstaufen), Holy Roman Emperor, 356, 357

Frederick III, Elector of Saxony, 445–446

Frederick William, Elector of Brandenburg, 559–560, 592

Frederick William I, King of Prussia, 593–595

Frederick William III, King of Prussia, 721

Freemasonry, 625–626

French and Indian War, 610, 612–613

French language, 356; as international language, 591, 624

French literature: essays, 524; in late seventeenth century, 532–533, 575–578; popular, in eighteenth century, 629; in Enlightenment, 633

French Revolution, 540, 636, 671–682, 686–703, 709–710; British reactions to, 670; origins, 671–672; fiscal crisis before, 672–674; third estate in, 674–675; oath of the tennis court, 675; Great Fear, 675–676; feudalism abolished, 676; Declaration of the Rights of Man, 676; constitutions, 676–680, 691, 695, 702; Church reforms, 677–680; paper money (assignats), 677, 690; counterrevolution, 680, 682; Jacobins, 680, 687–693, 695, 700–702; National Convention, 682, 686–693, 696–703; Girondists, 687–691; the Mountain and the Plain, 689, 691, 695, 697, 701; sans-culottes, 690–691, 694–697, 700–702; Committee of Public Safety, 691, 692, 698–700, 709; Reign of Terror, 692–693, 701; turning points, list, 694; calendar, 695–696, 711; democracy, 696–697; foreign policy, 697; armies, 699–700; Thermidorian reaction, 700–703

Friedland, Battle of, 716

Fronde, 487, 490–492

Fugger family, 404

Galen, 507, 508

Galileo Galilei, 393, 394, 508, 511–516, 518, 579; astronomical theories, 512–514; before Inquisition, 514

Gama, Vasco da, 399

Geneva, 698; Calvinists in, 452, 453; government reform, 669

Genoa, 493, 716

Gentleman's Magazine, 627

George I, King of Great Britain, 569, 588, 601

George II, King of Great Britain, 601

George III, King of Great Britain, 582, 636, 669, 671

German literature: in eighteenth century, 633, 634

Germany: in Holy Roman Empire, 356– 357; population decline, 335; in fourteenth and fifteenth centuries, 339, 425; Peasants' War (1524), 346, 448, 449; religious brotherhoods, 436; Lutheranism, 448; in Thirty Years' War, 472, 474, 475, 477; in seventeenth century, 559–562, 572, 573; industries, 665; in Napoleonic Wars, 714–716, 721–722

Ghent, 346

Gibbon, Edward, 95, 159, 620, 625

Giotto, 390

Girondists, 687–691, 701

Glassmaking, 404

Godoy, Manuel de, 719

Goethe, Johann Wolfgang von, 633

Gold, in currency, 403

Golden Bull, 357

Goldsmith, Oliver, 629

Goya y Lucientes, Francisco, 719

Granada, 419

Grand Alliance, 554

Great Britain: England and Scotland united (1707), 569; international relations in eighteenth century, 588, 589, 596–598, 609; government in eighteenth century, 600–602; Dutch financial relations with, 603; rivalry with France in colonial development, 603–608, 610–612; French and Indian War, 610, 612–613; naval battles with France (1759), 612; Enlightenment in, 617, 619–621, 640; publishing in eighteenth century, 627–630; Industrial Revolution, 647, 660–664; preconditions of industrialization, 649–651; aristocracy (gentry), 650; foreign trade, 651, 653; banking, 653; taxes, 653; prices in eighteenth century, 653–654; population in eighteenth century, 655; agriculture, 656–658; land enclosure, 657–658; parliamentary reform movement, 669–670; and French Revolution, 670; and American Revolution, 671; war with France (1778), 674; allied with Austria against France, 689; Napoleon hopes to invade, 707, 715; in coalition against Napoleon, 707, 714–715; in Napoleon's Continental system, 717–718; Peninsular War, 719, 720. *See also* England; English literature; Parliament

Great Britain, colonies, and industrialization, 651. *See also* American colonies

Great Lakes, French and British forts on, 612, 613

Great Northern War, 571–572

Great Schism, 362–364

Great War for Empire, 608, 612–613

Greco, El, 524

Greece (ancient): Classicism derived from, 531–533; eighteenth-century interest in, 620, 625. *See also* entries under Greek

Greek language, in Western culture, 374, 376, 378

Greek Orthodox Church, *see* Eastern Orthodox Church

Gregory XI, Pope, 362

Gregory XIII, Pope, 510

Greuze, Jean Baptiste, 636

Groote, Gerhard, 386

Grotius, Hugo, 466

Grünewald, Mathias, *Temptation of St. Anthony*, 438–440

Guarino da Verona, 377

Guatemala, 494

Guericke, Otto von, 663

Guicciardini, Francesco, *History of Italy*, 429

Guilds, 649; abolished, 649

Guise, Henri I de Lorraine, Duke of, 470

Guise family, 456, 469–470

Gulf of St. Lawrence, 610
Gustavus III, King of Sweden, 666–667, 673
Gustavus Adolphus (Gustavus II), King of Sweden, 464–466, 474–475, 498–499, 571
Gutenberg, Johannes, 342

Haarlem, 603
Halifax, 610
Hals, Frans, portrait of Descartes, 517
Hamburg, 339, 436
Hanover, 609
Hanoverian dynasty, 569, 588, 601
Hapsburg dynasty, 356–357, 419, 423, 425, 428, 500, 529, 608, 700; in Italy, 413, 426, 559; in Holy Roman Empire, 424, 557–559; in Thirty Years' War, 474, 475, 477; in Spain, 559; in eighteenth century, 588, 589, 595–598, 636; in Napoleonic wars, 714–716
Hargreaves, James, 662
Harvey, William, 514
Haydn, Franz Joseph, 634, 635
Hébert, Jacques René, 692, 701
Hebrew language, 378, 440
Heidelberg, university, 440, 453
Heinsius, Antonius, 570
Helvétius, Claude Adrien, 619
Henry II, King of France, 416, 469
Henry III, King of France, 470
Henry IV, King of France (Henry of Navarre), 466, 469–470, 487–488
Henry V, King of England, 354
Henry VII, King of England, 356, 409–410
Henry VIII, King of England, 410–411, 428, 441
Henry the Navigator, Prince of Portugal, 399
Heresy: suppression of, 387–388; in fourteenth and fifteenth centuries, 387–388
Hermeticism, 507
Hero of Alexandria, 663
Hispaniola, 401
Hobbes, Thomas, 519–520, 522, 523, 582
Hoche, Lazare, 699, 700
Hogarth, William, 633, 636; *Gin Lane*, 632
Hohenlinden, Battle of, 714
Hohenzollern family, 559–562, 594–595
Holbach, Paul Henri Dietrich, Baron d', 619, 625
Holbein, Hans, *The Ambassadors*, 427, 440
Holland (province), 497, 570. *See also* Netherlands
Holy Roman Empire, 416, 551; in fourteenth and fifteenth centuries, 356–357, 364; in sixteenth century, 424–425; Reformation in, 447–449; in Thirty Years' War, 472–477, 557; in seventeenth century, 557; in eighteenth century, 589, 659; end of, 716
Hooke, Robert, 579
Huguenots, 454, 469, 470, 472, 489–490, 555

Huizinga, Johan, 379–380, 382, 389
Humanism, 358, 372–379; in Renaissance, 374–377, 386, 394; heritage of, 378–379; Christian, 387, 440–441, 457; literary criticism, 394; in Reformation, 440–441; Loyola influenced by, 457
Hume, David, 619, 621
Hundred Years' War, 348, 350–356, 382, 387; effects of, 354–356
Hungary, 340, 348, 447, 454, 500, 557, 559; Turks capture, 425; kingdom, 425, 596. *See also* Austrian Empire
Huss, John, 388, 435, 436
Hussites, 388
Hutten, Ulrich von, 440–441

Iberian Peninsula, kingdoms, 416
Ignatius Loyola, *see* Loyola, St. Ignatius
Illyria, 716
Imperialism, in eighteenth century, 603–608
Incas, 402
Index of Forbidden Books, 455
India: search for routes to, 398–399; British in, 480, 613; trade with, 661, 662
Indians, American: Spanish use of, 493–494; in French and Indian War, 610
Indulgences: sale of, 362, 435; controversy on, 444–446
Industrial economy, characteristics of, 647–649
Industrialization, preconditions of, 648–652
Industrial Revolution, 646–647, 659–665; agriculture in, 647, 651, 656–659; steam power, 647, 660, 663–664; preconditions for, 648–652; coal and iron, 660
Industries: in sixteenth century, 404; in seventeenth century, 480; cottage (putting-out) system, 541, 647
Inflation: in sixteenth century, 403, 404; in eighteenth century, 654, 702
Innocent VIII, Pope, 378
Innocent X, Pope, 477
Inquisition, 455, 457, 467; Spanish, 419, 454, 620; Roman, 454, 620; Galileo before, 514
Insurance, origin of, 344
Ionian Islands, 716
Ireland, 485, 698; English in, 479; population increase, 656; Parliament, autonomy, 670–671; Protestants, 670–671
Iron: mining, 499; in Industrial Revolution, 660–661, 665; smelting with coke, 660, 665
Isabella I, Queen of Spain, 400, 416–417, 419
Italy: in Holy Roman Empire, 356, 357; commerce and trade, 404–405; Byzantine scholars in, 376; business institutions in fourteenth and fifteenth centuries, 344; taxes, 349; history in fourteenth and fifteenth centuries, 356–359, 368–372; Renaissance, *see* Renaissance; city-states, 357–358, 426–428; cities, 368–369; family size and structure, 369–371; life expectancy, 371–372; French wars with, 413, 415, 416, 419, 426; Hapsburg rulers of, 413,

426, 559, 596; Spanish war with, 419, 423, 426; international relations, 427, 589; operas, 634; population in eighteenth century, 655; Napoleon in, 705–707, 714, 715; Napoleonic kingdom, 716
Ivan IV (the Terrible), Tsar, 501

Jacobins (Jacobin Club), 680, 687–693, 695, 700–702, 709; under Directoire, 703–705, 708
Jacobites, 568, 569
Jagellon dynasty, 425
Jamaica, 487
James I, King of England (James VI of Scotland), 479–482
James II, King of England, 567–568, 582
Jansen, Cornelis, 520
Jansenism, 520, 555
Jason, 380 *n.*
Jefferson, Thomas, 620
Jemappes, Battle of, 687
Jerome, St., 455
Jerusalem, 457
Jesuits (Society or Company of Jesus), 457, 459, 467, 472, 500, 501, 514, 520, 627
Jews: in Spain, 419; in Netherlands, 497; in Austria, 638
Joanna (wife of Archduke Philip of Austria), 419
Joan of Arc, St., 354
John, King of Bohemia, 380
John II (the Good), King of France, 352, 356
John III Sobieski, King of Poland, 573
Johnson, Samuel, 625; *Dictionary,* 629
Joseph II, Holy Roman Emperor, 598, 638–639, 667–668
Journal des Savants, 627
Julius II, Pope, 365, 427
Junkers, 560
Jury, trial by, 482

Kant, Immanuel, 619, 621
Kaunitz, Count Wenzel Anton von, 589, 608–609
Kay, John, 662, 664
Kepler, Johannes, 511–514, 579, 580
Knights: chivalry, 379–380; Lutheranism attacked by, 447–448
Knights of the Garter, 380
Knights of the Golden Fleece, 380
Knights Templars, *see* Templars
Königsberg, 560
Kutuzov, Gen. Mikhail I., 721 *n.*

Labor (working class), in fourteenth and fifteenth centuries, 338–340, 346–348; in sixteenth century, 407; and industrialization, 647; Napoleon's regulation of, 713
Laissez faire, 621
Lancashire, cotton manufacture, 662
Langland, William, *Vision of Piers Plowman,* 382
Languedoc, 346

La Rochelle, 489
Latin America: conquest and colonization, 401–403, 421, 423; Spanish trade with, 492–493
Latin language, in Humanism, 372–374, 378
Lavoisier, Antoine Lourent, 617
Law, John, 599, 601, 652
Laws: Common Law, 409, 482; English, 409, 482; Napoleonic Code, 713–714, *See also* names of countries
League of Augsburg, 551, 554
Lefebvre, Georges, 694
Lefèvre d'Étaples, Jacques, 441
Legion of Honor, 711, 713
Leibniz, Gottfried Wilhelm von, 563, 579
Leiden, 603
Leipzig, Battle of, 722
Lely, Sir Peter, 575
Lenin, Vladimir Ilyich, 704
Leo X, Pope, 445, 454
Leonardo da Vinci, 370, 392–393; cannon foundry, 340; *Last Supper,* 393; *Mona Lisa,* 393
Leopold I, Holy Roman Emperor, 477, 554, 557–561
Leopold II, Holy Roman Emperor, 668–669
Lepanto, Battle of, 466
Lessing, Gotthold Ephraim, 619, 624
Levellers, 485, 486
Liberalism, in Englightenment, 639–643
Libraries, circulating and lending, 627
Liège, 346
Life expectancy, in fourteenth and fifteenth centuries, 371–372; in seventeenth century, 537–538
Lille, 664
Lincean Academy, 521–522
Lithuania, 565
Liverpool, 662
Locke, John, 581–582, 617, 620, 640, 671
Loire River (valley), 354
Lollards, 388
Lombardy, 368–369, 596, 698; French conquest of, 707; in Napoleonic wars, 714
Loménie de Brienne, Étienne Charles, 674
London, 573; Peasants' War in 346; population growth, sixteenth and seventeenth centuries, 404; social conditions in seventeenth century, 536, 570; St. Paul's Cathedral, 570
London Chronicle, 628
Lorraine, 477, 589. *See also* Alsace-Lorraine
Louis X, King of France, 350
Louis XI, King of France, 413, 419
Louis XII, King of France, 415
Louis XIII, King of France, 489, 491
Louis XIV, King of France, 464, 490–492, 522, 558, 561, 568–571, 573, 578, 587, 591, 598, 618, 637; reign of, 549–557
Louis XV, King of France, 599–600, 673

Louis XVI, King of France, 600, 641; and French Revolution, 668, 671, 675, 680, 682; in financial crisis, 673–674; execution, 687
Louisbourg, 610
Louisiana, 599, 610, 719
Louvois, Marquis de, 551
Low Countries, 413, 422–424, 454, 492; Renaissance art and music, 391–392. *See also* Flanders; Netherlands
Loyola, St. Ignatius, 456–457; *Spiritual Exercises*, 457
Lübeck, 339
Luther, Martin, 386, 441, 456, 457; in Reformation, 443–449; Zwingli and, 450–451
Lutheranism: doctrine and practice, 446–447; disorders in establishment of, 447–449; Calvinism compared with, 452–453
Lützen, Battle of, 475
Lyons, 488, 556; Academy, 627; silk manufacture, 665; in French Revolution, 690, 691, 693–694

Mably, Gabriel Bonnet de, 621
Machiavelli, Niccolò, *The Prince*, 428–429
Mâconnais, 675
Madrid, 529
Magazines, in eighteenth century, 627
Magellan, Ferdinand, 401
Magyars, 596
Maine (French province), 413
Manchester, 662
Mannerism, 393, 523–524
Mantua, Casa Giocosa, 377
Manutius, Aldus, 342
Marat, Jean Paul, 689
Marengo, Battle of, 714
Maria Louisa, Queen of Spain, 719
Maria Theresa, Archduchess of Austria, 592, 596–598
Marie Antoinette, Queen of France, 671, 673
Marie de Médicis, Queen of France, 489, 490
Marie Louise (wife of Napoleon), 716
Marlborough, John Churchill, Duke of, 555
Marranos, 419
Marseillaise, 681, 682
Marseilles, 488, 652; in French Revolution, 690, 691
Marsilius of Padua, *Defender of Peace*, 385
Martin V, Pope, 358, 364
Martinique, 613
Marx, Karl, 704
Marxism, French Revolution interpreted by, 672
Mary I, Queen of England (Mary Tudor), 411
Mary II, Queen of England (wife of William III), 568
Mary of Burgundy, 356, 413
Maryland, 480
Masaccio, *Holy Trinity with the Virgin and St. John*, 390
Mathematics, in scientific revolution, 515, 518, 520
Matthias Corvinus, King of Hungary, 425

Maupeou, René Nicolas de, 600, 673
Maurice of Nassau, Stadholder, 464, 468, 497
Maximilian I, Elector of Bavaria, 474
Mayas, 402
Mazarin, Giulio, Cardinal, 490–491, 551
Medici, Cosimo de', 358, 359, 378
Medici, Lorenzo de' (the Magnificent), 358
Medici bank, 344
Medici family, 426, 428
Mediterranean Sea, trade in, 477, 479, 493
Melanchthon, Philipp, 446
Melchiorites, 451
Mercantilism, 488–489, 604, 621
Mersenne, Marin, 522
Mesmerism, 617
Messina, plague in, 335
Metternich, Prince Klemens von, 721
Mexico: Cortés conquers, 402, 421; Indians in, 494
Michelangelo, 365, 378, 392, 393, 456, 524, 529
Middle class, British, 601
Mikhail Feodorovich, Tsar, 502
Milan, duchy of, 357–359, 426
Milan, French capture, 707
Military tactics: firearms and cannons, 340, 342; in Hundred Years' War, 354; in sixteenth century, 428; in seventeenth century, 462–464, 466
Milton, John, 486
Mining: in fifteenth and sixteenth centuries, 340; copper and iron in Sweden, 499
Minorca, 612
Mississippi River, 610
Mohammed; Mohammedans, *see* Muhammad
Molière, Jean Baptiste Poquelin, 533, 577, 578
Moluccas (Spice Islands), 400, 401
Monck, Gen. George, 487
Montaigne, Michel Eyquem de, 523, 524, 532
Montcalm, Gen. Louis Joseph, 612
Montesquieu, Charles de Secondat, Baron de, 619, 625, 633, 636, 667; *The Spirit of Laws*, 640–641
Monteverdi, Claudio, 531
Monthly Review, 627
Montreal, 612
Moors, *see* Muslims
Moravia, 665
More, Sir Thomas, 387, 442, 450; *Utopia*, 441, 516
Moriscos, 419
Morning Post, London, 670
Mozart, Wolfgang Amadeus, 634
Munich, 529
Münster, 451
Murat, Joachim, 716
Music: of Church, 388, 389; in Renaissance, 388–392; opera, 531, 634; in seventeenth century, 531, 577–578; in eighteenth century, 634–635; symphony, 634–635

Muslims: in Spain, 416; final expulsion from Spain (1492), 401, 417, 419; Spanish war with, 466
Mysticism, 385–387; in Spain, 456, 492

Nantes, 690; *noyades* (drownings), 693
Naples, 522
Naples and Sicily, Kingdom of (Kingdom of the Two Sicilies), 348, 359, 426; Spanish control of, 419, 422, 492; revolt against Spain, 494, 495; in coalition against Napoleon, 707; Napoleonic kingdom, 716
Napoleon, French Emperor, 655, 677, 700, 704; early career, 705–707; with Directory, 705–709; in Egypt, 707; Brumaire coup, 707–709; empire, 709–722; government, 710–711, 713; and Catholic Church, 711; Napoleonic Code, 713–714; war against allied coalition, 714–716; Continental system, 717–718, 720; Spanish campaign, 718–720; Russian campaign, 720–721; exiled to Elba, 722
Napoleonic Code, 713–714
Narva, Battle of, 571
Naseby, Battle of, 485
Natural history in eighteenty century, 617–618
Navigation, improvements in, 343
Necker, Jacques, 674, 675
Nelson, Adm. Horatio, 707, 715
Neoclassicism: in literature, 631, 634; in art, 636
Neoplatonism, 378, 393, 508, 510
Netherlands: Spanish rule of, 466; revolt against Spain, 467–469, 474, 493; dikes, 467 *n.*; United Provinces, 468–469, 477, 495–498, 531, 602; economic leadership, 477, 496–497; in seventeenth century, 495–498; banking and finance, 496, 603; art and intellectual life, 497, 531–532; Estates General, 497, 570–571; Reformed Church, 497, 531; colonies in seventeenth century, 535, 536; cottage industries, 541; French war with, in 1670s, 551, 570–571; aristocracy, 570–571; in eighteenth century, 588, 602–603; agriculture, 658; in French Revolution, 698, 699; Batavian Republic, 705, 708, 715, 716; Napoleonic kingdom, 716, 718
Netherlands, Austrian, 559, 596, 665; under Joseph II, 667–669; annexed by France, 698–700, 716
Newcomen, Thomas, engines, 663
New England colonies, 480, 536
Newfoundland fisheries, 410, 479
New Jersey, 569
New Orleans, 610
Newspapers: in eighteenth century, 627–628, 670; Napoleon's suppression of, 710
Newton, Sir Isaac, 393, 512, 579–581, 616–617, 620; laws of motion, 580, 581
Nicholas V, Pope, 364, 365
Nile, Battle of the, 707
Nocera, 358
Nominalism, 383–384, 394, 446

Normandy, 337; industries, 664; in French Revolution, 675, 690
North, Lord, 671
North America, *see* America
Nuremberg, 449

Ockham, William of, 383–384
Ohio Company of Virginia, 610
Ohio valley, 610, 613
Oldenbarneveldt, Jan van, 497
Olivares, Count de, 494–495
Operas, 634
Orange, House of, 497, 498
Order of the Black Eagle, 562
Orléans, 354
Orléans, Philippe II, Duke of, 599
Orry, Philibert, 652
Ottoman Empire, 398, 421, 425; sultan's power, 500; in seventeenth century, 500, 551; siege of Vienna, 554, 557, 558, 573; in eighteenth century, 589; in coalition against Napoleon, 707
Oxenstierna, Axel, 498–499
Oxford, Invisible College, 522

Pacific Ocean, discovery of, 401
Padua, 358, 373; university, 508
Palladio, Andrea, 391
Papacy: Avignon, 358–359, 361–362, 387; and Holy Roman Empire, 357; in fourteenth and fifteenth centuries, 359, 361–365; fiscal crisis, 361–362; Great Schism, 362–364, 435; popes as patrons of arts, 364–365; Wycliffe's heresy against, 387; loss of influence, 435; Luther's attack on, 444–445; in Catholic Reformation, 455, 456
Papal infallibility, dogma of, 455 *n.*, Papal States, 358–359, 362, 365, 426
Paracelsus, 507
Paris, 346, 624; University of, 394, 451; as cultural center, 573, 574; fall of Bastille, 675; Invalides, 675; in French Revolution, 675, 676, 680, 682, 688–690, 696–697; Napoleon surrenders in, 722
Parlement of Paris, 350, 412, 491, 555, 673, 674
Parliament (English): origins of, 349; after Hundred Years' War, 354–356; and king's power, 408–409, 482–483, 487, 565, 567, 569; under Henry VIII, 410–411; in seventeenth century, 479–482; Petition of Right, 482; Charles I and, 482–483, 485; under Cromwell, 486–487; gentry in House of Commons, 566–567; under William III, 568; distribution of seats for borough, 600; in eighteenth century, 600–601; European admiration of, 640; and joint-stock companies, 653; and enclosure of land, 658; reform movement in late eighteenth century, 669–670
Parmigianino, 524
Pascal, Blaise, 515, 520, 523, 524, 663

Paul, St., 441

Paul III, Pope, 454, 455, 457

Peace of Amiens (1801), 714–715

Peace of Brétigny (1360), 352

Peace of Hubertusburg (1763), 609

Peace of Lodi (1454), 359

Peace of Utrecht, see Treaties of Utrecht

Peace of Westphalia (1648), 468, 475, 477–478, 497, 559

Peasants: in sixteenth century, 407; in seventeenth century, 536; Russian, 564; Austrian, under Joseph II, 639; in French Revolution, 675–676, 689, 694

Peasants' revolts, 407, 540; in England, 346, 347; in Germany, sixteenth century, 346, 448, 449; in France, seventeenth century, 490

Peninsular War, 719, 720

Pepys, Samuel, 569, 578

Peru, Spanish conquest of, 402, 423

Perugia, 358

Perugino, 365

Peter I (the Great), Tsar, 503, 562–565, 571

Peter III, Tsar, 609

Peter's pence, 387

Petrarch, 372, 374–375, 387

Pfefferkorn, Johannes, 440

Philip II, King of Spain, 423, 469, 492–493, 637; campaign against Muslims, 466; relations with England, 466–467; Dutch revolt against, 467–469

Philip III, King of Spain, 493

Philip IV (the Fair), King of France, 355, 359

Philip IV, King of Spain, 494, 495

Philip V, King of France, 350

Philip V, King of Spain, 554

Philip VI (of Valois), King of France, 350, 352

Philip, Archduke of Austria, 419

Philip the Bold, Duke of Burgundy, 356

Philosophes, 619–621, 625, 637, 640, 641, 643–644, and French Revolution, 671–672

Philosophy: Neoplatonism, 378; in Renaissance, 378, 383–384; in Enlightenment, see Philosophes

Physics: of Newton, 579–581

Physiocrats, 621, 649

Pico della Mirandola, Giovanni, 378

Piedmont, 689, 700, 716

Pilgrimages: Christian, 382

Pinturicchio, 365

Pisa, 358; Council of (1409), 364

Pistoia, 335

Pitt, William, the Elder, 589, 601–602, 609, 612

Pius II, Pope, 365

Pius VII, Pope, 711

Pizarro, Francisco, 402

Plague, 407, 426; and life expectancy, 371; in seventeenth century, 494, 537. See also Black Death

Plato: Renaissance influenced by, 378, 394

Poggio Bracciolini, Giovanni Francesco, 370, 375

Poitiers: Battle of, 352

Poland, 349, 447, 498, 565; Kingdom of, 425; in seventeenth century, 500–501, 572, 573; in eighteenth century, 588, 589, 659; partition of, 590, 591; under Napoleon, 716

Polo, Marco, 398, 400, 401

Poltava, Battle of, 565, 571

Pomerania, 477, 609

Pompadour, Marquise de, 625

Pomponne, Simon de, 551

Ponthieu, 350, 352

Pope, Alexander, 581

Popes, see Papacy; names of popes

Population of Europe: decline, 1300–1450, 335–338; growth, sixteenth and seventeenth centuries, 404; demographic patterns in seventeenth century, 536–538; and birth rate, 655–656; growth in eighteenth century, 655–656

Po River (valley), 335, 357, 658

Port-Royal Abbey, 521, 555

Portugal, 416, 492, 603; trade with Asia and Africa, 405, 416; exploration and discovery by, 399–401; revolt against Spain, 494, 495; colonies, 535, 536

Potosi, silver mine, 403

Poussin, Nicolas, 531, 532

Pragmatic Sanction, 596

Prague, 529, 721

Presbyterians, 485

Prester John, 399

Prices: fourteenth and fifteenth centuries, 338–339; sixteenth century, 403, 404; eighteenth century, 653–655. See also Inflation

Priestley, Joseph, 617

Printing, 404, 440; invention of, 342–343; religious works and Bible, 436–438, 447, 453

Pro Aris et Focis, 668

Protestantism, 500, 543; Lutheranism, 443–449; of Zwingli, 449–451; radical sects, 450–451; of Calvin, 451–454; in religious wars, 466, 467, 469, 472, 474

Provence, 335, 413

Prussia, 447, 559–562; Estates General, 560; Junkers, see Junkers; serfs, 560, 639; kingdom established, 561; in eighteenth century, 588, 591–597, 612, 659; army, 591, 593–594; in Seven Years' War, 608–609; enlightened absolutism, 636–639; with Austria in wars against France, 680, 682, 687, 689, 700; in Napoleonic wars, 715–716, 721

Ptolemy (astronomer), 507, 509, 510

Publishing in eighteenth century, 627–630. See also Magazines; Newspapers; Printing

Purcell, Henry, 575

Puritans, 480–481; in English Civil War, 482–484; under Cromwell, 485–486

Pym, John, 482–484
Pyrenees Mountains, 700
Pythagoras, 394

Quakers (Society of Friends), 486
Quebec, Battle of, 612
Quebec (province), 610

Rabelais, François, 438
Racine, Jean, 533, 555, 575–576
Ranke, Leopold von, 587 *n.*
Raphael, 392, 393
Razin, Stenka, 502
Reformation, 365, 416, 425, 443–454; Henry VIII compromises with, 411; dissatisfaction with Church, 434–436; protest in literature and art, 436–440; Humanism in, 440–441; Luther and Lutheranism, 443–449. *See also* Catholic Reformation; Protestantism
Reformed Church (Dutch), 497, 531
Reims, 354
Rembrandt, 532; *The Anatomy Lesson of Dr. Nicholas Tulp,* 521
Renaissance, 368–396; popes as art patrons, 365; Italian society and culture, 368–372; learning and literature, 372–379; in Northern Europe, 379–383, 391–392; religious thought, 383–388; arts and music, 388–393; science, 393–395; technology, 394–395
Reuchlin, Johann, 440, 441
Reynolds, Sir Joshua, 636
Rhine River (valley), 356, 424, 440, 658, 698–700; mysticism, 386–387; industries, 665; French campaigns, 706, 707
Rhone River (valley), 356
Richard II, King of England, 346
Richardson, Samuel, *Pamela* 631, 633
Richelieu, Armand du Plessis, Cardinal de, 489–490, 532, 573
Robespierre, Maximilien, 672, 689, 691–692, 696, 698, 701
Roman Empire: Classicism derived from, 531; eighteenth-century interest in, 620, 625
Romanov dynasty, 502
Romanticism, in literature, 634; in music, 634; in art, 636
Rome (city), 624; and papacy, 357, 362, 364; St. Peter's Church, 365, 444, 529; Baroque art, 526, 529
Rossbach, Battle of, 609
Rouen, 354, 664
Rouget de Lisle, Claude Joseph, *Marseillaise,* 681, 682
Rousseau, Jean Jacques, 636, 641–644, 669; *The Social Contract,* 642–643
Royal Academy of Arts (British), 636
Royal Academy of Sciences (French), 522
Royal Society (London), 517, 522, 523, 574, 579
Rubens, Peter Paul, 529, 531, 532
Rudolf I (Hapsburg), Holy Roman Emperor, 356

Rudolf II, Holy Roman Emperor, 472, 474, 512
Russia, 479, 498, 769; boyars, 501, 502; Eastern Orthodox Church in, 502, 562, in seventeenth century, 501–503; serfs, 501, 502, 564, 638–639; Time of Troubles, 501; under Peter the Great, 562–565; aristocracy, 564–565; war with Sweden, 571–572; in eighteenth century, 588–591, 608, 609, 659; under Catherine the Great, 637, 638; population, 655; in coalition against Napoleon, 707, 715, 716, 721; Napoleon's campaign against, 720–721

Sacraments, 445 *n.,* 446
Sagres, 399
St. Bartholomew's Day Massacre, 469, 470, 619
Saint Gotthard Pass, 357
St. Lawrence, Gulf of, 610
St. Petersburg, 562, 564
Saint-Simon, Louis de Rouvroy, Duke de, 556
Salons (French), 574, 625
Salutati, Coluccio, 370, 375–376
San Gimignano, 335
Sans-culottes, 690–691, 694–697, 700–702, 710
Savery, Thomas, 660, 663
Savonorola, Girolamo, 436
Savoy, 474, 698
Saxony, 609; Napoleonic kingdom, 716
Scandinavia, 349
Scarlatti, Alessandro, 634
Schiller, Friedrich von, 634
Schmalkalden, 449
Scholasticism, 372, 383, 435
Schwyzz, 357
Science: in Renaissance, 393–395; in late seventeenh century, 578–581; in Enlightenment, 616–618, 622–623
Scientific revolution, 507–523; inventions and technology, 508; astronomy 509–514; scientific method, 514–515; societies, 521–523
Scotland: Calvinism in, 454, 482; England invaded by, 482, 483; in Civil War, 484, 485; union with England, 569
Sebond, Raymond, 524
Seneca, 374
Serfs, 347, 348, 407; in Russia, 501, 502, 564, 638–639, in Prussia, 560, 639; in Austria under Joseph II, 639; in France, abolished, 674
Seven Years' War, 588, 602, 608–609, 613
Seville, 423, 492, 493
Shakespeare, William, 523, 525–526
Sheep raising, 338, 404, 416, 493, 541
Ships: improvements in, 343; Dutch, 496
Sicily, in Kingdom of Naples and Sicily, 359; *See also* Naples and Sicily
Siena, 358
Sieyès, Emmanuel Joseph, 666, 708, 709
Sigismund II, King of Poland, 425
Sigismund III, King of Poland, 500, 501

Silesia, 608, 609, 665; Prussian conquest of, 595–597

Silk manufacture, 664–665

Silver: mining and metallurgy, 340; from Latin America, 403, 423, 493

Sistine Chapel, *see* Vatican, Sistine Chapel

Sixtus IV, Pope, 365

Slavery: in West Indies, 604, 606

Slave trade: Portuguese, 399, 400; in eighteenth century, 603, 605–608

Slavs, 596

Sluys, 352

Smith, Adam, 619, 621, 649

Soboul, Albert, 672

Social classes: nobles in fourteenth century, 350; in England, 408, 479, 480, 601, 650; in seventeenth century, 533, 535–536. *See also* Aristocracy; Labor; Middle class

Social sciences: in Enlightenment, 621, 623

Society of Jesus, *see* Jesuits

Sophocles, 575

South Sea Bubble, 601, 653

Spain, Jews in, 419; Muslims in, 416; Cortes, 416, 417, 421, 422, 720; Church in, 364, 417, 419, 426, 454, 456, 492; exploration and discovery by, 399–401; last Muslims conquered (1492), 401, 417, 419; American conquest and colonization by, 401–403, 421, 423; in late fifteenth and sixteenth centuries, 403, 404, 408, 416–424; union of kingdoms, 416; aristocracy, 417, 559; judicial systems, 417; taxes, 417, 494; war in Italy, 419, 423, 426; military tactics in seventeenth century, 463–464; war with Muslims, 466; war with England, 466–467; Dutch revolt against, 467–469, 474, 493, 494; in French religious war, 469–470, 493; in Thirty Years' War, 474, 475, 494; France invaded by, 490; in seventeenth century, 492–495, 559; colonies in seventeenth century, 492–493, 535–536; Union of Arms, 494–495; Hapsburg rulers of, 559; international relations in eighteenth century, 589, 596, 603; population in eighteenth century, 655; with Austria in war against France, 689, 700; Napoleon's campaign against, 718–720; Dos de Mayo rebellion, 719

Spanish America, *see* Latin America

Spanish Armada, 466–467, 471

Spanish Succession, 554; War of the, 551, 553–555, 559, 561

Spectator, 627

Speyer, Diet of (1529), 448

Spice Islands (Moluccas), 400, 401

Spinola, Ambrogio di, 494

Spinoza, Baruch, 617

Spoleto, 358

Sports, 631

Stalin, Joseph, 701 *n.*

Statute of Laborers (English), 339, 346

Steam power: in Industrial Revolution, 647, 660, 663–664

Steele, Richard, 627

Sterne, Laurence, 588, 633

Stockholm, 498

Strasbourg, 346, 551

Straw, Jack, 346

Stuart kings, 484

Subiaco, 180

Suleiman II (the Magnificent), Sultan, 428

Swabia, 357

Sweden, 230, 565, 588; Lutheranism in, 447, 448; in Thirty Years' War, 474–475, 477, 498; in seventeenth century, 498–500, 571–573; Riksdag, 499, 500, 572, 666; aristocracy, 571–573; war with Russia, 571–572; under Gustavus III, 666–667, 673

Swift, Jonathan, 519, 633

Switzerland; 698, 741, autonomy, 357; Protestants and Catholics in, 450; independence, 477; industrial growth, 665; Helvetic Republic, 705, 708, 715, 716

Taxes: in fourteenth and fifteenth centuries, 349, 354–355; in seventeenth century, 464; *See also* names of countries

Telescope, 395, 508, 512

Tell, William, 357

Templars (Knights Templars), 348

Tetzel, Johann, 444

Textile manufacture, 404, 410; in Industrial Revolution, 660–662, 664–665

Theresa of Avila, St. 492

Thirty Years' War, 472–477, 494, 498, 537–538, 557, 559, 592

Thomas à Kempis, *The Imitation of Christ*, 386, 387

Thomas Aquinas, *see* Aquinas, St. Thomas

Times, London, 670

Titian, 524

Tolstoy, Leo, 565

Tories, 567–568, 601

Townsend, Charles ("Turnip"), 657

Toynbee, Arnold, 647, 649

Toynbee, Arnold J., 647 *n.*

Trafalgar, Battle of, 715, 719

Treaties of Utrecht (1713, 1714), 555, 587–589, 600, 603

Treaty of Aix-la-Chapelle (1748), 610

Treaty of Campo Formio (1797), 707

Treaty of Copenhagen (1660), 477

Treaty of Kardia (1661), 477

Treaty of Lodi (1458), 426, 428

Treaty of Lunéville (1801), 714

Treaty of Oliva (1660), 477

Treaty of Paris, (1763), 613, 670

Treaty of Prague (1635), 475

Treaty of Pressburg (1805), 715

Treaty of the Pyrenees (1659), 477, 491

Treaty of Tilsit (1807), 716

Treaty of Tordesilas (1494), 399, 401

Treaty of Troyes (1420), 354

Trent, Council of (1545–1563), 455–456, 459
Trial by jury, see Jury, trial by
Trier, archbishop of, 448
Tripoli, 381
Troyes, 674
Tull, Jethro, 657
Turenne, Henri, Vicomte de, Marshal, 491, 555
Turgot, Jacques, 619, 641, 673–674
Tuscany, 368–369, 596, 716
Two Sicilies, see Naples and Sicily, Kingdom of
Tyler, Wat, 346

Ukraine, 501
Uniate Church, 500–501
United Provinces, see Netherlands
United States, 690, 705: Constitution, 640, 701 n.
Unterwalden, 357
Urban VIII, Pope, 529
Uri, 357

Valencia, 416
Valla, Lorenzo, 377
Valmy, Battle of, 687, 699
Valois dynasty, 412–416, 428
Valtellina, 474, 475
van Eyck, Jan, 391
Vatican: Library, 365; Sistine Chapel, 393, 456
Vatican Council (Vatican I, 1869–1870), 455 n.
Vatican Council (Vatican II, 1962), 455
Vauban, Sébastien Le Prestre, Marquis de, 556
Velásquez, Diego Rodríguez de Silva, 529, 531; The Surren-
    der of Breda, 527, 529
Vendée rebellion, 689–690, 693, 701
Venice, population, 369; Arsenal, 508, 512
Venice, republic, 358, 359, 426; Austria cedes to France,
    715
Verden, 477
Verdi, Giuseppe, The Masked Ball, 667
Vergil, 374
Verona, 358, 359
Versailles, 549, 556; women's march to, 676, 677
Vesalius, Andreas, 508–509, 514
Vicenza, 358
Vienna, 425, 598, 624, 638, 714, 715; Turkish siege of, 554,
    557, 558, 573; Schönbrunn, 557; university, 638
Villages in seventeenth century, 541, 543
Virginia (colony), 480, 536
Visconti, Gian Galeazzo, 357–358, 377
Vittorino da Feltre, 377
Volga River, 501, 502
Voltaire, François Marie Arouet, 595, 619–621, 625, 636,
    637, 640–644, 650; scientific interests, 617; Philosophical
    Dictionary, Candide, 633

Wages: fourteenth and fifteenth centuries, 339–340, 348;
    sixteenth century, 407; eighteenth century, 654
Wales, 600, 777
Wallenstein, Albrecht von, 474–475
Walpole, Sir Robert, 569, 601
War of the Austrian Succession, 588, 596–597, 610
War of the Roses, 348, 355–356, 409
War of the Spanish Succession, 551, 553–555, 559, 561
Wars of religion, 466–468
Warsaw, duchy of, 716
Wartburg castle, 446, 447
Water power, 664
Watt, James, 660, 663–664
Watteau, Antoine, 575
West Indies: British in, 480, 603, 613; French in, 603, 604,
    613; trade in, 604–605
Westphalia, Kingdom of, 716
Weyden, Rogier van der, Descent from the Cross, 391
Whigs, 568–569, 601, 669
White Mountain, Battle of the, 474
Whitney, Eli, 662
Wilkes, John, 670
Wilkinson, John, 660
William II of Orange, Stadholder (William the Silent), 467,
    468, 497
William III, King of England (Stadholder of Netherlands),
    497, 498, 554, 570; in England, 554, 568
Winckelmann, Johann, 625
Windmills, 664
Witchcraft, 381–382, 540–541
Witt, Jan de, 497–498, 570
Wittenberg, 444, 447; university, 443
Wolfe, Gen. James, 612
Wolsey, Thomas, Cardinal, 410
Women: readers and writers in eighteenth century, 627; in
    Napoleonic Code, 714
Wordsworth, William, 634
Workers, see Labor
Worms, Diet of (1521), 445
Wren, Sir Christopher, 522, 570
Wycliffe, John, 387–388, 435, 436

Ximenes de Cisneros, Francisco, Cardinal, 436

York, 346

Zeeland, 497
Zurich, 449
Zwickau, 447
Zwingli, Ulrich, 449–451; doctrines compared with Calvin-
    ism, 542–543

17/ Scala New York/Florence 18/ Staatliche Museen Preussischer Kulturbesitz Gemäldegalerie Berlin (West) 19/ Scala New York/Florence 20/ Alberto Augusto de Abreu Nunes 21/ Scala New York/Florence 22/ The Frick Collection, New York 23–28/ Scala New York/Florence 29/ Museum of Fine Arts, Boston, Isaac Sweetser Fund 30–31/ Scala New York/Florence 32/ Alte Pinakothek, München 33–35/ Scala New York/Florence 36/ Eberhard Zwicker, Würzburg 37/ Verlag Joachim Blauel, München 38/ Scala New York/Florence 39/ Rijksmuseum, Amsterdam 40/ Giraudon 41/ National Gallery of Art, Washington, D.C. 42/ Service de Documentation Photographie de la Réunion des Musées Nationaux 43/ Giraudon 44–45/ Service de Documentation Photographie de la Réunion des Musées Nationaux 46/ Scala New York/Florence 47/ Giraudon 48/ MAS

COLOR
ILLUSTRATION
SOURCES